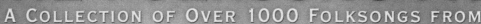

THE FOLKSONG FA
A COLLECTION OF OVER 1000 FOLKSONGS FROM

MELODY • LYRICS • CHORDS

The Folksong Fake Book

3   CONTENTS

12   SONGS INDEXED BY ORIGIN

536   GUITAR CHORDS

ISBN 0-634-01270-3

HAL•LEONARD®
CORPORATION

7777 W. BLUEMOUND RD. P.O. BOX 13819 MILWAUKEE, WI 53213

Visit Hal Leonard Online at
www.halleonard.com

Through the years, many folksongs have been altered in various ways for the sake of modern perceptions. In this book, however, we have made every effort to retain the original versions whenever possible. We have also attempted to include all known verses with each song, except in those rare cases where more than twelve exist.

–The Editors

THE FOLKSONG FAKE BOOK

CONTENTS

22	A-Hunting We Will Go
22	A-Roving
23	A-Tisket A-Tasket
23	Abdul Abulbul Amir
24	Ach du lieber Augustin (O My Dearest Augustine)
24	Acres of Clams
25	Across the Fields
25	Across the Hall
25	Across the Western Ocean
26	Adam in the Garden Pinnin' Leaves
26	Ah, Poor Bird
26	Ain't No More Cane on the Brazis
27	All Day Long
27	All God's Children Got Shoes
28	All My Trials
28	All Night, All Day
29	All Night Long
29	All Over This World
30	All Quiet Along the Potomac Tonight
30	All the Pretty Little Horses
33	All Through the Night
31	Aloha Oe
31	Alouette
32	Amazing Grace
32	Angel Band
33	Animal Fair
34	Annabel Lee
35	Annie Laurie
35	Are You Sleeping?
34	Arkansas Traveler
36	As I Roved Out
36	As I Was Going to Ballynure
36	The Ash Grove (Llwyn On)
37	At the Foot of Yonder Mountain
38	Auld Lang Syne
38	Aunt Dinah's Quilting Party
38	Aura Lee
39	Baa Baa Black Sheep
40	Babe of Bethlehem
41	Bad Company
42	The Bad Girl
44	The Bailiff's Daughter of Islington
43	The Ballad of Ned Kelly
39	The Ballad of the Tea Party
42	Baloo Baleerie
44	Baloo, Lammy
46	Baltimore Fire
46	The Bamboo Flute
47	Banana Boat Loader's Song (Day Oh)
47	The Banks of the Don
48	Banks of the Ohio
45	The Banks of the Sweet Primroses
48	Barbara Allen
48	Barnyard Song (I Had a Rooster)
50	The Barnyards of Delgaty
40	Batchelor's Walk
50	The Battle on Shiloh's Hill
51	Battleship of Maine
52	Be Present at Our Table, Lord
51	Be Thou My Vision
52	The Bear Went Over the Mountain
52	Beautiful Brown Eyes
53	Beautiful Dreamer
54	Bedlam
54	The Beggar
55	Believe Me, If All Those Endearing Young Charms
55	Bendemeer's Stream
56	Beware, Oh, Take Care
56	The Big Corral
57	Big Road Blues
49	The Big Rock Candy Mountain
56	Bile Them Cabbage Down
58	Bill Groggin's Goat
58	Billy Barlow
59	Billy Boy
57	Billy Broke Locks
59	Billy the Kid
60	Bingo
60	Birmingham Bull
61	Black-Eyed Susie
61	Black Is the Color of My True Love's Hair
62	Blackbirds and Thrushes
63	Blood on the Saddle
62	The Blooming Bright Star of Belle Isle
63	Blow Away the Morning Dew
64	Blow the Candles Out
64	Blow the Man Down
65	Blow the Wind Southerly
66	Blow, Ye Winds, in the Morning
66	Blow, Ye Winds, Westerly
68	The Blue Tail Fly (Jimmy Crack Corn)
67	The Blue Bells of Scotland
68	Blue Mountain Lake
69	Boatman Dance
69	Bobby Shaftoe
70	The Bold Fenian Men
71	Bold Fisherman
74	Bold Robert Emmet
72	The Bold Soldier
73	The Bold Tenant Farmer
72	The Boll Weevil
71	Boney Was a Warrior
74	The Bonniest Lass
75	The Bonny Bunch of Roses
76	The Bonny Earl of Murray
76	The Bonny Lighter Boy
76	The Bonny Ship the Diamond
77	Boothbay Whale
78	Boston Burglar
78	Boston Tea Tax Song
79	Botany Bay
67	Bound for South Australia

80	Bound for the Rio Grande
80	Bow and Balance
81	The Bowld Soger Boy
82	Bowling Green
82	The Brass Mounted Army
83	Brennan on the Moor
84	Bright Phoebe
85	The Brisk Young Bachelor
86	The British Grenadiers
84	Broke and Hungry
84	Brown Eyes
86	Brown Gal in de Ring
87	Brown's Ferry Blues
87	Bruton Town
85	Buckeye Jim
88	Buffalo Gals (Won't You Come Out Tonight)
88	The Buffalo Skinners
90	Bulldog and the Bullfrog
90	Bury Me Beneath the Willow
91	Bury Me Not on the Lone Prairie
83	Bye, Baby Bunting
89	Byker Hill
92	The Calton Weaver
92	Calvary
91	The Campbells Are Coming
93	Camptown Races
94	Canada-I-O
94	Canoe Song
95	Cape Ann
96	Cape Cod Girls
95	Captain Jinks of the Horse Marines
96	Captain Kidd
97	Captains and Ships
98	The Card Song
97	Careless Love
98	Carnival of Venice
100	Carrion Crow (I)
100	Carrion Crow (II)
102	Carry Me Back to Old Virginny
99	Casey Jones
101	The Cat Came Back
104	Charles Guiteau
102	Charlie Is My Darling
103	Charlie Mopps
104	Chester
105	Chewing Gum
104	Chiapanecas
106	The Chivalrous Shark
106	Cider Through a Straw
107	Cielito Lindo (My Pretty Darling)
108	Cindy
108	Clare's Dragoons
110	Clear the Track, Let the Bulgine Run
110	Clementine
111	Click Go the Shears
109	The Coasts of High Barbary
112	Cock-A-Doodle-Doo

112	Cock Robin
113	Cod-Liver Oil
113	Cold Water
114	Cole Younger
103	The Colorado Trail
115	Columbus Stockade Blues
115	Come All Ye Fair and Tender Maidens
116	Come and Go with Me
116	Come, Aurora
117	Come Follow
116	Come, My Dearest (Pjesma)
117	Come, O My Love
118	Come, Thou Fount of Every Blessing
118	Come, Ye Sinners, Poor and Needy
120	Comin' Through the Rye
118	Cordelia Brown
119	The Cork Leg
120	Cosher Bailey's Engine
117	Cotton-Eyed Joe
120	Cotton Field Song
121	Country Gardens
122	The County of Mayo
121	The Cowboy
122	The Cowboy's Dream
123	A Cowboy's Life Is a Dreary Life
124	Cradle Hymn
124	Cradle Song (Kehto Laula)
124	The Crawdad Song
125	Cripple Creek
125	The Croppy Boy
126	The Cruel Mother
126	The Cruel War Is Raging
127	The Cruel Youth
128	Cryderville Jail
127	The Cuckoo
128	The Cumberland Crew
129	Cumberland Gap
130	The Cutty Wren
130	Dabbling in the Dew
131	Dance to Your Daddy
132	Danny Boy
133	Danville Girl
134	Darlin' Corey
134	Darling Maiden, Hark, I Ask Thee (Krakowiak)
132	Darling Nelly Gray
136	Daughter, Will You Marry?
136	David of the White Rock
137	Days of Forty-Nine
138	Deadheads and Suckers
138	Death and the Lady
139	Deep Blue Sea
135	Deep River
139	The Deer Song
140	Delia's Gone
140	The Derby Ram
141	The Devil's Questions
141	Devilish Mary

142	Dick Darby	176	Every Night When the Sun Goes In
142	Didn't It Rain	178	Every Time I Feel the Spirit
143	Didn't My Lord Deliver Daniel?	177	Everybody Loves Saturday Night
144	Died for Love	178	Exultation
144	The Dingle Puck Goat	178	Ezekiel Saw the Wheel
139	Dink's Song	180	The Factory Girl
146	Dixie	180	Fair Harvard
146	Do As I'm Doing	179	The Fair Maid of Sorrento (La Vera Sorrentina)
147	The Dodger Song	181	Farewell, Nancy
145	Don't I Wish I Was a Single Girl Again	182	The Farmer in the Dell
148	Don't Let Your Deal Go Down	181	The Farmer Is the Man
148	Don't Sing Love Songs	182	The Farmer's Daughter
149	Don't You Weep After Me	183	Father Murphy
150	Doney Gal	183	Father's Whiskers
150	Donkey Riding	186	Felix, the Soldier
151	The Dowie Dens of Yarrow	184	The Fenian Man O' War
152	Down by the Riverside	185	The Fenians of Cahirciveen
152	Down by the Salley Gardens	184	Ferryland Sealer
154	Down by the Station	185	Filimiooriooriay
153	Down in My Heart	186	Finnegan's Wake
154	Down in That Valley	188	Fire Down Below
154	Down in the Valley	187	Fix Me, Jesus
156	Down in the Willow Garden	188	Flash Jack from Gundagai
156	Down the River	187	Flow Gently, Sweet Afton
157	The Dreary Black Hills	189	Flower So White (Flor, Blanca Flor)
158	Drill, Ye Tarriers, Drill	190	The Flying Cloud
157	Drink to Me Only with Thine Eyes	191	Fod
155	The Drover's Dream	191	The Foggy Dew
158	The Drummer and the Cook	192	The Foggy, Foggy Dew
162	The Drunkard's Doom	192	Foggy Mountain Top
160	The Drunken Sailor	193	Follow the Drinkin' Gourd
159	Dry Bones	194	For He's a Jolly Good Fellow
160	Dry Weather Houses	193	For Kansas
161	Du, Du Liegst Mir im Herzen (You, You Weigh on My Heart)	194	The Four Marys
162	Dublin City	195	Four Nights Drunk
163	Dumbarton's Drums	196	Four Pence a Day
163	Dumplins	196	The Fox
164	Duncan and Brady	197	Frankie and Johnny
164	Dunderbeck	198	Free at Last
166	The Dying Ranger	195	Free Little Bird
165	The Dying Stockman	198	Freedom
167	E-ri-e Canal	197	Freight Train
168	Early One Morning	198	The Frog in the Bog
169	East Virginia	199	Frog Went A-Courtin'
170	The Easter Rebellion	200	From Erin's Shores
170	The Ebenezer	200	Fuller and Warren
168	The Eddystone Light	202	Funiculi, Funicula!
169	Edward	201	The Gal That Got Stuck on Everything She Saw
167	Eensy, Weensy Spider	201	The Gallows Pole
172	Eggs and Marrowbone	203	The Galway Piper
171	Eileen Oge	203	Garryowen
172	Elanoy	204	Gee, Ma, I Want to Go Home
174	Empty Bed Blues	204	Geordie
173	Engine 143	204	George Collins
175	Equinoxial and Phoebe	205	Get Up, Jack!
174	The Erie Canal	206	Gin I Were
176	Erin's Lovely Home	205	The Girl I Left Behind Me
		206	Git Along, Little Dogies

207	Give Me That Old Time Religion		233	He Is King of Kings
207	Go Down, Moses		234	He Never Said a Mumbalin' Word
208	Go In and Out the Village		235	He Paid a Debt
208	Go Tell Aunt Rhody		235	He's Gone Away
208	Go, Tell It on the Mountain		234	He's Got the Whole World in His Hands
209	Go to Sleep My Little Baby (Duérmete Niño Chiquito)		231	Hear Lullabies and Sleep Now (A La Nanita Nana)
209	Go 'Way from My Window		236	Heave Away
210	God Save the King		238	The Hell-Bound Train
210	Goin' Across the Mountain		236	Henry Martin
212	Goin' Down to Town		237	Hey Diddle Diddle
210	Goin' to Germany		237	Hey, Ho! Nobody Home
211	Golden Slumbers		237	Hey Lolly, Lolly
212	The Golden Vanity		240	Hickory Dickory Dock
211	Goober Peas		239	Hieland Laddie
213	The Good Boy		239	High Barbaree
213	Good Morning, Mister Railroadman		238	High Germany
214	Good News		240	A Highland Lad My Love Was Born
214	Good Night Ladies		240	Hill and Gully Rider
214	The Good Old Rebel		242	Hinky Dinky Parley Voo
215	Goodbye, Old Paint		243	Home in That Rock
215	Goosey, Goosey Gander		242	Home on the Range
216	Gospel Plow		243	Home Sweet Home
216	The Gospel Train		244	Homeward from the Mountains (Hjemreise Fra Saeteren)
217	Grandfather's Clock		241	The Honest Ploughman
218	Great Day		244	Hoosen Johnny
217	Great Gettin' Up Mornin'		245	A Horse Named Bill
218	The Great Silkie		246	Hot Cross Buns
219	The Great Speckled Bird		246	The Hounds of Filemore
219	The Green Bushes		245	The House Carpenter
220	Green Corn		247	House of the Rising Sun
220	Green Gravel		248	The Housewife's Lament
220	Green Grow the Lilacs		247	How Can I Keep from Singing?
221	Green Grow the Rashes, O		249	How Can I Leave Thee?
221	Green Grows the Laurel		250	How Firm a Foundation
222	Greenland Fisheries		248	How Should I Your True Love Know
223	Greensleeves		250	How Old Are You, My Pretty Little Miss?
224	The Grey Goose		251	Hudson River Steamboat
222	Grizzly Bear		249	Hullaballoo-Balay
225	Groundhog		252	The Hunters of Kentucky
223	Guantanamera		251	Hunting the Hare (Hela'r 'Sgyvarnog)
225	Guide My Feet		249	Hurree Hurroo
224	Gypsy Davey		252	Hurry Up, Liza Jane
226	Hail, Hail, the Gang's All Here		253	Hush, Little Baby
226	Hallelujah, I'm a Bum!		253	I Am a Pilgrim
226	Hand Me Down My Walking Cane		254	I Can't Feel at Home in This World Anymore
227	Hard, Ain't It Hard		254	I Don't Want to Get Adjusted
227	Hard Is the Fortune of All Womankind (The Wagoner's Lad)		254	I Gave My Love a Cherry (The Riddle Song)
228	Hard Luck		255	I Know My Love
228	Hares on the Mountain		255	I Know Where I'm Going
229	The Harp That Once		256	I Never Will Marry
229	Hatikva		256	I Ride an Old Paint
230	Haul Away, Joe		256	I Shall Not Be Moved
229	Haul on the Bowline		258	I Walk the Road Again
232	Hauling Song		258	I Want Jesus to Walk with Me
230	Hava Nagila		257	I Will Feed My Baby
232	Have You Seen but a White Lily Grow?		259	I Wish I Was a Mole
233	He Arose		259	I Wish I Was Single Again

260	I'd Like to Be in Texas
261	I'll Give My Love an Apple
260	I'm a Roaring Repeater
262	I'm Gonna Sing When the Spirit Says Sing
262	I'm On My Way
263	I'm Sad and I'm Lonely
264	I'm Seventeen Come Sunday
265	I'se the B'y That Builds the Boat
262	I've Been Working on the Railroad
264	I've Got No Use for Women
265	I've Got Peace Like a River
266	I've Got Sixpence
266	If He'd Be a Buckaroo
267	If You're Happy and You Know It
267	Ilkley Moor
268	In Good Old Colony Times
268	In the Forest Grew a Tiny Birch Tree (Vo Pole Berëzyn'ka Stoiala)
269	In the Good Old Summertime
270	In the Pines
270	In the Shade of the Old Apple Tree
270	The Intoxicated Rat
272	Irish Astronomy
272	The Irish Girl
271	The Irish Washerwoman
273	The Irishman's Epistle
271	Iroquois Lullaby
273	It Was a Lover and His Lass
274	It Was a Mouse
274	It's the Same the Whole World Over
275	Jack Was Ev'ry Inch a Sailor
275	Jackson
277	Jacob's Ladder
276	The Jam on Gerry's Rocks
280	Jay Gould's Daughter
277	Jeanie with the Light Brown Hair
278	Jefferson and Liberty
280	Jenny Jenkins
281	Jerry Ryan
278	Jesse James
279	Jesus Born in Beth'ny
281	Jesus Loves Me
282	Jesus, the Christ, Is Born
283	Jim Fisk
284	Joe Bowers
282	John Brown's Body
285	John Hardy
286	John Henry
283	John Jacob Jingleheimer Schmidt
285	John Peel
288	John Riley (I)
288	John Riley (II)
286	Johnny, Come Down to Hilo
284	Johnny Has Gone for a Soldier
287	Johnny I Hardly Knew Ye
289	Johnny Todd
289	Johnson Boys
290	Join the British Army
289	The Jolly Miller
290	Jordan Ain't a Hard Road to Travel
291	Joshua (Fit the Battle of Jericho)
292	Jug of Punch
291	The Juniper Tree
293	Just a Closer Walk with Thee
292	Just Before the Battle, Mother
294	Katy Cline
294	Katy Cruel
296	Kentucky Babe
296	Kevin Barry
297	The Keys to Canterbury
298	Kitty Alone and I (I)
298	Kitty Alone and I (II)
295	Kitty of Coleraine
299	The Knight and the Shepherd's Daughter
293	Krishna
295	Kumbaya
300	La Cucaracha
300	Ladies of Brisbane
301	Lady Gay
302	Lady Isabel and the Elf Knight
302	Lady of Carlisle
303	Landlord, Fill the Flowing Bowl
303	The Lark in the Clear Air
304	The Lark in the Morn
304	The Last Request
301	Lavender's Blue
304	Lazy Mary, Will You Get Up?
305	Leatherwing Bat
305	Let Erin Remember the Days of Old
306	Let Me Fly
307	Let Us All Be Joyful Now (Gaudeamus Igitur)
308	Let Us Break Bread Together
308	Li'l Liza Jane
308	Life's Railway to Heaven
306	Likes Likker Better Than Me
307	Lily of the West
309	Limerick Is Beautiful
310	The Lincolnshire Poacher
310	Linstead Market
311	Listen to the Mockingbird
309	Little Annie Rooney
312	Little Brown Dog
312	Little Brown Jug
313	Little David Play on Your Harp
314	Little Joe, The Wrangler
311	Little Maggie
314	Little Mohee
316	Little Old Sod Shanty on My Claim
313	The Little Orphan Girl
316	Little Sandy Girl
317	The Little Saucepan (Sospan Vach)
318	Little Snowball Bush (Kalinka)
315	Liza Jane
318	Loch Lomond
317	London Bridge
320	Lonesome Valley

8

319	Looby Loo
320	Look Down That Lonesome Road
320	Lord, I Want to Be a Christian
321	Lord Rendal
321	The Low, Low Lands of Holland
322	Lullaby (Komoriuta)
322	Lullaby, My Baby (Arroro Mi Niño)
322	MacPherson's Farewell
324	The Maid Freed from the Gallows
323	The Maid on the Shore
324	Make Me a Bed on the Floor
325	Mama Don't 'Low
325	Mama, Have You Heard the News
325	Man Goin' Round
326	The Man on the Flying Trapeze
327	A Man Without a Woman
328	Mandolina
328	Marching Through Georgia
329	Marianne
327	Mary Ann
330	Mary Had a Baby
329	Mary Had a Little Lamb
331	Mary Hamilton
332	Matilda
330	May Song (Canción de Maja)
334	McCaffery
332	Me Father's a Lawyer in England
333	Men of Harlech (Rhyfelgyrch Gwyr Harlech)
334	The Men of the West
335	Mermaid Song
331	Merrily We Roll Along
336	Michael Finnegan
333	Michael Row the Boat Ashore
336	Michael Roy of Brooklyn City
338	Midnight Special
338	Mighty Day
339	The Miller's Daughter (La Fille de la Meunière)
339	The Minstrel Boy
340	Miss Lilian
337	Mrs. McGrath
340	Mrs. Murphy's Chowder
342	Mister Rabbit
335	Molly Bann
341	Molly Brannigan
342	Molly Malone (Cockles and Mussels)
343	More Pretty Girls Than One
344	Morrissey and the Russian Sailor
343	Motherless Children
344	Mountain Dew
345	Mountains of Mourne
346	Mowing the Barley
341	The Muffin Man
348	The Mulberry Bush
347	Must I Go Bound?
346	My Bonnie Lies Over the Ocean
348	My Dame Had a Lame Tame Crane
349	My Days Have Been So Wondrous Free
349	My Heart's Tonight in Texas
350	My Home's Across the Smoky Mountains
350	My Lord, What a Morning
352	My Love Is a Rider
350	My Luve Is Like a Red Red Rose
352	My Mother Chose My Husband
351	My Mother's Old Red Shawl
353	My Old Hen
347	My Old Kentucky Home
351	My Sweetheart's a Mule
353	My White Horse (Mi Caballo Blanco)
354	My Wild Irish Rose
355	Nassau Bound
356	Nearby to My Dear One (Auprès de ma Blonde)
357	Nelly Was a Lady
358	New River Train
357	New York Girls (Can't You Dance the Polka?)
358	The Next Market Day
359	Night Herding Song
355	Nightingale with the Dark Beak (Rouxinol do Pico Preto)
360	Nine Hundred Miles
360	Nine Miles from Gundagai
361	Nine Pound Hammer
359	No Hiding Place
362	No Irish Need Apply
361	No More Booze
364	Nobody Knows the Trouble I've Seen
364	Nobody's Business
363	None Can Love Like an Irishman
362	Norah O'Neale
365	O How I Love Jesus
366	O No, John!
365	O Soldier
366	O Waly, Waly (The Water Is Wide)
367	O'Donnell Aboo
367	The Oak and the Ash
368	Oats, Peas, Beans and Barley Grow
368	Oh, Brandy, Leave Me Alone
368	Oh, Daddy Be Gay
369	Oh Dear! What Can the Matter Be?
370	Oh, Freedom
370	Oh How Lovely Is the Evening
370	Oh Mary, Don't You Weep
372	Oh Rowan Tree
372	Oh, Sinner Man
369	Oh! Susanna
371	Oh, Them Golden Slippers
373	Oh Where, Oh Where Has My Little Dog Gone
374	Oh, Won't You Sit Down?
374	The Old Ark's A-Moverin'
375	Old Aunt Kate
373	The Old Bark Hut
376	Old Black Joe
375	Old Blue
376	The Old Chisholm Trail
376	The Old Cow Died
378	Old Dan Tucker

378	Old Dog Tray
379	Old Folks at Home
380	The Old Gospel Ship
379	The Old Gray Mare
380	Old Joe Clark
381	Old MacDonald Had a Farm
382	Old Oaken Bucket
382	The Old Orange Flute
383	Old Rattler
384	Old Soldiers Never Die
384	The Old Turf Fire
384	The Old Woman Who Went to Market
385	The Ole Grey Goose
385	Oleanna
386	Omie Wise
377	On a Crystal Throne (Necken's Polska)
383	On a Monday
386	On Jordan's Stormy Banks
387	On Mondays I Never Go to Work
389	On the Banks of Allan Water
388	On the Paris Way (Passant par Paris)
390	On Top of Old Smoky
387	Once I Had a Sweetheart
390	One Man Shall Mow My Meadow
392	One More Day
391	One More River
393	One Morning in May
389	Ophelia Letter Blow 'Way
394	Otto Wood
393	Outward and Homeward Bound
392	Over the Mountains (Love Will Find Out the Way)
394	Over the River and Through the Woods
395	Over the Waves
396	The Ox-Driving Song
396	Paddy and the Whale
397	Paper of Pins
398	The Parting Glass
398	Pat-A-Pan (Willie, Take Your Little Drum)
397	The Paw Paw Patch
399	Pay Me My Money Down
399	Peanut Sat on a Railroad Track
399	Peter, Peter, Pumpkin Eater
400	Po' Boy
400	Polly, Put the Kettle On
400	Polly Wolly Doodle
402	Poor Boy
402	Poor Lazarus
403	Poor Lonesome Cowboy
404	Pop Goes the Weasel
404	The Praties, They Grow Small
401	Preguntales a Las Estrellas
404	The Pretty Girl Milking Her Cow
405	Pretty Little Girl with the Red Dress On
403	Pretty Polly
405	Pretty Saro
406	Prison Bound
406	A Prisoner for Life

407	Putting on the Style
407	Queen Jane
408	Queen of Hearts
408	The Queensland Drover
409	Railroad Bill
409	A Railroader for Me
410	Raise a Ruckus Tonight
410	Rake and Rambling Boy
411	Rambling Blues
411	The Rambling Sailor
412	Real Old Mountain Dew
412	The Rebel Soldier
413	Red Apple Juice
413	Red Iron Ore
414	The Red Light Saloon
414	Red River Valley
415	The Regular Army, Oh!
408	Reuben and Rachel
416	Reuben's Train
416	Revolutionary Tea
417	A Rich Irish Lady
418	Richmond Is a Hard Road to Travel
415	Riding in a Buggy
420	The Rifle
417	Rig-A-Jig Jig
420	Ring Around the Rosie
421	Rise and Shine
419	Rise Up, Shepherd, and Follow
421	The Rising of the Moon
422	The River in the Pines
423	Rivers of Babylon
422	The Road to Gundagai
423	The Road to the Isles
424	Robin Redbreast
425	Rock-A-Bye, Baby
424	Rock-A-My Soul
425	Rock About My Saro Jane
426	The Rock Island Line
427	Rocks and Gravel
426	Roddy McCorley
427	Roll, Alabama, Roll
428	Roll Down the Line
428	Roll in My Sweet Baby's Arms
429	Roll on the Ground
429	Roll Over
430	Rolling Home
430	Rosa
432	The Rose of Tralee
431	Rose, Rose
431	Rosewood Casket
432	Rosin the Beau
433	Round the Bay of Mexico
433	The Roving Gambler
434	Row, Row, Row Your Boat
434	Rue
434	Run, Children, Run
435	Russian Lullaby

435	Rye Whiskey		461	Skillet Good and Greasy
435	Sable Island Song		463	Skip to My Lou
436	Sacramento		464	Skye Boat Song
437	Sail Away, Ladies		464	Sledgehammer Song (Dubinushka)
436	Sailing in the Boat		465	Sleep, Baby, Sleep
436	Sailing, Sailing		459	Sleep, My Baby, Precious Darling
437	Sailor on the Deep Blue Sea			(Duerme Niño Pequeñito)
438	Sailor's Hornpipe		463	Sleep, My Child (Aïnte)
438	St. James Infirmary		466	Snake Baked a Hoecake
438	Sakura (Cherry Blossoms)		465	So Early in the Morning
439	Sal Got a Meatskin		466	Soldier Boy
439	Sally Ann		466	Soldier, Soldier, Will You Marry Me?
440	Sally Brown		467	Somebody's Knocking at Your Door
440	Sally Goodin		467	Sometimes I Feel Like a Motherless Child
441	Sally in Our Alley		468	The Son of a Gambolier
442	Salty Dog		468	Song of the Volga Boatman
443	Sam Bass		469	The Sons of Liberty
441	Sam Hall		470	Soon Ah Will Be Done
442	Samson		471	Sourwood Mountain
444	Santa Lucia		473	South Australia
444	Santy Anna		474	The Sow Took the Measles
446	Scarborough Fair		471	Sowing on the Mountain
445	School Days		472	The Sporting Bachelors
446	Scotland's Burning		469	Springfield Mountain
446	Scots Wha Hae		475	The Squid-Jiggin' Ground
447	Seeing Nellie Home		470	Standing in the Need of Prayer
447	Set Down, Servant		472	Star in the East
448	The Seven Irishmen		473	The Star of County Down
450	Shady Grove		474	Starving to Death on My Government Claim
449	Shall We Gather at the River?		475	The State of Arkansas
450	Shalom Chaveyrim (Shalom, My Friend)		479	Steal Away
450	The Shan Van Vocht		478	Stir the Pudding
449	The Shanty-Man's Life		476	The Strawberry Roan
448	Shake That Little Foot		478	The Streets of Glory
451	The Shaver		477	The Streets of Laredo
451	She Moved Through the Fair		479	Sugar Baby
452	She Wore a Yellow Ribbon		478	Sumer Is Icumen In (Summer Is A-Coming In)
452	She'll Be Comin' 'Round the Mountain		480	Sun Don't Set in the Mornin'
453	She's Like a Swallow		480	The Sun Hangs High (Charki Hidjaz)
453	Shenandoah		484	Swannanoa Tunnel
454	The Ship That Never Returned		481	Sweet and Low
454	Shoo Fly, Don't Bother Me		481	Sweet Betsy from Pike
456	Shoot the Buffalo		482	Sweet Rosie O'Grady
458	Short'nin' Bread		483	Sweet the Evening Air of May
459	Shuckin' of the Corn		482	Swing a Lady
460	Shule Agra		483	Swing and Turn, Jubilee
455	The Sign of the Bonny Blue Bell		484	Swing Low, Sweet Chariot
461	Silkie		484	The Tailor and the Mouse
455	The Silver Dagger		485	Take Me Out to the Ball Game
460	Simple Gifts		486	Take This Hammer
456	Since I've Been in the Army		485	Taking Gair in the Night
460	Sing a Song of Sixpence		486	Tam Pierce
462	Sing an' Jump Up for Joy		487	The Tanyard Side
459	Single Girl		488	Tarantella
457	The Sioux Indians		488	The Tarry Trousers
462	Six Questions		489	Tell Me Why
458	Skibbereen		487	Ten Little Indians

490 Ten Thousand Cattle
489 Tenting Tonight
491 The Texas Rangers
490 The Tex-i-an Boys
492 That Crazy War
490 There Is a Balm in Gilead
492 There Is a Tavern in the Town
493 There Was an Old Soldier
494 There's a Hole in the Bottom of the Sea
495 There's a Hole in the Bucket
495 There's a Little Wheel A-Turning in My Heart
496 These Bones Goin' to Rise Again
    (Dese Bones Gwine to Rise Again)
496 This Little Light of Mine
497 This Old Man
497 This Train
498 Three Blind Mice
498 Three Lilies (Drei Lilien)
498 The Three Ravens
500 Timber (Jerry the Mule)
500 Times A-Getting Hard, Boys
501 Tipperary Recruiting Song
501 'Tis the Last Rose of Summer
502 The Titanic
502 To All Good Cheer (Ein Prosit der Gemütlichkeit)
502 Tobacco Union
503 Tobacco's but an Indian Weed
504 Told My Captain
503 Tom Cat Blues
504 Tom Dooley
505 Tom, Tom, the Piper's Son
505 Tom's Gone to Hilo
499 The Trail to Mexico
505 Tramp! Tramp! Tramp!
506 Trav'lin' Man
506 The Trees Are Getting High
507 Troika Rushing (Troika Mchitsia)
508 The Trooper and the Maid
507 The True Lover's Farewell
509 Tum Balalaika
508 Turkey in the Straw
510 Turkey Song
510 The Turtle Dove
510 Twelve Gates to the City
512 Twinkle, Twinkle, Little Star
    (Ah! Vous Dirai-je, Maman?)
512 Two Maids Went A-Milking One Day
513 Tyin' a Knot in the Devil's Tail
514 The Unquiet Grave
514 Unto a Poor Blind Lover (A Un Niño Ciegocito)
511 The Utah Iron Horse
515 The Vicar of Bray
516 Vicksburg Blues
516 Vine and Fig Tree
516 The Wabash Cannon Ball
518 Wae's Me for Prince Charlie
519 Wanderin'
520 Water Come a Me Eye

520 Water in Me Rum
520 Wayfaring Stranger
521 We Gather Together
518 The Wearing of the Green
521 Weaving Lilt
522 Weel May the Keel Row
522 Were You There?
523 What Time Is It? (Hoe Laat Is't?)
524 When Adam Was Created
523 When Cockleshells Turn Silverbells
524 When I Can Read My Title Clear
525 When Johnny Comes Marching Home
526 When the Saints Go Marching In
525 Whiskey Johnny!
517 Whiskey, You're the Devil
526 Whistle, Daughter, Whistle
522 White Coral Bells
526 The Wild Colonial Boy
527 Will the Circle Be Unbroken
528 Will Ye Go, Lassie?
529 Will Ye No' Come Back Again?
530 Willie Moore
528 Willie the Weeper
530 With My Swag All on My Shoulder
529 Wondrous Love
527 Wooing (Werbung)
531 The Work of the Weavers
531 Worried Man Blues
532 Wrap Me Up in My Tarpaulin Jacket
532 Yankee Doodle
533 Ye Banks and Braes O' Bonnie Doon
534 Ye Parliaments of England
533 The Yellow Rose of Texas
534 Yonder Stands a Handsome Lady
535 The Young Man Who Wouldn't Hoe Corn
534 Zacchaeus
535 Zum Gali Gali

SONGS INDEXED BY ORIGIN

AFRICA
295 Kumbaya
368 Oh, Brandy, Leave Me Alone

AFRICAN-AMERICAN
26 Adam in the Garden Pinnin' Leaves
27 All Day Long
27 All God's Children Got Shoes
28 All My Trials
28 All Night, All Day
29 All Night Long
29 All Over This World
32 Angel Band
92 Calvary
110 Clear the Track, Let the Bulgine Run
124 The Crawdad Song
134 Darlin' Corey
135 Deep River
142 Didn't It Rain
143 Didn't My Lord Deliver Daniel?
139 Dink's Song
152 Down by the Riverside
159 Dry Bones
178 Every Time I Feel the Spirit
178 Ezekiel Saw the Wheel
187 Fix Me, Jesus
193 Follow the Drinkin' Gourd
198 Free at Last
208 Go, Tell It on the Mountain
214 Good News
216 Gospel Plow
216 The Gospel Train
218 Great Day
217 Great Gettin' Up Mornin'
225 Guide My Feet
226 Hand Me Down My Walking Cane
233 He Arose
233 He Is King of Kings
234 He Never Said a Mumbalin' Word
234 He's Got the Whole World in His Hands
253 I Am a Pilgrim
258 I Want Jesus to Walk with Me
262 I'm Gonna Sing When the Spirit Says Sing
262 I'm On My Way
277 Jacob's Ladder
286 Johnny, Come Down to Hilo
291 Joshua (Fit the Battle of Jericho)
306 Let Me Fly
308 Let Us Break Bread Together
313 Little David Play on Your Harp
320 Lord, I Want to Be a Christian
330 Mary Had a Baby
343 Motherless Children
350 My Lord, What a Morning

364 Nobody Knows the Trouble I've Seen
370 Oh, Freedom
372 Oh, Sinner Man
374 Oh, Won't You Sit Down?
374 The Old Ark's A-Moverin'
410 Raise a Ruckus Tonight
424 Rock-A-My Soul
447 Set Down, Servant
467 Somebody's Knocking at Your Door
467 Sometimes I Feel Like a Motherless Child
470 Soon Ah Will Be Done
471 Sowing on the Mountain
470 Standing in the Need of Prayer
479 Steal Away
484 Swing Low, Sweet Chariot
490 There Is a Balm in Gilead
496 These Bones Goin' to Rise Again
      (Dese Bones Gwine to Rise Again)
496 This Little Light of Mine
522 Were You There?

ANTIGUA
118 Cordelia Brown
462 Sing an' Jump Up for Joy

ARGENTINA
322 Lullaby, My Baby (Arroro Mi Niño)

AUSTRALIA
43 The Ballad of Ned Kelly
79 Botany Bay
67 Bound for South Australia
111 Click Go the Shears
155 The Drover's Dream
188 Flash Jack from Gundagai
300 Ladies of Brisbane
360 Nine Miles from Gundagai
373 The Old Bark Hut
408 The Queensland Drover
422 The Road to Gundagai
526 The Wild Colonial Boy
530 With My Swag All on My Shoulder

AUSTRIA
527 Wooing (Werbung)

BAHAMAS
140 Delia's Gone
255 Nassau Bound

BRAZIL
355 Nightingale with the Dark Beak
      (Rouxinol do Pico Preto)

CANADA
31 Alouette
47 The Banks of the Don
62 The Blooming Bright Star of Belle Isle
66 Blow, Ye Winds, Westerly
84 Bright Phoebe
97 Captains and Ships
100 Carrion Crow (I)
100 Carrion Crow (II)
184 Ferryland Sealer
198 The Frog in the Bog
204 Geordie
261 I'll Give My Love an Apple
265 I'se the B'y That Builds the Boat
271 Iroquois Lullaby
274 It Was a Mouse
275 Jack Was Ev'ry Inch a Sailor
281 Jerry Ryan
327 Mary Ann
396 Paddy and the Whale
435 Sable Island Song
453 She's Like a Swallow
475 The Squid-Jiggin' Ground
485 Taking Gair in the Night
488 The Tarry Trousers

CARIBBEAN
160 Dry Weather Houses
163 Dumplins
198 Freedom
399 Pay Me My Money Down
520 Water in Me Rum

CENTRAL EUROPE
249 How Can I Leave Thee?

CHILE
353 My White Horse (Mi Caballo Blanco)

CHINA
46 The Bamboo Flute

COLOMBIA
459 Sleep, My Baby, Precious Darling
(Duerme Niño Pequeñito)

CUBA
223 Guantanamera

ENGLAND
26 Ah, Poor Bird
44 The Bailiff's Daughter of Islington
45 The Banks of the Sweet Primroses
52 Be Present at Our Table, Lord
54 Bedlam
54 The Beggar
60 Bingo
62 Blackbirds and Thrushes
63 Blow Away the Morning Dew
64 Blow the Candles Out
65 Blow the Wind Southerly
69 Bobby Shaftoe
71 Bold Fisherman
72 The Bold Soldier
76 The Bonny Lighter Boy
80 Bound for the Rio Grande
80 Bow and Balance
85 The Brisk Young Bachelor
86 The British Grenadiers
87 Bruton Town
95 Captain Jinks of the Horse Marines
103 Charlie Mopps
109 The Coasts of High Barbary
112 Cock Robin
116 Come, Aurora
121 Country Gardens
126 The Cruel Mother
127 The Cuckoo
130 The Cutty Wren
130 Dabbling in the Dew
136 David of the White Rock
138 Death and the Lady
140 The Derby Ram
144 Died for Love
150 Donkey Riding
157 Drink to Me Only with Thine Eyes
158 The Drummer and the Cook
162 Dublin City
168 Early One Morning
168 The Eddystone Light
169 Edward
176 Erin's Lovely Home
182 The Farmer's Daughter
192 The Foggy, Foggy Dew
194 For He's a Jolly Good Fellow
196 Four Pence a Day
201 The Gallows Pole
204 George Collins
210 God Save the King
211 Golden Slumbers
212 The Golden Vanity
219 The Green Bushes
223 Greensleeves
224 Gypsy Davey
228 Hares on the Mountain
229 Haul on the Bowline
232 Have You Seen but a White Lily Grow?
236 Henry Martin
238 High Germany
245 The House Carpenter
248 How Should I Your True Love Know

14

264 I'm Seventeen Come Sunday
266 I've Got Sixpence
267 Ilkley Moor
273 It Was a Lover and His Lass
274 It's the Same the Whole World Over
285 John Peel
289 Johnny Todd
290 Join the British Army
289 The Jolly Miller
297 The Keys to Canterbury
299 The Knight and the Shepherd's Daughter
302 Lady Isabel and the Elf Knight
302 Lady of Carlisle
303 Landlord, Fill the Flowing Bowl
304 The Lark in the Morn
310 The Lincolnshire Poacher
321 Lord Rendal
321 The Low, Low Lands of Holland
324 The Maid Freed from the Gallows
323 The Maid on the Shore
331 Mary Hamilton
332 Me Father's a Lawyer in England
346 Mowing the Barley
366 O No, John!
365 O Soldier
366 O Waly, Waly (The Water Is Wide)
367 The Oak and the Ash
387 On Mondays I Never Go to Work
390 One Man Shall Mow My Meadow
393 Outward and Homeward Bound
392 Over the Mountains (Love Will Find Out the Way)
407 Queen Jane
408 Queen of Hearts
411 The Rambling Sailor
420 Ring Around the Rosie
430 Rolling Home
431 Rose, Rose
434 Rue
438 Sailor's Hornpipe
441 Sally in Our Alley
441 Sam Hall
446 Scarborough Fair
446 Scotland's Burning
455 The Sign of the Bonny Blue Bell
455 The Silver Dagger
478 Sumer Is Icumen In (Summer Is A-Coming In)
483 Sweet the Evening Air of May
484 The Tailor and the Mouse
492 There Is a Tavern in the Town
497 This Old Man
498 The Three Ravens
501 'Tis the Last Rose of Summer
503 Tobacco's but an Indian Weed
505 Tom's Gone to Hilo
506 The Trees Are Getting High
507 The True Lover's Farewell

512 Two Maids Went A-Milking One Day
514 The Unquiet Grave
515 The Vicar of Bray
522 Weel May the Keel Row
523 When Cockleshells Turn Silverbells

FINLAND
124 Cradle Song (Kehto Laula)

FRANCE
35 Are You Sleeping?
339 The Miller's Daughter (La Fille de la Meunière)
356 Nearby to My Dear One (Auprès de ma Blonde)
388 On the Paris Way (Passant par Paris)
398 Pat-A-Pan (Willie, Take Your Little Drum)
512 Twinkle, Twinkle, Little Star
(Ah! Vous Dirai-je, Maman?)

GERMANY
24 Ach du lieber Augustin (O My Dearest Augustine)
161 Du, Du Liegst Mir im Herzen
(You, You Weigh on My Heart)
307 Let Us All Be Joyful Now (Gaudeamus Igitur)
498 Three Lilies (Drei Lilien)
502 To All Good Cheer (Ein Prosit der Gemütlichkeit)

INDIA
293 Krishna

IRELAND
23 Abdul Abulbul Amir
25 Across the Western Ocean
36 As I Roved Out
36 As I Was Going to Ballynure
40 Batchelor's Walk
51 Be Thou My Vision
55 Believe Me, If All Those Endearing Young Charms
55 Bendemeer's Stream
70 The Bold Fenian Men
74 Bold Robert Emmet
73 The Bold Tenant Farmer
71 Boney Was a Warrior
75 The Bonny Bunch of Roses
83 Brennan on the Moor
89 Byker Hill
108 Clare's Dragoons
119 The Cork Leg
122 The County of Mayo
125 The Croppy Boy
132 Danny Boy
142 Dick Darby
144 The Dingle Puck Goat
149 Don't You Weep After Me
152 Down by the Salley Gardens
170 The Easter Rebellion
171 Eileen Oge

180	Fair Harvard
181	Farewell, Nancy
183	Father Murphy
186	Felix, the Soldier
184	The Fenian Man O' War
185	The Fenians of Cahirciveen
186	Finnegan's Wake
190	The Flying Cloud
191	The Foggy Dew
200	From Erin's Shores
203	The Galway Piper
203	Garryowen
205	The Girl I Left Behind Me
221	Green Grows the Laurel
229	The Harp That Once
246	The Hounds of Filemore
255	I Know My Love
256	I Never Will Marry
272	The Irish Girl
271	The Irish Washerwoman
273	The Irishman's Epistle
288	John Riley (I)
287	Johnny I Hardly Knew Ye
292	Jug of Punch
296	Kevin Barry
295	Kitty of Coleraine
303	The Lark in the Clear Air
305	Let Erin Remember the Days of Old
309	Limerick Is Beautiful
334	McCaffery
334	The Men of the West
335	Mermaid Song
336	Michael Roy of Brooklyn City
339	The Minstrel Boy
337	Mrs. McGrath
340	Mrs. Murphy's Chowder
341	Molly Brannigan
342	Molly Malone (Cockles and Mussels)
344	Morrissey and the Russian Sailor
345	Mountains of Mourne
354	My Wild Irish Rose
358	The Next Market Day
362	No Irish Need Apply
363	None Can Love Like an Irishman
362	Norah O'Neale
367	O'Donnell Aboo
382	The Old Orange Flute
384	The Old Turf Fire
398	The Parting Glass
404	The Praties, They Grow Small
404	The Pretty Girl Milking Her Cow
410	Rake and Rambling Boy
412	Real Old Mountain Dew
417	A Rich Irish Lady
421	The Rising of the Moon
426	Roddy McCorley

432	The Rose of Tralee
432	Rosin the Beau
448	The Seven Irishmen
450	The Shan Van Vocht
451	She Moved Through the Fair
460	Shule Agra
456	Since I've Been in the Army
458	Skibbereen
468	The Son of a Gambolier
469	The Sons of Liberty
473	The Star of County Down
487	The Tanyard Side
501	Tipperary Recruiting Song
518	The Wearing of the Green
517	Whiskey, You're the Devil
528	Will Ye Go, Lassie?

ISRAEL
229	Hatikva
230	Hava Nagila
450	Shalom Chaveyrim (Shalom, My Friend)
509	Tum Balalaika
516	Vine and Fig Tree
535	Zum Gali Gali

ITALY
179	The Fair Maid of Sorrento (La Vera Sorrentina)
202	Funiculi, Funicula!
444	Santa Lucia
488	Tarantella

JAMAICA
47	Banana Boat Loader's Song (Day Oh)
237	Hey Lolly, Lolly
240	Hill and Gully Rider
310	Linstead Market
329	Marianne
364	Nobody's Business
423	Rivers of Babylon
520	Water Come a Me Eye

JAPAN
322	Lullaby (Komoriuta)
438	Sakura (Cherry Blossoms)

LATIN-AMERICA
401	Preguntales a Las Estrellas

MEXICO
26	Ain't No More Cane on the Brazis
104	Chiapanecas
107	Cielito Lindo (My Pretty Darling)
189	Flower So White (Flor, Blanca Flor)
300	La Cucaracha
328	Mandolina

NETHERLANDS
430 Rosa
521 We Gather Together
523 What Time Is It? (Hoe Laat Is't?)

NIGERIA
177 Everybody Loves Saturday Night
257 I Will Feed My Baby

NORWAY
244 Homeward from the Mountains
      (Hjemreise Fra Saeteren)
385 Oleanna

RUSSIA
268 In the Forest Grew a Tiny Birch Tree
      (Vo Pole Berëzyn'ka Stoiala)
318 Little Snowball Bush (Kalinka)
464 Sledgehammer Song (Dubinushka)
468 Song of the Volga Boatman
507 Troika Rushing (Troika Mchitsia)

SCOTLAND
38 Auld Lang Syne
42 Baloo Baleerie
44 Baloo, Lammy
48 Barbara Allen
50 The Barnyards of Delgaty
67 The Blue Bells of Scotland
74 The Bonniest Lass
76 The Bonny Earl of Murray
76 The Bonny Ship the Diamond
92 The Calton Weaver
91 The Campbells Are Coming
102 Charlie Is My Darling
120 Comin' Through the Rye
151 The Dowie Dens of Yarrow
163 Dumbarton's Drums
187 Flow Gently, Sweet Afton
194 The Four Marys
206 Gin I Were
218 The Great Silkie
221 Green Grow the Rashes, O
239 Hieland Laddie
240 A Highland Lad My Love Was Born
249 Hurree Hurroo
255 I Know Where I'm Going
318 Loch Lomond
322 MacPherson's Farewell
346 My Bonnie Lies Over the Ocean
350 My Luve Is Like a Red Red Rose
372 Oh Rowan Tree
389 On the Banks of Allan Water
423 The Road to the Isles
446 Scots Wha Hae
461 Silkie

486 Tam Pierce
508 The Trooper and the Maid
518 Wae's Me for Prince Charlie
521 Weaving Lilt
529 Will Ye No' Come Back Again?
531 The Work of the Weavers
533 Ye Banks and Braes O' Bonnie Doon

SERBIA
116 Come, My Dearest (Pjesma)

SPAIN
231 Hear Lullabies and Sleep Now (A la Nanita Nana)
330 May Song (Canción de Maja)
514 Unto a Poor Blind Lover (A Un Niño Ciegocito)

SWEDEN
377 On a Crystal Throne (Necken's Polska)

SYRIA
463 Sleep, My Child (Aïnte)

TOBAGO
316 Little Sandy Girl
340 Miss Lilian

TRINIDAD
389 Ophelia Letter Blow 'Way
86 Brown Gal in de Ring

TURKEY
480 The Sun Hangs High (Charki Hidjaz)

UNITED STATES OF AMERICA
22 A-Hunting We Will Go
23 A-Tisket A-Tasket
24 Acres of Clams
25 Across the Fields
25 Across the Hall
30 All Quiet Along the Potomac Tonight
30 All the Pretty Little Horses
31 Aloha Oe
32 Amazing Grace
33 Animal Fair
34 Annabel Lee
35 Annie Laurie
34 Arkansas Traveler
37 At the Foot of Yonder Mountain
38 Aunt Dinah's Quilting Party
38 Aura Lee
40 Babe of Bethlehem
41 Bad Company
42 The Bad Girl
39 The Ballad of the Tea Party
46 Baltimore Fire

48	Banks of the Ohio
48	Barnyard Song (I Had a Rooster)
50	The Battle on Shiloh's Hill
51	Battleship of Maine
52	The Bear Went Over the Mountain
52	Beautiful Brown Eyes
53	Beautiful Dreamer
56	Beware, Oh, Take Care
56	The Big Corral
57	Big Road Blues
49	The Big Rock Candy Mountain
56	Bile Them Cabbage Down
58	Bill Groggin's Goat
58	Billy Barlow
59	Billy Boy
57	Billy Broke Locks
59	Billy the Kid
60	Birmingham Bull
61	Black-Eyed Susie
61	Black Is the Color of My True Love's Hair
63	Blood on the Saddle
64	Blow the Man Down
66	Blow, Ye Winds, in the Morning
68	The Blue Tail Fly (Jimmy Crack Corn)
68	Blue Mountain Lake
69	Boatman Dance
72	The Boll Weevil
77	Boothbay Whale
78	Boston Burglar
78	Boston Tea Tax Song
81	The Bowld Soger Boy
82	Bowling Green
82	The Brass Mounted Army
84	Broke and Hungry
84	Brown Eyes
87	Brown's Ferry Blues
85	Buckeye Jim
88	Buffalo Gals (Won't You Come Out Tonight)
88	The Buffalo Skinners
90	Bulldog and the Bullfrog
90	Bury Me Beneath the Willow
91	Bury Me Not on the Lone Prairie
83	Bye, Baby Bunting
93	Camptown Races
94	Canada-I-O
94	Canoe Song
95	Cape Ann
96	Cape Cod Girls
96	Captain Kidd
98	The Card Song
97	Careless Love
102	Carry Me Back to Old Virginny
99	Casey Jones
101	The Cat Came Back
104	Charles Guiteau
104	Chester

105	Chewing Gum
106	Cider Through a Straw
108	Cindy
110	Clementine
113	Cod-Liver Oil
113	Cold Water
112	Cock-A-Doodle-Doo
113	Cod-Liver Oil
113	Cold Water
114	Cole Younger
103	The Colorado Trail
115	Columbus Stockade Blues
115	Come All Ye Fair and Tender Maidens
116	Come and Go with Me
117	Come Follow
117	Come, O My Love
118	Come, Thou Fount of Every Blessing
118	Come, Ye Sinners, Poor and Needy
117	Cotton-Eyed Joe
120	Cotton Field Song
121	The Cowboy
122	The Cowboy's Dream
122	A Cowboy's Life Is a Dreary Life
124	Cradle Hymn
125	Cripple Creek
126	The Cruel War Is Raging
127	The Cruel Youth
128	Cryderville Jail
128	The Cumberland Crew
129	Cumberland Gap
131	Dance to Your Daddy
133	Danville Girl
132	Darling Nelly Gray
136	Daughter, Will You Marry?
137	Days of Forty-Nine
138	Deadheads and Suckers
139	Deep Blue Sea
139	The Deer Song
141	The Devil's Questions
141	Devilish Mary
146	Dixie
146	Do As I'm Doing
147	The Dodger Song
145	Don't I Wish I Was a Single Girl Again
148	Don't Let Your Deal Go Down
148	Don't Sing Love Songs
150	Doney Gal
153	Down in My Heart
154	Down in That Valley
154	Down in the Valley
156	Down in the Willow Garden
156	Down the River
157	The Dreary Black Hills
158	Drill, Ye Tarriers, Drill
162	The Drunkard's Doom
160	The Drunken Sailor

164	Duncan and Brady
164	Dunderbeck
166	The Dying Ranger
165	The Dying Stockman
167	E-ri-e Canal
169	East Virginia
167	Eensy, Weensy Spider
172	Eggs and Marrowbone
172	Elanoy
174	Empty Bed Blues
173	Engine 143
175	Equinoxial and Phoebe
174	The Erie Canal
176	Every Night When the Sun Goes In
178	Exultation
180	The Factory Girl
182	The Farmer in the Dell
181	The Farmer Is the Man
183	Father's Whiskers
185	Filimiooriooriay
191	Fod
192	Foggy Mountain Top
193	For Kansas
195	Four Nights Drunk
196	The Fox
197	Frankie and Johnny
195	Free Little Bird
197	Freight Train
199	Frog Went A-Courtin'
200	Fuller and Warren
201	The Gal That Got Stuck on Everything She Saw
204	Gee, Ma, I Want to Go Home
205	Get Up, Jack!
206	Git Along, Little Dogies
207	Give Me That Old Time Religion
207	Go Down, Moses
208	Go In and Out the Village
208	Go Tell Aunt Rhody
209	Go 'Way from My Window
210	Goin' Across the Mountain
212	Goin' Down to Town
210	Goin' to Germany
211	Goober Peas
213	The Good Boy
213	Good Morning, Mister Railroadman
214	Good Night Ladies
214	The Good Old Rebel
215	Goodbye, Old Paint
215	Goosey, Goosey Gander
217	Grandfather's Clock
219	The Great Speckled Bird
220	Green Corn
220	Green Gravel
220	Green Grow the Lilacs
222	Greenland Fisheries
224	The Grey Goose
222	Grizzly Bear
225	Groundhog
226	Hallelujah, I'm a Bum!
227	Hard, Ain't It Hard
227	Hard Is the Fortune of All Womankind (The Wagoner's Lad)
228	Hard Luck
230	Haul Away, Joe
235	He Paid a Debt
235	He's Gone Away
236	Heave Away
238	The Hell-Bound Train
239	High Barbaree
242	Hinky Dinky Parley Voo
243	Home in That Rock
242	Home on the Range
243	Home Sweet Home
241	The Honest Ploughman
244	Hoosen Johnny
245	A Horse Named Bill
247	House of the Rising Sun
248	The Housewife's Lament
247	How Can I Keep from Singing?
250	How Firm a Foundation
250	How Old Are You, My Pretty Little Miss?
251	Hudson River Steamboat
252	The Hunters of Kentucky
252	Hurry Up, Liza Jane
253	Hush, Little Baby
254	I Can't Feel at Home in This World Anymore
254	I Don't Want to Get Adjusted
254	I Gave My Love a Cherry (The Riddle Song)
256	I Ride an Old Paint
256	I Shall Not Be Moved
258	I Walk the Road Again
259	I Wish I Was a Mole
259	I Wish I Was Single Again
260	I'd Like to Be in Texas
260	I'm a Roaring Repeater
263	I'm Sad and I'm Lonely
262	I've Been Working on the Railroad
264	I've Got No Use for Women
265	I've Got Peace Like a River
266	If He'd Be a Buckaroo
267	If You're Happy and You Know It
268	In Good Old Colony Times
269	In the Good Old Summertime
270	In the Pines
270	In the Shade of the Old Apple Tree
270	The Intoxicated Rat
272	Irish Astronomy
275	Jackson
276	The Jam on Gerry's Rocks
280	Jay Gould's Daughter
277	Jeanie with the Light Brown Hair
278	Jefferson and Liberty

280	Jenny Jenkins
278	Jesse James
279	Jesus Born in Beth'ny
281	Jesus Loves Me
282	Jesus, the Christ, Is Born
283	Jim Fisk
284	Joe Bowers
282	John Brown's Body
285	John Hardy
286	John Henry
283	John Jacob Jingleheimer Schmidt
288	John Riley (II)
284	Johnny Has Gone for a Soldier
289	Johnson Boys
290	Jordan Ain't a Hard Road to Travel
291	The Juniper Tree
293	Just a Closer Walk with Thee
292	Just Before the Battle, Mother
294	Katy Cline
294	Katy Cruel
296	Kentucky Babe
298	Kitty Alone and I (I)
298	Kitty Alone and I (II)
301	Lady Gay
304	The Last Request
301	Lavender's Blue
301	Leatherwing Bat
308	Li'l Liza Jane
308	Life's Railway to Heaven
306	Likes Likker Better Than Me
307	Lily of the West
311	Listen to the Mockingbird
309	Little Annie Rooney
312	Little Brown Dog
312	Little Brown Jug
314	Little Joe, The Wrangler
311	Little Maggie
314	Little Mohee
316	Little Old Sod Shanty on My Claim
313	The Little Orphan Girl
315	Liza Jane
320	Lonesome Valley
319	Looby Loo
320	Look Down That Lonesome Road
324	Make Me a Bed on the Floor
325	Mama Don't 'Low
325	Mama, Have You Heard the News
325	Man Goin' Round
326	The Man on the Flying Trapeze
327	A Man Without a Woman
328	Marching Through Georgia
331	Merrily We Roll Along
336	Michael Finnegan
333	Michael Row the Boat Ashore
338	Midnight Special
338	Mighty Day
342	Mister Rabbit
335	Molly Bann
343	More Pretty Girls Than One
344	Mountain Dew
341	The Muffin Man
348	The Mulberry Bush
347	Must I Go Bound?
348	My Dame Had a Lame Tame Crane
349	My Days Have Been So Wondrous Free
349	My Heart's Tonight in Texas
350	My Home's Across the Smoky Mountains
352	My Love Is a Rider
352	My Mother Chose My Husband
351	My Mother's Old Red Shawl
353	My Old Hen
347	My Old Kentucky Home
351	My Sweetheart's a Mule
357	Nelly Was a Lady
358	New River Train
357	New York Girls (Can't You Dance the Polka?)
359	Night Herding Song
360	Nine Hundred Miles
361	Nine Pound Hammer
359	No Hiding Place
361	No More Booze
365	O How I Love Jesus
368	Oats, Peas, Beans and Barley Grow
368	Oh, Daddy Be Gay
369	Oh Dear! What Can the Matter Be?
370	Oh How Lovely Is the Evening
370	Oh Mary, Don't You Weep
369	Oh! Susanna
371	Oh, Them Golden Slippers
373	Oh Where, Oh Where Has My Little Dog Gone
375	Old Aunt Kate
376	Old Black Joe
375	Old Blue
376	The Old Chisholm Trail
376	The Old Cow Died
378	Old Dan Tucker
378	Old Dog Tray
379	Old Folks at Home
380	The Old Gospel Ship
379	The Old Gray Mare
380	Old Joe Clark
381	Old MacDonald Had a Farm
382	Old Oaken Bucket
383	Old Rattler
384	Old Soldiers Never Die
384	The Old Woman Who Went to Market
385	The Ole Grey Goose
386	Omie Wise
383	On a Monday
386	On Jordan's Stormy Banks
390	On Top of Old Smoky
387	Once I Had a Sweetheart

391	One More River
393	One Morning in May
394	Otto Wood
394	Over the River and Through the Woods
396	The Ox-Driving Song
397	Paper of Pins
397	The Paw Paw Patch
399	Peanut Sat on a Railroad Track
400	Po' Boy
400	Polly, Put the Kettle On
400	Polly Wolly Doodle
402	Poor Boy
402	Poor Lazarus
403	Poor Lonesome Cowboy
404	Pop Goes the Weasel
405	Pretty Little Girl with the Red Dress On
403	Pretty Polly
405	Pretty Saro
406	Prison Bound
406	A Prisoner for Life
407	Putting on the Style
409	Railroad Bill
409	A Railroader for Me
411	Rambling Blues
412	The Rebel Soldier
413	Red Apple Juice
413	Red Iron Ore
414	The Red Light Saloon
414	Red River Valley
415	The Regular Army, Oh!
408	Reuben and Rachel
416	Reuben's Train
416	Revolutionary Tea
418	Richmond Is a Hard Road to Travel
415	Riding in a Buggy
420	The Rifle
417	Rig-A-Jig Jig
421	Rise and Shine
419	Rise Up, Shepherd, and Follow
422	The River in the Pines
424	Robin Redbreast
425	Rock-A-Bye, Baby
425	Rock About My Saro Jane
426	The Rock Island Line
427	Rocks and Gravel
427	Roll, Alabama, Roll
428	Roll Down the Line
428	Roll in My Sweet Baby's Arms
429	Roll on the Ground
429	Roll Over
431	Rosewood Casket
433	The Roving Gambler
434	Row, Row, Row Your Boat
434	Run, Children, Run
435	Russian Lullaby
435	Rye Whiskey
437	Sail Away, Ladies
436	Sailing in the Boat
436	Sailing, Sailing
437	Sailor on the Deep Blue Sea
438	St. James Infirmary
439	Sal Got a Meatskin
439	Sally Ann
440	Sally Goodin
442	Salty Dog
443	Sam Bass
442	Samson
445	School Days
447	Seeing Nellie Home
450	Shady Grove
449	Shall We Gather at the River?
449	The Shanty-Man's Life
448	Shake That Little Foot
452	She Wore a Yellow Ribbon
452	She'll Be Comin' 'Round the Mountain
453	Shenandoah
454	The Ship That Never Returned
454	Shoo Fly, Don't Bother Me
456	Shoot the Buffalo
458	Short'nin' Bread
459	Shuckin' of the Corn
460	Simple Gifts
459	Single Girl
457	The Sioux Indians
462	Six Questions
461	Skillet Good and Greasy
463	Skip to My Lou
465	Sleep, Baby, Sleep
466	Snake Baked a Hoecake
465	So Early in the Morning
466	Soldier Boy
466	Soldier, Soldier, Will You Marry Me?
471	Sourwood Mountain
474	The Sow Took the Measles
472	The Sporting Bachelors
469	Springfield Mountain
472	Star in the East
474	Starving to Death on My Government Claim
475	The State of Arkansas
478	Stir the Pudding
476	The Strawberry Roan
478	The Streets of Glory
477	The Streets of Laredo
479	Sugar Baby
480	Sun Don't Set in the Mornin'
484	Swannanoa Tunnel
481	Sweet and Low
481	Sweet Betsy from Pike
482	Sweet Rosie O'Grady
482	Swing a Lady
483	Swing and Turn, Jubilee
485	Take Me Out to the Ball Game

486 Take This Hammer
489 Tell Me Why
487 Ten Little Indians
490 Ten Thousand Cattle
489 Tenting Tonight
491 The Texas Rangers
490 The Tex-i-an Boys
492 That Crazy War
493 There Was an Old Soldier
494 There's a Hole in the Bottom of the Sea
495 There's a Hole in the Bucket
495 There's a Little Wheel A-Turning in My Heart
497 This Train
500 Timber (Jerry the Mule)
500 Times A-Getting Hard, Boys
502 The Titanic
502 Tobacco Union
504 Told My Captain
503 Tom Cat Blues
504 Tom Dooley
499 The Trail to Mexico
505 Tramp! Tramp! Tramp!
506 Trav'lin' Man
508 Turkey in the Straw
510 Turkey Song
510 The Turtle Dove
510 Twelve Gates to the City
513 Tyin' a Knot in the Devil's Tail
511 The Utah Iron Horse
516 Vicksburg Blues
516 The Wabash Cannon Ball
519 Wanderin'
520 Wayfaring Stranger
524 When Adam Was Created
524 When I Can Read My Title Clear
525 When Johnny Comes Marching Home
526 When the Saints Go Marching In
525 Whiskey Johnny!
526 Whistle, Daughter, Whistle
522 White Coral Bells
527 Will the Circle Be Unbroken
530 Willie Moore
528 Willie the Weeper
529 Wondrous Love
531 Worried Man Blues
532 Wrap Me Up in My Tarpaulin Jacket
532 Yankee Doodle
534 Ye Parliaments of England
533 The Yellow Rose of Texas
534 Yonder Stands a Handsome Lady
535 The Young Man Who Wouldn't Hoe Corn
534 Zacchaeus

VENEZUELA
209 Go to Sleep My Little Baby
       (Duérmete Niño Chiquito)

WALES
33   All Through the Night
36   The Ash Grove (Llwyn On)
120 Cosher Bailey's Engine
251 Hunting the Hare (Hela'r 'Sgyvarnog)
317 The Little Saucepan (Sospan Vach)
333 Men of Harlech (Rhyfelgyrch Gwyr Harlech)

WEST INDIES
332 Matilda

A-HUNTING WE WILL GO

Early American Game Song

A - hunt - ing we will go! A - hunt - ing we will

go! We'll catch a fox and put him in a box! A - hunt - ing we will go!

goat
cat   *boat*
             hat

A-ROVING

18th Century Sea Chantey

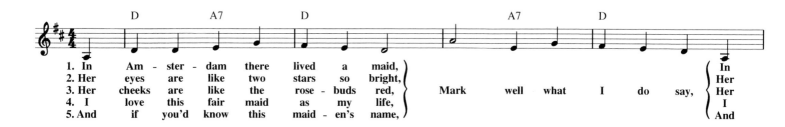

1. In Am - ster - dam there lived a maid,
2. Her eyes are like two stars so bright,
3. Her cheeks are like the rose - buds red,
4. I love this fair maid as my life,
5. And if you'd know this maid - en's name,
Mark well what I do say,
{ In
Her
Her
I
And

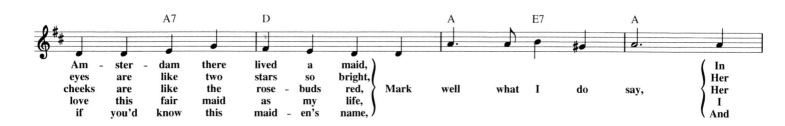

Am - ster - dam there lived a maid,
eyes are like two stars so bright,
cheeks are like the rose - buds red,
love this fair maid as my life,
if you'd know this maid - en's name,
Mark well what I do say,
{ In
Her
Her
I
And

Am - ster - dam there lived a maid, And she was mis - tress of her trade;
eyes are like two stars so bright, Her face is fair, her step is light;
cheeks are like the rose - buds red, There's wealth of hair up - on her head;
love this fair maid as my life, And soon she'll be my lit - tle wife;
if you'd know this maid - en's name, Why soon like mine 'twill be the same;
{ I'll

go no more a - rov - ing with you, fair maid, A - rov - ing, a - rov - ing, Since

rov - ing's been my ru - in, I'll go no more a - rov - ing with you, fair maid.

A-TISKET A-TASKET

Early American Game Song

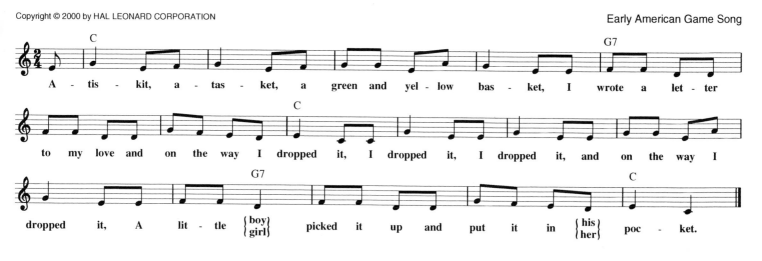

A - tis - kit, a - tas - ket, a green and yel - low bas - ket, I wrote a let - ter
to my love and on the way I dropped it, I dropped it, I dropped it, and on the way I
dropped it, A lit - tle {boy}{girl} picked it up and put it in {his}{her} poc - ket.

ABDUL ABULBUL AMIR

Words and Music by
William Percy French
1877

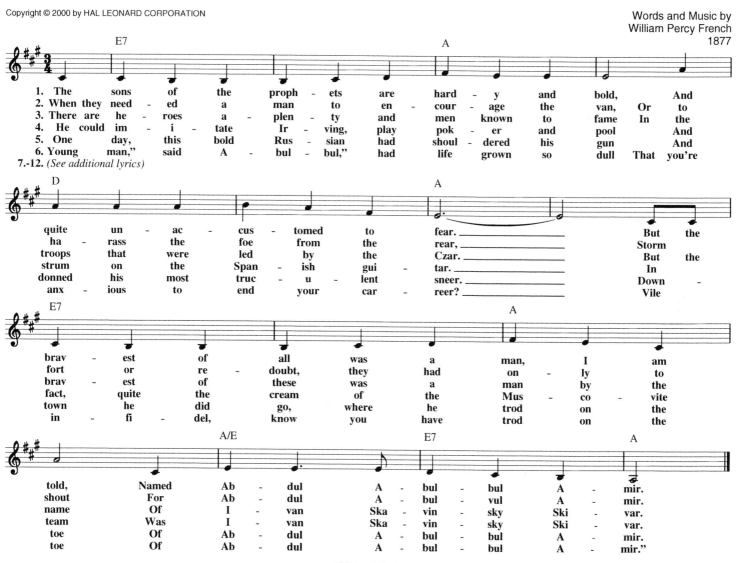

1. The sons of the proph - ets are hard - y and bold, And
2. When they need - ed a man to en - cour - age the van, Or
3. There are he - roes a - plen - ty and men known to fame In
4. He could im - i - tate Ir - ving, play pok - er and pool And
5. One day, this bold Rus - sian had shoul - dered his gun And
6. Young man," said A - bul - bul," had life grown so dull That you're

7.-12. *(See additional lyrics)*

quite un - ac - cus - tomed to fear. But the
ha - rass the foe from the rear, Storm
troops that were led by the Czar. But the
strum on the Span - ish gui - tar. In
donned his most truc - u - lent sneer. Down -
anx - ious to end your car - reer? Vile

brav - est of all was a man, I am
fort or re - doubt, they had on - ly to
brav - est of these was a man by the
fact, quite the cream of the Mus - co - vite
town he did go, where he trod on the
in - fi - del, know you have trod on the

told, Named Ab - dul A - bul - bul A - mir.
shout For Ab - dul A - bul - vul A - mir.
name Of I - van Ska - vin - sky Ski - var.
team Was I - van Ska - vin - sky Ski - var.
toe Of Ab - dul A - bul - bul A - mir.
toe Of Ab - dul A - bul - bul A - mir."

Additional Lyrics

7. Quoth Ivan, "My friend, your remarks, in the end,
Will avail you but little, I fear,
For you ne'er will survive to repeat them alive,
Mr. Abdul Abulbul Amir!"

8. They fought all that night, 'neath the pale yellow moon;
The din, it was heard from afar;
And great multitudes came, so great was the fame
of Abdul and Ivan Skivar.

9. As Abdul's long knife was extracting the life -
In fact, he was shouting "Huzzah!"
He felt himself struck by that wily Kalmuck,
Count Ivan Skavinsky Skivar.

10. The sultan drove by in his red-breasted fly,
Expecting the victor to cheer;
But he only drew nigh to hear the last sigh
Of Abdul Abulbul Amir.

11. There's a tomb rises up where the blue Danube flows;
Engraved there in characters clear;
"Ah stranger, when passing, please pray for the soul
Of Abdul Abulbul Amir."

12. A Muscovite maiden her lone vigil keeps,
'Neath the light of the pale polar star;
And the name that she murmurs as oft as she weeps
Is Ivan Skavinsky Skivar.

ACH DU LIEBER AUGUSTIN
(O My Dearest Augustine)

18th Century German

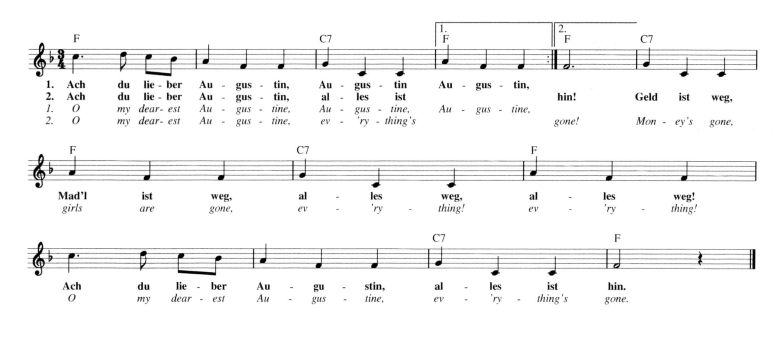

1. Ach du lie-ber Au - gus - tin, Au - gus - tin Au - gus - tin,
2. Ach du lie-ber Au - gus - tin, al - les ist hin! Geld ist weg,
1. O my dear-est Au - gus - tine, Au - gus - tine, Au - gus - tine,
2. O my dear-est Au - gus - tine, ev - 'ry - thing's gone! Mon - ey's gone,

Mad'l ist weg, al - les weg, al - les weg!
girls are gone, ev - 'ry - thing! ev - 'ry - thing!

Ach du lie - ber Au - gu - stin, al - les ist hin.
O my dear - est Au - gus - tine, ev - 'ry - thing's gone.

ACRES OF CLAMS

19th Century American

1. I've wan - der'd all o - ver this coun - try, _____ Pros -
2. For one who gets wealth - y by min - ing _____ I
3. No long - er the slave of am - bi - tion, _____ No
4. The time that you know you have am - ple, _____ That's

pect - ing and dig - ging for gold. _____ I've tun - nelled, hy -
know man - y hun - dred get poor. _____ I made up my
lead - er just one of the lambs, _____ I sing of my
when ev - 'ry care quick - ly scrams, _____ Take heart in my

drau - licked and cra - dled, And near - ly was froze in the
mind to go dig - ging For some - thing a lit - tle more
hap - py con - di - tion Sur - round - ed by a - cres of
fate for ex - am - ple, Con - tent on my a - cres of

cold. _____
sure. _____
clams. _____ And so I de - part - ed for Pu - get Sound, A -
clams. _____

way from a world full of shams, _____ I sing of my

hap - py con - di - tion, Sur - round - ed by a - cres of clams. _____

ACROSS THE FIELDS

19th Century American Round

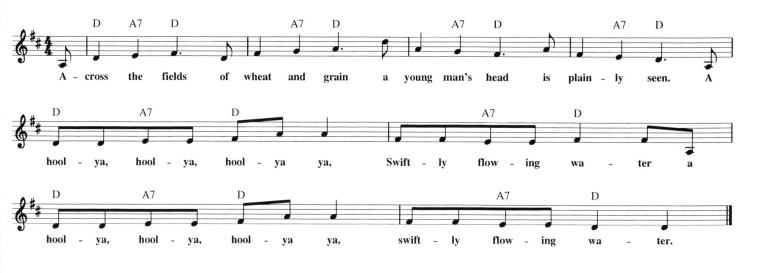

A - cross the fields of wheat and grain a young man's head is plain - ly seen. A

hool - ya, hool - ya, hool - ya ya, Swift - ly flow - ing wa - ter a

hool - ya, hool - ya, hool - ya ya, swift - ly flow - ing wa - ter.

ACROSS THE HALL

Children's Song from Tennessee

1. First } old gent a - cross the hall _____ swing her by the right hand. Swing
2. Next }

all your part - ners by the left, and prom - 'nade _ girl be - hind you.

Oh the girl, that pret - ty lit - tle girl, the girl I left be - hind me; I

wept and cried the day I died for the girl I _____ left be - hind me.

ACROSS THE WESTERN OCEAN

Irish Sea Chantey

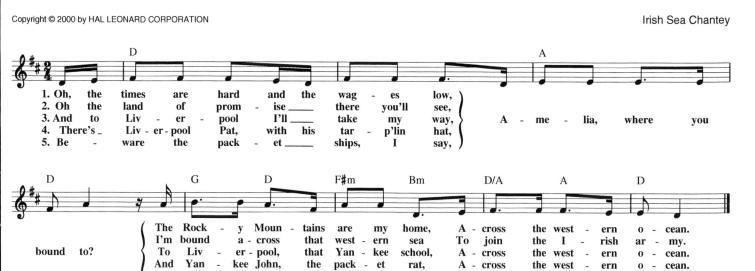

1. Oh, the times are hard and the wag - es low,
2. Oh the land of prom - ise _____ there you'll see,
3. And to Liv - er - pool I'll _____ take my way,   A - me - lia, where you
4. There's _ Liv - er - pool Pat, with his tar - p'lin hat,
5. Be - ware the pack - et _____ ships, I say,

bound to?   The Rock - y Moun - tains are my home,   A - cross the west - ern o - cean.
          I'm bound a - cross that west - ern sea   To join the I - rish ar - my.
          To Liv - er - pool, that Yan - kee school,   A - cross the west - ern o - cean.
          And Yan - kee John, the pack - et rat,   A - cross the west - ern o - cean.
          They steal your stores and clothes a - way,   A - cross the west - ern o - cean.

ADAM IN THE GARDEN PINNIN' LEAVES

African-American Spiritual

Oh Eve, _ where's Ad-am? Oh Eve, _ where's Ad-am? Oh Eve, _ where's Ad-am?

Ad-am in the gar-den, pin-nin' leaves. _

1. Well I know my God is a
2. Well the first time God called,
3. And the next time God called,

man of war.
Ad-am re-fused to an-swer. } Ad-am in the gar-den, pin-nin' leaves. _
God called loud-er.

He
The
The

fought the bat-tle at the Jer-i-cho wall.
first time God called, Ad-am re-fused to an-swer. } Ad-am in the gar-den,
next time God called, God called loud-er.

1-3
pin-nin' leaves. _

4
pin-nin' leaves. _ Oh Eve, _ where's Ad-am? Oh Eve, _

where's Ad-am? Oh Eve, _ where's Ad-am? Ad-am in the gar-den, pin-nin' leaves. _

AH, POOR BIRD

18th Century English Round

Ah, poor bird, take your flight far a-bove the sor-rows of this sad night.

AIN'T NO MORE CANE ON THE BRAZIS

Prison Work Song from Mexico

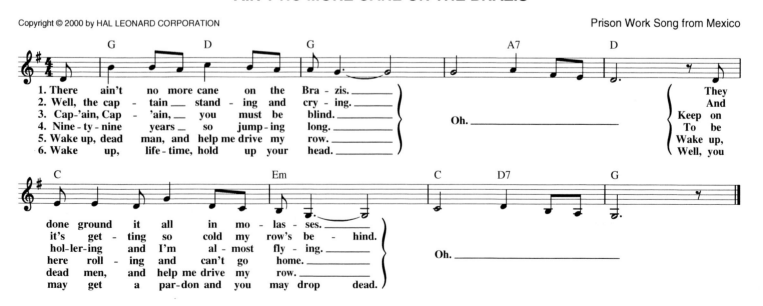

1. There ain't no more cane on the Bra-zis. _____
2. Well, the cap-tain stand-ing and cry-ing. _____
3. Cap-'ain, Cap-'ain, _ you must be blind. _____
4. Nine-ty-nine years _ so jump-ing long. _____
5. Wake up, dead man, and help me drive my row. _____
6. Wake up, life-time, hold up your head. _____

Oh. _____

They
And
Keep on
To be
Wake up,
Well, you

done ground it all in mo-las-ses.
it's get-ting so cold my row's be-hind.
hol-ler-ing and I'm al-most fly-ing. _____
here roll-ing and can't go home. _____
dead men, and help me drive my row.
may get a par-don and you may drop dead.

Oh. _____

ALL DAY LONG

African-American Spiritual

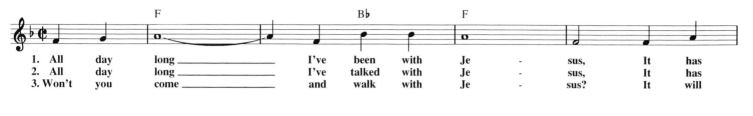

1. All   day   long _____ I've been with Je - sus, It has
2. All   day   long _____ I've talked with Je - sus, It has
3. Won't you come _____ and walk with Je - sus? It will

been _____ a glo - rious day. _____ I've just moved _____ up one step
been _____ a glo - rious day. _____ It just moved _____ me one step
be _____ a glo - rious day. _____ You can leave _____ your sin and

high - er, And I'm walk - ing on the King's high - way. _____
high - er, On my walk a - long the King's high - way. _____
sor - row, You can walk up - on the King's high - way. _____

ALL GOD'S CHILDREN GOT SHOES

African-American Spiritual

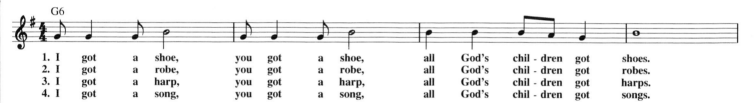

1. I got a shoe, you got a shoe, all God's chil - dren got shoes.
2. I got a robe, you got a robe, all God's chil - dren got robes.
3. I got a harp, you got a harp, all God's chil - dren got harps.
4. I got a song, you got a song, all God's chil - dren got songs.

When I get to heav - en gon - na put on my shoes, I'm gon - na tromp)
When I get to heav - en gon - na put on my robe, I'm gon - na shout } all o - ver God's
When I get to heav - en gon - na play on my harp, I'm gon - na play
When I get to heav - en gon - na sing out my song, I'm gon - na sing)

heav - en, _____ heav - en, _____ heav - en. _____

Ev - 'ry - bod - y talk - in' 'bout heav - en ain't a - go - in' there, Heav - en, _____

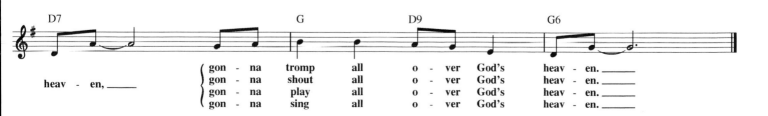

heav - en, _____   gon - na tromp all o - ver God's heav - en. _____
                    gon - na shout all o - ver God's heav - en. _____
                    gon - na play all o - ver God's heav - en. _____
                    gon - na sing all o - ver God's heav - en. _____

ALL MY TRIALS

African-American Spiritual

1. If re - li - gion was a thing that mon - ey could buy, _____ the
2. Go to sleep, my lit - tle ba - by, and don't you cry, _____ your
3. Oh I have a lit - tle book that sets me free, _____ my
4. Yes, a man was born to suf - fer ag - o - ny, _____ his

rich would live _____ and the poor would die. _____
dad was born _____ just to live and die. _____
Bi - ble, _____ it spells "Li - ber - ty." _____
will to live _____ spells "Vic - to - ry." _____

All _____ my

tri - als, Lord, _____ will soon _____ be o - ver. ___ Too late my

broth - ers, _____ too late, but nev - er mind. _____ All _____ my

tri - als, Lord, _____ will soon _____ be o - ver. _____

ALL NIGHT, ALL DAY

African-American Spiritual

1. Day is dy - in' in _____ the west, An - gels watch-in' o - ver me, my Lord. __
2. Now I lay me down __ to sleep, An - gels watch-in' o - ver me, my Lord. __
3. Thy love stay with me through _ the night, An - gels watch-in' o - ver me, my Lord. __ And

Sleep, my child, and take __ your rest, An - gels watch - in' o - ver me.
Pray the Lord my soul __ to keep, An - gels watch - in' o - ver me.
wake me with the morn - ing light, An - gels watch - in' o - ver me.

All _____ night, all _____ day, An - gels watch - in' o - ver me, my Lord. __

All _____ night, all _____ day, An - gels watch - in' o - ver me.

ALL NIGHT LONG

19th Century African-American Spiritual

ALL OVER THIS WORLD

African-American Spiritual

ALL QUIET ALONG THE POTOMAC TONIGHT

Words by Ethel Lynn Beers
Music by John H. Hewitt
1863

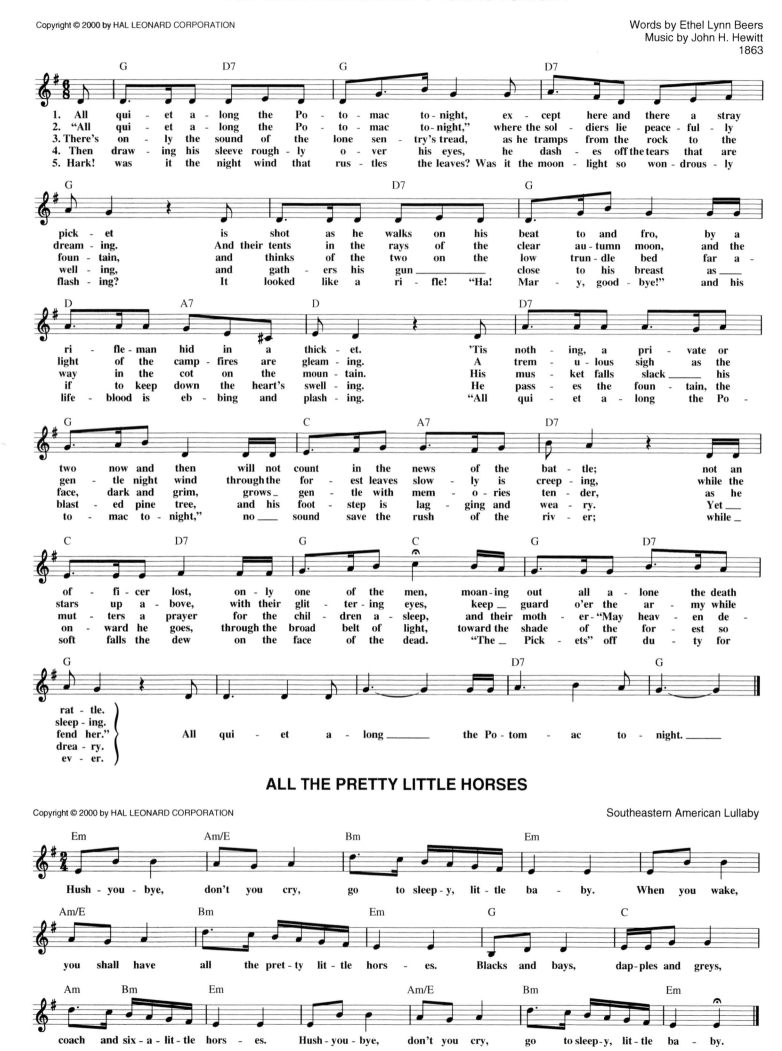

ALL THE PRETTY LITTLE HORSES

Southeastern American Lullaby

ALOHA OE

Hawaiian
Words and Music attributed to Queen Liliuokalani

ALOUETTE

French-Canadian Game Song

AMAZING GRACE

American
Music from Carrell and Clayton's *Virginia Harmony*
Words by John Newton v. 1-4
v. 5 from *A Collection of Sacred Ballads*, 1790

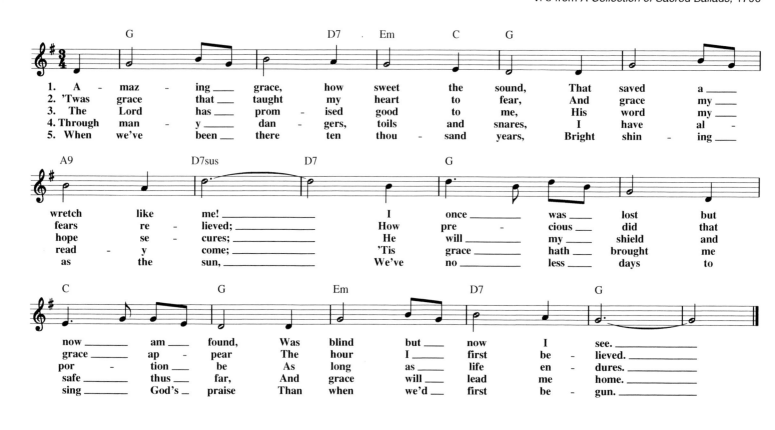

1. A - maz - ing ____ grace, how sweet the sound, That saved a ____
2. 'Twas grace that ____ taught my heart to fear, And grace my ____
3. The Lord has ____ prom - ised good to me, His word my ____
4. Through man - y ____ dan - gers, toils and snares, I have al -
5. When we've been ____ there ten thou - sand years, Bright shin - ing ____

wretch like me! _____ I once _____ was ____ lost but ____
fears re - lieved; _____ How pre - cious ____ did that
hope se - cures; _____ He will _____ my ____ shield and
read - y come; _____ 'Tis grace _____ hath ____ brought me
as the sun, _____ We've no _____ less ____ days to

now _____ am ____ found, Was blind but ____ now I see. _____
grace _____ ap - pear The hour I ____ first be - lieved. _____
por - tion ____ be As long as ____ life en - dures. _____
safe _____ thus ____ far, And grace will ____ lead me home. _____
sing _____ God's ____ praise Than when we'd ____ first be - gun. _____

ANGEL BAND

African-American Spiritual

1. My eve - ning sun is sink - ing fast, My race ____ is al - most
2. I know I'm join - ing ho - ly ranks Of friends ____ and loved ____ ones

run. _____ My strong - est tri - als now are past, My
dear. _____ I brushed the dew on Jor - dan's banks, I

tri - umph is ____ be - gun. _____ Oh, come, ____
know ____ the cross - ing's near. _____

an - gel band. Come, and ____ a - round me stand. Oh bear me a -

way on your snow white wings To my im - mor - tal home. _____ Oh

bear me a - way on your snow white wings To my im - mor - tal home.

ALL THROUGH THE NIGHT

Welsh Lullaby

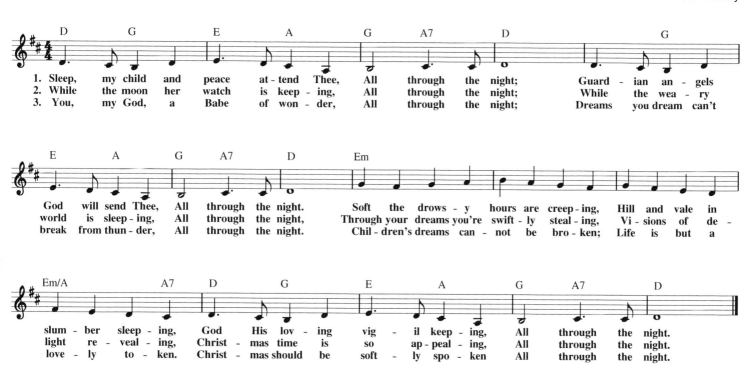

1. Sleep, my child and peace at-tend Thee, All through the night; Guard - ian an - gels
2. While the moon her watch is keep - ing, All through the night; While the wea - ry
3. You, my God, a Babe of won - der, All through the night; Dreams you dream can't

God will send Thee, All through the night. Soft the drows - y hours are creep-ing, Hill and vale in
world is sleep-ing, All through the night, Through your dreams you're swift - ly steal - ing, Vi - sions of de -
break from thun - der, All through the night. Chil - dren's dreams can - not be bro - ken; Life is but a

slum - ber sleep - ing, God His lov - ing vig - il keep - ing, All through the night.
light re - veal - ing, Christ - mas time is so ap - peal - ing, All through the night.
love - ly to - ken. Christ - mas should be soft - ly spo - ken All through the night.

ANIMAL FAIR

American Children's Song

I went to the an - i - mal fair, _____ The birds and beasts were

there, _____ The big ba - boon, by the light of the moon Was

comb - ing his au - burn hair. _____ The mon - key, he got

drunk, _____ And sat on the el - e - phant's trunk, _____ The

el - e - phant sneezed, And fell on his knees, And

what be - came of the monk, the monk, the monk, the monk?

ANNABEL LEE

American
Based on the 1849 poem by
Edgar Allan Poe

1. It was man—y and man—y a year a—go, In a king—dom __
   I was a child and __ she was a child, In this king—dom __
   this is the rea—son that long, long a—go, In this king—dom __
   love, it was strong—er by far than the love of the ones who were
   moon nev—er beams with—out bring—ing me dreams In this king—dom __

by the __ sea, __ That a maid—en there lived whom you may know by
by the __ sea, __ But we loved with a love that was great—er than
by the __ sea, __ There a—rose a strong wind blow—ing out of a
old—er than we, __ Of the man—y far old—er and wis—er than
by the __ sea, __ And the stars nev—er rise but I feel the bright

name, by the name of __ An—na—bel Lee. __ And this maid—en
love, So loved I and my An—na—bel Lee. __ With a love so
cloud, Chilled and killed my dear An—na—bel Lee. __ And her high—born
we, Of those old—er and wis—er than we. __ Ah but neith—er
eyes Of the beau—ti—ful An—na—bel Lee. __ Thru the night I

lived with no oth—er thought __ Than to love and be loved by
strong that the an—gels watched, __ E—ven cov—et—ed her and
kins—men, they quick—ly came, __ And they bore her a—way from
an—gel in sky a—bove, __ Nor the de—mons be—neath the
lie by my dear—est one, __ By the side of my bride to

me. __ Oh this maid—en she lived with no oth—er __ thought Than to
me. __ With a love so __ strong that the an—gels __ watched, E—ven
me. __ And they sealed her re—mains in a se—pul—cher deep, In this
sea, __ Could __ sev—er my soul from the soul of my love Of my
be, __ Though she lies in her se—pul—cher si—lent and cold Oh my

1-4
love and be loved by me! __ 2. For __
cov—et—ed her and me! __ 3. And __
king—dom __ be the sea! __ 4. But our
beau—ti—ful Ann'—bel Lee! __ 5. And the
beau—ti—ful

5
An—na—bel Lee! __

ARKANSAS TRAVELER

Southern American

ANNIE LAURIE

Words and Music by William Douglas
and Lady John Douglas Scott
1685

1. Max - wel - ton's braes are bon - nie, Where ear - ly fa's the ____ dew. And it's there that An - nie Lau - rie Gave me her prom - ise true,
2. Her ____ brow is like the snaw - drift, Her neck is like the ____ swan. Her ____ face it is the fair - est That e'er the sun shone on,
3. Like ____ dew on the gow - an ly - ing Is the fa' o' her fair - y feet. And like winds in sum - mer sigh - ing, Her voice is low an'

Gave me her prom - ise true, Which ne'er for - got will be.
That e'er the sun shone on, An' dark blue is her e'e.
Her voice is low an' sweet, An' she's a' the world to me.

And for bon - nie An - nie ____ Lau - rie ____ I'd ____ lay ____ me doon and die.

ARE YOU SLEEPING?
(Frère Jacques)

French

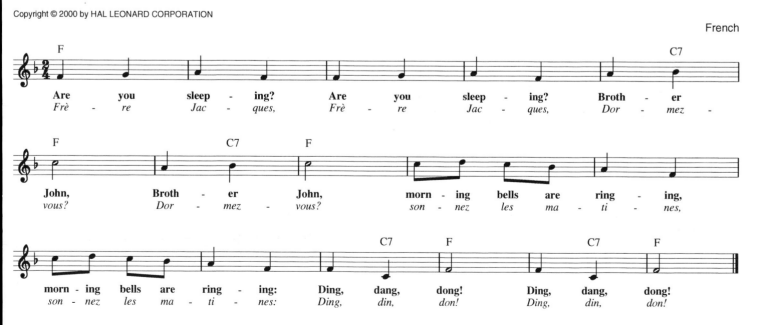

Are you sleep - ing? Are you sleep - ing? Broth - er
Frè - re Jac - ques, Frè - re Jac - ques, Dor - mez -

John, Broth - er John, morn - ing bells are ring - ing,
vous? Dor - mez vous? son - nez les ma - ti - nes,

morn - ing bells are ring - ing: Ding, dang, dong! Ding, dang, dong!
son - nez les ma - ti - nes: Ding, din, don! Ding, din, don!

AS I ROVED OUT

19th Century Irish Ballad

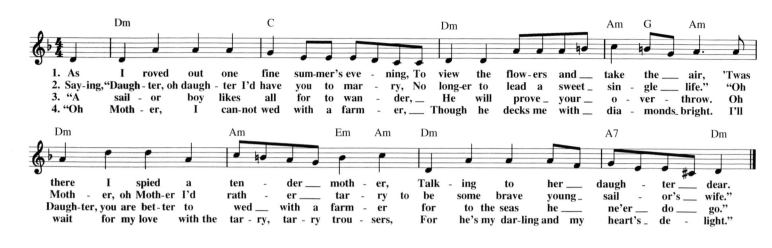

1. As I roved out one fine sum-mer's eve - ning, To view the flow-ers and __ take the __ air, 'Twas
2. Say-ing,"Daugh - ter, oh daugh - ter I'd have you to mar - ry, No long-er to lead a sweet __ sin - gle __ life." "Oh
3. "A sail - or boy likes all for to wan - der, __ He will prove __ your o - ver - throw. Oh
4. "Oh Moth - er, I can-not wed with a farm - er, __ Though he decks me with __ dia - monds_ bright. I'll

there I spied a ten - der __ moth - er, Talk - ing to her __ daugh - ter __ dear.
Moth - er, oh Moth-er I'd rath - er __ tar - ry to be some brave young_ sail - or's __ wife."
Daugh-ter, you are bet-ter to wed __ with a farm - er for to the seas he __ ne'er __ do __ go."
wait for my love with the tar - ry, tar - ry trou - sers, For he's my dar-ling and my heart's_ de - light."

AS I WAS GOING TO BALLYNURE

17th Century Irish Ballad

1. As I was go - in' to Bal - ly - nure, The day I well _____ re -
2. As I was go - in' a - long the road, When home - ward I _____ was
3. Said the wee lad to the wee _____ lass, "It's will ye let _____ me
4. This cor - dial that __ ye talk a - bout, There's ver - y few _____ that

mem - ber, _____ For to view the lads and lass - es On _____ the
walk - ing, _____ I heard a wee lad be - hind a ditch To his
kiss ye _____ For it's I have got the cor - dial eye _____ That
gets it, _____ For there's noth - in' now but crook - ed crumbs __ And

fifth day of No - vem - ber, } With a ma - ring - doo - a -
wee lass he was talk - ing, }
far ex - ceeds the whis - key, }
mus - lin gowns can catch it, }

day, With a ma - ring a - doo - a - dad - dy - o. _____

THE ASH GROVE
(Llwyn On)

Welsh

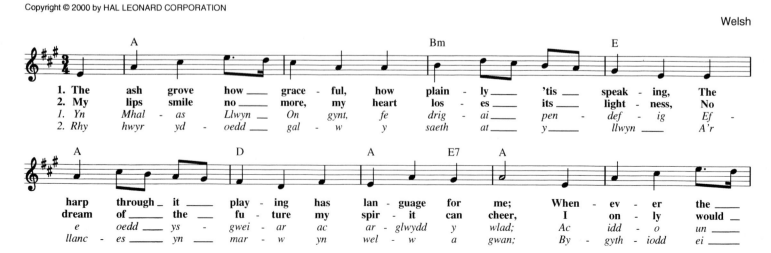

1. The ash grove how __ grace - ful, how plain - ly __ 'tis __ speak - ing, The
2. My lips smile no __ more, my heart los - es __ its __ light - ness, No
1. *Yn Mhal - as Llwyn __ On gynt, fe drig - ai __ pen - def - ig Ef -*
2. *Rhy hwyr yd - oedd __ gal - w y saeth at __ y __ llwyn __ A'r*

harp through __ it __ play - ing has lan - guage for me; When - ev - er the __
dream of __ the __ fu - ture my spir - it can cheer, I on - ly would __
e oedd __ ys - gwei - ar ac ar - glwydd y wlad; Ac idd - o un __
llanc - es __ yn __ mar - w yn wel - w a gwan; By - gyth - iodd ei __

light through its branch - es ___ is ___ break - ing, A host of ___ kind ___ fa - ces is
brood on the past and ___ its ___ bright - ness, The dead I ___ have ___ mourn'd are a -
en - eth a an - wyd ___ yn ___ un - ig A hi' nol ___ yr ___ han - es oedd
gledd - yf trwy gal - on ___ y ___ llenc - yn; Ond ni red - ai ___ Car - iad un

gaz - ing on me. The friends of my child ___ hood a - gain are be -
gain liv - ing here. From ev' - ry dark nook they press for - ward to
aer - es ei thad. Aeth Car - iad i'w gwel - ed, yn lân a phur
fod - fedd o'r fan. 'Roedd Gol - ud, ei "dar - par" yn hên ac an -

fore me, Each step wakes a mem - 'ry, as free - ly I roam, With
meet me, I lift up my eyes to the broad leaf - y dome, And
lenc - yn, Ond cod - ai'r ys gwei - ar yn af - ar ac erch, I
yn - ad, A geir - iau di - wedd - af yr Aer - es hardd hon, Oedd,

soft whis - pers ___ la - den, its leaves rus - tle ___ o'er me, The
oth - ers are ___ there look - ing down - ward ___ to ___ greet me, The
saeth - u'r bach - gen - yn, ond gwŷr - odd ___ ei ___ lin - yn, A'i
"gwell gen - yf ___ far - w trwy Er - gyd ___ fy Nghar - iad, Na

ash grove, ___ the ___ ash grove a - lone is my home.
ash grove, ___ the ___ ash grove a - lone is my home.
er - gyd ___ yn ___ wyr - gam i fyn - wes ei ferch.
byw gyd - a ___ Gol - ud yn Mhal - as Llwyn On."

AT THE FOOT OF YONDER MOUNTAIN

Copyright © 2000 by HAL LEONARD CORPORATION

Southern American

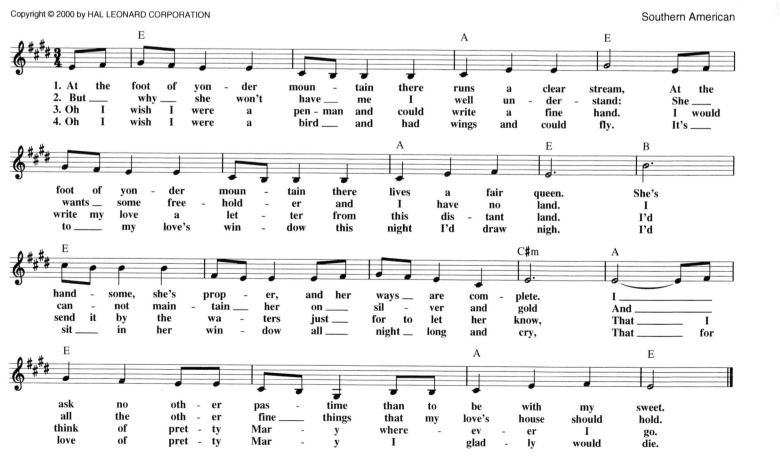

1. At the foot of yon - der moun - tain there runs a clear stream, At the
2. But ___ why ___ she won't have ___ me I well un - der - stand: She ___
3. Oh I wish I were a pen - man and could write a fine hand. I would
4. Oh I wish I were a bird ___ and had wings and could fly. It's ___

foot of yon - der moun - tain there lives a fair queen. She's
wants ___ some free - hold - er and I have no land. I
write my love a let - ter from this dis - tant land. I'd
to ___ my love's win - dow this night I'd draw nigh. I'd

hand - some, she's prop - er, and her ways ___ are com - plete. I ___
can - not main - tain ___ her on ___ sil - ver and gold And ___
send it by the wa - ters just ___ for to let her know, That ___ I
sit ___ in her win - dow all ___ night ___ long and cry, That ___ for

ask no oth - er pas - time than to be with my sweet.
all the oth - er fine ___ things that my love's house should hold.
think of pret - ty Mar - y where - ev - er I go.
love of pret - ty Mar - y I glad - ly would die.

AULD LANG SYNE

18th Century Scottish
Words by Robert Burns

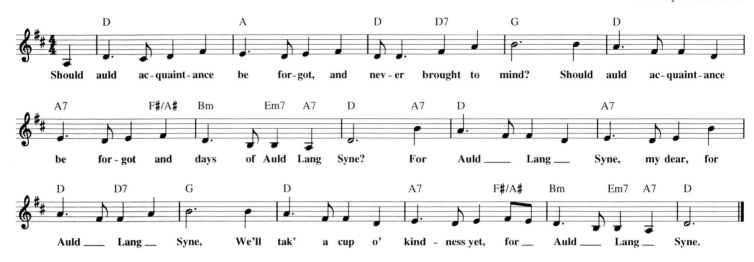

Should auld ac-quaint-ance be for-got, and nev-er brought to mind? Should auld ac-quaint-ance

be for-got and days of Auld Lang Syne? For Auld ___ Lang ___ Syne, my dear, for

Auld ___ Lang ___ Syne, We'll tak' a cup o' kind - ness yet, for ___ Auld ___ Lang ___ Syne.

AUNT DINAH'S QUILTING PARTY

American

1. In the sky the bright stars glit - tered, ___ On the bank the pale moon shone,
2. On my arm a soft hand rest - ed, ___ Rest ed like as o - cean foam
3. On my lips a whis - per trem - bled, ___ Trem-bled till it dared to come,
4. On my life new hopes were dawn - ing, ___ And those hopes have lived and grown,

And 'twas

from Aunt Di - nah's quilt - ing par - ty, I was see - ing Nel - lie home. I was

see - ing Nel - lie home, ___ I was see - ing Nel - lie home, And 'twas

from Aunt Di - nah's quilt - ing par - ty, I was see - ing Nel - lie home.

AURA LEE

Words by W.W. Fosdick
Music by George R. Poulton
First published in 1861

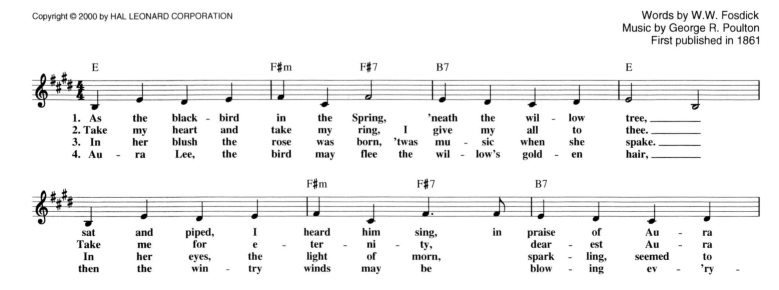

1. As the black - bird in the Spring, 'neath the wil - low tree, ___
2. Take my heart and take my ring, I give my all to thee. ___
3. In her blush the rose was born, 'twas mu - sic when she spake. ___
4. Au - ra Lee, the bird may flee the wil - low's gold - en hair, ___

sat and piped, I heard him sing, in praise of Au - ra
Take me for e - ter - ni - ty, dear - est Au - ra
In her eyes, the light of morn, spark - ling, seemed to
then the win - try winds may be blow - ing ev - 'ry -

Lee.
Lee! } Au - ra Lee, Au - ra Lee, maid with gold - en hair,
break. }
where. Yet if thy blue eyes I see, gloom will soon de - part.

sun - shine came a - long with thee, and swal - lows in the air.
For to me, sweet Au - ra Lee is sun - shine to the heart.

BAA BAA BLACK SHEEP

Nursery Rhyme Song

Baa! Baa! Black sheep have you an - y wool! Yes, Sir,

Yes, Sir, Three bags full. One for my mas - ter and

one for my dame, But none for the lit - tle boy that cries in the lane.

THE BALLAD OF THE TEA PARTY

18th Century American
From the Revolutionary War

1. Tea ships near to Bos - ton ly - ing, On the wharf a nu - mer-ous crew. Sons of free - dom,
2. Armed with ham - mers, ax - es, chis - els, Weap - ons new for war - like deed, Toward the tax - ed,
3. O - ver board she goes my boys, heave - Ho where dar - ling wa - ters roar. We love our cup of
4. Deep in - to the sea de - scend - ed Curs - ed weed of Chi - na's coast. Thus at once our

nev - er dy - ing, Then ap - peared in view! }
freight - ed ves - sels On they came with speed. } With a rink - tum, dink - tum, fa la link - tum,
tea full well, but Love our free - dom more. }
fears were end - ed, Rights shall ne'er be lost.

Then ap - peared in view, With a rink - tum, dink - tum, fa la link - tum, Then ap - peared in view!

BABE OF BETHLEHEM

Southern American Hymn

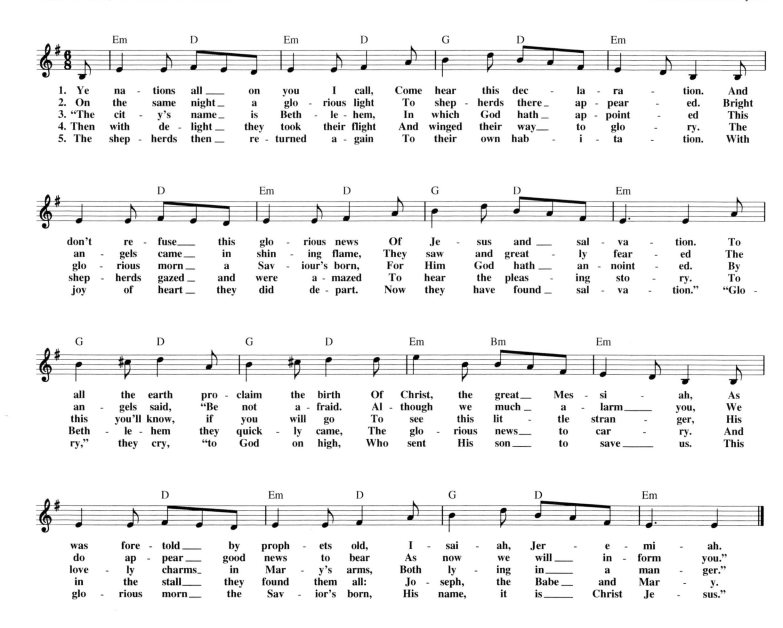

1. Ye nations all __ on you I call, Come hear this dec - la - ra - tion. And
2. On the same night __ a glo - rious light To shep - herds there __ ap - pear - ed. Bright
3. "The cit - y's name __ is Beth - le - hem, In which God hath __ ap - point - ed This
4. Then with de - light __ they took their flight And winged their way __ to glo - ry. The
5. The shep - herds then __ re - turned a - gain To their own hab - i - ta - tion. With

don't re - fuse __ this glo - rious news Of Je - sus and __ sal - va - tion. To
an - gels came __ in shin - ing flame, They saw and great - ly fear - ed The
glo - rious morn __ a Sav - iour's born, For Him God hath __ an - noint - ed. By
shep - herds gazed __ and were a - mazed To hear the pleas - ing sto - ry. To
joy of heart __ they did de - part. Now they have found __ sal - va - tion." "Glo -

all the earth pro - claim the birth Of Christ, the great __ Mes - si - ah, As
an - gels said, "Be not a - fraid. Al - though we much __ a - larm __ you, We
this you'll know, if you will go To see this lit - tle stran - ger, His
Beth - le - hem they quick - ly came, The glo - rious news __ to car - ry. And
ry," they cry, "to God on high, Who sent His son __ to save __ us. This

was fore - told __ by proph - ets old, I - sai - ah, Jer - e - mi - ah.
do ap - pear __ good news to bear As now we will __ in - form you."
love - ly charms __ in Mar - y's arms, Both ly - ing in __ a man - ger."
in the stall __ they found them all: Jo - seph, the Babe __ and Mar - y.
glo - rious morn __ the Sav - ior's born, His name, it is __ Christ Je - sus."

BATCHELOR'S WALK

Irish, circa 1914

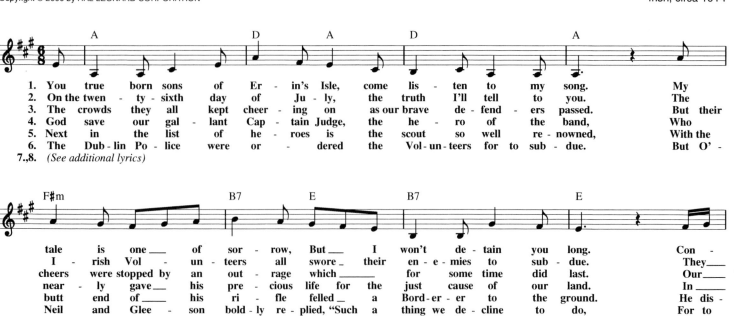

1. You true born sons of Er - in's Isle, come lis - ten to my song. My
2. On the twen - ty - sixth day of Ju - ly, the truth I'll tell to you. The
3. The crowds they all kept cheer - ing on as our brave de - fend - ers passed. But their
4. God save our gal - lant Cap - tain Judge, the he - ro of the band, Who
5. Next in the list of he - roes is the scout so well re - nowned, With the
6. The Dub - lin Po - lice were or - dered the Vol - un - teers for to sub - due. But O' -
7.,8. *(See additional lyrics)*

tale is one __ of sor - row, But __ I won't de - tain you long. Con -
I - rish Vol - un - teers all swore __ their en - e - mies to sub - due. They __
cheers were stopped by an out - rage which __ for some time did last. Our __
butt end of __ his ri - fle felled __ a Bord - er - er to the ground. In __
Neil and Glee - son bold - ly re - plied, "Such a thing we de - cline to do, For to

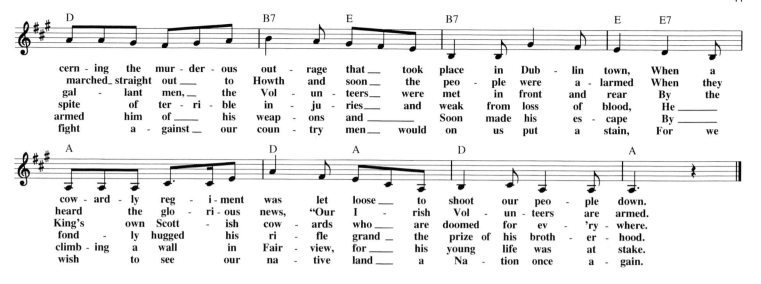

Additional Lyrics

7. On Batchelor's Walk a scene took place, which I'm sure had just been planned,
For the cowardly Scottish Borderers turned and fired without command.
With bayonets fixed they charged the crowd and left them in their gore,
But their deeds will be remembered in Irish hearts for evermore.

8. God rest the souls of those who sleep apart from earthly sin,
Including Mrs. Duffy, James Brennan and Patrick Quinn;
But we will yet avenge them and the time will surely come,
That we'll make the Scottish Borderers pay for the cowardly deeds they done.

BAD COMPANY

19th Century American

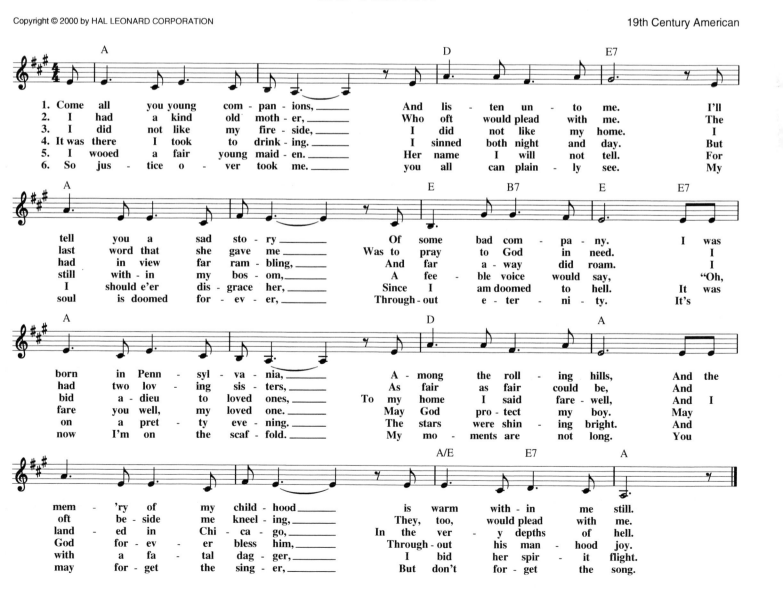

THE BAD GIRL

19th Century American

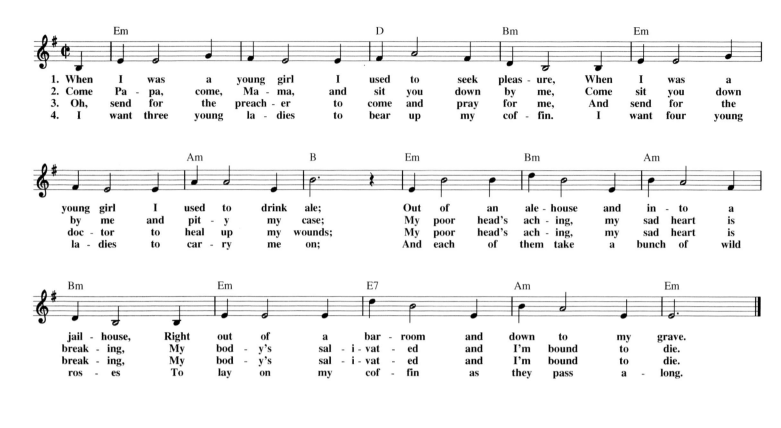

1. When I was a young girl I used to seek pleas - ure, When I was a
2. Come Pa - pa, come, Ma - ma, and sit you down by me, Come sit you down
3. Oh, send for the preach - er to come and pray for me, And send for the
4. I want three young la - dies to bear up my cof - fin. I want four young

young girl I used to drink ale; Out of an ale - house and in - to a
by me and pit - y my case; My poor head's ach - ing, my sad heart is
doc - tor to heal up my wounds; My poor head's ach - ing, my sad heart is
la - dies to car - ry me on; And each of them take a bunch of wild

jail - house, Right out of a bar - room and down to my grave.
break - ing, My bod - y's sal - i - vat - ed and I'm bound to die.
break - ing, My bod - y's sal - i - vat - ed and I'm bound to die.
ros - es To lay on my cof - fin as they pass a - long.

BALOO BALEERIE

Scottish

Ba - loo ba - lee - rie, ba - loo ba -

lee - rie, ba - loo ba - lee - rie, Ba - loo ba -

lee.

1. Gang a - wa' pee - rie fair - ies, gang a - wa' pee - rie
2. Down come the bon - ny an - gels, down come the bon - ny
3. Sleep saft my ba - by, sleep saft my

fair - ies. Gang a - wa' pee - rie
an - gels. Down come the bon - ny
ba - by. Sleep saft my

fair - ies. Frae oor ben noo.
an - gels. Tae oor ben noo.
ba - by. In oor ben noo.

THE BALLAD OF NED KELLY

19th Century Australian

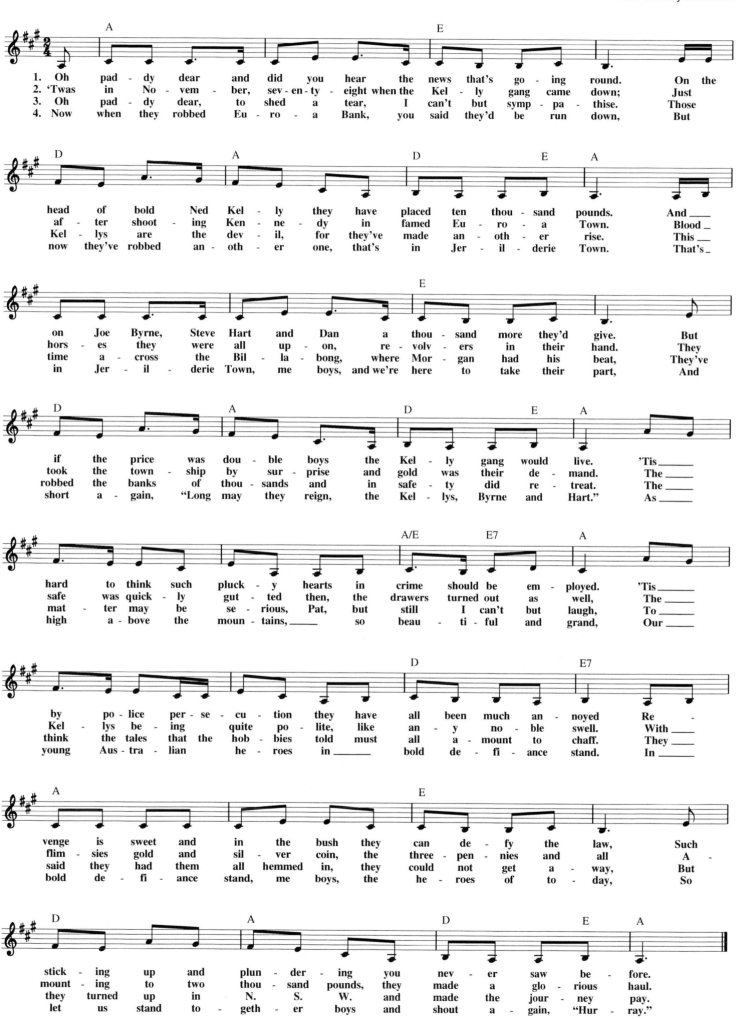

THE BAILIFF'S DAUGHTER OF ISLINGTON

18th Century English

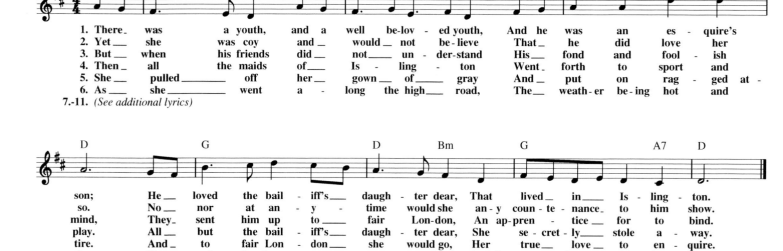

1. There was a youth, and a well belov-ed youth, And he was an es-quire's
2. Yet she was coy and would not be-lieve That he did love her
3. But when his friends did not un-der-stand His fond and fool-ish
4. Then all the maids of Is-ling-ton Went forth to sport and
5. She pulled off her gown of gray And put on rag-ged at-
6. As she went a-long the high road, The weath-er be-ing hot and

7.-11. *(See additional lyrics)*

son; He loved the bail-iff's daugh-ter dear, That lived in Is-ling-ton.
so. No nor at an-y time would she an-y coun-te-nance to him show.
mind, They sent him up to fair Lon-don, An ap-pren-tice for to bind.
play. All but the bail-iff's daugh-ter dear, She se-cret-ly stole a-way.
tire. And to fair Lon-don she would go, Her true love to en-quire.
dry. She sat her down up-on a green bank And her true love came rid-ing by.

Additional Lyrics

7. She started up with a color so red,
Catching hold of his bridle rein:
"One penny, one penny, kind sir," she said,
"Will ease me of much pain."

8. "Before I give you one penny, sweetheart,
Pray tell me where you were born."
"At Islington, kind sir," she said,
"Where I've had many a scorn."

9. "I prithee, sweetheart, tell to me,
O tell me whether you know
The bailiff's daughter of Islington."
"She's dead, sir, long ago."

10. "If she be dead, then take my horse,
My saddle and bridle also;
For I will into some far country,
Where no man shall me know."

11. "O stay, o stay, thou goodly youth,
She standeth by thy side.
She is here alive, she is not dead,
And ready to be your bride."

BALOO, LAMMY

17th Century Scottish

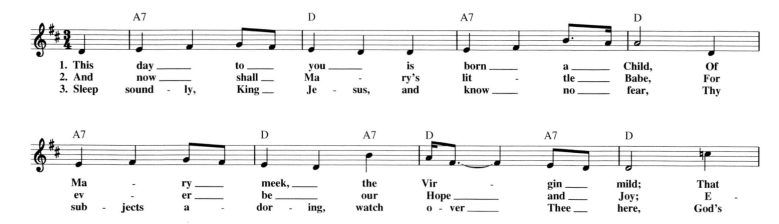

1. This day to you is born a Child, Of
2. And now shall Ma-ry's lit-tle Babe, For
3. Sleep sound-ly, King Je-sus, and know no fear, Thy

Ma-ry meek, the Vir-gin mild; That
ev-er be our Hope and Joy; E-
sub-jects a-dor-ing, watch o-ver Thee here, God's

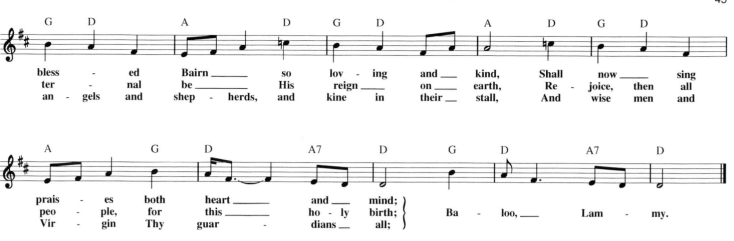

THE BANKS OF THE SWEET PRIMROSES

English

BALTIMORE FIRE

Eastern American, circa 1904

1. It was on a sil-ver falls by a nar-row   That I heard the cry I ev-er will re-mem-ber   The
2. A - mid an aw-ful strug-gle of com-mo-tion,   The_ wind blew a gale from the o - cean.   Brave

fire sent and cast its burn-ing em - bers   On an-oth-er fat-ed cit-y of our land ⎱   Fire, fire, I
fire-men_ strug-gled with de - vo - tion,   But their ef - forts_ all_ proved in vain. ⎰

heard the cry From ev - 'ry breeze that pass-es by   All the world_ was one sad cry of _

pit - y _   Strong men in an-guish prayed Call - ing loud_ to heav'n for aid

While the fire_ in ruin was laying Fair_ Bal - ti-more the beau-ti - ful cit - y. _

THE BAMBOO FLUTE

Chinese

BANANA BOAT LOADER'S SONG
(Day Oh)

Jamaican Work Song

Day Oh Day ____ Oh Day da light __ an' me wan' go home.

1. Come Mis-ter Tall-y-man, Come tall-y me ba-na-na Day da light __ an' me wan' go home.

shout!   *shout!*

2. Six hand, sev-en hand, eight hand bunch! Six hand, sev-en hand eight hand bunch!
3. We load ba-na-nas till the ear-ly light. Sleep all day and work all night.
4. Some men work some men make love. We load ba-na-na while the moon a-bove.

Day da light __ an' me wan' go home. Day Oh Day __ Oh Day da light __ an' me wan' go home.

THE BANKS OF THE DON

19th Century Canadian

1. On the banks of the Don, there's a dear lit-tle spot; A
2.,5. So turn out ev-'ry man of you, all in a line, From the
3. If you want to get in-to that pal-ace so neat, Take
4. Our ___ board-ers are hon-est; not one of them steals. For

board-ing house prop-er, Where you get your meals hot. You get
call to the stone-yard you ___ all must keep time. You ___
tan-gle-foot whis-ky and get drunk in the street. You'll __
we count all their knives and forks af-ter each meal. Our ___

fine bread and wa-ter and you won't pay a cent. Your
work like a Turk till the bell, it strikes one, In that
have a fine car-riage to drive you from town To that
win-dows are air-y and barred up be-side, To

tax-es are paid for, your board and your rent.
grand in-sti-tu-tion just o-ver the Don.
grand in-sti-tu-tion just o-ver the Don.
keep our good board-ers from fall-ing out-side.

BANKS OF THE OHIO

19th Century Western American

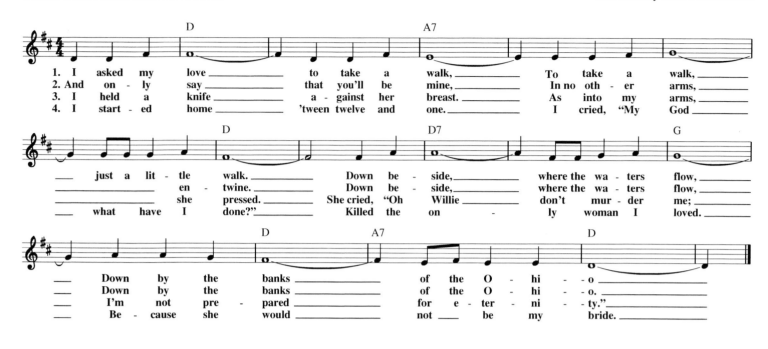

BARBARA ALLEN

Scottish

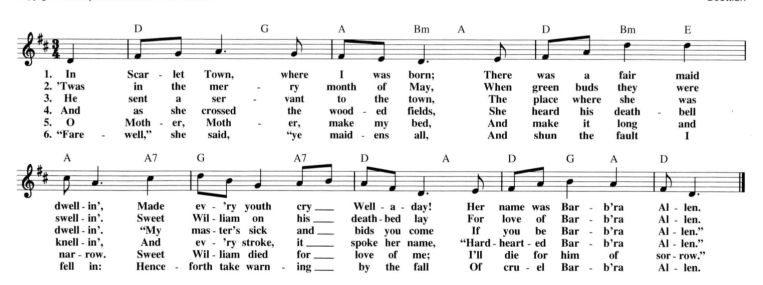

BARNYARD SONG
(I Had a Rooster)

19th Century Southeastern American

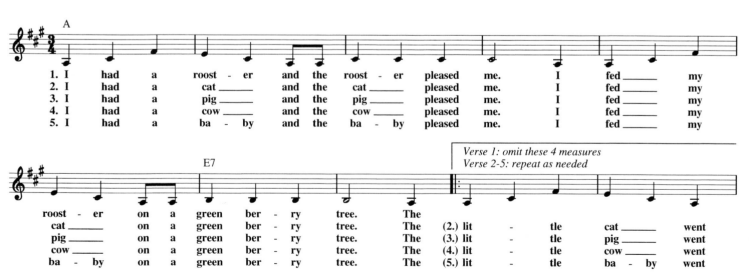

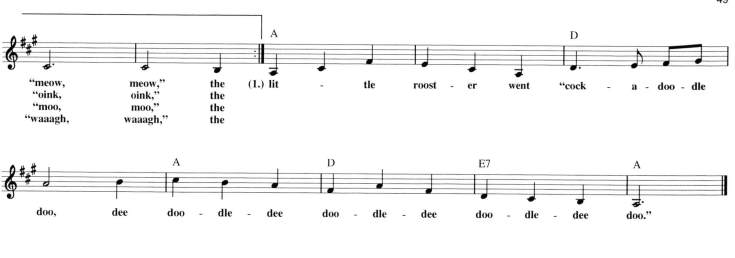

"meow,   meow,"   the   (1.) lit - tle roost - er went "cock - a - doo - dle
"oink,   oink,"   the
"moo,   moo,"   the
"waaagh,   waaagh,"   the

doo,   dee   doo - dle - dee   doo - dle - dee   doo - dle - dee   doo."

THE BIG ROCK CANDY MOUNTAIN

American Hobo Song
Attributed to Harry McClintock

1. On a sum - mer day in the month of May, A ___ bur - ly bum came hik - ing. Down a
2. In the Big Rock Can - dy ___ Moun - tain, boys, You ___ nev - er change your socks. ___ And ___
3. In the Big Rock Can - dy ___ Moun - tain, boys, The ___ cops have wood - en legs. ___ The ___
4. In the Big Rock Can - dy ___ Moun - tain, boys, The ___ jails are made of tin. ___ And ___

shad - y lane through the sug - ar cane, He was look - ing for his lik - ing. As he
lit - tle streams of ___ al - ky - hol Come ___ trick - ling down the rocks. ___ All the
bull dogs all have ___ rub - ber teeth, And the hens lay soft - boiled eggs. ___ The ___
you can slip right ___ out a - gain, Soon ___ as they put you in. ___ There ___

roamed a - long he sang this song of the land of milk and hon - ey, ___ Where a
sher - iffs have to tip their hats, And the rail - road bulls are blind. ___ There's a
box - cars are all emp - ty there, And the sun shines ev - 'ry day. ___ I'm ___
ain't no short han - dled shov - els there, No ax - es, saws, nor picks. ___ I'm ___

bum can stay for ___ man - y a day, And he won't need an - y mon - ey. ⎫
lake of stew, and ___ whis - key, too, In the Big Rock Can - dy Moun - tain. ⎬ Oh, the
bound to go where there ain't no snow, In the Big Rock Can - dy Moun - tain. ⎭
bound to stay where they sleep all day, In the Big Rock Can - dy Moun - tain.

buzz - in' of the bees in the cig - a - rette trees, The so - da wa - ter foun - tain, By the

lem - on - ade springs where the blue - bird sings, In the Big Rock Can - dy Moun - tain.

THE BARNYARDS OF DELGATY

18th Century Scottish

1. As I cam' in by Tur-ra mar-ket, Tur-ra mar-ket for to fee,
2. He prom-ised me the ae best pair That ev-er I set my e'en up-on.
3. The auld black horse sat on its rump, The auld white mare lay on her wime.
4. When I gae to the kirk on Sun-day, Mon-y's the bon-nie lass I see
5. I can drink and no' be drunk. I can fecht and no' be slain.
6. Noo my can-nle is brunt oot, My snot-ter's fair-ly on the wane.

I fell in wi' a fair-mer chiel, The Barn-yards o' Del-ga-ty.
When I gaed to the Barn-yards There was nae - thing but skin and bone.
And for a'that I could "Hup" and crack, They would-na rise at yok-in' time.
Sit-tin' by her fa-ther's side, And wink-in' owre the pews at me.
I can lie wi' an-ith-er man's lass, And aye-be wel-come to my ain.
Sae fare ye weel, ye Barn-yards, Ye nev-er catch me here a-gain.

Lin - ten a - die too - rin a - die, Lin - ten a - die too - rin ee;

Lin - ten low - rin, low - rin low - rin, the Barn - yards o' Del - ga - ty.

THE BATTLE ON SHILOH'S HILL

From the American Civil War

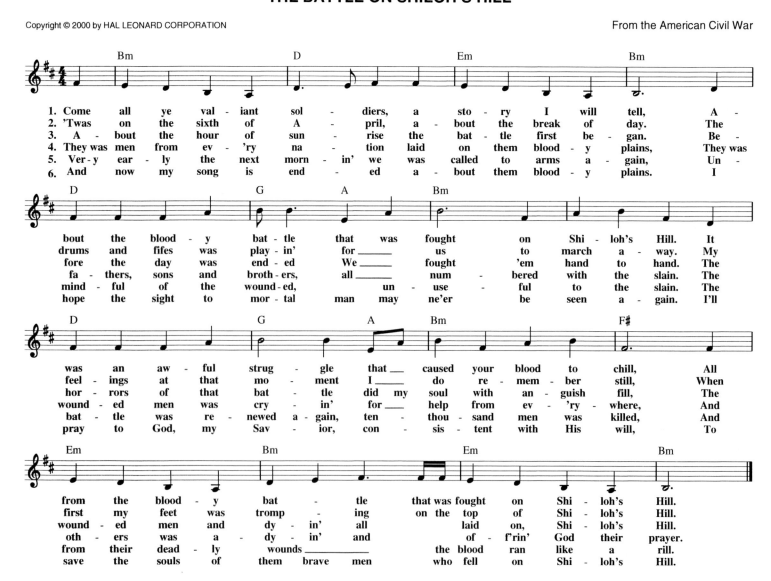

1. Come all ye val - iant sol - diers, a sto - ry I will tell, A-
2. 'Twas on the sixth of A - pril, a - bout the break of day. The
3. A - bout the hour of sun - rise the bat - tle first be - gan. Be -
4. They was men from ev - 'ry na - tion laid on them blood - y plains, They was
5. Ver - y ear - ly the next morn - in' we was called to arms a - gain, Un -
6. And now my song is end - ed a - bout them blood - y plains. I

bout the blood - y bat - tle that was fought on Shi - loh's Hill. It
drums and fifes was play - in' for _____ us to march a - way. My
fore the day was end - ed We _____ fought 'em hand to hand. The
fa - thers, sons and broth - ers, all _____ num - bered with the slain. The
mind - ful of the wound - ed, un - use - ful to the slain. The
hope the sight to mor - tal man may ne'er be seen a - gain. I'll

was an aw - ful strug - gle that __ caused your blood to chill, All
feel - ings at that mo - ment I _____ do re - mem - ber still, When
hor - rors of that bat - tle did my soul with an - guish fill, The
wound - ed men was cry - in' for __ help from ev - 'ry - where, And
bat - tle was re - newed a - gain, ten - thou - sand men was killed, And
pray to God, my Sav - ior, con - sis - tent with His will, To

from the blood - y bat - tle that was fought on Shi - loh's Hill.
first my feet was tromp - ing on the top of Shi - loh's Hill.
wound - ed men and dy - in' all laid on, Shi - loh's Hill.
oth - ers was a dy - in' and of - f'rin' God their prayer.
from their dead - ly wounds _____ the blood ran like a rill.
save the souls of them brave men who fell on Shi - loh's Hill.

BATTLESHIP OF MAINE

From the Spanish-American War
1898

1. Mc - Kin - ley called for vol - un - teers, Then I got my gun. First Span - iard I saw com - ing, I
2. Why are you run - ning, Are you a - fraid to die? The rea - son that I'm run - ning Is be -
3. The blood was a - run - ning And I was run - ning too. I give my feet good ex - er - cise, I had
4. When they were a - chas - ing me, I fell down on my knees. First thing I cast my eyes up - on Was a
5. The peas, they was greas - y. The meat, it was fat. The boys was fight - ing Span - iards, While

dropped my gun and run,
cause I can - not fly,
noth - ing else to do,   } It was all a - bout__ that Bat - tle - ship of Maine. At war with that great na - tion
great big pot of peas.
I was fight - ing that.

Spain, When I get back from Spain I want to hon - or my name, It was all a - bout_ that Bat - tle - ship of Maine.

BE THOU MY VISION

Traditional Irish melody
Ancient Irish poem
Translation by Mary E. Byrne, 1905

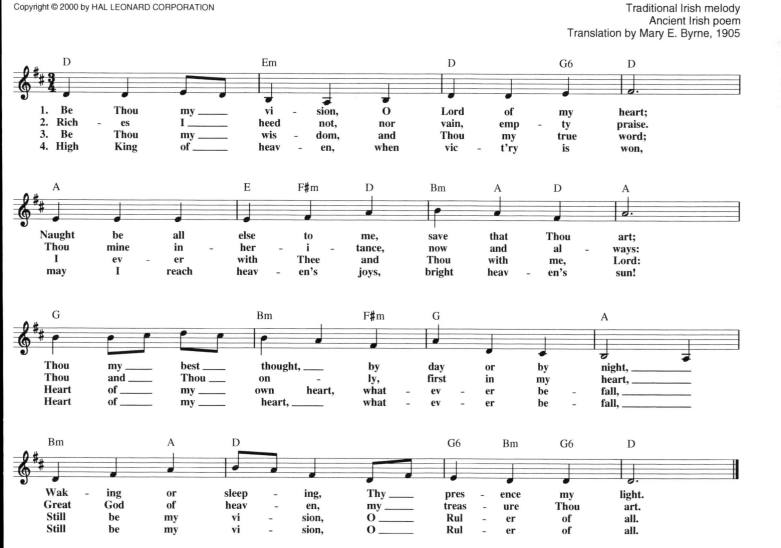

1. Be Thou my _____ vi - sion, O Lord of my heart;
2. Rich - es I _____ heed not, nor vain, emp - ty praise.
3. Be Thou my _____ wis - dom, and Thou my true word;
4. High King of _____ heav - en, when vic - t'ry is won,

Naught be all else to me, save that Thou art;
Thou mine in - her - i - tance, now and al - ways;
I ev - er with Thee and Thou with me, Lord:
may I reach heav - en's joys, bright heav - en's sun!

Thou my _____ best _____ thought, _____ by day or by night, _____
Thou and _____ Thou _____ on - ly, first in my heart, _____
Heart of _____ my _____ own heart, what - ev - er be - fall, _____
Heart of _____ my _____ heart, what - ev - er be - fall, _____

Wak - ing or sleep - ing, Thy _____ pres - ence my light.
Great God of heav - en, my _____ treas - ure Thou art.
Still be my vi - sion, O _____ Rul - er of all.
Still be my vi - sion, O _____ Rul - er of all.

BE PRESENT AT OUR TABLE, LORD

Music attributed to Louis Bourgeois, 1551
Words by John Cennick, 1741

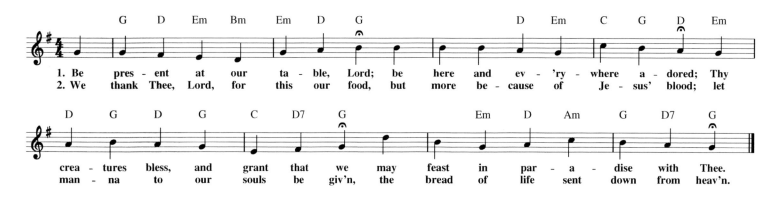

1. Be pres - ent at our ta - ble, Lord; be here and ev - 'ry - where a - dored; Thy
2. We thank Thee, Lord, for this our food, but more be - cause of Je - sus' blood; let

crea - tures bless, and grant that we may feast in par - a - dise with Thee.
man - na to our souls be giv'n, the bread of life sent down from heav'n.

THE BEAR WENT OVER THE MOUNTAIN

19th Century American

Oh, the bear went o - ver the moun - tain, the bear went o - ver the
moun - tain, the bear went o - ver the moun - tain to see what he could
see.

1. To see what he could see, _____ to see what he could see. Oh, the
2. He saw the oth - er side, _____ he saw the oth - er

side. Oh, the bear went o - ver the moun - tain, the bear went o - ver the
moun - tain, the bear went o - ver the moun - tain to see what he could see.

BEAUTIFUL BROWN EYES

From the Ozarks

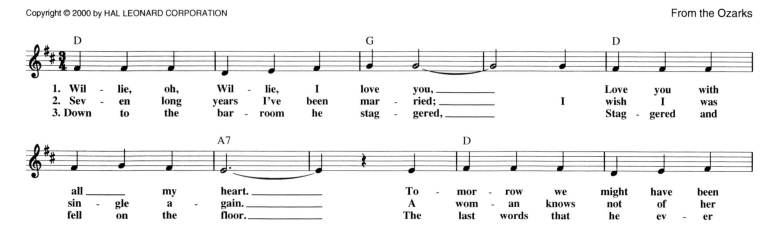

1. Wil - lie, oh, Wil - lie, I love you, _____ Love you with
2. Sev - en long years I've been mar - ried; _____ I wish I was
3. Down to the bar - room he stag - gered, _____ Stag - gered and

all _____ my heart. _____ To - mor - row we might have been
sin - gle a - gain. _____ A wom - an knows not of her
fell on the floor. _____ The last words that he ev - er

BEAUTIFUL DREAMER

Words and Music by
Stephen C. Foster, 1861

54

BEDLAM

18th Century English

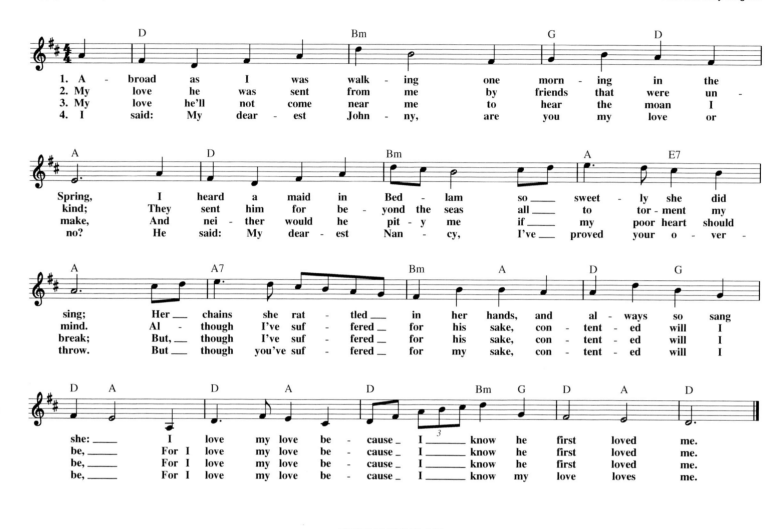

1. A - broad as I was walk - ing one morn - ing in the Spring, I heard a maid in Bed - lam so ___ sweet - ly she did sing; Her ___ chains she rat - tled ___ in her hands, and al - ways so sang she: _____ I love my love be - cause _ I _____ know he first loved me.

2. My love he was sent from me by friends that were un - kind; They sent him for be - yond the seas all ___ to tor - ment my mind. Al - though I've suf - fered ___ for his sake, con - tent - ed will I be, _____ For I love my love be - cause _ I _____ know he first loved me.

3. My love he'll not come near me to hear the moan I make, And nei - ther would he pit - y me if ___ my poor heart should break; But, ___ though I've suf - fered ___ for his sake, con - tent - ed will I be, _____ For I love my love be - cause _ I _____ know he first loved me.

4. I said: My dear - est John - ny, are you my love or no? He said: My dear - est Nan - cy, I've ___ proved your o - ver - throw. But ___ though you've suf - fered ___ for my sake, con - tent - ed will I be, _____ For I love my love be - cause _ I _____ know my love loves me.

THE BEGGAR

English

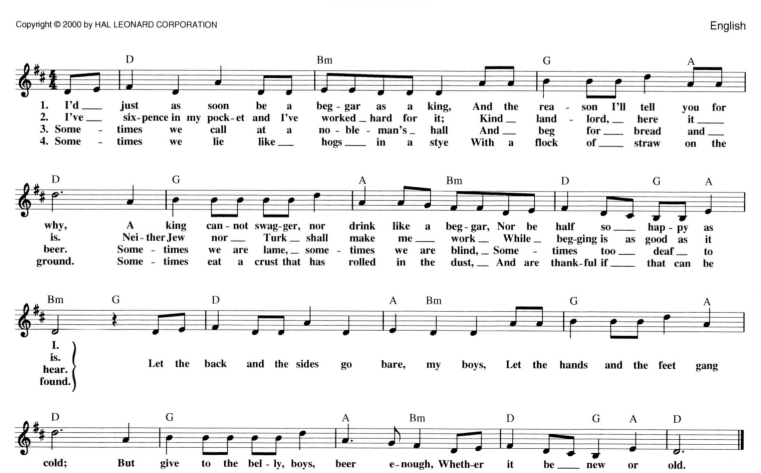

1. I'd ___ just as soon be a beg - gar as a king, And the rea - son I'll tell you for why, A king can - not swag - ger, nor drink like a beg - gar, Nor be half so ___ hap - py as is.

2. I've ___ six - pence in my pock - et and I've worked ___ hard for it; Kind ___ land - lord, ___ here it ___ Nei - ther Jew nor ___ Turk shall make me ___ work ___ While ___ beg - ging is as good as it is.

3. Some - times we call at a no - ble - man's ___ hall And ___ beg for ___ bread and ___ Some - times we are lame, ___ some - times we are blind, ___ Some - times too ___ deaf ___ to hear.

4. Some - times we lie like ___ hogs ___ in a stye With a flock of ___ straw on the ground. Some - times eat a crust that has rolled in the dust, ___ And are thank - ful if _____ that can be found.

I.
is.
hear.
found.
Let the back and the sides go bare, my boys, Let the hands and the feet gang cold; But give to the bel - ly, boys, beer e - nough, Wheth - er it be ___ new or old.

BELIEVE ME, IF ALL THOSE ENDEARING YOUNG CHARMS

18th Century Irish
Words by Thomas Moore, 1808

1. Be - lieve me, if all those en - dear - ing young charms which I gaze on so fond - ly to -
2. It is not that while beau - ty and youth are thine own And thy cheeks un - pro - faned by a

day,_____ Were to change by to - mor - row and fleet in my arms, like the fair - y gifts fad - ing a -
tear,_____ That the fer - vor and faith of a soul can be known To which time will but make thee more

way._____ Thou wouldst still be a - dored As this mo - ment thou art, Let thy love - li - ness fade as it
dear._____ No, the heart that has tru - ly loved nev - er for - gets, But as tru - ly loves on to the

will,_____ And a - round the dear ru - in each wish of my heart Would en - twine it - self ver - dant - ly still._____
close,_____ As the sun - flow - er turns on her god when he sets, The same look which she turned when he rose._____

BENDEMEER'S STREAM

Irish
Words by Thomas Moore

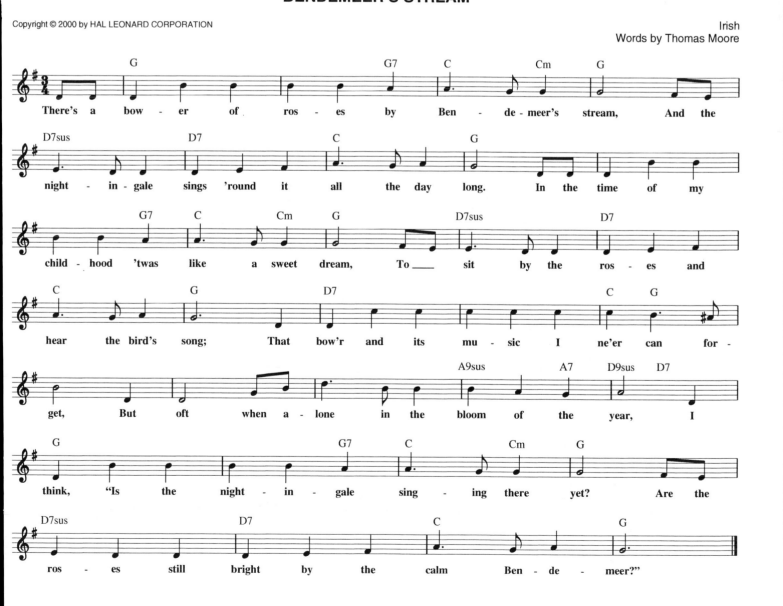

There's a bow - er of ros - es by Ben - de - meer's stream, And the

night - in - gale sings 'round it all the day long. In the time of my

child - hood 'twas like a sweet dream, To ____ sit by the ros - es and

hear the bird's song; That bow'r and its mu - sic I ne'er can for -

get, But oft when a - lone in the bloom of the year, I

think, "Is the night - in - gale sing - ing there yet? Are the

ros - es still bright by the calm Ben - de - meer?"

BEWARE, OH, TAKE CARE

19th Century American

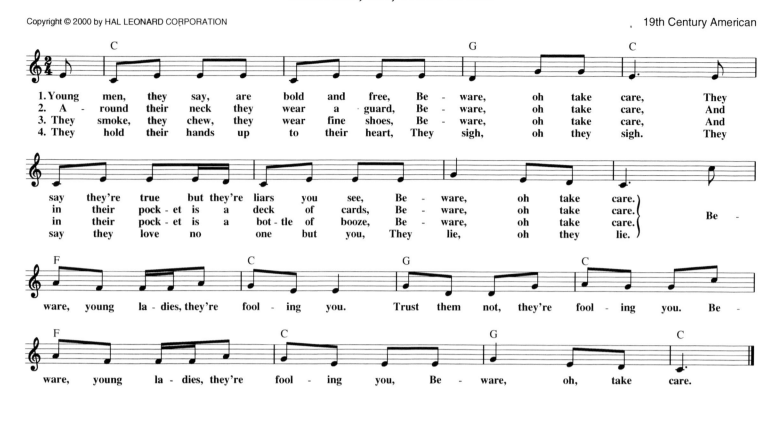

1. Young men, they say, are bold and free, Be - ware, oh take care, They
2. A - round their neck they wear a guard, Be - ware, oh take care, And
3. They smoke, they chew, they wear fine shoes, Be - ware, oh take care, And
4. They hold their hands up to their heart, They sigh, oh they sigh. They

say they're true but they're liars you see, Be - ware, oh take care.
in their pock - et is a deck of cards, Be - ware, oh take care.
in their pock - et is a bot - tle of booze, Be - ware, oh take care.
say they love no one but you, They lie, oh they lie.

Be -

ware, young la - dies, they're fool - ing you. Trust them not, they're fool - ing you. Be -

ware, young la - dies, they're fool - ing you, Be - ware, oh, take care.

THE BIG CORRAL

American Cowboy Song

1. This bon - ney brute from the cat - tle chute.
2. The chuck we get ain't fit to eat.
3. Ear - ly in the morn - in' 'bout half past four.
Press a - long to the big cor - ral.

He
There's
You

should be brand - ed on the snoot.
rocks in the beans and sand in the meat.
hear him o - pen his face to roar.
Press a - long to the big cor - ral. Press a -

long, cow - boy, press a - long, press a - long with a cow - boy yell. Press a -

long with a noise, big noise, press a - long to the big cor - ral.

BILE THEM CABBAGE DOWN

19th Century American

Bile them cab - bage down, down, Turn them hoe cakes 'round. The

on - ly song that I could sing was bile them cab - bage down.

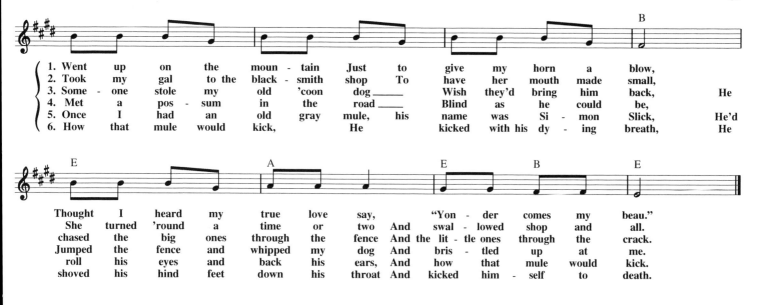

1. Went up on the moun - tain Just to give my horn a blow,
2. Took my gal to the black - smith shop To have her mouth made small,
3. Some - one stole my old 'coon dog Wish they'd bring him back, He
4. Met a pos - sum in the road Blind as he could be,
5. Once I had an old gray mule, his name was Si - mon Slick, He'd
6. How that mule would kick, He kicked with his dy - ing breath, He

Thought I heard my true love say, "Yon - der comes my beau."
She turned 'round a time or two And swal - lowed shop and all.
chased the big ones through the fence And the lit - tle ones through the crack.
Jumped the fence and whipped my dog And bris - tled up at me.
roll his eyes and whipped back his ears, And how that mule would kick.
shoved his hind feet down his throat And kicked him - self to death.

BIG ROAD BLUES

American

1. I ain't goin' down that big road by my - self. Why don't you hear me,
2. Cry - in,' sun goin' shine in my back door some - day. Now don't you hear me
3. Ba - by, what makes you do, like you do, do, do, like you do, do,

talk - in' pret - ty ma - ma, Lord, Ain't goin' down that big road by my - self.
talk - in', pret - ty ma - ma, Lord. Sun goin' to shine in my back door some - day.
do. Don't you hear me now. What makes you do me, like you do, do, do.

If I don't car - ry you, goin' car' some - bod - y else.
And the wind goin' to change, goin' to blow my blues a - way.
Now you say you goin' to do me like you done poor cher - ry Red.

BILLY BROKE LOCKS

From the American Revolutionary War

1. There were nine to hold the Brit - ish ranks, And five to guard the town a - bout, And
2. Bil - ly broke locks and Bil - ly broke bolts And Bil - ly broke all that he came nigh, Un -
3. There was eight - y weight of good Span - ish i - ron Be - tween his neck - bone and his knee, But
4. They mount - ed their hors - es and a - way did ride, And who but they rode man - full - y, Un -
5. And then they called for a room to dance, And who but they danced mer - ri - ly And

two to stand at ei - ther hand, And one to let the Old Ten - or out.
til he came to the dun - geon door, And that he broke quite man - full - y.
Bil - ly took John up un - der his arm And lugged him a - way right man - full - y.
til they came to the riv - er bank And there they a - light - ed right man - full - y.
the last danc - er a - mongst them all Was old John Webb who was just set free.

BILL GROGGIN'S GOAT

Southern Appalachian Folksong

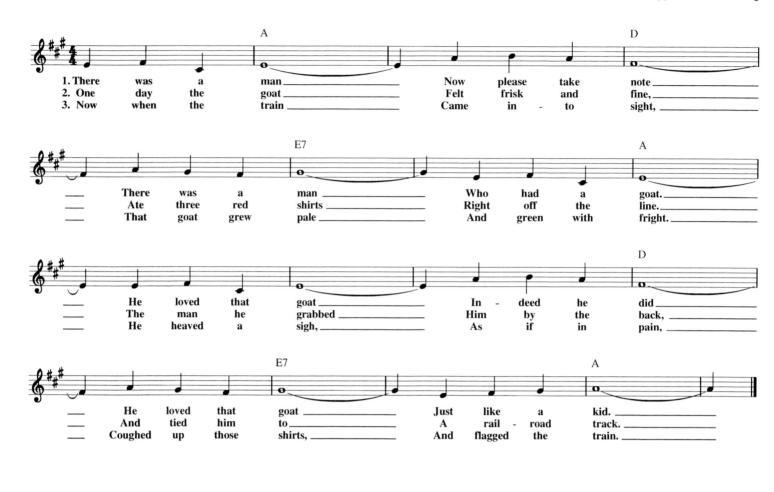

BILLY BARLOW

American Children's Game Song

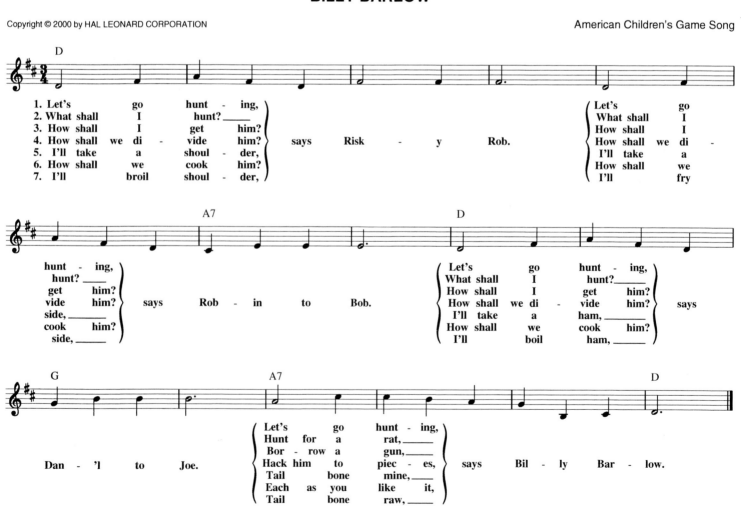

BILLY BOY

19th Century American

1. Oh___ where have you been,
2. Did she bid you come in,
3. Did she set for you a chair,
4. Can she bake a cher-ry pie,
5. How___ old is she,
6. Can she sing a pret-ty song,

Bil-ly Boy, Bil-ly Boy,

Oh___ where have you
Did she bid you come
Did she set for you a
Can she bake a cher-ry
How___ old is
Can she sing a pret-ty

been,
in,
chair,
pie,
she,
song,

charm-ing Bil-ly?___

I have been to seek a wife, She's the
Yes, she bade me to come in, Let me
Yes, she set for me a chair, But the
She can bake a cher-ry pie Quick as a
Three times six and four times sev-en, Twen-ty
She can sing a pret-ty song, But she

joy___ of my life.
kiss her on the chin.
bot-tom was-n't there.
cat can wink her eye.
eight___ and e-lev-en.
gets the words all wrong.

She's a young thing and can-not leave her moth - er.

She's a moth - er and can-not leave her young thing.

BILLY THE KID

American Cowboy Song

1. I'll sing you a true song of Bil-ly the Kid.
2. When Bil-ly the Kid was a ver-y young lad,
3. Fair Mex-i-can maid-ens play gui-tars and sing
4. It was on the same night when poor Bil-ly died,
5. Now this is how Bil-ly the Kid met his fate,
6. There's man-y a young lad with face fine and fair,

Sing of the
In old Sil-ver
Songs a-bout
Said he to his
The bright moon was
Who starts out in

des - per - ate deeds that he did.
Cit - y, he went to the bad.
Bil - ly, their boy-ban-dit king,
friends, "I'm not sat - is - fied.
shin - ing, the hour___ was late.
life with a chance to be square.

Way out in New Mex-i-co
Way out in the West with a
How there's a young lad who had
There are twen-ty-one men I have
Shot down by Pat Gar-rett who
But just like poor Bil-ly they

long, long a - go, Where a man's on - ly friend was his old for - ty - four.
gun in his hand, At the age of twelve years he killed his first man.
reached his sad end, Had a notch on his pis-tol for twen-ty-one men.
put bul-lets through And now Sher-iff Pat Gar-rett must make twen-ty-two.
once was his friend, The young out-law's life had now come to its end.
wan-der a-stray, They lose their own life in the ver-y same way.

BINGO

18th Century English Game Song

Note: Each time a letter of BINGO is deleted
in the lyric, clap your hands in place of singing
the letter.

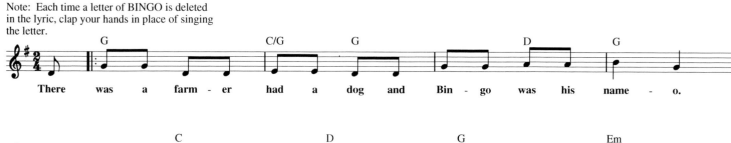

There was a farm-er had a dog and Bin-go was his name-o.

B - I - N - G - O, B - I - N - G - O, B - I -
__ - __ - N - G - O, __ - __ - N - G - O, __ - __ -
__ - __ - __ - __ - O, __ - __ - __ - __ - O, __ - __ -

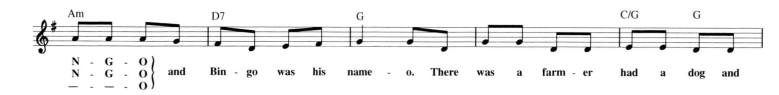

N - G - O, and Bin-go was his name-o. There was a farm-er had a dog and
N - G - O,
__ - __ - O,

Bin-go was his name-o.   __ - I - N - G - O, __ - I - N - G - O,
                         __ - __ - __ - G - O, __ - __ - __ - G - O,
                         __ - __ - __ - __ - __, __ - __ - __ - __ - __,

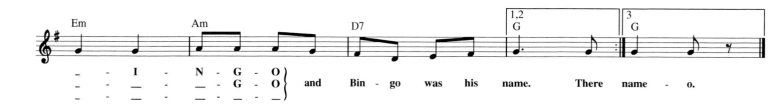

__ - __ - I - N - G - O, and Bin-go was his name. There name - o.
__ - __ - __ - __ - G - O,
__ - __ - __ - __ - __ - __,

BIRMINGHAM BULL

Southern American Comic Song

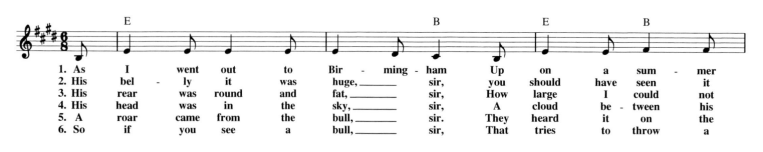

1. As I went out to Bir-ming-ham Up on a sum-mer
2. His bel-ly it was huge, _____ sir, you should have seen it
3. His rear was round and fat, _____ sir, How large I could not
4. His head was in the sky, _____ sir, A cloud be-tween his
5. A roar came from the bull, _____ sir. They heard it on the
6. So if you see a bull, _____ sir, That tries to throw a

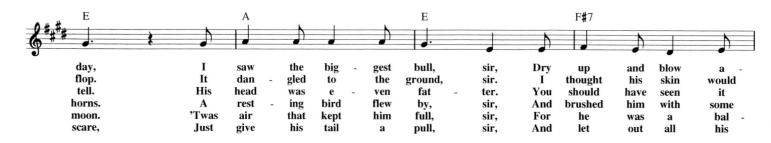

day, I saw the big-gest bull, sir, Dry up and blow a-
flop. It dan-gled to the ground, sir. I thought his skin would
tell. His head was e-ven fat-ter. You should have seen it
horns. A rest-ing bird flew by, sir, And brushed him with some
moon. 'Twas air that kept him full, sir, For he was a bal-
scare, Just give his tail a pull, sir, And let out all his

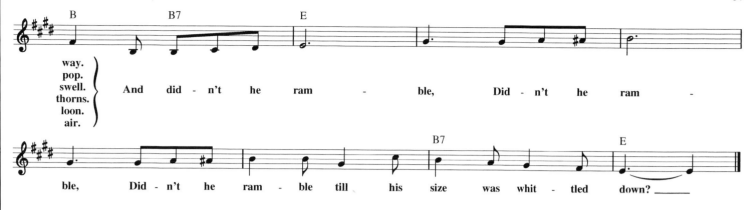

way.
pop.
swell.
thorns.
loon.
air.

And did - n't he ram - ble, Did - n't he ram -

ble, Did - n't he ram - ble till his size was whit - tled down?

BLACK-EYED SUSIE

19th Century American

1. Black - eyed Su - sie 'bout half grown, Jumps on a boy like a
2. All I want in this cre - a - tion, Pret - ty lit - le wife and a
3. All I need to keep me hap - py, Two lit - le boys to
4. I asked her to be my wife, She come at me with a

dog on a bone.
big plan - ta - tion.
call me Pap - py.
Bar - low knife.

Hey, black - eyed Su - sie.

Hey, pret - ty lit - tle black - eyed Su - sie. Hey, black - eyed Su - sie, hey.

BLACK IS THE COLOR OF MY TRUE LOVE'S HAIR

Southern Appalachian

Black, black, black is the col - or of my true love's hair.

{ 1. Her
2. Her
3. A -

lips are like a rose so fair. And the pret - ti - est face and the
face is some - thing tru - ly rare. Oh I do love my love and so
lone, my life would be so bare. I would sigh, I would weep, I would

neat - est hands. I love the grass where -
well she knows, I love the ground where -
nev - er fall a - sleep. My love is way be -

on she stands,
on she goes, } she with the won - drous hair.
yond com - pare,

62

BLACKBIRDS AND THRUSHES

English

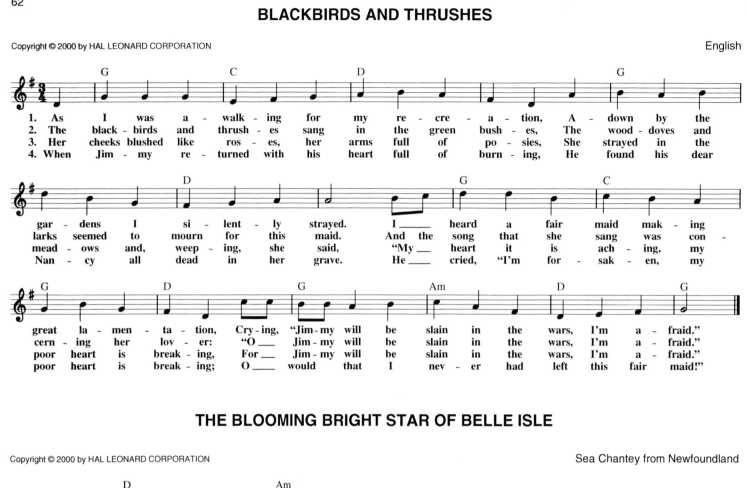

1. As I was a-walk-ing for my re-cre-a-tion, A-down by the gar-dens I si-lent-ly strayed. I ___ heard a fair maid mak-ing great la-men-ta-tion, Cry-ing, "Jim-my will be slain in the wars, I'm a-fraid."
2. The black-birds and thrush-es sang in the green bush-es, The wood-doves and larks seemed to mourn for this maid. And the song that she sang was con-cern-ing her lov-er: "O ___ Jim-my will be slain in the wars, I'm a-fraid."
3. Her cheeks blushed like ros-es, her arms full of po-sies, She strayed in the mead-ows and, weep-ing, she said, "My ___ heart it is ach-ing, my poor heart is break-ing, For ___ Jim-my will be slain in the wars, I'm a-fraid."
4. When Jim-my re-turned with his heart full of burn-ing, He found his dear Nan-cy all dead in her grave. He ___ cried, "I'm for-sak-en, my poor heart is break-ing; O ___ would that I nev-er had left this fair maid!"

THE BLOOMING BRIGHT STAR OF BELLE ISLE

Sea Chantey from Newfoundland

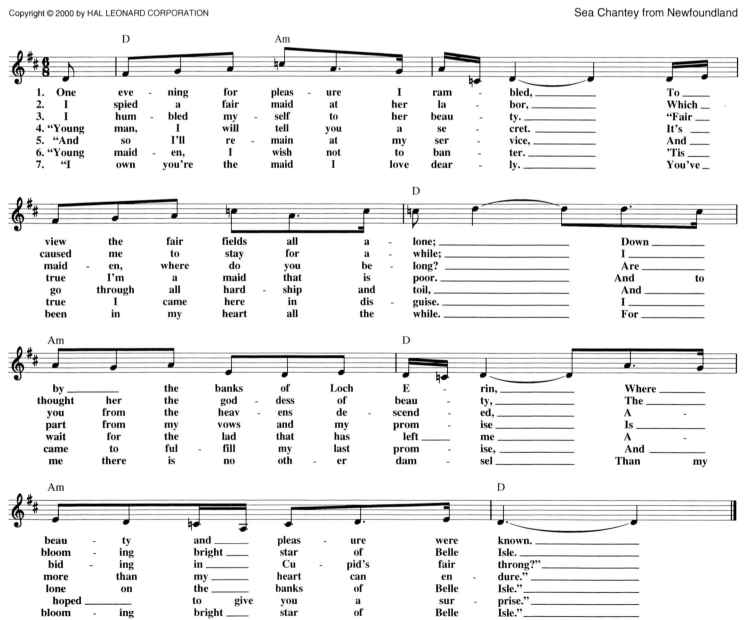

1. One eve-ning for pleas-ure I ram-bled, To ___ view the fair fields all a-lone; ___ Down ___ by ___ the banks of Loch E-rin, ___ Where ___ beau-ty and ___ pleas-ure were known. ___
2. I spied a fair maid at her la-bor, Which ___ caused me to stay for a-while; ___ I ___ thought her the god-dess of beau-ty, ___ The ___ bloom-ing bright ___ star of Belle Isle. ___
3. I hum-bled my-self to her beau-ty. ___ "Fair ___ maid-en, where do you be-long? ___ Are ___ you from the heav-ens de-scend-ed, ___ A-bid-ing in ___ Cu-pid's fair throng?" ___
4. "Young man, I will tell you a se-cret. ___ It's ___ true I'm a maid that is poor. ___ And to part from my vows and my prom-ise ___ Is ___ more than my ___ heart can en-dure." ___
5. "And so I'll re-main at my ser-vice, ___ And ___ go through all hard-ship and toil. ___ I ___ wait for the lad that has left ___ me ___ A-lone on the ___ banks of Belle Isle." ___
6. "Young maid-en, I wish not to ban-ter. ___ 'Tis ___ true I came here in dis-guise. ___ I ___ came to ful-fill my last prom-ise, ___ And ___ hoped ___ to give you a sur-prise." ___
7. "I own you're the maid I love dear-ly. ___ You've ___ been in my heart all the while. ___ For ___ me there is no oth-er dam-sel ___ Than my ___ bloom-ing bright ___ star of Belle Isle." ___

BLOOD ON THE SADDLE

Western American

1. There was blood on the sad - dle,_____ And blood on the ground,_____
2. The____ cow - boy lay in it,_____ All cov - ered with gore,_____
3. Oh____ pit - y the cow - boy,_____ All blood - y and red,_____

____ And a great big pud - dle_____ Of blood all a - round._____
____ And he won't go rid - ing_____ No bron - cos no more._____
____ For his bron - co fell on him_____ And mashed in his head._____

BLOW AWAY THE MORNING DEW

17th Century English

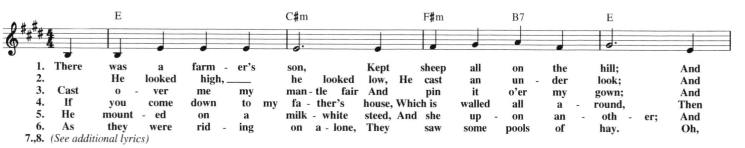

1. There was a farm - er's son, Kept sheep all on the hill; And
2. He looked high, ____ he looked low, He cast an un - der look; And
3. Cast o - ver me my man - tle fair And pin it o'er my gown; And
4. If you come down to my fa - ther's house, Which is walled all a - round, Then
5. He mount - ed on a milk - white steed, And she up - on an - oth - er; And
6. As they were rid - ing on a - lone, They saw some pools of hay. Oh,

7.,8. *(See additional lyrics)*

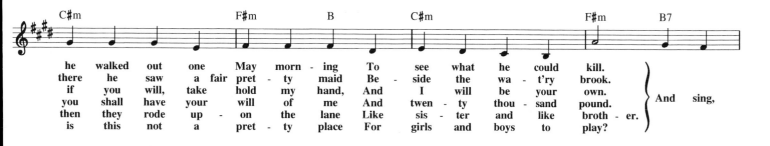

he walked out one May morn - ing To see what he could kill.
there he saw a fair pret - ty maid Be - side the wa - t'ry brook.
if you will, take hold my hand, And I will be your own.
you shall have your will of me And twen - ty thou - sand pound.
then they rode up - on the lane Like sis - ter and like broth - er.
is this not a pret - ty place For girls and boys to play?

} And sing,

blow a - way the morn - ing dew, The dew and the dew.

Blow a - way the morn - ing dew, How sweet the winds do blow.

Additional Lyrics

7. But when they came to her father's gate,
So nimble she popped in,
And said: There is a fool without,
And here's a maid within.

8. We have a flower in our garden;
We call it marigold,
And if you will not when you may,
You shall not when you wolde.

BLOW THE CANDLES OUT

18th Century English

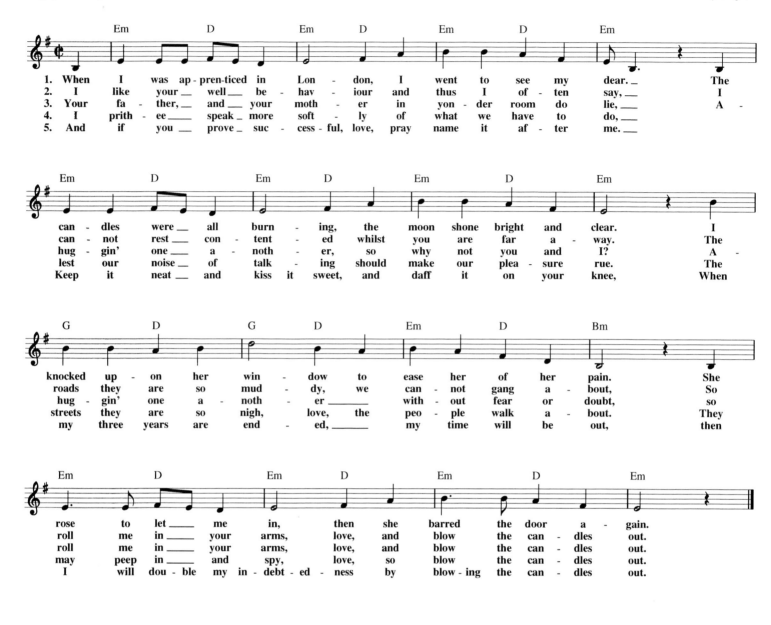

1. When I was ap-pren-ticed in Lon-don, I went to see my dear. _ The
2. I like your _ well _ be-hav-iour and thus I of-ten say, _ I
3. Your fa-ther, _ and _ your moth-er in yon-der room do lie, _ A-
4. I prith-ee _ speak _ more soft-ly of what we have to do, _ I
5. And if you _ prove _ suc-cess-ful, love, pray name it af-ter me. _ And

can-dles were _ all burn-ing, the moon shone bright and clear. I
can-not rest _ con-tent-ed whilst you are far a-way. The
hug-gin' one _ a-noth-er, so why not you and I? A-
lest our noise _ of talk-ing should make our plea-sure rue. The
Keep it neat _ and kiss it sweet, and daff it on your knee, When

knocked up-on her win-dow to ease her of her pain. She
roads they are so mud-dy, we can-not gang a-bout, So
hug-gin' one a-noth-er with-out fear or doubt, so
streets they are so nigh, love, the peo-ple walk a-bout. They
my three years are end-ed, my time will be out, then

rose to let _ me in, then she barred the door a-gain.
roll me in _ your arms, love, and blow the can-dles out.
roll me in _ your arms, love, and blow the can-dles out.
may peep in _ and spy, love, so blow the can-dles out.
I will dou-ble my in-debt-ed-ness by blow-ing the can-dles out.

BLOW THE MAN DOWN

18th Century American Sea Chantey

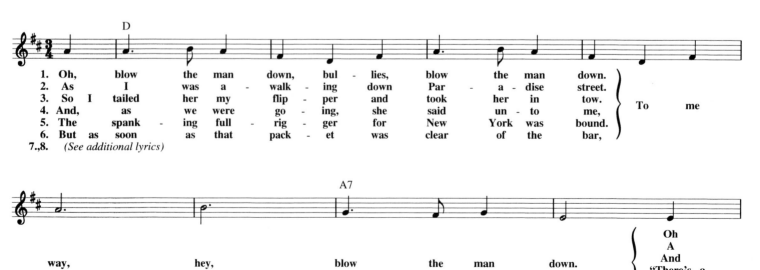

1. Oh, blow the man down, bul-lies, blow the man down.
2. As I was a-walk-ing down Par-a-dise street.
3. So I tailed her my flip-per and took her in tow.
4. And, as we were go-ing, she said un-to me,
5. The spank-ing full rig-ger for New York was bound.
6. But as soon as that pack-et was clear of the bar,
7.,8. *(See additional lyrics)*

To me

way, hey, blow the man down.

Oh
A
And
"There's a
She was
The

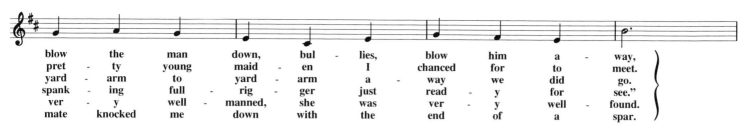

blow the man down, bul - lies, blow him a - way,
pret - ty young maid - en I chanced for to meet.
yard - arm to yard - arm a - way we did go.
spank - ing full - rig - ger just read - y for see."
ver - y well - manned, she was ver - y well - found.
mate knocked me down with the end of a spar.

Give me some time to blow the man down.

Additional Lyrics

7. And as soon as that packet was out on the sea,
To me way, hey, blow the man down.
'Twas dev'lish hard treatment of every degree.
Give me some time to blow the man down.

8. So I give you fair warning before we belay.
To me way, hey, blow the man down.
Don't never take heed of what pretty girls say.
Give me some time to blow the man down.

BLOW THE WIND SOUTHERLY

English
Words by John Stobbs

Blow the wind South - er - ly, South - er - ly, South - er - ly, Blow the wind South o'er the

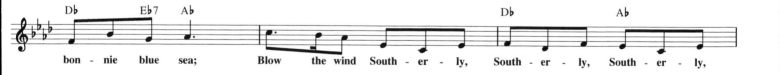

bon - nie blue sea; Blow the wind South - er - ly, South - er - ly, South - er - ly,

Blow bon - nie breeze, __ my lov - er to me. They told me last night there were

ships in the off - ing, And I hur - ried down to the deep roll - ing sea; But my

eye could not see it wher - ev - er might be it, The bark that is bear - ing my lov - er to me.

BLOW, YE WINDS, WESTERLY

Sea Chantey from Newfoundland

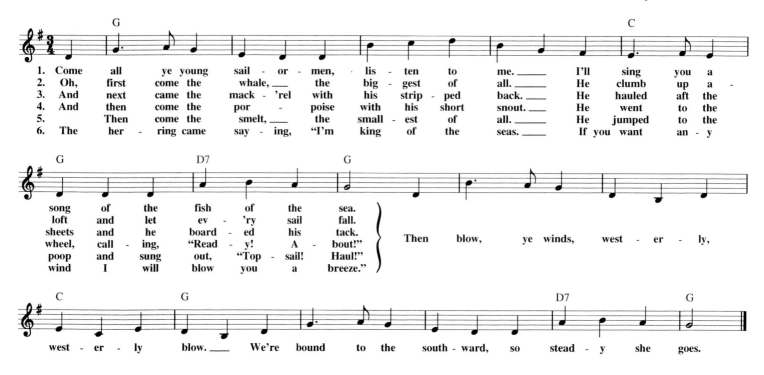

1. Come all ye young sail - or - men, lis - ten to me. _____ I'll sing you a
2. Oh, first come the whale, ___ the big - gest of all. _____ He clumb up a -
3. And next came the mack - 'rel with his strip - ped back. ___ He hauled aft the
4. And then come the por - poise with his short snout. ___ He went to the
5. Then come the smelt, ___ the small - est of all. _____ He jumped to the
6. The her - ring came say - ing, "I'm king of the seas. ___ If you want an - y

song of the fish of the sea.
loft and let ev - 'ry sail fall.
sheets and he board - ed his tack.
wheel, call - ing, "Read - y! A - bout!"
poop and sung out, "Top - sail! Haul!"
wind I will blow you a breeze."

Then blow, ye winds, west - er - ly,

west - er - ly blow. ___ We're bound to the south - ward, so stead - y she goes.

BLOW, YE WINDS, IN THE MORNING

18th Century American Sea Chantey

1. 'Tis ad - ver - tised in Bos - ton, New York and Buf - fa - lo, Five
2. They send you to New Bed - ford, That fa - mous whal - ing port, And
3. They tell you of the clip - per ships A - go - ing in and out, And
4. It's now we're out to se, my boys, The winds be - gin to blow. One
5. The skip - per's on the quar - ter deck A - squint - ing at the sails, When
6. Now clear a - way the boats, my boys, And af - ter him we'll trav - el. But
7., 8. (See additional lyrics)

hun - dred brave A - mer - i - cans, A - whal - ing for to go. _____
give you to some land - sharks ___ To board and fit you out. _____
say you'll take five hun - dred sperm Be - fore you're six months out. _____
half the watch is sick on deck, The oth - er sick be - low. _____
up a - loft the look - out Sights a school of whales. _____
if you get too near his fluke, He'll kick you to the dev - il. __

Sing - ing,

blow, ye winds, in the morn - ing, And blow ye winds, high - o!

Clear a - way the run - ning gear, And blow, ye winds, high - o!

Additional Lyrics

7. Now we've got him turned up,
   We tow him alongside,
   We over with our blubber hooks
   And rob him of his hide.

8. When we get home, our ship made fast,
   And we get through our sailing,
   A winding glass around we'll pass
   And damn this blubber-whaling.

THE BLUE BELLS OF SCOTLAND

Scottish
Attributed to a Mrs. Jordon, circa 1800

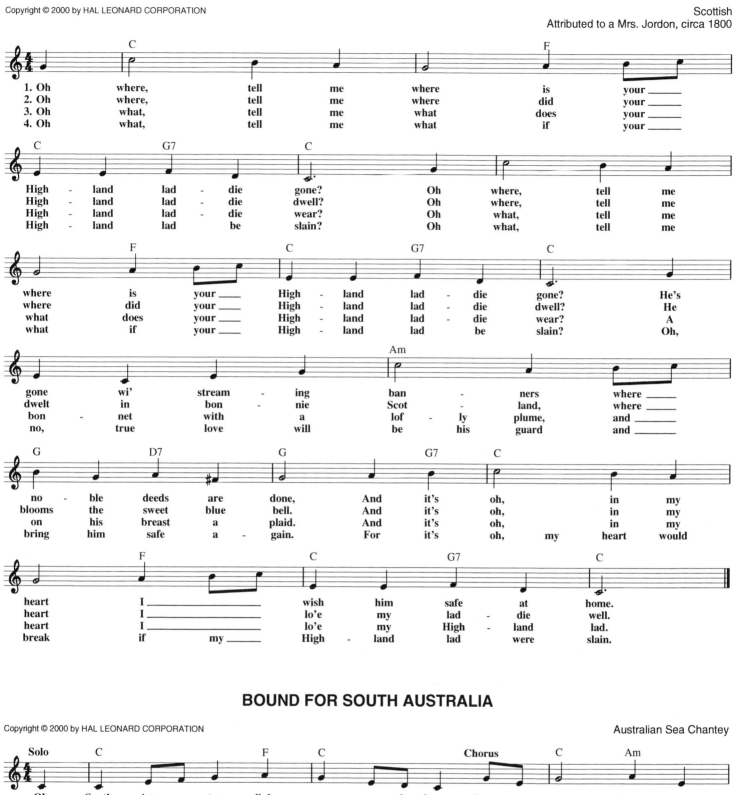

BOUND FOR SOUTH AUSTRALIA

Australian Sea Chantey

BLUE MOUNTAIN LAKE

19th Century American

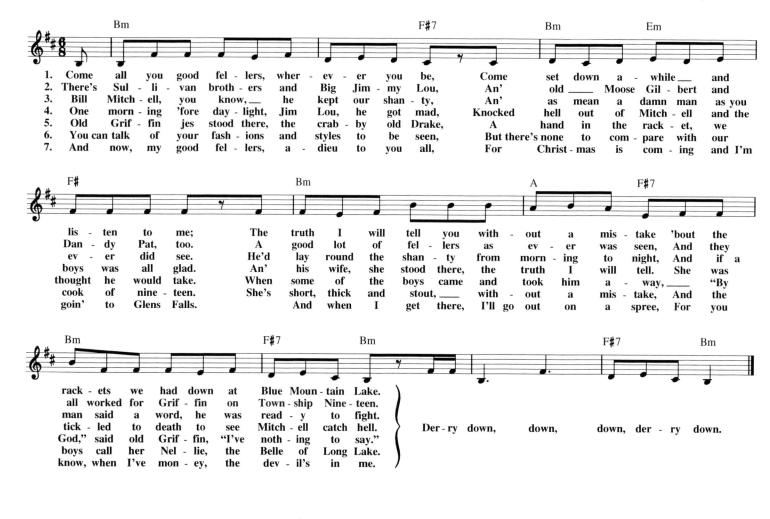

THE BLUE TAIL FLY
(Jimmy Crack Corn)

19th Century American
Based on a minstrel song by Dan Emmett

BOATMAN DANCE

19th Century American

BOBBY SHAFTOE

English Sea Chantey

THE BOLD FENIAN MEN

Irish
Words by Michael Scanlan

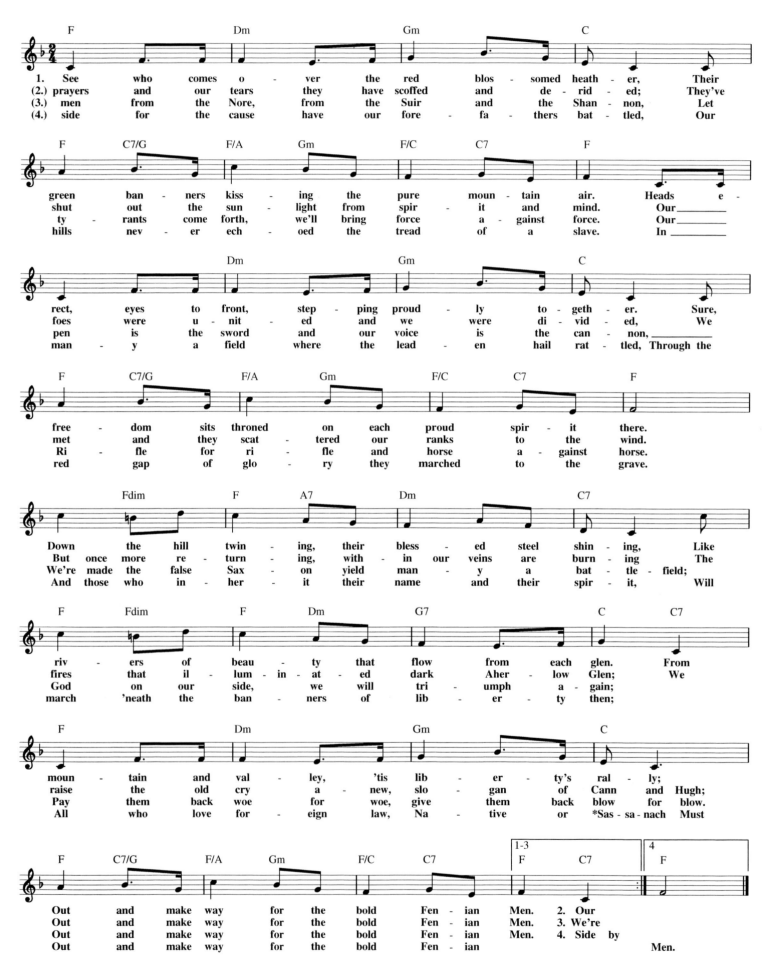

* derogatory term for the English

BOLD FISHERMAN

19th Century English Sea Chantey

1. There was a bold fish - er - man who sailed out from Pim - li - co To
2. He wrig - gled and scrig - gled in the wa - ter so brin - y - o. He
3. His ghost walked at mid - night to the bed - side of his Mar - i - Jane. He

slew the wild cod - fish and the bold mack - er - el. When he ar - rived off
yel - lowed and bel - lowed for ____ help but in vain. Then down - ward he did
told her how dead he was, said she, "I'll go mad." "Since my love - ly is so

Pim - li - co the storm - y winds did wild - ly blow. His lit - tle boat went
gent - ly glide to the bot - tom of the sil - v'ry tide; But pre - vi - ous - ly
dead," said she, "All joy on earth has fled for me. I nev - er - more will

wib - ble, wob - ble, and o - ver-board sprang he. }
to this he cried, "Fare thee well, Mar - i - Jane. } Twink - i, doo - dle, dum, twink - i,
hap - py be." ____ And she went rav - ing mad. }

doo - dle, dum, 'Twas the high - ly in - ter - est - ing song he sung. Twink - i

doo - dle, dum, twink - i, doo - dle, dum, sang the bold fish - er - man.

BONEY WAS A WARRIOR

19th Century Irish Sea Chantey

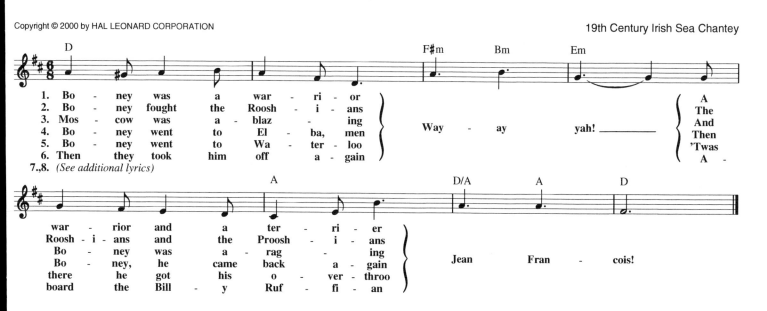

1. Bo - ney was a war - ri - or } Way - ay yah! ____ { A
2. Bo - ney fought the Roosh - i - ans } The
3. Mos - cow was a - blaz - ing } And
4. Bo - ney went to El - ba, men } Then
5. Bo - ney went to Wa - ter - loo } 'Twas
6. Then they took him off a - gain } A -
7.,8. (See additional lyrics)

war - rior and a ter - ri - er } Jean Fran - cois!
Roosh - i - ans and the Proosh - i - ans }
Bo - ney was a - rag - ing }
Bo - ney, he came back a - gain }
there he got his o - ver - throo }
board the Bill - y Ruf - fi - an }

Additional Lyrics

7. He went to Saint Helena
   Way-ay yah!
   There he was a prisona
   Jean Francois!

8. Boney broke his heart and died
   Way-ay yah!
   Away off in Saint Helena
   Jean Francois!

THE BOLD SOLDIER

17th Century English

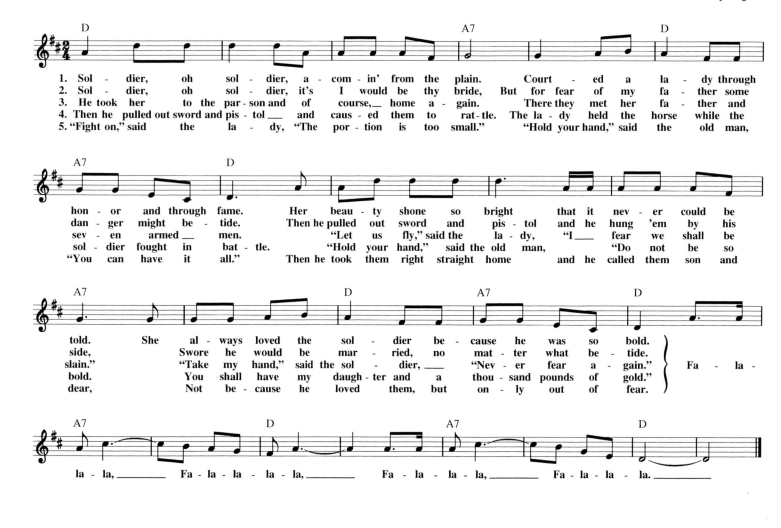

1. Sol - dier, oh sol - dier, a - com - in' from the plain. Court - ed a la - dy through
2. Sol - dier, oh sol - dier, it's I would be thy bride, But for fear of my fa - ther some
3. He took her to the par - son and of course,__ home a - gain. There they met her fa - ther and
4. Then he pulled out sword and pis - tol __ and caus - ed them to rat - tle. The la - dy held the horse while the
5. "Fight on," said the la - dy, "The por - tion is too small." "Hold your hand," said the old man,

hon - or and through fame. Her beau - ty shone so bright that it nev - er could be
dan - ger might be - tide. Then he pulled out sword and pis - tol and he hung 'em by his
sev - en armed __ men. "Let us fly," said the la - dy, "I__ fear we shall be
sol - dier fought in bat - tle. "Hold your hand," said the old man, "Do not be so
"You can have it all." Then he took them right straight home and he called them son and

told. She al - ways loved the sol - dier be - cause he was so bold.
side, Swore he would be mar - ried, no mat - ter what be - tide.
slain." "Take my hand," said the sol - dier, ___ "Nev - er fear a - gain." } Fa - la -
bold. You shall have my daugh - ter and a thou - sand pounds of gold."
dear, Not be - cause he loved them, but on - ly out of fear. }

la - la, _____ Fa - la - la - la - la, _____ Fa - la - la - la, _____ Fa - la - la - la. _____

THE BOLL WEEVIL

Folksong from Texas
circa 1890

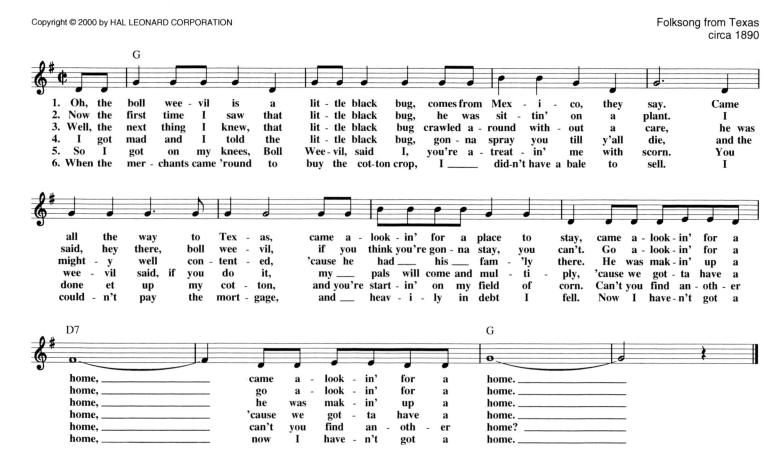

1. Oh, the boll wee - vil is a lit - tle black bug, comes from Mex - i - co, they say. Came
2. Now the first time I saw that lit - tle black bug, he was sit - tin' on a plant. I
3. Well, the next thing I knew, that lit - tle black bug crawled a - round with - out a care, he was
4. I got mad and I told the lit - tle black bug, gon - na spray you till y'all die, and the
5. So I got on my knees, Boll Wee - vil, said I, you're a - treat - in' me with scorn. You
6. When the mer - chants came 'round to buy the cot - ton crop, I _____ did-n't have a bale to sell. I

all the way to Tex - as, came a - look - in' for a place to stay, came a - look - in' for a
said, hey there, boll wee - vil, if you think you're gon - na stay, you can't. Go a - look - in' for a
might - y well con - tent - ed, 'cause he had __ his __ fam - 'ly there. He was mak - in' up a
wee - vil said, if you do it, my __ pals will come and mul - ti - ply, 'cause we got - ta have a
done et up my cot - ton, and you're start - in' on my field of corn. Can't you find an - oth - er
could - n't pay the mort - gage, and __ heav - i - ly in debt I fell. Now I have - n't got a

home, _____ came a - look - in' for a home. _____
home, _____ go a - look - in' for a home. _____
home, _____ he was mak - in' up a home. _____
home, _____ 'cause we got - ta have a home. _____
home, _____ can't you find an - oth - er home? _____
home, _____ now I have - n't got a home. _____

THE BOLD TENANT FARMER

19th Century Irish

* Let us leave that as it is.

BOLD ROBERT EMMET

Irish
circa 1803

1. The strug-gle is o-ver, the boys are de-feat-ed. Old Ire-land's sur-round-ed with sad-ness and gloom, We were de-feat-ed and shame-ful-ly treat-ed, And I, Rob-ert Em-met, a-wait now my doom. Hung, drawn,and quar-tered, sure that was my sen-tence, But soon I will show them no cow-ard am I. My crime is the love of the land I was born in.

2. The barque lay at an-chor a wait-ing to bring me O-ver the bil-lows to the land of the free. But I must see my sweet-heart for I know she will cheer me, And with her I will sail far o-ver the sea. But I was ar-rest-ed and cast in-to pris-on, Tried as a trai-tor, a reb-el, a spy. But no man can call me a knave or a cow-ard.

3. Hark, the bell's toll-ing, I well know its mean-ing. My poor heart tells me it is my death knell. In come the cler-gy, the ward-er is lead-ing. I have no friends here to bid me fare-well. Good-bye, old Ire-land, my par-ents and sweet-heart. Com-pan-ions in arms to for-get you must try. I am proud of the hon-our, it was on-ly my du-ty.

A he-ro I lived and a he-ro I'll die. Bold Rob-ert Em-met, the dar-ling of Ire-land, Bold Rob-ert Em-met will die with a smile. Fare-well, com-pan-ions both loy-al and dar-ing. I'll lay down my life for the Em-er-ald Isle.

THE BONNIEST LASS

Scottish
Based on a poem by Robert Burns

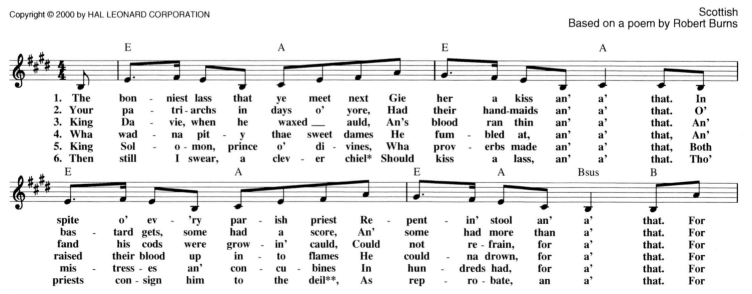

1. The bon-niest lass that ye meet next Gie her a kiss an' a' that. In spite o' ev-'ry par-ish priest Re-pent-in' stool an' a' that. For
2. Your pa-tri-archs in days o' yore, Had their hand-maids an' a' that. O' bas-tard gets, some had a score, An' some had more than a' that. For
3. King Da-vie, when he waxed auld, An's blood ran thin an' a' that. An' fand his cods were grow-in' cauld, Could not re-frain, for a' that. For
4. Wha wad-na pit-y thae sweet dames He fum-bled at, an' a' that, An' raised their blood up in-to flames He could-na drown, for a' that. For
5. King Sol-o-mon, prince o' di-vines, Wha prov-erbs made an' a' that, Both mis-tress-es an' con-cu-bines In hun-dreds had, for a' that. For
6. Then still I swear, a clev-er chiel* Should kiss a lass, an' a' that. Tho' priests con-sign him to the deil**, As rep-ro-bate, an a' that. For

*young man
**devil

a'_____ that an' a'_____ that, Their hol - low sangs an' a' that. In
a'_____ that an' a'_____ that, Your old - time saints an' a' that, Were
a'_____ that an' a'_____ that, To keep him warm an' a' that, The
a'_____ that an' a'_____ that, He, want - ed strength, an' a' that, For,
a'_____ that an' a'_____ that, Tho'a preach - er wise, an' a' that, The
a'_____ that an' a'_____ that, Their cant - ing stuff, an' a' that. They

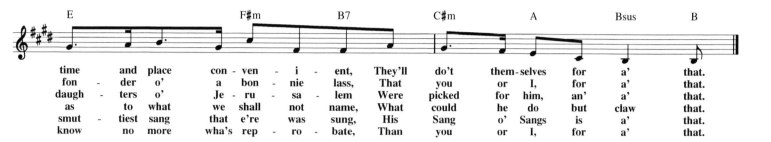

time and place con - ven - i - ent, They'll do't them-selves for a' that.
fon - der o' a bon - nie lass, That you or I, for a' that.
daugh - ters o' Je - ru - sa - lem Were picked for him, an' a' that.
as to what we shall not name, What could he do but claw that.
smut - tiest sang that e're was sung, His Sang o' Sangs is a' that.
know no more wha's rep - ro - bate, Than you or I, for a' that.

THE BONNY BUNCH OF ROSES

Irish
Based on an English tune

1. By the mar - gin___ of the o - cean, one___ morn - ing___ in___ the month of June, The___
2. Then_ up steps_ young Na - po - le - on and___ takes his___ moth - er by the hand, Say-ing,
3. The first time I saw young Na - po - le - on, down_ on his___ bend - ed knee fell he. He___
4. He___ took three_ hun - dred thou - sand men, with___ kings like - wise_ to bear his train. He___
5. Oh___ son, don't_ speak so ven - ture-some, for in Eng - land_ are___ the hearts of oak. There is
6. Now_ do be - lieve me dear-est moth - er; now___ I lie___ on___ my dy - ing bed. If I'd

feath - ered warb - ling song - sters their charm - ing notes___ did___ sweet - ly sing. There
"Moth - er___ dear, have pa - tience un - til I'm a - ble to___ take com - mand. I'll
asked the___ par - don of his fa - ther, who grant - ed it___ most mourn - ful - ly. "Dear
was so___ well pro - vid - ed for, that he could sweep_ the___ world a - lone. But
Eng - land,_ Ire - land, Scot - land, their u - ni - ty___ was___ nev - er - broke. Oh
lived, I___ would have been clev - er - er, but now I droop_ my___ youth - ful head. But

I es - pied a___ fe - male, she seemed to be in grief and woe, Con -
raise a ter - ri - ble ar - my, and through tre - men - dous dan - gers go, And in
son," he said, "I'll take an ar - my, and o - ver the fro - zen Alps will go, Then _
when he came to___ Mos - cow, he was o - ver - pow-ered by the driv - en snow, When_
son, think on thy___ fa - ther, on the Isle of Saint Hel - en - a his bod - y lies low, And you
whilst our bod - ies lie mould-er - ing, and weep - ing wil - lows o - ver our bod-ies grow, The

sult - ing with young_ Bon - a - parte con - cern - ing the bon - ny bunch of ros - es, oh.
spite_ of all the___ u - ni - verse, I'll con - quer the bon - ny bunch of ros - es, oh."
I___ will con - quer_ Mos - cow, and re - turn to the bon - ny bunch of ros - es, oh."
Mos - cow was a - blaz - ing, so he lost his___ bon - ny bunch of ros - es, oh.
may_ soon fol - low af - ter him, so be-ware of the bon - ny bunch of ros - es, oh.
deeds_ of great Na - po - le - on shall sing the___ bon - ny bunch of ros - es oh

THE BONNY EARL OF MURRAY

18th Century Scottish

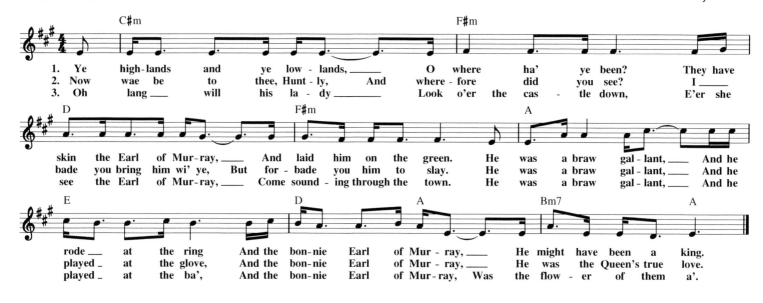

1. Ye high-lands and ye low-lands,____ O where ha' ye been? They have
2. Now wae be to thee, Hunt-ly, And where-fore did you see? I____
3. Oh lang____ will his la-dy_____ Look o'er the cas-tle down, E'er she

skin the Earl of Mur-ray,____ And laid him on the green. He was a braw gal-lant,____ And he
bade you bring him wi' ye, But for-bade you him to slay. He was a braw gal-lant,____ And he
see the Earl of Mur-ray,____ Come sound-ing through the town. He was a braw gal-lant,____ And he

rode____ at the ring And the bon-nie Earl of Mur-ray,____ He might have been a king.
played _ at the glove, And the bon-nie Earl of Mur-ray,____ He was the Queen's true love.
played _ at the ba', And the bon-nie Earl of Mur-ray, Was the flow-er of them a'.

THE BONNY LIGHTER BOY

English

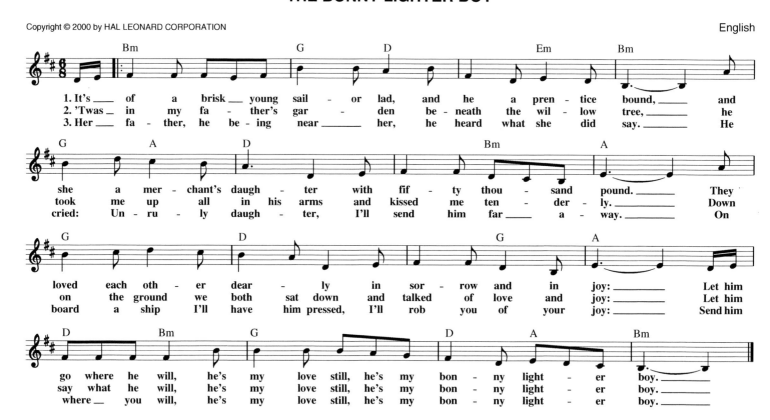

1. It's ____ of a brisk____ young sail-or lad, and he a pren-tice bound,____ and
2. 'Twas _ in my fa-ther's gar-den be-neath the wil-low tree,_____ he
3. Her____ fa-ther, he be-ing near_____ her, he heard what she did say._____ He

she a mer-chant's daugh-ter with fif-ty thou-sand pound._____ They
took me up all in his arms and kissed me ten-der-ly._____ Down
cried: Un-ru-ly daugh-ter, I'll send him far____ a-way._____ On

loved each oth-er dear-ly in sor-row and in joy:____ Let him
on the ground we both sat down and talked of love and joy:____ Let him
board a ship I'll have him pressed, I'll rob you of your joy:____ Send him

go where he will, he's my love still, he's my bon-ny light-er boy.____
say what he will, he's my love still, he's my bon-ny light-er boy.____
where____ you will, he's my love still, he's my bon-ny light-er boy.____

THE BONNY SHIP THE DIAMOND

Scottish Sea Chantey
circa 1820

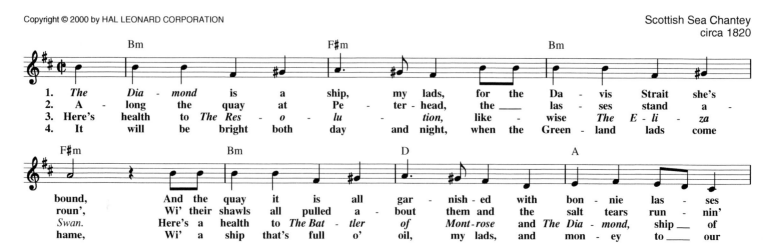

1. *The* *Dia* - *mond* is a ship, my lads, for the Da - vis Strait she's
2. A - long the quay at Pe - ter-head, the ____ las - ses stand a -
3. Here's health to *The Res* - *o* - *lu* - *tion*, like - wise *The E* - *li* - *za*
4. It will be bright both day and night, when the Green - land lads come

bound, And the quay it is all gar - nish-ed with bon - nie las - ses
roun', Wi' their shawls all pulled a - bout them and the salt tears run - nin'
Swan. Here's a health to *The Bat* - *tler* of *Mont-rose* and *The Dia* - mond, ship __ of
hame, Wi' a ship that's full o' oil, my lads, and mon - ey to ____ our

round. | Cap-tain Thom-son gives the or - der to sail the o-cean
down. | Don't you weep my bon-nie lass, _____ though you be left be
fame. | We ___ wear the trou-sers of the white and the jack-ets of the
name. | We'll ___ make the cra-dles for to rock, and the blan-kets for to

wide, | Where the sun it nev-er sets, my lad, no dark-ness dims ___ the
hind, | For the rose will grow on Green-land's ice be-fore we change ___ our
blue. | When ___ we re-turn to Pe - ter-head we'll ha'e sweet-hearts ___ e-
tear, | And ___ ev-'ry lass in Pe - ter-head sing, "Hush - a - bye, ___ my

sky.
mind. } So it's cheer up, my lads, let your hearts nev - er
noo.
dear."

fail, | While the bon-nie ship *The Dia-mond* goes a - fish-ing for the whale.

BOOTHBAY WHALE

Folksong from Maine
circa 1850

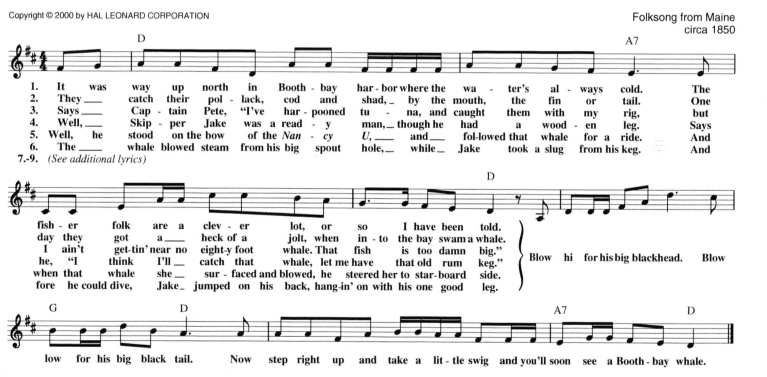

1. It was way up north in Booth - bay har-bor where the wa - ter's al - ways cold. The
2. They ___ catch their pol - lack, cod and shad, _ by the mouth, the fin or tail. One
3. Says ___ Cap - tain Pete, "I've har - pooned tu - na, and caught them with my rig, but
4. Well, ___ Skip - per Jake was a read - y man, _ though he had a wood - en leg. Says
5. Well, he stood on the bow of the *Nan* - cy U, ___ and ___ fol-lowed that whale for a ride. And
6. The ___ whale blowed steam from his big spout hole, _ while _ Jake took a slug from his keg. And
7.-9. *(See additional lyrics)*

fish - er folk are a clev - er lot, or so I have been told.
day they got a ___ heck of a jolt, when in - to the bay swam a whale.
I ain't get-tin' near no eight-y foot whale. That fish is too damn big." } Blow hi for his big blackhead. Blow
he, "I think I'll ___ catch that whale, let me have that old rum keg."
when that whale she _ sur - faced and blowed, he steered her to star-board side.
fore he could dive, Jake _ jumped on his back, hang-in' on with his one good leg.

low for his big black tail. Now step right up and take a lit - tle swig and you'll soon see a Booth-bay whale.

Additional Lyrics

7. Well, Jake took his keg and used it like a plug,
   Pushed it tight in the old whale's spout.
   He kicked it hard, then jumped on board
   Sayin', "Boys, it will never come out."

8. Well, the whale he blew, he puffed, he heaved,
   And the boys all gave a shout;
   And the very next time he 'rose to blow,
   He blew his brains right out.

9. You bold seafarin' whalermen, you've wasted all these years,
   With race boats, harpoons, ropes and hooks, and all that other gear.
   All you need is a big ol' plug; next time you see him spout,
   Just kick it in, sit back and rest, while he blows his brains right out.

BOSTON BURGLAR

Irish-American
circa 1910

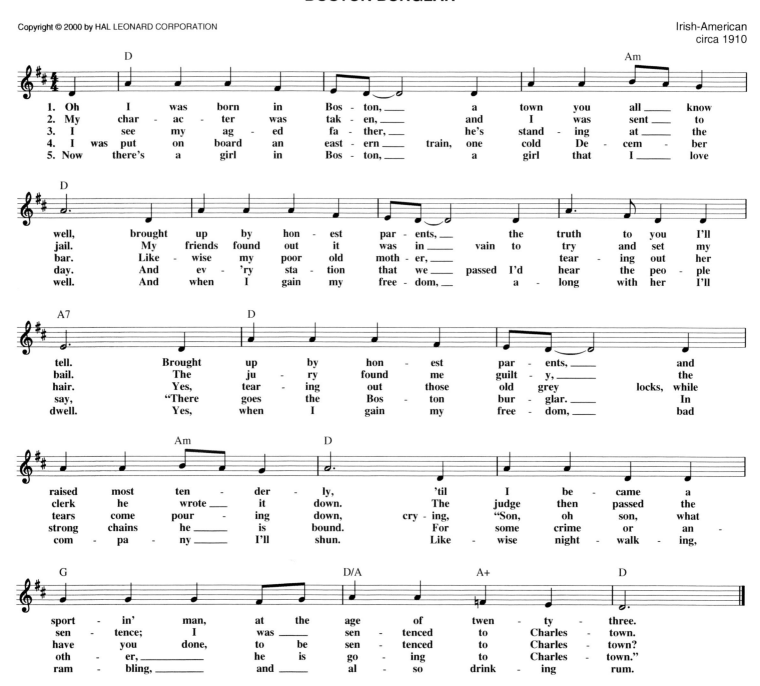

1. Oh I was born in Bos - ton, ___ a town you all ___ know
2. My char - ac - ter was tak - en, ___ and I was sent ___ to
3. I see my ag - ed fa - ther, ___ he's stand - ing at ___ the
4. I was put on board an east - ern ___ train, one cold De - cem - ber
5. Now there's a girl in Bos - ton, ___ a girl that I ___ love

well, brought up by hon - est par - ents, ___ the truth to you I'll
jail. My friends found out it was in ___ vain to try and set my
bar. Like - wise my poor old moth - er, ___ tear - ing out her
day. And ev - 'ry sta - tion that we ___ passed I'd hear the peo - ple
well. And when I gain my free - dom, ___ a - long with her I'll

tell. Brought up by hon - est par - ents, ___ and
bail. The ju - ry found me guilt - y, ___ the
hair. Yes, tear - ing out those old grey locks, while
say, "There goes the Bos - ton bur - glar. ___ In
dwell. Yes, when I gain my free - dom, ___ bad

raised most ten - der - ly, 'til I be - came a
clerk he wrote ___ it down. The judge then passed the
tears come pour - ing down, cry - ing, "Son, oh son, what
strong chains he ___ is bound. For some crime or an -
com - pa - ny ___ I'll shun. Like - wise night - walk - ing,

sport - in' man, at the age of twen - ty - three.
sen - tence; I was ___ sen - tenced to Charles - town.
have you done, to be sen - tenced to Charles - town?
oth - er, ___ he is go - ing to Charles - town."
ram - bling, ___ and ___ al - so drink - ing rum.

BOSTON TEA TAX SONG

From the American Revolutionary War

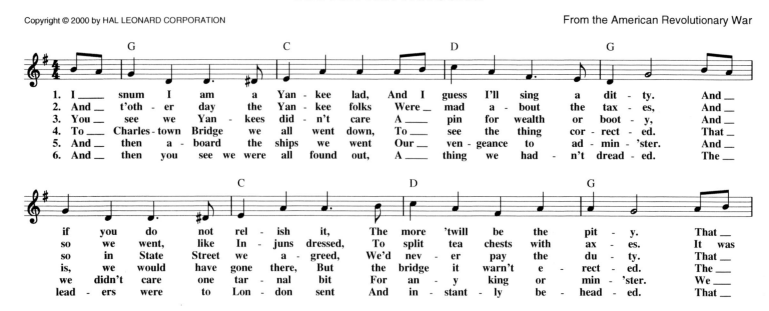

1. I ___ snum I am a Yan - kee lad, And I guess I'll sing a dit - ty. And ___
2. And ___ t'oth - er day the Yan - kee folks Were ___ mad a - bout the tax - es, And ___
3. You ___ see we Yan - kees did - n't care A ___ pin for wealth or boot - y, And ___
4. To ___ Charles - town Bridge we all went down, To ___ see the thing cor - rect - ed. That ___
5. And ___ then a - board the ships we went Our ___ ven - geance to ad - min - 'ster. And ___
6. And ___ then you see we were all found out, A ___ thing we had - n't dread - ed. The ___

if you do not rel - ish it, The more 'twill be the pit - y. That ___
so we went, like In - juns dressed, To split tea chests with ax - es. It was
so in State Street we a - greed, We'd nev - er pay the du - ty. That ___
is, we would have gone there, But the bridge it warn't e - rect - ed. The ___
we didn't care one tar - nal bit For an - y king or min - 'ster. We ___
lead - ers were to Lon - don sent And in - stant - ly be - head - ed. That ___

BOTANY BAY

Australian

BOUND FOR THE RIO GRANDE

19th Century English Sea Chantey

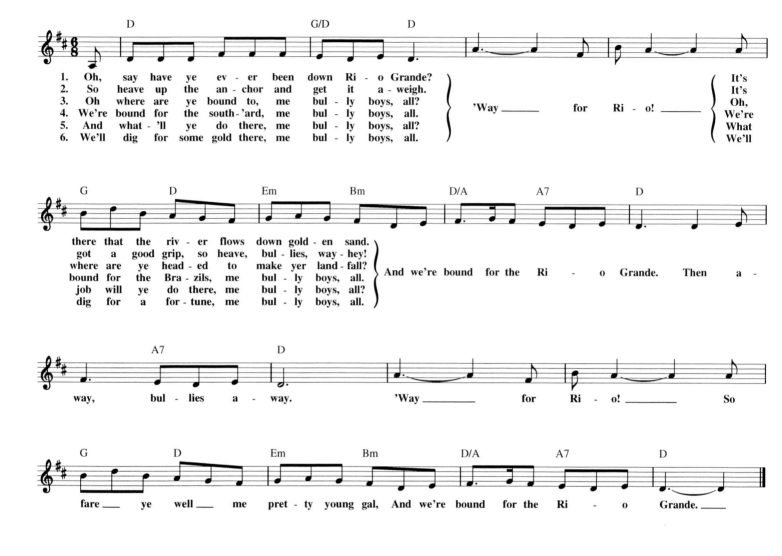

1. Oh, say have ye ev-er been down Ri-o Grande?
2. So heave up the an-chor and get it a-weigh.
3. Oh where are ye bound to, me bul-ly boys, all?
4. We're bound for the south-'ard, me bul-ly boys, all.
5. And what-'ll ye do there, me bul-ly boys, all?
6. We'll dig for some gold there, me bul-ly boys, all.

'Way _____ for Ri - o! _____

It's
It's
Oh,
We're
What
We'll

there that the riv-er flows down gold-en sand.
got a good grip, so heave, bul-lies, way-hey!
where are ye head-ed to make yer land-fall?
bound for the Bra-zils, me bul-ly boys, all.
job will ye do there, me bul-ly boys, all?
dig for a for-tune, me bul-ly boys, all.

And we're bound for the Ri - o Grande. Then a-

way, bul - lies a - way. 'Way _____ for Ri - o! _____ So

fare _____ ye well _____ me pret-ty young gal, And we're bound for the Ri - o Grande. _____

BOW AND BALANCE

17th Century English
Based on Child Ballad No. 10

1. There was an old wom-an lived on the sea-shore.
2. There was a young man who came there to see them.
3. He bought for the young-est a bea - ver hat.
4. "Oh sis - ter, oh sis - ter, let's walk the sea - shore."
5. And while these two sis - ters were walk - ing the shore,
6. "Oh sis - ter, oh sis - ter, please lend me your hand."

7.-12. *(See additional lyrics)*

Bow and bal - ance to me. _____

There was an old
There was a young
He bought for the
"Oh sis - ter, oh
And while these two
"Oh sis - ter, oh

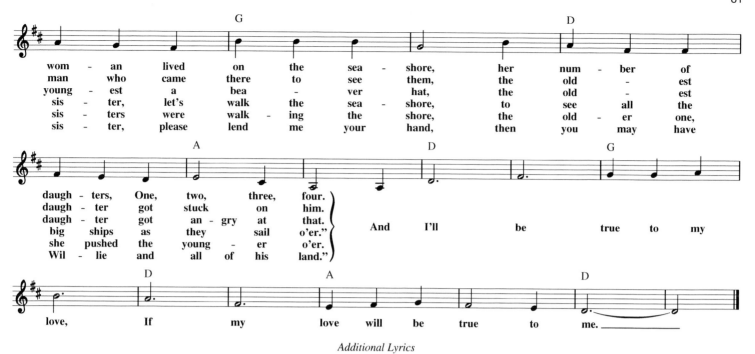

wom - an lived on the sea - shore, her num - ber of
man who came there to see them, the old - est
young - est a bea - ver hat, the old - est
sis - ter, let's walk the sea - shore, to see all the
sis - ters were walk - ing the shore, the old - er one,
sis - ter, please lend me your hand, then you may have

daugh - ters, One, two, three, four.
daugh - ter got stuck on him.
daugh - ter got an - gry at that.
big ships as they sail o'er."
she pushed the young - er o'er.
Wil - lie and all of his land."
And I'll be true to my

love, If my love will be true to me. ____

Additional Lyrics

7. "I never, I never will lend you my hand...
But I will have Willie and all of his land."
Chorus

8. Sometimes she sank and sometimes she swam...
Until she came to the old mill dam.
Chorus

9. The miller, he got his fishing hook...
And fished the maiden out of the brook.
Chorus

10. "Oh miller, oh miller, here's five gold rings...
If you'll put me safe on shore again."
Chorus

11. The miller received those five gold rings...
And pushed the maiden in again.
Chorus

12. The sister was hung on the gallows high...
And the miller was burned at the stake nearby.
Chorus

THE BOWLD SOGER BOY

By Samuel Lover
American Civil War Song

1. Oh, there's not a trade that's go - ing worth show - ing, or know - ing, like
2. But ____ when we get the route, how they pout and they shout, while ____

that from glo - ry grow - ing for a bowld so - ger boy! Where
to the right a - bout ____ goes the bowld so - ger boy! Tis

right or left we go, sure you know, friend or foe, will have the hand or toe from the
then that las - sies fair, in de - spair tear their hair. But "The dev - il a one I care," says the

bowld so - ger boy. There's not a town we march through, but the la - dies look - ing arch though the
bowld so - ger boy. For the world is all be - fore us, where the land - la - dies a - dore us, and

win - dow panes will sarch through the ranks to find their joy. While up the street each girl you meet, with
ne'er re - fuse to score us but chalk us up with joy. We taste her tap, we tear her cap. "Oh

look so sly will cry, "My eye! oh, is - n't he the dar - ling, the bowld so - ger boy!"
that's the chap for me," says she. "Oh is - n't he a dar - ling, the bowld so - ger boy."

BOWLING GREEN

19th Century Southeastern American

1. Wish I was in Bowl-ing Green, sit-tin' in a chair, one arm 'round my
2. If you see that gal of mine, tell her once for me, if she love an-
3. Wish I was a bum-ble bee, sail-ing through the air, sail right down to my
4. Go-in' through this whole wide world, go-in' through a-lone, go-in' through this

pret-ty lit-tle miss, t'oth-er 'round my dear, t'oth-er 'round my
oth-er boy, yes I'll set her free, yes I'll set her
true love's side, touch her if you dare, touch her if you
whole wide world, I ain't got no home, I ain't got no

dear.
free.
dare.
home.

Bowl-ing Green, hey, good old Bowl-ing Green.

THE BRASS MOUNTED ARMY

American Civil War Song

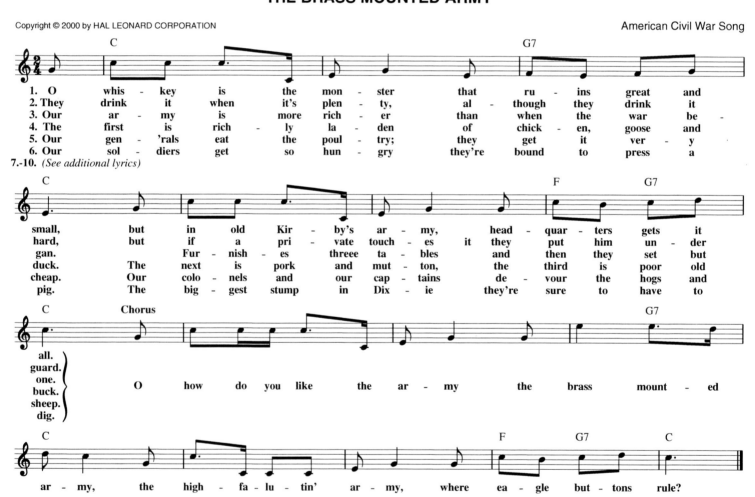

1. O whis-key is the mon-ster that ru-ins great and
2. They drink it when it's plen-ty, al-though they drink it
3. Our ar-my is more rich-er than when the war be-
4. The first is rich-ly la-den of chick-en, goose and
5. Our gen-'rals eat the poul-try; they get it ver-y
6. Our sol-diers get so hun-gry they're bound to press a
7.-10. *(See additional lyrics)*

small, but in old Kir-by's ar-my, head-quar-ters gets it
hard, but if a pri-vate touch-es it they put him un-der
gan. Fur-nish-es threee ta-bles and then they set but
duck. The next is pork and mut-ton, the third is poor old
cheap. Our colo-nels and our cap-tains de-vour the hogs and
pig. The big-gest stump in Dix-ie they're sure to have to

all.
guard.
one.
buck.
sheep.
dig.

Chorus

O how do you like the ar-my the brass mount-ed

ar-my, the high-fa-lu-tin' ar-my, where ea-gle but-tons rule?

Additional Lyrics

7. But when we are a-marchin';
The order number blank,
It makes the private soldier
Forever stay in rank.

8. On every big plantation
Or a nigger-holder's yard,
Just to save his property,
Our generals place a guard.

9. An' now my song is ended,
It's beautiful an' true;
The pore men an' the widders
Must have a line or two.

10. But there no guard is stationed,
Their fence is often burned;
Their property's molested,
As long ago we learned.

BRENNAN ON THE MOOR

19th Century Irish

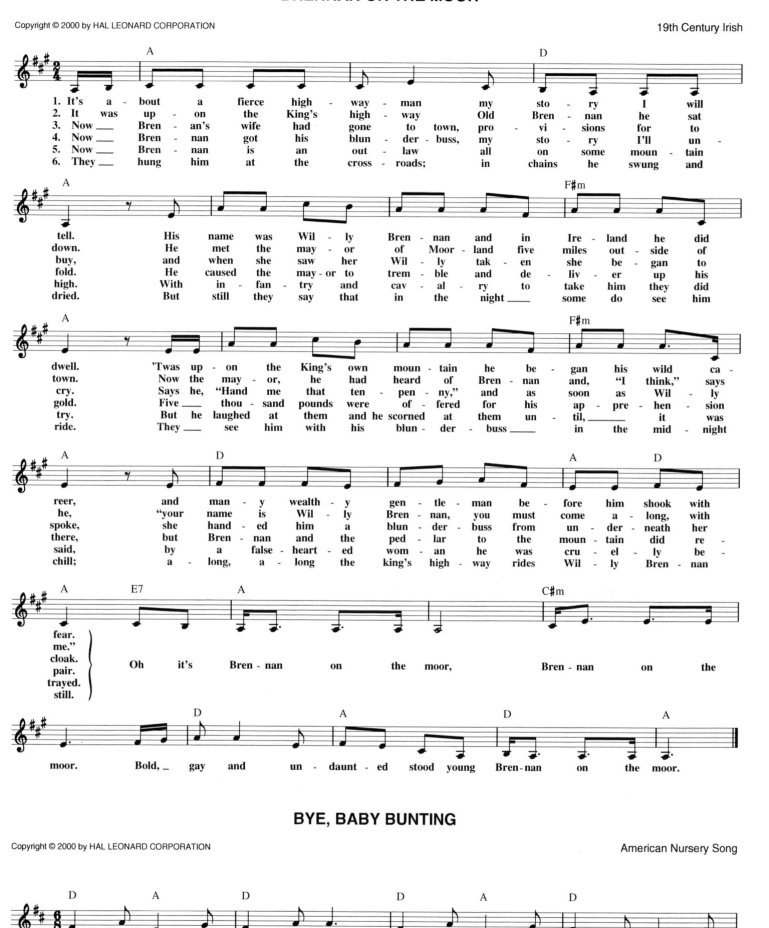

BYE, BABY BUNTING

American Nursery Song

BRIGHT PHOEBE

Canadian

1. Bright Phoe - be was my true love's name, so fair a
2. Oh, she and I we did a - gree that mar - ried
3. Be - fore I did re - turn from sea my love - ly
4. I am for - sak - en I am for - lorn. I wish to
5. I will go down to some si - lent place where no oth - er

girl that ev - er was seen, So fair a girl that
short - ly we would be. As soon as I re -
dam - sel was slain from me. The pride and glo - ry
God I'd nev - er been born. I'd have died be - fore the
man shall be - hold my face. I'll spend the re - main - der

ev - er was seen, If you'd trav - el the wide world o - ver.
turned from sea we would set - tle that sol - emn bar - gain.
of my heart in her cold grave lay moul - d'ring.
bil - lows' roar since for - tune had proved so cru - el.
of my days la - ment - ing for bright Phoe - be.

BROKE AND HUNGRY

American

1. I am broke and hun - gry, rag - ged and dirt - y, too, I say I'm broke and hun - gry,
2.-6. *(See additional lyrics)*

rag-ged and dirt - y too, Ma - ma, if I clean up can I go home with you?

Additional Lyrics

2. I am motherless, fatherless, sister— and brotherless too,
I am motherless, fatherless, sister— and brotherless too,
Reason I tried so hard to make this trip with you.

3. You miss me, woman, count the days I'm gone.
You miss me, woman, count the days I'm gone.
I'm goin' away to build me a railroad of my own.

4. I feel like jumpin' through the keyhole in your door,
I feel like jumpin' through the keyhole in your door
If you jump this time, baby, you won't jump no more.

5. I believe my good gal has found my black cat bone,
I believe my good gal has found my black cat bone,
I can leave Sunday morning; Monday morning I'm stickin' 'round home.

6. I want to show you woman what careless love has done,
I want to show you woman what careless love has done,
Caused a man like me to be a great long way from home.

BROWN EYES

19th Century American

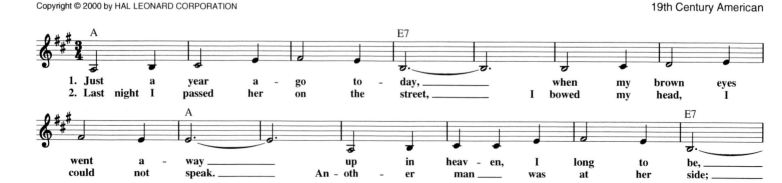

1. Just a year a - go to - day, when my brown eyes
2. Last night I passed her on the street, I bowed my head, I

went a - way up in heav - en, I long to be,
could not speak. An - oth - er man was at her side;

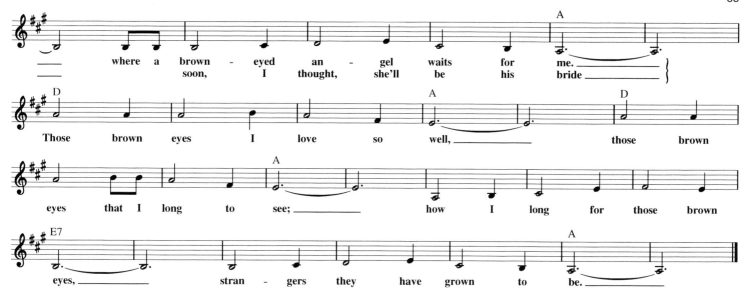

where a brown - eyed an - gel waits for me. _____
soon, I thought, she'll be his bride _____

Those brown eyes I love so well, _____ those brown

eyes that I long to see; _____ how I long for those brown

eyes, _____ stran - gers they have grown to be. _____

BUCKEYE JIM

American Frontier Song

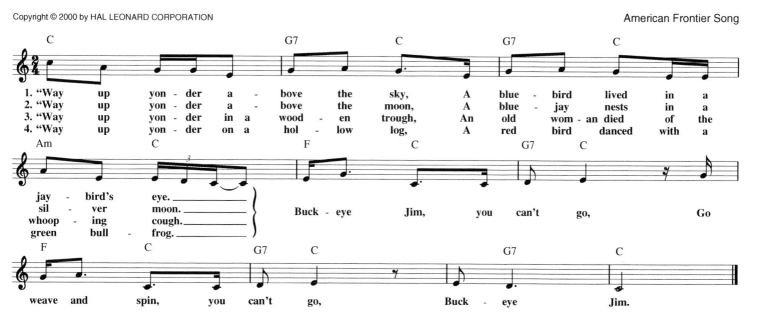

1. "Way up yon - der a - bove the sky, A blue - bird lived in a
2. "Way up yon - der a - bove the moon, A blue - jay nests in a
3. "Way up yon - der in a wood - en trough, An old wom - an died of the
4. "Way up yon - der on a hol - low log, A red bird danced with a

jay - bird's eye. _____
sil - ver moon. _____
whoop - ing cough. _____
green bull - frog. _____

Buck - eye Jim, you can't go, Go

weave and spin, you can't go, Buck - eye Jim.

THE BRISK YOUNG BACHELOR

16th Century English

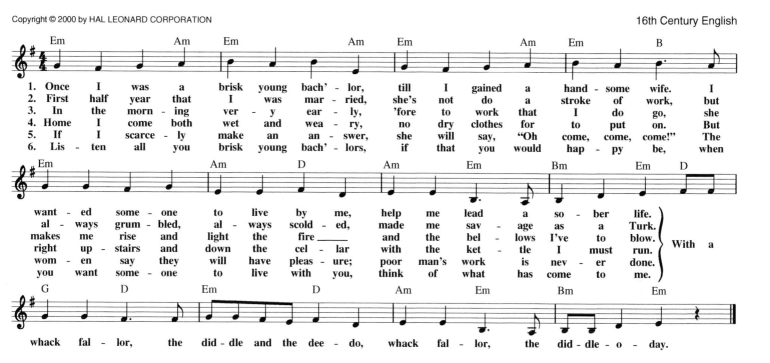

1. Once I was a brisk young bach' - lor, till I gained a hand - some wife. I
2. First half year that I was mar - ried, she's not do a stroke of work, but
3. In the morn - ing ver - y ear - ly, 'fore to work that I do go, she
4. Home I come both wet and wea - ry, no dry clothes for to put on. But
5. If I scarce - ly make an an - swer, she will say, "Oh come, come, come!" The
6. Lis - ten all you brisk young bach' - lors, if that you would hap - py be, when

want - ed some - one to live by me, help me lead a so - ber life.
al - ways grum - bled, al - ways scold - ed, made me sav - age as a Turk.
makes me rise and light the fire _____ and the bel - lows I've to blow.
right up - stairs and down the cel - lar with the ket - tle I must run.
wom - en say they will have pleas - ure; poor man's work is nev - er done.
you want some - one to live with you, think of what has come to me.

With a

whack fal - lor, the did - dle and the dee - do, whack fal - lor, the did - dle - o - day.

THE BRITISH GRENADIERS

17th Century English

BROWN GAL IN DE RING

Courting Song from Trinidad and Tobago

BROWN'S FERRY BLUES

19th Century American

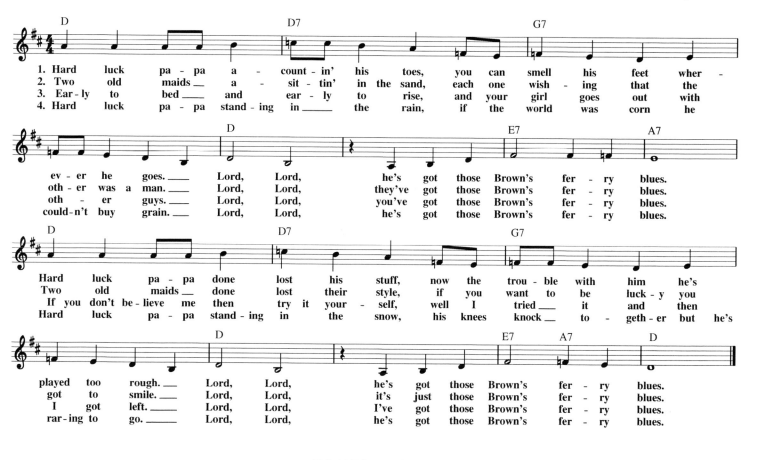

1. Hard luck pa - pa a - count - in' his toes, you can smell his feet wher -
2. Two old maids __ a - sit - tin' in the sand, each one wish - ing that the
3. Ear - ly to bed ___ and ear - ly to rise, and your girl goes out with
4. Hard luck pa - pa stand - ing in ___ the rain, if the world was corn he

ev - er he goes. ___ Lord, Lord, he's got those Brown's fer - ry blues.
oth - er was a man. ___ Lord, Lord, they've got those Brown's fer - ry blues.
oth - er guys. ___ Lord, Lord, you've got those Brown's fer - ry blues.
could - n't buy grain. ___ Lord, Lord, he's got those Brown's fer - ry blues.

Hard luck pa - pa done lost his stuff, now the trou - ble with him he's
Two old maids __ done lost their style, if you want to be luck - y you
If you don't be - lieve me then try it your - self, well I tried ___ it and then
Hard luck pa - pa stand - ing in the snow, his knees knock __ to - geth - er but he's

played too rough. __ Lord, Lord, he's got those Brown's fer - ry blues.
got to smile. __ Lord, Lord, it's just those Brown's fer - ry blues.
I got left. ___ Lord, Lord, I've got those Brown's fer - ry blues.
rar - ing to go. ___ Lord, Lord, he's got those Brown's fer - ry blues.

BRUTON TOWN

15th Century English

1. In Bru - ton Town there lived a ___ farm - er Who had two sons and one daugh - ter __ dear. By
2. If he our ser - vant courts our ___ sis - ter, That maid from such a ___ shame I'll __ save. I'll
3. Now wel - come home, my dear young _ broth - ers, Our ser - vant man is ___ he be - hind? We've
4. You rise up ear - ly to - mor - row ___ morn - ing And straight-way to the ___ brake you _ know, And
5. She took her ker - chief from her ___ pock - et, And wiped his eyes though _ he was _ blind; Be -

day and night they were a - con - triv - ing To fill their par - ents' __ hearts with fear. One
put an end to all their _ court - ship, And send him si - lent __ to his grave. A
left him where we've been a - hunt - ing, We've left him where no ___ man can find. She
then you'll find my bod - y ___ ly - ing All cov - er'd o'er in a gore of blood. Then
cause he was my own true _ lov - er, My own _ true lov - er and friend of mine. And

told his se - cret in none _ oth - er, But to his broth - er this he __ said: I
day of hunt - ing was pre - par - ed In thorn - y woods where bri - ars _ grew. And
went to bed cry - ing and la - ment - ing, La - ment - ing for her own true _ love. She
she rose ear - ly the ver - y next morn - ing, Un - to the gar - den brake she _ went, And
since my broth - ers have been so ___ cru - el To take your ten - der sweet life a - way, One

think our ser - vant courts our ___ sis - ter, I think _ they have a ___ mind to wed.
there they did that your man a - mur - der, And in ___ the brake his fair bod - y threw.
slept. She dream'd. She saw him _ by her All cov - er'd o'er in a gore of blood.
there she found her own dear _ jew - el, All cov - er'd o'er in a gore of blood.
grave shall hold us both to - geth - er, And a - long _ with you in __ death I'll stay.

BUFFALO GALS
(Won't You Come Out Tonight)

Words and Music by
Cool White (John Hodges)
1844

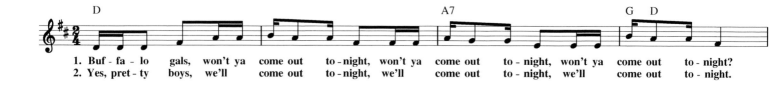

1. Buf - fa - lo gals, won't ya come out to - night, won't ya come out to - night, won't ya come out to - night?
2. Yes, pret - ty boys, we'll come out to - night, we'll come out to - night, we'll come out to - night.

Buf - fa - lo gals, won't ya come out to - night and dance by the light of the moon?
Yes, pret - ty boys, we'll come out to - night and dance by the light of the moon.
I

danced with a gal with a hole in her stock-ing and her heel kept a - rock-in' and her toe kept a-knock-in'. I

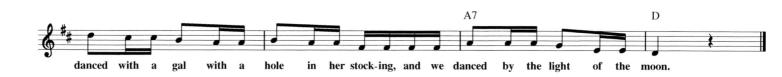

danced with a gal with a hole in her stock-ing, and we danced by the light of the moon.

THE BUFFALO SKINNERS

American Cowboy Song
Tune based on a Lumberjack song from Maine

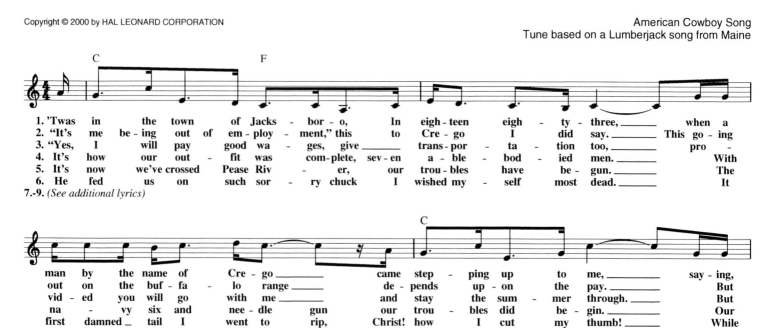

1. 'Twas in the town of Jacks - bor - o, In eigh - teen eigh - ty - three, _____ when a
2. "It's me be - ing out of em - ploy - ment," this to Cre - go I did say. _____ This go - ing
3. "Yes, I will pay good wa - ges, give _____ trans - por - ta - tion too, _____ pro -
4. It's how our out - fit was com - plete, sev - en a - ble - bod - ied men. _____ With
5. It's now we've crossed Pease Riv - er, our trou - bles have be - gun. _____ The
6. He fed us on such sor - ry chuck I wished my - self most dead. _____ It

7.-9. *(See additional lyrics)*

man by the name of Cre - go _____ came step - ping up to me, _____ say - ing,
out on the buf - fa - lo range _____ de - pends up - on the pay. _____ But
vid - ed you will go with me _____ and stay the sum - mer through. _____ But
na - vy six and nee - dle gun our trou - bles did be - gin. _____ Our
first damned _ tail I went to rip, Christ! how I cut my thumb! _____ While
was _____ old jerked _ beef _ cro - ton cof - fee and sour bread. _____ Pease

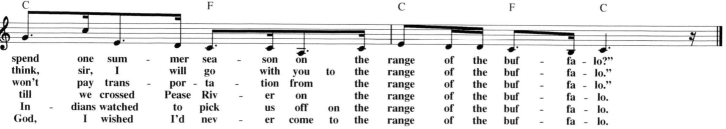

Additional Lyrics

7. Our meat it was buffalo rump and iron wedge bread,
And all we had to sleep on was a buffalo robe for a bed;
The fleas and graybacks worked on us, oh, boys, it was not slow,
I'll tell you there's no worse hell on earth than the range of the buffalo.

8. The season being near over, old Crego he did say
The crowd had been extravagant, was in debt to him that day.
We coaxed him and we begged him, and still it was no go—
We left his damned old bones to bleach on the range of the buffalo.

9. Oh, it's now we've crossed Pease River and homeward we are bound,
No more in that hell-fired country shall ever we be found.
Go home to our wives and sweethearts, tell others not to go,
For God's forsaken the buffalo range and the damned old buffalo.

BYKER HILL

Irish

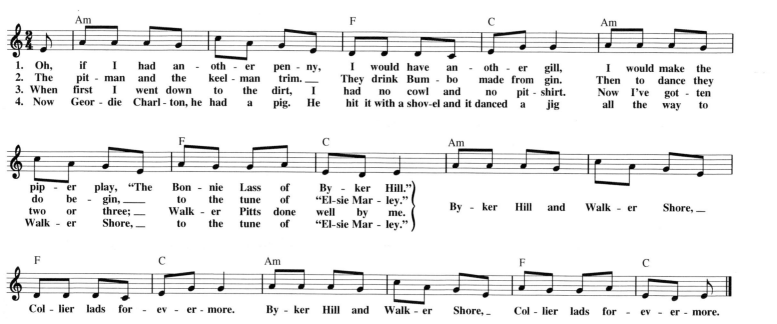

BULLDOG AND THE BULLFROG

Southern American

1. Oh, the bull - dog on the bank and the bull - frog in the
pool, the bull - dog on the bank and the bull - frog in the
pool; the _____ bull - dog called the bull - frog a green old wa - ter
fool.) Sing - ing tra la la la la la la la la la la,
tra la la la la la la. _____ Sing - ing
tra la la la la, sing - ing tra la la la la.
Tra la la la, tra la la la, tra la la la la la.

2. Oh, the bull - dog stooped to catch him and the snap - per caught his
paw, oh, the bull - dog stooped to catch him and the snap - per caught his
paw; the _____ pol - ly - wog died a - laugh - ing to see him wag his
jaw.)

BURY ME BENEATH THE WILLOW

Southeastern American

1. My heart is sad and I am lone - ly, think - ing of the one I love. I know I nev - er
2. They told me that he loved an - oth - er; how could I be - lieve them true, un - til an an - gel
3. To - mor - row was to be our wed - ding, Lord, oh Lord where can he be. He's gone a - way to

more shall see him, till we meet in heav'n a - bove.)
soft - ly whis - pered he has pro - ven his love un - true.) So bur - y me be - neath the wil - low;
wed an - oth - er, and no more he cares for me.)

'Neath the weep - ing wil - low tree. And when he knows where I am sleep - ing, then per - haps he'll weep for me.

BURY ME NOT ON THE LONE PRAIRIE

Cowboy Ballad, circa 1870s
Attributed to H. Clemens
Based on "The Ocean Burial" (1849)
Words by the Rev. Edwin H. Chapin
Music by Ossian N. Dodge

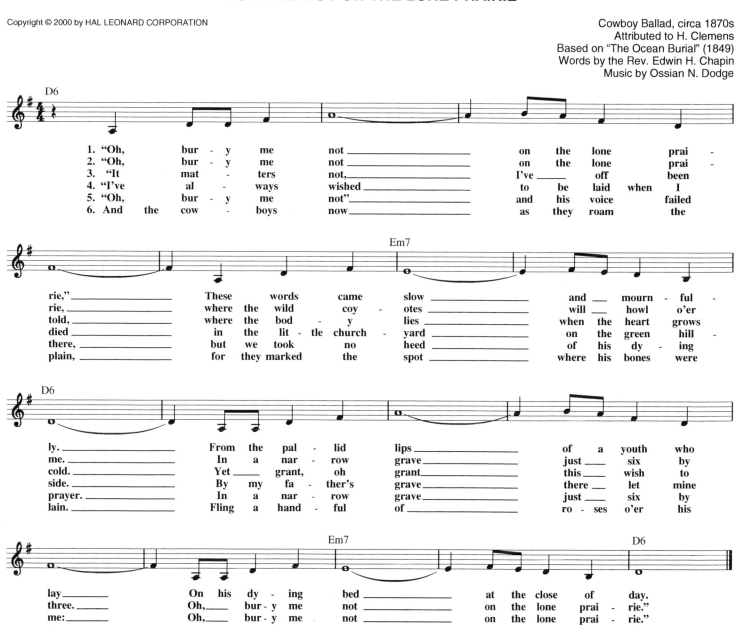

THE CAMPBELLS ARE COMING

Scottish

THE CALTON WEAVER

Scottish

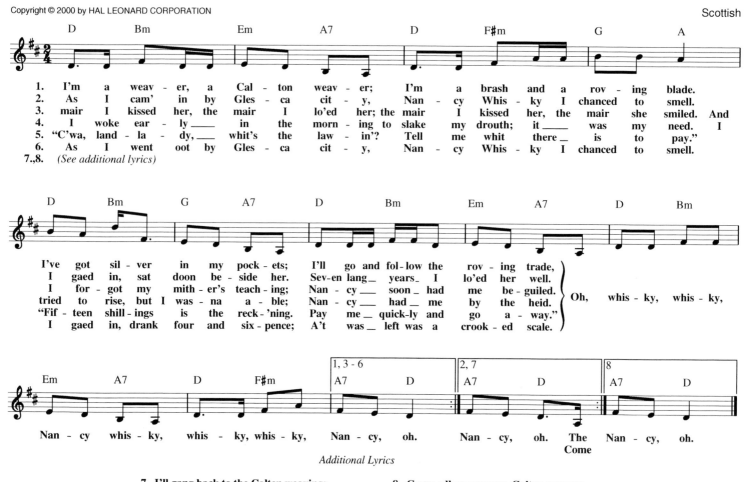

1. I'm a weav-er, a Cal-ton weav-er; I'm a brash and a rov-ing blade.
2. As I cam' in by Gles-ca cit-y, Nan-cy Whis-ky I chanced to smell.
3. mair I kissed her, the mair I lo'ed her; the mair I kissed her, the mair she smiled. And
4. I woke ear-ly ____ in the morn-ing to slake my drouth; it ____ was my need. I
5. "C'wa, land-la-dy, ____ whit's the law-in'? Tell me whit there ____ is to pay."
6. As I went oot by Gles-ca cit-y, Nan-cy Whis-ky I chanced to smell.

7., 8. *(See additional lyrics)*

I've got sil-ver in my pock-ets; I'll go and fol-low the rov-ing trade,
I gaed in, sat doon be-side her. Sev-en lang ____ years ____ I lo'ed her well.
I for-got my mith-er's teach-ing; Nan-cy ____ soon had me be-guiled.
tried to rise, but I was-na a - ble; Nan-cy ____ had ____ me by the heid.
"Fif-teen shill-ings is the reck-'ning. Pay me ____ quick-ly and go a - way."
I gaed in, drank four and six-pence; A't was ____ left was a crook-ed scale.

Oh, whis-ky, whis-ky,

Nan-cy whis-ky, whis-ky, whis-ky, Nan-cy, oh. |1, 3 - 6| Nan-cy, oh. |2, 7| The Come |8| Nan-cy, oh.

Additional Lyrics

7. I'll gang back to the Calton weaving;
   I'll surely mak' the shuttles fly.
   I'll mak' mair at the Calton weaving.
   Than ever I did in a roving way.

8. Come, all ye weavers, Calton weavers,
   A' ye weavers where'er ye be.
   Beware of whisky, Nancy whisky;
   She'll ruin you as she ruined me.

CALVARY

African-American Spiritual

Cal - va - ry, ____ Cal - va - ry, ____ Cal - va - ry, ____

____ Cal - va - ry, ____ Cal - va - ry, ____ Cal - va -

ry, ____ Sure - ly He died on ____ Cal - va - ry, ____

1. Ev - 'ry time I ____ think ____ a - bout Je - sus, Ev - 'ry ____
2. Don't you hear the ____ ham - mer ring - ing? Don't you ____
3. Don't you hear Him ____ call - ing His Fa - ther? Don't you ____
4. Don't you hear Him ____ say, ____ "It is fin - ished"? Don't you

time I _____ think ____ a - bout Je - sus, _____ Ev - 'ry time I _____
hear the _____ ham - mer ring - ing? _____ Don't you hear the _____
hear Him _____ call - ing His Fa - ther? _____ Don't you hear Him _____
hear Him _____ say, ____ "It is fin - ished"? _____ Don't you hear Him _____

D.C. *(3 times)*
D.C. al Fine *(4th time)*

____ think ____ a - bout Je - sus, _____
____ ham - mer ring - ing? _____ } Sure - ly He died on _____ Cal - va - ry.
____ call - ing His Fa - ther? _____
____ say, ____ "It is fin - ished"? _____ }

CAMPTOWN RACES

Words and Music by
Stephen C. Foster

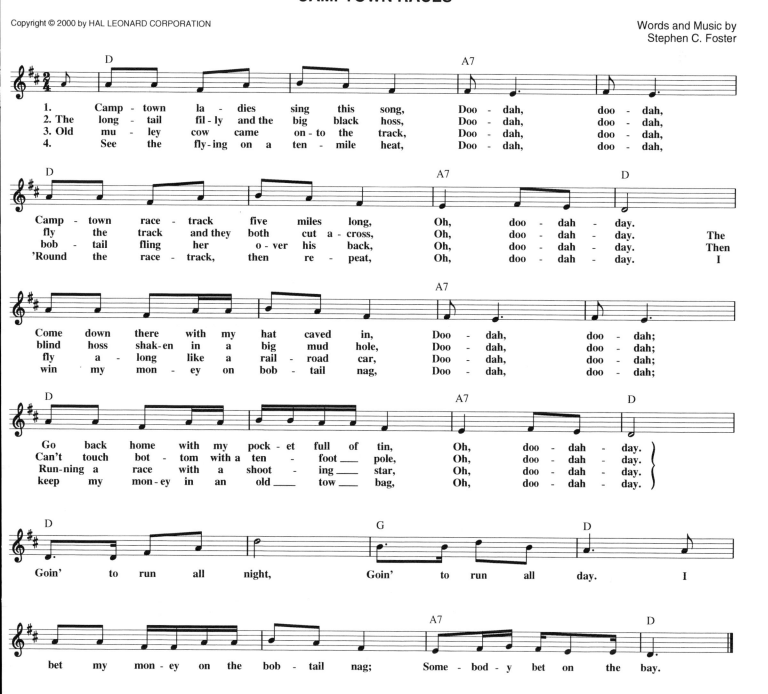

1. Camp - town la - dies sing this song, Doo - dah, doo - dah,
2. The long - tail fil - ly and the big black hoss, Doo - dah, doo - dah,
3. Old mu - ley cow came on - to the track, Doo - dah, doo - dah,
4. See the fly - ing on a ten - mile heat, Doo - dah, doo - dah,

Camp - town race - track five miles long, Oh, doo - dah - day. The
fly the track and they both cut a - cross, Oh, doo - dah - day.
bob - tail fling her o - ver his back, Oh, doo - dah - day. Then
'Round the race - track, then re - peat, Oh, doo - dah - day. I

Come down there with my hat caved in, Doo - dah, doo - dah;
blind hoss shak - en in a big mud hole, Doo - dah, doo - dah;
fly a - long like a rail - road car, Doo - dah, doo - dah;
win my mon - ey on bob - tail nag, Doo - dah, doo - dah;

Go back home with my pock - et full of tin, Oh, doo - dah - day.
Can't touch bot - tom with a ten - foot ____ pole, Oh, doo - dah - day.
Run-ning a race with a shoot - ing ____ star, Oh, doo - dah - day. }
keep my mon - ey in an old ____ tow ____ bag, Oh, doo - dah - day.)

Goin' to run all night, Goin' to run all day. I

bet my mon - ey on the bob - tail nag; Some - bod - y bet on the bay.

CANADA-I-O

19th Century Lumberjack song from Maine

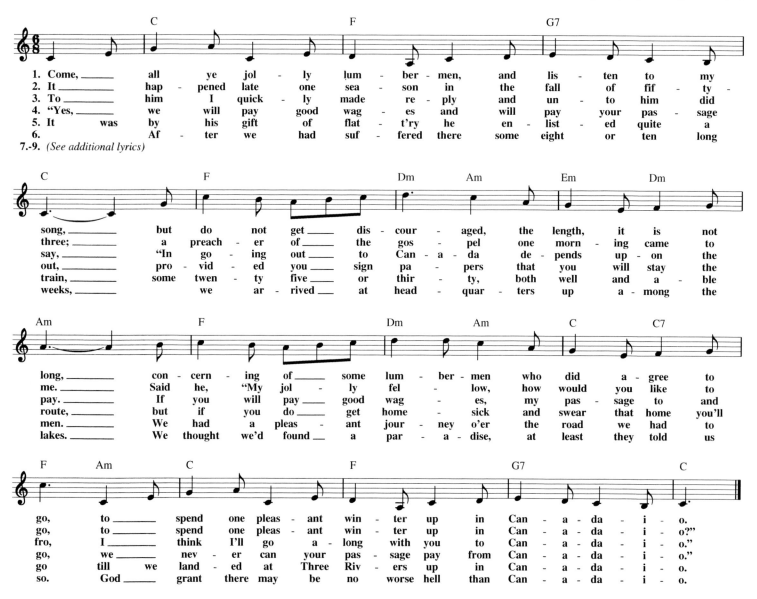

1. Come, _____ all ye jol - ly lum - ber - men, and lis - ten to my
2. It _____ hap - pened late one sea - son in the fall of fif - ty -
3. To _____ him I quick - ly made re - ply and un - to him did
4. "Yes, _____ we will pay good wag - es and will pay your pas - sage
5. It was by his gift of flat - t'ry he en - list - ed quite a
6. _____ Af - ter we had suf - fered there some eight or ten long

7.-9. *(See additional lyrics)*

song, _____ but do not get _____ dis - cour - aged, the length, it is not
three; _____ a preach - er of _____ the gos - pel one morn - ing came to
say, _____ "In go - ing out _____ to Can - a - da de - pends up - on the
out, _____ pro - vid - ed you _____ sign pa - pers that you will stay the
train, _____ some twen - ty five _____ or thir - ty, both well and a - ble
weeks, _____ we ar - rived _____ at head - quar - ters up a - mong the

long, _____ con - cern - ing of _____ some lum - ber - men who did a - gree to
me. _____ Said he, "My jol - ly fel - low, how would you like to
pay. _____ If you will pay _____ good wag - es, my pas - sage to and
route, _____ but if you do _____ get home - sick and swear that home you'll
men. _____ We had a pleas - ant jour - ney o'er the road we had to
lakes. _____ We thought we'd found _____ a par - a - dise, at least they told us

go, to _____ spend one pleas - ant win - ter up in Can - a - da - i - o.
go, to _____ spend one pleas - ant win - ter up in Can - a - da - i - o?"
fro, I _____ think I'll go a - long with you to Can - a - da - i - o."
go, we _____ nev - er can your pas - sage pay from Can - a - da - i - o."
go till we _____ land - ed at Three Riv - ers up in Can - a - da - i - o.
so. God _____ grant there may be no worse hell than Can - a - da - i - o.

Additional Lyrics

7. To describe what we have suffered is past the art of man,
   But to give a fair description, I will do the best I can.
   Our food, the dogs would snarl at it, our beds were on the snow;
   We suffered worse than murderers up in Canada-i-o.

8. Our hearts were made of iron and our souls were cased in steel;
   The hardships of that winter could never make us yield
   Field, Philips, and Norcross, they found their match, I know,
   Among the boys that went from Maine to Canada-i-o.

9. But now our lumbering is over and we are returning home
   To greet our wives and sweethearts, and never more to roam,
   To greet our wives and sweethearts, and never more to go
   Unto the God-forsaken place called Canada-i-o.

CANOE SONG

American Camp Song

My pad - dle's keen and bright, Flash - ing with sil - ver. Fol - low the wild goose flight: Dip dip and swing.
Dip, dip and swing her back, Flash - ing with sil - ver. Swift as the wild goose flies; Dip, dip and swing.

* This song can be sung as a 4-part round.

CAPE ANN

American

1. We hunt-ed and we hal-loed, and the first thing that we found was a barn in the mead-ow, and
2. So we hunt-ed and we hal-loed, and the next thing we did find was the man in the el - e - ment, and
3. So we hunt-ed and we hal-loed, and the next thing we did find was the light - house in Cape Ann, and
4. So we hunt-ed and we hal-loed, and the last thing we did find was the owl in the o - live bush, and

that we left be-hind. Look ye there! One said it was a barn, but the
that we left be-hind. Look ye there! One said it was the moon, but the
that we left be-hind. Look ye there! One said it was the light-house, but the
that we left be-hind. Look, ye there! One said it was an owl, the

oth - er said nay; he said it was a meet-ing-house with the stee - ple blown a-way. Look ye there!
oth - er said nay; he said it was a Yan-kee cheese with the one half cut a-way. Look ye there!
oth - er said nay; he said it was a sug - ar loaf with the pa - per blown a-way. Look ye there!
oth - er said nay; he said it was the E - vil One and we all three ran a-way. Look ye there!

CAPTAIN JINKS OF THE HORSE MARINES

19th Century English

1. I'm _ Cap - tain Jinks of the Horse Ma - rines, I feed my horse on corn and beans, and
2. I ___ joined my corps _ when twen - ty-one; of course I thought it cap - i - tal fun. When the
3. The _ first time I ____ went out for drill, the bug - ler sound - ing made me ill; of the

sport young la - dies in their teens, tho' a cap - tain in the Ar - my, I
en - e - my comes of course I run, for I'm not cut out for the Ar - my. When
bat - tle-field I'd had my fill, for I'm not cut out for the Ar - my. The

teach young la - dies how to dance, how to dance, how to dance. I
I left home, ma - ma she cried, ma - ma she cried, ma - ma she cried. When
of - fi - cers they all did shout, they all did shout, they all did shout. The

teach young la - dies how to dance, for I'm the pet of the Ar - my.
I left home, ma - ma she cried, "He's not cut out for the Ar - my!" I'm _
of - fi - cers they all did shout, "Why, kick him out of the Ar - my!"

Cap - tain Jinks of the Horse Ma - rines, I feed my horse on corn and beans, and

of - ten live be - yond my means, for that's the style of the Ar - my.

CAPE COD GIRLS

American

1. O, Cape Cod girls they have no combs; } heave a - way, heave a - way! { They
2. O, Cape Cod boys they have no sleds; } heave a - way, heave a - way! { They
3. O, Cape Cod cats they have no tails; } heave a - way, heave a - way! { They

comb their hair with cod - fish bones; } heave a - way, heave a - way! Heave a -
slide down - hill on cod - fish heads; } heave a - way, heave a - way! Heave a -
blew a - way in heav - y gales; } heave a - way, heave a - way! Heave a -

way, you bul - ly, bul - ly boys! Heave a - way, heave a - way! Heave a -

way, and don't you make a noise, for we're bound for Aus - tral - ia.

CAPTAIN KIDD

18th Century American

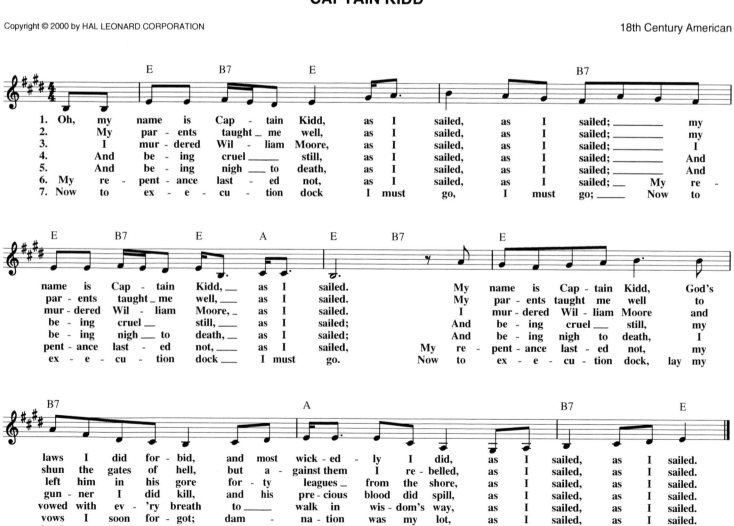

1. Oh, my name is Cap - tain Kidd, as I sailed, as I sailed; _____ my
2. My par - ents taught _ me well, as I sailed, as I sailed; _____ my
3. I mur - dered Wil - liam Moore, as I sailed, as I sailed; _____ I
4. And be - ing cruel _____ still, as I sailed, as I sailed; _____ And
5. And be - ing nigh ___ to death, as I sailed, as I sailed; _____ And
6. My re - pent - ance last - ed not, as I sailed, as I sailed; __ My re -
7. Now to ex - e - cu - tion dock I must go, I must go; _____ Now to

name is Cap - tain Kidd, ___ as I sailed. My name is Cap - tain Kidd, God's
par - ents taught _ me well, ___ as I sailed. My par - ents taught me well to
mur - dered Wil - liam Moore, _ as I sailed. I mur - dered Wil - liam Moore and
be - ing cruel ___ still, ___ as I sailed; And be - ing cruel ___ still, my
be - ing nigh ___ to death, ___ as I sailed; And be - ing nigh to death, I
pent - ance last - ed not, ____ as I sailed, My re - pent - ance last - ed not, my
ex - e - cu - tion dock ___ I must go. Now to ex - e - cu - tion dock, lay my

laws I did for - bid, and most wick - ed - ly I did, as I sailed, as I sailed.
shun the gates of hell, but a - gainst them I re - belled, as I sailed, as I sailed.
left him in his gore for - ty leagues _ from the shore, as I sailed, as I sailed.
gun - ner I did kill, and his pre - cious blood did spill, as I sailed, as I sailed.
vowed with ev - 'ry breath to _____ walk in wis - dom's way, as I sailed, as I sailed.
vows I soon for - got; dam - na - tion was my lot, as I sailed, as I sailed.
head up - on the block; no _____ more the laws I'll mock, as I sailed, as I sailed.

CAPTAINS AND SHIPS

Sea Chantey from Newfoundland

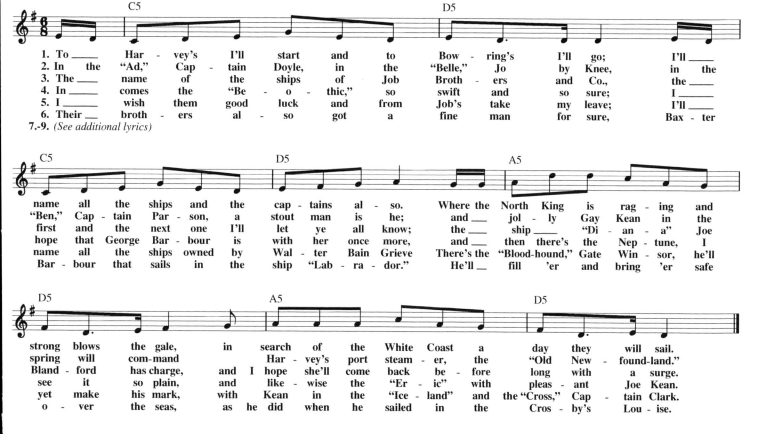

1. To ____ Har - vey's I'll start and to Bow - ring's I'll go; I'll ____
2. In the "Ad," Cap - tain Doyle, in the "Belle," Jo by Knee, in the
3. The ____ name of the ships of Job Broth - ers and Co., the ____
4. In ____ comes the "Be - o - thic," so swift and so sure; I ____
5. I ____ wish them good luck and from Job's take my leave; I'll ____
6. Their ___ broth - ers al - so got a fine man for sure, Bax - ter

7.-9. *(See additional lyrics)*

name all the ships and the cap - tains al - so. Where the North King is rag - ing and
"Ben," Cap - tain Par - son, a stout man is he; and ___ jol - ly Gay Kean in the
first and the next one I'll let ye all know; the ___ ship ___ "Di - an - a" Joe
hope that George Bar - bour is with her once more, and ___ then there's the Nep - tune, I
name all the ships owned by Wal - ter Bain Grieve There's the "Blood-hound," Gate Win - sor, he'll
Bar - bour that sails in the ship "Lab - ra - dor." He'll ___ fill 'er and bring 'er safe

strong blows the gale, in search of the White Coast a day they will sail.
spring will com-mand Har - vey's port steam - er, the "Old New - found-land."
Bland - ford has charge, and I hope she'll come back be - fore long with a surge.
see it so plain, and like - wise the "Er - ic" with pleas - ant Joe Kean.
yet make his mark, with Kean in the "Ice - land" and the "Cross," Cap - tain Clark.
o - ver the seas, as he did when he sailed in the Cros - by's Lou - ise.

Additional Lyrics

7. Next it is Bowring's, the firm that's well-known
    For the pluck, push and enterprise and all it has shown
    By building that steamer, ye all know it well,
    Even Kean, her commander, the new "Florizel."

8. The "Kite", Captain Carrol, I wish him good luck;
    Once more in the "Eagle" Joe Kean showed his pluck.
    And Bartlett the "Viking" I pray ye will fill;
    Dear old Dan Green, may he make the big bill.

9. The "Ranger" Sam Windsor be fleetingly seen;
    Likewise Noah Bishop and the "Algerine"
    My song is concluded by captains and ships,
    And may they come in with big beards on their lips.

CARELESS LOVE

American

1. Love, oh love, oh care - less love; love, oh love, oh care - less
2. cried last night and the night be - fore; to - night I'll cry, then cry no

love. }
more. }
Love, oh love, oh care - less love, oh,

see what love has done to me. ____ I me. ____

THE CARD SONG

American

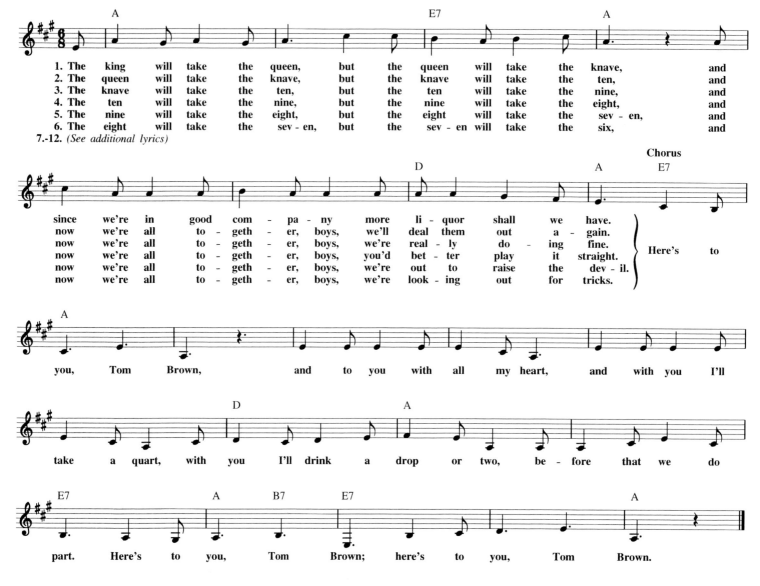

1. The king will take the queen, but the queen will take the knave, and
2. The queen will take the knave, but the knave will take the ten, and
3. The knave will take the ten, but the ten will take the nine, and
4. The ten will take the nine, but the nine will take the eight, and
5. The nine will take the eight, but the eight will take the sev-en, and
6. The eight will take the sev-en, but the sev-en will take the six, and
7.-12. (See additional lyrics)

since we're in good com-pa-ny more li-quor shall we have.
now we're all to-geth-er, boys, we'll deal them out a-gain.
now we're all to-geth-er, boys, we're real-ly do-ing fine.
now we're all to-geth-er, boys, you'd bet-ter play it straight.
now we're all to-geth-er, boys, we're out to raise the dev-il.
now we're all to-geth-er, boys, we're look-ing out for tricks.

Here's to

you, Tom Brown, and to you with all my heart, and with you I'll

take a quart, with you I'll drink a drop or two, be-fore that we do

part. Here's to you, Tom Brown; here's to you, Tom Brown.

Additional Lyrics

7. The seven will take the six,
   But the six will take the five,
   And now we're all together, boys,
   I'll skin you all alive.

8. The six will take the five,
   But the five will take the four,
   And now we're all together, boys,
   I'll knock you on the floor.

9. The five will take the four,
   But the four will take the trey,
   And now we're all together, boys,
   We'll never go home 'til day.

10. The four will take the trey,
    But the trey will take the deuce,
    And now we're all together, boys,
    We'll never call a truce.

11. The trey will take the deuce,
    But the ace will take them all,
    And now we're all together, boys,
    We'll never go home at all.

12. The ace will take them all,
    The ace will take the king,
    And now we're all together, boys,
    We've just begun to sing.

CARNIVAL OF VENICE

By Julius Benedict

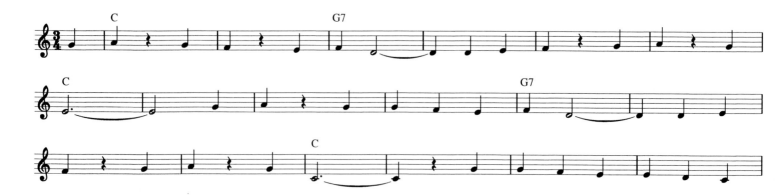

CASEY JONES

Lyrics by T. Lawrence Seibert
Music by Eddie Newton

CARRION CROW (I)

Folksong from Nova Scotia

CARRION CROW (II)

Folksong from Nova Scotia

THE CAT CAME BACK

American

1. Old Mis-ter John-son had trou-bles of his own; he had a yel-low cat which
2. The man a-round the cor-ner swore he'd kill the cat on sight; he load-ed up his shot-gun with
3. He gave it to a lit-tle boy with a dol-lar note; he told him for to take it up the
4. He gave it to a man___ go-ing up in a bal-loon; he told him for to take it to the
5. He gave it to a man___ go-ing way___ out___ west; he told him for to take it to the
6. The cat, it had some com-pa-ny one night out in the yard; some-one threw a boot-jack and they

7.-9. *(See additional lyrics)*

would-n't leave its home. He tried and he tried to give the cat a-way; He
nails and dy-na-mite. He wait-ed and he wait-ed for the cat to come a-round;
riv-er in a boat. They tied a rope a-round its neck, it must have weighed a pound;
man___ in the moon. the bal-loon came down a-bout nine-ty miles a-way;
one he loved the best. first the train___ hit the curve, then it jumped the rail;
threw it might-y hard. It caught the cat be-hind the ear, she thought it rath-er slight, when a-

gave it to a man go-ing far, far a-way.
nine-ty-sev-en piec-es of the man is all they found.
now they drag the riv-er for a lit-tle boy that's drowned.
where___ he is now, well I dare not___ say.
not a soul was left be-hind to tell the grue-some tale.
long came a brick-bat and knocked the cat out of sight.

Chorus
But the cat came back the

ver-y next day, the cat came back, they thought he was a gon-er but the

cat came back; it just could-n't stay a-way.

Additional Lyrics

7. Away across the ocean they did send the cat at last;
   Vessel only out a day and making the water fast.
   People all began to pray, the boat began to toss,
   A great big gust of wind came by and every soul was lost.
   Chorus

8. On a telegraph wire, sparrows sitting in a bunch,
   The cat was feeling hungry, thought she'd like 'em for a lunch.
   Climbing softly up the pole, and when she reached the top,
   Put her foot upon the electric wire, which tied her in a knot.
   Chorus

9. The cat was a possessor of a family of its own,
   With seven little kittens, till there came a cyclone.
   Blew the houses all apart and tossed the cat around;
   The air was full of kittens, and not a one was ever found.
   Chorus

CARRY ME BACK TO OLD VIRGINNY

Words and Music by James Bland
1878

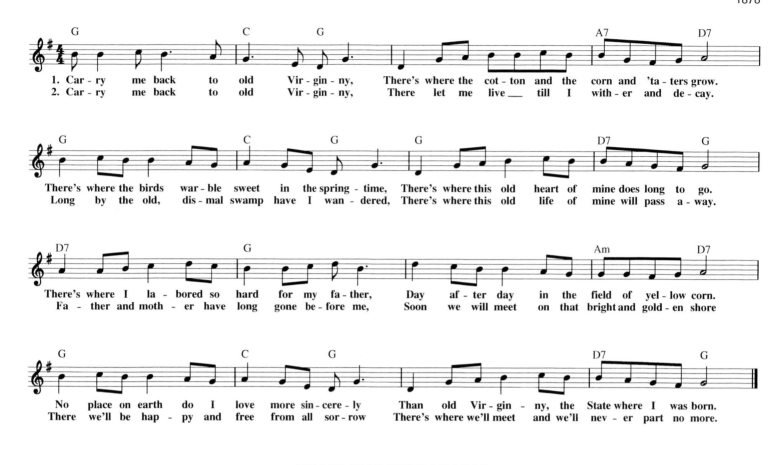

1. Car - ry me back to old Vir - gin - ny, There's where the cot - ton and the corn and 'ta - ters grow.
2. Car - ry me back to old Vir - gin - ny, There let me live ___ till I with - er and de - cay.

There's where the birds war - ble sweet in the spring - time, There's where this old heart of mine does long to go.
Long by the old, dis - mal swamp have I wan - dered, There's where this old life of mine will pass a - way.

There's where I la - bored so hard for my fa - ther, Day af - ter day in the field of yel - low corn.
Fa - ther and moth - er have long gone be - fore me, Soon we will meet on that bright and gold - en shore

No place on earth do I love more sin - cere - ly Than old Vir - gin - ny, the State where I was born.
There we'll be hap - py and free from all sor - row There's where we'll meet and we'll nev - er part no more.

CHARLIE IS MY DARLING

Scottish
Words variously attributed to
James Hogg or Lady Carolina Nairne

Oh! Char - lie is my dar - ling, my dar - ling my dar - ling! Oh! Char - lie is my dar - ling, the

young chev - a - lier.

1. 'Twas on a Mon - day morn - ing, Right ear - ly in the year, When
2. As he cam' march - in' up the street, The pipes played loud and clear; And
3. Wi' High - land bon - nets on their heads, And clay - mores bright and clear, They
4. They've left their bon - nie High - land hills, Their wives and bairn - ies dear, To
5. Oh! there were mon - y beat - ing hearts, And mon - y a hope and fear; And

Char - lie came to our ___ town, The ___ young ___ chev - a - lier.
a' the folk cam' rin - nin' out To ___ meet the chev - a - lier.
cam' to fight for Scot - land's right And the young ___ chev - a - lier.
draw the sword for Scot - land's lord, The ___ young ___ chev - a - lier.
mon - y were the prayers put up for the young ___ chev - a - lier.

Oh! Char - lie is my dar - ling, my

dar - ling, my dar - ling! Oh, Char - lie is my dar - ling, the young chev - a - lier.

CHARLIE MOPPS

English

1. A long time a - go, way back in his - to-
2. Ab - bey, the Con - naught, the Hole In The Wall as
3. bush - el of hops and a bar - rel of malt and stir it a - round with a

ry, when all they had to drink was noth - ing but cups of tea, a -
well, one thing you can be sure, it's Char - lie's beer they sell. So
stick; the sort of lu - bri - ca - tion to make your en - gine tick.

long came a man by the name of Char - lie Mopps, and he in - vent - ed a
come on, all you luck - y lads, at ten o' - clock she stops; for five short
Twen - ty pints of wol - lop a day will keep a - way the quacks. It's on - ly four-pence ha'

won - der - ful drink and he gave it the name of hops.
sec - onds, re - mem - ber Char - lie Mopps. Oh, he
pen - ny a pint and a shil - ling and tup - pence in tax.

ought - a been an ad - m'ral, a sul - tan or a king, and to his prais - es

we should al - ways sing. Oh, look what he has done for us, he's filled us up with

cheer. Lord bless Char - lie Mopps, the man who in - vent - ed beer, beer,

1,2	3

beer, did - dle - y, beer, beer, beer. { (2.) Oh, the beer, did - dle - y, beer.
{ (3.) Oh, a

THE COLORADO TRAIL

American

Weep, all ye lit - tle rains, Wail, wind, wail, All a - long, a - long, a - long the Col - o - rad - o trail.

Eyes like a morn - ing star, lips like a rose, Jen - nie was a pret - ty gal, God Al - might - y knows!

Weep, all ye lit - tle rains, Wail, wind, wail, All a - long, a - long, a - long the Col - o - rad - o trail.

CHARLES GUITEAU

19th Century American

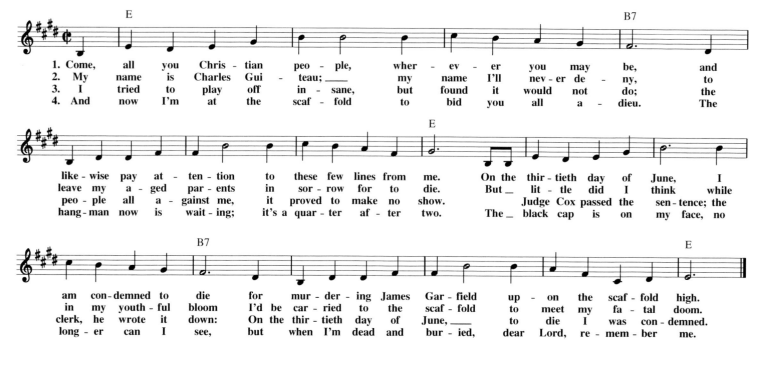

1. Come, all you Christian people, wherever you may be, and
2. My name is Charles Guiteau; my name I'll never deny, to
3. I tried to play off insane, but found it would not do; the
4. And now I'm at the scaffold to bid you all adieu. The

like-wise pay at-ten-tion to these few lines from me. On the thir-tieth day of June, I
leave my a-ged par-ents in sor-row for to die. But lit-tle did I think while
peo-ple all a-gainst me, it proved to make no show. Judge Cox passed the sen-tence; the
hang-man now is wait-ing; it's a quar-ter af-ter two. The black cap is on my face, no

am con-demned to die for mur-der-ing James Gar-field up-on the scaf-fold high.
in my youth-ful bloom I'd be car-ried to the scaf-fold to meet my fa-tal doom.
clerk, he wrote it down: On the thir-tieth day of June, to die I was con-demned.
long-er can I see, but when I'm dead and bur-ied, dear Lord, re-mem-ber me.

CHESTER

Words and Music by William Billings
from *The New England Psalm-Singer*, 1771

1. Let ty-rants shake their i-ron rod, and slav-'ry
2. Howe and Bur-goyne and Clin-ton, too, with Pres-cott
3. When God in-spired us for the fight, their ranks were
4. The foe comes on with haugh-ty stride. Our troops ad-
5. What grate-ful of-f'ring shall we bring? What shall we

clank her gall-ing chain. We'll fear them not; we trust in
and Corn-wal-lis join'd, to-geth-er plot our o-ver-
broke, their lines were forced, their ships were shel-tered in our
vance with mar-tial noise. Their vet-'rans flee be-fore our
ren-der to the Lord? Loud hal-le-lu-jahs let us

God: New Eng-land's God for-ev-er reigns.
throw, in one in-fer-nal league com-bined.
sight, or swift-ly driv-en from our coast.
youth, and gen-'rals yield to beard-less boys.
sing, and praise His name on ev-'ry chord.

CHIAPANECAS

Mexican

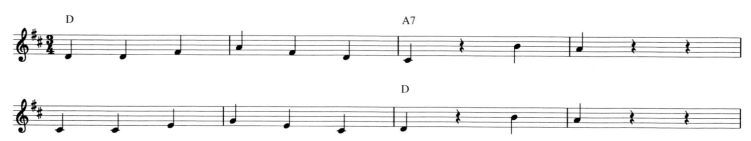

CHEWING GUM

American

CIDER THROUGH A STRAW

American Popular Song
Based on a Cowboy Song

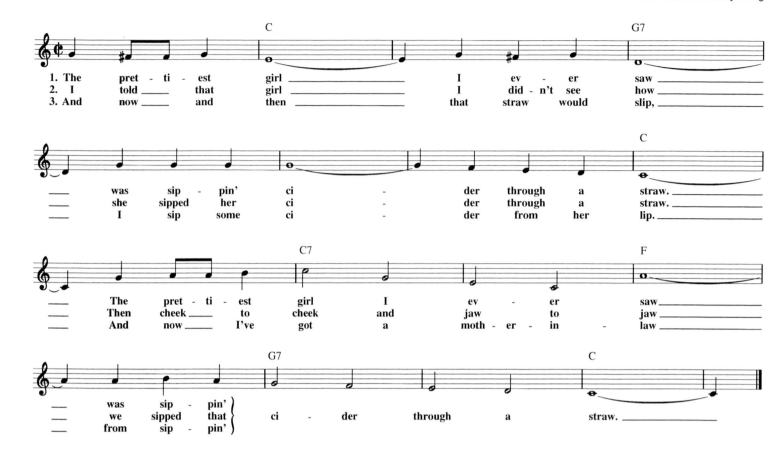

1. The pret-ti-est girl _____ I ev-er saw _____
2. I told _____ that girl _____ I did-n't see how _____
3. And now _____ and then _____ that straw would slip, _____

_____ was sip-pin' ci - der through a straw. _____
_____ she sipped her ci - der through a straw. _____
_____ I sip some ci - der from her lip. _____

The pret-ti-est girl I ev-er saw _____
Then cheek _____ to cheek and jaw to jaw _____
And now _____ I've got a moth-er-in - law _____

_____ was sip-pin' }
_____ we sipped that } ci - der through a straw. _____
_____ from sip-pin' }

THE CHIVALROUS SHARK

Words and Music by
Wallace Irwin

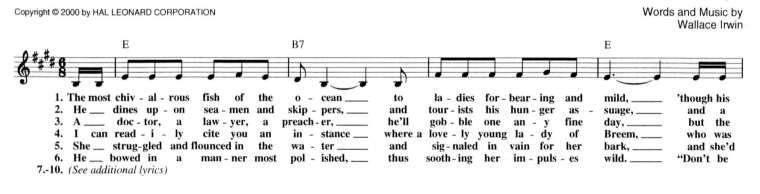

1. The most chiv-al-rous fish of the o-cean _____ to la-dies for-bear-ing and mild, _____ 'though his
2. He ___ dines up-on sea-men and skip-pers, _____ and tour-ists his hun-ger as-suage, _____ and a
3. A ___ doc-tor, a law-yer, a preach-er, _____ he'll gob-ble one an-y fine day, _____ but the
4. I can read-i-ly cite you an in-stance _____ where a love-ly young la-dy of Breem, _____ who was
5. She ___ strug-gled and flounced in the wa-ter _____ and sig-naled in vain for her bark, _____ and she'd
6. He ___ bowed in a man-ner most pol-ished, _____ thus sooth-ing her im-puls-es wild. _____ "Don't be

7.-10. *(See additional lyrics)*

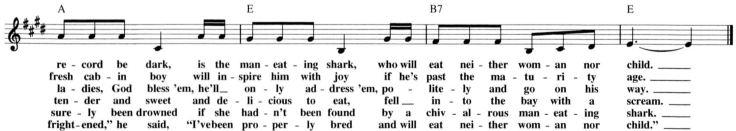

re-cord be dark, is the man-eat-ing shark, who will eat nei-ther wom-an nor child. _____
fresh cab-in boy will in-spire him with joy if he's past the ma-tu-ri-ty age. _____
la-dies, God bless 'em, he'll on-ly ad-dress 'em, po-lite-ly and go on his way. _____
ten-der and sweet and de-li-cious to eat, fell in-to the bay with a scream. _____
sure-ly been drowned if she had-n't been found by a chiv-al-rous man-eat-ing shark. _____
fright-ened," he said, "I've been pro-per-ly bred and will eat nei-ther wom-an nor child." _____

Additional Lyrics

7. Then he proffered his fin and she took it –
Such a gallantry none can dispute –
While the passengers cheered
As the vessel they neared,
And a broadside was fired in salute.

8. And they stood alongside the vessel,
When a life-saving dinghy was lowered,
With the pick of the crew,
And her relatives, too,
And the mate and the skipper aboard.

9. So they took her aboard in a jiffy,
And the shark stood at attention the while;
Then he raised on his flipper
And ate up the skipper
And went on his way with a smile.

10. And this shows that the prince of the ocean,
To ladies forbearing and mild.
Though his record be dark,
He's the man-eating shark
Who will eat neither woman nor child.

CIELITO LINDO
(My Pretty Darling)

Mexican

CINDY

Southern Appalachian Folksong

1. You ought to see my Cin - dy, she lives a - way down
2. I wish I was an ap - ple a - hang - in' on a
3. I wish I had a nee - dle as fine as I could
4. I wish I had a nick - el. I wish I had a
5. Cin - dy in the spring - time, Cin - dy in the

south, and she's so sweet the hon - ey - bees _____ swarm a - round her
tree, and ev - 'ry time my Cin - dy passed she'd take a bite of
sew, I'd sew that gal to my coat - tail, and down the road I'd
dime, I wish I had my Cin - dy girl to love me all the
fall; if I can't have my Cin - dy, _____ I'll have no girl at

mouth.
me.
go.   Get a - long home, Cin - dy, Cin - dy, get a - long home, Cin - dy,
time.
all.

Cin - dy, get a - long home, Cin - dy, Cin - dy, I'll mar - ry you some - day.

CLARE'S DRAGOONS

18th Century Irish

1. When_ on Ram - il - lies' blood - y field The baf - fled French were forced _ to _ yield, The _
2. An - oth - er Clare is here to lead, Though wor - thy fan of such _ a _ breed; the _
3. Oh,_ com - rades, think how Ire - land pines, Her ex - iled lords, her ri - fled _ shrines, Her_

vic - tor Sax - on back - ward reeled Be - fore the charge of Clare's dra - goons. The
French ex - pect some fa - mous deed When Clare leads on his bold dra - goons. Our
dear - est hope, the or - dered lines, And burst - ing charge of Clare's dra - goons. Then

flags we con - quered in that fray Look lone in Y - pres' choir, _ they _ say We'll
colo - nel comes from Bri - an's race, His wounds are in his breast _ and _ face; The _
fling your green flag to the sky, Be Lim - er - ick your bat - tle _ cry, And _

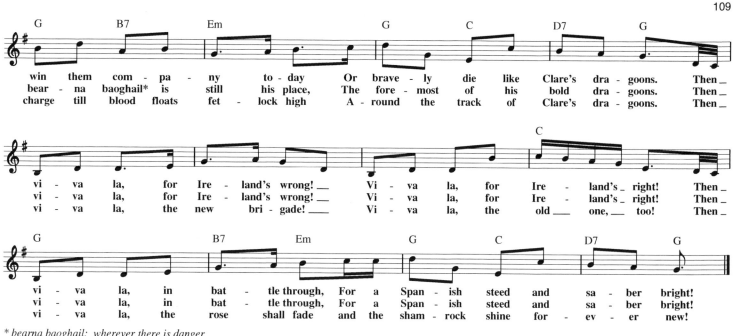

win them com - pa - ny to - day Or brave - ly die like Clare's dra - goons. Then __
bear - na baoghail* is still his place, The fore - most of his bold dra - goons. Then __
charge till blood floats fet - lock high A - round the track of Clare's dra - goons. Then __

vi - va la, for Ire - land's wrong! __ Vi - va la, for Ire - land's __ right! Then __
vi - va la, for Ire - land's wrong! __ Vi - va la, for Ire - land's __ right! Then __
vi - va la, the new bri - gade! __ Vi - va la, the old __ one, __ too! Then __

vi - va la, in bat - tle through, For a Span - ish steed and sa - ber bright!
vi - va la, in bat - tle through, For a Span - ish steed and sa - ber bright!
vi - va la, the rose shall fade and the sham - rock shine for - ev - er new!

bearna baoghail: wherever there is danger

THE COASTS OF HIGH BARBARY

16th Century English Sea Chantey

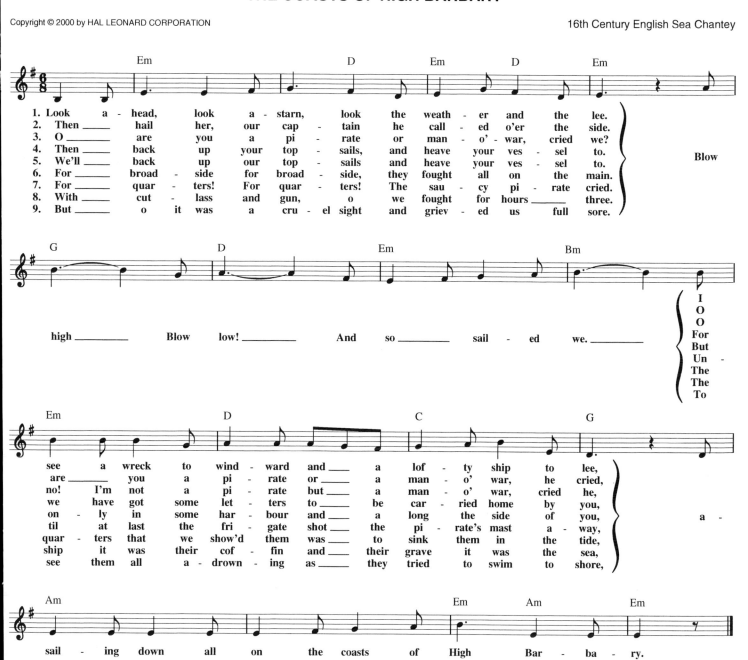

1. Look a - head, look a - starn, look the weath - er and the lee.
2. Then ___ hail her, our cap - tain he call - ed o'er the side.
3. O ___ are you a pi - rate or man - o' - war, cried we?
4. Then ___ back up your top - sails, and heave your ves - sel to.
5. We'll ___ back up our top - sails and heave your ves - sel to.
6. For ___ broad - side for broad - side, they fought all on the main.
7. For ___ quar - ters! For quar - ters! The sau - cy pi - rate cried.
8. With ___ cut - lass and gun, o we fought for hours ___ three.
9. But ___ o it was a cru - el sight and griev - ed us full sore.

Blow

high ___ Blow low! ___ And so ___ sail - ed we. ___

I
O
O
For
But
Un
The
The
To

see a wreck to wind - ward and ___ a lof - ty ship to lee,
are ___ you a pi - rate or ___ a man - o' war, he cried,
no! I'm not a pi - rate but ___ a man - o' war, cried he,
we have got some let - ters to ___ be car - ried home by you,
on - ly in some har - bour and ___ a long the side of you,
til at last the fri - gate shot ___ the pi - rate's mast a - way,
quar - ters that we show'd them was ___ to sink them in the tide,
ship it was their cof - fin and ___ their grave it was the sea,
see them all a - drown - ing as ___ they tried to swim to shore,

a -

sail - ing down all on the coasts of High Bar - ba - ry.

CLEAR THE TRACK, LET THE BULGINE RUN

African-American Capstan Chantey
Based on an Irish Tune

1. Oh the smart-est pack-et you can find,
2. Oh the Mar-g'ret Ev-ans of the Blue Star line,
3. When we've showed our freight at the West Street pier,
4. When we all get back to Liv-er-pool town,
5. Oh ___ Li - za Lee, will you be mine?
6. And ___ when I'm home a - gain from sea,

Ah hey, ah ho, are you most done?

Is the
She's ___
It's ___
I'll ___
I'll ___
Oh ___

Marg'-ret Ev-ans of the Blue Star ___ line,
nev-er a day ___ be - hind her ___ time,
home to Liv-er-pool ___ then we'll ___ steer,
stand ye whis-kies ___ all a - round,
dress you up ___ in ___ silk so ___ fine,
Li - za, you ___ shall mar-ry ___ me,

So clear the track, let the bul - gine run. To me

aye, rig - a - gig in a low - backed car, ah hey, ah ho, are you most done? With

Li - za Lee all on my ___ knee, So clear the track, let the bul - gine run.

CLEMENTINE

American
Mining song probably from California
Attributed to Percy Montrose, 1863 or 1883

1. In a cav - ern, in a can - yon, Ex - ca - vat - ing for a
2. Light she was, and like a fair - y, and her shoes were num - ber
3. Drove she duck - lings to the wa - ter ev - 'ry morn - ing just at
4. Ru - by lips a - bove the wa - ter, blow - ing bub - bles soft and

mine, Dwelt a min - er, for - ty - nin - er, And his daugh - ter, Clem - en -
nine. Her - ring box - es with - out top - ses, san - dals were for Clem - en -
nine. Hit her foot a - gainst a splin - ter, fell in - to the foam - ing
fine. A - las for me! I was no swim - mer, so I lost my Clem - en -

tine.
tine.
brine.
tine.

Oh my dar - ling, oh my dar - ling, oh my dar - ling Clem - en -

tine. You are lost and gone for - ev - er, dread - ful sor - ry, Clem - en - tine.

CLICK GO THE SHEARS

20th Century Australian

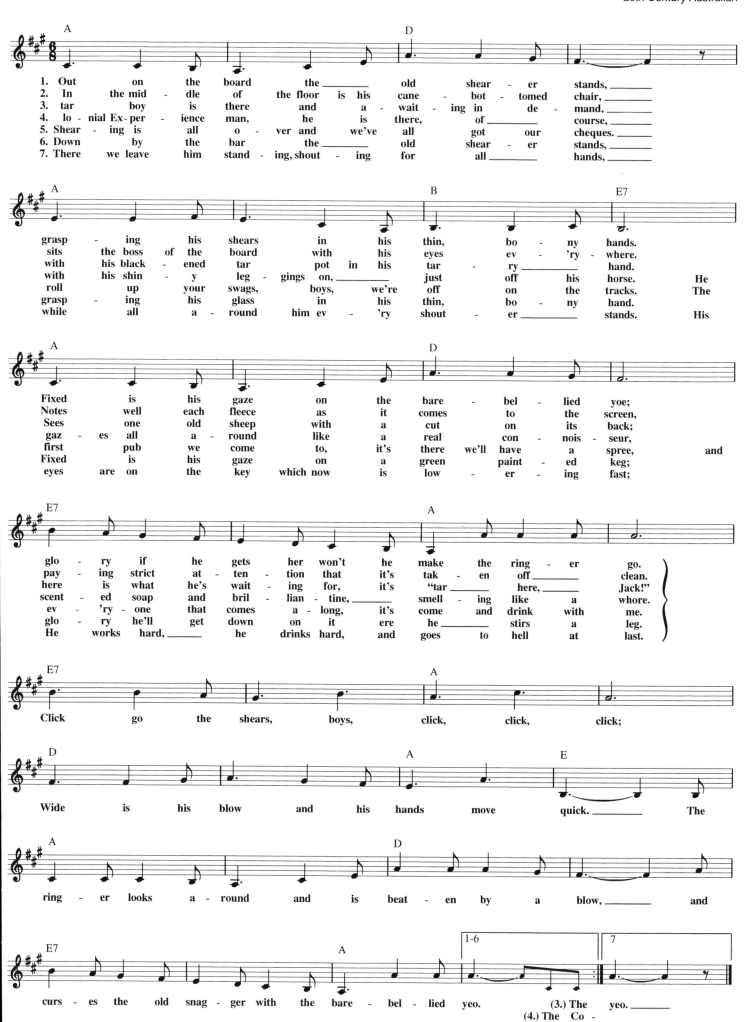

1. Out on the board the _____ old shear - er stands, _____
2. In the mid - dle of the floor is his cane - bot - tomed chair, _____
3. tar boy is there and a - wait - ing in de - mand, _____
4. lo - nial Ex - per - ience man, he is there, of _____ course, _____
5. Shear - ing is all o - ver and we've all got our cheques. _____
6. Down by the bar the _____ old shear - er stands, _____
7. There we leave him stand - ing, shout - ing for all _____ hands,

grasp - ing his shears in his thin, bo - ny hands.
sits the boss of the board with his eyes ev - 'ry - where.
with his black - ened tar pot in his tar - ry _____ hand.
with his shin - y leg - gings on, _____ just off his horse. He
roll up your swags, boys, we're off on the tracks. The
grasp - ing his glass in his thin, bo - ny hand.
while all a - round him ev - 'ry shout - er _____ stands. His

Fixed is his gaze on the bare - bel - lied yoe;
Notes well each fleece as it comes to the screen,
Sees one old sheep with a cut on its back;
gaz - es all a - round like a real con - nois - seur,
first pub we come to, it's there we'll have a spree, and
Fixed is his gaze on a green paint - ed keg;
eyes are on the key which now is low - er - ing fast;

glo - ry if he gets her won't he make the ring - er go.
pay - ing strict at - ten - tion that it's tak - en off _____ clean.
here is what he's wait - ing for, it's "tar _____ here, _____ Jack!"
scent - ed soap and bril - lian - tine, _____ smell - ing like a whore.
ev - 'ry - one that comes a - long, it's come and drink with me.
glo - ry he'll get down on it ere he _____ stirs a leg.
He works hard, _____ he drinks hard, and goes to hell at last.

Click go the shears, boys, click, click, click;

Wide is his blow and his hands move quick. _____ The

ring - er looks a - round and is beat - en by a blow, _____ and

curs - es the old snag - ger with the bare - bel - lied yeo. (3.) The yeo. _____
(4.) The Co -

COCK-A-DOODLE-DOO

American Nursery Song

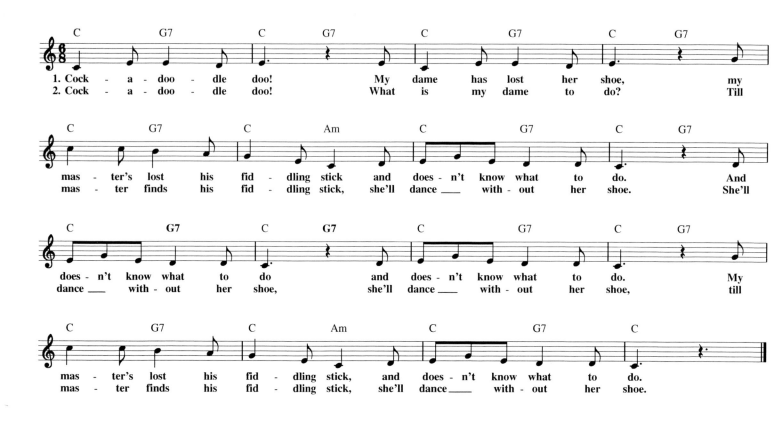

1. Cock - a - doo - dle doo! My dame has lost her shoe, my
2. Cock - a - doo - dle doo! What is my dame to do? Till

mas - ter's lost his fid - dling stick and does - n't know what to do. And
mas - ter finds his fid - dling stick, she'll dance ___ with - out her shoe. She'll

does - n't know what to do and does - n't know what to do. My
dance ___ with - out her shoe, she'll dance ___ with - out her shoe, till

mas - ter's lost his fid - dling stick, and does - n't know what to do.
mas - ter finds his fid - dling stick, she'll dance ___ with - out her shoe.

COCK ROBIN

English

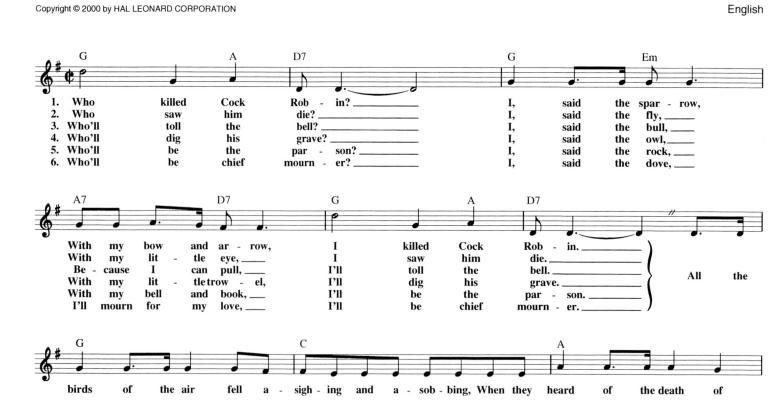

1. Who killed Cock Rob - in? ___ I, said the spar - row,
2. Who saw him die? ___ I, said the fly, ___
3. Who'll toll the bell? ___ I, said the bull, ___
4. Who'll dig his grave? ___ I, said the owl, ___
5. Who'll be the par - son? ___ I, said the rock, ___
6. Who'll be chief mourn - er? ___ I, said the dove, ___

With my bow and ar - row, I killed Cock Rob - in. ___
With my lit - tle eye, ___ I saw him die. ___
Be - cause I can pull, ___ I'll toll the bell. ___
With my lit - tle trow - el, I'll dig his grave. ___
With my bell and book, ___ I'll be the par - son. ___
I'll mourn for my love, ___ I'll be chief mourn - er.

All the

birds of the air fell a - sigh - ing and a - sob - bing, When they heard of the death of

poor Cock Rob - in, when they heard of the death of ___ poor Cock Rob - in.

COD-LIVER OIL

American

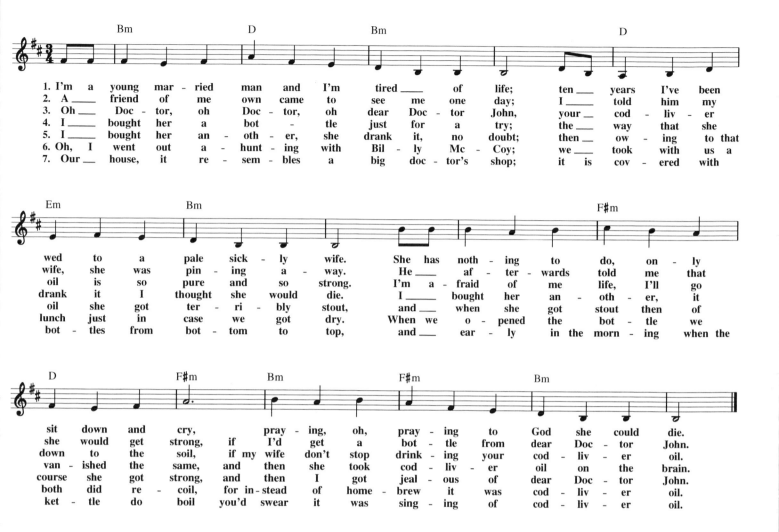

1. I'm a young mar - ried man and I'm tired ___ of life; ten ___ years I've been
2. A ___ friend of me own came to see me one day; I ___ told him my
3. Oh ___ Doc - tor, oh Doc - tor, oh dear Doc - tor John, your ___ cod - liv - er
4. I ___ bought her a bot - tle just for a try; the ___ way that she
5. I ___ bought her an - oth - er, she drank it, no doubt; then ___ ow - ing to that
6. Oh, I went out a - hunt - ing with Bil - ly Mc - Coy; we ___ took with us a
7. Our ___ house, it re - sem - bles a big doc - tor's shop; it is cov - ered with

wed to a pale sick - ly wife. She has noth - ing to do, on - ly
wife, she was pin - ing a - way. He ___ af - ter - wards told me that
oil is so pure and so strong. I'm a - fraid of me life, I'll go
drank it I thought she would die. I ___ bought her an - oth - er, it
oil she got ter - ri - bly stout, and ___ when she got stout then of
lunch just in case we got dry. When we o - pened the bot - tle we
bot - tles from bot - tom to top, and ___ ear - ly in the morn - ing when the

sit down and cry, pray - ing, oh, pray - ing to God she could die.
she would get strong, if I'd get a bot - tle from dear Doc - tor John.
down to the soil, if my wife don't stop drink - ing your cod - liv - er oil.
van - ished the same, and then she took cod - liv - er oil on the brain.
course she got strong, and then I got jeal - ous of dear Doc - tor John.
both did re - coil, for in - stead of home - brew it was cod - liv - er oil.
ket - tle do boil you'd swear it was sing - ing of cod - liv - er oil.

COLD WATER

American

1. Cold wa - ter, cold wa - ter for me; there's noth - ing so
2. There's noth - ing like wa - ter to give the strength that we

pure and so free. ___ } I'll go to the brook and I'll go to the
need for to live. ___

spring, and o - ver the bub - bles I mer - ri - ly sing, "Cold wa -

ter, cold wa - ter, cold wa - ter, cold wa - ter for me." ___

COLE YOUNGER

19th Century American

7.-9. *(See additional lyrics)*

Additional Lyrics

7. But I stationed out my pickets and up to the bank did go.
   And there upon the counter I struck my fatal blow.
   "Just hand us over your money and make no further delay.
   We are the famous Younger boys; we spend no time in play."

8. The cashier, being as true as steel, refused our noted band;
   'Twas Jesse James that pulled the trigger that killed this noble man.
   We run for life, for death was near, four hundred on our trail.
   We soon were overtaken, and landed safe in jail.

9. I am a noted highwayman; Cole Younger is my name.
   My crimes and depredations have brought my mane to shame.
   And now in the Stillwater Jail I lie, a-wearin' my life away;
   Two James boys live to tell the tale of that sad and fatal day.

COLUMBUS STOCKADE BLUES

Southern American

COME ALL YE FAIR AND TENDER MAIDENS

Folksong from Kentucky

COME AND GO WITH ME

American

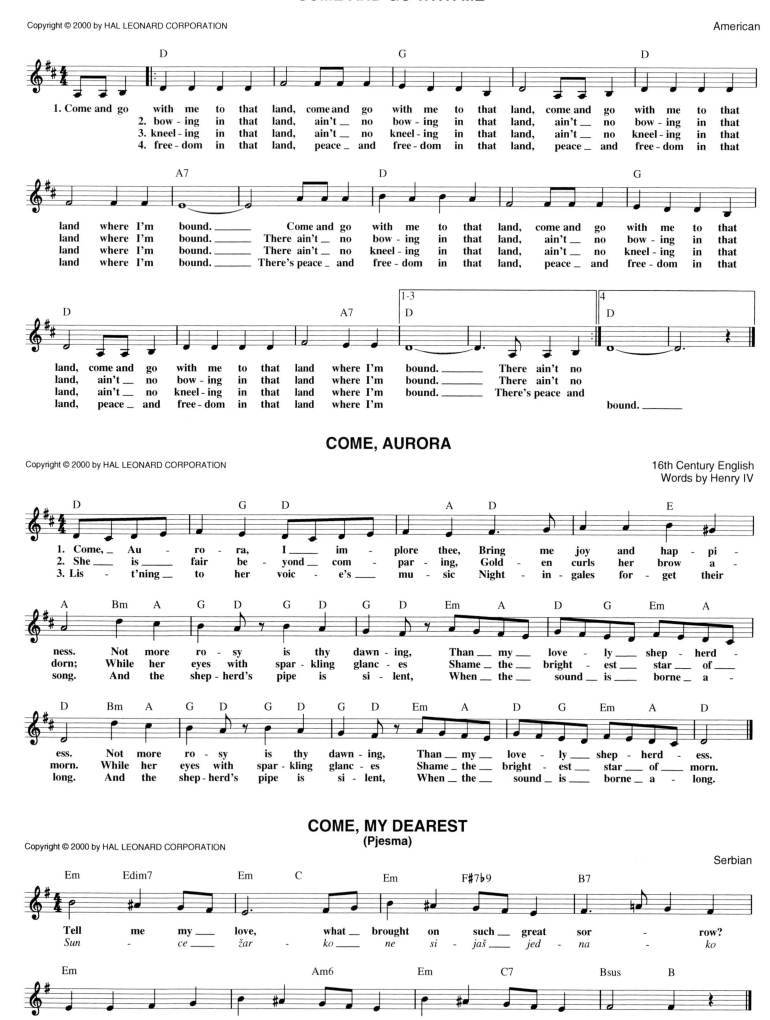

1. Come and go with me to that land, come and go with me to that land, come and go with me to that
2. bow-ing in that land, ain't __ no bow-ing in that land, ain't __ no bow-ing in that
3. kneel-ing in that land, ain't __ no kneel-ing in that land, ain't __ no kneel-ing in that
4. free-dom in that land, peace __ and free-dom in that land, peace __ and free-dom in that

land where I'm bound. _____ Come and go with me to that land, come and go with me to that
land where I'm bound. _____ There ain't __ no bow-ing in that land, ain't __ no bow-ing in that
land where I'm bound. _____ There ain't __ no kneel-ing in that land, ain't __ no kneel-ing in that
land where I'm bound. _____ There's peace __ and free-dom in that land, peace __ and free-dom in that

land, come and go with me to that land where I'm bound. _____ There ain't no
land, ain't __ no bow-ing in that land where I'm bound. _____ There ain't no
land, ain't __ no kneel-ing in that land where I'm bound. _____ There ain't no
land, peace __ and free-dom in that land where I'm bound. There's peace and

bound. _____

COME, AURORA

16th Century English
Words by Henry IV

1. Come, _ Au - ro - ra, I _____ im - plore thee, Bring me joy and hap - pi -
2. She ___ is _____ fair be - yond _____ com - par - ing, Gold - en curls her brow a -
3. Lis - t'ning _ to her voic - e's ____ mu - sic Night - in - gales for - get their

ness. Not more ro - sy is thy dawn - ing, Than __ my __ love - ly _____ shep - herd -
dorn; While her eyes with spar - kling glanc - es Shame __ the __ bright - est ___ star __ of __
song. And the shep - herd's pipe is si - lent, When __ the __ sound __ is ____ borne __ a -

ess. Not more ro - sy is thy dawn - ing, Than __ my __ love - ly _____ shep - herd - ess.
morn. While her eyes with spar - kling glanc - es Shame __ the __ bright - est ___ star __ of __ morn.
long. And the shep - herd's pipe is si - lent, When __ the __ sound __ is ____ borne __ a - long.

COME, MY DEAREST
(Pjesma)

Serbian

Tell me my ___ love, what __ brought on such __ great sor - row?
Sun - ce ___ žar - ko ___ ne si - jaš ___ jed - na - ko

Do you fear the love I give __ you, love you will __ not bor - row?
sun - ce žar - ko (i - me mo - je) ne si - jaš ___ jed - na - ko.

COME FOLLOW

English

* This song can be sung as a 3-part round.

COME, O MY LOVE

Southern Mountain Prison Song

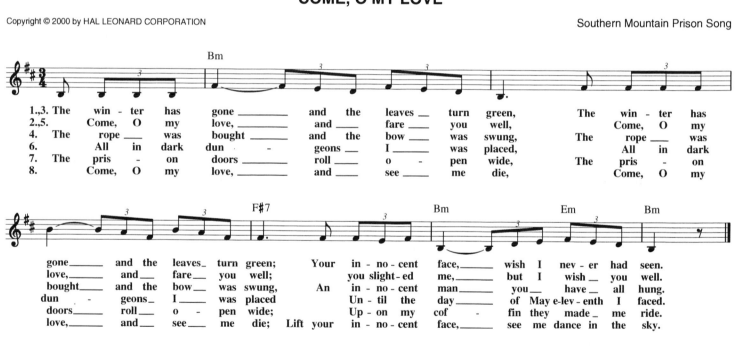

COTTON-EYED JOE

Folksong from Tennessee

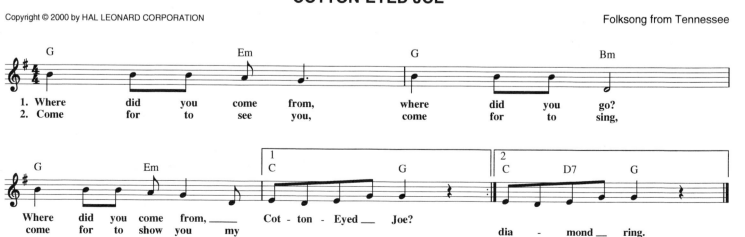

COME, THOU FOUNT OF EVERY BLESSING

American
Music from Wyeth's *Repository of Sacred Music,* 1813
Words by Robert Robinson, 1758

1. Come, Thou Fount of ev-'ry bless-ing, Tune my heart to sing Thy grace; Streams of mer-cy, nev-er
2. Here I raise mine Eb-e-ne-zer, Hith-er by Thy help I'm come; And I hope, by Thy good
3. O to grace how great a debt-or Dai-ly I'm con-strained to be! Let Thy good-ness, like a

ceas-ing, Call for songs of loud-est praise. Teach me some me-lo-dious son-net, Sung by flam-ing tongues a-
plea-sure, Safe-ly to ar-rive at home. Je-sus sought me when a strang-er, Wan-d'ring from the fold of
fet-ter, Bind my wan-d'ring heart to Thee. Prone to wan-der, Lord, I feel it, Prone to leave the God I

bove; Praise the mount, I'm fixed up-on it, Mount of Thy re-deem-ing love.
God; He, to res-cue me from dan-ger, In-ter-posed His pre-cious blood.
love; Here's my heart, O take and seal it, Seal it for Thy courts a-bove.

COME, YE SINNERS, POOR AND NEEDY

American
Music from Walker's *Southern Harmony,* 1835
Words by Joseph Hart

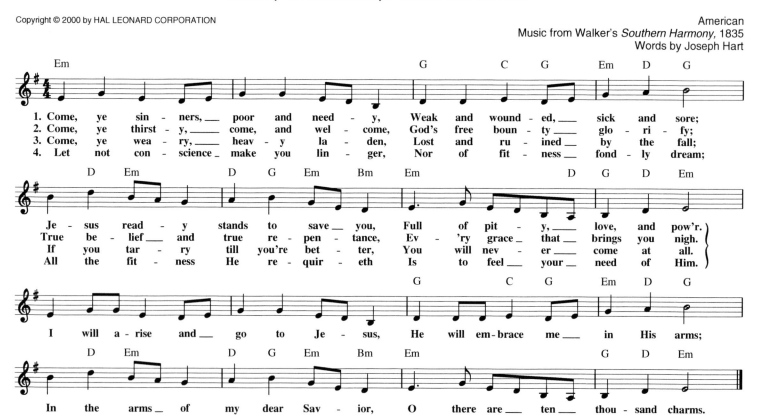

1. Come, ye sin-ners, poor and need-y, Weak and wound-ed, sick and sore;
2. Come, ye thirst-y, come, and wel-come, God's free boun-ty glo-ri-fy;
3. Come, ye wea-ry, heav-y la-den, Lost and ru-ined by the fall;
4. Let not con-science make you lin-ger, Nor of fit-ness fond-ly dream;

Je-sus read-y stands to save you, Full of pit-y, love, and pow'r.
True be-lief and true re-pen-tance, Ev-'ry grace that brings you nigh.
If you tar-ry till you're bet-ter, You will nev-er come at all.
All the fit-ness He re-quir-eth Is to feel your need of Him.

I will a-rise and go to Je-sus, He will em-brace me in His arms;

In the arms of my dear Sav-ior, O there are ten thou-sand charms.

CORDELIA BROWN

Folksong from Antigua

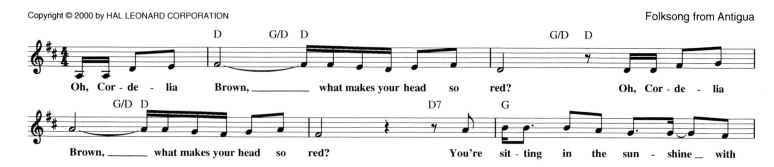

Oh, Cor-de-lia Brown, what makes your head so red? Oh, Cor-de-lia

Brown, what makes your head so red? You're sit-ting in the sun-shine with

THE CORK LEG

Irish

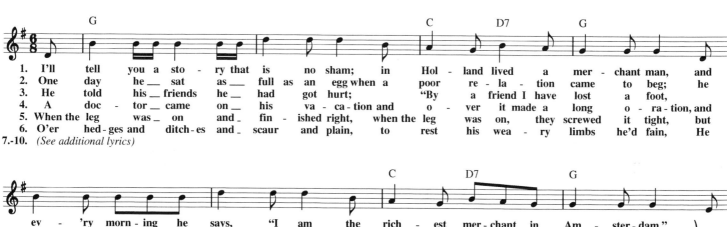

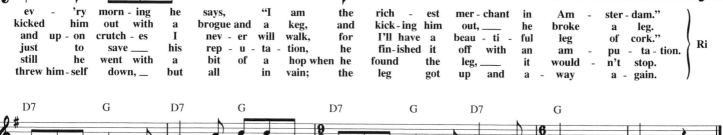

Additional Lyrics

7. He called to them that were in sight,
"Stop me or I'm wounded quite."
Although their aid he did invite,
In less than a minute he was out of sight.

8. And he kept running from place to place;
The people thought he was running a race.
He clung to a post for to stop the pace,
But the leg, it still kept up the chase.

9. Over hedges and ditches and plain and scaur,
And Europe he has travelled o'er.
Although he's dead and is no more,
The leg goes on as it did before.

10. So often you see in broad daylight
A skeleton on a cork leg tight.
Although the artist did him invite,
He never was paid, and it served him right.

COMIN' THROUGH THE RYE

Words and Music by
Robert Burns

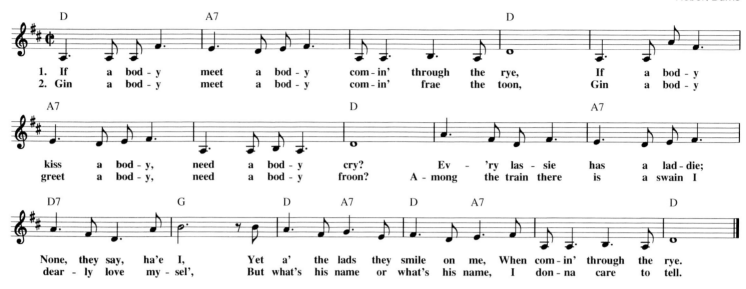

1. If a bod-y meet a bod-y com-in' through the rye, If a bod-y
2. Gin a bod-y meet a bod-y com-in' frae the toon, Gin a bod-y

kiss a bod-y, need a bod-y cry? Ev-'ry las-sie has a lad-die;
greet a bod-y, need a bod-y froon? A-mong the train there is a swain I

None, they say, ha'e I, Yet a' the lads they smile on me, When com-in' through the rye.
dear-ly love my-sel', But what's his name or what's his name, I don-na care to tell.

COTTON FIELD SONG

Southern American Folksong

1. Rac-coon an' a pos-sum, rack-in' 'cross de prai-rie;
2. Pos-sum in a 'sim-mon tree, rac-coon on de groun';
3. Met a rab-bit in de road, ask him whar he's gwine.
4. "Say, Mis-ter Rab-bit, your ears might-y thin."
5. "Say, Mis-ter Rab-bit, your fur might-y gray."
6. Hog an' a sheep a-go-in' to de pas-tor;
7. Thou-sand vers-es to my song, Hope I've sung them all;

rac-coon asked de pos-sum, does she want to mar-ry?
rac-coon ask de pos-sum, to shake dem 'sim-mons down.
"Ain't got no time to tell you now, de ol' gray houn's be-hin'."
"Yas, bless a God, they been a-split-tin' de win'."
"Yas, bless a God, seen a ha'nt 'fore day."
hog tol' de sheep, "Cain-cha trot a lit-tle fast-er?"
'Fore I'd sing 'em all a-gain, I'd soon-er jump de wall.

COSHER BAILEY'S ENGINE

Welsh

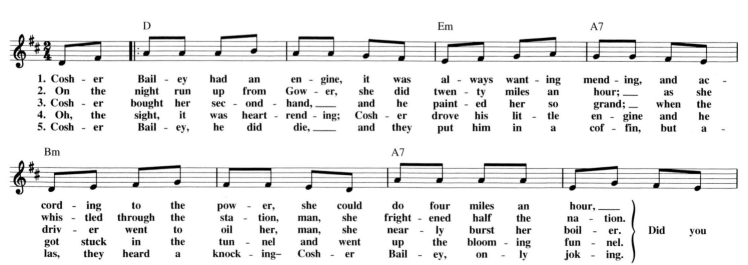

1. Cosh-er Bail-ey had an en-gine, it was al-ways want-ing mend-ing, and ac-
2. On the night run up from Gow-er, she did twen-ty miles an hour; as she
3. Cosh-er bought her sec-ond-hand, and he paint-ed her so grand; when the
4. Oh, the sight, it was heart-rend-ing; Cosh-er drove his lit-tle en-gine and he
5. Cosh-er Bail-ey, he did die, and they put him in a cof-fin, but a-

cord-ing to the pow-er, she could do four miles an hour,
whis-tled through the sta-tion, man, she fright-ened half the na-tion.
driv-er went to oil her, man, she near-ly burst her boil-er. } Did you
got stuck in the tun-nel and went up the bloom-ing fun-nel.
las, they heard a knock-ing— Cosh-er Bail-ey, on-ly jok-ing.

ev - er see, did you ev - er see, did you

ev - er see such a fun - ny thing be - fore?

COUNTRY GARDENS

English

THE COWBOY

American

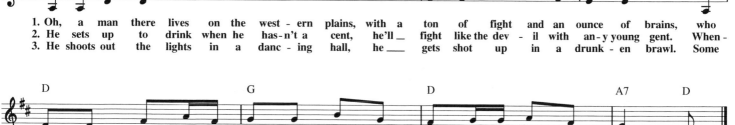

1. Oh, a man there lives on the west - ern plains, with a ton of fight and an ounce of brains, who
2. He sets up to drink when he has-n't a cent, he'll __ fight like the dev - il with an - y young gent. When -
3. He shoots out the lights in a danc - ing hall, he __ gets shot up in a drunk - en brawl. Some

herds the cows and __ robs the trains And goes by the name of cow - boy.
ev - er he makes love he __ goes it hell - bent. Oh, he's some __ lov - er, this cow - boy.
cor - o - ner's ju - ry then ends it all, and that's the __ last of the cow - boy.

THE COUNTY OF MAYO

Irish
Words by Thomas La Nelle

THE COWBOY'S DREAM

American

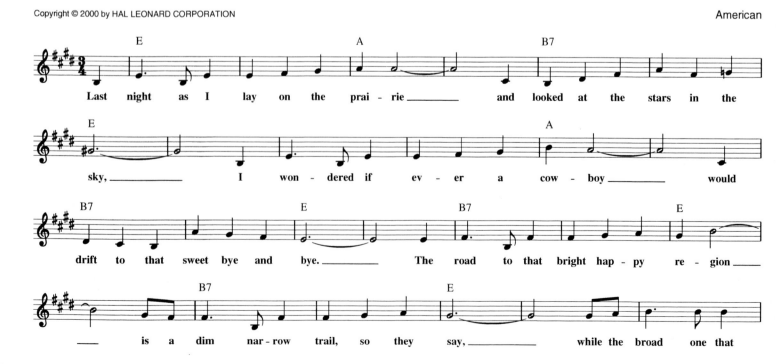

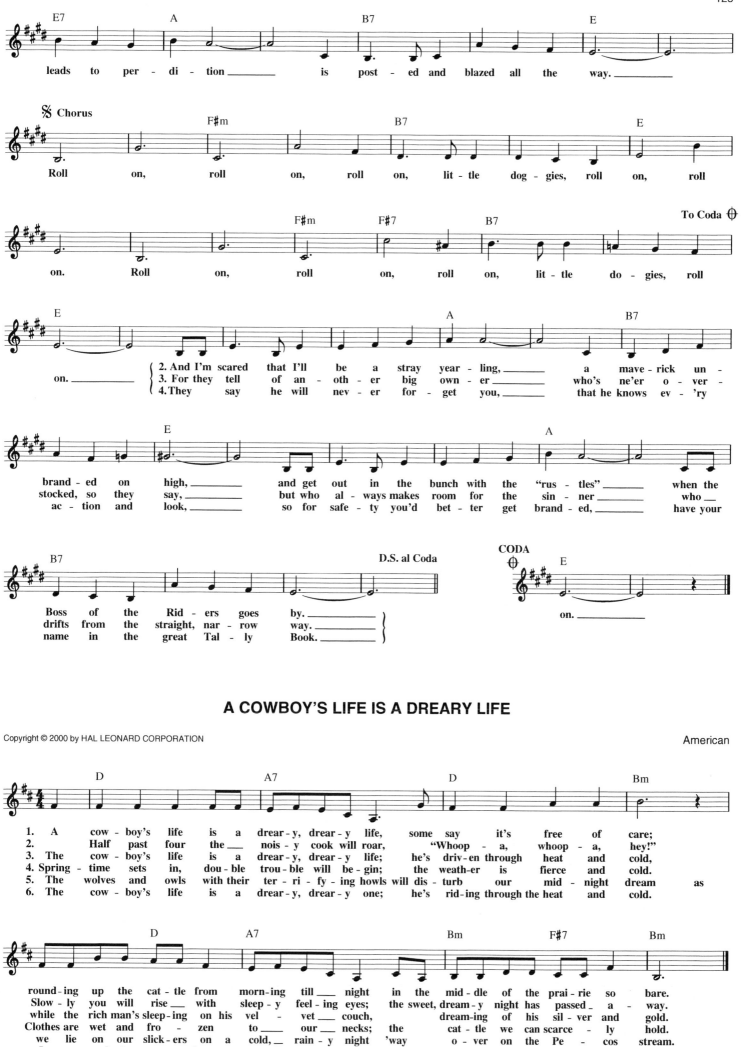

A COWBOY'S LIFE IS A DREARY LIFE

American

CRADLE HYMN

Folk Hymn from Kentucky

1. Hush, my babe, lie still and slum - ber; Ho - ly an - gels guard thy bed.
2. How much bet - ter thou art tend - ed Than the Son of God could be,
3. Soft and eas - y is thy cra - dle, Coarse and hard the Sav - ior lay,

Heav'n - ly bless - ings with - out ___ num - ber Gen - tly steal - ing on thy head.
When from heav - en He de - scend - ed and be - came a child like thee.
When his birth - place was a ___ sta - ble and his soft - est bed was hay.

CRADLE SONG
(Kehto Laula)

Finnish

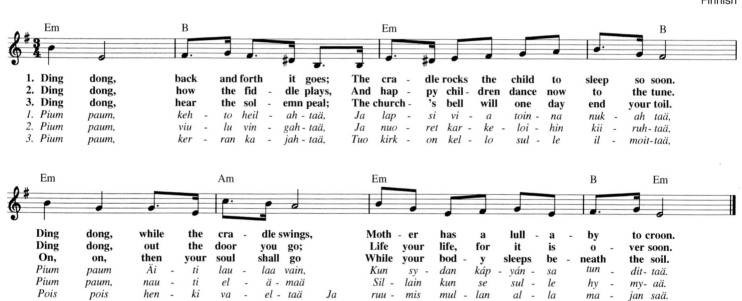

1. Ding dong, back and forth it goes; The cra - dle rocks the child to sleep so soon.
2. Ding dong, how the fid - dle plays, And hap - py chil - dren dance now to the tune.
3. Ding dong, hear the sol - emn peal; The church - 's bell will one day end your toil.
1. Pium paum, keh - to heil - ah - taä, Ja lap - si vi - a toin - na nuk - ah taä,
2. Pium paum, viu - lu vin - gah - taä, Ja nuo - ret kar - ke - loi - hin kii - ruh - taä,
3. Pium paum, ker - ran ka - jah - taä, Tuo kirk - on kel - lo sul - le il - moit - taä,

Ding dong, while the cra - dle swings, Moth - er has a lull - a - by to croon.
Ding dong, out the door you go; Life your life, for it is o - ver soon.
On, on, then your soul shall go While your bod - y sleeps be - neath the soil.
Pium paum Äi - ti lau - laa vain, Kun sy - dan káp - yán - sa tun - dit - taä.
Pium paum, nau - ti el - ä - maä Sil - lain kun se sul - le hy - my - aä.
Pois pois hen - ki va - el - taä Ja ruu - mis mul - lan al - la ma - jan saä.

THE CRAWDAD SONG

African-American

1. You get a line and I'll get a pole, ___ hon - ey. ___
2. Get up, old ___ man, you slept too ___ late, ___ hon - ey. ___
3. Get up, old ___ wom - an you slept too ___ late, ___ hon - ey. ___
4. A - long come a man with a sack on his back, ___ hon - ey. ___ A -
5. What you gon - na do when the lake goes ___ dry, ___ hon - ey. ___

You get a line and I'll get a pole, ___ babe. ___
Get up, old ___ man, you slept too ___ late, ___ babe. ___
Get up, old ___ wom - an, you slept too ___ late, ___ babe. ___
long came a man with a sack on his back, ___ babe. ___ A -
What you gon - na do when the lake goes ___ dry, ___ babe? ___

You get a line and I'll get a pole, and we'll go down to the craw-dad hole, ___
Get up, old ___ man, you slept too ___ late; ___ last piece of craw - dad's ___ on your plate, ___
Get up, old ___ wom-an, you slept too ___ late; ___ craw-dad man done ___ passed your gate, ___
long come a man with a sack on his back, pack-in' all the craw - dads ___ he can pack, ___
What you gon - na do when the lake goes ___ dry? Sit on the bank and watch the craw-dads die, ___

hon - ey, su - gar ba - by, mine. ___
hon - ey, su - gar ba - by, mine. ___
hon - ey, su - gar ba - by, mine. ___
hon - ey, su - gar ba - by, mine. ___
hon - ey, su - gar ba - by, mine. ___

CRIPPLE CREEK

American

1. I got a gal at the head of the creek; Go up to see her 'bout the mid - dle of the week.
2. Girls on the Crip-ple Creek ___ 'bout half ___ grown, jump on a boy ___ like a dog ___ on a bone.
3. Crip-ple Creek's ___ wide and ___ Crip-ple Creek's ___ deep; I'll wade old Crip-ple Creek a - fore ___ I ___ sleep.

Kiss her on the mouth, just as sweet as an - y wine; wraps her - self a - round me like a sweet per - ta - ter vine.
Roll ___ my ___ brit - ches ___ up ___ to my knees; I'll ___ wade old Crip-ple Creek ___ when ___ I ___ please.
Roads ___ are ___ rock-y and the hill - side's ___ mud-dy, and I'm ___ so ___ drunk ___ that I can't ___ stand ___ stud - y.*

Go - in' up Crip-ple Creek, go - in' in a run, go - in' up Crip-ple Creek to have a lit - tle fun.
Go - in' up Crip-ple Creek, go - in' in a whirl, go - in' up Crip-ple Creek to see ___ my ___ girl.

steady

THE CROPPY BOY

18th Century Irish

1. 'Twas ear - ly, ear - ly in the Spring, The birds did
2. 'Twas ear - ly, ear - ly in the night, the yeo - man
3. 'Twas in the guard - house where I was laid, and in the
4. As I was pass - ing my fa - ther's door, my broth - er
5. As I was go - ing up Wex - ford Hill, who could
6. As I was mount - ed on the scaf - fold high, my ag - ed
7. 'Twas in the Dun - gan - non this young man died, and in Dun -

whis - tle and sweet - ly sing, ___ Chang - ing their notes from
cav - al - ry gave me a fright. ___ The yeo - man cav - al - ry
par - lor where I was tried. ___ My sen - tence passed and my
Wil - liam stood at the door. ___ My ag - ed fa - ther stood
blame me to cry my fill? ___ I looked be - hind and I
fa - ther was stand - ing by. ___ My ag - ed fa - ther did
gan - non his bod - y lies. ___ And you good peo - ple that

tree to tree, ___ And the song they sang ___ was "Old Ire - land Free."
was my down - fall, ___ and ___ ta - ken was I ___ by the Lord Corn - wall.
cour - age low, ___ when to Dun - gan - non ___ I was forced to go.
there al - so, ___ my ___ ten - der moth - er I shall see no more.
looked be - fore, ___ my ___ ag - ed moth - er her hair she tore.
me de - ny, ___ and the name he gave me was the Crop - py Boy.
do pass by, ___ oh ___ shed a tear ___ for the Crop - py Boy.

THE CRUEL MOTHER

English

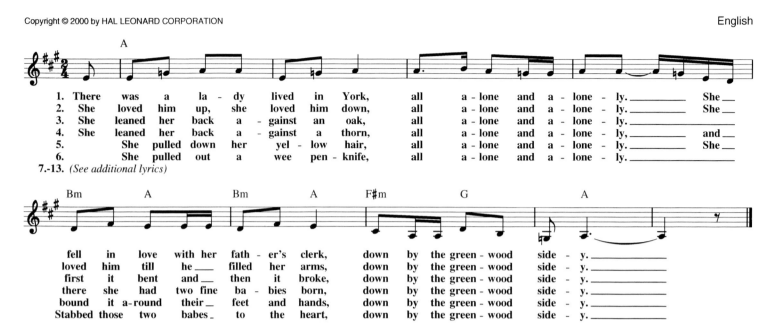

1. There was a la - dy lived in York, all a - lone and a - lone - ly. _____ She __
2. She loved him up, she loved him down, all a - lone and a - lone - ly. _____ She __
3. She leaned her back a - gainst an oak, all a - lone and a - lone - ly. _____ She __
4. She leaned her back a - gainst a thorn, all a - lone and a - lone - ly, _____ and __
5. She pulled down her yel - low hair, all a - lone and a - lone - ly. _____ She __
6. She pulled out a wee pen - knife, all a - lone and a - lone - ly. _____

7.-13. *(See additional lyrics)*

fell in love with her fath - er's clerk, down by the green - wood side - y. _____
loved him till he ___ filled her arms, down by the green - wood side - y. _____
first it bent and ___ then it broke, down by the green - wood side - y. _____
there she had two fine ba - bies born, down by the green - wood side - y. _____
bound it a-round their ___ feet and hands, down by the green - wood side - y. _____
Stabbed those two babes _ to the heart, down by the green - wood side - y. _____

Additional Lyrics

7. She laid them under a marble stone...
   Then she turned as a fair maid home...

8. One day she was sitting in her father's hall...
   She saw two babes come playing at ball...

9. Babes, oh, babes, if you was mine...
   I'd dress you up in scarlet fine...

10. Mother, oh, mother, it's we was yours...
    Scarlet fine was our own heart's blood...

11. You wiped your penknife on your shoe...
    The more you wiped, more red it grew...

12. You laid us under a marble stone...
    Now you sit as a fair maid home...

13. Babes, oh, babes, it's Heaven for you...
    Mother, oh, mother, it's Hell for you...

THE CRUEL WAR IS RAGING

American, from the Civil War

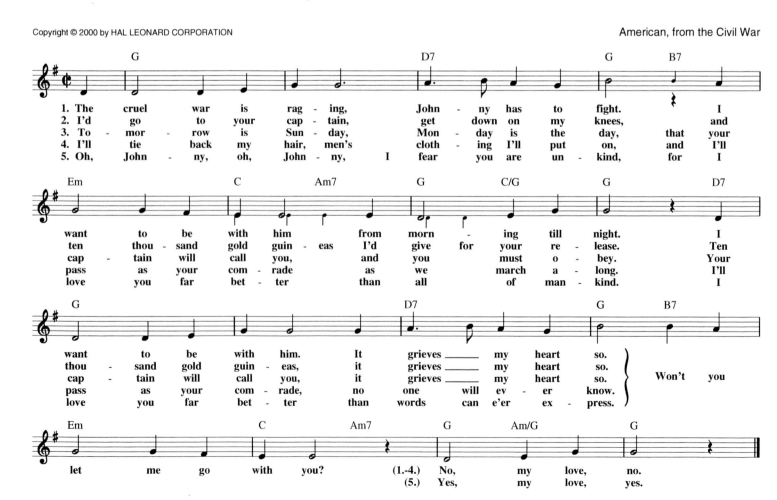

1. The cruel war is rag - ing, John - ny has to fight. I
2. I'd go to your cap - tain, get down on my knees, and
3. To - mor - row is Sun - day, Mon - day is the day, that your
4. I'll tie back my hair, men's cloth - ing I'll put on, and I'll
5. Oh, John - ny, oh, John - ny, I fear you are un - kind, for I

want to be with him from morn - ing till night. I
ten thou - sand gold guin - eas I'd give for your re - lease. Ten
cap - tain will call you, and you must o - bey. Your
pass as your com - rade as we march a - long. I'll
love you far bet - ter than all of man - kind. I

want to be with him. It grieves _____ my heart so.
thou - sand gold guin - eas, it grieves _____ my heart so.
cap - tain will call you, it grieves _____ my heart so.
pass as your com - rade, no one will ev - er know.
love you far bet - ter than words can e'er ex - press.

Won't you

let me go with you? (1.-4.) No, my love, no.
(5.) Yes, my love, yes.

THE CRUEL YOUTH

17th Century American

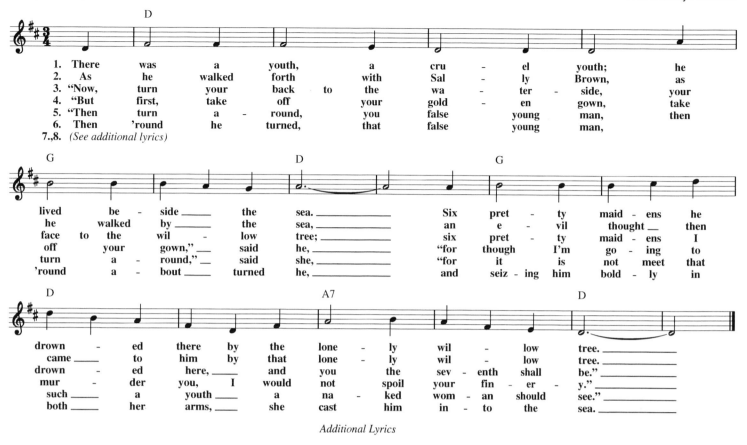

1. There was a youth, a cru - el youth; he lived be - side ___ the sea. ___ Six pret - ty maid - ens he drown - ed there by the lone - ly wil - low tree. ___

2. As he walked forth with Sal - ly Brown, as he walked by ___ the sea, ___ an e - vil thought ___ then came ___ to him by that lone - ly wil - low tree. ___

3. "Now, turn your back to the wa - ter - side, your face to the wil - low tree; ___ six pret - ty maid - ens I drown - ed here, ___ and you the sev - enth shall be." ___

4. "But first, take off your gold - en gown, take off your gown," ___ said he, ___ "for though I'm go - ing to mur - der you, I would not spoil your fin - er - y." ___

5. "Then turn a - round, you false young man, then turn a - round," ___ said she, ___ "for it is not meet that such ___ a youth ___ a na - ked wom - an should see." ___

6. Then 'round he turned, that false young man, 'round a - bout ___ turned he, ___ and seiz - ing him bold - ly in both ___ her arms, ___ she cast him in - to the sea. ___

7.,8. *(See additional lyrics)*

Additional Lyrics

7. "Lie there, lie there, you false young man,
   Lie there, lie there," said she,
   "For six pretty maidens you've drowned here;
   Go keep them company."

8. He sank beneath the icy waves,
   He sank down into the sea;
   No living thing wept a tear for him
   Save that lonely willow tree.

THE CUCKOO

English

1. The cuck - oo is a fun - ny bird; she sings as she flies. She'll bring you glad tid - ings, she'll tell you no lies. She sips from the pret - ty flow - ers to make her voice clear, and she'll nev - er sing cuck - oo till the spring of the year.

2. A - walk - ing and a - talk - ing and a - wan - d'ring go I, a - wait - ing for my true ___ love; he'll come by and by. She meet him ___ in the morn - ing, for he's all my de - light. I'll walk with my true ___ love from ___ morn - ing to night.

3. Come, all you fair ___ maid - ens, take warn - ing from me; don't place your af - fec - tions on a young man too free, leaves they ___ do ___ with - er and roots they do die, and your love, he will leave ___ you and he'll nev - er say why.

4. But if he will ___ leave ___ me I'll not be for - lorn, and if he'll for - swear ___ me I'll not be for - sworn. I'll get my - self ___ up in my best fin - er - y and I'll walk as proud by ___ him as ___ he walks by me.

CRYDERVILLE JAIL

American

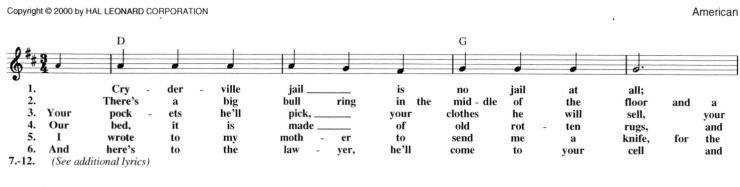

1. Cry - der - ville jail _____ is no jail at all;
2. There's a big bull ring in the mid - dle of the floor and a
3. Your pock - ets he'll pick, _____ your clothes he will sell, your
4. Our bed, it is made _____ of old rot - ten rugs, and
5. I wrote to my moth - er to send me a knife, for the
6. And here's to the law - yer, he'll come to your cell and

7.-12. *(See additional lyrics)*

lice in that jail _____ are chew - in' the wall.
damned _____ old jail - er to o - pen the door.
hands he will hand - cuff; god - damn him to hell.
when we lie down, we are cov - ered with bugs.
lice and the chinch - es have threat - ened my life.
swear he will clear you in spite of all hell.

} It's a -

hard times _____ in the Cry - der - ville jail; _____ It's hard

times, _____ poor boy. _____

Additional Lyrics

7. Get all your money
Before he will rest,
Then say, "Plead guilty,
For I think it the best."

8. Old Judge Simpkins
Will read us the law,
The damndest fool judge
That you ever saw.

9. And there sits the jury,
A devil of a crew;
They'll look a poor prisoner
Clean through and through.

10. And here's to the sheriff,
I like to forgot,
The damndest old rascal
We have in the lot.

11. Your privileges he'll take,
Your clothes he will sell;
Get drunk on the money
Goddamn him to hell!

12. And now I have come
To the end of my song;
I'll leave it to the boys
As I go along.

THE CUMBERLAND CREW

Civil War Song

1. Oh ship - mates, come _ gath - er and join in my dit - ty of a ter - ri - ble bat - tle that
2. That ill - fat - ed _____ day, a - bout ten in the morn - ing, the _ sky, it was cloud - less and
3. They fought us three _ hours _____ with stern res - o - lu - tion till those reb - els found can - non could
4. Oh, slow - ly she _ sank in the dark, roll - ing wa - ters; their _ voic - es on earth will be

hap - pened of late. Let each Un - ion _____ tar shed, a tear of his pit - y when he
bright shone the sun. The drums of the _____ Cum - ber - land sound - ed a warn - ing that _____
nev - er de - cide, for the flag of Se - ces - sion had no pow'r to quell them, though the
heard nev - er more. They'll be wept by Co - lum - bia's brave sons and fair daugh - ters; may their

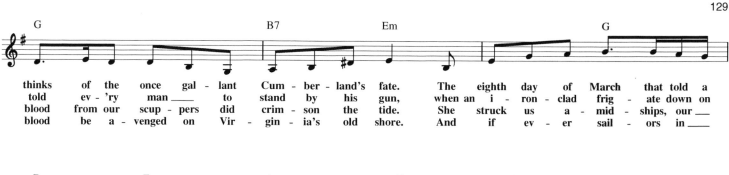

thinks   of   the   once   gal - lant   Cum - ber - land's   fate.   The   eighth   day   of   March   that   told   a
told   ev - 'ry   man____   to   stand   by   his   gun,   when   an   i - ron - clad   frig - ate   down   on
blood   from   our   scup - pers   did   crim - son   the   tide.   She   struck   us   a - mid - ships,   our ___
blood   be   a - venged   on   Vir - gin - ia's   old   shore.   And   if   ev - er   sail - ors   in ___

ter - ri - ble   sto - ry,   when   man - y   a   brave   tar   to   this   world   bid   "a - dieu;"   our
us ____   came   bear - ing,   high   up ___   in   the   air   her   base ___   reb - el   flag   flew;   an
planks   she   did   sev - er,   her   sharp _   i - ron   prow   pierced   our ___   no - ble   ship   through,   and
bat - tle   as - sem - ble,   God   bless ___   our   dear   ban - ner,   the ___   red,   white   and   blue;   be -

flag   was ___   wrapped   in   a   man - tle   of   glo - ry   by   the   he - ro - ic   deeds   of   the   Cum - ber - land's   crew.
em - blem   of   trea - son   she   proud - ly   was   wear - ing,   de - ter - mined   to   con - quer   the   Cum - ber - land   crew.
slow - ly   we   sank   in   Vir - gin - ia's   dark   wa - ters.   "We'll _   die   by   our   guns,"   cried   the   Cum - ber - land   crew.
neath   its   proud   folds   we'll   cause   ty - rants   to   trem - ble   or ____   sink   at   our   guns   like   the   Cum - ber - land   crew.

CUMBERLAND GAP

Southern American

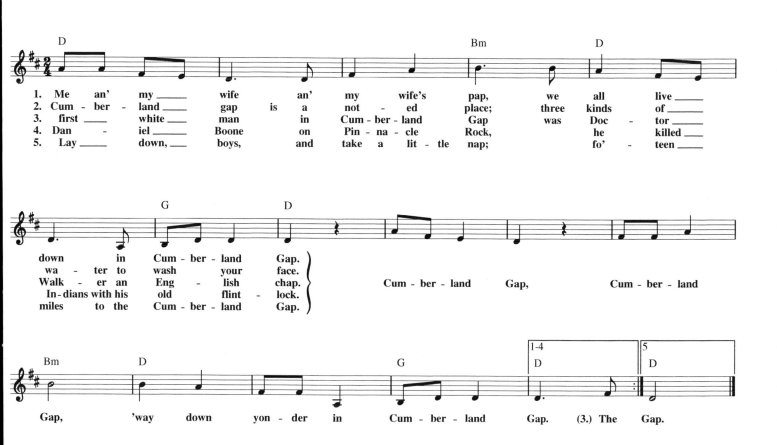

1. Me   an'   my ____   wife   an'   my   wife's   pap,   we   all   live ____
2. Cum - ber - land ____   gap   is   a   not - ed   place;   three   kinds   of ____
3. first ____   white ____   man   in   Cum - ber - land   Gap   was   Doc - tor ____
4. Dan - iel ____   Boone   on   Pin - na - cle   Rock,   he   killed ____
5. Lay ____   down, ____   boys,   and   take   a   lit - tle   nap;   fo' - teen ____

down   in   Cum - ber - land   Gap.
wa - ter   to   wash   your   face.
Walk - er   an   Eng - lish   chap.   Cum - ber - land   Gap,   Cum - ber - land
In - dians   with   his   old   flint - lock.
miles   to   the   Cum - ber - land   Gap.

Gap,   'way   down   yon - der   in   Cum - ber - land   Gap.   (3.) The   Gap.

THE CUTTY WREN

English

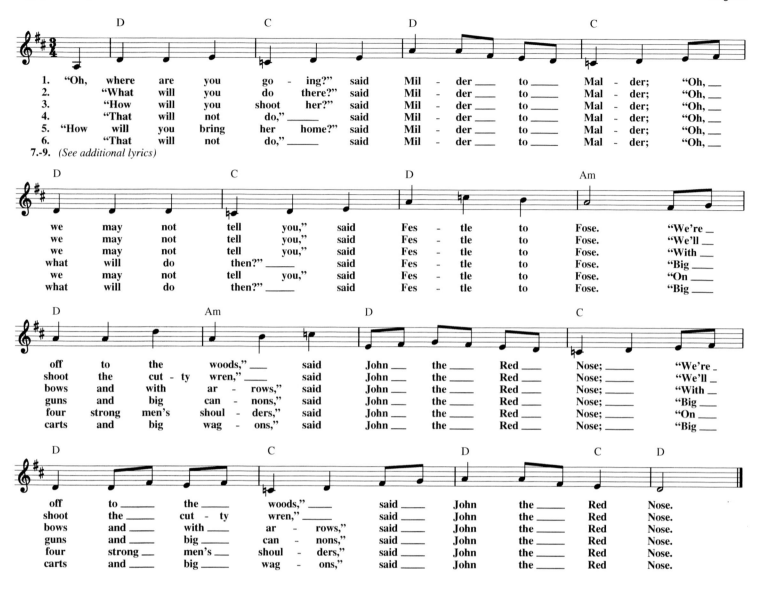

1. "Oh, where are you go - ing?" said Mil - der to Mal - der; "Oh,
2. "What will you do there?" said Mil - der to Mal - der; "Oh,
3. "How will you shoot her?" said Mil - der to Mal - der; "Oh,
4. "That will not do," said Mil - der to Mal - der; "Oh,
5. "How will you bring her home?" said Mil - der to Mal - der; "Oh,
6. "That will not do," said Mil - der to Mal - der; "Oh,
7.-9. (See additional lyrics)

we may not tell you," said Fes - tle to Fose. "We're
we may not tell you," said Fes - tle to Fose. "We'll
we may not tell you," said Fes - tle to Fose. "With
what will do then?" said Fes - tle to Fose. "Big
we may not tell you," said Fes - tle to Fose. "On
what will do then?" said Fes - tle to Fose. "Big

off to the woods," said John the Red Nose; "We're
shoot the cut - ty wren," said John the Red Nose; "We'll
bows and with ar - rows," said John the Red Nose; "With
guns and big can - nons," said John the Red Nose; "Big
four strong men's shoul - ders," said John the Red Nose; "On
carts and big wag - ons," said John the Red Nose; "Big

off to the woods," said John the Red Nose.
shoot the cut - ty wren," said John the Red Nose.
bows and with ar - rows," said John the Red Nose.
guns and big can - nons," said John the Red Nose.
four strong men's shoul - ders," said John the Red Nose.
carts and big wag - ons," said John the Red Nose.

Additional Lyrics

7. "How will you cut her up?" said Milder to Malder;
   "Oh, we may not tell you," said Festle to Fose.
   "With knives and with forks," said John the Red Nose. (2x)

8. "That will not do," said Milder to Malder;
   "Oh, what will do then?" said Festle to Fose.
   "Big hatchets and cleavers," said John the Red Nose. (2x)

9. "Who'll get the spare ribs?" said Milder to Malder;
   "Oh, we may not tell you," said Festle to Fose.
   "We'll give it all to the poor," said John the Red Nose. (2x)

DABBLING IN THE DEW

English

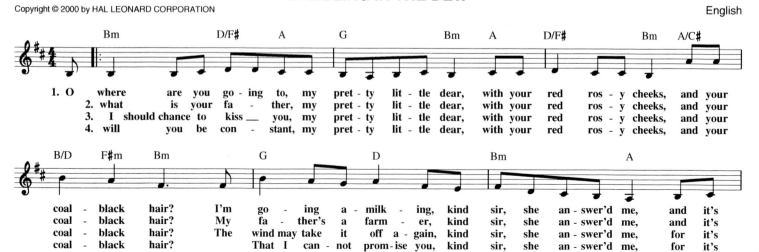

1. O where are you go - ing to, my pret - ty lit - tle dear, with your red ros - y cheeks, and your
2. what is your fa - ther, my pret - ty lit - tle dear, with your red ros - y cheeks, and your
3. I should chance to kiss you, my pret - ty lit - tle dear, with your red ros - y cheeks, and your
4. will you be con - stant, my pret - ty lit - tle dear, with your red ros - y cheeks, and your

coal - black hair? I'm go - ing a - milk - ing, kind sir, she an - swer'd me, and it's
coal - black hair? My fa - ther's a farm - er, kind sir, she an - swer'd me, and it's
coal - black hair? The wind may take it off a - gain, kind sir, she an - swer'd me, for it's
coal - black hair? That I can - not prom-ise you, kind sir, she an - swer'd me, for it's

dab - bling in the dew makes the milk - maids fair. O
dab - bling in the dew makes the milk - maids fair. And
dab - bling in the dew makes the milk - maids fair. O
dab - bling in the dew makes the milk - maids fair. Then

may I go with you, my pret - ty lit - tle dear, with your red ros - y cheeks, and your
what is your moth - er, my pret - ty lit - tle dear, with your red ros - y cheeks, and your
say, will you mar - ry me, my pret - ty lit - tle dear, with your red ros - y cheeks, and your
I won't __ mar - ry you, my pret - ty lit - tle dear, with your red ros - y cheeks, and your

coal - black hair? O you may go with me, kind sir, she an - swered me, for it's
coal - black hair? My moth - er's a dairy - maid, kind sir, she an - swer'd me, and it's
coal - black hair? O yes, if you please, ___ kind sir, she an - swer'd me, for it's
coal - black hair? No - bod - y ask'd you, kind sir, she an - swer'd me, and it's

dab - bling in the dew makes the milk - maids fair. (2.) And
dab - bling in the dew makes the milk - maids fair. (3.) If
dab - bling in the dew makes the milk - maids fair. (4.) O
dab - bling in the dew makes the milk - maids fair.

DANCE TO YOUR DADDY

English

Dance to your dad - dy, my lit - tle lad - die; dance to your dad - dy,

my ___ lit - tle man.
1. Thou shalt have a fish and thou shalt have a fin,
2. When thou art a man and come to take a wife,

thou shalt have a cod - lin' when the boat comes in. Thou shalt have a had - dock
thou shalt wed a lass and love her all your life. She shall be your lass and

boiled ___ in a pan. Dance to your dad - dy, my ___ lit - tle man.
thou shall be her man. Dance to your dad - dy, my ___ lit - tle man.

DANNY BOY

Words by Frederick Edward Weatherly
Irish folk melody, "Londonderry Air"

DARLING NELLY GRAY

Words and Music by
Benjamin R. Harby

D / **G**

sitting and a - singing by the little cottage door, where ___
taken her to Georgia for to wear her life away as she

D / **A7** / **D**

lived my ___ darling Nelly Gray. }
toils in the cotton and the cane. }

Oh, my

A7 / **D**

poor Nelly Gray, they have taken you away, and I'll never see my darling any

A7 / **D**

more. I'm a - sitting by the river and I'm

G / **D** / **A7** / **D**

weeping all the day, for you've gone from the old Kentucky shore.

DANVILLE GIRL

American

E / **A**

1. My pocket - book was empty, my heart was
2. I was standing on the platform, smoking a
3. When I got off at Danville, got stuck on a
4. She took me to her kitchen; she treated me
5. She wore her hat on the back of her head like high - tone
6. I pulled my cap down over my eyes, walked down to the

E / **A**

full of pain; ___ ten thousand miles a -
cheap cigar, ___ waiting for the next
Danville girl. ___ You can bet your life she was
nice and fine. ___ She got me out of the
people do, ___ but the very next train come
railroad tracks. ___ There I caught the next

E / **B7** / **E**

way from home, bumming a railroad train. ___
freight ___ train to carry an empty car. ___
out of sight; she wore ___ those Danville curls. ___
no - tion of bumming all the time. ___
down the line, I bid ___ that girl a - dieu. ___
freight ___ train, never to come back. ___

DARLIN' COREY

African-American

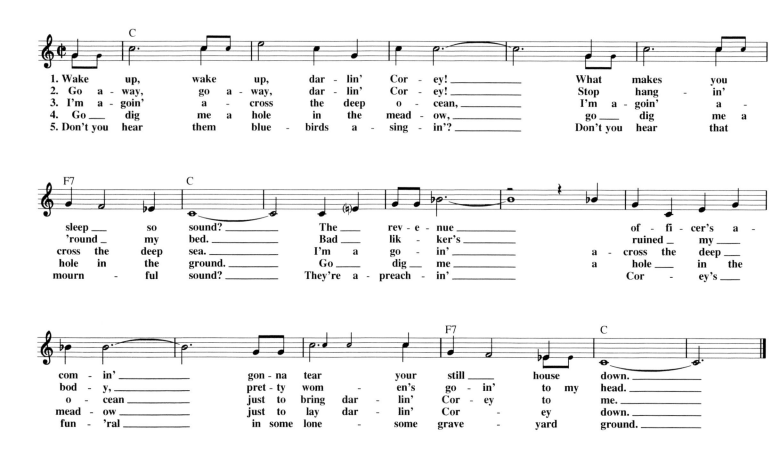

1. Wake up, wake up, dar-lin' Cor-ey! _____ What makes you
2. Go a-way, go a-way, dar-lin' Cor-ey! _____ Stop hang-in'
3. I'm a-goin' a-cross the deep o-cean, _____ I'm a-goin' a-
4. Go ___ dig me a hole in the mead-ow, _____ go ___ dig me a
5. Don't you hear them blue-birds a-sing-in'? _____ Don't you hear that

sleep ___ so sound? _____ The ___ rev-e-nue _____ of-fi-cer's a-
'round ___ my bed. _____ Bad ___ lik-ker's _____ ruined ___ my ___
cross the deep sea. _____ I'm a-go-in' _____ a-cross the deep
hole in the ground. _____ Go ___ dig ___ me _____ a hole ___ in the
mourn-ful sound? _____ They're a-preach-in' _____ Cor-ey's ___

com-in' _____ gon-na tear your still ___ house down. _____
bod-y, _____ pret-ty wom-en's go-in' to my head. _____
o-cean _____ just to bring dar-lin' Cor-ey to me. _____
mead-ow _____ just to lay dar-lin' Cor-ey down. _____
fun-'ral _____ in some lone-some grave-yard ground. _____

DARLING MAIDEN, HARK, I ASK THEE
(Krakowiak)

Polish

1. Dar-ling maid-en, hark, I ask thee. I would like to make a bar-gain.
2. Light-ly laughs the pret-ty wom-an. From her red lips comes no an-swer.
1. U-ktad ze mną zrób, dzie-wecz-ko, z o-czy-wi-stym two-im zys-kiem
2. Dzie-wcze się na to u-śmie-cha nic nie mó-wi, więc ze-zwa-la;

I'll sing you some love _____ songs if you will kiss ___ me ___
With my pas-sion-lad-en sing-ing, I will cap-ture the
ja dam piosn-ke za pio-snecz-ke ty mi u-ścisk ___
ja za-czy-nam śpie-wać z ci-cha tra la la _____

sweet-ly and gen-tly. Nev-er was there such a fine trade,
heart of this wom-an. I will sing till her eyes dark-en,
za u-ścis-kiem. Przy u-ktad-zie tym ob-sta-waj
tra la _____ la la. Śpie-wam cią-gle, o-na stu-cha

songs __ of __ pas - sion for man - y kiss - es. Can I claim my
filled __ with __ love __ and __ sweet af - fec - tion. So that we may
a __ wa - ru - jac __ so - bie zy - ski ty mi pio - snek
są - dze __ wiec __ o __ tej fi - lu - tce Że gdy mi nad -

songs a - gain and sing __ them __ for more kiss - es from my sweet maid? __
share these pleas - ures, please, __ I __ ask __ thee, __ maid - en, hark - en. __
nie od - da - waj ja __ ci __ od - dam __ twe u - ści - ski. __
sta - wia u - cha od - da __ mi __ i __ ser - ce w krót - ce. __

DEEP RIVER

African-American Spiritual

Deep __ riv - er, my home is o - ver Jor - dan,

Deep __ riv - er, Lord, I want to cross o - ver in - to camp - ground.

Oh, don't you want to go o - ver to that gos - pel __ feast, __ that

prom - ised land __ where all __ is peace. Oh,

deep __ riv - er, my home is o - ver Jor - dan,

Deep __ riv - er, Lord, I want to cross o - ver in - to

camp - ground. I want to cross o - ver in - to camp - ground.

DAUGHTER, WILL YOU MARRY?

Pennsylvania Dutch Folksong

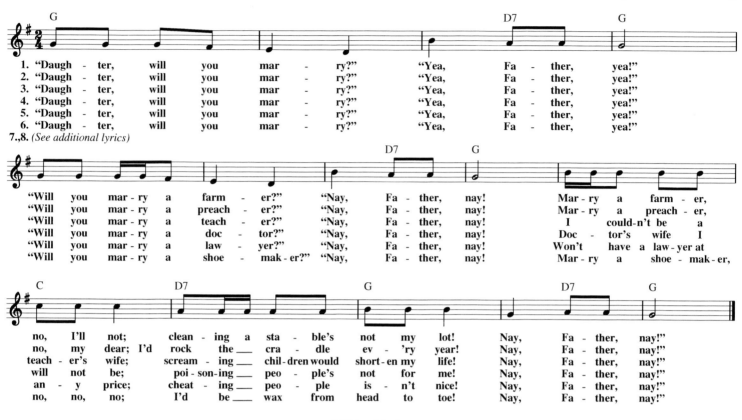

Additional Lyrics

7. "Daughter, will you marry?"
"Yea, Father, yea!"
"Will you marry a carpenter?"
"Nay, Father, nay!
I can't do a thing like that;
Pounding nails would drive me mad!
Nay, Father, nay!"

8. "Daughter, will you marry?"
"Yea, Father, yea!"
"Will you marry a fiddler?"
"Yea, Father, yea!
I want to be a fiddler's wife,
Singing and dancing are the joy of my life!
Yea, Father, yea!"

DAVID OF THE WHITE ROCK

English

DAYS OF FORTY-NINE

19th Century American

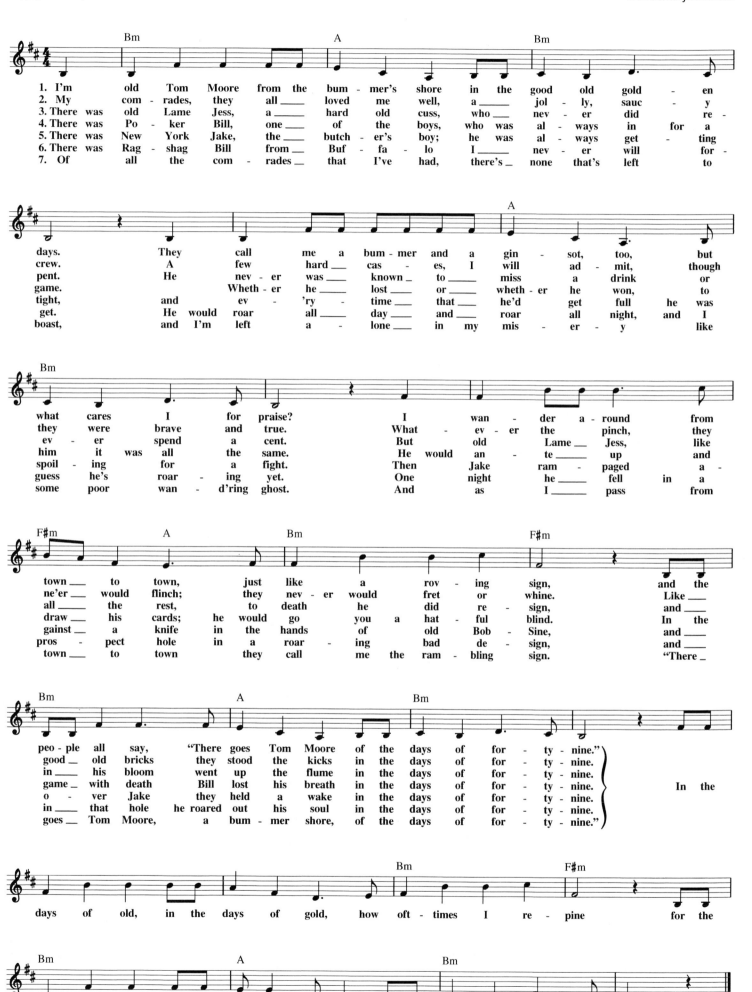

DEADHEADS AND SUCKERS

American

DEATH AND THE LADY

English

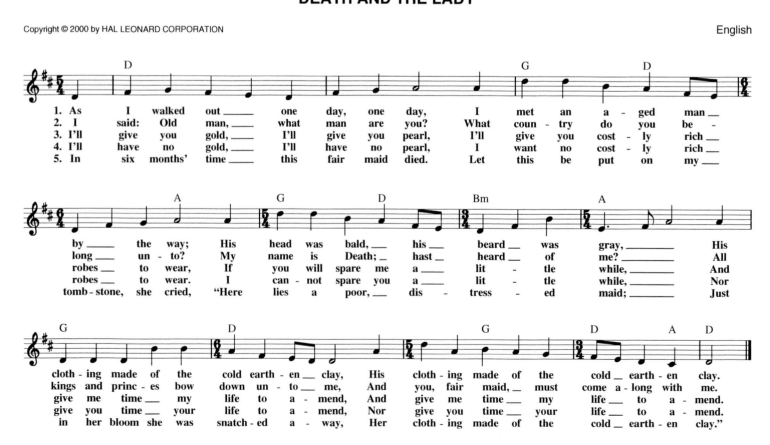

DEEP BLUE SEA

American

THE DEER SONG

North Carolina Folksong

DINK'S SONG

African-American

Additional Lyrics

7. Now my aprons up to my chin,
You pass my door an' you won' come in.

8. Ef I had listened to whut my mama said,
I'd be at home in my mama's bed.

DELIA'S GONE

Bahamian

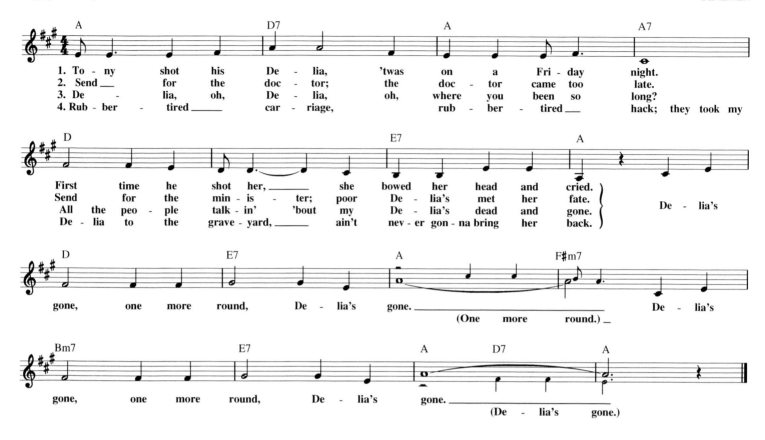

1. To- ny shot his De - lia, 'twas on a Fri- day night.
2. Send __ for the doc - tor; the doc - tor came too late.
3. De - lia, oh, De - lia, oh, where you been so long?
4. Rub - ber - tired ____ car - riage, rub - ber - tired __ hack; they took my

First time he shot her, ____ she bowed her head and cried.
Send for the min - is - ter; poor De - lia's met her fate.
All the peo - ple talk- in' 'bout my De - lia's dead and gone.
De - lia to the grave- yard, ____ ain't nev- er gon- na bring her back.

De - lia's gone, one more round, De - lia's gone. (One more round.) De - lia's
gone, one more round, De - lia's gone. (De - lia's gone.)

THE DERBY RAM

English

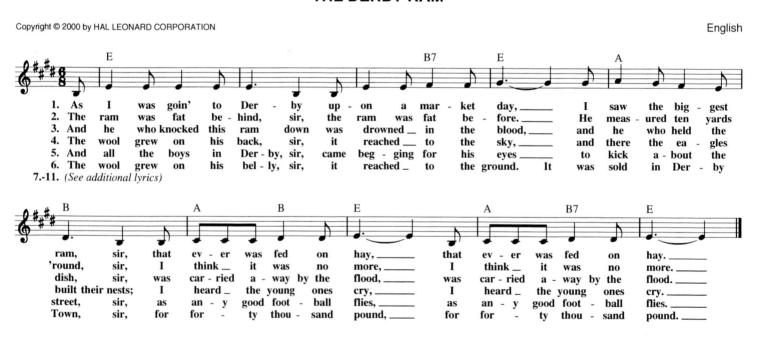

1. As I was goin' to Der - by up - on a mar - ket day, ____ I saw the big- gest
2. The ram was fat be - hind, sir, the ram was fat be - fore. ____ He meas - ured ten yards
3. And he who knocked this ram down was drowned __ in the blood, ____ and he who held the
4. The wool grew on his back, sir, it reached __ to the sky, ____ and there the ea - gles
5. And all the boys in Der - by, sir, came beg - ging for his eyes ____ to kick a - bout the
6. The wool grew on his bel - ly, sir, it reached __ to the ground. It was sold in Der - by
7.-11. *(See additional lyrics)*

ram, sir, that ev - er was fed on hay, ____ that ev - er was fed on hay. ____
'round, sir, I think __ it was no more, ____ I think __ it was no more. ____
dish, sir, was car - ried a - way by the flood, ____ was car - ried a - way by the flood. ____
built their nests; I heard __ the young ones cry, ____ I heard __ the young ones cry. ____
street, sir, as an - y good foot - ball flies, ____ as an - y good foot - ball flies. ____
Town, sir, for for - ty thou - sand pound, ____ for for - ty thou - sand pound. ____

Additional Lyrics

7. The wool upon his tail, sir,
Filled more than fifty bags.
You'd better keep away, sir,
When that tail shakes and wags.

8. The horns upon his head, sir,
As high as a man could reach,
And there they built a pulpit, sir,
The Quakers for to preach.

9. And one of this ram's teeth, sir,
Was hollow as a horn,
And when they took its measure, sir,
It held a bushel of corn.

10. The mutton that the ram made
Gave the whole Army meat,
And what was left, I'm told, sir,
Was served out to the fleet.

11. The man who owned this ram, sir,
Was considered mighty rich,
But the man who told this story, sir,
Was a lyin' son of a bitch.

THE DEVIL'S QUESTIONS

Folksong from North Carolina
Based on an English Folksong

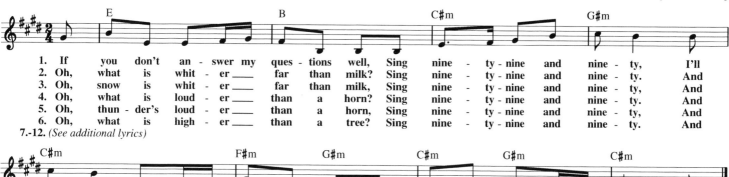

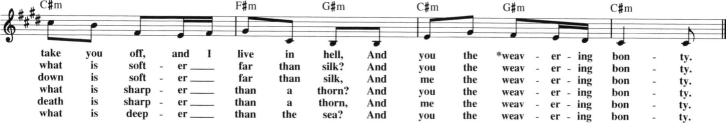

7.-12. (See additional lyrics)

*weaver's bonny

Additional Lyrics

7. Oh, heaven's higher than a tree,
Sing ninety-nine and ninety,
And hell is deeper than the sea,
And me the weavering bonty.

8. Oh, what red fruit September grows?
Sing ninety-nine and ninety.
And what thing 'round the whole world goes?
And you the weavering bonty.

9. The apple in September grows,
Sing ninety-nine and ninety,
And air around the whole world goes,
And me the weavering bonty.

10. Oh, what is wicked man's repay?
Sing ninety-nine and ninety,
And what is worse than woman's way?
And you the weavering bonty.

11. Now hell is wicked man's repay,
Sing ninety-nine and ninety,
And a she-devil's worse than woman's way,
And me the weavering bonty.

12. Oh, you have answered my questions well,
Sing ninety-nine and ninety,
But I'll take you off 'cause I live in hell,
And you the weavering bonty.

DEVILISH MARY

American

DICK DARBY

Irish

1. Oh, me name is Dick Dar - by, I'm a cob - bler; I ser - ved me time at old
2. Now, my fa - ther was hung for sheep steal - ing, me moth - er was burned for a
3. Ah, it's for - ty long years I have trav - eled, all by the con - tents of me
4. Oh, my wife she is hump - y, she's lump - y; my wife she's the dev - il, she's
5. It was ear - ly one fine sum - mer's morn - ing, a lit - tle be - fore it was

camp. Some call me an old ag - i - ta - tor, but now I'm re - solved to re -
witch, my sis - ter's a dan - dy house - keep - er, and I'm a me - chan - i - cal
pack. Me ham - mers, me awls and me pinch - es, I car - ry them all on me
black, and no mat - ter what I may do with her, her tongue it goes click - et - y -
day. I dipped her three times in the riv - er and care - less - ly bade her good

pent.
switch.
lack.   With me ing - twing of an ing - thing of an i - day, with me
clack.
day.

ing - twing of an ing - thing of an i - day, with me roo - boo - boo - roo - boo - boo

ran - dy, and me lab stone keeps beat - ing a - way.

DIDN'T IT RAIN

African-American

Now, did - n't it rain, _____ chil - lun; _____ God's gon - na 'stroy this

world with wa - ter. Now did - n't it rain, my Lord, now did - n't it rain, rain, _

rain. Well, it rained for - ty days and it rained for - ty nights; there
Well, it rained for - ty days 'n' for - ty nights with - out stop - pin'.
They __ knocked at the win - dow and they knocked at the door. They

was - n't no land no - where in sight. God sent a ra - ven to
No - ah was glad when the rain stopped a - drop - pin'. God sent __ No - ah a
cried, _ "Oh No - ah, please take me on board." No - ah ___ cried, _ "You're

car - ry the news; he histe his wings and a - way ___ he flew. __
rain - bow sign; says, "No more wa - ter but fire ___ next time." __
full ___ of sin. The Lord's got the key and you can't __ get in." __

DIDN'T MY LORD DELIVER DANIEL?

African-American Spiritual

DIED FOR LOVE

English

1. A bold young farm - er court - ed me, He
2. I wish, I wish, but it's all in vain, I
3. I wish my ba - by lit - tle was born, And
4. There is a house in yon - der town, Where
5. Go dig my grave long, wide, _____ and deep, Put a

gained my heart and my lib - er - ty; He's gained my heart with a
wish I was _____ a maid a - gain; But a maid a - gain I nev -
smil - ing on _____ its fa - ther's knee; And I, poor girl, _____ was
my love goes _____ and sits him down, And takes some strange _____ girl
mar - ble stone at my head and feet, Put o - ver and above _____ a

free good will, And I must _____ con - fess that I love _____ him still.
er shall be, _____ Since that _____ young farm - er lay still _____ with me.
dead and gone, And the green _____ grass grow - ing o - ver me.
on his knee, And he tells _____ her things that he won't _____ tell me.
pure white dove, _____ To let the world know that I died _____ for love.

THE DINGLE PUCK GOAT

Irish

C

1. I am a young job - ber both fool - ish and air - y; the green hills of Ker - ry I
2. dar - ing old fel - low I stood for to stare him, al - though I feared he was a
3. made my ap - proach to the own - er that held him; a bar - gain we struck _____ with -
4. old man de - part - ed and I was for start - ing. Those words that he told me put
5. came near to Bran - don I thought it was Lon - don; I re - gret - ted my jour - ney when
6. came on the strand _____ now quick - ly he ran; _____ towards Clones _____ or Cas - tle - maine

7.,8. *(See additional lyrics)*

D7   G7   C

came for to see. I went back to Din - gle to buy up some cat - tle, and I
mon - ster to see. He wore a long meg - gal as gray as a badg - er that would
out much de - lay. He said, "If you pay me down twen - ty - two shill - ings, some ad -
me in des - pair. The first jump he gave, well, he near broke my left arm. I _____
I saw the sea. He jumped in - to the wa - ter and swam right a - cross it _____
sure he did steer. To Mill - town, Kil - lor - gin and like - wise Kil - lar - ney, and _____

F   C   G7   C   Em   Am

want you to lis - ten what hap - pened to me. As I en - tered the fair on a
reach _____ from Din - gle to Ca - hir - ci - veen, with a pair of long horns _____ like
vice I will give you be - fore go - ing a - way. This _____ dar - ing young he - ro was
jumped on his back and got hold of his hair. Says _____ I, "My bold he - ro, on
towards Cas - tle Greg - or - y o - ver the way. The _____ waves of the o - cean they
nev - er cried stop till he came to Ken - mare. At _____ length then he spoke: "We have

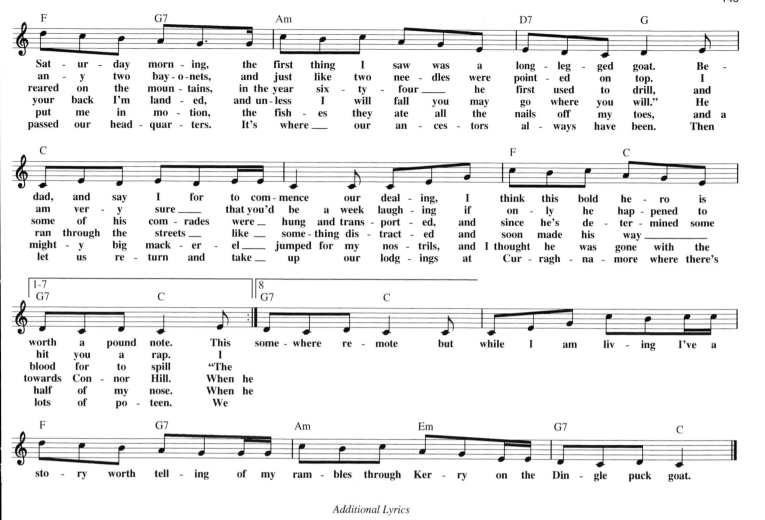

F | G7 | Am | D7 | G

Sat-ur-day morn-ing,	the first thing I saw was a	long-leg-ged goat.	Be-
an-y two bay-o-nets,	and just like two nee-dles were	point-ed on top.	I
reared on the moun-tains,	in the year six-ty-four ___ he	first used to drill,	and
your back I'm land-ed,	and un-less I will fall you may	go where you will."	He
put me in mo-tion,	the fish-es they ate all the	nails off my toes,	and a
passed our head-quar-ters.	It's where ___ our an-ces-tors	al-ways have been.	Then

C | F | C

dad, and say I for	to com-mence our deal-ing,	I think this bold he-ro is
am ver-y sure ___	that you'd be a week laugh-ing	if on-ly he hap-pened to
some of his com-rades	were ___ hung and trans-port-ed,	and since he's de-ter-mined some
ran through the streets ___	like ___ some-thing dis-tract-ed	and soon made his way ___
might-y big mack-er-el ___	jumped for my nos-trils,	and I thought he was gone with the
let us re-turn and take ___	up our lodg-ings	at Cur-ragh-na-more where there's

1-7 G7 | C || 8 G7 | C

worth a pound note.	This some-where re-mote	but while I am liv-ing I've a
hit you a rap.	I "The	
blood for to spill	towards Con-nor Hill. When he	
half of my nose.	When he	
lots of po-teen.	We	

F | G7 | Am | Em | G7 | C

sto-ry worth tell-ing of my ram-bles through Ker-ry on the Din-gle puck goat.

Additional Lyrics

7. We done our returns and stopped there till morning;
It's during the night I sat up on his back.
As the day it was dawning he jumped from the corner,
And t'wards Castle Island he went in a crack.
To the town of Tralee we next took our rambles.
I think he was anxious to see some more sport.
Outside of the town we met some Highlanders.
He up with his horns and he tore all their clothes.

8. The Highlanders shouted and bawled, "Meela murder!
Send for the polis and get him to jail."
But the louder they shouted the faster my goat ran,
And over the Basin he gave them legbail.
On crossing the Basin I fell on the footway;
Away went the goat and I saw him no more.
Sure if he's in Ireland he's in Camp or in Brandon,
Or away in the mountains somewhere remote.

DON'T I WISH I WAS A SINGLE GIRL AGAIN

American

E | A7 | E | C#m

1. When I was sin-gle,	I went dressed	so fine.	
2. Dish-es to wash, ___	spring to	go to;	
3. When I was sin-gle,	my shoes they	did squeak.	
4. Three lit-tle ba-bies ___	ly-ing in the	bed,	
5. Wash their lit-tle feet ___	and ___ send them	to school;	a-
6. When I was sin-gle,	I eat bis-cuit	and pie.	

E | A7 | E

Now I am mar-ried,	go ___ rag-ged all the	time.
When you're mar-ried, Lord,	you've ___ got it all to	do.
Now I am mar-ried,	my ___ shoes ___ they do	leak.
All of them so hun-gry	they ___ can't raise up their	head.
long comes the drunk-ard	and ___ calls ___ them a	fool.
Now I am mar-ried, Lord,	it's ___ eat corn-bread or	die.

A | A7 | E

Lord, don't I wish I was a sin-gle girl a-gain.

DIXIE

Words and Music by
Daniel Decatur Emmett
American

1. I _____ wish I was _____ in the land of cot - ton, old times there are
2. Old _____ Mis - sus mar - ry _____ Will the Weav - er, Wil - liam was a
3. His face was sharp _____ as a butch - er's cleav - er, but that did not
4. Now _____ here's a health _____ to the next old Mis - sus and all the girls that

not for - got - ten. Look a - way, look a - way, look a - way, Dix - ie Land! In _____
gay de - ceiv - er. Look a - way, look a - way, look a - way, Dix - ie Land! But _____
seem to grieve her. Look a - way, look a - way, look a - way, Dix - ie Land! Old _____
want to kiss us. Look a - way, look a - way, look a - way, Dix - ie Land! But _____

Dix - ie Land _____ where _____ I was born in _____ ear - ly on _____ one
when he put _____ his _____ arm a - round her, he smiled as fierce as a
Mis - sus act - ed the fool - ish part and died for a man _____ that

frost - y morn - in'. Look a - way, look a - way, look a - way, Dix - ie Land!
for - ty-pound-er. Look a - way, look a - way, look a - way, Dix - ie Land!
broke her heart. _____ Look a - way, look a - way, look a - way, Dix - ie Land!
song to - mor-row. Look a - way, look a - way, look a - way, Dix - ie Land!

I

wish I was in Dix - ie. Hoo - ray! Hoo - ray! In Dix - ie Land I'll

take my stand to live and die in Dix - ie. A - way, a - way, a -

way down south in Dix - ie. A - way, a - way, a - way down south in Dix - ie.

DO AS I'M DOING

American Play Party Song

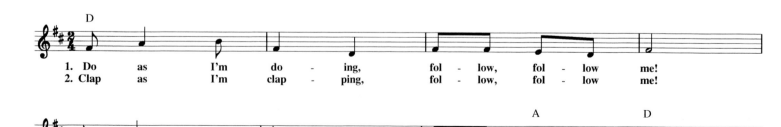

1. Do as I'm do - ing, fol - low, fol - low me!
2. Clap as I'm clap - ping, fol - low, fol - low me!

Do as I'm do - ing, fol - low, fol - low me!
Clap as I'm clap - ping, fol - low, fol - low me!

If I do it high or low, If I do it fast or slow,

Do as I'm do - ing, fol - low, fol - low me!
Clap as I'm clap - ping, fol - low, fol - low me!

Do as I'm do - ing, fol - low, fol - low me!
Clap as I'm clap - ping, fol - low, fol - low me!

THE DODGER SONG

American

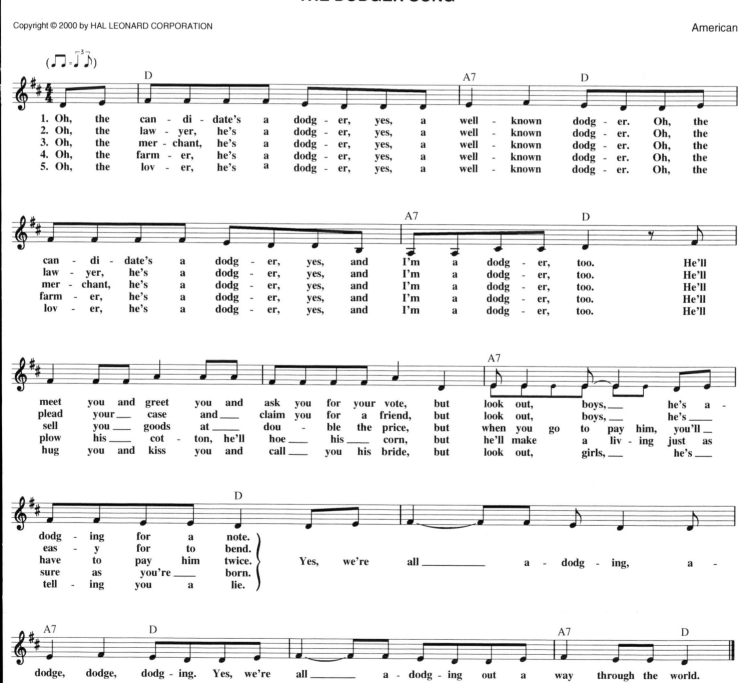

1. Oh, the can - di - date's a dodg - er, yes, a well - known dodg - er. Oh, the
2. Oh, the law - yer, he's a dodg - er, yes, a well - known dodg - er. Oh, the
3. Oh, the mer - chant, he's a dodg - er, yes, a well - known dodg - er. Oh, the
4. Oh, the farm - er, he's a dodg - er, yes, a well - known dodg - er. Oh, the
5. Oh, the lov - er, he's a dodg - er, yes, a well - known dodg - er. Oh, the

can - di - date's a dodg - er, yes, and I'm a dodg - er, too. He'll
law - yer, he's a dodg - er, yes, and I'm a dodg - er, too. He'll
mer - chant, he's a dodg - er, yes, and I'm a dodg - er, too. He'll
farm - er, he's a dodg - er, yes, and I'm a dodg - er, too. He'll
lov - er, he's a dodg - er, yes, and I'm a dodg - er, too. He'll

meet you and greet you and ask you for your vote, but look out, boys,___ he's a -
plead your___ case and___ claim you for a friend, but look out, boys,___ he's___
sell you___ goods at___ dou - ble the price, but when you go to pay him, you'll___
plow his___ cot - ton, he'll hoe___ his___ corn, but he'll make a liv - ing just as
hug you and kiss you and call___ you his bride, but look out, girls, ___ he's___

dodg - ing for a note.
eas - y for to bend.
have to pay him twice.   Yes, we're all_____ a - dodg - ing, a -
sure as you're___ born.
tell - ing you a lie.

dodge, dodge, dodg - ing. Yes, we're all_____ a - dodg - ing out a way through the world.

DON'T SING LOVE SONGS

American

1. Don't sing love songs, _____ you'll wake my moth- er; ___ she's sleep- in'
2. All men are false, _____ says my moth- er; ___ they'll tell you
3. My fa- ther is _____ a hand- some dev- il; ___ he's got a
4. Wish that I was _____ some lit- tle spar- row; ___ yes, one of
5. On his breast _____ I'd light and flut- ter ___ with my
6. Go court some oth - er ten- der la- dy, _____ and I hope that

close _____ by __ my side, _____ and in her right hand _____ she holds a
wick - ed, love- ly lies, _____ and the ver- y next eve - ning court an- oth-
chain _____ that's five _ miles long, _____ and ev- 'ry link _____ a heart does
those _____ that flies _ so high. _____ I'd fly __ a - way _____ to my false true
lit - tle ten- der wings. _____ I'd ask __ him who _____ he meant to
she _____ will be _ you wife, _____ 'cause I've _ been warned _____ and I've de-

dag - ger, _____ and says that _____ I _____ can't be your bride.
oth - er, _____ leav-ing you a - lone _____ to pine and sigh.
dan - gle _____ of some poor _____ maid _____ he's loved and wronged.
lov - er, _____ and when he'd _____ speak, _____ I would de - ny.
flat - ter _____ or who he _____ meant _____ to de - ceive.
cid - ed _____ to sleep a - lone _____ all of my life.

DON'T LET YOUR DEAL GO DOWN

American

1. I've been all a - round this whole wide world, way down in
2. When __ I __ left my love be - hind, she's stand - in'
3. who's gon - na shoe your pret - ty lit - tle feet? Who's gon - na
4. "Pa - pa _____ will shoe my pret - ty lit - tle feet, Ma - ma will

Mem - phis, Ten - nes - see. _____ An - y old place I hang my
in _____ the _____ door. _____ She throwed her lit - tle arms a - round my
glove _ your _ hand? _____ Who's gon - na kiss your ru - by
glove _ my _ hand. _____ You _____ can kiss my ros - y

hat seems like home __ to me. _____
neck and said, "Sweet Dad - dy, please __ don't go." _____
lips? _____ Hon - ey, who's gon - na be _____ your man? _____
lips _____ when you get back _____ a - gain." _____

Don't let your deal go down, _____ boys, don't let your deal go

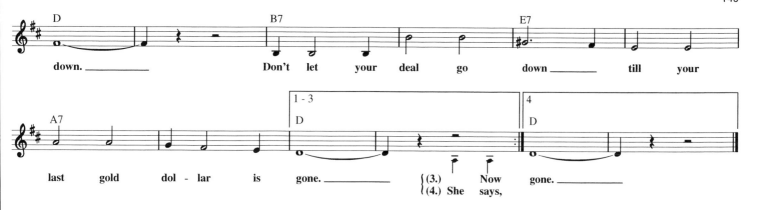

down. _____ Don't let your deal go down _____ till your
last gold dol - lar is gone. _____ (3.) Now gone. _____
(4.) She says,

DON'T YOU WEEP AFTER ME

Irish

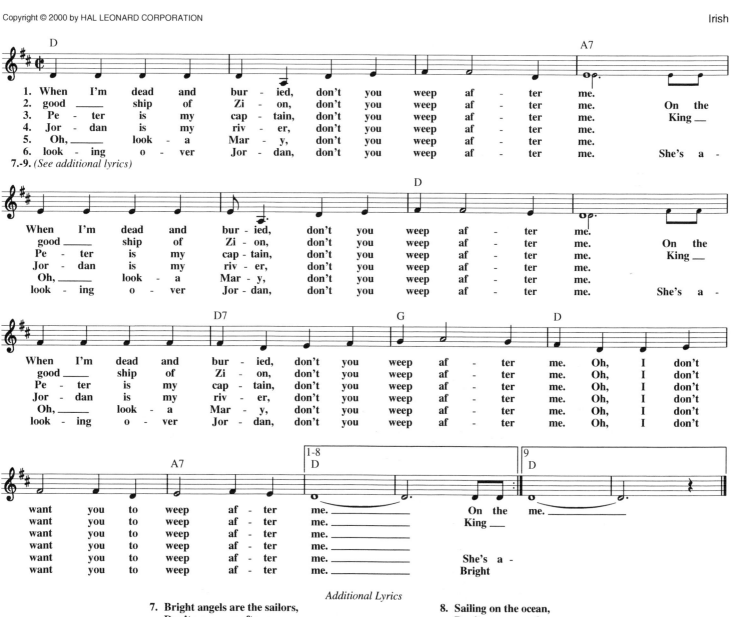

1. When I'm dead and bur - ied, don't you weep af - ter me. On the
2. good ___ ship of Zi - on, don't you weep af - ter me. On the
3. Pe - ter is my cap - tain, don't you weep af - ter me. King ___
4. Jor - dan is my riv - er, don't you weep af - ter me.
5. Oh, ___ look - a Mar - y, don't you weep af - ter me.
6. look - ing o - ver Jor - dan, don't you weep af - ter me. She's a -

7.-9. *(See additional lyrics)*

When I'm dead and bur - ied, don't you weep af - ter me. On the
good ___ ship of Zi - on, don't you weep af - ter me. On the
Pe - ter is my cap - tain, don't you weep af - ter me. King ___
Jor - dan is my riv - er, don't you weep af - ter me.
Oh, ___ look - a Mar - y, don't you weep af - ter me.
look - ing o - ver Jor - dan, don't you weep af - ter me. She's a -

When I'm dead and bur - ied, don't you weep af - ter me. Oh, I don't
good ___ ship of Zi - on, don't you weep af - ter me. Oh, I don't
Pe - ter is my cap - tain, don't you weep af - ter me. Oh, I don't
Jor - dan is my riv - er, don't you weep af - ter me. Oh, I don't
Oh, ___ look - a Mar - y, don't you weep af - ter me. Oh, I don't
look - ing o - ver Jor - dan, don't you weep af - ter me. Oh, I don't

want you to weep af - ter me. _____ On the me. _____
want you to weep af - ter me. _____ King ___
want you to weep af - ter me. _____
want you to weep af - ter me. _____
want you to weep af - ter me. _____ She's a -
want you to weep af - ter me. _____ Bright

Additional Lyrics

7. Bright angels are the sailors,
Don't you weep after me.
Bright angels are the sailors,
Don't you weep after me.
Bright angels are the sailors,
Don't you weep after me.
Oh, I don't want you to weep after me.

8. Sailing on the ocean,
Don't you weep after me.
Sailing on the ocean,
Don't you weep after me.
Sailing on the ocean,
Don't you weep after me.
Oh, I don't want you to weep after me.

9. When I do cross over,
Don't you weep after me.
When I do cross over,
Don't you weep after me.
When I do cross over,
Don't you weep after me.
Oh, I don't want you to weep after me.

DONEY GAL

19th Century American Cowboy Song

1. We ride the range from sun to sun, for a cow - boy's
2. A cow - boy's life is a drear - y thing, for it's rope and
3. We trav - el down that lone - some trail, where a man and his
4. Tired and hun - gry, far from home, I'm just a poor cow -
5. Drift - ing my Don - ey Gal 'round and 'round; steers are a -
6. Swim - ming riv - er's a - long the way, push - ing for the
7.,8. (See additional lyrics)

work is nev - er done. We're up and gone at the break of day,
brand and ride and sing. Yes, day or night, in __ rain or hail, we'll
horse sel - dom ev - er fail. We laugh at storms, _____ sleet and snow
boy and bound to roam. Star - less nights and __ light - ning glare,
North Star day by day. Storm clouds break, and at break - neck speed we

driv - ing the do - gies on their wea - ry way.
stay with the do - gies __ on the trail.
when we __ camp near San An - to - ni - o.
dan - ger and dark - ness __ ev - 'ry - where.   It's rain or shine,
sing - ing __ soft - ly a __ cow - boy song.
fol - low the steers in a wild stam - pede.

sleet or snow, me and my Don - ey Gal are bound to go. Yes, rain or

shine, sleet or snow, me and my Don - ey Gal are on the go.

Additional Lyrics

7. Over the prairies lean and brown
   And on through wastes where there ain't no town.
   Bucking dust storms, wind, and hail,
   Pushing the longhorns up the trail.

8. Trailing the herd through mountains green,
   We pen all the cattle at Abilene.
   Then round the campfire's flickering glow
   We sing the songs of long ago.

DONKEY RIDING

Sea Chantey from Lancashire

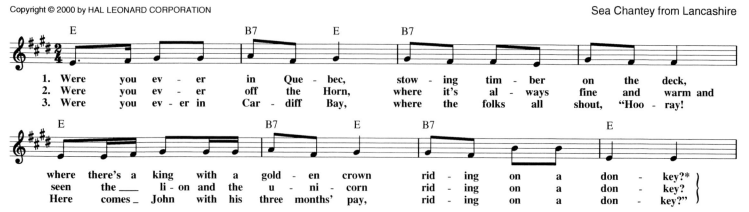

1. Were you ev - er in Que - bec, stow - ing tim - ber on the deck,
2. Were you ev - er off the Horn, where it's al - ways fine and warm and
3. Were you ev - er in Car - diff Bay, where the folks all shout, "Hoo - ray!

where there's a king with a gold - en crown rid - ing on a don - key?*
seen the __ li - on and the u - ni - corn rid - ing on a don - key?
Here comes __ John with his three months' pay, rid - ing on a don - key?"

* donkey: a dock engine used in handling cargo

Hey! ho! a - way we go, don - key rid - ing, don - key rid - ing;

Hey! ho! a - way we go, rid - ing on a don - key.

THE DOWIE DENS OF YARROW

17th Century Scottish

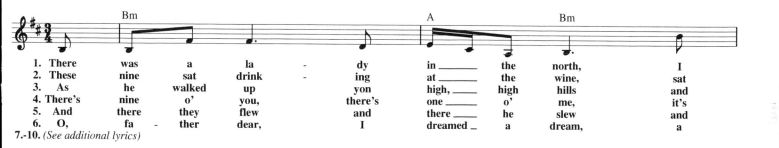

1. There was a la - dy in ___ the north, I
2. These nine sat drink - ing at ___ the wine, sat
3. As he walked up yon high, ___ high hills and
4. There's nine o' you, there's one ___ o' me, it's
5. And there they flew and there ___ he slew and
6. O, fa - ther dear, I dreamed ___ a dream, a

7.-10. *(See additional lyrics)*

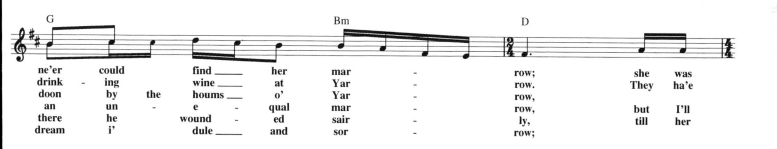

ne'er could find ___ her mar - row; she was
drink - ing the wine ___ at Yar - row. They ha'e
doon by the houms ___ o' Yar - row,
an un - e - qual mar - row, but I'll
there he wound - ed sair - ly, till her
dream i' dule ___ and sor - row;

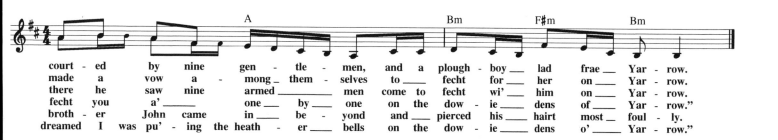

court - ed by nine gen - tle - men, and a plough - boy lad frae ___ Yar - row.
made a vow a - mong ___ them - selves to ___ fecht for ___ her on ___ Yar - row.
there he saw nine armed ___ men come to fecht wi' ___ him on ___ Yar - row.
fecht you a' ___ one ___ by ___ one on the dow - ie ___ dens of ___ Yar - row."
broth - er John came in ___ be - yond and ___ pierced his ___ hairt most ___ foul - ly.
dreamed I was pu' - ing the heath - er ___ bells on the dow - ie ___ dens o' ___ Yar - row."

Additional Lyrics

7. "O, dochter dear, I read your dream,
   I doubt it will bring sorrow,
   For your lover John lies pale and wan
   On the dowie dens o' Yarrow."

8. As she walked up yon high, high hill
   And doon by the houms o' Yarrow,
   There she saw her lover dear
   Lying pale and wan on yarrow.

9. Her hair it being three-quarters long,
   The colour it was yellow,
   She wrappit it roond his middle sae sma'
   And bore him doon to Yarrow.

10. "O, father dear, ye've seiven sons,
    Ye may wed them a tomorrow,
    But the fairest flooer amang them a'
    Was the lad I wooed on Yarrow."

DOWN BY THE RIVERSIDE

African-American Spiritual

DOWN BY THE SALLEY GARDENS

Irish
Words by William Butler Yeats, 1889

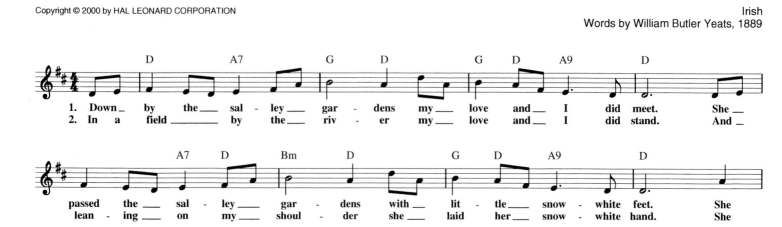

bid me ___ take love eas - y, as the leaves grow ___ on ___ the ___ tree. But ___
bid me ___ take life eas - y, as the grass grows ___ on ___ the ___ weirs. But ___

I, be - ing young and ___ fool - ish, with ___ her did ___ not a - gree.
I was ___ young and ___ fool - ish, and ___ now am ___ full of tears.

DOWN IN MY HEART

Traditional Christian Children's Song

I've got the joy, joy, joy, joy down in my heart, down in my heart,

down in my heart! I've got the joy, joy, joy, joy down in my heart, down in my heart to

stay! I've got the peace that pass - eth un - der-stand-ing down in my heart, down in my heart,

down in my heart! I've got the peace that pass - eth un - der - stand - ing down in my heart,

down in my heart to stay! I've got the won - der - ful love of my bless - ed re - deem - er way

down in my heart, down in my heart, down in my heart! I've got the

won-der-ful love of my bless-ed re-deem-er way down in my heart, down in my heart to stay! ___

DOWN BY THE STATION

Traditional Round

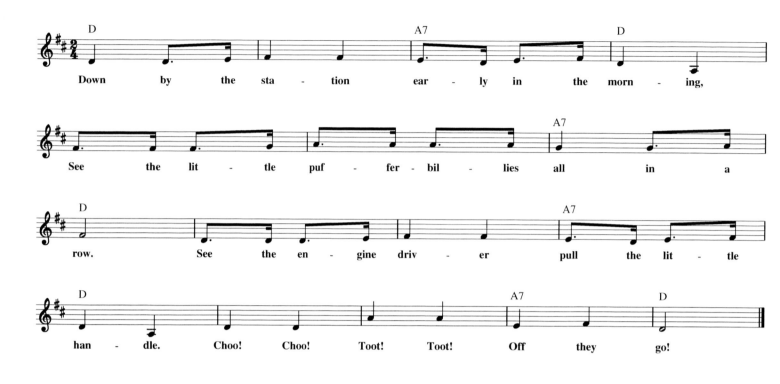

Down by the sta - tion ear - ly in the morn - ing,

See the lit - tle puf - fer - bil - lies all in a

row. See the en - gine driv - er pull the lit - tle

han - dle. Choo! Choo! Toot! Toot! Off they go!

DOWN IN THAT VALLEY

Folksong from Kentucky

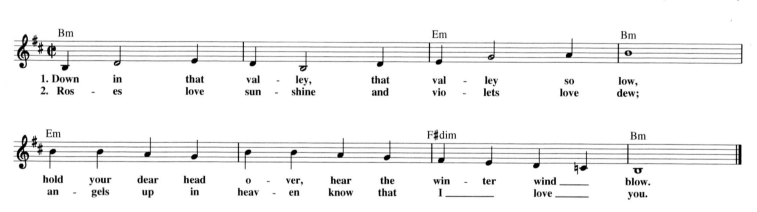

1. Down in that val - ley, that val - ley so low,
2. Ros - es love sun - shine and vio - lets love dew;

hold your dear head o - ver, hear the win - ter wind _____ blow.
an - gels up in heav - en know that I _____ love _____ you.

DOWN IN THE VALLEY

19th Century American
Words by an anonymous inmate at
Raleigh State Prison
(later variously altered)

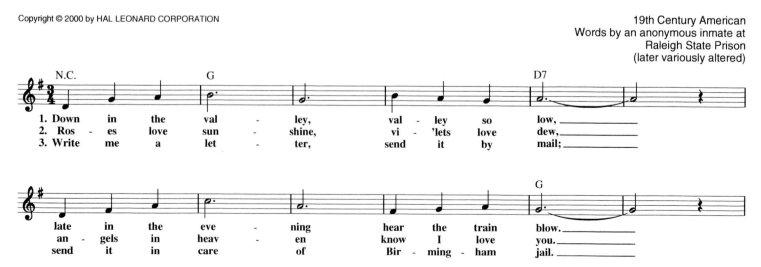

1. Down in the val - ley, val - ley so low, _____
2. Ros - es love sun - shine, vi - 'lets love dew, _____
3. Write me a let - ter, send it by mail; _____

late in the eve - ning hear the train blow. _____
an - gels in heav - en know I love you. _____
send it in care of Bir - ming - ham jail. _____

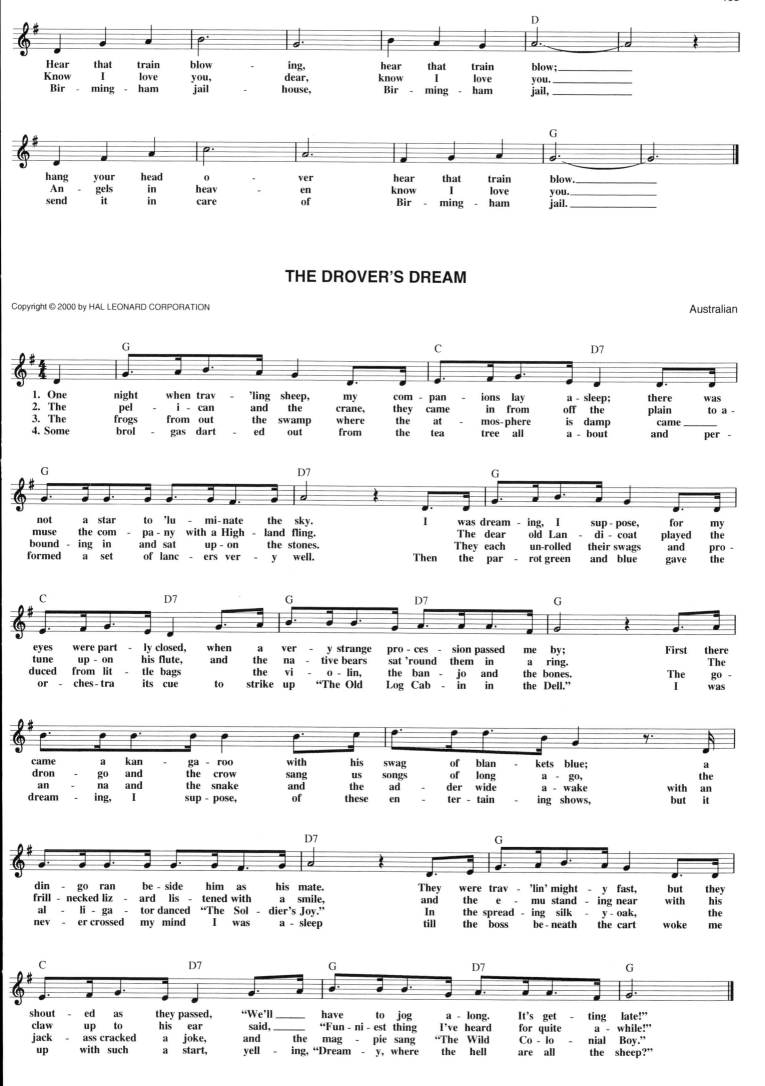

Hear that train blow - ing, hear that train blow;_____
Know I love you, dear, know I love you._____
Bir - ming - ham jail - house, Bir - ming - ham jail,_____

hang your head o - ver hear that train blow._____
An - gels in heav - en know I love you._____
send it in care of Bir - ming - ham jail._____

THE DROVER'S DREAM

Australian

1. One night when trav - 'ling sheep, my com - pan - ions lay a - sleep; there was
2. The pel - i - can and the crane, they came in from off the plain to a -
3. The frogs from out the swamp where the at - mos-phere is damp came_____
4. Some brol - gas dart - ed out from the tea tree all a - bout and per -

not a star to 'lu - mi-nate the sky. I was dream - ing, I sup - pose, for my
muse the com - pa - ny with a High - land fling. The dear old Lan - di - coat played the
bound - ing in and sat up - on the stones. They each un-rolled their swags and pro -
formed a set of lanc - ers ver - y well. Then the par - rot green and blue gave the

eyes were part - ly closed, when a ver - y strange pro - ces - sion passed me by; First there
tune up - on his flute, and the na - tive bears sat 'round them in a ring. The
duced from lit - tle bags the vi - o - lin, the ban - jo and the bones. The go -
or - ches-tra its cue to strike up "The Old Log Cab - in in the Dell." I was

came a kan - ga - roo with his swag of blan - kets blue; a
dron - go and the crow sang us songs of long a - go, the
an - na and the snake and the ad - der wide a - wake with an
dream - ing, I sup - pose, of these en - ter - tain - ing shows, but it

din - go ran be - side him as his mate. They were trav - 'lin' might - y fast, but they
frill - necked liz - ard lis - tened with a smile, and the e - mu stand - ing near with his
al - li - ga - tor danced "The Sol - dier's Joy." In the spread - ing silk - y - oak, the
nev - er crossed my mind I was a - sleep till the boss be - neath the cart woke me

shout - ed as they passed, "We'll_____ have to jog a - long. It's get - ting late!"
claw up to his ear said,_____ "Fun - ni - est thing I've heard for quite a - while!"
jack - ass cracked a joke, and the mag - pie sang "The Wild Co - lo - nial Boy."
up with such a start, yell - ing, "Dream - y, where the hell are all the sheep?"

DOWN IN THE WILLOW GARDEN

American

1. Down in the wil - low gar - den, where me and my true love did meet, 'twas there we sat a - court - ing, my love dropped off to sleep. I had a bot - tle of bur - gun - dy wine which my true love did not know, and there I poi - soned that dear lit - tle girl, down un - der the bank be - low.

2. I stabbed her with my dag - ger, which was a blood - y knife. I threw her in the riv - er, which was a dread - ful sight. My fa - ther of - ten told me that mon - ey would set me free. If I would mur - der that dear lit - tle girl, whose name was Rose Con - nel - ly.

3. And now he sits in his cot - tage door, a - wip - ing his weep - ing eye, and now he waits for his own dear son up - on the scaf - fold high. My race is run be - neath the sun, cruel Hell's now wait - ing for me, for I have mur - dered my own true love, whose name was Rose Con - nel - ly.

DOWN THE RIVER

Party song from Ohio

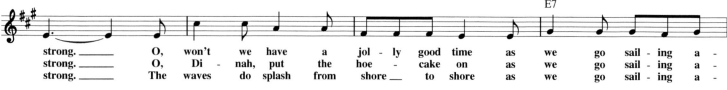

1. The riv - er is up and the chan - nel is deep, the wind is stead - y and strong. O, won't we have a jol - ly good time as we go sail - ing a - long.

2. The riv - er is up and the chan - nel is deep, the wind is stead - y and strong. O, Di - nah, put the hoe - cake on as we go sail - ing a - long.

3. The riv - er is up and the chan - nel is deep, the wind is stead - y and strong. The waves do splash from shore to shore as we go sail - ing a - long.

Down the riv - er, O, down the riv - er, O, down the riv - er we go.

Down the riv - er, O, down the riv - er, O, down the O - hi - o.

THE DREARY BLACK HILLS

American

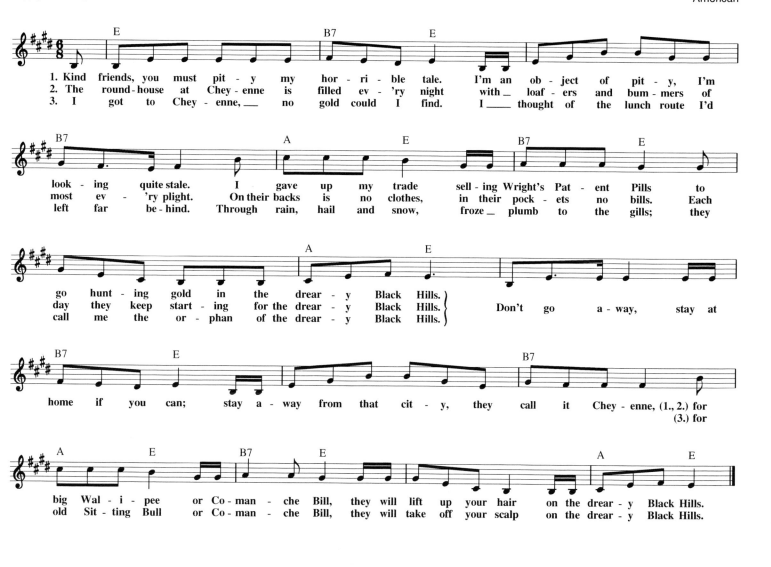

1. Kind friends, you must pit - y my hor - ri - ble tale. I'm an ob - ject of pit - y, I'm
2. The round - house at Chey - enne is filled ev - 'ry night with _ loaf - ers and bum - mers of
3. I got to Chey - enne, ___ no gold could I find. I ___ thought of the lunch route I'd

look - ing quite stale. I gave up my trade sell - ing Wright's Pat - ent Pills to
most ev - 'ry plight. On their backs is no clothes, in their pock - ets no bills. Each
left far be - hind. Through rain, hail and snow, froze _ plumb to the gills; they

go hunt - ing gold in the drear - y Black Hills.)
day they keep start - ing for the drear - y Black Hills.) Don't go a - way, stay at
call me the or - phan of the drear - y Black Hills.)

home if you can; stay a - way from that cit - y, they call it Chey - enne, (1., 2.) for
(3.) for

big Wal - i - pee or Co - man - che Bill, they will lift up your hair on the drear - y Black Hills.
old Sit - ting Bull or Co - man - che Bill, they will take off your scalp on the drear - y Black Hills.

DRINK TO ME ONLY WITH THINE EYES

Words by Ben Jonson
Music based on an English Folksong

1. Drink to me on - ly with ___ thine eyes, ___ and I ___ will pledge with mine; ___
2. I sent thee late a ros - y wreath, _ Not so ___ much hon - 'ring thee, ___

or leave a kiss with - in ___ the cup ___ and I'll ___ not ask for wine. ___ The
As giv - ing it a hope ___ that there ___ It could ___ not with - ered be. ___ But

thirst ___ that from the soul ___ doth rise, Doth ask a drink ___ di - vine, ___
thou ___ there - on didst on - ly breathe And sent it back ___ to me, ___

But might I of Jove's nec - tar sip, ___ I would ___ not ask for wine. ___
Since when it grows and smells, _ I swear, _ Not of ___ it - self, but thee. ___

DRILL, YE TARRIERS, DRILL

American

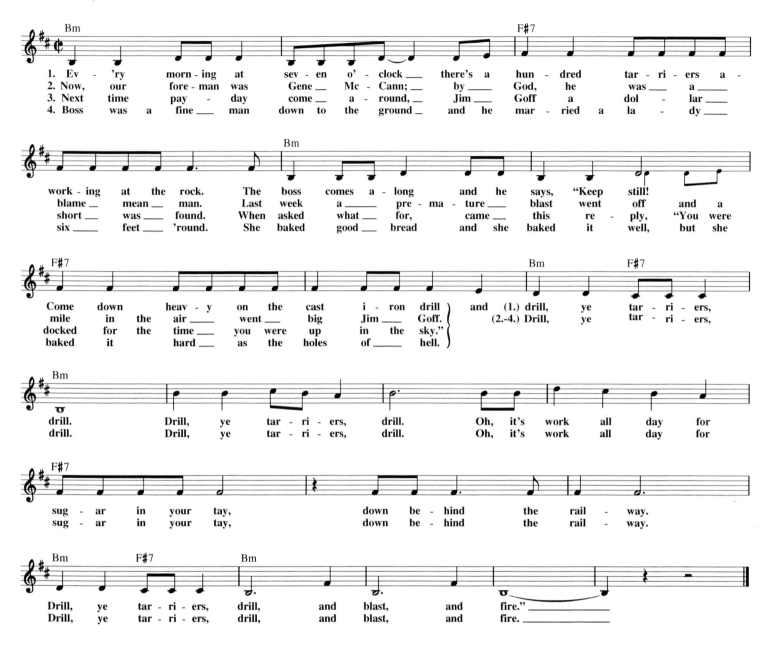

THE DRUMMER AND THE COOK

English

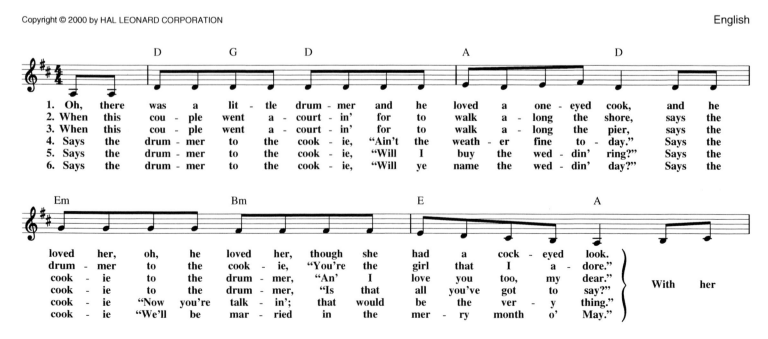

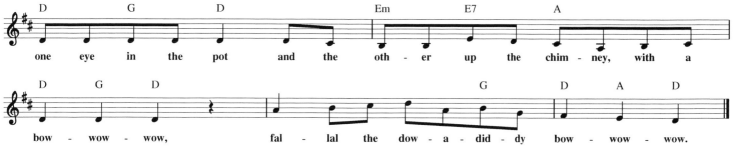

one eye in the pot and the oth - er up the chim - ney, with a

bow - wow - wow, fal - lal the dow - a - did - dy bow - wow - wow.

DRY BONES

Copyright © 2000 by HAL LEONARD CORPORATION

African-American Spiritual

E - ze - kiel cried, "Them dry bones!" { E - ze - kiel cried, "Them dry bones!" { Oh,

hear the word of the Lord! The foot bone con-nect - ed to the leg bone, the

leg bone con-nect - ed to the knee bone, The knee bone con-nect - ed to the thigh bone, The

thigh bone con-nect - ed to the back bone, The back bone con-nect - ed to the neck bone, The

neck bone con-nect - ed to the head bone, Oh, hear the word of the Lord! Them

bones, them bones gon - na walk a - roun', { them bones, them bones gon - na walk a - roun', Them { Oh,

hear the word of the Lord! The head bone con-nect - ed to the neck bone, the

neck bone con-nect - ed to the back bone, The back bone con-nect - ed to the thigh bone, The

thigh bone con-nect - ed to the knee bone, The knee bone con-nect - ed to the leg bone, The

leg bone con-nect - ed to the foot bone, Oh, hear the word of the Lord! _____

THE DRUNKEN SAILOR

19th Century American Sea Chantey

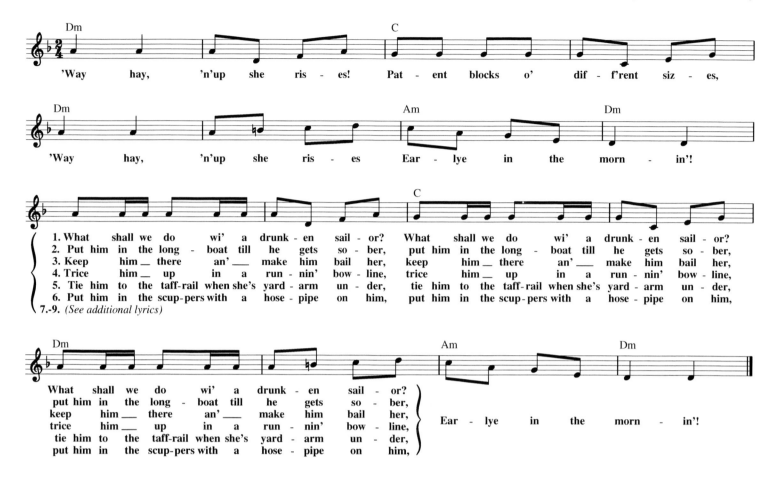

'Way hay, 'n'up she ris - es! Pat - ent blocks o' dif - f'rent siz - es,

'Way hay, 'n'up she ris - es Ear - lye in the morn - in'!

1. What shall we do wi' a drunk - en sail - or? What shall we do wi' a drunk - en sail - or?
2. Put him in the long - boat till he gets so - ber, put him in the long - boat till he gets so - ber,
3. Keep him — there an' — make him bail her, keep him — there an' — make him bail her,
4. Trice him — up in a run - nin' bow - line, trice him — up in a run - nin' bow - line,
5. Tie him to the taff-rail when she's yard - arm un - der, tie him to the taff-rail when she's yard - arm un - der,
6. Put him in the scup-pers with a hose - pipe on him, put him in the scup-pers with a hose - pipe on him,
7.-9. *(See additional lyrics)*

What shall we do wi' a drunk - en sail - or?
put him in the long - boat till he gets so - ber,
keep him — there an' — make him bail her,
trice him — up in a run - nin' bow - line,
tie him to the taff-rail when she's yard - arm un - der,
put him in the scup-pers with a hose - pipe on him,

Ear - lye in the morn - in'!

Additional Lyrics

7. Take him an' shake 'im, an' try an' wake 'im,
   Earlye in the mornin'!

8. Give him a dose o' salt an' water,
   Earlye in the mornin'!

9. Give him a taste o' the bosun's rope-end,
   Earlye in the mornin'!

DRY WEATHER HOUSES

Caribbean

1. One Mon - day morn - ing, a land - lord went to a ten - ant to get some
2. "Look at the room you rent me to live, the whole of the roof is just like a
3. "Some of the rooms, the way them so small, you can't e - ven turn 'round in them at

rent, but the ten - ant say, "Mas - sa, — me no fool, me no pay no
sieve. If it rain at night and I — sleep too sound, so help me,
all. When you want to turn you got - ta — go out - side, turn your

rent for no — swim - min' pool.
King, I sure — would-a drowned.
back and go — back in - side.

I tell you, dry weath - er hous - es are not

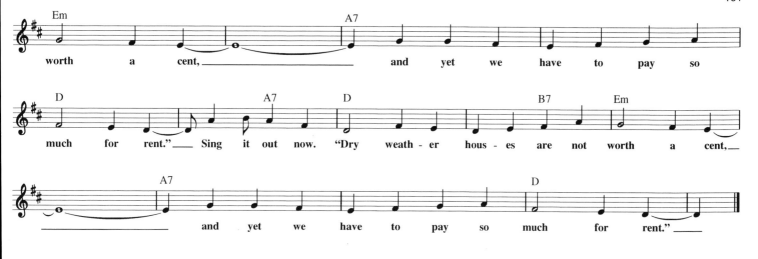

worth a cent,_____ and yet we have to pay so

much for rent."____ Sing it out now. "Dry weath-er hous-es are not worth a cent,__

_____ and yet we have to pay so much for rent." ____

DU, DU LIEGST MIR IM HERZEN
(You, You Weigh on My Heart)

German

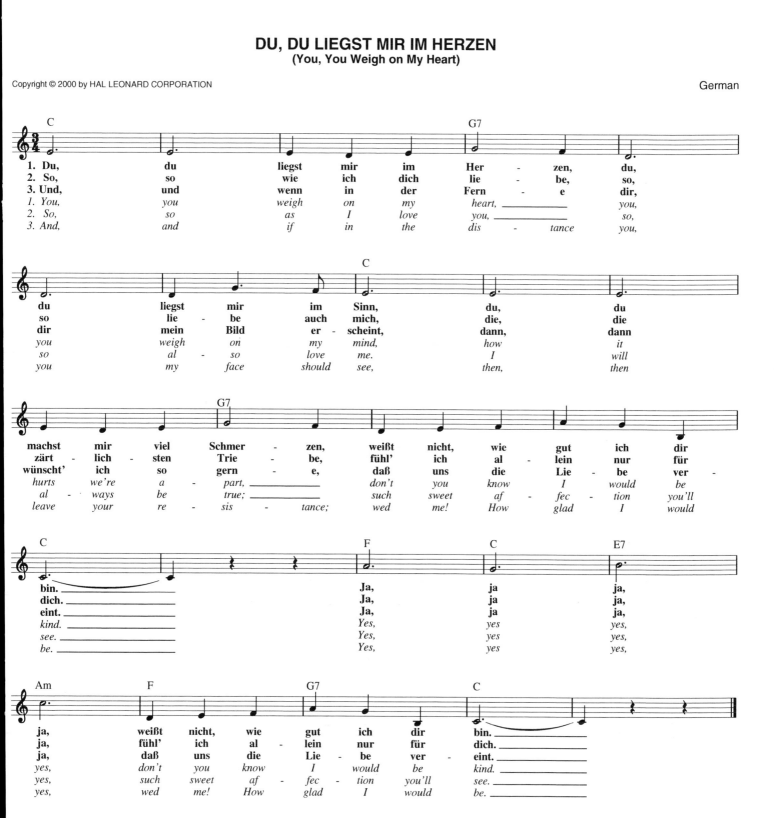

1. Du, du liegst mir im Her - zen, du,
2. So, so wie ich dich lie - be, so,
3. Und, und wenn in der Fern - e dir,
1. You, you weigh on my heart,_____ you,
2. So, so as I love you,_____ so,
3. And, and if in the dis - tance you,

du liegst mir im Sinn, du, du
so lie - be auch mich, die, die
dir mein Bild er - scheint, dann, dann
you weigh on my mind, how it
so al - so love me. I will
you my face should see, then, then

machst mir viel Schmer - zen, weißt nicht, wie gut ich dir
zärt - lich - sten Trie - be, fühl' ich al - lein nur für
wünsch' ich so gern gern - e, daß uns die Lie - be ver -
hurts we're a - part,_____ don't you know I would be
al - ways be true;_____ such sweet af - fec - tion you'll
leave your re - sis - tance; wed me! How glad I would

bin._____ Ja, ja ja,
dich._____ Ja, ja ja,
eint._____ Ja, ja ja,
kind._____ Yes, yes yes,
see._____ Yes, yes yes,
be._____ Yes, yes yes,

ja, weißt nicht, wie gut ich dir bin._____
ja, fühl' ich al - lein nur für dich._____
ja, daß uns die Lie - be ver - eint._____
yes, don't you know I would be kind._____
yes, such sweet af - fec - tion you'll see._____
yes, wed me! How glad I would be._____

THE DRUNKARD'S DOOM

American

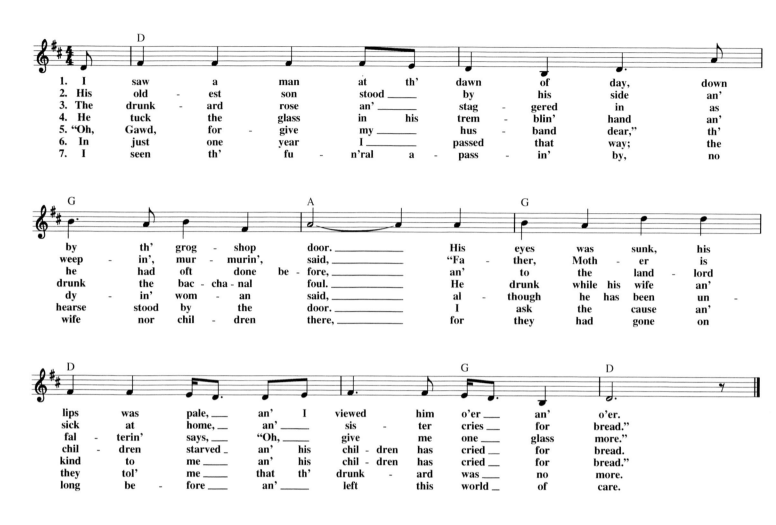

1. I saw a man at th' dawn of day, down
2. His old-est son stood _____ by his side an'
3. The drunk-ard rose an' _____ stag-gered in as
4. He tuck the glass in his trem-blin' hand an'
5. "Oh, Gawd, for-give my _____ hus-band dear," th'
6. In just one year I _____ passed that way; the
7. I seen th' fu-n'ral a pass-in' by, no

by th' grog-shop door. _____ His eyes was sunk, his
weep-in', mur-murin', said, _____ "Fa-ther, Moth-er is
he had oft done be-fore, _____ an' to the land-lord
drunk the bac-cha-nal foul. _____ He drunk while his wife an'
dy-in' wom-an said, _____ al-though he has been un-
hearse stood by the door. _____ I ask the cause an'
wife nor chil-dren there, _____ for they had gone on

lips was pale, _____ an' I viewed him o'er _____ an' o'er.
sick at home, _ an' _____ sis-ter cries _____ for bread."
fal-terin' says, _ "Oh, _____ give me one _____ glass more."
chil-dren starved _ an' his chil-dren has cried _ for bread.
kind to me _____ an' his chil-dren has cried _ for bread."
they tol' me _____ that th' drunk-ard was _ no more.
long be-fore _____ an' _____ left this world _ of care.

DUBLIN CITY

English

1. As I was a-walk-in' through Dub-lin Cit-y, a-
2. First she _____ washed them and then she dried them;
3. She had twen-ty, _____ eight--een, six-teen, four-teen,
4. 'Round, _____ 'round _ the wheel of for-tune;

bout the hour of twelve at night, 'twas there I saw a
'round her shoul-ders she pegged a towel, and in all me life I
twelve, ten, eight, six, four, two, none. She had nine-teen, sev-en-teen,
where it stays wea-ries me. Fair maids they are

fair, pret-ty maid _____ wash-in' her feet by can-dle-light.
ne'er did _____ see such a fine _____ young girl up-on my soul.
fif-teen, _____ thir-teen, e-lev-en, nine, sev-en, five, three and one.
so de-ceiv-in', sad _____ ex-pe-ri-ence teach-es me.

DUMBARTON'S DRUMS

Scottish

1. Dum - bar - ton's drums, _____ they sound so bon - nie _____ when they re -
2. A - cross the fields _____ of bound - ing heath - er, _____ Dum - bar - ton
3. 'Tis he a - lone _____ that can de - light me, _____ his grace - ful
4. My love he is _____ a hand - some lad - die, _____ and though he

mind _____ me of my John - nie; _____ what fond de - light _____ can steal up -
tolls _____ the hour of pleas - ure, _____ A song of love _____ that has no
eye _____ it doth in - vite me, _____ and when his ten - der arms en -
is _____ Dum - bar - ton's cad - die, _____ some - day I'll be _____ a cap - tain's

on me _____ when John - nie kneels _____ and kiss - es me. _____
meas - ure _____ when John - nie kneels _____ and sings to me. _____
fold me, _____ the black - est night _____ doth turn and see. _____
la - dy _____ when John - nie tends _____ his vow to me. _____

DUMPLINS

Caribbean

*(1.) Leader: Des - mond, you see no - bod - y pass here? Desmond: No, me friend.
(last time) Leader: Chil - lun, you see no - bod - y pass here? Children: No, me friend.

Leader: Li - sa, you see no - bod - y pass here? Lisa: No, me friend. Leader: Well,
Leader: Chil - lun, you see no - bod - y pass here? Children: No, me friend. Leader: Well,

{ one / two / three / etc. } of me dum - plins gone, don't tell __ me so, { one / two / three / etc. } of me dum - plins gone. Desmond & Lisa: Don't tell __ me so.
all of me dum - plins gone, don't tell __ me so, all of me dum - plins gone. Children: Don't tell __ me so.

One of your dum - plins gone. Leader: Yes, { one! / two! / three! / etc. } { One / Two / Three / etc. } of me dum - plins gone.
All of your dum - plins gone. Leader: Yes, all! All of me dum - plins gone.

*Substitute the names of children in your group for Desmond and Lisa.
Repeat the song as needed until everyone has had a chance to sing.

DUNCAN AND BRADY

19th Century American

1. Down in St. Lou-is at Twelfth __ and Carr, Big Bill
2. Dun-can and his broth-er was play - ing pool when Bra - dy came
3. Bra-dy went to hell look - in' might - y cur - i - ous. The dev - il says,
4. When all the girls heard Bra-dy was dead they went up

Bra-dy was a-tend-in' bar. In came old Dun-can a
in _____ act - ing a fool. He shot him once;
"Where you from?" "East St. Lou-is." "Well, pull off your coat and
home and put on red, and came down town

star on his chest. Dun-can says, "Bra-dy you're un-der ar - rest."
he shot him twice, say-ing, "I don't make my liv-ing by shoot-ing dice."
step this way, for I've been ex-pect-ing you ev-'ry day!"
sing-in' this song: "Bra-dy's strut-tin' in hell with his Stet-son on."

(1.-4.) Bra - dy, _____ why did - n't you run? Bra - dy, _____ you
(5.) Bra - dy, _____ where you at? Bra - dy, _____

should a - run! Bra - dy, _____ why did - n't you
where you at? Bra - dy, _____ where you

run, When you seen Black Dun-can with his gat - ling gun.
at? Strut-tin' in hell with his gat Stet - son hat.

DUNDERBECK

19th Century American

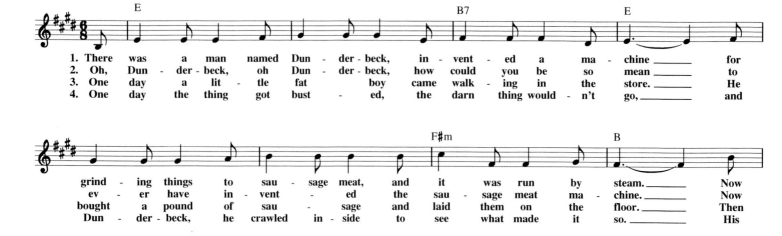

1. There was a man named Dun - der - beck, in - vent - ed a ma - chine _____ for
2. Oh, Dun - der - beck, oh Dun - der - beck, how could you be so mean _____ to
3. One day a lit - tle fat boy came walk - ing in the store. _____ He
4. One day the thing got bust - ed, the darn thing would - n't go, _____ and

grind - ing things to sau - sage meat, and it was run by steam. _____ Now
ev - er have in - vent - ed the sau - sage meat ma - chine. _____ Now
bought a pound of sau - sage and laid them on the floor. _____ Then
Dun - der - beck, he crawled in - side to see what made it so. _____ His

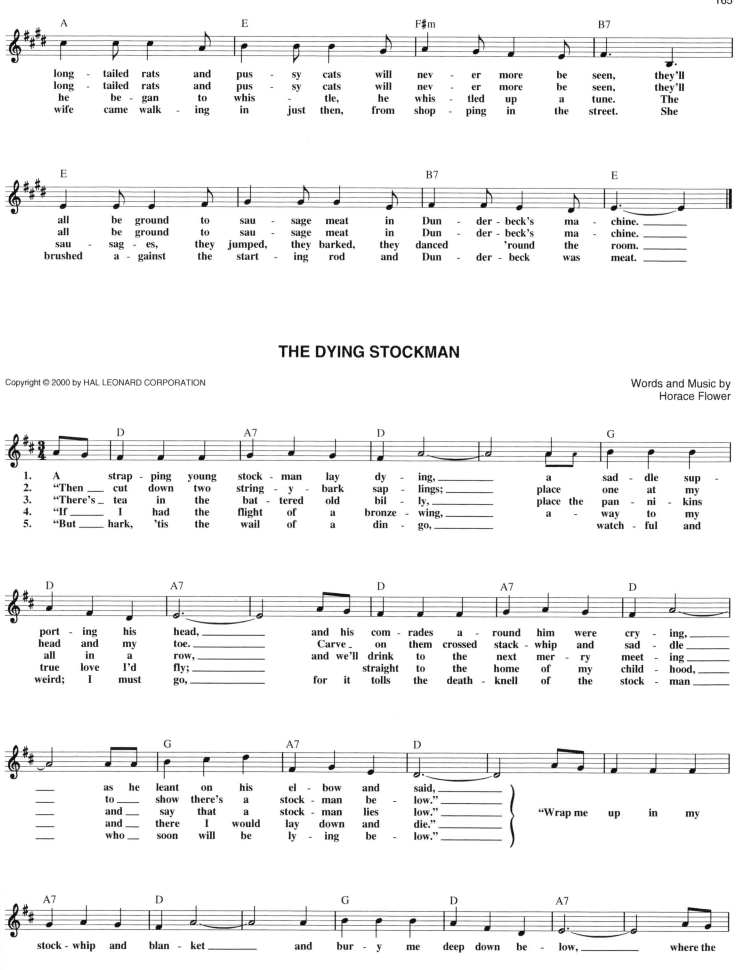

long - tailed rats and pus - sy cats will nev - er more be seen, they'll
long - tailed rats and pus - sy cats will nev - er more be seen, they'll
he be - gan to whis - tle, he whis - tled up a tune. The
wife came walk - ing in just then, from shop - ping in the street. She

all be ground to sau - sage meat in Dun - der - beck's ma - chine. ____
all be ground to sau - sage meat in Dun - der - beck's ma - chine. ____
sau - sag - es, they jumped, they barked, they danced 'round the room. ____
brushed a - gainst the start - ing rod and Dun - der - beck was meat. ____

THE DYING STOCKMAN

Words and Music by
Horace Flower

1. A strap - ping young stock - man lay dy - ing, ____ a sad - dle sup -
2. "Then __ cut down two string - y - bark sap - lings; ____ place one at my
3. "There's _ tea in the bat - tered old bil - ly, ____ place the pan - ni - kins
4. "If ____ I had the flight of a bronze - wing, ____ a - way to my
5. "But ____ hark, 'tis the wail of a din - go, ____ watch - ful and

port - ing his head, ____ and his com - rades a - round him were cry - ing, ____
head and my toe. ____ Carve _ on them crossed stack - whip and sad - dle ____
all in a row, ____ and we'll drink to the next mer - ry meet - ing ____
true love I'd fly; ____ straight to the home of my child - hood, ____
weird; I must go, ____ for it tolls the death - knell of the stock - man ____

____ as he leant on his el - bow and said, ____
____ to __ show there's a stock - man be - low." ____
____ and __ say that a stock - man lies low." ____ "Wrap me up in my
____ and __ there I would lay down and die." ____
____ who __ soon will be ly - ing be - low." ____

stock - whip and blan - ket ____ and bur - y me deep down be - low, ____ where the

din - goes and crows will not find me, ____ in the shade where the coo - li - bahs grow."

THE DYING RANGER

American

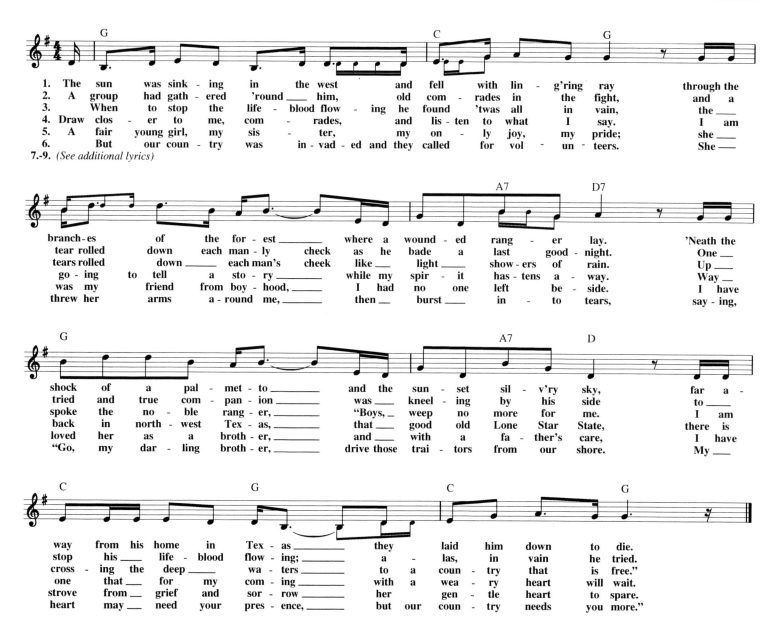

1. The sun was sink - ing in the west and fell with lin - g'ring ray through the
2. A group had gath - ered 'round ___ him, old com - rades in the fight, and a
3. When to stop the life - blood flow - ing he found 'twas all in vain, the
4. Draw clos - er to me, com - rades, and lis - ten to what I say. I am
5. A fair young girl, my sis - ter, my on - ly joy, my pride; she ___
6. But our coun - try was in - vad - ed and they called for vol - un - teers. She ___

7.-9. *(See additional lyrics)*

branch - es of the for - est ___ where a wound - ed rang - er lay. 'Neath the
tear rolled down each man - ly check as he bade a last good - night. One ___
tears rolled down ___ each man's cheek like ___ light ___ show - ers of rain. Up ___
go - ing to tell a sto - ry ___ while my spir - it has - tens a - way. Way ___
was my friend from boy - hood, ___ I had no one left be - side. I have
threw her arms a - round me, ___ then ___ burst ___ in - to tears, say - ing,

shock of a pal - met - to ___ and the sun - set sil - v'ry sky, far a -
tried and true com - pan - ion ___ was ___ kneel - ing by his side to ___
spoke the no - ble rang - er, ___ "Boys, _ weep no more for me. I am
back in north - west Tex - as, ___ that ___ good old Lone Star State, there is
loved her as a broth - er, ___ and ___ with a fa - ther's care, I have
"Go, my dar - ling broth - er, ___ drive those trai - tors from our shore. My ___

way from his home in Tex - as ___ they laid him down to die.
stop his ___ life - blood flow - ing; a - las, in vain he tried.
cross - ing the deep ___ wa - ters ___ to a coun - try that is free."
one that ___ for my com - ing ___ with a wea - ry heart will wait.
strove from ___ grief and sor - row ___ her gen - tle heart to spare.
heart may ___ need your pres - ence, ___ but our coun - try needs you more."

Additional Lyrics

7. It is true I love my country,
For her I gave my all.
If it hadn't been for my sister,
I would be content to fall.
I am dying, comrades, dying,
She will never see me more,
But in vain she'll wait my coming
By our little cabin door.

8. Comrades, gather closer
And hear my dying prayer.
Who'll be to her a brother,
Shield her with a brother's care?
Up spake the noble rangers,
They answered one and all,
"We will be to her as brothers
Till the last one does fall."

9. One glad smile of pleasure
O'er the ranger's face was spread;
One dark, convulsive shadow,
And the ranger was dead.
Far from his darling sister
We laid him down to rest,
With his saddle for a pillow
And his gun across his breast.

E-RI-E CANAL

19th Century American

1. We were for - ty miles from Al - ba - ny, For - get it I nev - er
2. We were load - ed down with bar - ley, We were chock __ full up on
3. The __ cap - tain he came up on deck With a spy - glass in his
4. Two days out of Syr - a - cuse Our ves - sel struck a
5. Our __ cook, she was a grand old gal, She wore __ a rag - ged
6. The __ cap - tain, he got mar - ried; And the cook, __ she went to

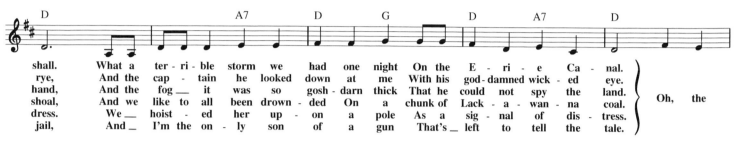

shall. What a ter - ri - ble storm we had one night On the E - ri - e Ca - nal.
rye, And the cap - tain he looked down at me With his god - damned wick - ed eye.
hand, And the fog __ it was so gosh - darn thick That he could not spy the land.
shoal, And we like to all been drown - ded On a chunk of Lack - a - wan - na coal.
dress. We __ hoist - ed her up - on a pole As a sig - nal of dis - tress.
jail, And __ I'm the on - ly son of a gun That's __ left to tell the tale.

Oh, the

E - ri - e was a - ris - in', and the gin was a - get - tin' low. And I scarce - ly think we'll

get a drink till we get to Buf - fa - lo - o - o, till we get to Buf - fa - lo.

EENSY, WEENSY SPIDER

North Carolina Children's Song

Een - sy, ween - sy spi - der went up the wa - ter spout.

Down came the rain and washed the spi - der out.

Out came the sun and dried up all the rain, And the

een - sy, ween - sy spi - der went up the spout a - gain.

EARLY ONE MORNING

English

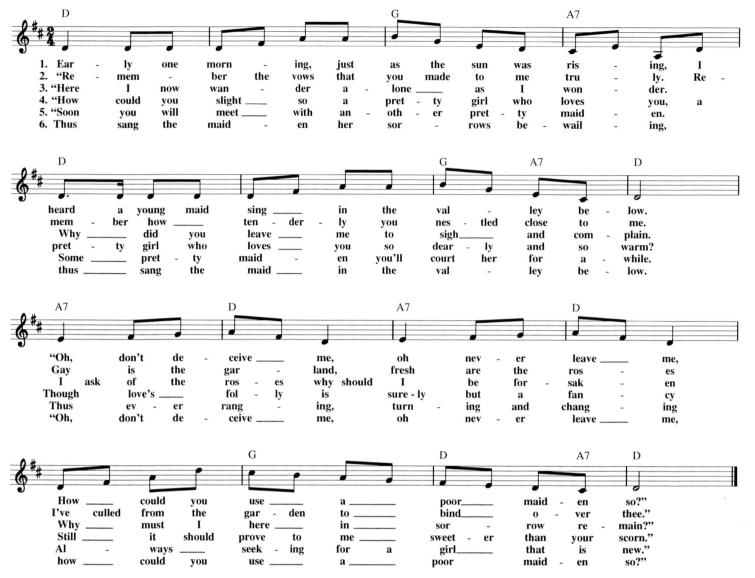

1. Ear - ly one morn - ing, just as the sun was ris - ing, I
2. "Re - mem - ber the vows that you made to me tru - ly. Re -
3. "Here I now wan - der a - lone as I won - der.
4. "How could you slight so a pret - ty girl who loves you, a
5. "Soon you will meet with an - oth - er pret - ty maid - en.
6. Thus sang the maid - en her sor - rows be - wail - ing,

heard a young maid sing in the val - ley be - low.
mem - ber how ten - der - ly you nes - tled close to me.
Why did you leave me to sigh and com - plain.
pret - ty girl who loves you so dear - ly and so warm?
Some pret - ty maid - en you'll court her for a - while.
thus sang the maid in the val - ley be - low.

"Oh, don't de - ceive me, oh nev - er leave me,
Gay is the gar - land, fresh are the ros - es
I ask of the ros - es why should I be for - sak - en
Though love's fol - ly is sure - ly but a fan - cy
Thus ev - er rang - ing, turn - ing and chang - ing
"Oh, don't de - ceive me, oh nev - er leave me,

How could you use a poor maid - en so?"
I've culled from the gar - den to bind o - ver thee."
Why must I here in sor - row re - main?"
Still it should prove to me sweet - er than your scorn."
Al - ways seek - ing for a girl that is new."
how could you use a poor maid - en so?"

THE EDDYSTONE LIGHT

English Sea Chantey

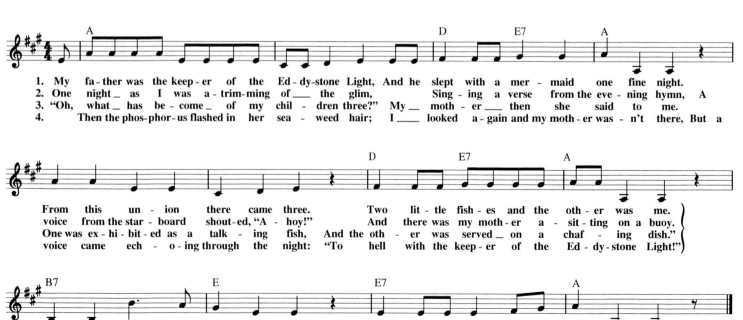

1. My fa - ther was the keep - er of the Ed - dy-stone Light, And he slept with a mer - maid one fine night.
2. One night as I was a - trim - ming of the glim, Sing - ing a verse from the eve - ning hymn, A
3. "Oh, what has be - come of my chil - dren three?" My moth - er then she said to me.
4. Then the phos-phor-us flashed in her sea - weed hair; I looked a - gain and my moth - er was - n't there, But a

From this un - ion there came three. Two lit - tle fish - es and the oth - er was me.
voice from the star - board shout-ed, "A - hoy!" And there was my moth - er a - sit - ting on a buoy.
One was ex - hi - bit - ed as a talk - ing fish, And the oth - er was served on a chaf - ing dish."
voice came ech - o - ing through the night: "To hell with the keep - er of the Ed - dy-stone Light!"

Yo ho ho, the wind blows free. Oh, for the life on the roll - ing sea!

EAST VIRGINIA

American

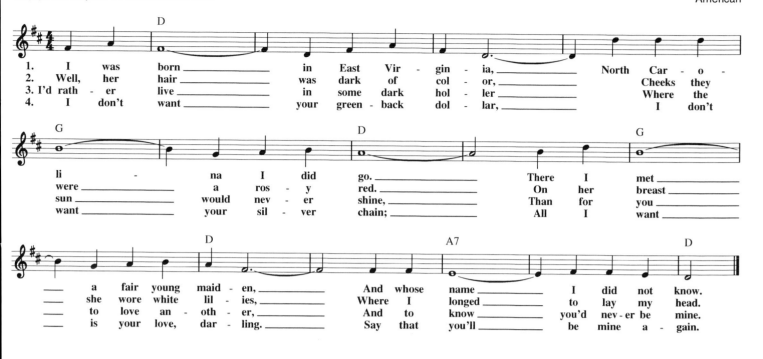

EDWARD

English Ballad

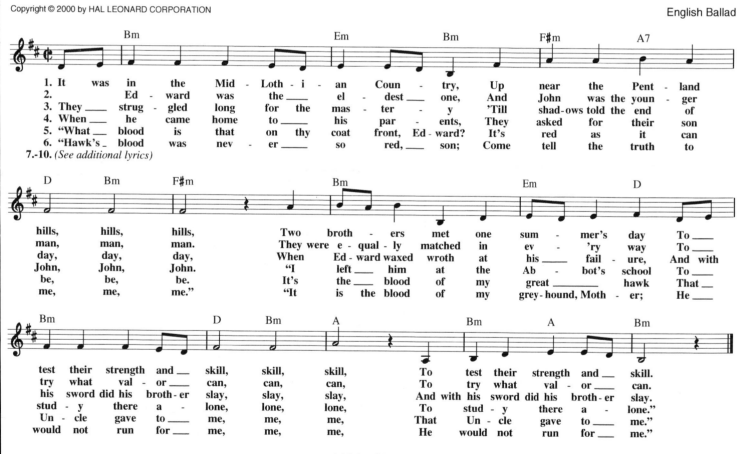

Additional Lyrics

7. "That's not the blood of a hound, son,
That is very plain to see.
Is it not the blood of thy brother John?
Come and tell the truth to me, me, me,
Come and tell the truth to me."

8. "It is the blood of brother John;
Oh mother, woe is me!
I slew him in a fit of rage,
Now the truth I have told to thee, thee, thee,
Now the truth I have told to thee."

9. "What penance will you do, son
To wipe away the stain?"
"I'll sail away across the seas
And never come home again, gain, gain,
And never come home again."

10. "What will you leave your mother, Edward,
Who has been so fond of thee?"
"I'll leave with her the memory of
Wrong counsel given me, me, me,
Wrong counsel given me."

THE EASTER REBELLION

Irish

1. As down the ___ glen one ___ Eas - ter morn to a cit - y ___
2. Right proud - ly ___ high o - ver Dub - lin town they ___ hung ___ out the
3. The brav - est ___ fell, and the sul - len bell rang ___ mourn - ful -
4. 'Twas Eng - land ___ bade our ___ "Wild Geese" go that ___ small ___ na - tions
5. Back to the ___ glen I ___ rode a - gain, and my heart ___ with ___

fair rode I, ___ There armed ___ lines of ___
flag of war. ___ 'Twas bet - ter to die 'neath an
ly and clear ___ For those who ___ died that ___
might be free, ___ But their lone - ly ___ graves are by
grief was sore, ___ For I part - ed ___ then with ___

march - ing men in ___ squad - rons ___ passed me by. ___ No
I - rish sky than at Suv - la or ___ Sud el Bar. ___ And
Eas - ter - tide in the spring - ing ___ of the year. ___ And the
Suv - la's waves and the fringe ___ of the grey North Sea. ___ Oh,
val - iant men I ___ nev - er would see no more. ___ But

pipes did hum, no ___ bat - tle ___ drum did ___ sound its
from the plains of ___ Roy - al ___ Meath, strong ___ men came
world did gaze with ___ deep a - maze on those fear - less
had they died by ___ Pear - se's ___ side or fought with De
to and fro in my dreams I ___ go, and I kneel and

dread ta - too, ___ But the an - gel - us bell o'er the
hur - rying ___ through, ___ While Brit - an - nia's ___ sons, with ___
men, but ___ few, ___ Who ___ bore the ___ fight that ___
Vale - ra ___ too, ___ Their ___ place we'd ___ keep, where the
pray for ___ you, ___ For ___ slav - er - y fled, oh, ___

Lif - fey's swell rang ___ out ___ in the fog - gy dew. ___
their great guns, sailed ___ in ___ by the fog - gy dew. ___
free - dom's light might ___ shine ___ through the fog - gy dew. ___
Fen - ian's sleep, 'neath the hills ___ of the fog - gy dew. ___
Reb - el dead, when you fell ___ in the fog - gy dew. ___

THE EBENEZER

Sea Chantey

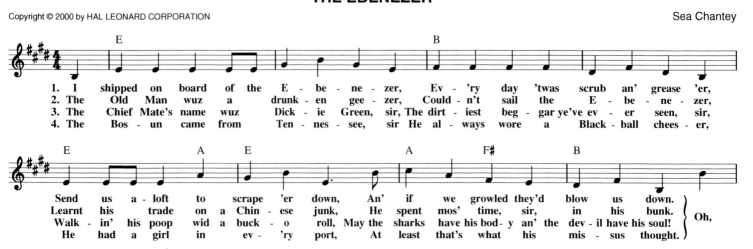

1. I shipped on board of the E - be - ne - zer, Ev - 'ry day 'twas scrub an' grease 'er,
2. The Old Man wuz a drunk - en gee - zer, Could - n't sail the E - be - ne - zer,
3. The Chief Mate's name wuz Dick - ie Green, sir, The dirt - iest beg - gar ye've ev - er seen, sir,
4. The Bos - un came from Ten - nes - see, sir He al - ways wore a Black - ball chees - er,

Send us a - loft to scrape 'er down, An' if we growled they'd blow us down.
Learnt his trade on a Chin - ese junk, He spent mos' time, sir, in his bunk.
Walk - in' his poop wid a buck - o roll, May the sharks have his bod - y an' the dev - il have his soul!
He had a girl in ev - 'ry port, At least that's what his mis - sus thought. } Oh,

git a - long boys, git a - long do, Hand - y, me boys, so hand - y!

Git a - long boys, git a - long do, Hand - y! me boys, so hand - y!

EILEEN OGE

Words by Percy French
Traditional Irish Melody

1. Ei - leen Oge! an' that the dar - lin's name is. Through the Bar - o - ny, her
2. Fri - day at the fair of Bal - lin - tub - ber, Ei - leen met _____ Mc -
3. So it went as 'twas in the be - gin - ning, Ei - leen Oge, _____ she was
4. Boys, O boys, with fate 'tis hard to grap - ple. Of his eye _____ 'tis Ei -

fea - tures they were fa - mous. If we loved her, who is there to blame us, For _____
Grath the cat - tle job - ber. I'd like to set me mark up - on the rob - ber, For he
bent up - on the win - ning. Big Mc - Grath con - tent - ed - ly was grin - ning, Be - ing
leen _____ was the ap - ple; And now to see her walk - in' to the chap - el With the

was - n't she the Pride of Pet - ra - vore? But her beau - ty made us all so shy,
stole a - way the Pride of Pet - ra - vore. He nev - er seemed to see the girl at all,
court - ed by the Pride of Pet - ra - vore. Says he, "I know a girl that could knock you in - to fits."
hard - est fea - tured man in Pet - ra - vore. And now, boys, this is all I have to say:

Not a man could look her in the eye. Boys, O boys! sure that's the rea - son why We're in
E - ven when she o - gled him un - der - neath her shawl. Look - in' big and mas - ter - ful when she was look - in' small, Most pro -
At that, Ei - leen near - ly lost her wits. The up - shot of the ruc - tion was that now the rob - ber sits With his
When you do your court - in', don't make a dis - play. If you want them to run af - ter you, just walk the oth - er way, For they're

mourn - in' for the Pride of Pet - ra - vore.
vok - ing for the Pride of Pet - ra - vore.
arm a - round the Pride of Pet - ra - vore.
most - ly like the Pride of Pet - ra - vore.

Ei - leen Oge! Me

heart is grow - in' grey, Ev - er since the day you wan - dered far a - way.

Ei - leen Oge! There's good fish in the say, But there's no one like the Pride of Pet - ra - vore.

EGGS AND MARROWBONE

American

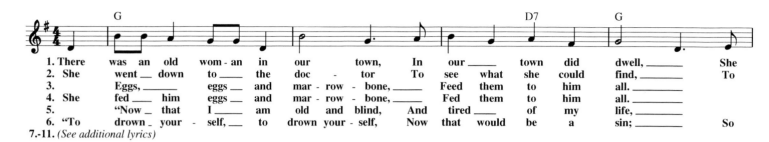

1. There was an old wom-an in our town, In our ____ town did dwell, ____ She
2. She went ___ down to ___ the doc - tor To see what she could find, ____ To
3. Eggs, ____ eggs ___ and mar - row - bone, ____ Feed them to him all. ____ She
4. She fed ___ him eggs ___ and mar - row - bone, ____ Fed them to him all. ____
5. "Now ___ that I ____ am old and blind, And tired ____ of my life, ____
6. "To drown ___ your - self, ___ to drown your - self, Now that would be a sin; ____ So

7.-11. *(See additional lyrics)*

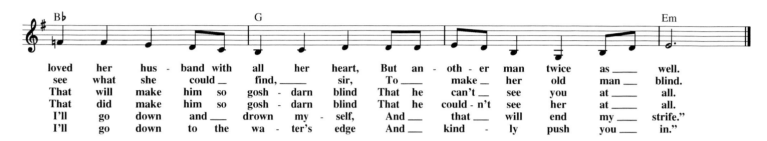

loved her hus - band with all her heart, But an - oth - er man twice as ____ well.
see what she could ___ find, ____ sir, To ____ make ___ her old man ___ blind.
That will make him so gosh - darn blind That he can't ___ see you at ____ all.
That did make him so gosh - darn blind That he could - n't see her at ____ all.
I'll go down and ___ drown my - self, And ___ that ___ will end my ___ strife."
I'll go down to the wa - ter's edge And ___ kind - ly push you ___ in."

Additional Lyrics

7. The old woman took a running jump
   For to push the old man in.
   The old man, he stepped to one side
   And the old woman, she fell in.

8. She cried for help, she screamed for help,
   Loudly did she bawl.
   The old man said, "I'm so goshdarn blind,
   I can't see you at all."

9. She swam along, she swam along,
   Till she came to the river's brim.
   The old man got a great long pole
   And pushed her further in.

10. Now the old woman is dead and gone,
    And the Devil's got her soul.
    Wasn't she a blamed old fool
    That she didn't grab the pole?

11. Eggs, eggs and marrowbone
    Won't make your old man blind:
    So if you want to push him in,
    You must sneak up from behind!

ELANOY

American

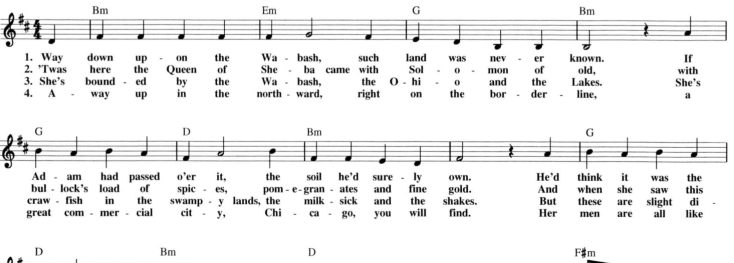

1. Way down up - on the Wa - bash, such land was nev - er known. If
2. 'Twas here the Queen of She - ba came with Sol - o - mon of old, with
3. She's bound - ed by the Wa - bash, the O - hi - o and the Lakes. She's
4. A - way up in the north - ward, right on the bor - der - line, a

Ad - am had passed o'er it, the soil he'd sure - ly own. He'd think it was the
bul - lock's load of spic - es, pom - e - gran - ates and fine gold. And when she saw this
craw - fish in the swamp - y lands, the milk - sick and the shakes. But these are slight di -
great com - mer - cial cit - y, Chi - ca - go, you will find. Her men are all like

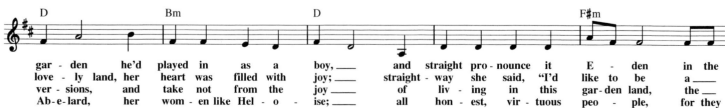

gar - den he'd played in as a boy, ____ and straight pro - nounce it E - den in the
love - ly land, her heart was filled with joy; ____ straight - way she said, "I'd like to be a ____
ver - sions, and take not from the joy ____ of liv - ing in this gar - den land, the ___
Ab - e - lard, her wom - en like Hel - o - ise; ____ all hon - est, vir - tuous peo - ple, for they

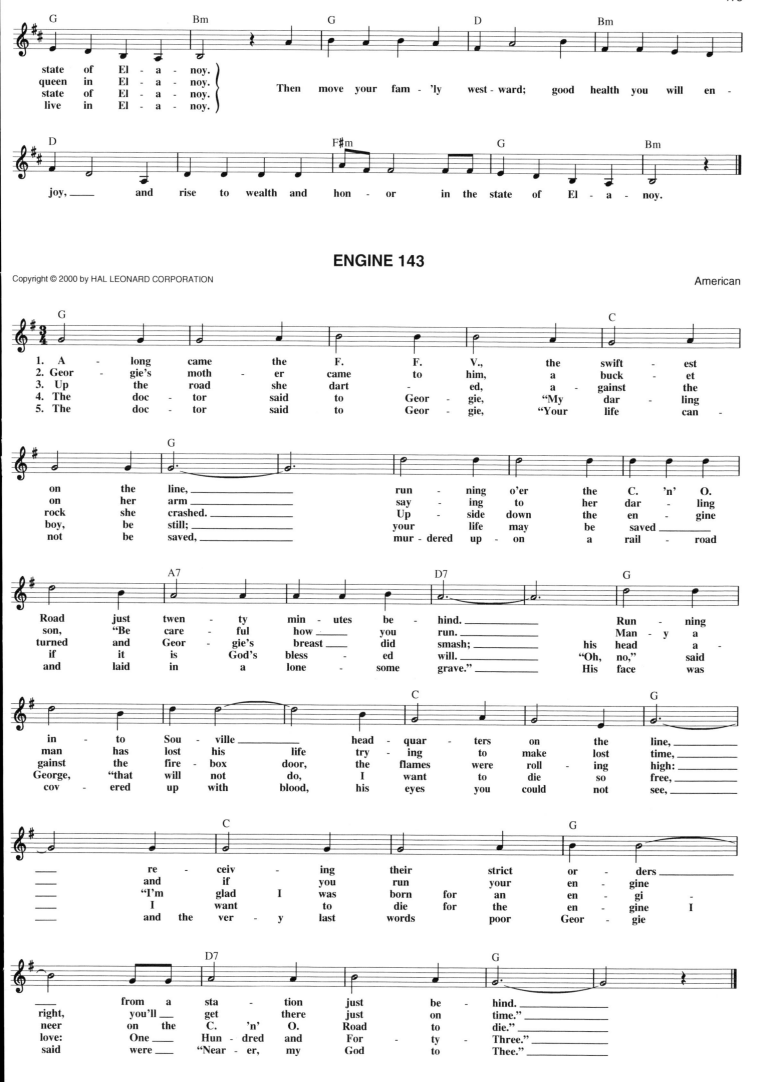

state of El - a - noy.
queen in El - a - noy.
state of El - a - noy.
live in El - a - noy.

Then move your fam - 'ly west - ward; good health you will en -

joy, ____ and rise to wealth and hon - or in the state of El - a - noy.

ENGINE 143

American

1. A - long came the F. F. V., the swift - est
2. Geor - gie's moth - er came to him, a buck - et
3. Up the road she dart - ed, a - gainst the
4. The doc - tor said to Geor - gie, "My dar - ling
5. The doc - tor said to Geor - gie, "Your life can -

on the line, ____ run - ning o'er the C. 'n' O.
on her arm ____ say - ing to her dar - ling
rock she crashed. ____ Up - side down the en - gine
boy, be still; ____ your life may be saved ____
not be saved, ____ mur - dered up - on a rail - road

Road just twen - ty min - utes be - hind. ____ Run - ning
son, "Be care - ful how ____ you run. ____ Man - y a
turned and Geor - gie's breast ____ did smash; ____ his head a -
if it is God's bless - ed will. ____ "Oh, no," said
and laid in a lone - some grave." ____ His face was

in - to Sou - ville ____ head - quar - ters on the line, ____
man has lost his life try - ing to make lost time, ____
gainst the fire - box door, the flames were roll - ing high: ____
George, "that will not do, I want to die so free, ____
cov - ered up with blood, his eyes you could not see, ____

____ re - ceiv - ing their strict or - ders ____
____ and if you run your en - gine
____ "I'm glad I was born for an en - gi -
____ I want to die for the en - gine I
____ and the ver - y last words poor Geor - gie

____ from a sta - tion just be - hind. ____
right, you'll ____ get there just on time." ____
neer on the C. 'n' O. Road to die." ____
love: One ____ Hun - dred and For - ty - Three." ____
said were ____ "Near - er, my God to Thee." ____

EMPTY BED BLUES

American

1. I woke up this morn-ing with an aw-ful ach-ing head. _____ I woke
2.-8. *(See additional lyrics)*

up this morn-ing with an aw-ful ach-ing head. _____ My

new man had left me just a room and an emp-ty bed. _____

Additional Lyrics

2. He's a coffee grinder— grinding all the time
He's a coffee grinder— grinding all the time
He can grind my coffee, 'cause he's got a brand-new grind.

3. He's a deep-sea diver with a stroke that can't go wrong
He's a deep sea diver with a stroke that can't go wrong
He can reach the bottom 'cause his breath holds out so long.

4. He came home one evening with his spirit 'way up high
He came home one evening with his spirit 'way up high
What he had to give me made me wring my hands and cry.

5. He taught me a lesson I never had before
He taught me a lesson I never had before
When he got through teaching, from my elbows down I was sore.

6. Well, he boiled my cabbage and he made it awful hot
Well, he boiled my cabbage and he made it awful hot
Then he put the bacon and overflowed the pot.

7. Well, he knows how to thrill me, and I told my girlfriend, Lou
Well, he knows how to thrill me, and I told my girlfriend, Lou
And the way she's raving she must have gone and tried it too.

8. If you get good loving, never go and spread the news
If you get good loving, never go and spread the news
Gals will doublecross you and leave you with the empty bed blues.

THE ERIE CANAL

New York Work Song, circa 1820

1. I've got a mule, ____ her name is Sal, fif-teen miles ____ on the E-rie Ca-nal, ____ she's a
2. up, old Sal, ___ let's pass the lock, fif-teen miles ____ on the E-rie Ca-nal, ___ in Sche-

good hard work-er and a real good pal! Fif-teen miles _ on the E-rie Ca-nal. ___ We've
nec-ta-dy ___ to-day at six o-'clock, fif-teen miles _ on the E-rie Ca-nal. ___ It's

hauled some barg-es in our day, filled with lum-ber, coal, and hay, from
all the time ___ the same old haul, glad to reach _ my port of call, a

Buf-fa-lo we're start-ing a trip, and it's a slow _ but a ver-y good ship. _ Hey! {
hun-dred friends will greet me "hel-lo," from Al-ba-ny ___ to ____ Buf-fa-lo. Hey! {

Low bridge, ev-'ry-bod-y down! Low bridge, we're a - com-in' to a town! And you'll al-ways know your neigh-bor, you'll

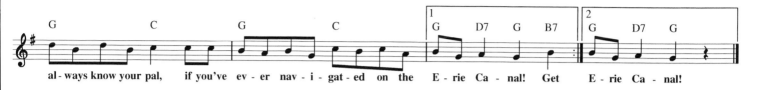

al - ways know your pal, if you've ev - er nav - i - gat - ed on the E - rie Ca - nal! Get E - rie Ca - nal!

EQUINOXIAL AND PHOEBE

American

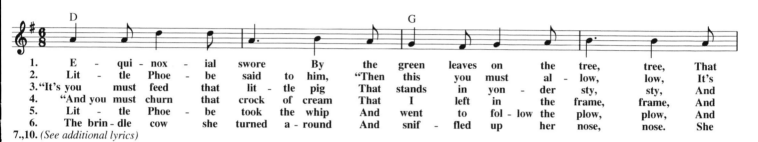

1. E - qui - nox - ial swore By the green leaves on the tree, tree, That
2. Lit - tle Phoe - be said to him, "Then this you must al - low, low, It's
3. "It's you must feed that lit - tle pig That stands in yon - der sty, sty, And
4. "And you must churn that crock of cream That I left in the frame, frame, And
5. Lit - tle Phoe - be took the whip And went to fol - low the plow, plow, And
6. The brin - dle cow she turned a - round And snif - fled up her nose, nose. She

7.,10. *(See additional lyrics)*

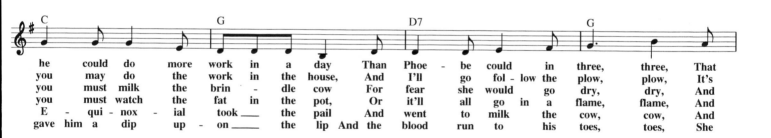

he could do more work in a day Than Phoe - be could in three, three, That
you may do the work in the house, And I'll go fol - low the plow, plow, It's
you must milk the brin - dle cow For fear she would go dry, dry, And
you must watch the fat in the pot, Or it'll all go in a flame, flame, And
E - qui - nox - ial took the pail And went to milk the cow, cow, And
gave him a dip up - on the lip And the blood run to his toes, toes, She

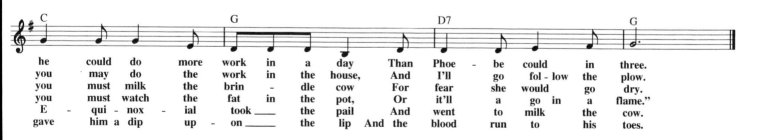

he could do more work in a day Than Phoe - be could in three.
you may do the work in the house, And I'll go fol - low the plow.
you must milk the brin - dle cow For fear she would go dry.
you must watch the fat in the pot, Or it'll a go in a flame."
E - qui - nox - ial took the pail And went to milk the cow.
gave him a dip up - on the lip And the blood run to his toes.

Additional Lyrics

7. He went to feed the little pig,
That stands in yonder sty.
He bumped his nose upon the beam,
And how the blood did fly, fly.
He bumped his nose upon the beam,
And how the blood did fly.

8. He went to churn that crock of cream
That she left in the frame,
And he forgot the fat in the pot
And it all went in a flame, flame.
And he forgot the fat in the pot,
And it all went in a flame.

9. He looked to the east and he looked to the west,
And he saw the setting sun.
He swore it'd been an awful long day
And Phoebe hadn't come, come.
He swore it'd been an awful long day,
And Phoebe hadn't come.

10. So Equinoxial swore
By all the stars in heaven,
That she could do more work in a day
Than he could do in seven, seven.
That she could do more work in a day
Than he could do in seven.

ERIN'S LOVELY HOME

English

1. When __ I was young and in my prime, my age just __ twen - ty - one, Then __
2. 'Twas __ in her fa - ther's gar - den, all in the __ month of June, A -
3. That __ ver - y night I gave con - sent a - long with __ her to go All __
4. But __ when we got to Bel - fast, 'twas at the __ break of day, My __
5. But __ of our great mis - for - tune I mean to __ let you hear; 'Twas __
6. And now when I heard my sen - tence it grieved my __ heart full sore; And __
7. (See additional lyrics)

I __ be - came a ser - vant un - to some gen - tle - man. I __
view - ing of those pret - ty flow'rs all __ in their youth - ful bloom, She __
from __ her fa - ther's dwell - ing place, which __ proved my o - ver - throw. The __
true __ love she got read - y a __ pas - sage for to pay; Five __
in __ a few hours af - ter - wards her __ fa - ther did ap - pear. He __
part - ing from my sweet - heart it __ grieved me ten times more. I'd __

served __ him true __ and hon - est, and __ that is ver - y well known, But __
said, __ "My dear - est John - nie, if __ with me you __ will roam, We'll __
night __ be - ing bright __ with moon - light, we __ both set off __ to roam, A -
hun - dred pounds __ she did pay down, say - ing, "That shall be __ your own, And __
marched __ me back __ to Ar - magh gaol, in the coun - ty of __ Ty - rone, And __
sev - en links __ all on my chain, and __ ev - 'ry link __ a year, Be -

cru - el - ly he ban - ish'd me from E - rin's __ love - ly home.
bid a - dieu to all our friends in E - rin's __ love - ly home."
think - ing we'd got safe a - way from E - rin's __ love - ly home.
nev - er mourn for the friends you've left in E - rin's __ love - ly home."
there I was trans - port - ed from E - rin's __ love - ly home."
fore I could re - turn a - gain to the girl I __ loved so dear.

Additional Lyrics

7. But when the rout came to the gaol to take us all away,
   My true love she came on to me, and this to me did say,
   "Bear up your heart, don't be dismayed, for it's you I'll never disown
   Until you do return again to Erin's lovely home."

EVERY NIGHT WHEN THE SUN GOES IN

Southern Appalachian

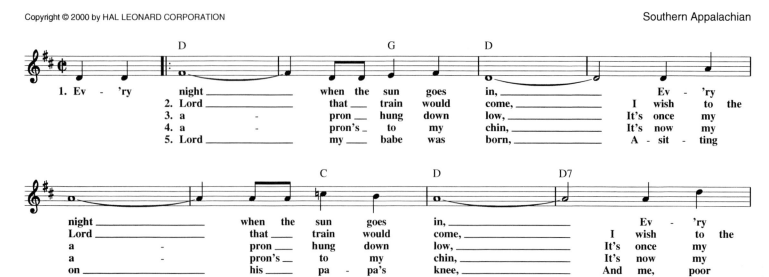

1. Ev - 'ry night __ when the sun goes in, __ Ev - 'ry
2. Lord __ that __ train would come, __ I wish to the
3. a - pron __ hung down low, __ It's once my
4. a - pron's __ to my chin, __ It's now my
5. Lord __ my __ babe was born, __ A - sit - ting

night __ when the sun goes in, __ Ev - 'ry
Lord __ that __ train would come, __ I wish to the
a - pron __ hung down low, __ It's once my
a - pron's __ to my chin, __ It's now my
on __ his __ pa - pa's knee, __ And me, poor

night _____ when the sun goes in, _____
Lord _____ that _____ train would come, _____
a - pron _____ hung down low, _____
a - pron's _____ to my chin, _____
girl, _____ was _____ dead and gone, _____

_____ I hang _____ my head _____ and mourn - ful
_____ To take _____ me back _____ to where I come
_____ He'd fol - low me _____ through sleet and
_____ He'll face _____ my door _____ and won't come
_____ And the _____ green grass _____ grow - ing o - ver

cry. _____ True love, don't weep, _____ true love, don't
from. _____
snow. _____ True love, don't weep, _____ true love, don't
in. _____
me. _____

mourn, _____ True love, don't weep, _____ true love, don't

mourn, _____ True love, don't weep _____ or mourn for me, _____ I'm go - ing a -

way _____ to Mar - ble - town. _____
(2.) I wish to the town. _____
(3.) It's once my __
(4.) It's now my __
(5.) I wish to the

EVERYBODY LOVES SATURDAY NIGHT

Nigerian

Ev - 'ry - bod - y loves Sat - ur - day night. _____

Ev - 'ry - bod - y loves Sat - ur - day night. _____

Ev - 'ry - bod - y, ev - 'ry - bod - y, ev - 'ry - bod - y,

ev - 'ry - bod - y, Ev - 'ry - bod - y loves Sat - ur - day night. _____

EVERY TIME I FEEL THE SPIRIT

African-American Spiritual

EXULTATION

Southern Folk Hymn

EZEKIEL SAW THE WHEEL

African-American Spiritual

THE FAIR MAID OF SORRENTO
(La Vera Sorrentina)

Italian from Naples

THE FACTORY GIRL

American

1. No more shall I work in the fac - t'ry, greas - y up my
2. No more shall I hear the ___ boss - es say, "Girls, you'd bet - ter
3. No more shall I hear the ___ drum - mer wheels a - roll - ing o - ver my
4. No more shall I hear the ___ whis - tle blow to call me up so
5. No more shall I see the ___ su - per come, all dressed up so
6. No more shall I wear the ___ old black dress, greas - y all a -

clothes; no more shall I work in the fac - t'ry with splin - ters in my toes.
daulf." No more shall I hear the ___ boss - es say, _____ "Spin - ners, you'd bet - ter clean off."
head. When fac - to - ries are ___ hard at work, _____ I'll be in my bed.
soon. No more shall I hear the ___ whis - tle blow to call me from my home.
proud, for I know I'll mar - ry a coun - try boy be - fore the year is out.
round; no more shall I wear the ___ old black bon - net with holes all in the crown.

Pit - y me, my dar - ling, pit - y me, I say;

Pit - y me, my dar - ling, and car - ry me a - way.

FAIR HARVARD

Words by Samuel Gilman, 1811
Traditional Irish Air

1. Fair ___ Har - vard! thy sons to thy ju - bi - lee throng, And with bless - ings sur - ren - der thee o'er, _____ By these
2. To thy bow'rs we were led in the bloom of our youth, From the home of our in - fan - tile years, _____ When our
3. When as pil - grims we come to re - vis - it thy halls, To what kin - dlings the sea - son gives birth! ___ Thy ___
4. Fare - well! be thy des - ti - nies on - ward and bright! To thy chil - dren the les - son still give, _____ With ___

fes - ti - val rites, from the age that is past, To the age that is wait - ing be - fore. _____ O
fa - thers had warned, and our moth - ers had prayed, And our sis - ters had blest, through their tears: _____ Thou
shades are more sooth - ing, thy sun - light more dear, Then de - scend on less priv - i - leged earth; _____ For the
free - dom to think, and with pa - tience to bear, And for right ev - er brave - ly to live. _____ Let not

rel - ic and type of our an - ces - tors worth, That has long kept their mem - o - ry warm, _____ First ___
then, wert our par - ent, the nurse of our souls, We were mold - ed to man - hood by thee, _____ Till ___
good and the great, in their beau - ti - ful prime, Through thy pre - cincts have mus - ing - ly trod, _____ As they
moss - cov - ered er - ror moor thee at its side As the world on truth's cur - rent glides by; _____ Be the

flow'r of their wil - der - ness, star of their night, Calm ___ ris - ing through change and through storm! _____
freight - ed with treas - ure thoughts, friend - ships and hopes, Thou didst launch us on Des - ti - ny's sea. _____
gird - ed their spir - its or deep - ened the streams That make glad the fair cit - y of God. _____
her - ald of light and the bear - er of love Till the stock of the Pu - ri - tans die. _____

FAREWELL, NANCY

19th Century Irish

1. Fare - well, my dear-est Nan - cy, since _ I must now _ leave you; Un - to the salt _
2. Like some pret - ty lit - tle sea - boy I will dress and go _ with you; In the deep - est of _
3. Your _ pret - ty lit - tle hands _ can't _ han - dle our _ tack - le, And your pret - ty lit - tle
4. So fare - well, my dear-est Nan - cy, since _ I must now _ leave you; Un - to the salt _

seas I _ am _ bound for to go. But let my long ab - sence be _
dan - ger, _ I _ shall stand your friend. In the cold storm - y weath - er when the
feet on _ our _ top - mast can't go. And the cold storm - y weath-er, Love, you _
seas. I _ am _ bound for to go Where the winds do blow high _ and the _

no trou - ble _ to you, For _ I shall re - turn in the spring, _ as you _ know.
winds are _ a - blow - ing, My _ dear, I shall be will - ing to wait _ on you _ then.
ne'er can _ en - dure; _ There - fore, dear - est Nan - cy, to the seas _ do not _ go.
seas loud _ do _ roar. _ So _ make your - self con - tent - ed, be kind _ and stay on shore.

THE FARMER IS THE MAN

American

1. When the farm - er comes to town with his wag - on bro - ken down, oh, the farm - er is the
2. When the law - yer stands a - round while the butch - er cuts a pound, he for - gets that it's the
3. When the bank - er says he's broke and the mer - chant's up in smoke, they for - get that it's the

man who feeds us all. _____ If we'd on - ly look and see, well, I
farm - er feeds 'em all. _____ And the preach - er and the cook go a -
farm - er feeds 'em all. _____ If he'd on - ly take a rest, he could

think that we'd a - gree that the farm - er is the man who feeds us all. _____
stroll - in' by the brook; they for - get that it's the farm - er feeds 'em all. _____
put 'em to the test, 'cause the farm - er is the man who feeds 'em all. _____

The farm - er is the man, _____ the farm - er is the man, lives on

cred - it till the fall. _____ Then they take him by the hand and they lead him from the
With the in - t'rest rates so high, it's a won - der he don't
His con - di - tion, it's a sin, 'cause his pants are get - tin'

land, and the mid - dle - man's the one who gets it all. _____
die, and the mid - dle - man's the one who gets it all. _____
thin; we for - get that he's the one who feeds us all. _____

THE FARMER IN THE DELL

Southern American

1. The farm - er in the dell, _____ The farm - er in the dell,
2. The farm - er takes a wife, _____ The farm - er takes a wife,
3. The wife _____ takes the child, _____ The wife _____ takes the child,
4. The child _____ takes the nurse, _____ The child _____ takes the nurse,
5. The nurse _____ takes the dog, _____ The nurse _____ takes the dog,
6. The dog _____ takes the cat, _____ The dog _____ takes the cat,

7.-9. *(See additional lyrics)*

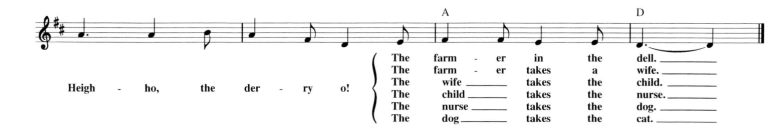

Heigh - ho, the der - ry o!

The farm - er in the dell. _____
The farm - er takes a wife. _____
The wife _____ takes the child. _____
The child _____ takes the nurse. _____
The nurse _____ takes the dog. _____
The dog _____ takes the cat. _____

Additional Lyrics

7. The cat takes the rat,
The cat takes the rat,
Heigh-ho, the derry o!
The cat takes the rat.

8. The rat takes the cheese,
The rat takes the cheese,
Heigh-ho, the derry o!
The rat takes the cheese.

9. The cheese stands alone,
The cheese stands alone,
Heigh-ho, the derry o!
The cheese stands alone.

THE FARMER'S DAUGHTER

English

1. A farm - er he lived in the west coun - try,
2. One day _____ they walked by the riv - er's brim,
3. "O sis - ter, O sis - ter, pray lend me your hand,
4. "I'll neith - er lend _____ you hand nor glove,
5. So down _____ the riv - er the maid - en swam,
6. The mil - ler, he took _____ his rod and hook,

Bow down, bow down,

A
One
O
I'll
So
The

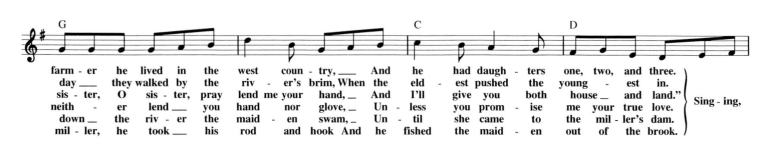

farm - er he lived in the west coun - try, _____ And he had daugh - ters one, two, and three.
day _____ they walked by the riv - er's brim, When the eld - est pushed the young - est in.
sis - ter, O sis - ter, pray lend me your hand, _ And I'll give you both house _ and land."
neith - er lend _____ you hand nor glove, _ Un - less you prom - ise me your true love.
down _ the riv - er the maid - en swam, _ Un - til she came to the mil - ler's dam.
mil - ler, he took _____ his rod and hook And he fished the maid - en out of the brook.

Sing - ing,

I will be true un - to my love if my love will be true un - to me." _____

FATHER MURPHY

Irish

1. At Boul - a - vogue, as the sun was set - ting O'er bright May mead - ows of Shel - ma - lier, A _____
2. He led us on 'gainst the com - ing sol - diers, The cow'r - dly Yeo - men we put to flight; 'Twas _
3. We took Cam - o - lin and En - nis - cor - thy, And Wex - ford storm - ing drove out our foes; 'Twas _
4. At Vin - e - gar Hill, o'er the pleas - ant Sla - ney, Our he - roes vain - ly stood back to back, And the

reb - el hand set the heath - er blaz - ing, And brought the neigh - bors from far and near. Then
at the Har - row the boys of Wex - ford Showed Book - ey's reg - i - ment how men could fight. Look
at Slieve Coil - lte our pikes were reek - ing With the crim - son stream _ of the beat - en Yeos. At
Yeos at Tul - low took Fa - ther Mur - phy And burned his bod - y up - on the rack. God

Fa - ther Mur - phy, from old Kil - cor - mack, Spurred up the rocks with a warn - ing cry: "Arm!
out for hire - lings, King George of En - gland, Search ev - 'ry king - dom where breathes a slave, For
Tub - ber - neer - ing and Bal - ly - el - lis, Full man - y a Hes - sian lay in his gore. Ah,
grant you glo - ry, brave Fa - ther Mur - phy, And o - pen Heav - en to all your men; The

Arm!" he cried, "for I've come to lead you; For Ire - land's free - dom we fight or die."
Fa - ther Mur - phy of the Coun - ty Wex - ford Sweeps o'er the land _ like a might - y wave.
Fa - ther Mur - phy, had aid come o - ver, The green flag float - ed from shore to shore!
cause that called you may call to - mor - row In an - oth - er fight _ for the green a - gain.

FATHER'S WHISKERS

American, circa 1920

1. We have a dear old dad - dy, for whom we dai - ly pray. He's
2. Fa - ther had a strong back; _____ now it's all caved in. He
3. We have a dear old moth - er; with him she night - ly sleeps. She
4. We have a dear old broth - er; he has a Ford ma - chine. He
5. Fa - ther fought in Flan - ders; he was - n't killed, you see. He
6. When Fa - ther goes in swim - ming, no bath - ing suit for him. He

got a set of whis - kers that are al - ways in the way.
stepped up - on his whis - kers and _ walked up to his chin.
wakes up in the morn - ing Eat - ing shred - ded wheat.
us - es Fa - ther's whis - kers to _ strain the gas - o - line.
hid be - hind his whis - kers and _ fooled the en - e - my.
ties his whis - kers 'round his waist And gai - ly plung - es in.

They're al - ways in the way, the

cow eats them for hay. They hide the dirt on dad - dy's shirt, they're al - ways in the way.

THE FENIAN MAN O' WAR

19th Century Irish

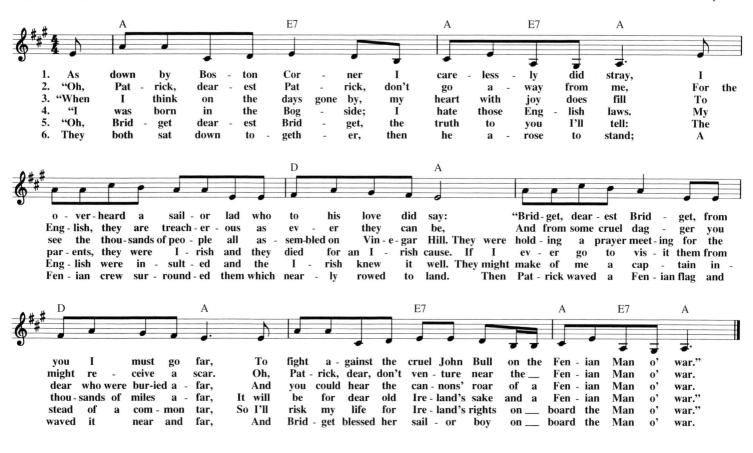

1. As down by Bos - ton Cor - ner I care - less - ly did stray, I
2. "Oh, Pat - rick, dear - est Pat - rick, don't go a - way from me, For the
3. "When I think on the days gone by, my heart with joy does fill To
4. "I was born in the Bog - side; I hate those Eng - lish laws. My
5. "Oh, Brid - get dear - est Brid - get, the truth to you I'll tell: The
6. They both sat down to - geth - er, then he a - rose to stand; A

o - ver - heard a sail - or lad who to his love did say: "Brid - get, dear - est Brid - get, from
Eng - lish, they are treach - er - ous as ev - er they can be, And from some cruel dag - ger you
see the thou - sands of peo - ple all as - sem - bled on Vin - e - gar Hill. They were hold - ing a prayer meet - ing for the
par - ents, they were I - rish and they died for an I - rish cause. If I ev - er go to vis - it them from
Fen - ian crew sur - round - ed them which near - ly rowed to land. Then Pat - rick waved a Fen - ian flag and

you I must go far, To fight a - gainst the cruel John Bull on the Fen - ian Man o' war."
might re - ceive a scar. Oh, Pat - rick, dear, don't ven - ture near the __ Fen - ian Man o' war.
dear who were bur - ied a - far, And you could hear the can - nons' roar of a Fen - ian Man o' war.
thou - sands of miles a - far, It will be for dear old Ire - land's sake and a Fen - ian Man o' war."
stead of a com - mon tar, So I'll risk my life for Ire - land's rights on __ board the Man o' war."
waved it near and far, And Brid - get blessed her sail - or boy on __ board the Man o' war.

FERRYLAND SEALER

Sea Chantey from Newfoundland

1. Oh, our schoo - ner and our sloop in Fer - ry - land they do lie, They are
2. We had vit - tles for to last more than two mouths at the least. And __
3. Oh, our cap - tain he cried out, __ "Come on, boys, bear a hand!" Our __
4. Oh, __ now __ we are load - ed and our schoo - ner she is sound. And the

all read - y rig - géd to be bound for the ice. All you
plen - ty of good rum, boys, stowed a - way in our chest. We will
cook he gets the break - fast and each man takes a dram. With their
ice it is o - pen and to Fer - ry - land we're bound. We all

lads of the South - ern we will have you to be - ware, She is
give her a ral - ly for to praise __ all our fan - cy. All our
bats in their hands __ it was ear - lye to go. Ev - 'ry
gave her a ral - ly for to praise __ all our fan - cy. Our __

going to the ice __ in the spring of the year. __
seals will be col - lect - ed by the Wil - liam and the Nan - cy.
man showed his ac - tion 'thout the miss - ing of a blow. __
seals they were col - lect - ed by the Wil - liam and the Nan - cy.

Lad - die

whack fall the lad - die, Lad - die whack fall the day. __

THE FENIANS OF CAHIRCIVEEN

Irish

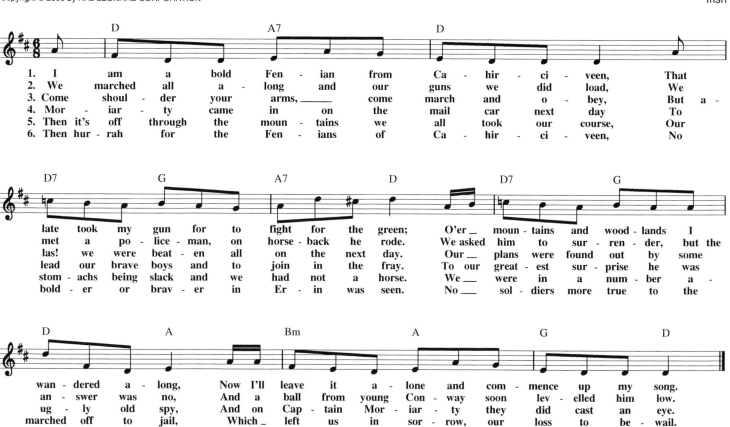

1. I am a bold Fenian from Cahirciveen, That late took my gun for to fight for the green; O'er_ mountains and woodlands I wandered along, Now I'll leave it alone and commence up my song.
2. We marched all along and our guns we did load, We met a policeman, on horseback he rode. We asked him to surrender, but the answer was no, And a ball from young Conway soon levelled him low.
3. Come shoulder your arms, _____ come march and obey, But alas! we were beaten, on all on the next day. Our _____ plans were found out by some ugly old spy, And on Captain Moriarty they did cast an eye.
4. Moriarty came in on the mail car next day To lead our brave boys and to join in the fray. To our greatest surprise he was marched off to jail, Which _ left us in sorrow, our loss to bewail.
5. Then it's off through the mountains we all took our course, Our stomachs being slack and we had not a horse. We _____ were in a number about sixty strong, surrounded by redcoats, for something went wrong.
6. Then hurrah for the Fenians of Cahirciveen, No bolder or braver in Erin was seen. No _____ soldiers more true to the banner of green Than the true-hearted Fenians of Cahirciveen.

FILIMIOORIOORIAY

Irish-American

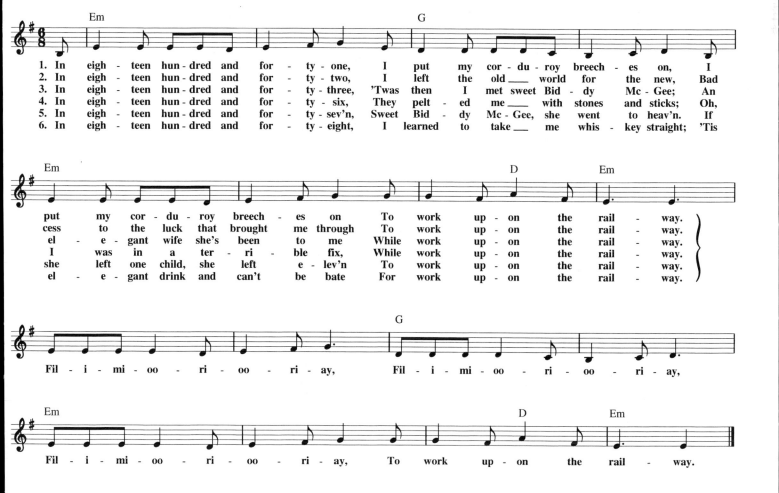

1. In eighteen hundred and forty-one, I put my corduroy breeches on, I put my corduroy breeches on To work upon the railway.
2. In eighteen hundred and forty-two, I left the old _____ world for the new, Bad cess to the luck that brought me through To work upon the railway.
3. In eighteen hundred and forty-three, 'Twas then I met sweet Biddy McGee; An elegant wife she's been to me While work upon the railway.
4. In eighteen hundred and forty-six, They pelted me _____ with stones and sticks; Oh, I was in a terrible fix, While work upon the railway.
5. In eighteen hundred and forty-sev'n, Sweet Biddy McGee, she went to heav'n. If she left one child, she left elev'n, To work upon the railway.
6. In eighteen hundred and forty-eight, I learned to take _____ me whiskey straight; 'Tis elegant drink and can't be bate For work upon the railway.

Fil-i-mi-oo-ri-oo-ri-ay, Fil-i-mi-oo-ri-oo-ri-ay,

Fil-i-mi-oo-ri-oo-ri-ay, To work upon the railway.

FELIX, THE SOLDIER

Irish
from the French and Indian War

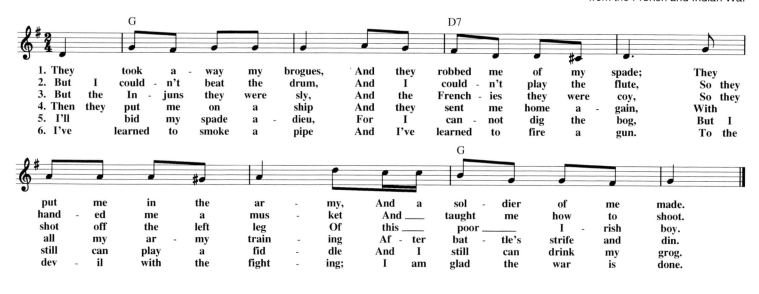

1. They took a way my brogues, And they robbed me of my spade; They
2. But I could n't beat the drum, And I could n't play the flute, So they
3. But the In - juns they were sly, And the French - ies they were coy, So they
4. Then they put me on a ship And they sent me home a - gain, With
5. I'll bid my spade a - dieu, For I can not dig the bog, But I
6. I've learned to smoke a pipe And I've learned to fire a gun. To the

put me in the ar - my, And a sol - dier of me made.
hand - ed me a mus - ket And __ taught me how to shoot.
shot off the left leg Of this __ poor __ I - rish boy.
all my ar - my train - ing Af - ter bat - tle's strife and din.
still can play a fid - dle And I still can drink my grog.
dev - il with the fight - ing; I am glad the war is done.

FINNEGAN'S WAKE

Irish Drinking Song

1. Tim Fin - ne - gan lived in Walk - in' Street, A gen - tle I - rish - man,
2. One morn - in' Tim was rath - er full; His head felt heav - y, which
3. His friends __ as - sem - bled at the wake, And Mrs. _____ Fin - ne - gan
4. Then Mag - gie O' - Con - nor took up the job, "Oh Bid - dy," says she, "you're
5. Then Mic - key Ma - lo - ney ducked his head When a nog - gin of whis - key

might - y odd. He had a brogue both rich and sweet, And to rise in the world he
made him shake. He fell from a lad - der and he broke his skull, And they car - ried him home, his
called for lunch. __ First they brought in tay and cake, Then pipes, to - bac - co, and
wrong, I'm sure." Bid - dy, she gave her a belt in the gob And __ left her __ spraw - lin'
flew at him. It missed, and fall - ing on the bed, The __ li - quor __ scat - tered

car - ried a hod. Now Tim had a sort o' the tip - plin' way, With a love for the liq - uor poor
corpse __ to wake. They rolled him __ up in a nice clean sheet And __ laid him __ out up -
whis - key punch. Bid - dy O' - Bri - en be - gan to cry, "Such a nice clean __ corpse did you
on _____ the floor. And then the __ war did __ soon en - gage, 'Twas __ wom - an to wom - an and
o - ver Tim! The corpse re - vives; see __ how he ri - ses! __ Tim - o - thy, ris - ing

Tim was born, To help him on with his work each day, He'd a "drop o' the cray - thur"
on the bed; A gal - lon of whis - key at his feet, And a bar - rel of por - ter
ev - er see? Oh Tim, mav - our - neen, why did you die?" "Arragh, __ hold __ your gob," said
man to man. Shil - le - laigh law was all the rage, And a row and a ruc - tion
from the bed, said, "Whirl your whis - key a - round like blaz - es, Than - um __ an Dhul! Do you

ev - 'ry morn.
at his head.
Pad - dy Mc - Ghee.   Whack fol the darn O, Dance to your part - ner Whirl the floor, your
soon be - gan.
think I'm dead?"

trot - ters shake; Was - n't it the truth I told you, Lots of fun at Fin - ne - gan's Wake.

FIX ME, JESUS

African-American Spiritual

Oh, _____ fix me, oh, _____ fix me, oh, _____ fix me;

fix me, Je - sus, fix me.
{ 1. Fix me for __ my long white robe,
{ 2. Fix me for __ my jour- ney home, } fix me, Je - sus, fix me.

{ Fix me for __ my star - ry crown,
{ Fix me for __ my dy - ing bed, } fix me, Je - sus, fix me.

fix me.

FLOW GENTLY, SWEET AFTON

Scottish
Words by Robert Burns
Melody by Alexander Hume

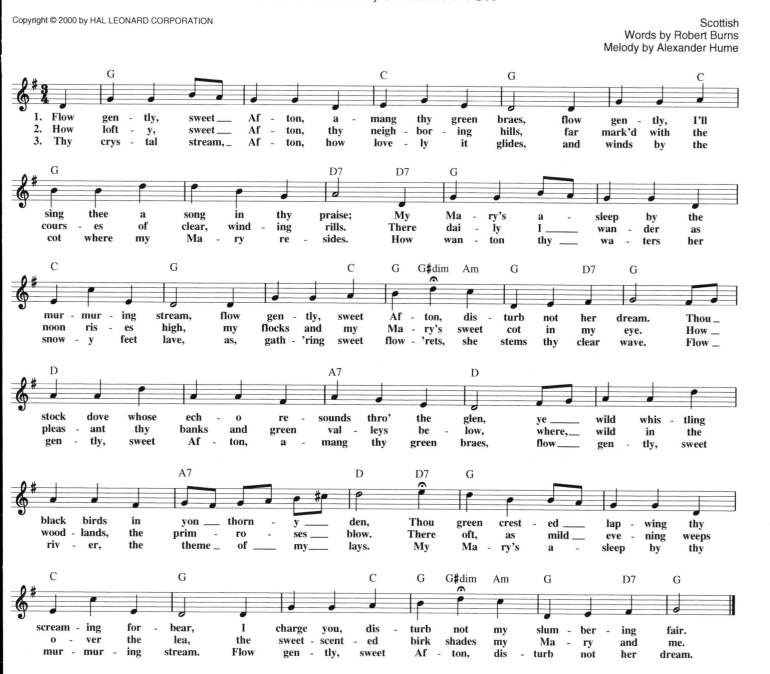

1. Flow gen - tly, sweet __ Af - ton, a - mang thy green braes, flow gen - tly, I'll
2. How loft - y, sweet __ Af - ton, thy neigh - bor - ing hills, far mark'd with the
3. Thy crys - tal stream, _ Af - ton, how love - ly it glides, and winds by the

sing thee a song in thy praise; My Ma - ry's a - sleep by the
cours - es of clear, wind - ing rills. There dai - ly I _____ wan - der as
cot where my Ma - ry re - sides. How wan - ton thy __ wa - ters her

mur - mur - ing stream, flow gen - tly, sweet Af - ton, dis - turb not her dream. Thou _
noon ris - es high, my flocks and my Ma - ry's sweet cot in my eye. How _
snow - y feet lave, as, gath - 'ring sweet flow - 'rets, she stems thy clear wave. Flow _

stock dove whose ech - o re - sounds thro' the glen, ye _____ wild whis - tling
pleas - ant thy banks and green val - leys be - low, where, _ wild in the
gen - tly, sweet Af - ton, a - mang thy green braes, flow _ gen - tly, sweet

black birds in yon __ thorn - y _____ den, Thou green crest - ed _____ lap - wing thy
wood - lands, the prim - ro - ses __ blow. There oft, as mild __ eve - ning weeps
riv - er, the theme _ of _____ my _ lays. My Ma - ry's a - sleep by thy

scream - ing for - bear, I charge you, dis - turb not my slum - ber - ing fair.
o - ver the lea, the sweet - scent - ed birk shades my Ma - ry and me.
mur - mur - ing stream. Flow gen - tly, sweet Af - ton, dis - turb not her dream.

FIRE DOWN BELOW

Sea Chantey

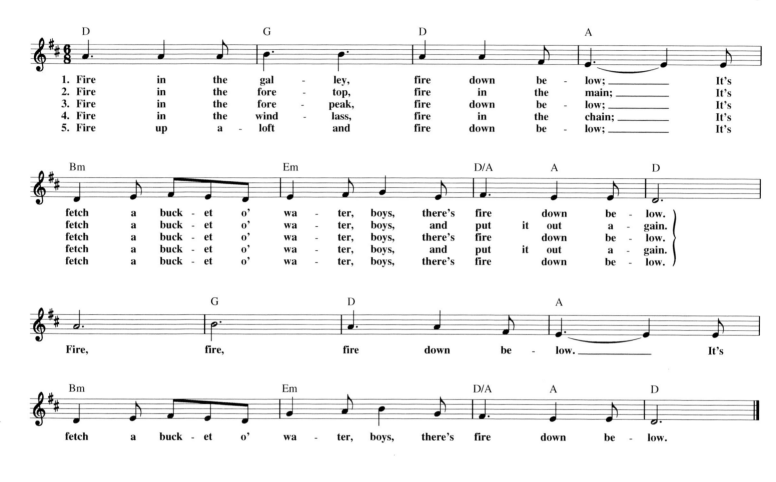

1. Fire in the gal - ley, fire down be - low; _____ It's
2. Fire in the fore - top, fire in the main; _____ It's
3. Fire in the fore - peak, fire down be - low; _____ It's
4. Fire in the wind - lass, fire in the chain; _____ It's
5. Fire up a - loft and fire down be - low; _____ It's

fetch a buck - et o' wa - ter, boys, there's fire down be - low.
fetch a buck - et o' wa - ter, boys, and put it out a - gain.
fetch a buck - et o' wa - ter, boys, there's fire down be - low.
fetch a buck - et o' wa - ter, boys, and put it out a - gain.
fetch a buck - et o' wa - ter, boys, there's fire down be - low.

Fire, fire, fire down be - low. _____ It's

fetch a buck - et o' wa - ter, boys, there's fire down be - low.

FLASH JACK FROM GUNDAGAI

Australian

1. I've shore at Bur - ra - bo - gie, and I've shore at To - gan - main, I've
2. I've shore at big Wil - lan - dra and I've shore at Til - be - roo, And
3. I've pinked 'em with the Wolse - leys and I've rushed with B - bows too, And
4. I've been whal - in' up the Lach - lan and I've dossed on Coop - er's Creek, And

shore at big Wil - lan - dra and on the old Cole - raine, But be -
once I drew my blades, my boys, up - on the famed Bar - coo, At
shaved 'em in the grease, my boys, with grass seed show - ing through. But I
once I rung Cud - jin - gie shed, and blued it in a week. But when

fore ___ the shear - in' was o - ver I've wished my - self back a - gain,
Cow - an Downs ___ and Tri - da, as far ___ as Mou - la - mein, But I
nev - er slummed ___ my pen, my lads, what - e'er ___ it might con - tain, While
Ga - briel blows ___ his trum - pet lads, I'll catch ___ the morn - ing train, And I'll

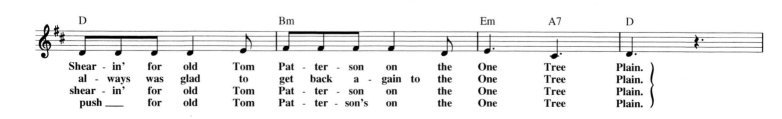

Shear - in' for old Tom Pat - ter - son on the One Tree Plain.
al - ways was glad to get back a - gain to the One Tree Plain.
shear - in' for old Tom Pat - ter - son on the One Tree Plain.
push ___ for old Tom Pat - ter - son's on the One Tree Plain.

189

FLOWER SO WHITE
(Flor, Blanca Flor)

Copyright © 2000 by HAL LEONARD CORPORATION

Mexican

THE FLYING CLOUD

19th Century Irish

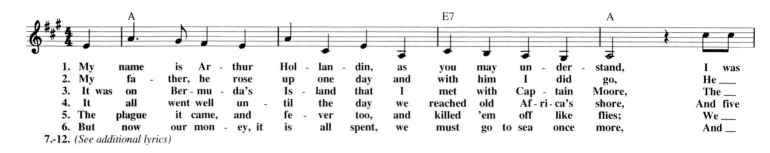

1. My name is Ar - thur Hol - lan - din, as you may un - der - stand, I was
2. My fa - ther, he rose up one day and with him I did go, He __
3. It was on Ber - mu - da's Is - land that I met with Cap - tain Moore, The __
4. It all went well un - til the day we reached old Af - ri - ca's shore, And five
5. The plague it came, and fe - ver too, and killed 'em off like flies; We __
6. But now our mon - ey, it is all spent, we must go to sea once more, And __

7.-12. *(See additional lyrics)*

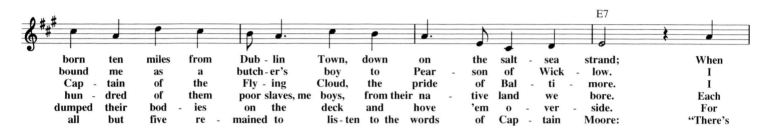

born ten miles from Dub - lin Town, down on the salt - sea strand; When
bound me as a butch - er's boy to Pear - son of Wick - low. I
Cap - tain of the Fly - ing Cloud, the pride of Bal - ti - more. I
hun - dred of them poor slaves, me boys, from their na - tive land we bore. Each
dumped their bod - ies on the deck and hove 'em o - ver - side. For
all but five re - mained to lis - ten to the words of Cap - tain Moore: "There's

I was young and come - ly, sure, good for - tune on me shone, My
wore the blood - y a - pron there for three long years and more, Till I
un - der - took to ship with him on a slav - ing voy - age to go, To the
man was load - ed down with chains as we made them walk be - low, Just
sure, the dead were the luck - y ones, for they'd have to weep no more, Nor
gold and sil - ver to be had if with me you'll re - main; Let's

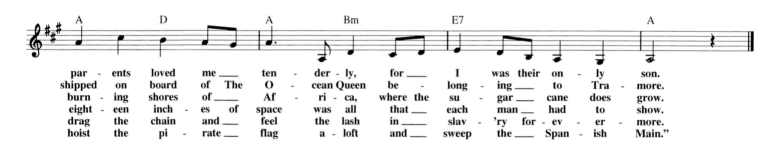

par - ents loved me __ ten - der - ly, for __ I was their on - ly son.
shipped on board of The O - cean Queen be - long - ing __ to Tra - more.
burn - ing shores of __ Af - ri - ca, where the su - gar __ cane does grow.
eight - een inch - es of space was all that __ each man __ had to show.
drag the chain and __ feel the lash in __ slav - 'ry for - ev - er - more.
hoist the pi - rate __ flag a - loft and __ sweep the __ Span - ish Main."

Additional Lyrics

7. The Flying Cloud was a Yankee ship, five hundred tons or more,
   She could outsail any clipper ship hailing out of Baltimore,
   With her canvas white as the driven snow and on it there's no specks,
   And forty men and fourteen guns she carried below her decks.

8. We plundered many a gallant ship down on the Spanish Main,
   Killed many a man and left his wife and children to remain,
   To none we showed no kindness but gave them watery graves,
   For the saying of our captain was: "Dead men tell no tales."

9. We ran and fought with many a ship both frigates and liners too,
   Till, at last a British Man-O'-War, the Dunmow, hove in view,
   She fired a shot across our bows as we ran before the wind,
   And a chainshot cut our mainmast down and we fell far behind.

10. They beat our crew to quarters as they drew up alongside,
    And soon across our quarterdeck there ran a crimson tide,
    We fought until they killed our captain and twenty of our men,
    Then a bombshell set our ship on fire, we had to surrender then.

11. It's now to Newgate we have come, bound down with iron chains,
    For the sinking and the plundering of ships on the Spanish Main,
    The judge he has condemned us and we are condemned to die.
    Young men a warning by me take and shun all piracy.

12. Farewell to Dublin City and the girl that I adore,
    I'll never kiss your cheek again nor hold your hand no more,
    Whisky and bad company have made a wretch of me,
    Young men, a warning by me take and shun all piracy.

FOD

Folksong from Oklahoma

1. As I went down to the mow - in' field, ___
2. Well, I fell down up - on the ground, ___
3. I set up - on a stump to take my rest, ___
4. The wood - chuck grinned a ___ ban - jo song, ___
5. The wood - chuck and skunk got in - to a fight, ___
6. They danced and played till the chim-ney be - gan to rust, ___

Hu - rye, tu - rye, fod - a - link - a - dye - do,

As I went down to the mow - in' field, ___ Fod!
Well, I fell down up - on the ground, ___ Fod!
I set up - on a stump to take my rest, ___ Fod!
The wood - chuck grinned a ___ ban - jo song, ___ Fod!
The wood - chuck and skunk got in - to a fight, ___ Fod!
They danced and played till the chim-ney be - gan to rust, ___ Fod!

As I went down to the
Well, I fell down up -
I set up - on a stump to
The wood-chuck grinned a ___
The wood-chuck and skunk got
They danced and played till the chim-ney

mow - in' field, A big black snake got me by the heel, ___
on the ground, I shut both eyes and looked all a-round, ___
take my rest, I looked like a wood-chuck on his nest, ___
ban - jo song, And up stepped a skunk with the britch-es on, ___
in - to a fight, The fumes was so strong they put out the light, ___
be - gan to rust, It was hard to tell which smelled the wust. ___

Tu - rol - ly day.

THE FOGGY DEW

Irish

1. O - ver the hills I ___ went one day; A ___ love - ly ___ maid I spied. ___
2. O - ver the hills I ___ went one morn, A - sing - ing ___ I did go. ___

___ With her coal - black ___ hair and her man - tle so green, An ___ im - age ___
___ Met this love - ly ___ maid with her coal - black hair, And she an - swered ___

to per - ceive. ___ Says I, "Dear girl, will you be my ___ bride?" And she
soft and low. ___ Said she, "Young man, I'll ___ be your ___ bride, If I

lift - ed her eyes of ___ blue. ___ She smiled and ___ said, "Young man,
know ___ that you'll be ___ true." ___ Oh, in my ___ arms, all ___

I'm to wed; I'm to meet him in the fog - gy dew. ___
of her charms Were ___ cast - ed in the fog - gy dew. ___

THE FOGGY, FOGGY DEW

English Ballad

1. When I was a bach-'lor, I lived all a-lone, I worked at the weav-er's trade: ___ And the
2. One night she knelt close __ by my __ side, When I was __ fast a-sleep. ___ She
3. A-gain I am a bach-'lor, I live with my son, We work at the weav-er's trade; ___ And __

on-ly, on-ly thing I did that was wrong Was to woo a fair young maid. I
threw __ her arms a-round my __ neck, And __ then be-gan to weep. She
ev-'ry sin-gle time I look in-to his eyes He re-minds me of the fair young maid. He re-

wooed her in the win-ter-time, And in the sum-mer, too, And the
wept, she cried, she tore her hair. Ah, me, what could I do? So ___
minds me of the win-ter-time, And of the sum-mer, too, And the

on-ly, on-ly thing I did that was wrong Was to keep her from the fog-gy, fog-gy dew.
all __ night __ long I held her in my arms, Just to keep her from the fog-gy, fog-gy dew.
man-y, man-y times that I held her in my arms, Just to keep her from the fog-gy, fog-gy dew.

FOGGY MOUNTAIN TOP

American Bluegrass

If I was on some fog-gy moun-tain top, I'd sail a-

way to the West; I'd sail all a-round this whole wide ___

world to the girl I love the best. Yo-del-lay-ee-

o, a-lay-ee-ay yay-ee-hee-ee-ee.

1. Now if you see that girl of ___ mine, there's
2. She caused me to weep and she caused me to moan, she
3. If I'd on-ly lis-tened to what my ma-ma said, I

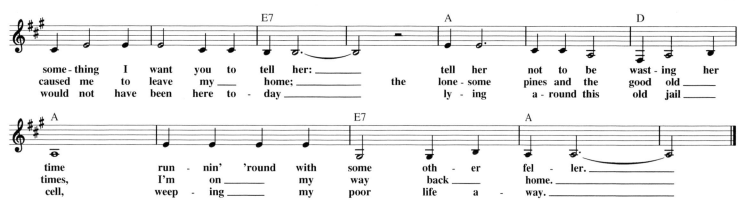

some-thing I want you to tell her:_____ tell her not to be wast-ing her
caused me to leave my____ home;_____ the lone-some pines and the good old____
would not have been here to - day_____ ly - ing a - round this old jail_____

time run - nin' 'round with some oth - er fel - ler._____
times, I'm on_____ my way back_____ home._____
cell, weep - ing_____ my poor life a - way._____

FOLLOW THE DRINKIN' GOURD

African-American Spiritual

1. When the sun comes back and the first quail calls,_____ Fol - low the drink - in' gourd, For the
2. Oh the riv - er bank makes a ve - ry true road.____ Dead trees will mark the way. The__
3. Where the riv - er ends in be - tween two hills,_____ Fol - low the drink - in' gourd. There the

Ole Man's wait - in' for to car - ry you to free - dom.⎫
left foot, peg - foot, trav - el - in' on.___ ⎬ Fol - low the drink - in' gourd.
Ole Man's wait - in' for to car - ry you to free - dom.⎭

Fol - low the drink - in' gourd,__ Fol - low the drink - in' gourd, For the

Ole Man is a - wait - in' for to car - ry you to free - dom. Fol - low the drink - in' gourd._____

FOR KANSAS

American

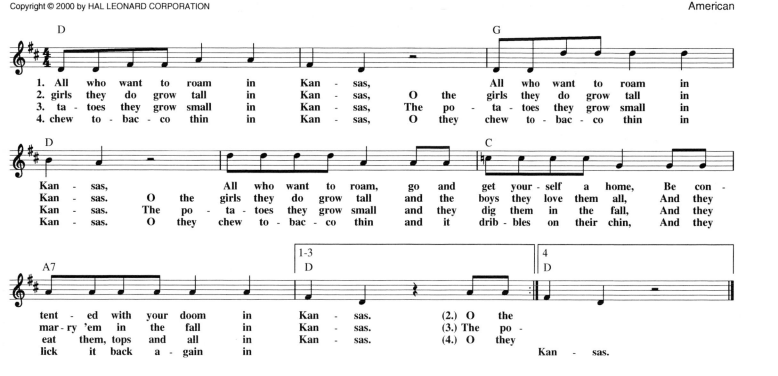

1. All who want to roam in Kan - sas, All who want to roam in
2. girls they do grow tall in Kan - sas, O the girls they do grow tall in
3. ta - toes they grow small in Kan - sas, The po - ta - toes they grow small in
4. chew to - bac - co thin in Kan - sas, O they chew to - bac - co thin in

Kan - sas, All who want to roam, go and get your - self a home, Be con -
Kan - sas. O the girls they do grow tall, and the boys they love them all, And they
Kan - sas. The po - ta - toes they grow small and they dig them in the fall, And they
Kan - sas. O they chew to - bac - co thin and it drib - bles on their chin, And they

tent - ed with your doom in Kan - sas. (2.) O the
mar - ry 'em in the fall in Kan - sas. (3.) The po -
eat them, tops and all in Kan - sas. (4.) O they
lick it back a - gain in Kan - sas.

FOR HE'S A JOLLY GOOD FELLOW

English

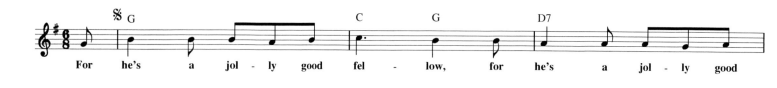

For he's a jol - ly good fel - low, for he's a jol - ly good

fel - low, for ___ he's a jol - ly good fel - low, which

no - bod - y can de - ny. ___ Which no - bod - y can de -

ny, ___ Which no - bod - y can de - ny. ___ For

THE FOUR MARYS

16th Century Scottish Ballad

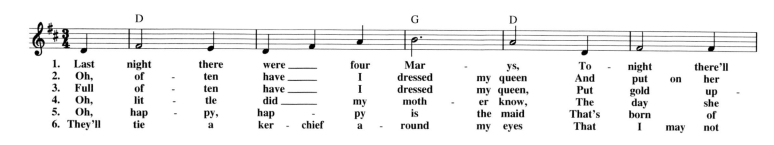

1. Last night there were ___ four Mar - ys, To - night there'll
2. Oh, of - ten have ___ I dressed my queen And put on her
3. Full of - ten have ___ I dressed my queen, Put gold up -
4. Oh, lit - tle did ___ my moth - er know, The day she
5. Oh, hap - py, hap - py is the maid That's born of
6. They'll tie a ker - chief a - round my eyes That I may not

be but three. ___ There was Mar - y Sea - ton and
braw silk gown, ___ But ___ all the thanks ___ I've
on her hair, ___ But ___ I have got ___ for
cra - dled me, ___ The ___ land I was ___ to
beau - ty free; ___ Oh, it was my ros - y,
see to dee, ___ And they'll nev - er tell my fa -

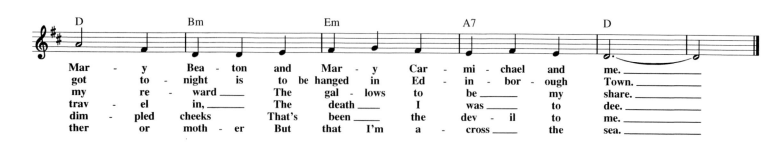

Mar - y Bea - ton and Mar - y Car - mi - chael and me. ___
got to - night is to be hanged in Ed - in - bor - ough Town. ___
my re - ward ___ The gal - lows to be ___ my share. ___
trav - el in, ___ The death ___ I was ___ to dee. ___
dim - pled cheeks That's been ___ the dev - il to me. ___
ther or moth - er But that I'm a - cross ___ the sea. ___

FOUR NIGHTS DRUNK

American

1. I came home the oth-er night as drunk as I could be. I saw a horse in the
2. I came home the sec-ond night as drunk as I could be. I saw a hat in the
3. I came home the third __ night as drunk as I could be. I saw some pants a -
4. I came home the fourth __ night as drunk as I could be. I saw a head on the

sta - ble where my horse ought to be.
clos - et where my hat ought to be.
hang - ing where my pants ought to be.
pil - low where my head ought to be.
So I said to my wife, my pret - ty lit - tle wife, "Now

won't you tell me, please: what's {this horse / this hat / these pants / this head} a - do - ing here where my {horse / hat / pants / head} ought to be?" She said, "You

darn fool, you drunk - en fool, can't you ev - er see? It's noth - ing but a

{milk - cow my cous - in / bed - pan my moth - er / ta - ble-cloth my un - cle / mel - on my fa - ther} gave to me." Well, I've trav-eled this wide world o - ver, ten

thou - sand miles or more, but a {sad - dle on a milk - cow, / bed-pan size sev-en and three quar - ters, / zip - per in a ta - ble-cloth, / mous - tache on a mel - on,} I nev - er seen be - fore.

FREE LITTLE BIRD

American

1. I'm as free a lit - tle bird as I can be, _____ I'm as free a lit - tle
2. Car-ry me home, lit - tle bird - ie, car-ry me home, _____ Car-ry me home, lit - tle
3. I'll _____ nev - er build my nest _____ on the ground, _____ Nei - ther in the

bird as I _____ can be. _____ I'm as free at my age as a
bird - ie, car - ry me home. _____ Car - ry me home to my wife, she's the
forks _____ of _____ a tree. _____ I'll build my nest in the

bird - ie in the cage, I'm as free a lit - tle bird as I can be. _____
joy of _____ my life, Car - ry me home, lit - tle bird - ie, car-ry me home. _____
ruf - fle of her dress, Where the bad boys _____ can nev - er both - er me. _____

FOUR PENCE A DAY

English

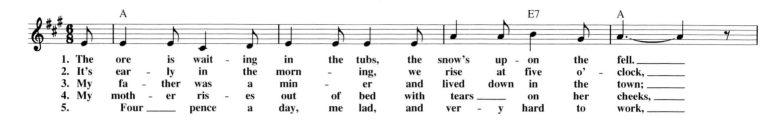

1. The ore is wait - ing in the tubs, the snow's up - on the fell. _____
2. It's ear - ly in the morn - ing, we rise at five o' - clock, _____
3. My fa - ther was a min - er and lived down in the town; _____
4. My moth - er ris - es out of bed with tears ____ on her cheeks, ____
5. Four ____ pence a day, me lad, and ver - y hard to work, _____

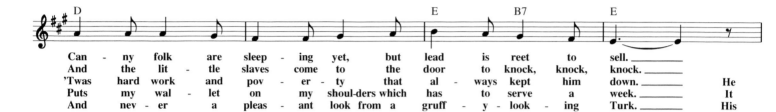

Can - ny folk are sleep - ing yet, but lead is reet to sell. _____
And the lit - tle slaves come to the door to knock, knock, knock. _____ He
'Twas hard work and pov - er - ty that al - ways kept him down. _____ He
Puts my wal - let on my shoul-ders which has to serve a week. _____ It
And nev - er a pleas - ant look from a gruff - y - look - ing Turk. _____ His

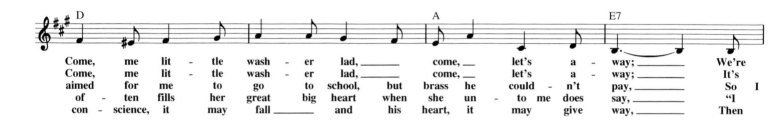

Come, me lit - tle wash - er lad, _____ come, __ let's a - way; _____ We're
Come, me lit - tle wash - er lad, _____ come, __ let's a - way; _____ It's
aimed for me to go to school, but brass he could - n't pay, _____ So I
of - ten fills her great big heart when she un - to me does say, _____ "I
con - science, it may fall _____ and his heart, it may give way, _____ Then

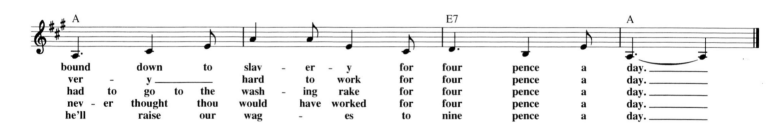

bound down to slav - er - y for four pence a day. _____
ver - y _____ hard to work for four pence a day. _____
had to go to the wash - ing rake for four pence a day. _____
nev - er thought thou would have worked for four pence a day. _____
he'll raise our wag - es to nine pence a day. _____

THE FOX

19th Century American

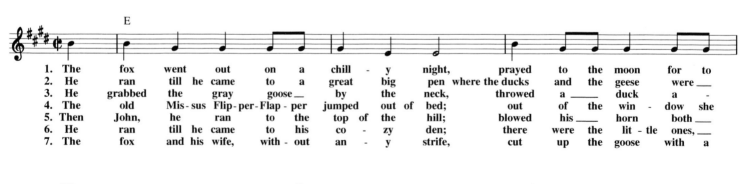

1. The fox went out on a chill - y night, prayed to the moon for to
2. He ran till he came to a great big pen where the ducks and the geese were __
3. He grabbed the gray goose __ by the neck, throwed a ____ duck a -
4. The old Mis - sus Flip-per-Flap-per jumped out of bed; out of the win - dow she
5. Then John, he ran to the top of the hill; blowed his ____ horn both __
6. He ran till he came to his co - zy den; there were the lit - tle ones, __
7. The fox and his wife, with - out an - y strife, cut up the goose with a

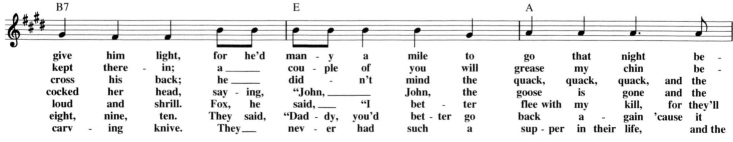

give him light, for he'd man - y a mile to go that night be -
kept there - in; a _____ cou - ple of you will grease my chin be -
cross his back; he _____ did - n't mind the quack, quack, quack, and the
cocked her head, say - ing, "John, _____ John, the goose is gone and the
loud and shrill. Fox, he said, ____ "I bet - ter flee with my kill, for they'll
eight, nine, ten. They said, "Dad - dy, you'd bet - ter go back a - gain 'cause it
carv - ing knive. They ____ nev - er had such a sup - per in their life, and the

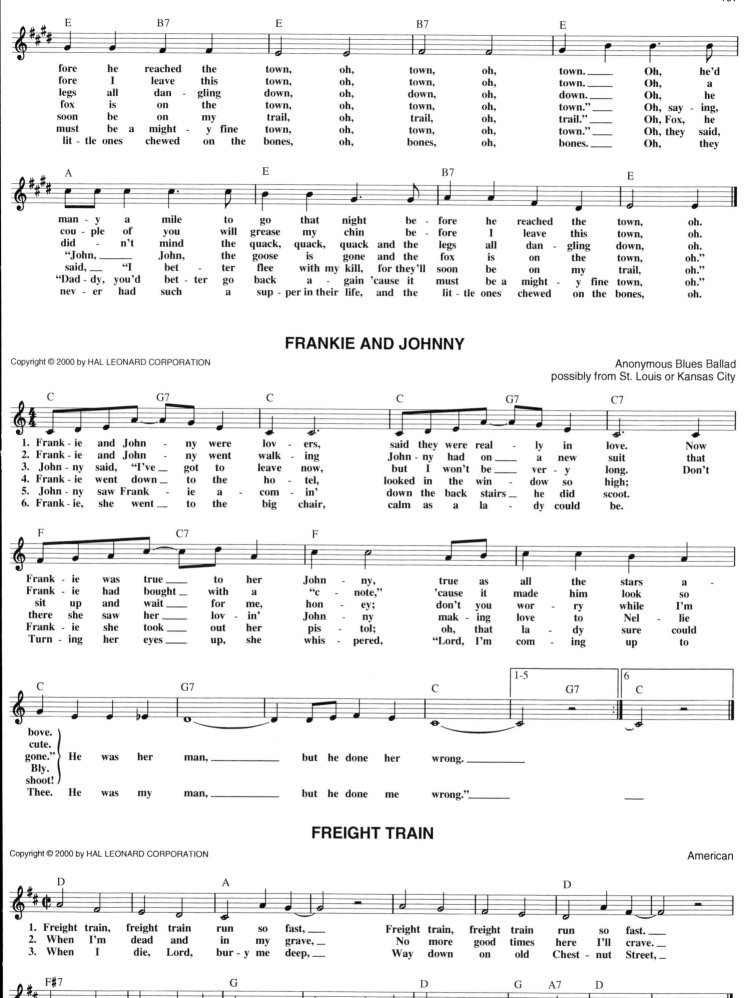

fore	he	reached	the	town,	oh,	town,	oh,	town.___	Oh, he'd
fore	I	leave	this	town,	oh,	town,	oh,	town.___	Oh, a
legs	all	dan -	gling	down,	oh,	down,	oh,	down.___	Oh, he
fox	is	on	the	town,	oh,	town,	oh,	town."___	Oh, say - ing,
soon	be	on	my	trail,	oh,	trail,	oh,	trail."___	Oh, Fox, he
must	be	a	might - y fine	town,	oh,	town,	oh,	town."___	Oh, they said,
lit - tle ones	chewed	on	the	bones,	oh,	bones,	oh,	bones.___	Oh, they

man - y a mile to go that night be - fore he reached the town, oh.
cou - ple of you will grease my chin be - fore I leave this town, oh.
did - n't mind the quack, quack, quack and the legs all dan - gling down, oh.
"John, ___ John, the goose is gone and the fox is on the town, oh."
said, ___ "I bet - ter flee with my kill, for they'll soon be on my trail, oh."
"Dad - dy, you'd bet - ter go back a - gain 'cause it must be a might - y fine town, oh."
nev - er had such a sup - per in their life, and the lit - tle ones chewed on the bones, oh.

FRANKIE AND JOHNNY

Copyright © 2000 by HAL LEONARD CORPORATION

Anonymous Blues Ballad
possibly from St. Louis or Kansas City

1. Frank - ie and John - ny were lov - ers, said they were real - ly in love. Now
2. Frank - ie and John - ny went walk - ing John - ny had on ___ a new suit that
3. John - ny said, "I've ___ got to leave now, but I won't be ___ ver - y long. Don't
4. Frank - ie went down ___ to the ho - tel, looked in the win - dow so high;
5. John - ny saw Frank - ie a - com - in' down the back stairs ___ he did scoot.
6. Frank - ie, she went ___ to the big chair, calm as a la - dy could be.

Frank - ie was true ___ to her John - ny, true as all the stars a -
Frank - ie had bought ___ with a "c - note," 'cause it made him look so
sit up and wait ___ for me, hon - ey; don't you wor - ry while I'm
there she saw her ___ lov - in' John - ny mak - ing love to Nel - lie
Frank - ie she took ___ out her pis - tol; oh, that la - dy sure could
Turn - ing her eyes ___ up, she whis - pered, "Lord, I'm com - ing up to

bove. }
cute. }
gone." } He was her man, _____ but he done her wrong. _____
Bly. }
shoot! }
Thee. He was my man, _____ but he done me wrong."_____

FREIGHT TRAIN

Copyright © 2000 by HAL LEONARD CORPORATION

American

1. Freight train, freight train run so fast, ___ Freight train, freight train run so fast. ___
2. When I'm dead and in my grave, ___ No more good times here I'll crave. ___
3. When I die, Lord, bur - y me deep, ___ Way down on old Chest - nut Street, ___

Please don't tell what ___ train I'm on, ___ They won't know what ___ route I've gone. _____
Place the stones at my head and feet, And tell them all that I've gone to sleep. _____
So I can hear old Num - ber Nine ___ As ___ she comes ___ roll - ing by.

FREEDOM

Caribbean Spiritual

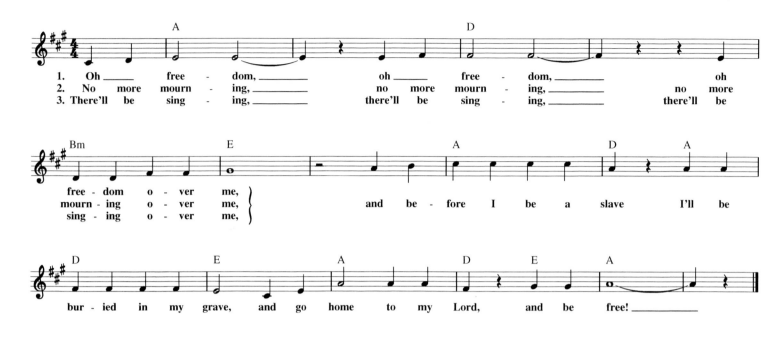

1. Oh ____ free - dom, _____ oh ____ free - dom, _____ oh
2. No more mourn - ing, _____ no more mourn - ing, _____ no more
3. There'll be sing - ing, _____ there'll be sing - ing, _____ there'll be

free - dom o - ver me,
mourn - ing o - ver me,   and be - fore I be a slave I'll be
sing - ing o - ver me,

bur - ied in my grave, and go home to my Lord, and be free! _____

THE FROG IN THE BOG

Canadian

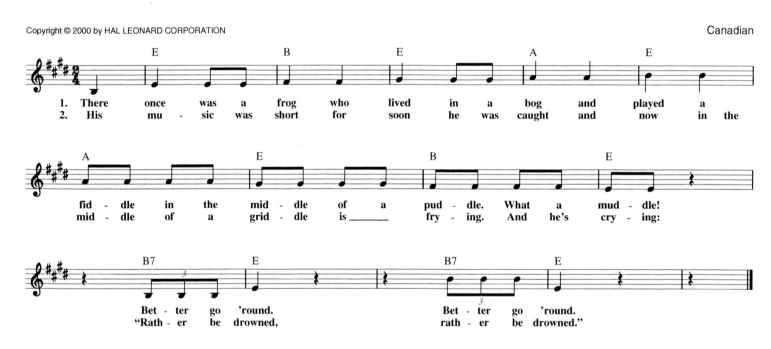

1. There once was a frog who lived in a bog and played a
2. His mu - sic was short for soon he was caught and now in the

fid - dle in the mid - dle of a pud - dle. What a mud - dle!
mid - dle of a grid - dle is ____ fry - ing. And he's cry - ing:

Bet - ter go 'round.   Bet - ter go 'round.
"Rath - er be drowned,   rath - er be drowned."

FREE AT LAST

African-American Spiritual

Free at last, free at last, I thank God I'm free at last; Free at last, free at last, ____

To Coda
I thank God I'm free at last. Oh free at last.

1. Way down yon - der in the
2. On my knees ____ when the
3. Some of these ____ morn - ings

grave - yard walk,)
light passed by, } I thank God I'm free at last,
bright and fair,)

Me and my Je - sus gon - na
Thought _ my soul _ would _
Gon - na meet my Je - sus in the

1st time D.C.
2nd time D.C. al Coda   CODA
(with repeats)

meet and talk, ___)
rise and fly, ___ } I thank God I'm free at last. Oh,
mid-dle of the air, ___)

free at last.

FROG WENT A-COURTIN'

Folksong from Kentucky

1. Frog went a-court-in' and he did ride, A - huh, a - huh, Frog went a-court-in' and
2.-15. *(See additional lyrics)*

he did ride, A sword and pis - tol _ by his side, A - huh, a - huh.

Additional Lyrics

2. Well, he rode down to Miss Mouses's door, a-huh, a-huh,
Well, he rode down to Miss Mouses's door,
Where he had often been before, a-huh, a-huh.

3. He took Miss Mousie on his knee, a-huh, a-huh,
He took Miss Mousie on his knee,
Said, "Miss Mousie will you marry me?" A-huh, a-huh.

4. "I'll have to ask my Uncle Rat, etc.
See what he will say to that.", etc.

5. "Without my Uncle Rat's consent,
I would not marry the President."

6. Well, Uncle Rat laughed and shook his fat sides,
To think his niece would be a bride.

7. Well, Uncle Rat rode off to town
To buy his niece a wedding gown.

8. "Where will the wedding supper be?"
"Way down yonder in a hollow tree."

9. "What will the wedding supper be?"
"A fried mosquito and a roasted flea."

10. First to come in were two little ants,
Fixing around to have a dance.

11. Next to come in was a bumble bee,
Bouncing a fiddle on his knee.

12. Next to come in was a fat sassy lad,
Thinks himself as big as his dad.

13. Thinks himself a man indeed,
Because he chews the tobacco weed.

14. And next to come in was a big tomcat,
He swallowed the frog and the mouse and the rat.

15. Next to come in was a big old snake,
He chased the party into the lake.

FROM ERIN'S SHORES

Words by Florence Hoare
Traditional Irish Melody
("The Flight of the Earls")

1. From Er - in's shores _ we ___ sailed a - way, while morn was sleep - ing ___
2. Though mem - o - ry ___ should _ smil - ing come to cheer the dis - tant ___
3. Yet sang the breez - es ___ in our ear like beat of mar - tial ___

yet. We saw our home _ a - cross the bay, and ev - 'ry eye ___ was
shore, the sim - ple joys _ of ___ hearth and home would be our own no ___
feet, and fame to Er - in's ___ heart is dear, am - bi - tion's paths _ are ___

wet. The flap - ping sails a wel - come threw, tri - um - phant sang the winds, but
more. As some dear face seems fair - er grown be - neath a lov - ing eye, So
sweet. And so we turned and sailed a - way while morn was sleep - ing yet, but

we looked back ___ o'er ___ vales we knew to loved ones left ___ be - hind.
Er - in wore ___ a ___ grace un - known the day we said ___ good - bye.
Er - in's Isle ___ and ___ Er - in's smile we nev - er shall ___ for - get.

FULLER AND WARREN

American

1. Ye sons of Co - lum - bia, your at - ten - tion I do crave while a sor - row-ful sto - ry I will
2. A gold ring he gave her as a to - ken of true love, and the flow'r was the im - age of a
3. When Ful - ler came to hear he was de - prived _ of his dear whom he'd vowed by the pow - ers to _____
4. Then War - ren re - plied, _ "Your re - quest must be de - nied, for my heart to your true _ love is
5. The time it drew nigh ___ when _ Ful - ler was to die; he ___ smiled _ and bid the world a -
6. The might - y God of love ___ looked with sor - row from a - bove; and the rope flew a - sun - der like the

tell, which hap - pened of late in the In - di - an - a state, of a he - ro that none _ could ex -
dove. They mu - tual - ly a - greed to be mar - ried in speed, and were prom-ised by the pow - ers a -
wed, with his heart full of woe, straight to War - ren he did go, and _ smil - ing, to War - ren he
dieu. Like an an - gel he did stand, for he was a hand-some man; on his breast he wore a rib - bon of
sand. Two doc - tors for the pay they did mur - der him, they say, and hung him by the main _ strength of

cel. Like Sam - son, he court - ed the choice of the fair and in -
bove. But, fick - le - mind - ed maid - en, she vowed she would wed young _
said: "Oh, War - ren, you've done a wrong to grat - i - fy your cause by _____
town." Then Ful - ler, in the pas - sion of love and an - ger bound, which at
blue. Ten thou - sand spec - ta - tors then smote up - on their breasts, and the
hand. But the corpse, it was bur - ied and the doc - tors lost their prey; oh, that

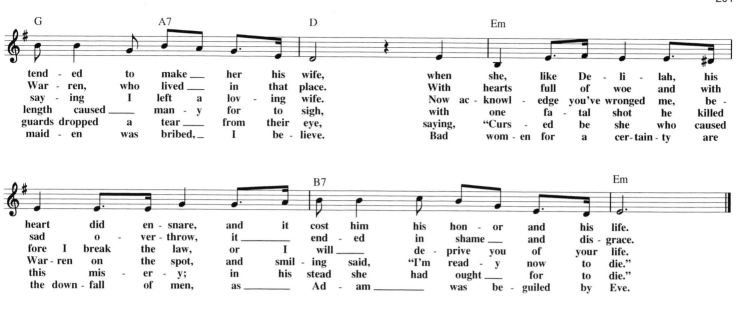

THE GAL THAT GOT STUCK ON EVERYTHING SHE SAW

By Uncle Dave Macon

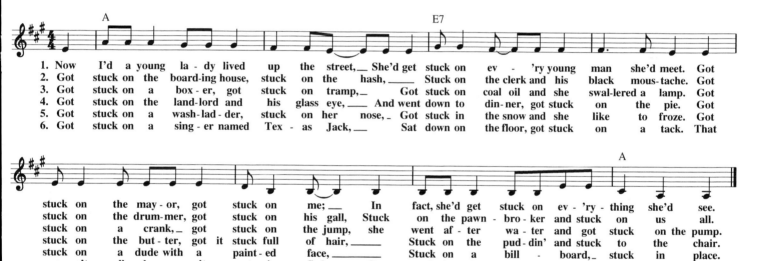

THE GALLOWS POLE

English Ballad

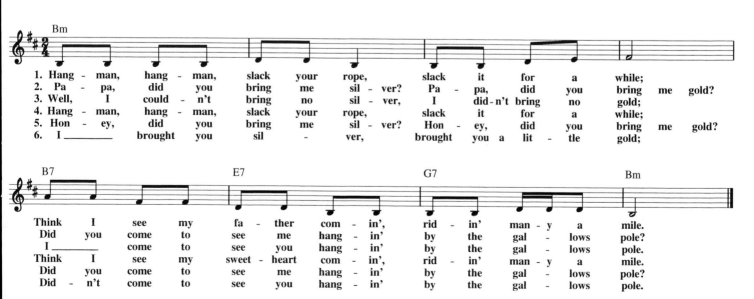

FUNICULI, FUNICULA!

Italian
Written by Luigi Denza, circa 1880

THE GALWAY PIPER

Irish

1. Ev - 'ry per - son in the na - tion or of great or hum - ble sta - tion
2. When the wed - ding bells are ring - ing, his the breath that stirs the sing - ing.
3. When he walks the high - way peal - ing, 'round his head the birds come wheel - ing.

holds in high - est es - ti - ma - tion, Pip - ing Tim of Gal - way.
Then in jigs the folks go swing - ing. What a splen - did pip - er!
Tim has car - ols worth the steal - ing, Pip - ing Tim of Gal - way.

Loud - ly he can play, or low. He can move you, fast or slow.
He will blow from eve to morn, count - ing sleep a thing of scorn.
Thrush and lin - net, finch and lark to each oth - er twit - ter "Hark!"

Touch your hearts or stir your toe. Pip - ing Tim of Gal - way.
Old is he, but not out - worn. Know you such a pip - er?
Soon they sing from light to dark. Pip - ings learnt in Gal - way.

GARRYOWEN

Irish

1. Let Bac - chus' sons be not dis - mayed, but join with me each
2. We are the boys that take de - light in smash - ing the lime - rick lights
3. We'll break the win - dows, we'll break the doors, the watch knock down by
4. We'll beat the bail - iffs out of fun, we'll make the may - ors and
5. Our hearts so stout have got us fame, for soon 'tis known from

jo - vi - al blade. Come booze and sing and lend your aid, to
when light - ing. Through all the streets like sport - ers fight - ing, and
threes and fours. Then let the doc - tors work their cures, and
sher - iffs run. We are the boys no man dares dun, if
whence we came. Wher - e'er we go they dread the name of

help me with the cho - rus.
tear - ing all be - fore us.
tink - er up our brui - ses. In - stead of spa we'll
he re - gards a whole skin.
Gar - ry - o - wen in glo - ry.

drink down ale and pay the reck - 'ning on the nail. No man for debt shall

go to jail from Gar - ry - o - wen in glo - ry.

GEE, MA, I WANT TO GO HOME

U.S. Army Song from World War I

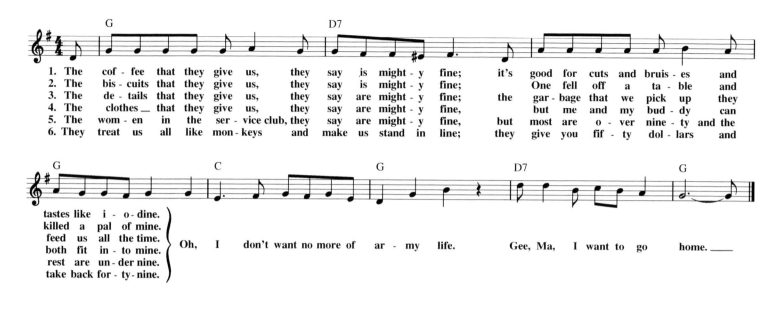

1. The cof-fee that they give us, they say is might-y fine; it's good for cuts and bruis-es and
2. The bis-cuits that they give us, they say is might-y fine; One fell off a ta-ble and
3. The de-tails that they give us, they say are might-y fine; the gar-bage that we pick up they
4. The clothes _ that they give us, they say are might-y fine, but me and my bud-dy can
5. The wom-en in the ser-vice club, they say are might-y fine, but most are o-ver nine-ty and the
6. They treat us all like mon-keys and make us stand in line; they give you fif-ty dol-lars and

tastes like i - o-dine.
killed a pal of mine.
feed us all the time.
both fit in - to mine. } Oh, I don't want no more of ar-my life.   Gee, Ma, I want to go home. _____
rest are un-der nine.
take back for-ty-nine.

GEORDIE

Canadian

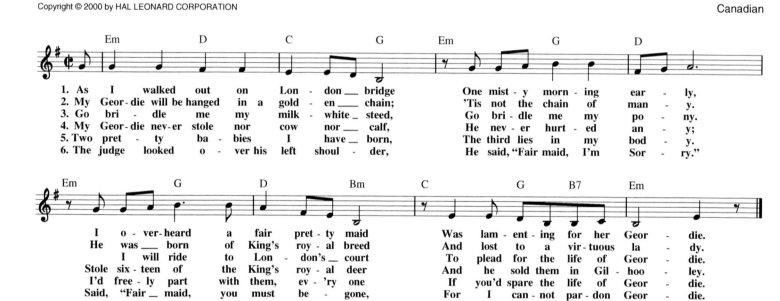

1. As I walked out on Lon-don _ bridge   One mist-y morn-ing ear - ly,
2. My Geor-die will be hanged in a gold - en _ chain;   'Tis not the chain of man - y.
3. Go bri - dle me my milk - white _ steed,   Go bri-dle me my po - ny.
4. My Geor-die nev-er stole nor cow nor _ calf,   He nev - er hurt - ed an - y;
5. Two pret - ty ba - bies I have _ born,   The third lies in my bod - y.
6. The judge looked o - ver his left shoul - der,   He said, "Fair maid, I'm Sor - ry."

I o-ver-heard a fair pret - ty maid   Was lam-ent-ing for her Geor - die.
He was _ born of King's roy - al breed   And lost to a vir - tuous la - dy.
I will ride to Lon - don's _ court   To plead for the life of Geor - die.
Stole six - teen of the King's roy - al deer   And he sold them in Gil - hoo - ley.
I'd free - ly part with them, ev - 'ry one   If you'd spare the life of Geor - die.
Said, "Fair _ maid, you must be - gone,   For I can - not par - don Geor - die.

GEORGE COLLINS

19th Century English Ballad

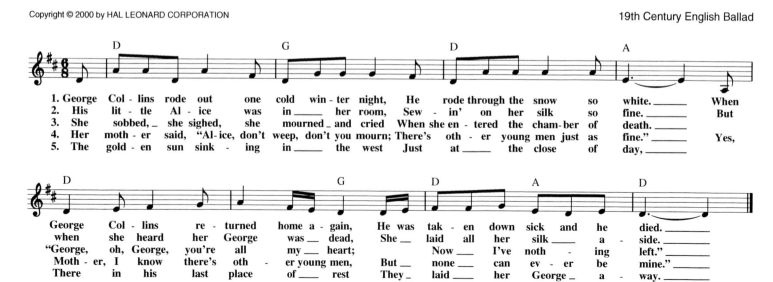

1. George Col - lins rode out one cold win - ter night, He rode through the snow so white. _____ When
2. His lit - tle Al - ice was in _ her room, Sew - in' on her silk so fine. _____ But
3. She sobbed, _ she sighed, she mourned _ and cried When she en - tered the cham-ber of death. _____
4. Her moth - er said, "Al-ice, don't weep, don't you mourn; There's oth - er young men just as fine." _____ Yes,
5. The gold - en sun sink - ing in _ the west Just at _ the close of day, _____

George Col - lins re - turned home a - gain, He was tak - en down sick and he died. _____
when she heard her George was _ dead, She _ laid all her silk _ a - side. _____
"George, oh, George, you're all my _ heart; Now _ I've noth - ing left." _____
Moth - er, I know there's oth - er young men, But _ none _ can ev - er be mine." _____
There in his last place of _ rest They _ laid _ her George _ a - way. _____

GET UP, JACK!

19th Century American

1. Ships may come and ships may go, as long as the sea does roll; Each sail - or lad, like -
2. Jack's a - shore, he beats his way ___ to some _ board - ing house; He's wel - comed in with
3. Jack is old and weath - er - beat - en, too old to knock a - bout, In some grog - shop they'll

wise his dad, he loves that flow - ing bowl. A lass a - shore he does a - dore,
rum and gin, like - wise with port and souse. He'll spend and spend and nev - er of - fend, till
let him stop, till eight bells he's turned out. Then he cries and sighs right up to the skies,

one that is plump and round, ___ But when his
he lies drunk on the ground, _ But when his } mon - ey is gone, it's the same old song: 'Get
"Good Lord, I'm home - ward bound," _ For when your

up, Jack! John, sit down!' Come a - long, come a - long, my jol - ly brave tars, There's lots of grog in the

| 1,2 D | 3 D |

jar, ___ We'll plough the brin - y o - cean With those jol - ly rov - ing tars. (2.,3.) When tars.

THE GIRL I LEFT BEHIND ME

19th Century Irish

1. The ___ hour was sad I left the maid, A lin - g'ring fare - well ___
2. Then ___ to the East we bore a - way To win a name ___ in ___
3. Full ___ man - y a name our ban - ners bore Of for - mer deeds ___ of ___
4. The ___ hope of fi - nal vic - to - ry With - in my bos - om ___
5. The ___ dames of France are fond and free, And Flem - ish lips ___ are ___

tak - ing, Her ___ sighs and tears my steps de - layed; I thought her heart was ___
sto - ry, And ___ there, where dawns the sun of day, There dawned our sun of ___
dar - ing, But ___ they were of the days of yore, In which we had no ___
burn - ing, Is ___ min - gled with sweet thoughts of thee, And of my fond re -
will - ing, And ___ soft the maids of It - a - ly, While Span - ish eyes are ___

break - ing. In ___ hur - ried words her name I blessed, I breathed the vows that
glo - ry. Both ___ blazed in noon on Al - ma's heights When, in the past as -
shar - ing. But ___ now our lau - rels fresh - ly won With the old ones shall en -
turn - ing. But ___ should I ne'er re - turn a - gain, Still worth thy love thou'lt
thrill - ing. Still ___ though I bask be - neath their smile, Their charms quite fail to

bind me, And ___ to my heart in an - guish pressed The girl I left be - hind me.
signed me, I ___ shared the glo - ry of that fight, Sweet girl I left be - hind me.
twined be, Still ___ wor - thy of his sire each son, Sweet girl I left be - hind me.
find me; Dis - hon - or's breath shall nev - er stain The name I leave be - hind me.
bind me, And my heart falls back to Er - in's Isle To the girl I left be - hind me.

GIN I WERE

Scottish

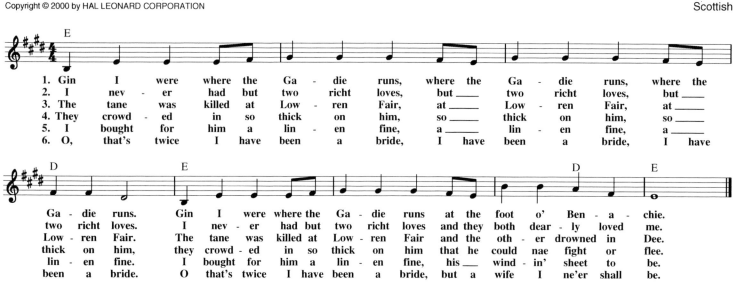

1. Gin I were where the Ga - die runs, where the Ga - die runs, where the
2. I nev - er had but two richt loves, but ____ two richt loves, but ____
3. The tane was killed at Low - ren Fair, at ____ Low - ren Fair, at ____
4. They crowd - ed in so thick on him, so ____ thick on him, so ____
5. I bought for him a lin - en fine, a ____ lin - en fine, a ____
6. O, that's twice I have been a bride, I have been a bride, I have

Ga - die runs. Gin I were where the Ga - die runs at the foot o' Ben - a - chie.
two richt loves. I nev - er had but two richt loves and they both dear - ly loved me.
Low - ren Fair. The tane was killed at Low - ren Fair and the oth - er drowned in Dee.
thick on him, they crowd - ed in so thick on him that he could nae fight or flee.
lin - en fine. I bought for him a lin - en fine, his ____ wind - in' sheet to be.
been a bride. O that's twice I have been a bride, but a wife I ne'er shall be.

GIT ALONG, LITTLE DOGIES

American Cowboy Song

1. As I was a - walk - ing one morn - ing for pleas - ure, I
2. Ear - ly in the spring we round up all the do - gies. We
3. whoop - ing and yell - ing and round - ing the do - gies from

saw a cow - punch - er come rid - ing a - long. His hat was throwed
mark 'em and brand 'em and bob off their tails. Round up our
sun - rise till sun - set and all the their night long. So come now, you

back and his spurs was a - jing - ling, and as he ap - proached he was
hors - es, load ____ up the chuck ____ wag - on. Throw all them do - gies right
young o - ver the ____ prai - rie and keep right on hear - ing my

sing - ing this song. }
up - on the trail. } Whoop - ee - ti - yi - yo, git a - long, lit - tle
beau - ti - ful song. }

do - gies! It's your mis - for - tune and none of my ____ own. Whoop - ee -

ti - yi - yo, git a - long, lit - tle do - gies! You know that Wy

o - ming will be your new home.

1. home.
2. home. Well, it's
3. home.

GIVE ME THAT OLD TIME RELIGION

Southern American

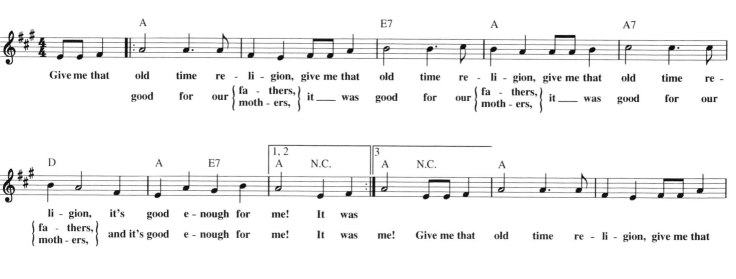

GO DOWN, MOSES

Traditional American Spiritual

GO IN AND OUT THE VILLAGE

Traditional American Ring Game Song

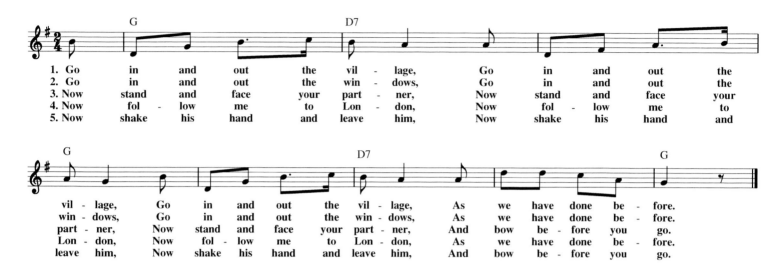

1. Go in and out the vil - lage, Go in and out the
2. Go in and out the win - dows, Go in and out the
3. Now stand and face your part - ner, Now stand and face your
4. Now fol - low me to Lon - don, Now fol - low me to
5. Now shake his hand and leave him, Now shake his hand and

vil - lage, Go in and out the vil - lage, As we have done be - fore.
win - dows, Go in and out the win - dows, As we have done be - fore.
part - ner, Now stand and face your part - ner, And bow be - fore you go.
Lon - don, Now fol - low me to Lon - don, As we have done be - fore.
leave him, Now shake his hand and leave him, And bow be - fore you go.

GO TELL AUNT RHODY

American

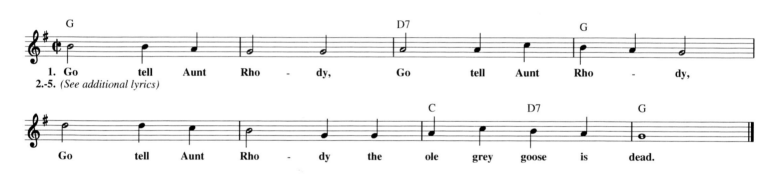

1. Go tell Aunt Rho - dy, Go tell Aunt Rho - dy,
2.-5. *(See additional lyrics)*

Go tell Aunt Rho - dy the ole grey goose is dead.

Additional Lyrics

2. The one she was saving, *(three times)*
   To make a feather bed.

3. The gander is weeping, *(three times)*
   Because his wife is dead.

4. The goslings are crying, *(three times)*
   Because their mama's dead.

5. She died in the water, *(three times)*
   With her heels above her head.

GO, TELL IT ON THE MOUNTAIN

African-American Spiritual
Verses by John W. Work, Jr., 1907

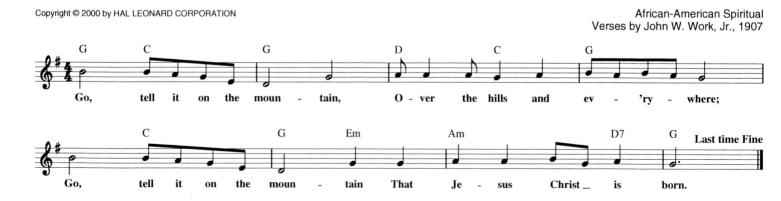

Go, tell it on the moun - tain, O - ver the hills and ev - 'ry - where;

Go, tell it on the moun - tain That Je - sus Christ is born.

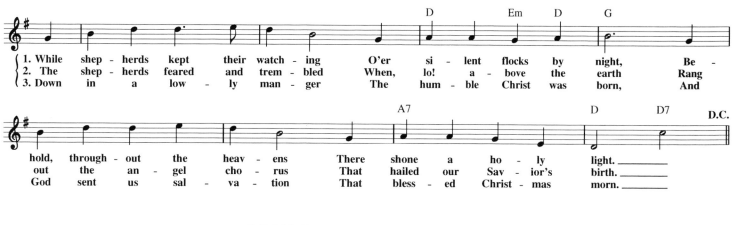

| D | Em | D | G |

1. While shep - herds kept their watch - ing O'er si - lent flocks by night, Be -
2. The shep - herds feared and trem - bled When, lo! a - bove the earth Rang
3. Down in a low - ly man - ger The hum - ble Christ was born, And

| A7 | | D | D7 | D.C. |

hold, through - out the heav - ens There shone a ho - ly light. _____
out the an - gel cho - rus That hailed our Sav - ior's birth. _____
God sent us sal - va - tion That bless - ed Christ - mas morn. _____

GO TO SLEEP MY LITTLE BABY
(Duérmete Niño Chiquito)

Venezuelan

E

1. Go to sleep my lit - tle ba - by _____
2. If this ba - by is not sleep - y, _____
1. *Duér - me - te ni - ño chi - qui - to _____*
2. *Si es - te ni - ño no se duer - me, _____*

Am / B / Em

For your moth - er is not here _____
If he will not close his eyes. _____
Que tu ma - dre no es - tá a - quí, _____
Que no - che pa - sa - ré yo! _____

Am / B / Em

She has gone to fetch some gua - vas _____
I shall pass the night in vig - il, _____
Que se fué a bus - car gua - ya - bas _____
Pa - sa - ré la no - che en ve - la, _____

Am / B / Em

All the best for you, my dear. _____
Sing - ing end - less lul - la - bies. _____
Las me - jo - res pa - ra tí. _____
Can - tán - do - le el a - rro - rro. _____

GO 'WAY FROM MY WINDOW

By John Jacob Niles

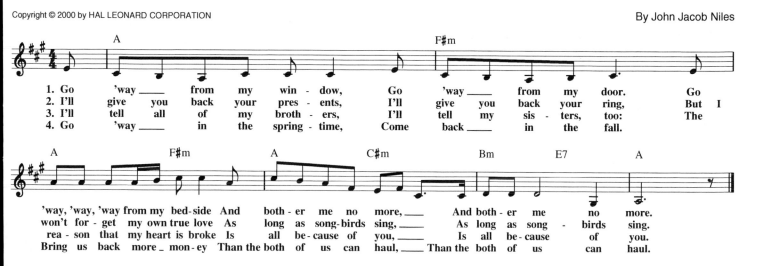

A / F#m

1. Go 'way _____ from my win - dow, Go 'way _____ from my door. Go
2. I'll give you back your pres - ents, I'll give you back your ring, But I
3. I'll tell all of my broth - ers, I'll tell my sis - ters, too: The
4. Go 'way _____ in the spring - time, Come back _____ in the fall.

A / F#m / A / C#m / Bm / E7 / A

'way, 'way, 'way from my bed - side And both - er me no more, _____ And both - er me no more.
won't for - get my own true love As long as song - birds sing, _____ As long as song - birds sing.
rea - son that my heart is broke Is all be - cause of you, _____ Is all be - cause of you.
Bring us back more _ mon - ey Than the both of us can haul, _____ Than the both of us can haul.

GOD SAVE THE KING

17th or 18th Century English
sometimes attributed to Henry Carey, 1740

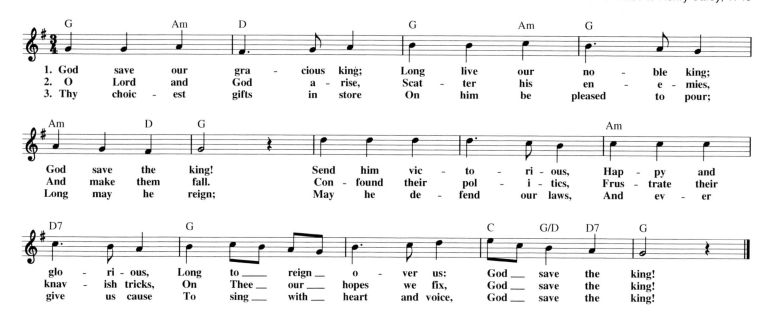

1. God save our gra - cious king; Long live our no - ble king;
2. O Lord and God a - rise, Scat - ter his en - e - mies,
3. Thy choic - est gifts in store On him be pleased to pour;

God save the king! Send him vic - to - ri - ous, Hap - py and
And make them fall. Con - found their pol - i - tics, Frus - trate their
Long may he reign; May he de - fend our laws, And ev - er

glo - ri - ous, Long to ___ reign ___ o - ver us: God ___ save the king!
knav - ish tricks, On Thee ___ our ___ hopes we fix, God ___ save the king!
give us cause To sing ___ with ___ heart and voice, God ___ save the king!

GOIN' ACROSS THE MOUNTAIN

American Civil War Song

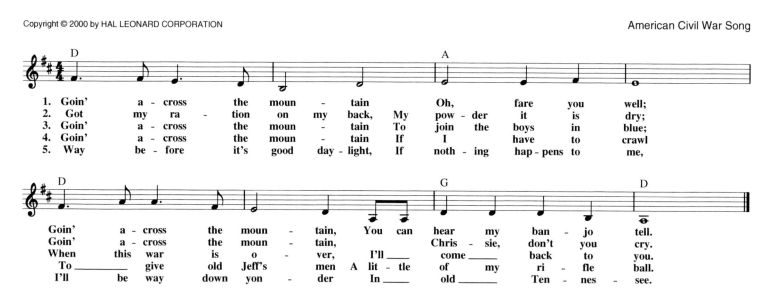

1. Goin' a - cross the moun - tain Oh, fare you well;
2. Got my ra - tion on my back, My pow - der it is dry;
3. Goin' a - cross the moun - tain To join the boys in blue;
4. Goin' a - cross the moun - tain If I have to crawl
5. Way be - fore it's good day - light, If noth - ing hap - pens to me,

Goin' a - cross the moun - tain, You can hear my ban - jo tell.
Goin' a - cross the moun - tain, Chris - sie, don't you cry.
When this war is o - ver, I'll ___ come back to you.
To ___ give old Jeff's men A lit - tle of my ri - fle ball.
I'll be way down yon - der In old ___ Ten - nes - see.

GOIN' TO GERMANY

American Folksong
from World War I

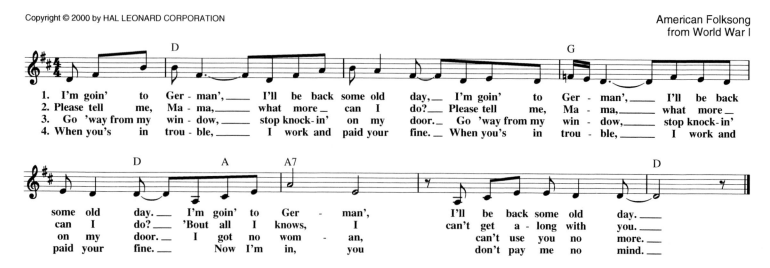

1. I'm goin' to Ger - man', ___ I'll be back some old day, ___ I'm goin' to Ger - man', ___ I'll be back
2. Please tell me, Ma - ma, ___ what more can I do? ___ Please tell me, Ma - ma, ___ what more
3. Go 'way from my win - dow, ___ stop knock - in' on my door. ___ Go 'way from my win - dow, ___ stop knock - in'
4. When you's in trou - ble, ___ I work and paid your fine. ___ When you's in trou - ble, ___ I work and

some old day. ___ I'm goin' to Ger - man', I'll be back some old day. ___
can I do? ___ 'Bout all I knows, I can't get a - long with you. ___
on my door. ___ I got no wom - an, can't use you no more. ___
paid your fine. ___ Now I'm in, you don't pay me no mind. ___

GOLDEN SLUMBERS

17th Century English

1. Gold - en slum - bers kiss your eyes, Smiles __ a - wake you
2. Care __ you know not, there - fore sleep, While __ I o'er you

when you rise: } Sleep, pret - ty dar - ling, do __ not cry, __ And
watch do keep: }

I will sing a lull - a - by. Lull - a -

by, _____ lull - a - by. _____

GOOBER PEAS

Words by P. Pindar
Music by P. Nutt
American, from the Civil War

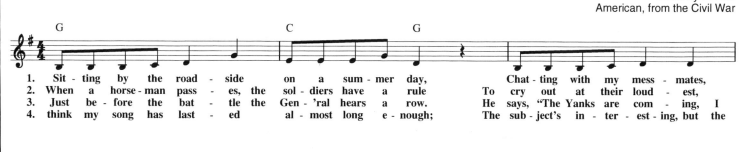

1. Sit - ting by the road - side on a sum - mer day, Chat - ting with my mess - mates,
2. When a horse - man pass - es, the sol - diers have a rule To cry out at their loud - est,
3. Just be - fore the bat - tle the Gen - 'ral hears a row. He says, "The Yanks are com - ing, I
4. think my song has last - ed al - most long e - nough; The sub - ject's in - ter - est - ing, but the

pass - ing time a - way, Ly - ing in the shad - ow un - der - neath the trees,
"Mis - ter, here's your mule!" But an - oth - er pleas - ure, en - chant - ing - er than these Is
hear their ri - fles now." He turns a - round in won - der and what do you think he sees? The
rhymes are might - y rough. I wish this war was o - ver, when free from rags and fleas, We'd

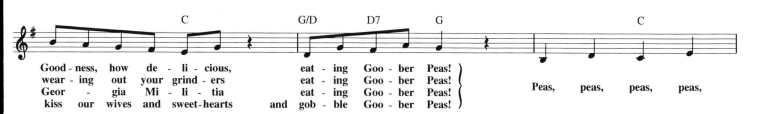

Good - ness, how de - li - cious, eat - ing Goo - ber Peas! }
wear - ing out your grind - ers eat - ing Goo - ber Peas! }
Geor - gia Mi - li - tia eat - ing Goo - ber Peas! }
kiss our wives and sweet-hearts and gob - ble Goo - ber Peas! }

Peas, peas, peas, peas,

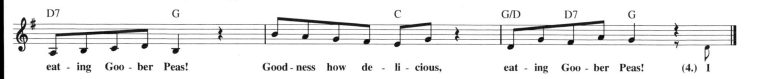

eat - ing Goo - ber Peas! Good - ness how de - li - cious, eat - ing Goo - ber Peas! (4.) I

GOIN' DOWN TO TOWN

Southern American

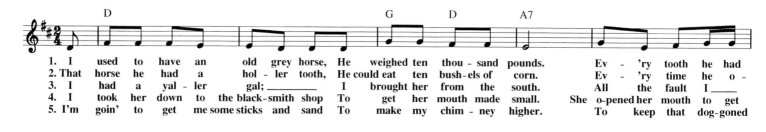

1. I used to have an old grey horse, He weighed ten thou-sand pounds. Ev - 'ry tooth he had
2. That horse he had a hol - ler tooth, He could eat ten bush-els of corn. Ev - 'ry time he o-
3. I had a yal - ler gal; I brought her from the south. All the fault I ____
4. I took her down to the black-smith shop To get her mouth made small. She o-pened her mouth to get
5. I'm goin' to get me some sticks and sand To make my chim - ney higher. To keep that dog-goned

in his head, Was eight - een inch-es a - round.
pened his mouth, Two bush - els and a half were gone.
had with her, She had too big a mouth.
a long breath, And swal-lowed black - smith, shop and all.
old tom cat From put - tin' out ___ my fire.

I'm a - go - in' down to town, I'm a -

go - in' down to town, I'm a - go - in' down to Lynch-burg town, To car - ry my to-bac - co down.

THE GOLDEN VANITY

17th Century English

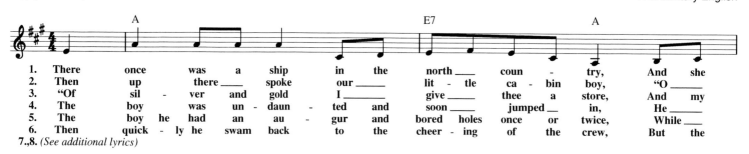

1. There once was a ship in the north ___ coun - try, And she
2. Then up there ___ spoke our ___ lit - tle ca - bin boy, "O ___
3. "Of sil - ver and gold I ___ give ___ thee a store, And my
4. The boy was un - daun - ted and soon ___ jumped ___ in, He ___
5. The boy he had an au - gur and bored holes once or twice, While ___
6. Then quick - ly he swam back to the cheer - ing of the crew, But the

7.,8. *(See additional lyrics)*

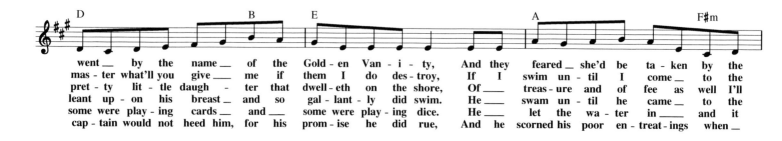

went ___ by the name ___ of the Gold - en Van - i - ty, And they feared ___ she'd be ta - ken by the
mas - ter what'll you give ___ me if them I do des - troy, If I swim un - til I come ___ to the
pret - ty lit - tle daugh - ter that dwell - eth on the shore, Of ___ treas - ure and of fee as well I'll
leant up - on his breast ___ and so gal - lant - ly did swim. He ___ swam un - til he came ___ to the
some were play - ing cards ___ and ___ some were play - ing dice. He ___ let the wa - ter in ___ and it
cap - tain would not heed him, for his prom - ise he did rue, And he scorned his poor en - treat-ings when ___

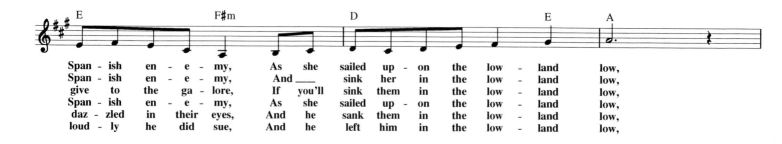

Span - ish en - e - my, As she sailed up - on the low - land low,
Span - ish en - e - my, And ___ sink her in the low - land low,
give to the ga - lore, If you'll sink them in the low - land low,
Span - ish en - e - my, As she sailed up - on the low - land low,
daz - zled in their eyes, And he sank them in the low - land low,
loud - ly he did sue, And he left him in the low - land low,

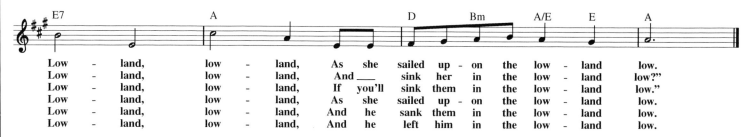

Low - land, low - land, As she sailed up - on the low - land low.
Low - land, low - land, And ___ sink her in the low - land low?"
Low - land, low - land, If you'll sink them in the low - land low."
Low - land, low - land, As she sailed up - on the low - land low.
Low - land, low - land, And he sank them in the low - land low.
Low - land, low - land, And he left him in the low - land low.

Additional Lyrics

7. Then the cabin boy did swim all to the larboard side,
His strength began to fail him, and bitterly he cried,
"O, messmates, take me up, for I'm drifting with the tide,
And I'm sinking in the lowland low,
Lowland, lowland,
And I'm sinking in the lowland low."

8. His messmates took him up, and on the deck he died,
And they wrapped his body up all in an old cow's hide;
And they threw him overboard to go with wind and tide,
And they sank him in the lowland low,
Lowland, lowland,
And they sank him in the lowland low.

THE GOOD BOY

American
By Lemuel F. Parton

1. I have led a good life, full of peace and qui - et, I shall have an old age
2. I have nev - er slit throats, e - ven when I yearned to, nev - er sang dir - ty songs

full of rum and ri - ot. I have been a good boy, wed to work and
that my fan - cy turned to. I have been a nice boy and done what was ex -

stud - y, I shall be an old man, ri - bald, coarse and blood - y.
pect - ed; I shall die an old bum, loved but un - re - spect - ed.

GOOD MORNING, MISTER RAILROADMAN

American

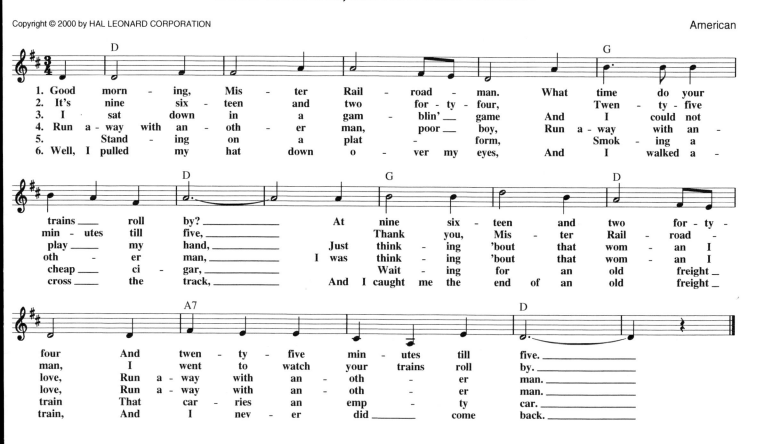

1. Good morn - ing, Mis - ter Rail - road - man. What time do your
2. It's nine six - teen and two for - ty - four, Twen - ty - five
3. I sat down in a gam - blin' ___ game And I could not
4. Run a - way with an - oth - er man, poor ___ boy, Run a - way with an -
5. Stand - ing on a plat - form, Smok - ing a
6. Well, I pulled my hat down o - ver my eyes, And I walked a -

trains ___ roll by? _____ At nine six - teen and two for - ty -
min - utes till five, _____ Thank you, Mis - ter Rail - road -
play ___ my hand, _____ Just think - ing 'bout that wom - an I
oth - er man, _____ I was think - ing 'bout that wom - an I
cheap ___ ci - gar, _____ Wait - ing for an old freight _
cross ___ the track, _____ And I caught me the end of an old freight _

four And twen - ty - five min - utes till five. _____
man, I went to watch your trains roll by. _____
love, Run a - way with an - oth - er man. _____
love, Run a - way with an - oth - er man. _____
train That car - ries an emp - ty car. _____
train, And I nev - er did ___ come back. _____

GOOD NIGHT LADIES

19th Century American
Words by E.P. Christy

THE GOOD OLD REBEL

Post-Civil War Song from the American South

GOOD NEWS

African-American Spiritual

peace and free-dom in this world, I know; peace and free-dom in this world, I know; peace and free-dom in this
long white robe _ in _ Heav'n, I know; long white robe _ in _ Heav'n, I know; long white robe _ in _
bet - ter land _ in this world, I know; bet - ter land _ in this world, I know; bet - ter land _ in this

1st and 2nd time D.S.
3rd time D.S. al Coda

A7 D CODA D

world, I know, and I don't want it to leave a - me be - hind.
Heav'n, I know, and I don't want it to leave a - me be - hind. Good hind.
world, I know, and I don't want it to leave a - me be - hind.

GOODBYE, OLD PAINT

Western American Cowboy Song

A E A

Good - bye, old Paint, I'm a - leav - in' Chey - enne. Good - bye, old

last time To Coda

E A D A D E

Paint, I'm a - leav - in' Chey - enne.
1. I'm a leav - in' Chey - enne, I'm off to Mon -
2. Old _ Paint's a good po - ny he pac - es when he
3. Oh, _ hitch up your hors - es and feed 'em some
4. My _ hors - es ain't hun - gry, they'll not eat your
5. My _ foot's in the stir - rup, the reins in my

A E A D.S. al Coda CODA A

tan', _ Good - bye, old Paint, I'm a - leav - in' Chey - enne. enne.
can, _ Good - bye, lit - tle An - nie, I'm _ off to Mon - tan'.
hay, _ And seat your-self by me as _ long as you stay. Good
hay, _ My wag - on is load - ed and _ roll - ing a - way.
hand, _ Good morn - in' young la - dy my _ hors - es won't stand.

GOOSEY, GOOSEY GANDER

American Nursery Rhyme Song

G D7 G

Goose - y, goose - y gan - der, gan - der, gan - der, goose - y, goose - y

C D7 G

gan - der, where do you go? I am go - ing walk - ing,

D7 G C D7 G

walk - ing, walk - ing, I am go - ing walk - ing if you must know.

GOSPEL PLOW

African-American Spiritual

1. Mar - y wore three links of chain, ev - 'ry link was Je - sus' name.
2. Pe - ter was so nice and neat, would - n't let Je - sus wash his feet.
3. Je - sus said "If I wash them not, you'll have no fa - ther in this lot." ⎫
4. Pe - ter got anx - ious and he said, "Wash me feet, ___ hands and head." ⎬ Keep your hand on - a that
5. Got my hand on the gos - pel plow, would - n't take noth - in' for my jour - ney now. ⎭

plow, Hold on. ___ Hold on, ___ Hold on, ___ Keep your hand on - a that plow, Hold on.

THE GOSPEL TRAIN

African-American Spiritual

1. The gos - pel train is a - com - in', I hear it just at hand. ___ I
2. I hear the bell and ___ whis - tle, she's com - in' 'round the curve. ___ She's
3. The fare is cheap and ___ all can go; the rich and poor are there. ___ No
4. She's near - ing now the ___ sta - tion. Oh, sin - ner, don't be vain, ___ but

hear the car ___ wheels mov - ing and rum - bling through the land. ___ ⎫
play - in' all ___ her steam and pow'r and strain - in' ev - 'ry nerve. ___ ⎬ Oh, get on
sec - ond class ___ a - board this train, no dif - f'rence in the fare. ___
come and get ___ your tick - et and be read - y for this train. ___ ⎭

board, lit - tle chil - dren, get on board, lit - tle chil - dren, get on

board, lit - tle chil - dren, there's room for man - y - a more. Oh, get on

board, lit - tle chil - dren, get on board, lit - tle chil - dren, get on

board, lit - tle chil - dren, there's room for man - y - a more.

GRANDFATHER'S CLOCK

American
Words and Music by
Henry Clay Work

1. My grand-fa-ther's clock was too large for the shelf so it stood nine-ty years on the floor. It was
2. In watch-ing its pen-du-lum swing to and fro man-y hours had he spent while a boy. And in
3. My grand-fa-ther said that of those he could hire, not a ser-vant so faith-ful he found, for it
4. It rang an a-larm in the dead of the night, an a-larm that for years had been dumb. And we

tall-er-by half than the old man him-shelf tho' it weighed not a pen-ny-weight more. It was
child-hood and man-hood the clock seemed to know and to share both his grief and his joy. For it
wast-ed-no time, and had but one de-sire, at the close of each week to be wound. And it
knew that his spir-it was plum-ing its flight, that his hour of de-par-ture had come. Still the

bought on the morn of the day that he was born and was al ways his treas-ure and pride.
struck twen-ty-four when he en-tered at the door, with a bloom-ing a beau-ti-ful bride. But it
kept in its place not a frown up-on its face, and its hands nev-er hung by its side.
clock kept the time, with a soft and muf-fled chime, as we si-lent ly stood by his side.

stopped short nev-er to go a-gain when the old man died. Nine-ty

years with-out slum-ber-ing, tick, tock, tick, tock, his life sec-onds num-ber-ing, tick, tock, tick, tock. It

stopped short nev-er to go a-gain when the old man died.

GREAT GETTIN' UP MORNIN'

African-American Spiritual

In that great get-tin' up morn-in', Fare thee well, ___ fare thee well. _

___ In that great get-tin' up morn-in', Fare thee well, ___ fare thee well. ___

1. Stop and lem-me tell you 'bout the com-ing of the Sav-ior,
2. God's _ gon-na up ___ and _ speak _ to ___ Ga-briel,
3. "Blow _ your _ trum-pet, ___ Ga - briel," ___
4. You ___ will ___ see ___ the ___ cof - fins ___ bust-ing,
5. Then ___ the ___ Chris-tians ___ will ___ be ___ ris-ing,
6. March-ing ___ home _ to ___ live ___ with _ Je-sus,

Fare thee well, ___ fare thee well. _

Last time D.C. al Fine

Stop and lem-me tell you 'bout the com-in' of the Sav-ior,
God's _ gon-na up ___ and _ speak _ to ___ Ga-briel,
"Blow _ your _ trum-pet, ___ Ga - briel," ___
You ___ will ___ see ___ the ___ cof - fins ___ bust-ing,
Then ___ the ___ Chris-tians ___ will ___ be ___ ris-ing,
March-ing ___ home _ to ___ live ___ with _ Je-sus,

Fare thee well, ___ fare thee well. ___

GREAT DAY

African-American Spiritual

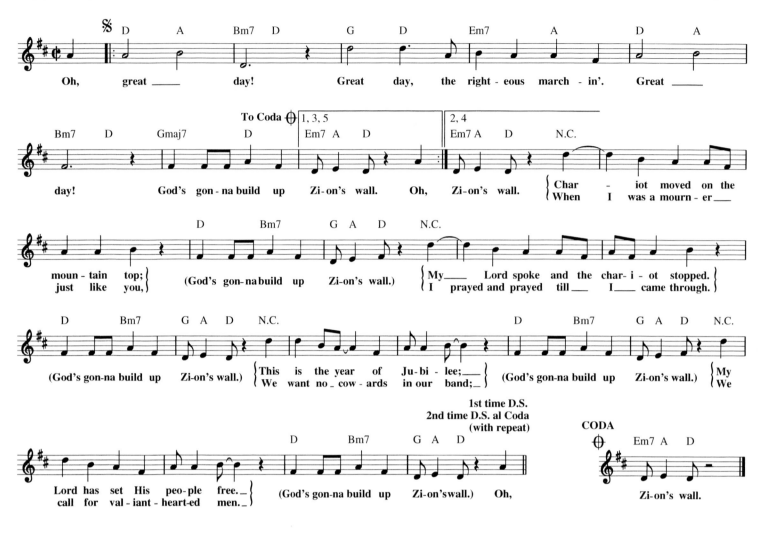

THE GREAT SILKIE

Scottish Ballad
From the Orkney Islands

THE GREAT SPECKLED BIRD

American

1. What a beau - ti - ful thought I am think - ing, _____ Con -
2. The _____ great speck - led bird sits in splen - dor, _____ All sur -
3. I am glad that I come to your meet - ing, _____ I'm
4. When He comes, if He comes, I will greet Him _____ On a

cern - ing the great speck - led bird. _____ Re - mem - ber his name is re -
round - ed and de - spised by the mob. _____ The great speck - led bird is the
proud that my name is of a bird, _____ For I want to be one nev - er
cloud that is float - ing in the Word. _____ I will rise up, my Sav - ior, to

cord - ed, _____ In the great Book of God's Ho - ly Word. _____
Bi - ble, _____ Re - pre - sent - ing the great Church of God. _____
fear - ing, _____ In the arms of my Sav - ior's true Word. _____
greet Him, _____ On the wings of a great speck - led bird. _____

THE GREEN BUSHES

English

1. As _____ I was a - walk - ing one morn - ing in May, To
2. "Oh, _____ why are you loi - ter - ing here, pret - ty maid?" "I am
3. "I will give you fine bea - vers and fine silk - en gowns, I will
4. "I want none of your bea - vers or fine silk - en hose, for
5. "Come _ let us be go - ing, kind sir if you please. Come,
6. And _____ when _____ he came there and found she was gone, he

hear the birds whis - tle and see lamb - kins play, I es -
wait - ing for my true love," soft - ly she said. "Shall _____
give you fine pet - ti - coats, flounced to the ground. I will
I'm not so poor as to mar - ry for clothes. But if
let us be go - ing from un - der these trees. For _____
looked ver - y fool - ish, and cried quite for - lorn. "She's _____

pied a young dam - sel, so sweet - ly sang she, Down _____
I be your true love, and will you a - gree, down _____
give you fine jew - els, and live but for thee, if you'll _____
you _____ be con - stant and true un - to me, I'll _____
yon - der is com - ing, my true love I see, down _____
gone with a lov - er, and for - sak - en me, and _____

by the green bush - es, where she chanced to meet me.
by the green bush - es to _____ tar - ry with me."
leave your own true love and _____ mar - ry with me."
leave my own true love, and _____ mar - ry with me."
by the green bush - es, where he thinks to meet me."
left the green bush - es, where she vowed to meet me."

GREEN CORN

American

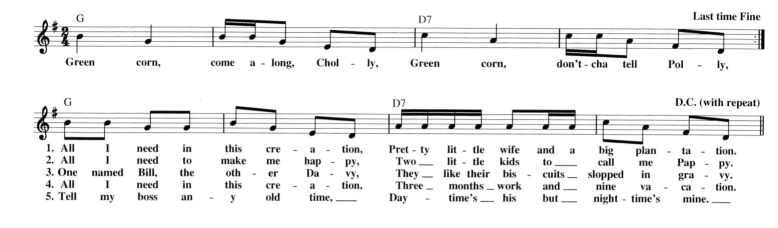

Green corn, come a-long, Chol-ly, Green corn, don't-cha tell Pol-ly,

1. All I need in this cre-a-tion, Pret-ty lit-tle wife and a big plan-ta-tion.
2. All I need to make me hap-py, Two __ lit-tle kids to __ call me Pap-py.
3. One named Bill, the oth-er Da-vy, They __ like their bis-cuits __ slopped in gra-vy.
4. All I need in this cre-a-tion, Three __ months __ work and __ nine va-ca-tion.
5. Tell my boss an-y old time, ___ Day-time's __ his but __ night-time's mine. ___

GREEN GRAVEL

American Children's Song

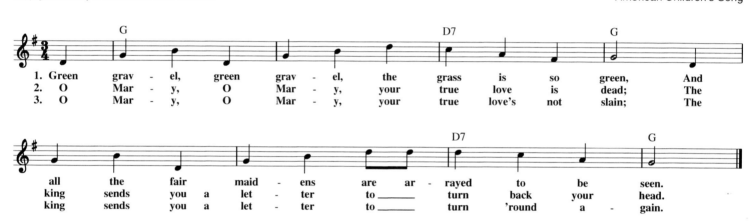

1. Green grav-el, green grav-el, the grass is so green, And
2. O Mar-y, O Mar-y, your true love is dead; The
3. O Mar-y, O Mar-y, your true love's not slain; The

all the fair maid-ens are ar-rayed to be seen.
king sends you a let-ter to ___ turn back your head.
king sends you a let-ter to ___ turn 'round a-gain.

GREEN GROW THE LILACS

American

1. Green grow the li-lacs all spark-ling with dew. I'm lone-ly, my
2. used to have a sweet-heart, but now I have none. Since she's gone and
3. passed my love's win-dow, both ear-ly and late; The look that she
4. wrote my love let-ters in ro-sy red lines; She sent me an

dar-ling, since part-ing with you. But by our next meet-ing I hope to prove
left me, I care not for one. Since she's gone and left me, con-tent-ed I'll
gave me, it made my heart ache. Oh, the look that she gave me was pain-ful to
an-swer all twist-ed in twines, Say-ing, "Keep your love let-ters and don't waste your

true, And change the green li-lacs to the red, white and blue. (2.) I
be, For she loves an-oth-er one __ bet-ter than me. (3.) I
see, For she loves an-oth-er one __ bet-ter than me. (4.) I
time, Just you write to your love and __ I'll write to mine."

GREEN GROW THE RASHES, O

Scottish
By Robert Burns

GREEN GROWS THE LAUREL

Irish

GREENLAND FISHERIES

American Sea Chantey

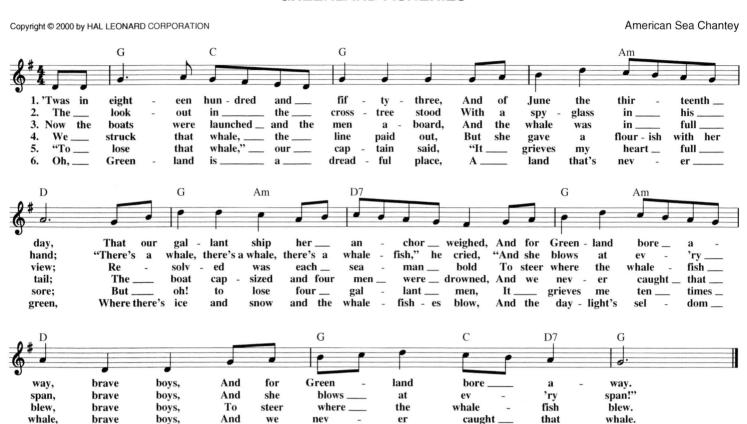

1. 'Twas in eight - een hun - dred and ___ fif - ty - three, And of June the thir - teenth ___
2. The ___ look - out in ___ the ___ cross - tree stood With a spy - glass in ___ his ___
3. Now the boats were launched _ and the men a - board, And the whale was in ___ full ___
4. We ___ struck that whale, ___ the ___ line paid out, But she gave a flour - ish with her
5. "To ___ lose that whale," ___ our ___ cap - tain said, "It ___ grieves my heart ___ full ___
6. Oh, ___ Green - land is ___ a ___ dread - ful place, A ___ land that's nev - er ___

day, That our gal - lant ship her ___ an - chor ___ weighed, And for Green - land bore ___ a ___
hand; "There's a whale, there's a whale, there's a whale - fish," he cried, "And she blows at ev - 'ry
view; Re - solv - ed was each ___ sea - man ___ bold To steer where the whale - fish
tail; The ___ boat cap - sized and four men ___ were ___ drowned, And we nev - er caught ___ that ___
sore; But ___ oh! to lose four ___ gal - lant ___ men, It ___ grieves me ten ___ times ___
green, Where there's ice and snow and the whale - fish - es blow, And the day - light's sel - dom ___

way, brave boys, And for Green - land bore ___ a - way.
span, brave boys, And she blows ___ at ev - 'ry span!"
blew, brave boys, To steer where ___ the whale - fish blew.
whale, brave boys, And we nev - er caught ___ that whale.
more, brave boys, It ___ grieves ___ me ten ___ times more."
seen, brave boys, And the day - light's sel - dom seen.

GRIZZLY BEAR

Southern American Chain-Gang Song

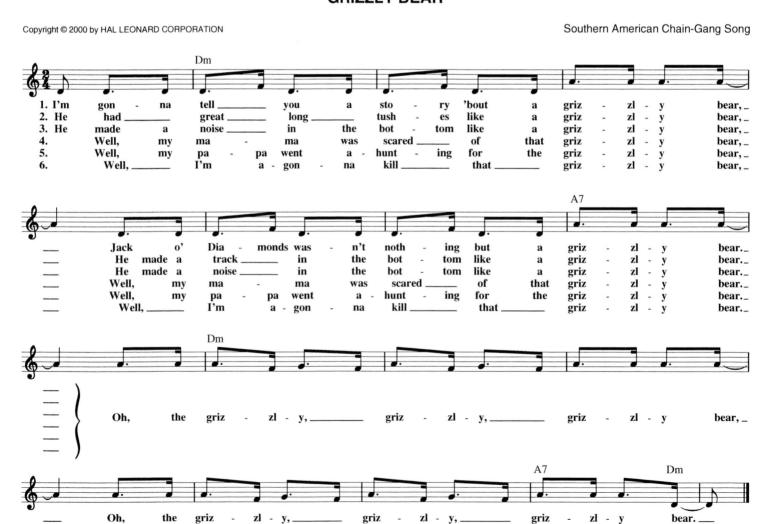

1. I'm gon - na tell ___ you a sto - ry 'bout a griz - zl - y bear,
2. He had ___ great ___ long ___ tush - es like a griz - zl - y bear, ___
3. He made a noise ___ in the bot - tom like a griz - zl - y bear, ___
4. Well, my ma - ma was scared ___ of that griz - zl - y bear, ___
5. Well, my pa - pa went a - hunt - ing for the griz - zl - y bear, ___
6. Well, ___ I'm a - gon - na kill ___ that ___ griz - zl - y bear, ___

___ Jack o' Dia - monds was - n't noth - ing but a griz - zl - y bear. ___
___ He made a track ___ in the bot - tom like a griz - zl - y bear. ___
___ He made a noise ___ in the bot - tom like a griz - zl - y bear. ___
___ Well, my ma - ma was scared ___ of that griz - zl - y bear. ___
___ Well, my pa - pa went a - hunt - ing for the griz - zl - y bear. ___
___ Well, ___ I'm a - gon - na kill ___ that ___ griz - zl - y bear. ___

___
___
___ Oh, the griz - zl - y, ___ griz - zl - y, ___ griz - zl - y bear,
___
___

___ Oh, the griz - zl - y, ___ griz - zl - y, ___ griz - zl - y bear. ___

GREENSLEEVES

16th Century English

GUANTANAMERA

Cuban

THE GREY GOOSE

Southern American

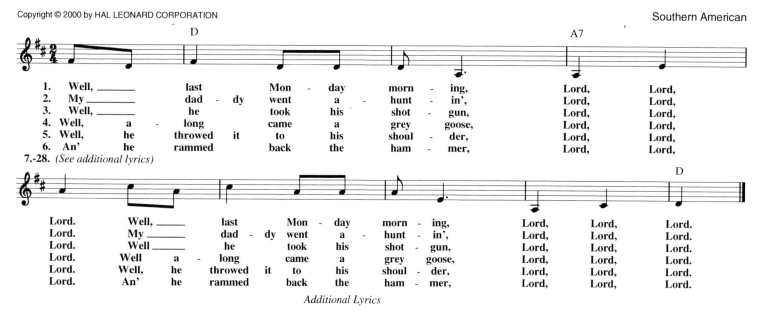

1. Well, _____ last Mon - day morn - ing, Lord, Lord,
2. My _____ dad - dy went a - hunt - in', Lord, Lord,
3. Well, _____ he took his shot - gun, Lord, Lord,
4. Well, a - long came a grey goose, Lord, Lord,
5. Well, he throwed it to his shoul - der, Lord, Lord,
6. An' he rammed back the ham - mer, Lord, Lord,

7.-28. *(See additional lyrics)*

Lord. Well, _____ last Mon - day morn - ing, Lord, Lord, Lord.
Lord. My _____ dad - dy went a - hunt - in', Lord, Lord, Lord.
Lord. Well _____ he took his shot - gun, Lord, Lord, Lord.
Lord. Well a - long came a grey goose, Lord, Lord, Lord.
Lord. Well, he throwed it to his shoul - der, Lord, Lord, Lord.
Lord. An' he rammed back the ham - mer, Lord, Lord, Lord.

Additional Lyrics

7. Well, he pulled on de trigger...

8. Well, down he come a-windin'...

9. He was six weeks a-fallin'...

10. He was six weeks a-findin'...

11. An' he put him on de wagon...

12. An' he taken him to de white house...

13. He was six weeks a-pickin'...

14. Lordy, your wife an' my wife...

15. Oh, dey give a feather pickin'...

16. An' dey put him on to parboil,...

17. He was six months a-parboil'...

18. An' dey out him on de table...

19. Now, de fork couldn' stick him...

20. An' de knife couldn't cut him...

21. An' dey throwed him in de hog-pen...

22. An' he broke de ol' sow's jaw-bone...

23. An' dey taken him to de saw-mill...

24. An' he broke de saw's teeth out...

25. An' de las' time I seed him...

26. Well, he's flyin' across de ocean...

27. Wid a long string o' goslin's...

28. An' dey all goin': Quank Quink-Quank...

GYPSY DAVEY

English

1. It was late last night when the boss came home a - ask - ing for his la - dy. The
2. Go _____ sad - de for me my buck - skin horse and my hun - dred - dol - lar sad - dle. Point
3. Well, he had not rode to the mid - night moon when he saw their camp - fire gleam - ing. He
4. There _____ in the light of the camp - ing fire he saw her fair face beam - ing, her
5. Have _____ you for - sak - en your house and home? Have you for - sak - en your ba - by? Have
6. Yes _____ I've for - sak - en my hus - band dear to go with the Gyp - sy Da - vey, And

on - ly an - swer _____ he re - ceived, "She's gone with the Gyp - sy Da - vey, she's gone with the Gyp - sy Dave."
out to me their _____ wag - on tracks and af - ter _____ them I'll trav - el, well, af - ter _____ them I'll ride.
heard the notes of the big gui - tar and the voice of the gyp - sies sing - ing that song of the Gyp - sy Dave.
heart in tune to the big gui - tar and the voice of the gyp - sies sing - ing that song of the Gyp - sy Dave.
you for - sak - en your hus - band dear to go with the Gyp - sy Da - vey, and sing with the Gyp - sy Dave?
I've for - sak - en my man - sion high, but not my _____ blue - eyed ba - by, my pret - ty lit - tle blue - eyed babe.

GUIDE MY FEET

African-American Spiritual

1. Guide my feet
2. Hold my hand
3. Stand by me
4. I'm Your child
5. Search my heart

while I run this race,

Guide my
Hold my
Stand by
I'm Your
Search my

feet
hand
me
child
heart

while I run this race,

Guide my feet
Hold my hand
Stand by me
I'm Your child
Search my heart

while I run this

race, For I don't want to run this race in vain!

GROUNDHOG

Folksong from North Carolina

1. Shoul-der up your gun and call your dog,
2. Too man-y rocks and too man-y logs,
3. He's in here, boys, the hole's wore slick,
4. Stand back, boys, and let's be wise,
5. Up jumped Sam with a ten-foot pole,
6. Stand back, boys, and let me get my breath,
7.-9. *(See additional lyrics)*

Shoul-der up your gun and
Too man-y rocks and
He's in here, boys, the
Stand back, boys, and
Up jumped Sam with a
Stand back, boys, and

call your dog, We're off to the woods to catch a ground-hog. Ground-hog!
too man-y logs, Too man-y rocks to catch ground-hogs. Ground-hog!
hole's wore slick, Run here, Sam, with your forked stick! Ground-hog!
let's be wise, For I think I see his bead-ed eyes. Ground-hog!
ten-foot pole, He roused it in that ground-hog's hole. Ground-hog!
let me get my breath, Catch-in' this ground-hog's might nigh death. Ground-hog!

Additional Lyrics

7. Here he comes right in a whirl,
   Here he comes right in a whirl,
   Biggest old groundhog in the world!
   Groundhog!

8. They put him in the pot and all begin to smile,
   They put him in the pot and all begin to smile,
   They eat that hog before he struck a boil,
   Groundhog!

9. The children screamed and the children cried,
   The children screamed and the children cried,
   They love groundhog cooked or fried.
   Groundhog!

HAIL, HAIL, THE GANG'S ALL HERE

Words by D.A. Esrom
Music by Theodore F. Morse and Arthur Sullivan
1917

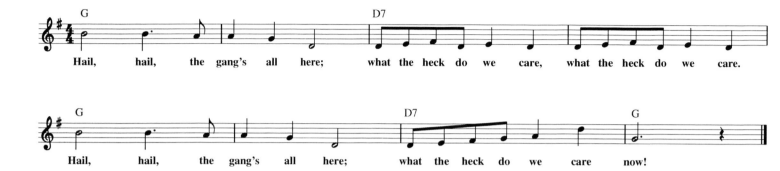

Hail, hail, the gang's all here; what the heck do we care, what the heck do we care.

Hail, hail, the gang's all here; what the heck do we care now!

HALLELUJAH, I'M A BUM!

American Hobo Song

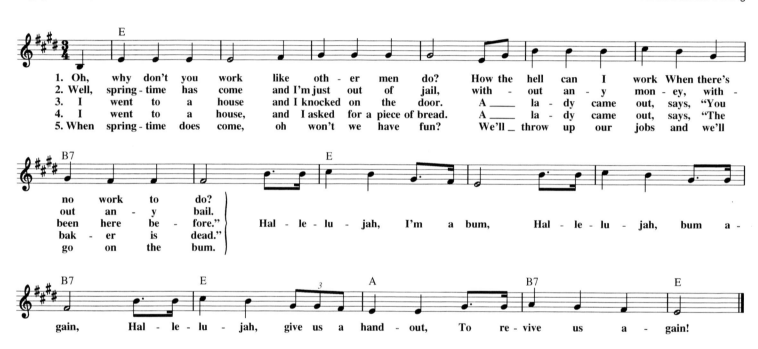

1. Oh, why don't you work like oth-er men do? How the hell can I work When there's
2. Well, spring-time has come and I'm just out of jail, with-out an-y mon-ey, with-
3. I went to a house and I knocked on the door. A ___ la-dy came out, says, "You
4. I went to a house, and I asked for a piece of bread. A ___ la-dy came out, says, "The
5. When spring-time does come, oh won't we have fun? We'll ___ throw up our jobs and we'll

no work to do?
out an-y bail.
been here be-fore." Hal-le-lu-jah, I'm a bum, Hal-le-lu-jah, bum a-
bak-er is dead."
go on the bum.

gain, Hal-le-lu-jah, give us a hand-out, To re-vive us a-gain!

HAND ME DOWN MY WALKING CANE

Words and Music by James A. Bland
African-American Minstrel Song, circa 1880

1. Hand me down _____ my walk-ing cane, _____ hand me down _____
2. Hand me down _____ my bot-tle of corn, _____ hand me down _____

___ my walk-ing cane. _____ Oh, hand me down my walk-ing cane, I'm a
___ my bot-tle of corn. _____ Oh, hand me down my bot-tle of corn, I'm a

goin' to leave on that mid-night train, 'cause all of my sins are tak-en a-way. _____
goin' to leave drunk as sure as you're born, 'cause all of my sins are tak-en a-way. _____

HARD, AIN'T IT HARD

Appalachian Folksong

1. There is a _____ house in this old town, That's where my true love lays a - round. Takes
2. Don't go to _____ drink - in' and to gam - blin', Don't go there your sor - rows to _____ drown. That
3. The first time I seen _____ my true love, He _____ was walk - in' by my door, And the

oth - er wom - en right down _ on his knee, Tells them a tale that he won't tell me. _____
hard _ liq - uor place is a low - down dis - grace, The mean - est damn place _____ in this town. _____ It's
last _ time I saw his _____ false heart - ed smile, He was dead on his bar _____ room _ board. _____

hard and it's hard, ain't it hard _____ To love one that nev - er did love you.

Hard and it's hard, ain't it hard, great God, To love one that nev - er will be true.

HARD IS THE FORTUNE OF ALL WOMANKIND
(The Wagoner's Lad)

American version of an 18th Century English Folksong

1. Oh, _____ hard is the for - tune of all wom - an - kind. They're
2. Oh, _____ I am a poor girl my for - tune is sad. I have
3. Your _____ par - ents don't like me be - cause I am poor. They
4. Your _____ hors - es are hun - gry, go feed them some hay. Come
5. Your _____ wag - on needs greas - ing, your whip is to mend. Come

al - ways con - trolled, _____ they're al - ways con - fined. Con -
al - ways been court - ed by the wag - on - er's lad. He
say I'm not wor - thy of en - t'ring your door. I
sit down be - side me as long as you may. My
sit down here by me as long as you can. My

trolled by their par - ents un - til they are wives, then _____
court - ed me dai - ly, by night and by day, and _____
work for my liv - ing my mon - ey's my own, and _____
hors - es ain't hun - gry, they won't eat your hay, so _____
wag - on is greas - y, my whip's in my hand, so _____

slaves to their hus - bands the rest of their lives.
now he is load - ed and go - ing a - way.
if they don't like me they can leave me a - lone.
fare thee well, dar - ling, I'll be on my way.
fare thee well, dar - ling, no long - er to stand.

HARD LUCK

, American Cowboy Song

Oh, rat - tle your bones, __ you skin - ny old cay - ute, We're gone out to ride the range. _____ You

can't get much lean - er, we'll roam where it's green - er, Some day our luck must change.

You've been a pal __ through hun - ger and cold, __ You're read - y to ride the range. _____ Just

like in the sto - ry, we'll round up in Glo - ry, Some day our luck must change. _____

HARES ON THE MOUNTAIN

English

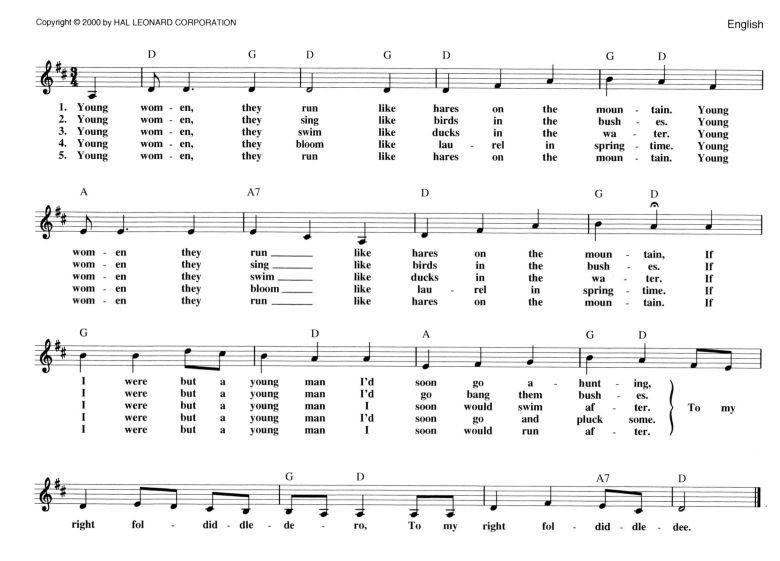

1. Young wom - en, they run like hares on the moun - tain. Young
2. Young wom - en, they sing like birds in the bush - es. Young
3. Young wom - en, they swim like ducks in the wa - ter. Young
4. Young wom - en, they bloom like lau - rel in spring - time. Young
5. Young wom - en, they run like hares on the moun - tain. Young

wom - en they run _____ like hares on the moun - tain, If
wom - en they sing _____ like birds in the bush - es. If
wom - en they swim _____ like ducks in the wa - ter. If
wom - en they bloom _____ like lau - rel in spring - time. If
wom - en they run _____ like hares on the moun - tain. If

I were but a young man I'd soon go a - hunt - ing,
I were but a young man I'd go bang them bush - es.
I were but a young man I soon would swim af - ter.
I were but a young man I'd soon go and pluck some.
I were but a young man I soon would run af - ter.
} To my

right fol - did - dle - de - ro, To my right fol - did - dle - dee.

THE HARP THAT ONCE

Irish
Words by Thomas Moore

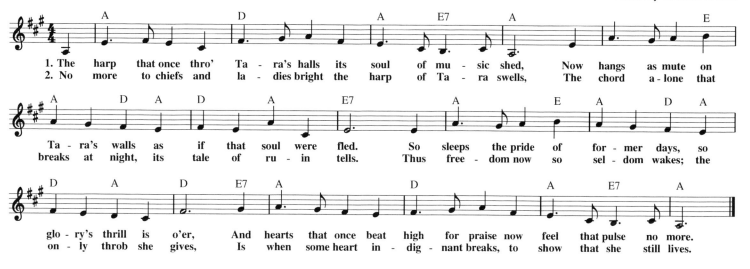

1. The harp that once thro' Ta - ra's halls its soul of mu - sic shed, Now hangs as mute on
2. No more to chiefs and la - dies bright the harp of Ta - ra swells, The chord a - lone that

Ta - ra's walls as if that soul were fled. So sleeps the pride of for - mer days, so
breaks at night, its tale of ru - in tells. Thus free - dom now so sel - dom wakes; the

glo - ry's thrill is o'er, And hearts that once beat high for praise now feel that pulse no more.
on - ly throb she gives, Is when some heart in - dig - nant breaks, to show that she still lives.

HATIKVA

Israeli National Anthem
Words by N.H. Imber
Folk Melody

Kol od ba - lé - vav p' - ni - ma ne - fesh Y' - hu - di ho - mi - ya. Ul' -

fa - a - té miz - rach ka - di - ma a - yin l' - tsi - yon tso - fi - ya.

Od lo av - da tik - va - té - nu, ha - tik - va bat sh'not al - pa - yim.

Li - yot am chof - shi b' - ar - tsé - nu e - rets Tsi - yon Y' - ru - sha - la - yim.

Li - yot am chof - shi b' - ar - tsé - nu e - rets Tsi - yon Y' - ru - sha - la - yim.

HAUL ON THE BOWLINE

English Sea Chantey

1. Haul on the bow - line, our bul - ley ship's a - roll - in'.
2. Haul on the bow - line, __ Kit - ty is my dar - ling.
3. Haul on the bow - line, __ Kit - ty lives in Liv - er - pool.
4. Haul on the bow - line, the old man is a growl - in'.
5. Haul on the bow - line, so ear - ly in the morn - in'.
6. Haul on the bow - line, __ it's a far cry to pay - day.

Haul on the bow - line, the bow - line haul.

HAUL AWAY, JOE

American version of an English Sea Chantey

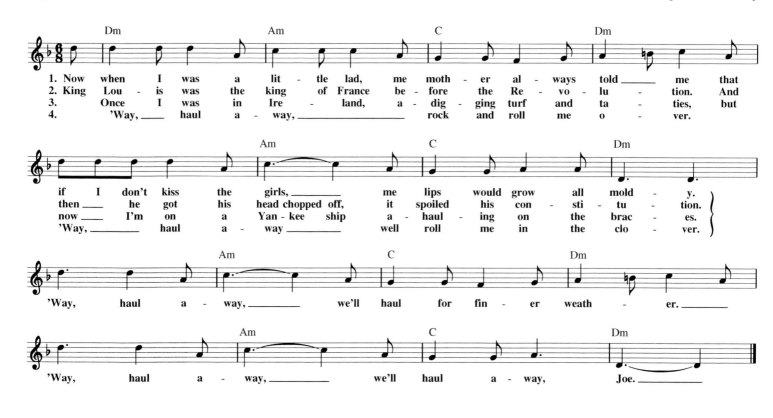

1. Now when I was a lit-tle lad, me moth-er al-ways told _____ me that
2. King Lou-is was the king of France be-fore the Re-vo-lu-tion. And
3. Once I was in Ire-land, a dig-ging turf and ta-ties, but
4. 'Way, _____ haul a-way, _____ rock and roll me o-ver.

if I don't kiss the girls, _____ me lips would grow all mold-y.
then ____ he got his head chopped off, it spoiled his con-sti-tu-tion.
now ____ I'm on a Yan-kee ship a-haul-ing on the brac-es.
'Way, _____ haul a-way _____ well roll me in the clo-ver.

'Way, haul a-way, _____ we'll haul for fin-er weath-er. _____

'Way, haul a-way, _____ we'll haul a-way, Joe. _____

HAVA NAGILA

Folksong from Israel
Words by Moshe Nathanson
Music by Abraham Z. Idelsohn

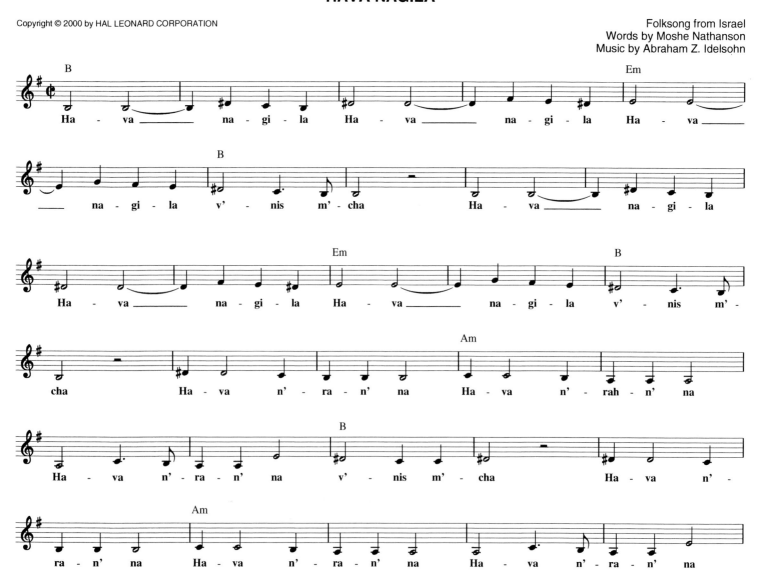

Ha-va _____ na-gi-la Ha-va _____ na-gi-la Ha-va _____

_____ na-gi-la v'-nis m'-cha Ha-va _____ na-gi-la

Ha-va _____ na-gi-la Ha-va _____ na-gi-la v'-nis m'-

cha Ha-va n'-ra-n'-na Ha-va n'-rah-n'-na

Ha-va n'-ra-n'-na v'-nis m'-cha Ha-va n'-

ra-n'-na Ha-va n'-ra-n'-na Ha-va n'-ra-n'-na

B ... **Em**

v' - nis m' - cha U - ru, U - ru a - chim,

U - ru a - chim B' - lev sa - mey - ach, U - ru a - chim B' - lev sa - mey - ach,

B7

U - ru a - chim B' - lev sa - mey - ach. U - ru a - chim B' - lev sa - mey - ach,

Em

U - ru a - chim, U - ru a - chim B'lev sa - mey - ach.

HEAR LULLABIES AND SLEEP NOW
(A la Nanita Nana)

Spanish

Em ... **Am** **Em** **Am** **Em**

1. Hear lul - la - bies and sleep now, yes, go to sleep now, yes, go to sleep.
2. My lit - tle bunch of ros - es, with face be - guil - ing, with face be - guil - ing,
3. Birds call - ing, foun - tains rush - ing, and blow - ing breez - es, and blow - ing breez - es:

1. A la na - ni - ta na - na, na - ni - ta e - a, na - ni - ta e - a,
2. Ma - no - ji - to de ro - sas y de_a - le - lí - es y de_a - le - lí - es,
3. Pa - ja - ri - llos y fuen - tes, au - ras y bri - sas, au - ras y bri - sas:

Am **Em** **B** **Em** **Fine**

My sleep - y Je - sus, may God your slum - ber keep, God your slum - ber keep.
What are you dream - ing now, that I see you smil - ing, I see you smil - ing.
Re - peat this smil - ing dream as my ba - by pleas - es, my ba - by pleas - es.

Mi Je - sús tie - ne sue - ño, ben - di - to se - a, ben - di - to se - a.
Qué_es lo que_es - tás so - ñan - do, qué te son - ri - es, qué te son - ri - es?
Re - pe - tad e - se sue - ño y_e - sas son - ri - sas, y_e - sas son - ri - sas.

E **C#m** **G#m** **A** **E** **C#m**

Hear how the foun - tain bab - bles, splash - ing its wa - ters. Night - in - gales in the
Fuen - te - ci - illa que cor - res cla - ra y so - no - ra, Rui - se - ñor de la

G#m **A** **E** **B** **Am**

woods call all sons and daugh - ters. {Rest as the cra - dle
{What do you see in
sel - va, can - tan - do llo - ras; {ca - llad mien - tras la
{Cuál - es son tus en -

Em **Am** **E** **Am**

calms you now with its swing - ing; Hear lul - la - bies and
dream - land? Tell me, my dear - est. What do you see in
cu - na se ba - lan - ce - a, A la na - ni - ta
sue - ños? di - lo_al - ma mi - a; Cuál - es son tus en -

Em **B7** **[1] E** **[2] E** **D.C. al Fine**

sleep now, while I am sing - ing.
dream - land? Tell me, my dear - est.
na - na, na - ni - ta e - a.
sue - ños? di - lo_al - ma mi - a.

HAULING SONG

Sea Chantey

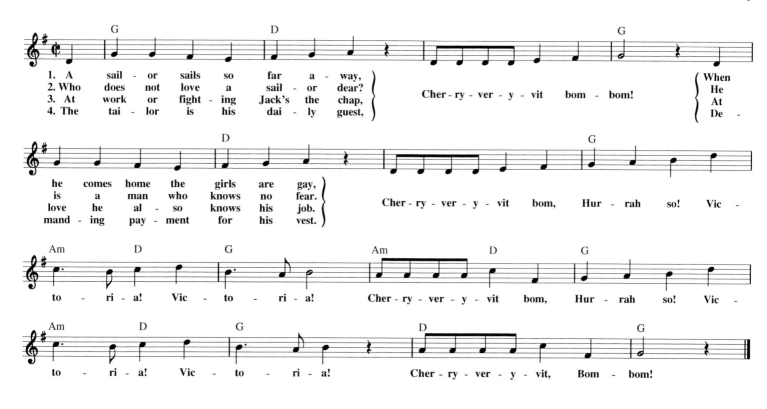

1. A sail - or sails so far a - way,
2. Who does not love a sail - or dear?
3. At work or fight - ing Jack's the chap,
4. The tai - lor is his dai - ly guest,

Cher - ry - ver - y - vit bom - bom!

When
He
At
De -

he comes home the girls are gay,
is a man who knows no fear.
love he al - so knows his job.
mand - ing pay - ment for his vest.

Cher - ry - ver - y - vit bom, Hur - rah so! Vic -

to - ri - a! Vic - to - ri - a! Cher - ry - ver - y - vit bom, Hur - rah so! Vic -

to - ri - a! Vic - to - ri - a! Cher - ry - ver - y - vit, Bom - bom!

HAVE YOU SEEN BUT A WHITE LILY GROW?

Words by Ben Johnson
17th Century English

Have you seen but a white lil - y grow ____ be - fore rude hands had

touch'd it? Have you mark'd __ but __ the __ fall of the snow Be - fore ____ the earth hath

smudged it? Have you felt the wool of bea - ver or swan's - down _____

ev - er, or have smelt of the bud of the bri - ar or the nard in the

fire or have tast - ed the bag of the bee? Oh, so white, Oh so

soft, Oh so sweet, so sweet, _____ so sweet is she!

HE AROSE

African-American Spiritual

1. They cru-ci-fied my Sav-ior and nailed Him to the cross, They cru-ci-fied my Sav-ior and
2. And Jo-seph begged His bod-y and laid it in the tomb, And Jo-seph begged His bod-y and
3. Sister Mar-y, she came run-ning, a-look-ing for my Lord, Sister Mar-y she came run-ning, a-
4. An an-gel came from heav-en and rolled the stone a-way, An an-gel came from heav-en and

nailed Him to the cross, They cru-ci-fied my Sav-ior and nailed Him to the cross, __ And the
laid it in the tomb, And Jo-seph begged His bod-y and laid it in the tomb, __ And the
look-ing for my Lord, Sister Mar-y, she came run-ning, a-look-ing for my Lord, __ And the
rolled the stone a-way, An an-gel came from heav-en and rolled the stone-a way, __ And the

Lord will bear my spir-it home.
Lord will bear my spir-it home.   He 'rose, He 'rose, He
Lord will bear my spir-it home.
Lord will bear my spir-it home.

'rose __ from the dead, He 'rose, He 'rose, He 'rose __ from the dead, He

'rose, He 'rose, He 'rose __ from the dead, __ And the Lord shall bear my spir-it home.

HE IS KING OF KINGS

African-American Spiritual

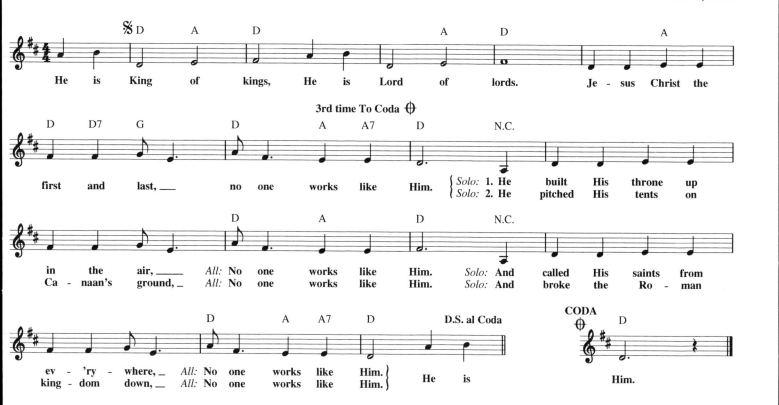

He is King of kings, He is Lord of lords. Je-sus Christ the

3rd time To Coda ⊕

first and last, __ no one works like Him.   Solo: 1. He built His throne up
                                            Solo: 2. He pitched His tents on

in the air, __ All: No one works like Him. Solo: And called His saints from
Ca-naan's ground, __ All: No one works like Him. Solo: And broke the Ro-man

D.S. al Coda   **CODA** ⊕ D

ev-'ry-where, __ All: No one works like Him.   He is   Him.
king-dom down, __ All: No one works like Him.

HE NEVER SAID A MUMBALIN' WORD

African-American Spiritual

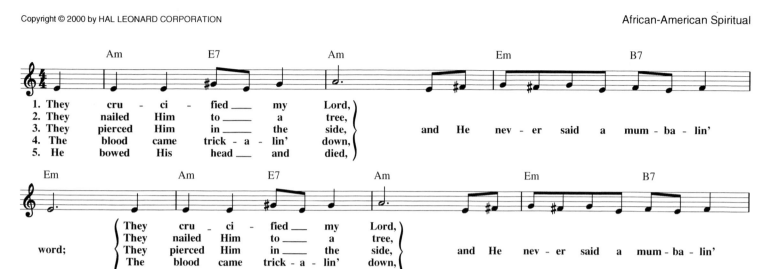

1. They cru - ci - fied ___ my Lord,
2. They nailed Him to ___ a tree,
3. They pierced Him in ___ the side,
4. The blood came trick - a - lin' down,
5. He bowed His head ___ and died,

and He nev - er said a mum - ba - lin'

word;
{
They cru - ci - fied ___ my Lord,
They nailed Him to ___ a tree,
They pierced Him in ___ the side,
The blood came trick - a - lin' down,
He bowed his head ___ and died,
}
and He nev - er said a mum - ba - lin'

word. Not a word, not a word, not a word.

HE'S GOT THE WHOLE WORLD IN HIS HANDS

African-American Spiritual

He's got the whole world ___ is His hands, ___ He's got the whole wide world ___ in His hands, ___ He's got the

whole world ___ in His hands, ___ He's got the whole world in His hands.
{
1. He's got the
2. He's got
3. He's got
}

lit - tle ti - ny ba - by in His hands, ___ He's got the lit - tle ti - ny ba - by
you and me, ___ broth - er, in His hands, ___ He's got you and me, ___ sis - ter,
ev - 'ry - bod - y here ___ in His hands, ___ He's got ev - 'ry - bod - y here ___

in His hands, ___ He's got the lit - tle ti - ny ba - by in His hands, ___
in His hands, ___ He's got you and me, ___ broth - er, in His hands, ___
in His hands, ___ He's got ev - 'ry - bod - y here ___ in His hands, ___
}
He's got the

whole world in His hands. He's got the hands. He's got the hands.

sau - sag - es, like - wise liv - er. _____
start - ed and ran a - way. _____
tru - ly an ob - ject of pit - y. _____

For Oh, _____ for Oh, _____ He was my dar - ling

boy, _____ for he was the lad with the au - burn hair and his name was Mi - chael Roy. _____

MRS. McGRATH

Irish

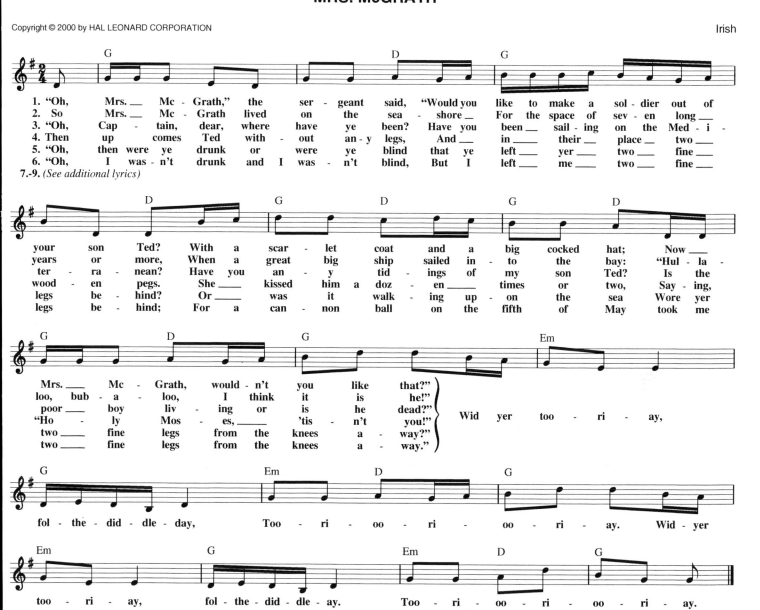

1. "Oh, Mrs. _____ Mc - Grath," the ser - geant said, "Would you like to make a sol - dier out of
2. So Mrs. _____ Mc - Grath lived on the sea - shore _____ For the space of sev - en long _____
3. "Oh, Cap - tain, dear, where have ye been? Have you been _____ sail - ing on the Med - i -
4. Then up comes Ted with - out an - y legs, And _____ in _____ their _____ place _____ two _____
5. "Oh, then were ye drunk or were ye blind that ye left _____ yer _____ two _____ fine _____
6. "Oh, I was - n't drunk and I was - n't blind, But I left _____ me _____ two _____ fine _____

7.-9. *(See additional lyrics)*

your son Ted? With a scar - let coat and a big cocked hat; Now _____
years or more, When a great big ship sailed in - to the bay: "Hul - la -
ter - ra - nean? Have you an - y tid - ings of my son Ted? Is the
wood - en pegs. She _____ kissed him a doz - en _____ times or two, Say - ing,
legs be - hind? Or _____ was it walk - ing up - on the sea Wore yer
legs be - hind; For a can - non ball on the fifth of May took me

Mrs. _____ Mc - Grath, would - n't you like that?"
loo, bub - a - loo, I think it is he!"
poor _____ boy liv - ing or is he dead?"
"Ho - ly Mos - es, _____ 'tis - n't you!"
two _____ fine legs from the knees a - way?"
two _____ fine legs from the knees a - way."

Wid yer too - ri - ay,

fol - the - did - dle - day, Too - ri - oo - ri - oo - ri - ay. Wid - yer

too - ri - ay, fol - the - did - dle - ay. Too - ri - oo - ri - oo - ri - ay.

Additional Lyrics

7. "Oh, then, Teddy me boy," the widow cried,
"Yer two fine legs were yer mama's pride.
Them stumps of a tree wouldn't do at all,
Why didn't ye run from the big cannon ball?"

8. "All foreign wars I do proclaim
Between Don John and the King of Spain.
But by Heavens I'll make them rue the time
That they swept the legs from a child of mine."

9. "Oh then, if I had ye back again,
I'd never let ye go to fight the King of Spain.
For I'd rather my Ted as he used to be
Than the King of France and his whole Navy."

MIDNIGHT SPECIAL

American

1. Well, you wake up in the morn - ing, _____ hear the ding _ dong ring, _____ You go march-ing to the
2. If you ev - er go to Hous - ton, _____ you'd _ bet - ter walk right, _____ And you bet - ter not _
3. Yon-der comes _ Miss _ Ros - ie, _____ tell me how do you know? _____ I ____ know her by her
4. Lord, _ Thel-ma said she loved me, but I be-lieve she told a lie, _____ 'Cause she has - n't been to
5. Well, the bis-cuits on the ta - ble, _____ just as hard as an - y rock; _____ If you try _ to _

ta - ble, _____ see the same _ damn _ thing. Well, it's on - a one ____ ta - ble, _____
stag - ger, _____ and you bet - ter not ____ fight, 'Cause the sher - iff will ar - rest you _____
a - pron _____ and the dress _ she wore, Um - brel - la on her shoul - der, _____
see me, _____ break a con - vict's _ heart. My ____ sis - ter wrote a let - ter, _____
eat them, _____ break a con - vict's _ heart. My ____ sis - ter wrote a let - ter, _____

— knife and fork and a pan, _____ And if you say an - y - thing a - bout it, _____
— and he'll car - ry you down, _____ And you can bet your _ bot - tom dol - lar _____
— piece of pa - per in her hand, _____ Well, I heard her _ tell the cap - tain, _____
— she brought me lit - tle tea, _____ She brought me near - ly _ ev - 'ry - thing _____
— my moth - er wrote a card: _____ "If you want to ____ come and see us, _____

— you're in trou-ble with the man.
— you're _ Sug - ar - land _ bound.
— "I ____ want _ my ____ man." } Let the Mid - night Spe - cial _____ shine her light _ on me, _____
— but the jail - house _ key.
— you'll _ have to ride the rods."

— Let the Mid - night Spe - cial _____ shine her ev - er - lov - in' light on me. __

MIGHTY DAY

American
Commemorating the great Galveston Flood of 1900

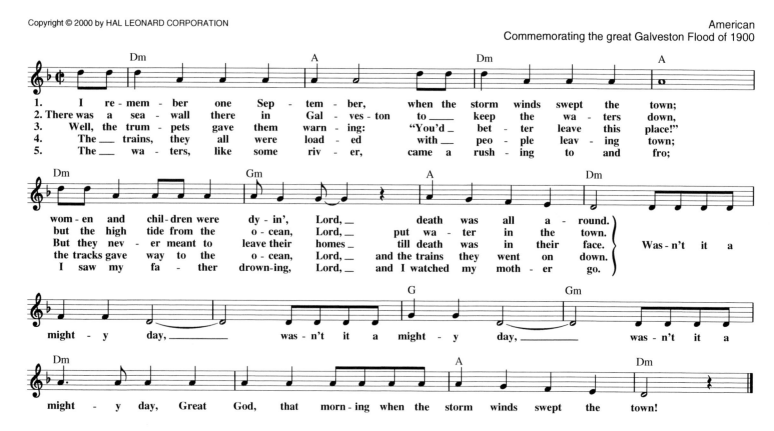

1. I re - mem - ber one Sep - tem - ber, when the storm winds swept the town;
2. There was a sea - wall there in Gal - ves - ton to ____ keep the wa - ters down,
3. Well, the trum - pets gave them warn - ing: "You'd _ bet - ter leave this place!"
4. The ____ trains, they all were load - ed with __ peo - ple leav - ing town;
5. The ____ wa - ters, like some riv - er, came a rush - ing to and fro;

wom - en and chil - dren were dy - in', Lord, _ death was all a - round.
but the high tide from the o - cean, Lord, _ put wa - ter in the town.
But they nev - er meant to leave their homes _ till death was in their face. } Was - n't it a
the tracks gave way to the o - cean, Lord, _ and the trains they went on down.
I saw my fa - ther drown-ing, Lord, _ and I watched my moth - er go.

might - y day, _____ was - n't it a might - y day, _____ was - n't it a

might - y day, Great God, that morn - ing when the storm winds swept the town!

THE MILLER'S DAUGHTER
(La Fille de la Meunière)

French from Auvergne

There she goes, the Mill-er's daugh-ter, Who is danc-ing there with
C'est la fill' de la Meu-niér-e Qui dan-se a-vec Tho-

Tom. You can see she's lost her gar-ter But her stock-ing's stay-ing
mas. Elle a per-du sa jarre-tiér-e, Mais ses bas ne tom-bent

on. **Refrain** Kick it up, kick it up, kick it up high-er. Kick it up, kick it up, kick it up
pas. Ah-lèv' donc, _ lèv' donc _ la gi-gue, Ah__ lèv' donc, _ lèv' donc _ plus

high. Kick it up, kick it up, kick it up high-er. Kick it up, kick it up, kick it up high.
haut. Ah__ lèv' donc, _ lèv' donc _ la gi-gue, Ah__ lèv' donc, _ lèv' donc _ plus haut.

THE MINSTREL BOY

Irish
Words by Thomas Moore

1. The min-strel boy __ to the war is gone, In the ranks of death _____ you'll
2. The min-strel fell, __ but the foe-man's chain Could not bring that proud __ soul __
3. The min-strel boy __ will re-turn, we pray; When we hear the news we all will

find him. His fa-ther's sword __ he has gird-ed on, And his
un-der. The harp he lov'd __ ne'er __ spoke a-gain, For he
cheer it. The min-strel boy __ will re-turn one day, Torn per-

wild harp slung _____ be-hind him. "Land of song!" said the
tore its chords __ a-sun-der; And said, "No chain shall __
haps in bod-y, not in spir-it. Then may he play on his

war-rior bard, "Though all the world be-trays _____ thee, One
sul-ly thee, Thou soul of love and brav-er-y. Thy
harp in peace In a world such as Heav'n has in-ten-ded, For

sword, at least, __ thy __ rights shall guard, One __ faith-ful harp __ shall __ praise thee."
songs were made __ for the pure and free; They shall nev-er sound __ in ____ slav-'ry."
all the bit-ter-ness of man must cease And __ ev-'ry bat-tle must be end-ed.

MISS LILIAN

Folksong from Tobago

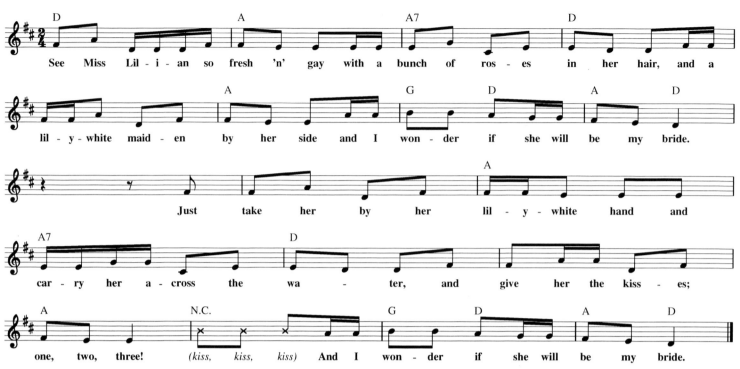

MRS. MURPHY'S CHOWDER

Irish

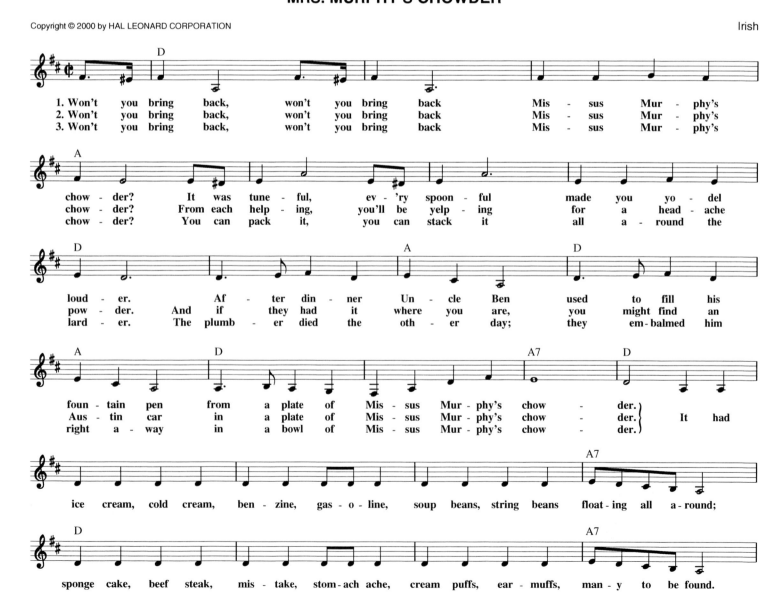

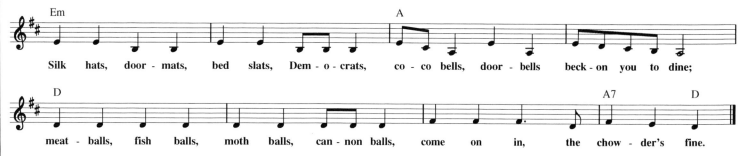

Silk hats, door-mats, bed slats, Dem-o-crats, co-co bells, door-bells beck-on you to dine;

meat-balls, fish balls, moth balls, can-non balls, come on in, the chow-der's fine.

MOLLY BRANNIGAN

Irish

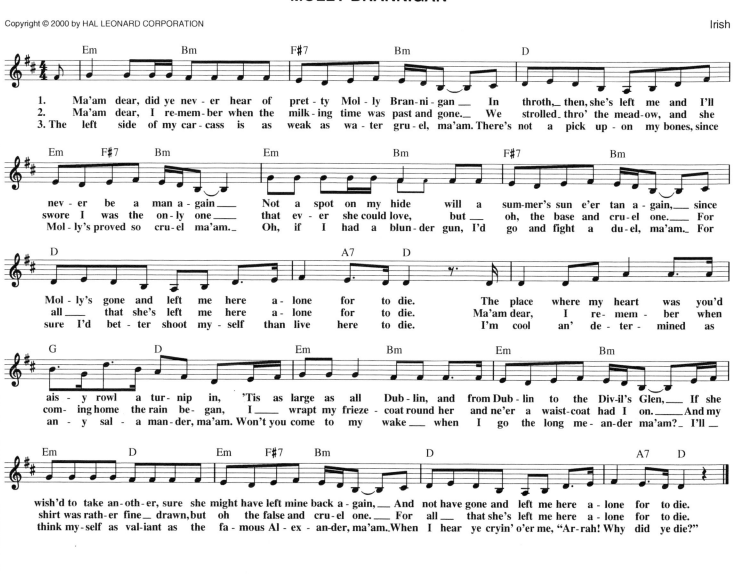

1. Ma'am dear, did ye nev-er hear of pret-ty Mol-ly Bran-ni-gan __ In throth,_ then, she's left me and I'll
2. Ma'am dear, I re-mem-ber when the milk-ing time was past and gone._ We strolled_ thro' the mead-ow, and she
3. The left side of my car-cass is as weak as wa-ter gru-el, ma'am. There's not a pick up-on my bones, since

nev-er be a man a-gain___ Not a spot on my hide will a sum-mer's sun e'er tan a-gain,__ since
swore I was the on-ly one___ that ev-er she could love, but __ oh, the base and cru-el one.__ For
Mol-ly's proved so cru-el ma'am._ Oh, if I had a blun-der gun, I'd go and fight a du-el, ma'am._ For

Mol-ly's gone and left me here a - lone for to die. The place where my heart was you'd
all __ that she's left me here a - lone for to die. Ma'am dear, I re-mem-ber when
sure I'd bet-ter shoot my-self than live here to die. I'm cool an' de-ter-mined as

ais- y rowl a tur-nip in, 'Tis as large as all Dub-lin, and from Dub-lin to the Div-il's Glen,__ If she
com-ing home the rain be-gan, I___ wrapt my frieze - coat round her and ne'er a waist-coat had I on.___ And my
an- y sal - a man-der, ma'am. Won't you come to my wake __ when I go the long me - an-der ma'am?_ I'll __

wish'd to take an-oth-er, sure she might have left mine back a - gain, __ And not have gone and left me here a - lone for to die.
shirt was rath-er fine_ drawn, but oh the false and cru-el one. __ For all __ that she's left me here a - lone for to die.
think my-self as val-iant as the fa - mous Al - ex - an-der, ma'am. When I hear ye cryin' o'er me, "Ar-rah! Why did ye die?"

THE MUFFIN MAN

American version of an English Folksong

Do you know the muf - fin man, the muf - fin man, the muf - fin man? Do you know the

muf - fin man who lives in Dru - ry Lane? Yes, we know the muf - fin man, the

muf - fin man, the muf - fin man. Yes, we know the muf - fin man who lives in Dru - ry Lane.

MISTER RABBIT

Southern American

1. "Mis - ter Rab - bit, Mis - ter Rab - bit, your tail's might - y white."
2. "Mis - ter Rab - bit, Mis - ter Rab - bit, your coat's might - y grey."
3. "Mis - ter Rab - bit, Mis - ter Rab - bit, your ears might - y long."
4. "Mis - ter Rab - bit, Mis - ter Rab - bit, your ears might - y thin."

"Yes, bless God, been get - tin' out - a sight." ____
"Yes, bless God, been out ____ all ____ day." ____
"Yes, bless God, been put ____ on ____ wrong." ____
"Yes, bless God, been split - ten' the ____ wind." ____

Ev - 'ry lit - tle soul gon - na shine, shine, ____

Ev - 'ry lit - tle soul gon - na shine a - long.

MOLLY MALONE
(Cockles and Mussels)

Irish

1. In Dub - lin's fair cit - y, where girls are so pret - ty, I
2. She was a fish - mon - ger, but sure 'twas no won - der, for
3. She died of a fe - ver, but and no one could save her, and

first set my eyes on sweet Mol - ly Ma - lone, as she pushed her wheel-
so were her fa - ther and moth - er be - fore. And they each wheeled their
that was the end of sweet Mol - ly Ma - lone. But her ghost wheels her

bar - row thro' streets broad and nar - row cry - ing "Cock - les and mus - sels, a -
bar - row thro' streets broad and nar - row cry - ing "Cock - les and mus - sels, a -
bar - row thro' streets broad and nar - row cry - ing "Cock - les and mus - sels, a -

live, a - live, oh!
live, a - live, oh!   A - live, a - live, oh! ____ A - live, a - live,
live, a - live, oh!

oh!" ____ Cry - ing "Cock - les and mus - sels, a - live, a - live, oh!"

HE PAID A DEBT

American

1. He paid a debt He did not owe, _____ I owed a debt I could not pay. _
2. He paid that debt at Cal - va - ry, _____ He cleansed my soul and set me free, _
3. One day He's com - ing back for me _____ To live with Him e - ter - nal - ly, _

_____ I need - ed some - one to wash my sins a - way. _____
_____ I'm glad that Je - sus did all my sins e - rase; _____
_____ Won't it be glo - ry to see Him on that day! _____

_____ And now I sing a brand new song: _____ } "A - maz - ing Grace." All day
_____ I now can sing a brand new song: _____
_____ I then will sing a brand new song: _____

long. Christ Je - sus paid the debt that I could nev - er pay. _____

HE'S GONE AWAY

American

1. I'm goin' a - way _____ for to stay a lit - tle while, but I'm
2. He's gone a - way _____ for to stay a lit - tle while, but he's

com - ing back, if I go ten thou - sand miles. Oh, who will tie your
com - ing back, if he goes ten thou - sand miles. Oh, it's dad - dy'll tie my

shoes? And who will glove your hand? And who will kiss those ru - by
shoes, and mom - my'll glove my hands. And you will kiss my ru - by

lips when I am gone? Look a - way, look a - way o - ver Yan - dro.
lips when you come back! Look a - way, look a - way o - ver Yan - dro.

HEAVE AWAY

American Slave Song

Heave a - way, _____ heave a - way! _____ I'd rath - er court a yel - low gal than
work for Hen - ry Clay. Heave a - way, _____ heave a - way! _____ Yel - low gal, I want to go, I'd
rath - er court a yel - low gal than work for Hen - ry Clay. Heave a - way! _____ Yel - low gal, I want to go.

HENRY MARTIN

English

1. There were ___ three broth - ers in mer - ry Scot - land, in Scot - land there lived broth - ers
2. The lot it fell first up - on Hen - ry Mar - tin, the young - est of all the
3. He had not been sail - ing but a long win - ter's night, and a part of a long win - ter's
4. "Hel - lo, ___ hel - lo," cried Hen - ry Mar - tin, "what makes __ you sail so
5. "Oh no, ___ oh no," cried Hen - ry Mar - tin, "that thing ___ it nev - er could
6. "Come low - er your top - sail and brail up your miz - zen, and bring your ship un - der my

7.-9. *(See additional lyrics)*

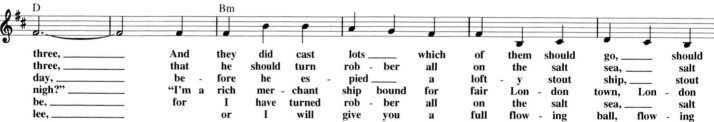

three, _____ And they did cast lots _____ which of them should go, _____ should
three, _____ that he should turn rob - ber all on the salt sea, _____ salt
day, _____ be - fore he es - pied _____ a loft - y stout ship, ___ stout
nigh?" _____ "I'm a rich mer - chant ship bound for fair Lon - don town, Lon - don
be, _____ for I have turned rob - ber all on the salt sea, _____ salt
lee, _____ or I will give you a full flow - ing ball, flow - ing

go, _____ should go, for to turn rob - ber all on the salt sea.
sea, _____ salt sea, for to main - tain his two broth - ers and he.
ship, _____ stout ship, come _____ a - bib - bing down on him straight way.
town, Lon - don town, there - fore I will you to let me pass free."
sea, _____ salt sea, for to main - tain my two broth - ers and me.
ball, flow - ing ball, and your dear bod - ies drown in the salt sea."

Additional Lyrics

7. With broadside and broadside, and at it they went,
   For fully two hours or three,
   When Henry Martin gave to her the death shot,
   The death shot, the death shot,
   Heavily listing to starboard went she.

8. The rich merchant ship she was wounded full sore;
   Right down to the bottom went she.
   And Henry Martin sailed away on the sea,
   Salt sea, salt sea,
   For to maintain my two brothers and me.

9. Bad news! bad news! unto fair London town,
   Bad news I will tell unto thee:
   They've robbed a rich vessel and she's cast away,
   Cast away, cast away,
   All the bold sailors drowned in the salt sea.

HEY DIDDLE DIDDLE

Nursery Rhyme Song

Hey did - dle did - dle, the cat and the fid - dle, The cow jumped o - ver the moon. _____ The

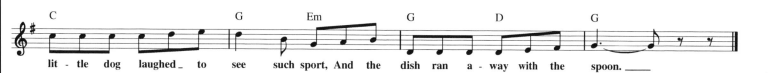

lit - tle dog laughed _ to see such sport, And the dish ran a - way with the spoon. _____

HEY, HO! NOBODY HOME

Traditional Round

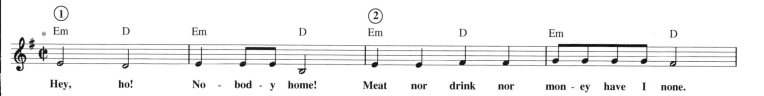

Hey, ho! No - bod - y home! Meat nor drink nor mon - ey have I none.

Still I will be ver - y mer - ry. _____ Hey, ho! No - bod - y home.

* This song may be sung as a 4-part round.

HEY LOLLY, LOLLY

Jamaican Calypso

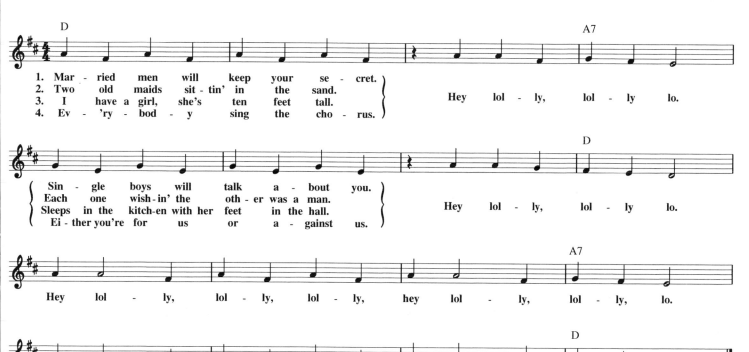

1. Mar - ried men will keep your se - cret.
2. Two old maids sit - tin' in the sand.
3. I have a girl, she's ten feet tall.
4. Ev - 'ry - bod - y sing the cho - rus.

Hey lol - ly, lol - ly lo.

Sin - gle boys will talk a - bout you.
Each one wish - in' the oth - er was a man.
Sleeps in the kitch - en with her feet in the hall.
Ei - ther you're for us or a - gainst us.

Hey lol - ly, lol - ly lo.

Hey lol - ly, lol - ly, lol - ly, hey lol - ly, lol - ly, lo.

Hey lol - ly, lol - ly, lol - ly, hey lol - ly, lol - ly lo.

THE HELL-BOUND TRAIN

American

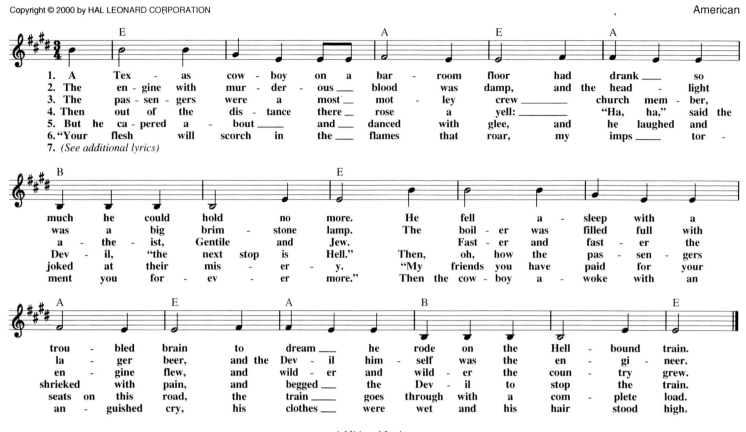

Additional Lyrics

7. And he prayed as he'd never prayed before
To be saved from Hell's front door.
His prayers and pleadings were not in vain,
For he never rode on the Hell-bound train.

HIGH GERMANY

18th Century English

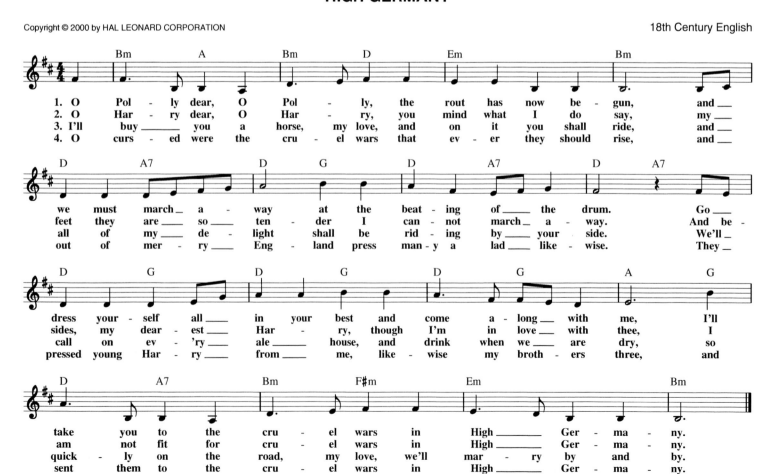

HIELAND LADDIE

Scottish Sea Chantey

1. Was you ev - er in Que - bec? __
2. Was you ev - er in Mer - a - shee? __
3. Was you ev - er in Balt - i - more? __
4. Was you ev - er on the Brum - ma - low? __
5. Was you ev - er in Dun - dee? __

Bon - nie Lad - die, Hie - land Lad - die.

Stow - ing tim - ber on the deck, __
Where you stayed fast to a tree, __
Danc - in' on that sand - ed floor, __
Where the girls are all the go, __
There some pret - ty ships you'll see, __

My bon - nie Hie - land Lad - die.

Hey, ho, and a - way we go. Bon - nie Lad - die, Hie - land Lad - die.

Hey, ho, a - way we go, my bon - nie Hie - land Lad - die.

HIGH BARBAREE

American Sea Chantey
attributed to Charles Dibdin

1. There were two loft - y ships from old Eng - land came,
2. "A - loft there, a - loft! our jol - ly boat - swain cries,
3. "O naught up - on the stern, there's naught up - on the lee,"
4. "O hail her! O hail her! our gal - lant cap - tain cried,"
5. "O I am not a man - o' - war or a priv - a - teer," said he,
6. "O 'twas broad - side to broad - side a long time we lay,
7. (See additional lyrics)

Blow

high! Blow low! An' so sailed we,

One
"But
"Are
"But
Un

was the Prince o' Luth - er an' the oth - er Prince o' Wales,
"Look a - head, look a - stern, look a - weath - er and a - lee,
there's a loft - y ship wind - ward, and she's sail - ing fast and free."
you a man - o' - war or a priv - a - teer," said he,
til the prince of Lu - ther shot the pi - rate's mast a - way.

All a -

cruis - in' down the coasts of the High Bar - ba - ree!

Additional Lyrics

7. "O quarter! O quarter!" those pirates then did cry,
Blow high! Blow low! An' so sailed we.
But the quarter that we gave them - we sunk them in the sea.
All a cruisin' down the coasts of the High Barbaree!

HICKORY DICKORY DOCK

Nursery Rhyme Song

Hick - o - ry dick - o - ry dock   The mouse ran up the clock.   The

clock struck one;   the mouse ran down,   Hick - o - ry dick - o - ry dock.

A HIGHLAND LAD MY LOVE WAS BORN

Words by Robert Burns
Scottish Folk Melody, "The White Cockade"

1. A ___ High - land lad my ___ love was born, The ___ Law - land laws ___ he ___
2. With his phi - la - beg and ___ tar - tan plaid, and gude clay - more ___ down ___
3. They ___ ban - ished him be - yond the sea, but ___ ere the bud ___ was ___
4. But ___ oh! they catched him ___ at the last, and bound him in ___ a ___
5. And ___ now a wid - ow ___ I must mourn the pleas - ures that ___ will ___

held in scorn; But he still was faith - fu' ___ to his clan, My ___
by his side. The la - dies' hearts ___ he ___ did tre - pan, my ___
on the tree. A - doun my cheeks ___ the ___ pearls they ran, em ___
dun - geon fast. My ___ curse up - on ___ them ___ ev - 'ry one, they've ___
ne'er re - turn; o ___ com - fort but ___ a ___ heart - y can, when ___

gal - lant ___ braw ___ John ___ High - land - man.
gal - lant ___ braw ___ John ___ High - land - man.
brac - ing ___ my ___ John ___ High - land - man. } Sing ___ hey, my braw John
hanged ___ my ___ braw ___ John ___ High - land - man.
I ___ think ___ on ___ John ___ High - land - man.

High - land - man, Sing ho, my braw John ___ High - land - man; There's ___

no' a lad ___ in ___ a' the lan' Was ___ match ___ wi' ___ my ___ John ___ High - land - man.

HILL AND GULLY RIDER

Jamaican

Hill an' gul - ly rid - er, hill an' gul - ly.   Hill an' gul - ly rid - er, hill an' gul - ly.   I was

walk - in' real slow down hill an' gul - ly, when I break my toe down hill an' gul - ly.   Ma - ma

told me don't	go	down	hill an'	gul - ly,	all the boys	walk the road down	hill an'	gul - ly.

{1. Wom - en
2. Me —
3. The hot

car - ry all the load down hill an' gul - ly, grass too green to be mowed down
don - key like to run down hill an' gul - ly, I chase him just for fun down
sun — is a - burn - in' down hill an' gul - ly, I'm a - wheel - in' and a - turn - in' down

hill an' gul - ly. Hill an' gul - ly rid - er, hill an' gul - ly.
hill an' gul - ly. When the work's all done down hill an' gul - ly.
hill an' gul - ly. My heart is a - yearn - in' down hill an' gul - ly.

THE HONEST PLOUGHMAN

American

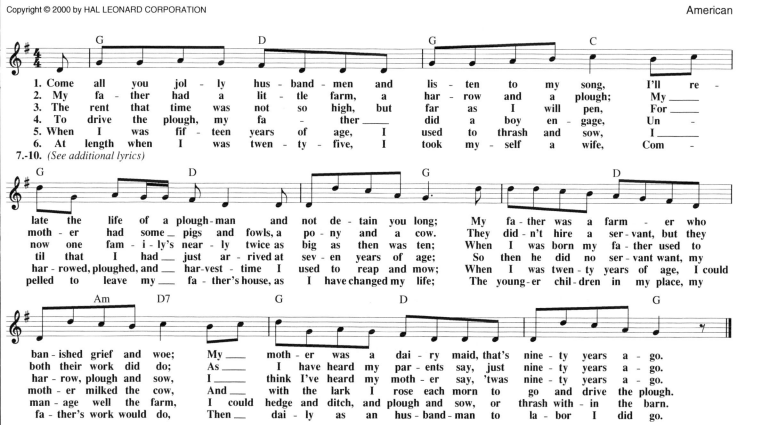

1. Come all you jol - ly hus - band - men and lis - ten to my song, I'll re -
2. My fa - ther had a lit - tle farm, a har - row and a plough; My _____
3. The rent that time was not so high, but far as I will pen, For _____
4. To drive the plough, my fa - ther _____ did a boy en - gage, Un -
5. When I was fif - teen years of age, I used to thrash and sow, I _____
6. At length when I was twen - ty - five, I took my - self a wife, Com -

7.-10. *(See additional lyrics)*

late the life of a plough-man and not de - tain you long; My fa - ther was a farm - er who
moth - er had some _ pigs and fowls, a po - ny and a cow. They did - n't hire a ser - vant, but they
now one fam - i - ly's near - ly twice as big as then was ten; When I was born my fa - ther used to
til that I had _ just ar - rived at sev - en years of age; So then he did no ser - vant want, my
har - rowed, ploughed, and _ har - vest - time I used to reap and mow; When I was twen - ty years of age, I could
pelled to leave my _ fa - ther's house, as I have changed my life; The young - er chil - dren in my place, my

ban - ished grief and woe; My _____ moth - er was a dai - ry maid, that's nine - ty years a - go.
both their work did do; As _____ I have heard my par - ents say, just nine - ty years a - go.
har - row, plough and sow, I _____ think I've heard my moth - er say, 'twas nine - ty years a - go.
moth - er milked the cow, And _____ with the lark I rose each morn to go and drive the plough.
man - age well the farm, I could hedge and ditch, and plough and sow, or thrash with - in the barn.
fa - ther's work would do, Then _____ dai - ly as an hus - band - man to la - bor I did go.

Additional Lyrics

7. My wife and me, tho' very poor, could keep a pig and cow,
   She could sit and knit, and spin, and I the land could plough;
   There nothing was upon a farm at all, but I could do,
   I feel things very different now - that's many years ago.

8. We lived along contented, and banished pain and grief,
   We had not occasion then to ask parish relief;
   But now my hairs are grown quite grey, I cannot well engage
   To work as I had used to do - I'm ninety years of age.

9. But now that I'm ninety years of age, and poverty do feel,
   If for relief do go, they shove me in a Whig Bastille,
   Where I may hang my weary head, and pine in grief and woe,
   My father did not see the like, just ninety years ago.

10. When a man has laboured all his life, to do his country good,
    He's respected just as much when old as a donkey in a wood,
    His days are gone and past, and he may weep in grief and woe,
    The times are very different now, to ninety years ago.

HINKY DINKY PARLEY VOO

American, from World War I

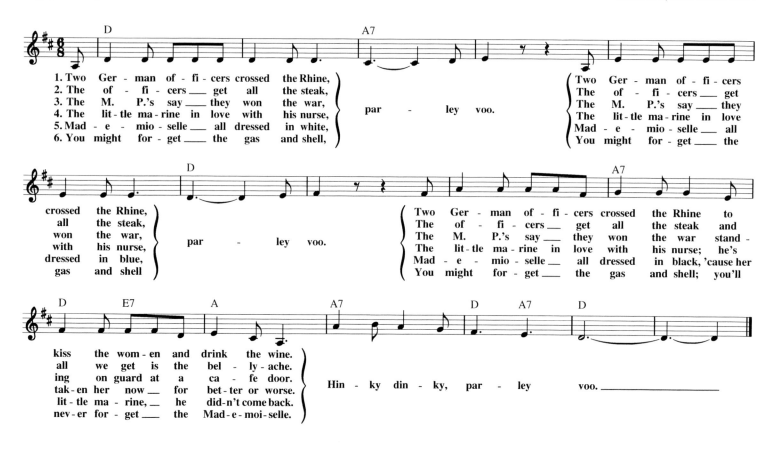

1. Two Ger - man of - fi - cers crossed the Rhine, par - ley voo. Two Ger - man of - fi - cers
2. The of - fi - cers __ get all the steak,
3. The M. P.'s say __ they won the war,
4. The lit - tle ma - rine in love with his nurse,
5. Mad - e - mio - selle __ all dressed in white,
6. You might for - get __ the gas and shell,

The of - fi - cers __ get
The M. P.'s say __ they
The lit - tle ma - rine in love
Mad - e - mio - selle __ all
You might for - get __ the

crossed the Rhine, par - ley voo. Two Ger - man of - fi - cers crossed the Rhine to
all the steak, The of - fi - cers __ get all the steak and
won the war, The M. P.'s say __ they won the war stand -
with his nurse, The lit - tle ma - rine in love with his nurse; he's
dressed in blue, Mad - e - mio - selle __ all dressed in black, 'cause her
gas and shell You might for - get __ the gas and shell; you'll

kiss the wom - en and drink the wine. Hin - ky din - ky, par - ley voo. __
all we get is the bel - ly - ache.
ing on guard at a ca - fe door.
tak - en her now __ for bet - ter or worse.
lit - tle ma - rine, __ he did - n't come back.
nev - er for - get __ the Mad - e - moi - selle.

HOME ON THE RANGE

Kansas, circa 1873
Attributed to Dr. Brewster Higley (words) and Dan Kelly (music)

1. Oh, give me a home where the buf - fa - lo roam, Where the deer and the
2. How oft - en at night when the heav - ens are bright, with the light from the
3. Where the air is so pure, the __ zeph - yrs so free, the __ breez - es so
4. Oh, I love those wild flow'rs in this dear land of ours. The __ cur - lew, I

an - te - lope play, __ Where sel - dom is heard a dis -
glit - ter - ing stars, __ have I stood there a - mazed and __
balm - y and light. __ That I would not ex - change my __
love to hear scream. __ And I love the white rocks and the

cour - ag - ing word, And the skies are not cloud - y all day. __
asked as I gazed, if their glo - ry ex - ceeds that of ours. __
home on the range for __ all of the cit - ies so bright. __
an - te - lope flocks, that __ graze on the moun - tain - tops green. __

Home, home on the range, __ Where the deer and the

an - te - lope play. _____ Where sel - dom is heard a dis-

cour - ag - ing word, And the skies are not cloud - y all day. _____

HOME IN THAT ROCK

Traditional Spiritual

1. I've got a home in - a that rock, don't you see? Don't you see? I've got a
2. Poor man Laz - a - ras, poor_ as I, don't you see? Don't you see? Poor man Laz -
3. Rich man Di - ves lived _ so well, don't you see? Don't you see? Rich man Di -
4. God gave No - ah the rain - bow sign, don't you see? Don't you see? God gave No -

home in - a that rock, don't you see? Don't you see? Be - tween the earth and sky, thought I
a - ras poor _ as I, don't you see? Don't you see? Poor man Laz-a-ras poor as I, when he
ves lived _ so well, don't you see? Don't you see? Rich man Di - ves lived so well, when he
ah the rain - bow sign, don't you see? Don't you see? God gave No - ah the rain-bow sign, no more

heard my Sav - ior cry: "You've got a home in - a that rock, don't you see? Don't you see?"
died he found a home on high. He had a home in - a that rock, don't you see? Don't you see?
died he found a home in Hell. He had no home in - a that rock, don't you see? Don't you see?
wa-ter - but fire next time. No - ah had a home in - a that rock, don't you see? Don't you see?

HOME SWEET HOME

Words by John Howard Payne
Music by Sir Henry Bishop
American Popular Song, 1823

1. 'Mid_ pleas - ures and pal - a - ces though_ we may roam, Be it ev - er so hum - ble, there's
2. An _ ex - ile from home, splen-dor daz - zles in vain, Oh,_ give me my low - ly thatched
3. To _ thee, I'll re - turn, o - ver - bur - dened with care, The _ hearts dear - est sol - ace will

no_____ place like home; A charm_ from the sky seems to hal - low us there, Which,
cot - tage a - gain; The birds _ sing - ing gai - ly, that come_ at my call; Give me
smile_ on me there. No more _ from that cot - tage a - gain _ will I roam, Be it

seek _ through the world, is ne'er met _ with else - where.)
them, _ with that peace of mind dear - er than all.) Home! Home! Sweet Home. _____ There's
ev - er so hum - ble, there's no _ place like home.)

no _____ place like home. Home! Home! Sweet Home. _____ There's no _ place like home.

HOMEWARD FROM THE MOUNTAINS
(Hjemreise Fra Saeteren)

Norwegian Shepherd's Song

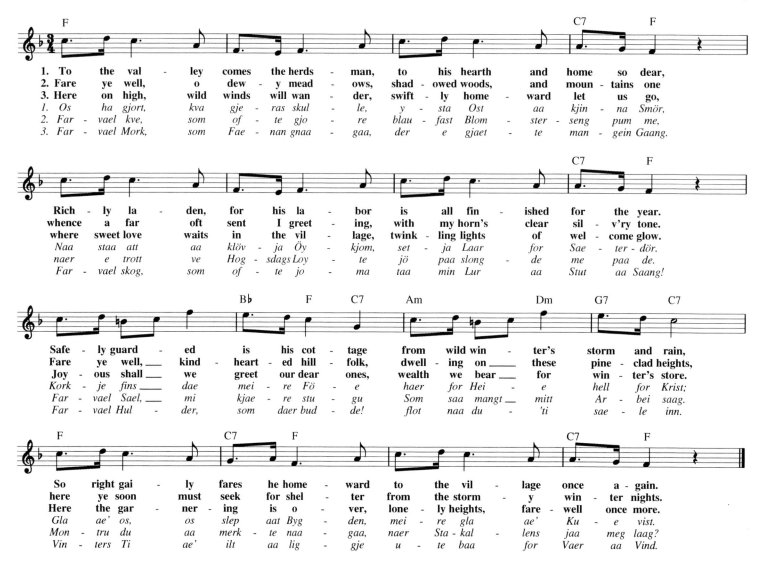

HOOSEN JOHNNY

Folksong from Illinois

A HORSE NAMED BILL

American Nonsense Song

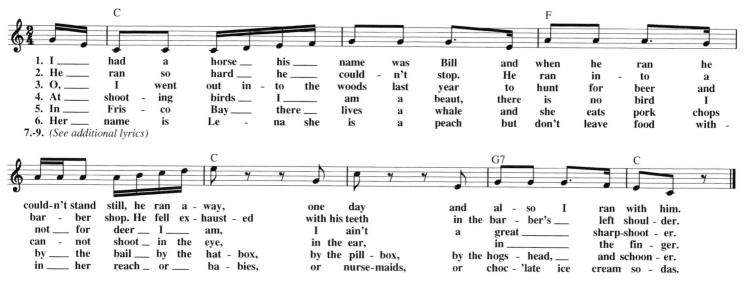

1. I _____ had a horse _____ his _____ name was Bill and when he ran he
2. He _____ ran so hard _____ he _____ could - n't stop. He ran in - to a
3. O, _____ I went out in - to the woods last year to hunt for beer and
4. At _____ shoot - ing birds _____ I _____ am a beaut, there is no bird I
5. In _____ Fris - co Bay _____ there _____ lives a whale and she eats pork chops
6. Her _____ name is Le - na she is a peach but don't leave food with -

7.-9. *(See additional lyrics)*

could-n't stand still, he ran a - way, one day and al - so I ran with him.
bar - ber shop. He fell ex - haust - ed with his teeth in the bar - ber's _____ left shoul - der.
not _____ for deer _____ I _____ am, I ain't a great _____ sharp-shoot - er.
can - not shoot _____ in the eye, in the ear, in _____ the fin - ger.
by _____ the bail _____ by the hat - box, by the pill - box, by the hogs - head, _____ and schoon - er.
in _____ her reach _____ or _____ ba - bies, or nurse-maids, or choc - 'late ice cream so - das.

Additional Lyrics

7. She loves to laugh and when she smiles
You just see teeth for miles and miles
And tonsils
And spareribs
And things too fierce to mention.

8. She knows no games so when she plays
She rolls her eyes for days and days
She vibrates
And yodels
And breaks the Ten Commandments.

9. O, what can you do in a case like that
O, what can you do but stamp on your hat
Or on an eggshell
Or a toothbrush
Or anything that's helpless.

THE HOUSE CARPENTER

English

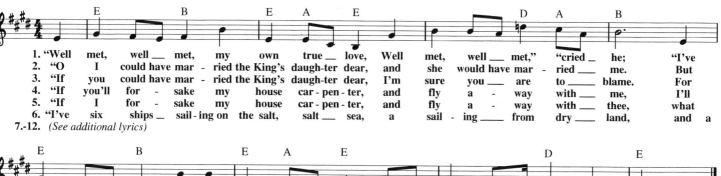

1. "Well met, well _____ met, my own true _____ love, Well met, well _____ met," "cried _____ he; "I've
2. "O I could have mar - ried the King's daugh-ter dear, and she would have mar - ried _____ me. But
3. "If you could have mar - ried the King's daugh-ter dear, I'm sure you _____ are to _____ blame. For
4. "If you'll for - sake my house car - pen - ter, and fly a - way with _____ me, I'll
5. "If I for - sake my house car - pen - ter, and fly a - way with _____ thee, what
6. "I've six ships _____ sail-ing on the salt, salt _____ sea, a sail - ing _____ from dry _____ land, and a

7.-12. *(See additional lyrics)*

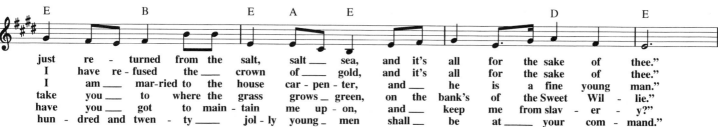

just re - turned from the salt, salt _____ sea, and it's all for the sake of thee."
I have re - fused the _____ crown of _____ gold, and it's all for the sake of thee."
I am _____ mar-ried to the house car - pen - ter, and _____ he is a fine young man."
take you _____ to where the grass grows _____ green, on the bank's of the Sweet Wil - lie."
have you _____ got to main - tain me up - on, and _____ keep me from slav - er - y?"
hun - dred and twen - ty _____ jol - ly young _____ men shall _____ be at _____ your com - mand."

Additional Lyrics

7. She picked up her poor little babe,
Her kisses were one two three;
And as she trod upon her way,
She shone like glittering gold.

8. They had not been at sea two weeks,
I'm sure it was not three,
When this poor maid began to weep,
And she sept most bitterly.

9. "O do you weep for your gold?" he said,
"Your houses, your land, or your store?
Or do you weep for your house carpenter,
That you never shall see anymore?"

10. "I do not weep for my gold," she said,
My houses, my land, or my store;
But I do weep for my poor little babe,
That I never shall see anymore."

11. They had not been at sea three weeks,
I'm sure it was not four,
When in the ship there sprang a leak,
And she sank, to rise no more.

12. "Farewell, farewell, my own true love,
Farewell, farewell," cried she;
"O I have deserted my house carpenter,
For a grave in the depths of the sea."

HOT CROSS BUNS

Nursery Rhyme Song

Hot cross buns! Hot cross buns!

One, a pen - ny, Two, a pen - ny, Hot cross buns!

THE HOUNDS OF FILEMORE

Irish

1. You lads and lass - es gay, And you with sport - ing fa - ces, If you
2. A drag hunt we will have, Swift hors - es and fine rid - ers. Gen -
3. A - round the course we'll go, To see who'll rouse the ech - o From
4. Come - ly struck it first. There was Ratt - ler Thade the Weav - er. Small
5. And now the hunt is o'er, The sun is near - ly set - ting.

live un - to next year, You will ne'er for - get the ra - ces. Such ra - ces we will
tle - men there will be, For to wield their swords and sa - bres. If a sin - gle man should
Car - han woods a - bove, To the moun - tains of Kim - e - go. Ken - mare will hear the
Tru - man from Tur - een, And Tau - ner was their lead - er, Ju - no Cof - fey of
In - to town we'll go, As tired our limbs are get - ting. In tap rooms we will

have, With out bri - dle, whip or sad - dle, And none of you will say, That it's
fall, We will all feel ver - y sor - ry, For a sign it is most sure, That
shock, And Din - gle will a - wak - en. Kil - lorg - lin will re - sound, And Val -
Coars, Like - wise Ju - no of Fo - ley. Ju - no Lynch in - deed, Were three
sit, Call for por - ter, ale and whis - ky. Then home - ward we will go, With

all a fid - dle fad - dle.)
year he will not mar - ry.
en - tia will be shak - en. Oh, File - more you're the place for mer - ry sport and
Ju - nos full of glo - ry.
spir - its light and frisk - y.)

sing - ing, And the chief a - mong them all is the charm - ing bea - gle hunt - ing.

HOUSE OF THE RISING SUN

American

Additional Lyrics

7. I'm going back to New Orleans,
    My race is almost run.
    Going back to end my life
    Beneath the Rising Sun.

HOW CAN I KEEP FROM SINGING?

19th Century Quaker Hymn

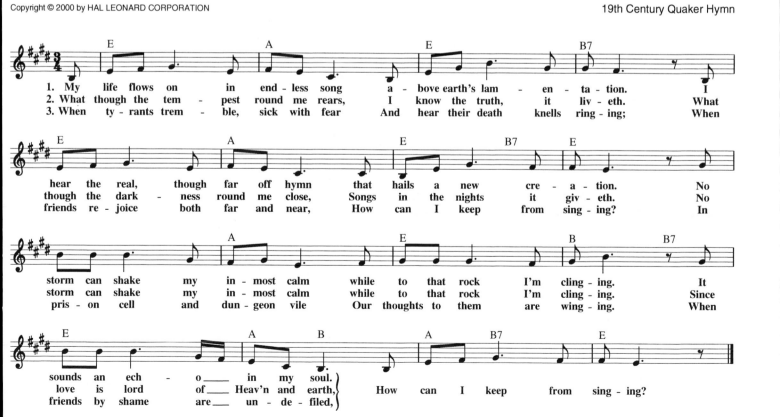

THE HOUSEWIFE'S LAMENT

American

1. One day I was walk-ing, I heard a com-plain-ing, and saw an old
2. There's too much of wor-ri-ment goes to a bon-net, there's too much of
3. In March it is mud, it is slush in De-cem-ber, the mid-sum-mer
4. There are worms on the cher-ries and slugs on the ros-es, and ants in the
5. It's sweep-ing at six and it's dust-ing at sev-en, it's vict-uals at
6. With grease and with grime ___ from cor-ner to cen-ter, for-ev-er at

7.,8. (*See additional lyrics*)

wom-an, the pic-ture of gloom. She gazed at the mud on her
i-ron-ing goes to a shirt. There's noth-ing that pays for the
bree-zes are load-ed with dust. In fall the leaves lit-ter, in
su-gar and mice in the pies. The rub-bish of spi-ders no
eight and it's dish-es at nine. It's pot-ting and pan-ning from
war and for-ev-er a-lert. No rest for a day lest the

door-step ('twas rain-ing) and this was her song as she wield-ed her broom.
time you waste on it, there's noth-ing that lasts us but trou-ble and dirt.
mud-dy Sep-tem-ber the wall-pa-per rots and the can-dle-sticks rust.
mor-tal sup-pos-es and rav-ag-es roach-es and dam-ag-ing flies.
ten to e-lev-en, we scarce break our fast till we plan how to dine.
en-e-my en-ter, I spend my whole life in the strug-gle with dirt.

} Oh,

Chorus

life is a toil, ___ and love is a trou-ble, ___ beau-ty will

fade ___ and rich-es will flee. Pleas-ures, they dwin-dle and pric-es, they

dou-ble, and noth-ing is as I would wish it to be.

Additional Lyrics

7. "Last night in my dreams I was stationed forever,
On a far little rock in the midst of the sea.
My one change of life was a ceaseless endeavor,
To sweep off the waves as they swept over me."
Chorus

8. "Alas! 'Twas no dream— ahead I behold it,
I see I am helpless my fate to avert."
She lay down her broom, her apron she folded,
She lay down and died and was buried in dirt.
Chorus

HOW SHOULD I YOUR TRUE LOVE KNOW

Words by William Shakespeare
Traditional English

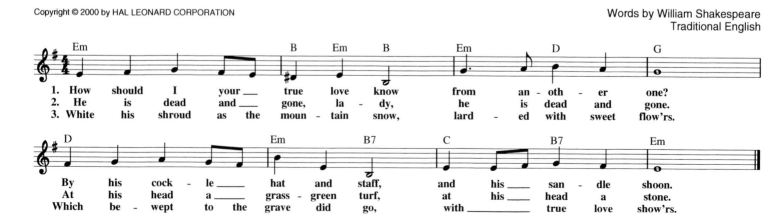

1. How should I your ___ true love know from an-oth-er one?
2. He is dead and ___ gone, la-dy, he is dead and gone.
3. White his shroud as the moun-tain snow, lard-ed with sweet flow'rs.

By his cock-le ___ hat and staff, and his ___ san-dle shoon.
At his head a ___ grass-green turf, at his ___ head a stone.
Which be-wept to the grave did go, with ___ true love show'rs.

HOW CAN I LEAVE THEE?

Folksong from Central Europe

1. How can I leave thee? How can I from thee part? Thou, on - ly,
2. Blue is a flow - 'ret Called the "For - get - me - not," Wear it up -

hath my heart, Dear one, be - lieve. Thou hath this soul of mine, So close - ly
on thy heart, And think of me! Flow - 'ret and hope may die. Yet love with

bound to thine, No oth - er can I love, Save thee a - lone.
us shall stay, That can - not pass a - way, Sis - ter, be - lieve.

HULLABALLOO-BALAY

Sea Chantey

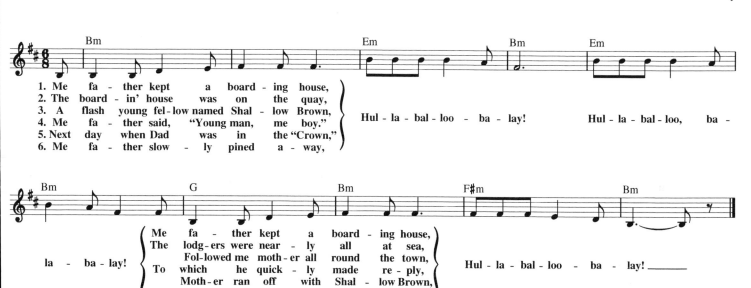

1. Me fa - ther kept a board - ing house,
2. The board - in' house was on the quay,
3. A flash young fel - low named Shal - low Brown,
4. Me fa - ther said, "Young man, me boy."
5. Next day when Dad was in the "Crown,"
6. Me fa - ther slow - ly pined a - way,

Hul - la - bal - loo - ba - lay! Hul - la - bal - loo, ba -

Me fa - ther kept a board - ing house,
The lodg - ers were near - ly all at sea,
Fol - lowed me moth - er all round the town,
To which he quick - ly made re - ply,
Moth - er ran off with Shal - low Brown,
For Moth - er came back on the fol - low - ing day,

la - ba - lay! Hul - la - bal - loo - ba - lay! _____

HURREE HURROO

Scottish

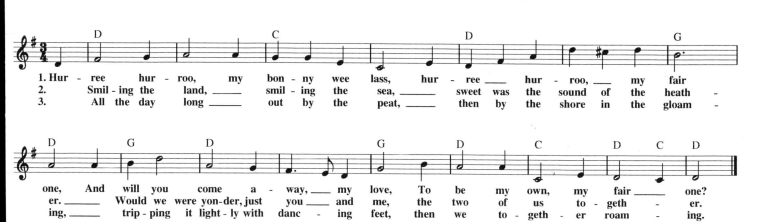

1. Hur - ree hur - roo, my bon - ny wee lass, hur - ree ____ hur - roo, ____ my fair
2. Smil - ing the land, ____ smil - ing the sea, ____ sweet was the sound of the heath -
3. All the day long ____ out by the peat, ____ then by the shore in the gloam -

one, And will you come a - way, ____ my love, To be my own, my fair ____ one?
er. ____ Would we were yon - der, just you ____ and me, the two of us to - geth - er.
ing, ____ trip - ping it light - ly with danc - ing feet, then we to - geth - er roam - ing.

HOW FIRM A FOUNDATION

Early American
Words by John Rippon

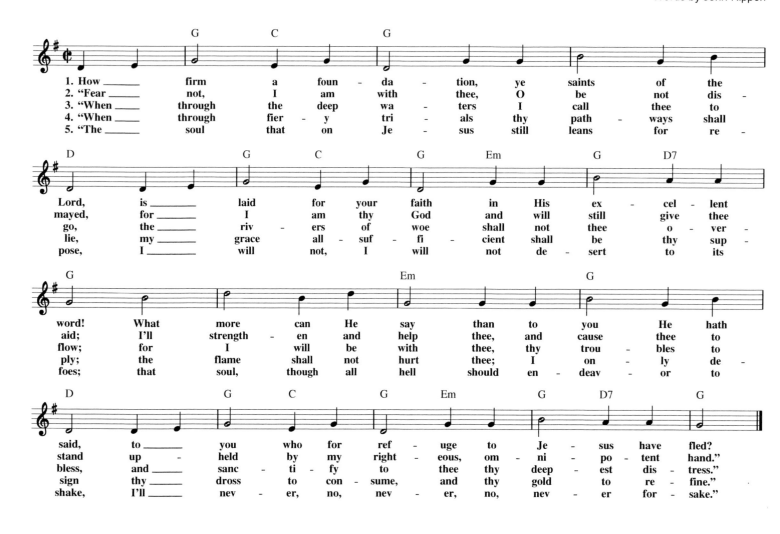

HOW OLD ARE YOU, MY PRETTY LITTLE MISS?

American

HUDSON RIVER STEAMBOAT

19th Century American

1. Hud - son Riv - er steam - boat, steam - ing up and down, New York to Al - ba - ny or
2. Shad __ boat, __ pick - le boat, ly - ing side by side, fish - er-folk and sail - or men, __
3. The Sedge - wick was rac - ing and she lost all hope, used up her steam __ on the

an - y riv - er town. Choo, choo to go a - head, choo, choo to slack 'er. The
wait - ing for the tide. Rain cloud, __ storm __ cloud o - ver yon - der hill. __
big cal - li - o - pe. But she hopped right a - long, she was hop - ping quick, __ all the

cap - tain and the first mate they both chew to - bac - co
Thun - der on the Dun - der-berg __ rum - bles in the kill. __ } Choo, choo to go a - head,
way from Sto - ny Point up to Po - pa - lo - pen Creek. __

choo, choo to slack 'er, pack - et boat, tow boat and a dou - ble stack - er. { 1.,2. Choo, choo to Tar - ry Town,
3. New York to Al - ba - ny,

Spuy - ten Duy - vil, all a - round, }
Round - out and Tiv - o - li, } choo, choo to go a - head, choo, choo to back 'er.

HUNTING THE HARE
(Hela'r 'Sgyvarnog)

Welsh

1. O - ver hill __ and plain they're bound - ing, Thro' the air __ they seem __ to fly,
2. When the day's __ glad sport is o - ver, Seat - ed in __ the Bar - on's hall,
1. Awn i hel - a'r ys - gyf - arn - og, Dym - a for - eu hyf - rhd iach;
2. Am ei by - wyd mae hi'n rhe - deg, E - for claw wd a god - rau'r llwyn:

Hark! the mer - ry horn is sound - ing, Hear the hunt - er's hap - py cry!
Round the fes - tive board dis - cov - er, Gal - lant hunt - ers one __ and all.
Cod - wyd hi __ ar graig eith - in - og: Hei! y cwn __ a'r gw - ta fach!
We - le fil - gi fel yn he - deg, Dy - na hi __ o flaen __ ei drwyn.

Now __ through din - gle, dell __ and hol - low, Dart __ they on __ at fear - less pace:
Laugh - ing loud - ly, jok - ing, sing - ing, As __ the wine __ goes round __ a - pace,
Fel __ y - gwynt, neu'n gynt __ na hy - ny, Gyd - a'r cwn __ a hith - au'r awn;
Hir __ y bydd - o mewn __ cad - wr - aeth, He - la gy - da gwledd - a chan:

Oh! what joy __ the hounds to fol - low, There's no pleas - ure like __ the chase.
While the an - cient roof is ring - ing With the glo - ries of __ the chase!
Ar y ffridd __ wrth fyn'd i fyn - y, Dy - na i - ddi dro - fa iawn.
O! am ddysg - u Naw Hel - wr - iaeth, Camp au gwled - ig Cym - ru lân!

THE HUNTERS OF KENTUCKY
THE HUNTERS OF KENTUCKY

Words by Samuel Woodworth
19th Century American

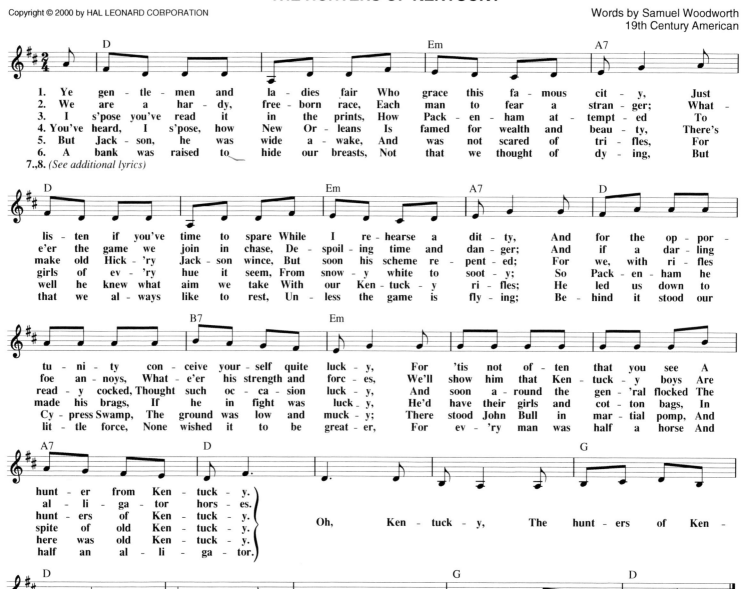

1. Ye gentlemen and ladies fair Who grace this famous city, Just
2. We are a hardy, free-born race, Each man to fear a stranger; What-
3. I s'pose you've read it in the prints, How Pack-en-ham attempted To
4. You've heard, I s'pose, how New Orleans Is famed for wealth and beauty, There's
5. But Jackson, he was wide awake, And was not scared of trifles, For
6. A bank was raised to hide our breasts, Not that we thought of dying, But

7.,8. *(See additional lyrics)*

listen if you've time to spare While I rehearse a ditty, And for the oppor-
e'er the game we join in chase, Despoiling time and danger; And if a darling
make old Hick-'ry Jackson wince, But soon his scheme repented; For we, with rifles
girls of ev-'ry hue it seem, From snow-y white to soot-y; So Pack-en-ham he
well he knew what aim we take With our Ken-tuck-y rifles; He led us down to
that we al-ways like to rest, Un-less the game is fly-ing; Be-hind it stood our

tu-ni-ty con-ceive your-self quite luck-y, For 'tis not of-ten that you see A
foe an-noys, What-e'er his strength and forc-es, We'll show him that Ken-tuck-y boys Are
read-y cocked, Thought such oc-ca-sion luck-y, And soon a-round the gen-'ral flocked The
made his brags, If he in fight was luck-y, He'd have their girls and cot-ton bags, In
Cy-press Swamp, The ground was low and muck-y, There stood John Bull in mar-tial pomp, And
lit-tle force, None wished it to be great-er, For ev-'ry man was half a horse And

hunt-er from Ken-tuck-y.
al-li-ga-tor hors-es.
hunt-ers of Ken-tuck-y.
spite of old Ken-tuck-y.
here was old Ken-tuck-y.
half an al-li-ga-tor.

Oh, Ken-tuck-y, The hunt-ers of Ken-

tuck-y. Oh, Ken-tuck-y, The hunt-ers of Ken-tuck-y.

Additional Lyrics

7. They did not let our patience tire,
Before they showed their faces;
We did not choose to waste our fire,
So snugly kept our places;
But when so near we saw them wink,
We thought it time to stop 'em,
And 'twould have done you good, I think,
To see Kentucky drop 'em.

8. They found, at last, 'twas vain to fight,
Where lead was all the booty,
And so they wisely took to flight,
And left us all our beauty;
And now, if danger e'er annoys,
Remember what our trade is,
Just send for us Kentucky boys,
And we'll protect ye, ladies.

HURRY UP, LIZA JANE

Appalachian Folksong

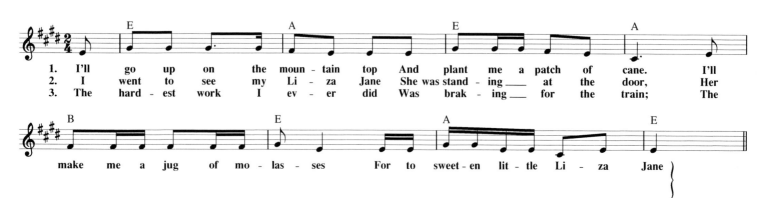

1. I'll go up on the moun-tain top And plant me a patch of cane. I'll
2. I went to see my Li-za Jane She was stand-ing at the door, Her
3. The hard-est work I ev-er did Was brak-ing for the train; The

make me a jug of mo-las-ses For to sweet-en lit-tle Li-za Jane

Hur - ry up, pret - ty lit - tle gal, Hur - ry up, Li - za Jane;

Hur - ry up, pret - ty lit - tle gal Or we will miss that train.

HUSH, LITTLE BABY

American, from the Carolinas

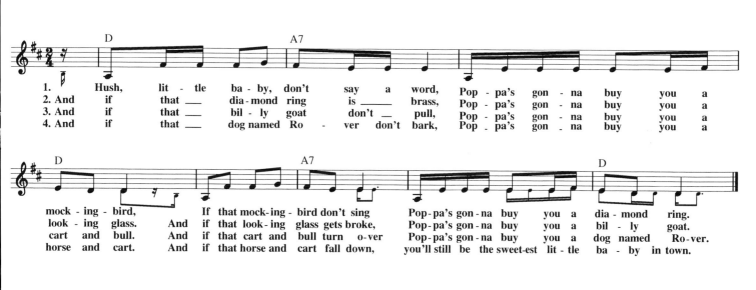

1. Hush, lit - tle ba - by, don't say a word, Pop - pa's gon - na buy you a
2. And if that __ dia - mond ring is __ brass, Pop - pa's gon - na buy you a
3. And if that __ bil - ly goat don't __ pull, Pop - pa's gon - na buy you a
4. And if that __ dog named Ro - ver don't bark, Pop - pa's gon - na buy you a

mock - ing - bird, If that mock - ing - bird don't sing Pop - pa's gon - na buy you a dia - mond ring.
look - ing glass. And if that look - ing glass gets broke, Pop - pa's gon - na buy you a bil - ly goat.
cart and bull. And if that cart and bull turn o - ver Pop - pa's gon - na buy you a dog named Ro - ver.
horse and cart. And if that horse and cart fall down, you'll still be the sweet - est lit - tle ba - by in town.

I AM A PILGRIM

African-American Spiritual

1. I am a Pil - grim, __ and a stran - ger, __ trav - 'ling through __
2. I got a moth - er, __ a sis - ter and broth - er, __ who have gone __
3. I'm go - ing down to __ that riv - er Jor - dan, __ just to bathe __

__ this wea - ri - some land. __ I got a home in __ that yon - der
__ to that __ sweet land. __ I'm de - ter - mined __ to go __ and
__ my wea - ry soul. __ If I could touch but __ the hem of His

cit - y, good Lord, and it's not made, __ not made __ by hand. __
see them, good Lord, __ all o - ver on that dis - tant shore. __
gar - ment, good Lord, well I be - lieve it would make __ me whole. __

I CAN'T FEEL AT HOME IN THIS WORLD ANYMORE

American Gospel Song

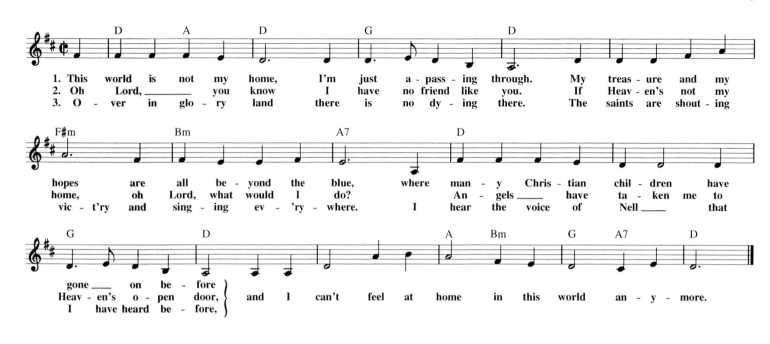

1. This world is not my home, I'm just a-pass-ing through. My treas-ure and my
2. Oh Lord, _____ you know I have no friend like you. If Heav-en's not my
3. O-ver in glo-ry land there is no dy-ing there. The saints are shout-ing

hopes are all be-yond the blue, where man-y Chris-tian chil-dren have
home, oh Lord, what would I do? An-gels have ta-ken me to
vic-t'ry and sing-ing ev-'ry-where. I hear the voice of Nell ____ that

gone ____ on be-fore
Heav-en's o-pen door, } and I can't feel at home in this world an-y-more.
I have heard be-fore,

I GAVE MY LOVE A CHERRY
(The Riddle Song)

Mountain Song from Kentucky

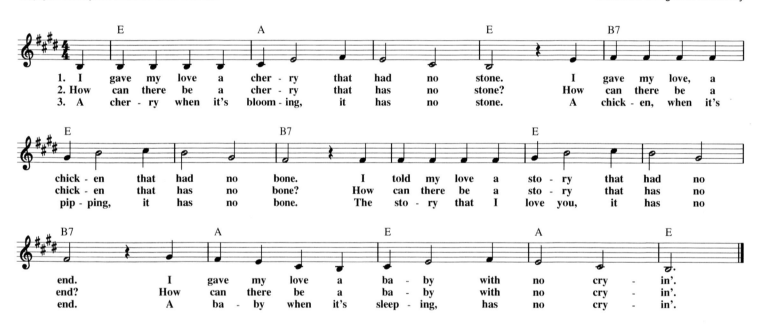

1. I gave my love a cher-ry that had no stone. I gave my love, a
2. How can there be a cher-ry that has no stone? How can there be a
3. A cher-ry when it's bloom-ing, it has no stone. A chick-en, when it's

chick-en that had no bone. I told my love a sto-ry that had no
chick-en that has no bone? How can there be a sto-ry that has no
pip-ping, it has no bone. The sto-ry that I love you, it has no

end. I gave my love a ba-by with no cry-in'.
end? How can there be a ba-by with no cry-in'.
end. A ba-by when it's sleep-ing, has no cry-in'.

I DON'T WANT TO GET ADJUSTED

Words and Music by Sanford J. Massengale
American Gospel Song

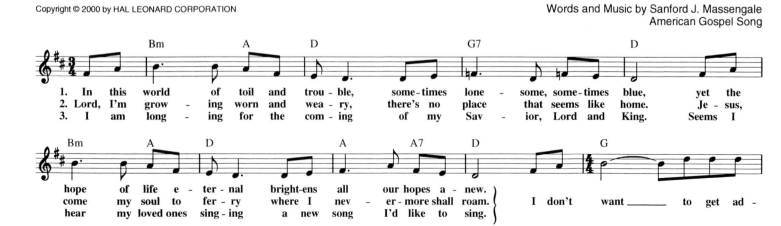

1. In this world of toil and trou-ble, some-times lone-some, some-times blue, yet the
2. Lord, I'm grow-ing worn and wea-ry, there's no place that seems like home. Je-sus,
3. I am long-ing for the com-ing of my Sav-ior, Lord and King. Seems I

hope of life e-ter-nal bright-ens all our hopes a-new.
come my soul to fer-ry where I nev-er-more shall roam. } I don't want ____ to get ad-
hear my loved ones sing-ing a new song I'd like to sing.

just - ed _____ to this world, to this world. I got a home that's so much bet - ter, I want to go to soon - er or la - ter I don't want to get ad - just - ed to this world.

I KNOW MY LOVE

Irish Ballad

1. I know my love by his way o' walk - in' and I know my love by his
2. There is a dance house in Mar - a - dyke, ____ and there my true love goes ____
3. If my love knew I could wash and wring, ____ if ____ my love knew I could
4. I know my love is an ar - rant rov - er, I ____ know he'll wan - der the

way o' talk - in' And I know my love in a suit of blue, and if
ev' - ry night. ____ He ____ takes a strange one up - on his knee, and ____
weave and spin, ____ I'd ____ make a coat of all the fin - est kind, but the
wild world o - ver. In ____ for - eign parts he may chance to stray, where ____

my love leaves me, what will I do? ____ } And still she cried, "I love
don't you know, now, that vex - es me? ____
love of mon - ey leaves me be - hind. ____
all the girls are so bright and gay. ____

him the best, And a trou - bled mind, sure, can know no rest." ____ And

still she cried, "Bon - ny boys are few, And if my love leaves me, what will I do?"

I KNOW WHERE I'M GOING

Scottish Ballad

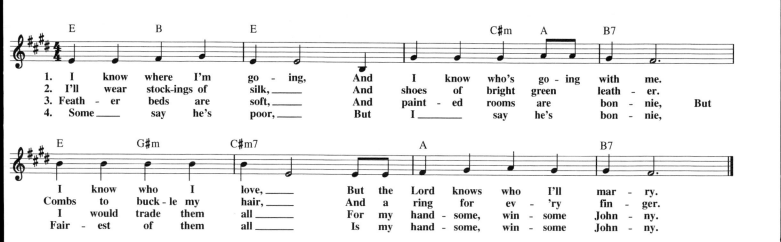

1. I know where I'm go - ing, And I know who's go - ing with me.
2. I'll wear stock-ings of silk, ____ And shoes of bright green leath - er.
3. Feath - er beds are soft, ____ And paint - ed rooms are bon - nie, But
4. Some ____ say he's poor, ____ But I ____ say he's bon - nie,

I know who I love, ____ But the Lord knows who I'll mar - ry.
Combs to buck - le my hair, ____ And a ring for ev - 'ry fin - ger.
I would trade them all ____ For my hand - some, win - some John - ny.
Fair - est of them all ____ Is my hand - some, win - some John - ny.

I NEVER WILL MARRY

Irish Ballad

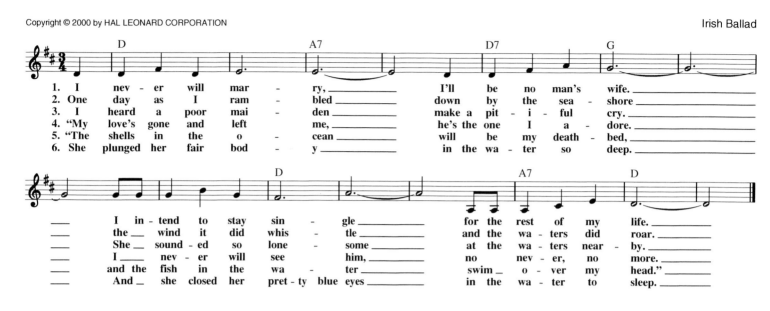

1. I nev-er will mar - ry, _____ I'll be no man's wife. _____
2. One day as I ram - bled _____ down by the sea - shore _____
3. I heard a poor mai - den _____ make a pit - i - ful cry. _____
4. "My love's gone and left me, _____ he's the one I a - dore. _____
5. "The shells in the o - cean _____ will be my death - bed, _____
6. She plunged her fair bod - y _____ in the wa - ter so deep. _____

___ I in - tend to stay sin - gle _____ for the rest of my life. _____
___ the __ wind it did whis - tle _____ and the wa - ters did roar. _____
___ She __ sound - ed so lone - some _____ at the wa - ters near - by. _____
___ I ___ nev - er will see him, _____ no nev - er, no more. _____
___ and the fish in the wa - ter _____ swim _ o - ver my head." _____
___ And _ she closed her pret - ty blue eyes _____ in the wa - ter to sleep. _____

I RIDE AN OLD PAINT

Cowboy Song

1. I ride an old Paint. __ I lead an old Dan. __ I'm goin' to Mon - tan - a to
2. Old ____ Bill Jones had a daugh - ter and a son. _____ One went to Den - ver, the
3. When ___ I die take my sad - dle from the wall. _____ Put it on my po - ny and

throw the hoo - li - han. They feed in the cou - lees, they wa - ter in the draw, their
oth - er went _ wrong. His wife _____ got killed in a pool room _ fight, but
lead him from _ stall. Tie my bones to his back, turn our fac - es to the west, and

tails are all mat - ted, their backs are all raw. }
still he keeps sing - ing from morn - ing 'til night. } Ride a - round, lit - tle do - gies, ride a -
we'll ride the prai - rie that we love the best. }

round _____ them _ slow, For the fier - y and snuf - fy are rar - in' to go.

I SHALL NOT BE MOVED

American
Words by Edward H. Boatner

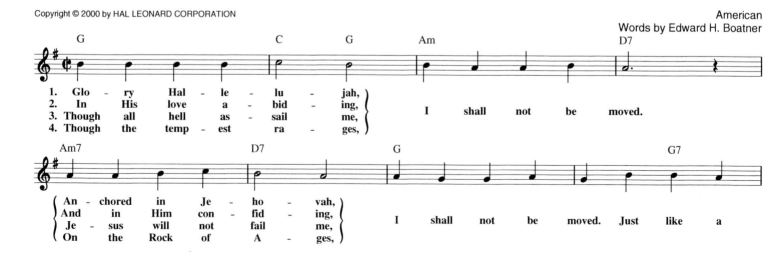

1. Glo - ry Hal - le - lu - jah, }
2. In His love a - bid - ing, } I shall not be moved.
3. Though all hell as - sail me, }
4. Though the temp - est ra - ges, }

{ An - chored in Je - ho - vah,
{ And in Him con - fid - ing, } I shall not be moved. Just like a
{ Je - sus will not fail me,
{ On the Rock of A - ges,

I WILL FEED MY BABY

Yoruba Lullaby, from Nigeria

I WANT JESUS TO WALK WITH ME

African-American Spiritual

I WALK THE ROAD AGAIN

American Hobo Song

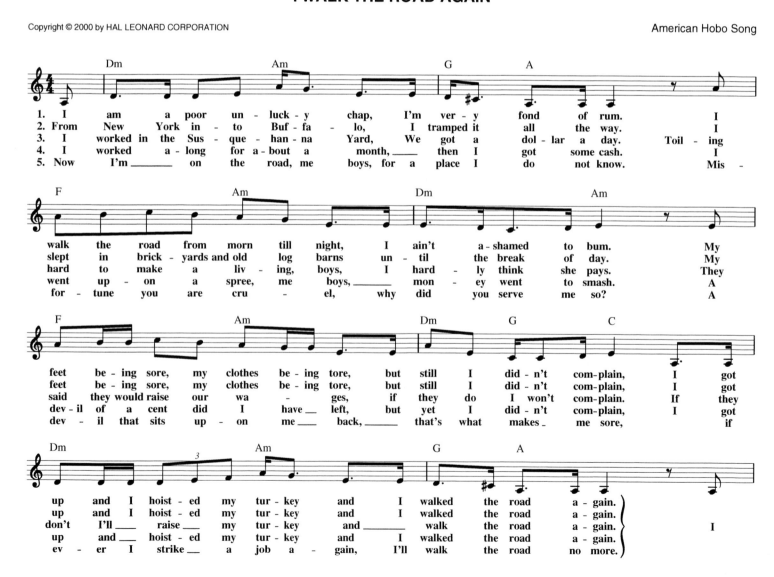

Dm walked the road a-gain, me boys, I walked the road a-gain. **Am** **G** **A** If the

Dm weath-er be fair I combed my hair and I walked the road a-gain. **Am** **G** **A**

I WISH I WAS A MOLE

Folksong from the American South

1. I wish I was a mole in the ground, I
2. I wish I was a liz-ard in the spring, I

wish I was a mole in the ground. If I was a mole in the ground I'd
wish I was a liz-ard in the spring, If I was a liz-ard in the spring I could

root that moun-tain down, I wish I was a mole in the ground.
hear my dar-lin' sing, I wish I was a liz-ard in the spring.

I WISH I WAS SINGLE AGAIN

J.C. Beckel
1871

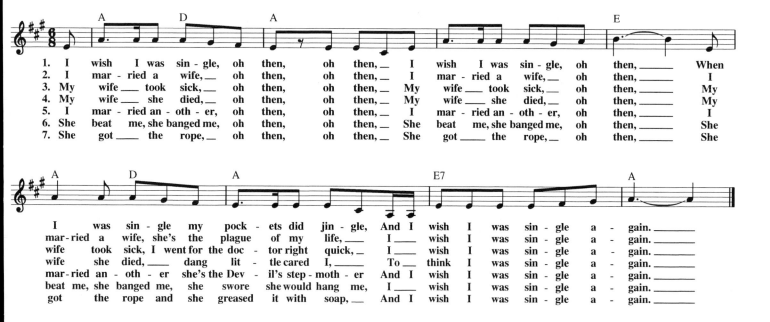

1. I wish I was sin-gle, oh then, oh then, I wish I was sin-gle, oh then, When
2. I mar-ried a wife, oh then, oh then, I mar-ried a wife, oh then, I
3. My wife took sick, oh then, oh then, My wife took sick, oh then, My
4. My wife she died, oh then, oh then, My wife she died, oh then, My
5. I mar-ried an-oth-er, oh then, oh then, I mar-ried an-oth-er, oh then, I
6. She beat me, she banged me, oh then, oh then, She beat me, she banged me, oh then, She
7. She got the rope, oh then, oh then, She got the rope, oh then, She

I was sin-gle my pock-ets did jin-gle, And I wish I was sin-gle a-gain.
mar-ried a wife, she's the plague of my life, I wish I was sin-gle a-gain.
wife took sick, I went for the doc-tor right quick, I wish I was sin-gle a-gain.
wife she died, dang lit-tle cared I, To think I was sin-gle a-gain.
mar-ried an-oth-er she's the Dev-il's step-moth-er And I wish I was sin-gle a-gain.
beat me, she banged me, she swore she would hang me, I wish I was sin-gle a-gain.
got the rope and she greased it with soap, And I wish I was sin-gle a-gain.

I'D LIKE TO BE IN TEXAS

American Cowboy Song

I'M A ROARING REPEATER

American Campaign Song
1884

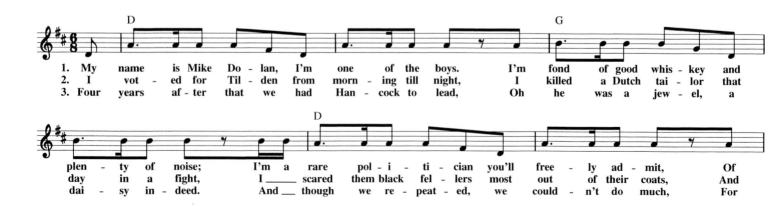

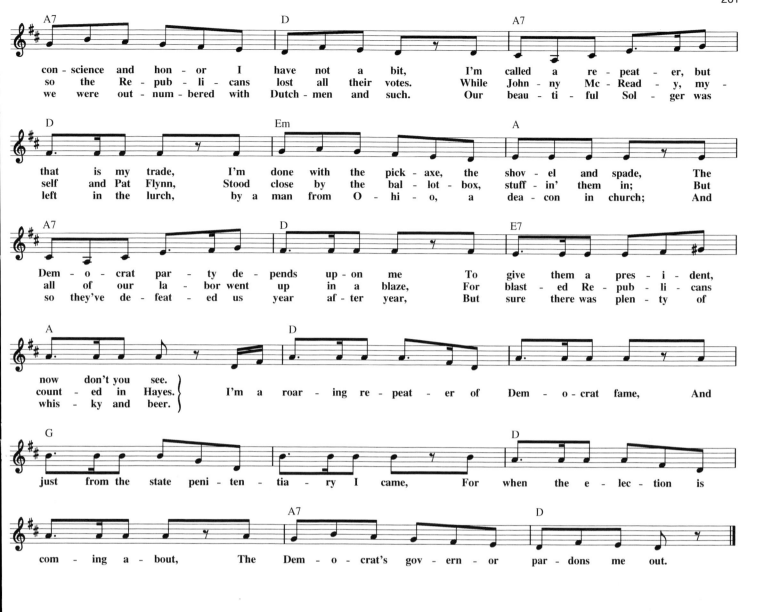

con - science and hon - or I have not a bit, I'm called a re - peat - er, but
so the Re - pub - li - cans lost all their votes. While John - ny Mc - Read - y, my -
we were out - num - bered with Dutch - men and such. Our beau - ti - ful Sol - ger was

that is my trade, I'm done with the pick - axe, the shov - el and spade, The
self and Pat Flynn, Stood close by the bal - lot - box, stuff - in' them in; But
left in the lurch, by a man from O - hi - o, a dea - con in church; And

Dem - o - crat par - ty de - pends up - on me To give them a pres - i - dent,
all of our la - bor went up in a blaze, For blast - ed Re - pub - li - cans
so they've de - feat - ed us year af - ter year, But sure there was plen - ty of

now don't you see.)
count - ed in Hayes. } I'm a roar - ing re - peat - er of Dem - o - crat fame, And
whis - ky and beer.)

just from the state peni - ten - tia - ry I came, For when the e - lec - tion is

com - ing a - bout, The Dem - o - crat's gov - ern - or par - dons me out.

I'LL GIVE MY LOVE AN APPLE

Canadian

1. I'll _____ give my love an ap - ple with - out _____ e'er a core. I'll _____ give my love a
2. How _____ can there be an ap - ple with - out _____ e'er a core? How _____ can there be a
3. My _____ head _____ is an ap - ple with - out _____ e'er a core. My _____ house _____ is a

dwell - ing with - out _____ e'er a door. I'll _____ give my love a pal - ace where -
dwell - ing with - out _____ e'er a door? How _____ can there be a pal - ace where -
dwell - ing with - out _____ e'er a door. My _____ heart _____ is a pal - ace where -

in she _____ might _ be, that _____ she might un - lock it with - out e'er _ a key.
in she _____ might _ be, that _____ she might un - lock it with - out e'er _ a key.
in she _____ might _ be, that _____ she might un - lock it with - out e'er _ a key.

I'M GONNA SING WHEN THE SPIRIT SAYS SING

African-American Spiritual

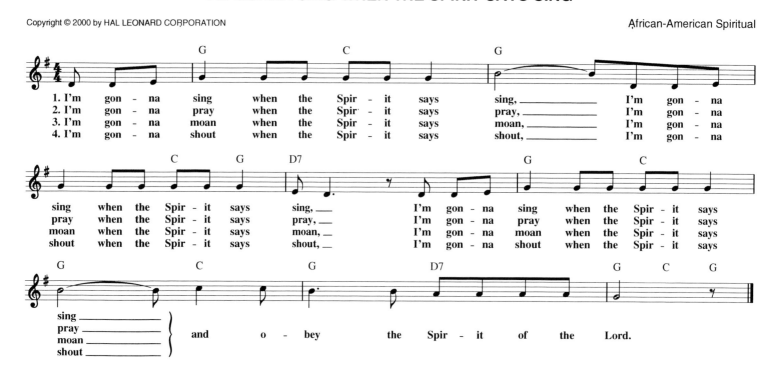

I'M ON MY WAY

African-American Slavery Song

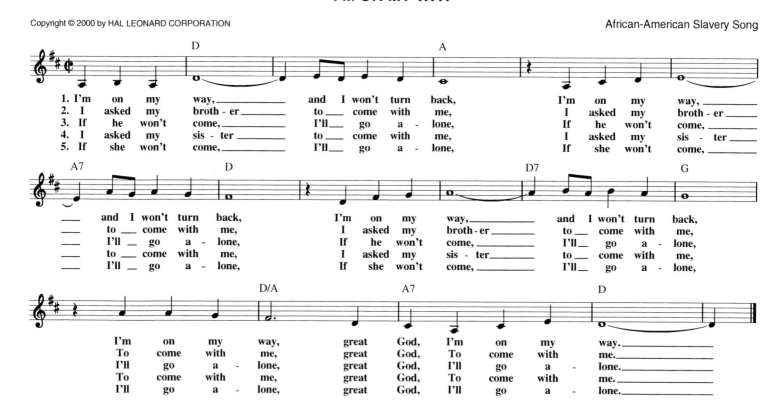

I'VE BEEN WORKING ON THE RAILROAD

19th Century American

Can't you hear the whis - tle blow - in'? Rise up so ear - ly in the morn.

Can't you hear the cap - tain shout - in' "Di - nah, blow your horn!"

Di - nah, won't you blow, Di - nah, won't you blow, Di - nah won't you blow your horn?_____

Di - nah, won't you blow, Di - nah, won't you blow, Di - nah won't you blow your horn?

Some-one's in the kitch - en with Di - nah, Some-one's in the kitch - en I know,_____

Some-one's in the kitch - en with Di - nah, Strum-min' on the old ban - jo and sing - in',

"Fee, fi, fid - dle - ee - i - o, Fee, fi, fid - dle - ee - i - o,_____

Fee, fi, fid - dle - ee - i - o," Strum-min' on the old ban - jo.

I'M SAD AND I'M LONELY

American

1. I'm sad and I'm lone - ly, my heart it will break. My
2. Young la - dies take warn - ing, take warn - ing from me. Don't
3. He'll hug you, he'll kiss you, he'll tell you more lies than the
4. My cheeks once were red_____ like the red,_____ red rose; but
5. I'll build me a cab - in on the moun - tain so high, where the
6. I'm trou - bled, I'm trou - bled, I'm trou - bled in my mind. If this

sweet - heart loves an - oth - er, Lord, I wish I wuz dead!
waste your af - fec - tions on a young man so free.
cross - ties on the_____ rail - road or the stars in the sky.
now they are_____ white_____ as the li - ly grows.
black - birds can't_____ find me or_____ hear my sad cry.
trou - ble don't_____ kill me I'll_____ live a long time.

I'M SEVENTEEN COME SUNDAY

English

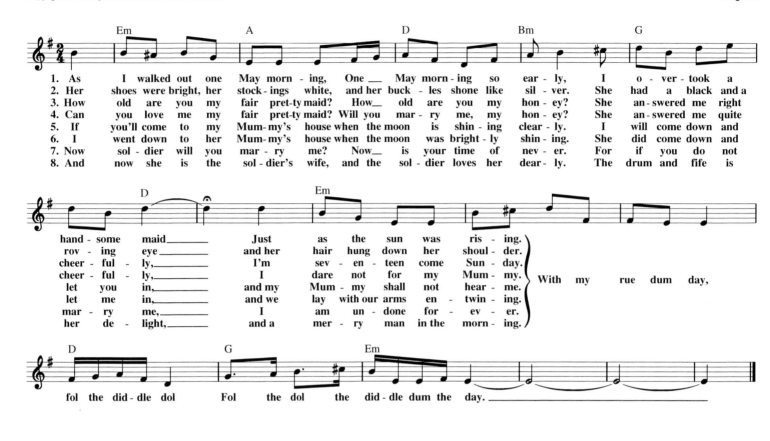

1. As I walked out one May morn - ing, One __ May morn - ing so ear - ly, I o - ver - took a
2. Her shoes were bright, her stock - ings white, and her buck - les shone like sil - ver. She had a black and a
3. How old are you my fair pret-ty maid? How __ old are you my hon - ey? She an - swered me right
4. Can you love me my fair pret-ty maid? Will you mar - ry me, my hon - ey? She an - swered me quite
5. If you'll come to my Mum-my's house when the moon is shin - ing clear - ly. I will come down and
6. I went down to her Mum-my's house when the moon was bright-ly shin - ing. She did come down and
7. Now sol - dier will you mar - ry me? Now __ is your time of nev - er. For if you do not
8. And now she is the sol - dier's wife, and the sol - dier loves her dear - ly. The drum and fife is

hand - some maid_____ Just as the sun was ris - ing.
rov - ing eye_____ and her hair hung down her shoul - der.
cheer - ful - ly,_____ I'm sev - en - teen come Sun - day.
cheer - ful - ly,_____ I dare not for my Mum - my.
let you in,_____ and my Mum - my shall not hear - me. } With my rue dum day,
let me in,_____ and we lay with our arms en - twin - ing.
mar - ry me,_____ I am un - done for - ev - er.
her de - light,_____ and a mer - ry man in the morn - ing.

fol the did - dle dol Fol the dol the did - dle dum the day. _____

I'VE GOT NO USE FOR WOMEN

American Cowboy Song

1. Now I've got no use ____ for wom - en, _____ A true one may nev - er be
2. My pal was a straight young cow - punch - er, _____ hon - est and up - right and
3. All through the long night __ they trailed him _____ through mes - quite and thick chap - ar -
4. Death's __ slow sting did not trou - ble, _____ his chanc - es for life were too
5. "Oh, bur - y me out on the prai - rie, _____ where the coy - otes may howl o'er my
6. So they bur - ried him out on the prai - rie, _____ and the coy - otes still how o'er his

found, _____ They'll stick by a man for his mon - ey; _____ When it's
square. _____ But he turned to a hard - shoot - ing gun - man, _____ and a
ral. _____ And I could - n't help curs - ing that wom - an, _____ as I
slim. _____ But where they were put - ting his bod - y _____ was a
grave. _____ Bur - y me out on the prai - rie, _____ and __
grave. _____ But his soul ____ is now ____ a - rest - ing, _____ from the

gone they'll turn him down. _____ They're all a - like at the
wom - an sent him there. _____ He fell in with e - vil com -
saw him pitch, stag - ger and fall. _____ If she'd been the pal that the
all that wor - ried him. _____ He lift - ed his head on his
some of my bones please save. _____ Wrap me up in my
un - kind cut she gave. _____ And man - y a sim - 'lar cow -

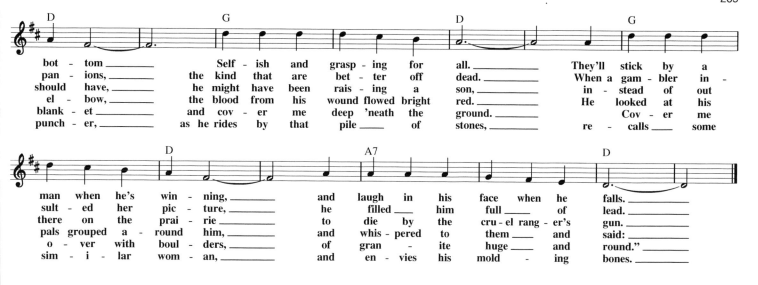

bot - tom _____ Self - ish and grasp - ing for all. _____ They'll stick by a
pan - ions, _____ the kind that are bet - ter off dead. _____ When a gam - bler in -
should have, _____ he might have been rais - ing a son, _____ in - stead of out
el - bow, _____ the blood from his wound flowed bright red. _____ He looked at his
blank - et _____ and cov - er me deep 'neath the ground. _____ Cov - er me
punch - er, _____ as he rides by that pile ____ of stones, _____ re - calls ____ some

man when he's win - ning, _____ and laugh in his face when he falls. _____
sult - ed her pic - ture, _____ he filled ____ him full ____ of lead. _____
there on the prai - rie _____ to die by the cru - el rang - er's gun. _____
pals grouped a - round him, _____ and whis - pered to them ____ and said: _____
o - ver with boul - ders, _____ of gran - ite huge ____ and round." _____
sim - i - lar wom - an, _____ and en - vies his mold - ing bones. _____

I'SE THE B'Y THAT BUILDS THE BOAT

Folksong from Newfoundland

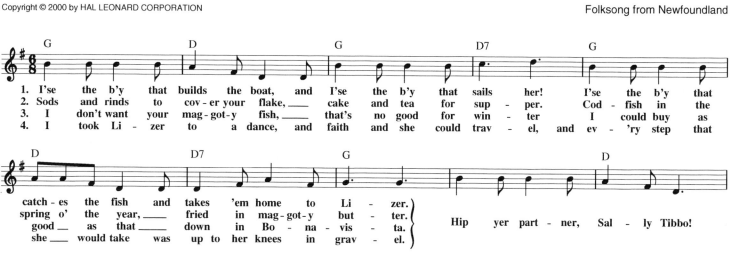

1. I'se the b'y that builds the boat, and I'se the b'y that sails her! I'se the b'y that
2. Sods and rinds to cov - er your flake, ____ cake and tea for sup - per. Cod - fish in the
3. I don't want your mag - got - y fish, ____ that's no good for win - ter I could buy as
4. I took Li - zer to a dance, and faith and she could trav - el, and ev - 'ry step that

catch - es the fish and takes 'em home to Li - zer.)
spring o' the year, ____ fried in mag - got - y but - ter.)
good ____ as that ____ down in Bo - na - vis - ta.} Hip yer part - ner, Sal - ly Tibbo!
she ____ would take was up to her knees in grav - el.)

Hip yer part - ner, Sal - ly Brown! Fo - go, Twil - lin - gate, Mor' - ton's Har - bour, all a - round the cir - cle!

I'VE GOT PEACE LIKE A RIVER

American

1. I've got peace like a riv - er, I've got peace like a riv - er, I've got
2. I've got love like an o - cean, I've got love like an o - cean, I've got
3. I've got joy like a foun - tain, I've got joy like a foun - tain, I've got

peace like a riv - er in my soul; _____ I've got peace like a riv - er, I've got
love like an o - cean in my soul; _____ I've got love like an o - cean, I've got
joy like a foun - tain in my soul; _____ I've got joy like a foun - tain, I've got

peace like a riv - er, I've got peace like a riv - er in my soul. _____
love like an o - cean, I've got love like an o - cean in my soul. _____
joy like a foun - tain, I've got joy like a foun - tain in my soul. _____

I'VE GOT SIXPENCE

English Marching Song
based on American Civil War Song

IF HE'D BE A BUCKAROO

American

IF YOU'RE HAPPY AND YOU KNOW IT

American Game Song

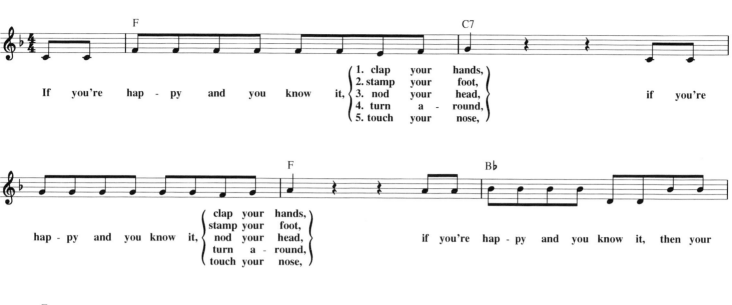

If you're hap - py and you know it,

1. clap your hands,
2. stamp your foot,
3. nod your head,
4. turn a - round,
5. touch your nose,

if you're

hap - py and you know it,

clap your hands,
stamp your foot,
nod your head,
turn a - round,
touch your nose,

if you're hap - py and you know it, then your

face will sure - ly show it, if you're hap - py and you know it,

clap your hands.
stamp your foot.
nod your head.
turn a - round.
touch your nose.

ILKLEY MOOR

English

1. Where hast thou been since I saw thee?
2. I've been a - court-ing Mar - y Jane,
3. Thou'll sure - ly catch thy death of cold,
4. Then we shall have to bur - y thee,
5. Then worms shall come and eat thee up,
6. Then ducks shall come and eat the worms,
7.,8. *(See additional lyrics)*

On Ilk - ley ___ Moor ___ baht ___ 'at. ___

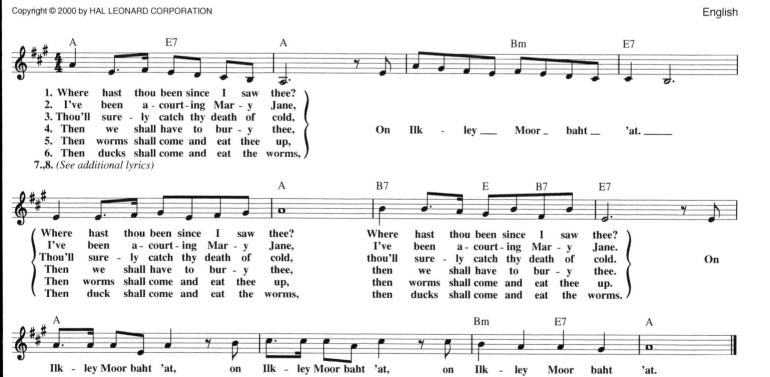

Where hast thou been since I saw thee?
I've been a - court-ing Mar - y Jane,
Thou'll sure - ly catch thy death of cold,
Then we shall have to bur - y thee,
Then worms shall come and eat thee up,
Then duck shall come and eat the worms,

Where hast thou been since I saw thee?
I've been a - court-ing Mar - y Jane,
thou'll sure - ly catch thy death of cold.
then we shall have to bur - y thee.
then worms shall come and eat thee up.
then ducks shall come and eat the worms.

On

Ilk - ley Moor baht 'at, on Ilk - ley Moor baht 'at, on Ilk - ley Moor baht 'at.

Additional Lyrics

7. Then we shall go and eat the ducks,
   On Ilkley Moor baht 'at.
   Then we shall go and eat the ducks,
   Then we shall go and eat the ducks.
   On Ilkley Moor baht 'at,
   On Ilkley Moor baht 'at,
   On Ilkley Moor baht 'at.

8. Then we shall all have eaten thee,
   On Ilkley Moor baht 'at.
   Then we shall all have eaten thee,
   Then we shall all have eaten thee.
   On Ilkley Moor baht 'at,
   On Ilkley Moor baht 'at,
   On Ilkley Moor baht 'at.

IN GOOD OLD COLONY TIMES

19th Century American

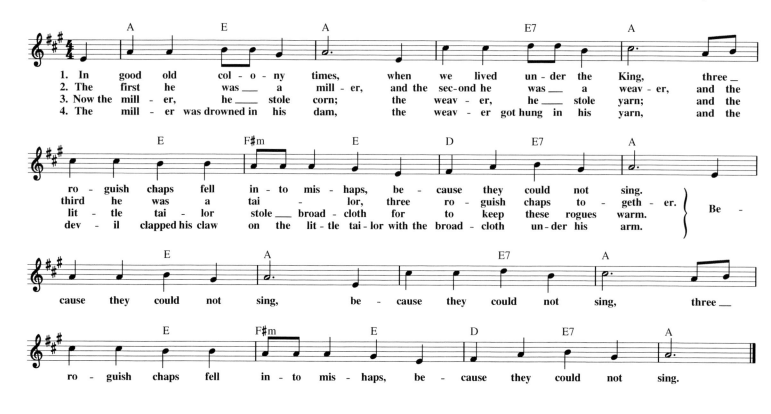

1. In good old col-o-ny times, when we lived un-der the King, three _
2. The first he was _ a mill - er, and the sec-ond he was _ a weav-er, and the
3. Now the mill - er, he _ stole corn; the weav - er, he _ stole yarn; and the
4. The mill - er was drowned in his dam, the weav - er got hung in his yarn, and the

ro - guish chaps fell in - to mis - haps, be - cause they could not sing.
third he was a tai - lor, three ro - guish chaps to - geth - er. } Be -
lit - tle tai - lor stole _ broad - cloth for to keep these rogues warm.
dev - il clapped his claw on the lit - tle tai-lor with the broad - cloth un - der his arm.

cause they could not sing, be - cause they could not sing, three _

ro - guish chaps fell in - to mis - haps, be - cause they could not sing.

IN THE FOREST GREW A TINY BIRCH TREE
(Vo Pole Berëzyn'ka Stoiala)

Russian

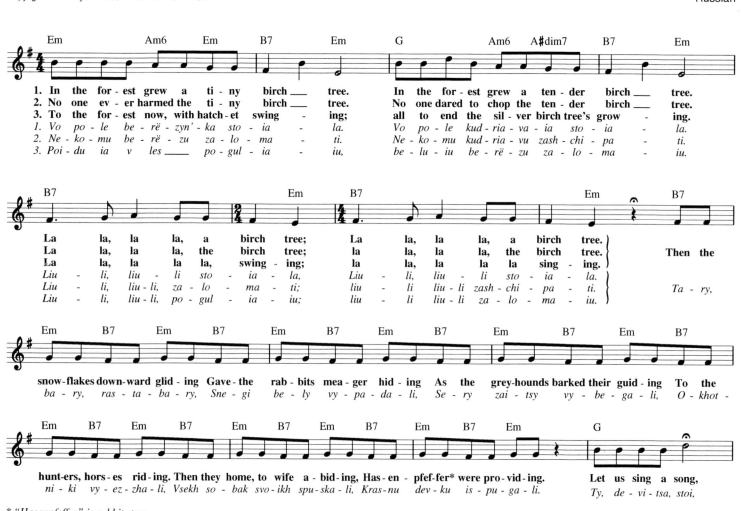

1. In the for - est grew a ti - ny birch _ tree. In the for - est grew a ten - der birch _ tree.
2. No one ev - er harmed the ti - ny birch _ tree. No one dared to chop the ten - der birch _ tree.
3. To the for - est now, with hatch - et swing - ing; all to end the sil - ver birch tree's grow - ing.
1. Vo po - le be - rë - zyn' - ka sto - ia - la. Vo po - le kud - ria - va - ia sto - ia - la.
2. Ne - ko - mu be - rë - zu za - lo - ma - ti. Ne - ko - mu kud - ria - vu zash - chi - pa - ti.
3. Poi - du ia v les _ po - gul - ia - iu, be - lu - iu be - rë - zu za - lo - ma - iu.

La la, la la, a birch tree; La la, la la, a birch tree.
La la, la la, the birch tree; la la, la la, the birch tree. } Then the
La la, la la la, swing - ing; la la, la la la sing - ing.
Liu - li, liu - li sto - ia - la, Liu - li, liu - li sto - ia - la.
Liu - li, liu - li, za - lo - ma - ti; liu - li liu - li zash - chi - pa - ti. } Ta - ry,
Liu - li, liu - li, po - gul - ia - iu; liu - li liu - li za - lo - ma - iu.

snow-flakes down-ward glid - ing Gave-the rab - bits mea - ger hid - ing As the grey-hounds barked their guid - ing To the
ba - ry, ras - ta - ba - ry, Sne - gi be - ly vy - pa - da - li, Se - ry zai - tsy vy - be - ga - li, O - khot -

hunt-ers, hors - es rid - ing. Then they home, to wife a - bid - ing, Has - en - pfef-fer* were pro - vid - ing. Let us sing a song,
ni - ki vy - ez - zha - li, Vsekh so - bak svo - ikh spu - ska - li, Kras - nu dev - ku is - pu - ga - li. Ty, de - vi - tsa, stoi,

* "Hasenpfeffer" is rabbit stew.

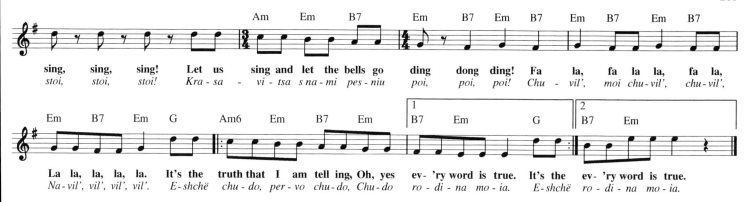

sing, sing, sing! Let us sing and let the bells go ding dong ding! Fa la, fa la la, fa la,
stoi, stoi, stoi! Kra - sa - vi - tsa s na - mi pes - niu poi, poi, poi! Chu - vil', moi chu - vil', chu - vil',

La la, la, la, la. It's the truth that I am tell ing, Oh, yes ev- 'ry word is true. It's the ev- 'ry word is true.
Na - vil', vil', vil', vil'. E - shchë chu - do, per - vo chu - do, Chu - do ro - di - na mo - ia. E - shchë ro - di - na mo - ia.

IN THE GOOD OLD SUMMERTIME

Words by Ren Shields
Music by George Evans
African-American Minstrel Song, 1902

1. There's a time in each year that we al - ways hold dear, Good old sum - mer - time, _____ With the
2. To ___ swim in the pool you'd play "hook-ey" from school, Good old sum - mer - time, _____ You'd _

birds and the trees __ and sweet scent - ed breez - es, Good old sum - mer - time, _____ When your
play "ring a - ros - ie" with Jim, Kate and Jo - sie, Good old sum - mer - time, _____ Those _

day's work is o - ver then you are in clo - ver, and life is one beau - ti - ful rhyme, _____ No
days full of pleas - ure we now fond - ly treas - ure, when we nev - er thought it a crime _____ To

trou - ble an - noy - ing, each one is en - joy - ing, The good old sum - mer - time. _____ } In the
go steal - ing cher - ries, with face brown as ber - ries, __ Good old sum - mer - time. _____ }

good old sum - mer - time, _____ In the good old sum - mer - time, _____

Stroll - ing thro' the shad - y lanes with your ba - by mine; _____ You

hold her hand and she holds yours, and that's a ver - y good sign _____ That

she's your toot - sey woot - sey in the good old sum - mer - time. _____

IN THE PINES

American

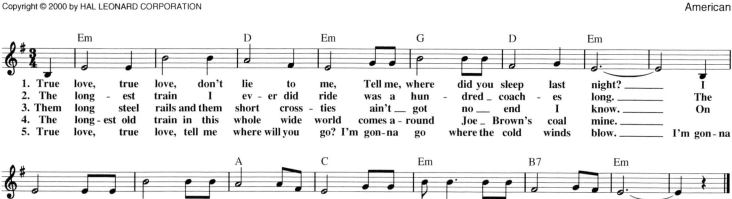

1. True love, true love, don't lie to me, Tell me, where did you sleep last night? _____ I
2. The long-est train I ev-er did ride was a hun-dred coach-es long. _____ The
3. Them long steel rails and them short cross-ties ain't got no end I know. _____ On
4. The long-est old train in this whole wide world comes a-round Joe Brown's coal mine. _____
5. True love, true love, tell me where will you go? I'm gon-na go where the cold winds blow. _____ I'm gon-na

slept in the pines where the sun nev-er shines, and I shiv-ered with a cold dead-ly cold. _____
on - ly wom-an I ev-er did love, she's on that _____ train and gone. _____
these long steel rails and short cross-ties I'm tramp-ing my way back home. _____
Head-light comes 'round when the sun comes up, the ca-boose when the sun goes down. _____
weep, gon-na cry, gon-na moan, gon-na sigh, gon-na dance in my good-time clothes. _____

IN THE SHADE OF THE OLD APPLE TREE

Words by Harry H. Williams
Music by Egbert Van Alstyne
American, 1905

In the shade of the old ap-ple tree, _____ Where the love in your eyes I could see, _____
hear the dull buzz of the bee. _____ In the blos-soms as you said to me, _____

— When the voice that I heard, Like the song of the bird, Seem'd to whis-per sweet mu-sic to me; _____
— With a heart that is

— I could true, I'll be wait-ing for you, In the shade of the old ap-ple tree. _____

THE INTOXICATED RAT

Southern American

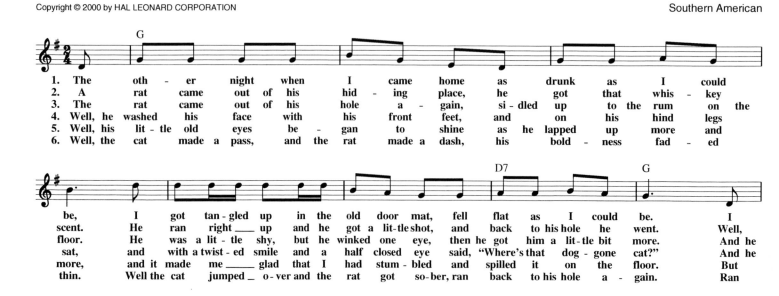

1. The oth-er night when I came home as drunk as I could
2. A rat came out of his hid-ing place, he got that whis-key
3. The rat came out of his hole a-gain, si-dled up to the rum on the
4. Well, he washed his face with his front feet, and on his hind legs
5. Well, his lit-tle old eyes be-gan to shine as he lapped up more and
6. Well, the cat made a pass, and the rat made a dash, his bold-ness fad-ed

be, I got tan-gled up in the old door mat, fell flat as I could be. I
scent. He ran right up and he got a lit-tle shot, and back to his hole he went. Well,
floor. He was a lit-tle shy, but he winked one eye, then he got him a lit-tle bit more. And he
sat, and with a twist-ed smile and a half closed eye said, "Where's that dog-gone cat?" And he
more, and it made me glad that I had stum-bled and spilled it on the floor. But
thin. Well the cat jumped o-ver and the rat got so-ber, ran back to his hole a-gain. Ran

had	me	a	lit -	tle		bot -	tle	of	rum		and	I		did -	n't	have	an -	y -
back				to		his	hole		he		went,		right		back	to	his	hole	he
did -	n't	go		back		to	his	hole		that	time,	but	he		stayed	by	that	pud -	dle of
did -	n't		go	back		to		his	hole,		he			said,		"Dog -	gone	my
soon	the		pud -	dle	of		rum		was	gone,	and	I		did -	n't	have	an - y -	more
back				to		his	hole		a -		gain,	ran		back	to	his	hole	a -

more.	The	cap	flew	off	when	I	went	down,	and	I	spilled	it	on	the	floor.
went.	He	ran	right	up	and he	got a	lit - tle	shot,	and		back	to	his hole	he	went.
soul,	I'm	on - ly	a	rat,	but	a	dog - gone	cat	can't		run	me	back to	my	hole."
gin.	And	the	old	rat	was a - hav - ing a	time	when the	old	tom - cat	walked	in.
gain.	Well the	cat	jumped	o - ver and the	rat	got	so - ber, ran	back	to his	hole	a - gain.

THE IRISH WASHERWOMAN

Copyright © 2000 by HAL LEONARD CORPORATION

Irish, circa 1785

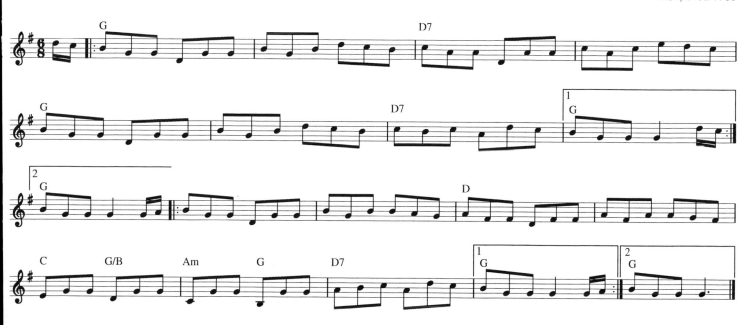

IROQUOIS LULLABY

Copyright © 2000 by HAL LEONARD CORPORATION

Canadian

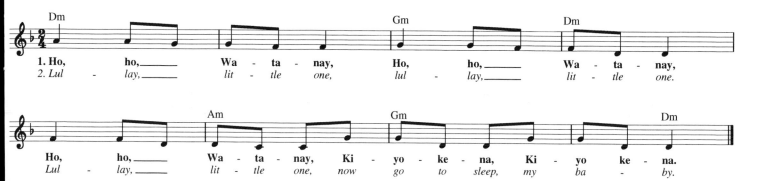

1. Ho, ho,___ Wa - ta - nay, Ho, ho,___ Wa - ta - nay,
2. Lul - lay,___ lit - tle one, lul - lay,___ lit - tle one.

Ho, ho,___ Wa - ta - nay, Ki - yo - ke - na, Ki - yo ke - na.
Lul - lay,___ lit - tle one, now go to sleep, my ba - by.

272

IRISH ASTRONOMY

C.G. Hapline

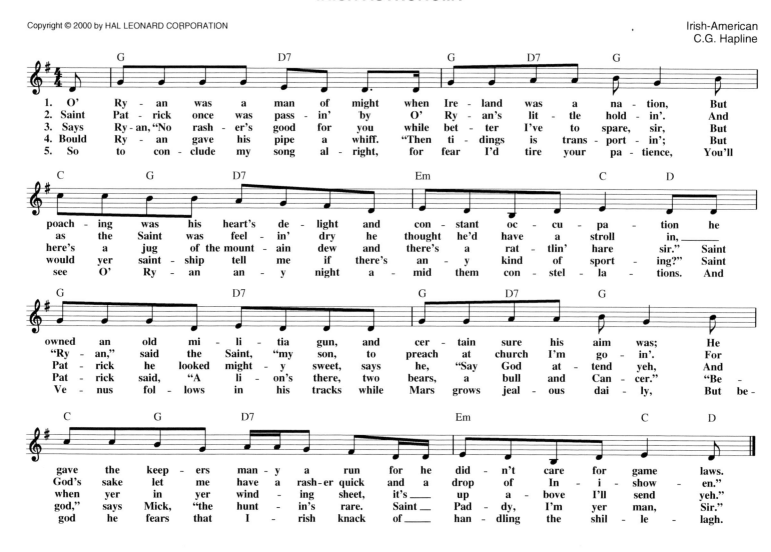

THE IRISH GIRL

Irish Love Song

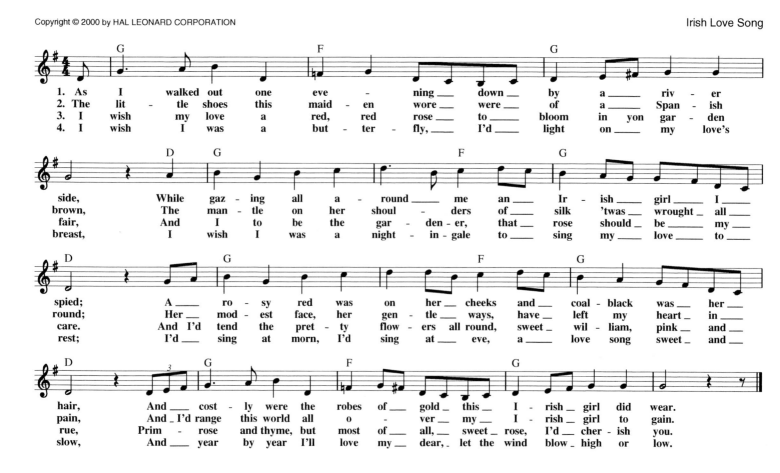

THE IRISHMAN'S EPISTLE

Irish

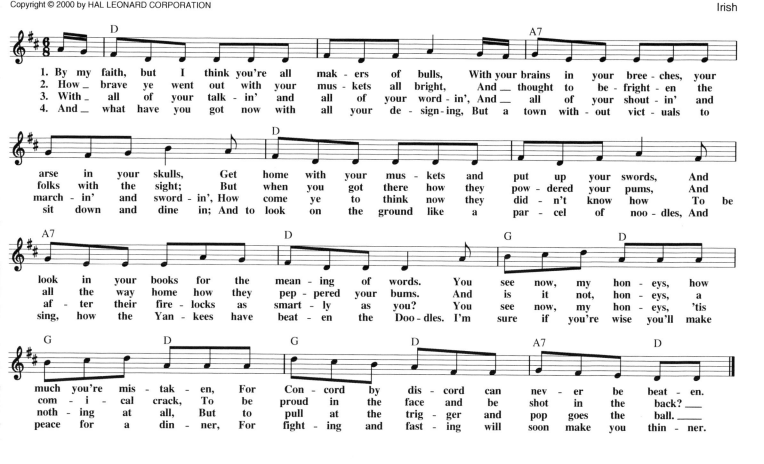

1. By my faith, but I think you're all mak-ers of bulls, With your brains in your bree-ches, your
2. How_ brave ye went out with your mus-kets all bright, And_ thought to be-fright-en the
3. With_ all of your talk-in' and all of your word-in', And_ all of your shout-in' and
4. And_ what have you got now with all your de-sign-ing, But a town with-out vict-uals to

arse in your skulls, Get home with your mus-kets and put up your swords, And
folks with the sight; But when you got there how they pow-dered your pums, And
march-in' and sword-in', How come ye to think now they did-n't know how To be
sit down and dine in; And to look on the ground like a par-cel of noo-dles, And

look in your books for the mean-ing of words. You see now, my hon-eys, how
all the way home how they pep-pered your bums. And is it not, hon-eys, a
af-ter their fire-locks as smart-ly as you? You see now, my hon-eys, 'tis
sit down and dine in; And to look on the ground like a par-cel of noo-dles, And

much you're mis-tak-en, For Con-cord by dis-cord can nev-er be beat-en.
com-i-cal crack, To be proud in the face and be shot in the back?
noth-ing at all, But to pull at the trig-ger and pop goes the ball._
peace for a din-ner, For fight-ing and fast-ing will soon make you thin-ner.

IT WAS A LOVER AND HIS LASS

Words from *As You Like It*,
by William Shakespeare
Music by Thomas Morley
16th Century English

1. It was a lov-er and his lass,
2. Be-tween the a-cres of the rye,
3. This car-ol they be-gan to sing,
4. And there-fore take the pre-sent time,

With a hey and a ho and a hey non-ni-

no, With a hey _____ non-ni non-ni no,

That o'er the green corn-
These pret-ty coun-try
How that a life was
for love is crown-

field did pass,
folks would lie,
but a flow-er,
with the prime,

In spring-time, in spring-time, _____ In spring-time, the

on-ly pret-ty ring time, When the birds do sing, Hey ding a ding a ding, Hey

ding a ding a ding, Hey ding a ding a ding, _____ Sweet lov-ers love the Spring.

IT WAS A MOUSE

Folksong from Nova Scotia

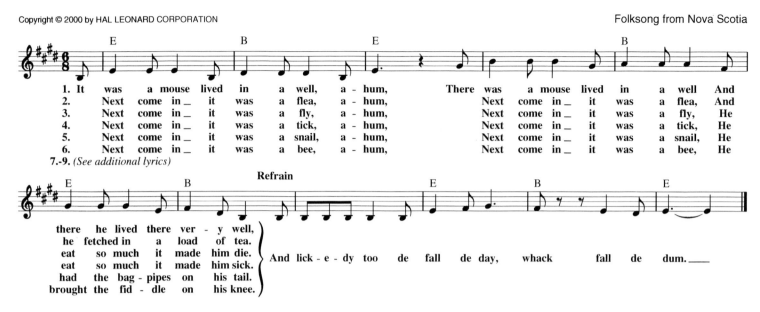

1. It was a mouse lived in a well, a - hum, There was a mouse lived in a well And
2. Next come in _ it was a flea, a - hum, Next come in _ it was a flea, And
3. Next come in _ it was a fly, a - hum, Next come in _ it was a fly, He
4. Next come in _ it was a tick, a - hum, Next come in _ it was a tick, He
5. Next come in _ it was a snail, a - hum, Next come in _ it was a snail, He
6. Next come in _ it was a bee, a - hum, Next come in _ it was a bee, He

7.-9. *(See additional lyrics)*

Refrain

there he lived there ver - y well,
he fetched in a load of tea.
eat so much it made him die.
eat so much it made him sick.
had the bag - pipes on his tail.
brought the fid - dle on his knee.

And lick - e - dy too de fall de day, whack fall de dum.___

Additional Lyrics

7. Next come in— it was a snake, a-hum,
Next come in— it was a snake,
And he fetched in a load of cake.
Refrain

8. The big black snake, he swamped the land, a-hum,
The big black snake, he swamped the land,
And he was killed by an overgrown man.
Refrain

9. The overgrown man, he went to France, a-hum,
The overgrown man, he went to France,
To learn the ladies how to dance.
Refrain

IT'S THE SAME THE WHOLE WORLD OVER

English Ballad

1. It's the same the whole world o - ver, ___ It's the poor what gets the blame, ___
2. She was poor, but she was hon - est, ___ Pure, un - stain - ed was her fame, ___
3. So she went a - way to Lon - don, ___ Just to hide her guilt - y shame. ___
4. Look at him with all his hors - es, ___ Drink-ing cham - pagne in his club, ___
5. Now he's in his rid - ing britch - es, ___ Hunt-ing fox - es in the chase, ___
6. Then there came a bloat - ed bish - op. ___ Mar-riage was the tale he told. ___

7.-9. *(See additional lyrics)*

___ While the rich has all the pleas - ures, ___ Now ain't that a blood - y shame? ___
___ Till a coun - try squire come court - ing, ___ And the poor girl lost her name. ___
___ There she met an ar - my chap - lain, ___ Once a - gain she lost her name. ___
___ While the vic - tim of his pas - sions ___ Drinks her Guin - ess in a pub. ___
___ While the vic - tim of his fol - ly ___ Makes her liv - ing by her vice. ___
___ There was no one else to take her, ___ So she sold her soul for gold. ___

Additional Lyrics

7. See her in her horse and carriage,
Driving daily through the park.
Though she made a wealthy marriage,
Still she hides a breaking heart.

8. In a cottage down in Sussex
Live her parents old and lame,
And they drink the wine she sends them,
But they never speak her name.

9. In their poor and humble dwelling,
There her grieving parents live.
Drinking champagne as she sends them
But they never can forgive.

Sea Chantey from Newfoundland

1. Now, 'twas twen-ty-five or thir-ty years since Jack first saw the light. He came in-to this world of woe one
2. When Jack grew up to be a man he went to Lab-ra-dor. He fished in In-dian Har-bour where his
3. The whale went straight for Baf-fin's Bay 'bout nine-ty knots an hour, and ev-'ry time he'd blow a spray he'd

dark and storm-y night. He was born on board his fa-ther's ship as she was ly-ing to 'bout twen-ty-five or thir-ty miles south-
fa-ther fished be-fore. On his re-turn-ing in the fog he met a heav-y gale, and Jack was swept in-to the sea and
send it in a shower. "Oh now," says Jack un-to him-self, "I must see what he's a-bout." He caught the whale all by the tail and

east of Bac-al-hao. swal-lowed by a whale. turned him in-side out. Jack was ev-'ry inch a sail-or, five and twen-ty years a

whal-er. Jack was ev-'ry inch a sail-or, He was born up-on the bright blue sea.

JACKSON

Folksong from the Ozarks

1. Jack-son is on sea. Jack-son is on shore. Jack-son's gone to
2. "How's full up, Jack-son?" "Ver-y poor," says he. "I lost all my
3. "Mar-y is not home, nor has she been to-day. And, if she were
4. Jack-son be-ing wea-ry, he hung down his head, ask-ing for a
5. Jack looked on the strang-ers, looked on them one and all. And then for his
6. See-ing all this mon-ey made the old wom-an rue. "Mar-y is at
7.,8. (See additional lyrics)

Mex-i-co to fight the bat-tle's war. "Wel-come home, dear Jack-son, oh
mon-ey_____ while sail-ing on the sea. Fetch your daugh-ter Mar-y and
at home, Jack, she would not let you stay. Mar-y's ver-y rich now, and
can-dle to_____ light his way to bed. "Our beds are full of strang-ers, and
reck-on-ing he all at once did call. Twen-ty shil-lings of the new and
home Jack,___ and she's been true to you. I hope you're not in ear-nest; I

wel-come home," said she. "Last night my daugh-ter Mar-y, lay dream-ing of thee."
bring her down to me. We'll drown our mel-an-chol-y, and mar-ried we will be."
you are ver-y poor, and if she were at home Jack, she'd show you to the door."
have been all this week, and so then for your lodg-ing, poor Jack, you'll have to seek."
twen-ty of the old, he took out from his pock-ets, his two hands full of gold.
on-ly spoke in jest. With-out an-y ex-cep-tion she loves___ you the best."

Additional Lyrics

7. At the sound of the money Mary came with a smiling face.
First a sweet kiss, and then a fond embrace
"Oh welcome home, dear Jackson. Welcome home, my dear.
The big bed is all empty, and we shall lie there."

8. "Before I'd lie within your bed, I'd lie within the street,
For when I had no money, my lodging I must seek,
But now I've plenty money, I'll make the taverns whirl.
A bottle of good brandy, and on each arm a girl."

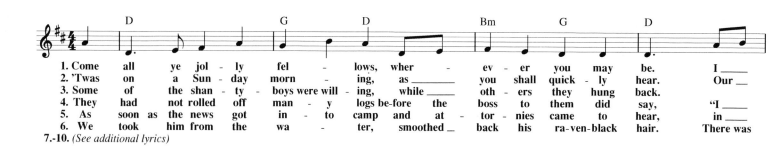

1. Come all ye jol - ly fel - lows, wher - ev - er you may be. I ____
2. 'Twas on a Sun - day morn - ing, as ____ you shall quick - ly hear. Our __
3. Some of the shan - ty - boys were will - ing, while ____ oth - ers they hung back.
4. They had not rolled off man - y logs be-fore the boss to them did say, "I ____
5. As soon as the news got in - to camp and at - tor - nies came to hear, in ____
6. We took him from the wa - ter, smoothed __ back his ra-ven-black hair. There was

7.-10. *(See additional lyrics)*

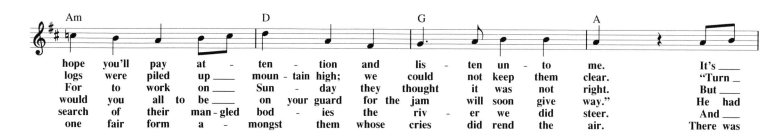

hope you'll pay at - ten - tion and lis - ten un - to me. It's ____
logs were piled up ____ moun - tain high; we could not keep them clear. "Turn __
For to work on ____ Sun - day they thought it was not right. But ____
would you all to be ____ on your guard for the jam will soon give way." He had
search of their man - gled bod - ies the riv - er we did steer. And ____
one fair form a - mongst them whose cries did rend the air. There was

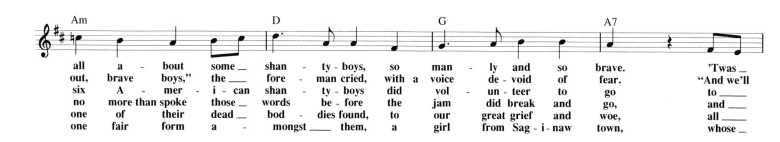

all a - bout some __ shan - ty - boys, so man - ly and so brave. 'Twas __
out, brave boys," the ____ fore - man cried, with a voice de - void of fear. "And we'll
six A - mer - i - can shan - ty - boys did vol - un - teer to go to ____
no more than spoke those __ words be - fore the jam did break and go, and ____
one of their dead __ bod - dies found, to our great grief and woe, all ____
one fair form a - mongst ____ them, a girl from Sag - i - naw town, whose __

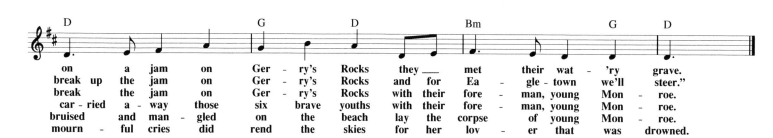

on a jam on Ger - ry's Rocks they ____ met their wat - 'ry grave.
break up the jam on Ger - ry's Rocks and for Ea - gle - town we'll steer."
break the jam on Ger - ry's Rocks with their fore - man, young Mon - roe.
car - ried a - way those six brave youths with their fore - man, young Mon - roe.
bruised and man - gled on the beach lay the corpse of young Mon - roe.
mourn - ful cries did rend the skies for her lov - er that was drowned.

Additional Lyrics

7. We buried him quite decently. 'Twas on the twelfth of May,
Come all you jolly shanty-boys, and for your comrade pray.
We engraved upon a hemlock tree that near his grave did grow—
The name, the age, the drownding date of the foreman, young Monroe.

8. His mother was a widow living down by the river side.
Miss Clark she was a noble girl, this young man's promised bride.
The wages of true love the firm to her did pay,
And liberal subscription she received from the shanty-boys that day.

9. She received their presents kindly and thanked them every one,
Though she did not survive him long, as you shall understand;
Scarcely three weeks after, and she was called to go,
And her last request was to be laid by her lover, young Monroe.

10. Come all you brave shanty-boys, I'd have you call and see
Two green graves by the river side where grows the hemlock tree;
The shanty-boys cut off the wood where lay those lovers low—
'Tis the handsome Clara Clark and her true love, brave Monroe.

JACOB'S LADDER

African-American Spiritual

1. We are climb - ing Ja - cob's lad - der. We are
2. Ev - 'ry rung goes high - er, high - er. Ev - 'ry
3. Sin - ner, do you love my Je - sus? Sin - ner,
4. If you love Him, why not serve Him? If you
5. We are climb - ing high - er, high - er. We are

climb - ing Ja - cob's lad - der. We are climb - ing
rung goes high - er, high - er. Ev - 'ry rung goes
do you love my Je - sus? Sin - ner, do you
love Him, why not serve Him? If you love Him,
climb - ing high - er, high - er. We are climb - ing

Ja - cob's lad - der, Sol - diers of the cross.
high - er, high - er, Sol - diers of the cross.
love my Je - sus? Sol - diers of the cross.
why not serve Him? Sol - diers of the cross.
high - er, high - er, Sol - diers of the cross.

JEANIE WITH THE LIGHT BROWN HAIR

Words and Music by
Stephen C. Foster

1. I dream of Jean - ie with the light brown hair, borne like a va - por
2. I long for Jean - ie with the day - dawn smile, ra - diant in glad - ness,
3. I sigh for Jean - ie, but her light form strayed far from the fond hearts

on the sum - mer air. I see her trip - ping where the bright streams play,
warm with win - ning guile. I hear her mel - o - dies, like joys gone by.
'round her na - tive glade. Her smiles have van - ished and her sweet songs flown,

hap - py as the dai - sies that dance on her way. Man - y were the wild notes her
sigh - ing 'round my heart o'er the fond hopes that die. Sigh - ing like the night wind and
flit - ting like the dreams that have cheered us and gone. How the nod - ding wild - flowers may

mer - ry voice would pour, man - y were the blithe birds that war - bled them o'er. I
sob - bing like the rain, wail - ing for the lost one that comes not a - gain. I
with - er on the shore, while her gen - tle fin - gers will cull them no more. I

dream of Jean - ie with the light brown hair, float - ing like a va - por on the soft sum - mer air.
long for Jean - ie, and my heart bows low, nev - er more to find her where the bright wa - ters flow.
sigh for Jean - ie with the light brown hair, float - ing like a va - por on the soft sum - mer air.

JEFFERSON AND LIBERTY

Early American
Based on an Irish Folksong

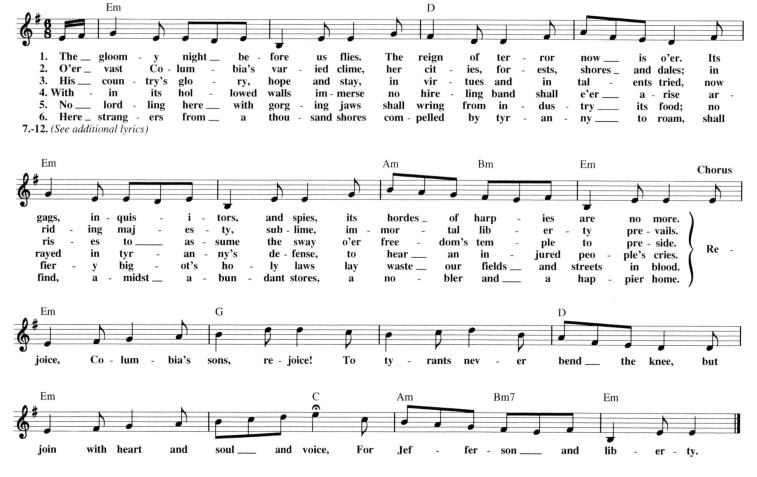

1. The gloom-y night be-fore us flies. The reign of ter-ror now is o'er. Its
2. O'er vast Co-lum-bia's var-ied clime, her cit-ies, for-ests, shores and dales; in
3. His coun-try's glo-ry, hope and stay, in vir-tues and in tal-ents tried, now
4. With-in its hol-lowed walls im-merse no hire-ling band shall e'er a-rise ar-
5. No lord-ling here with gorg-ing jaws shall wring from in-dus-try its food; no
6. Here strang-ers from a thou-sand shores com-pelled by tyr-an-ny to roam, shall

7.-12. *(See additional lyrics)*

gags, in-quis-i-tors, and spies, its hordes of harp-ies are no more.
rid-ing maj-es-ty, sub-lime, im-mor-tal lib-er-ty pre-vails.
ris-es to as-sume the sway o'er free-dom's tem-ple to pre-side.
rayed in tyr-an-ny's de-fense, to hear an in-jured peo-ple's cries.
fier-y big-ot's ho-ly laws lay waste our fields and streets in blood.
find, a-midst a-bun-dant stores, a no-bler and a hap-pier home.

Chorus

Re-

joice, Co-lum-bia's sons, re-joice! To ty-rants nev-er bend the knee, but

join with heart and soul and voice, For Jef-fer-son and lib-er-ty.

Additional Lyrics

7. Here art shall lift her laurel'd head
   Wealth industry and peace divine;
   And where dark forests lately spread
   Rich fields and lofty cities shine.
   Chorus

8. From Europe's wants and woes remote
   A dreary waste of waves between;
   Here plenty cheers the humble cot,
   And smiles on every village green.
   Chorus

9. Here, free as air's expanded space,
   To every soul and sect shall be;
   That sacred privilege of our race,
   The worship of the Deity.
   Chorus

10. These gifts, great liberty, are thine,
    Ten thousand more we owe to thee;
    Immortal may their mem'ries shine,
    Who fought and died for liberty.
    Chorus

11. What heart but hails a scene so bright
    What soul but inspiration draws;
    Who would not guard so dear a right
    Or die in such a glorious cause.
    Chorus

12. Let foes to freedom dread the name,
    But should they touch the sacred tree
    Twice fifty thousand swords would flame,
    For Jefferson and liberty.
    Chorus

JESSE JAMES

19th Century Folk Ballad from Missouri

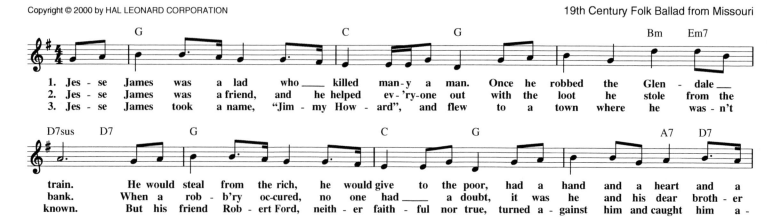

1. Jes-se James was a lad who killed man-y a man. Once he robbed the Glen-dale
2. Jes-se James was a friend, and he helped ev-'ry-one out with the loot he stole from the
3. Jes-se James took a name, "Jim-my How-ard", and flew to a town where he was-n't

train. He would steal from the rich, he would give to the poor, had a hand and a heart and a
bank. When a rob-b'ry oc-cured, no one had a doubt, it was he and his dear broth-er
known. But his friend Rob-ert Ford, neith-er faith-ful nor true, turned a-gainst him and caught him a-

brain.   Poor Jes - se had a wife to ____ mourn for his life, three chil - dren, they were brave.   But the)
Frank.   Then one day Rob - ert Ford, for the sake of re - ward, his word to the gov - 'nor gave.   Oh, the)
lone.   Poor Jes - se, he was mourned, and his kill - er was scorned how can friend - ship so be - have?   Oh, the)

dirt - y lit - tle cow - ard ____ who shot Jim - my How-ard ____ has laid poor Jes - se in his grave.

JESUS BORN IN BETH'NY

Hymn from Virginia

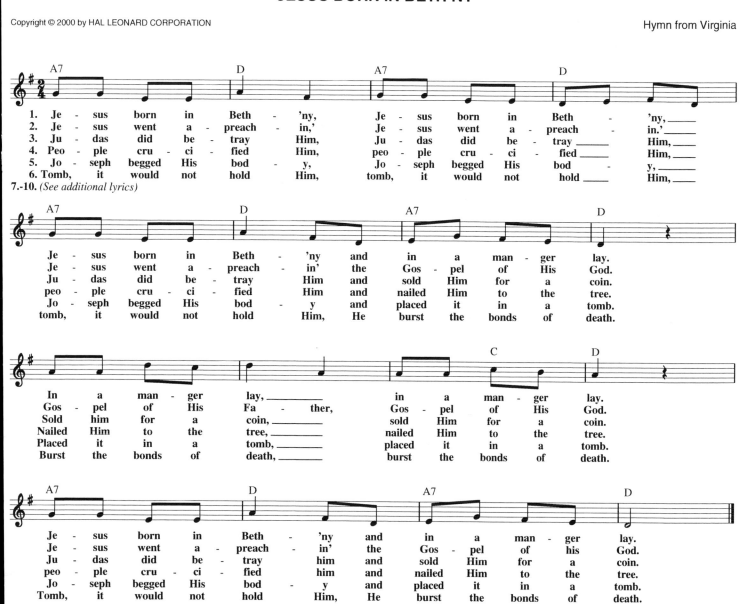

1. Je - sus born in Beth - 'ny,   Je - sus born in Beth - 'ny, _____
2. Je - sus went a - preach - in,'   Je - sus went a - preach - in.' _____
3. Ju - das did be - tray Him,   peo - ple cru - ci - fied _____ Him, ____
4. Peo - ple cru - ci - fied Him,   peo - ple cru - ci - fied _____ Him, ____
5. Jo - seph begged His bod - y,   Jo - seph begged His bod - y, _____
6. Tomb, it would not hold Him,   tomb, it would not hold ____ Him, ____

7.-10. *(See additional lyrics)*

Je - sus born in Beth - 'ny and in a man - ger lay.
Je - sus went a - preach - in' the Gos - pel of His God.
Ju - das did be - tray Him and sold Him for a coin.
peo - ple cru - ci - fied Him and nailed Him to the tree.
Jo - seph begged His bod - y and placed it in a tomb.
tomb, it would not hold Him, He burst the bonds of death.

In a man - ger lay, _____ in a man - ger lay.
Gos - pel of His Fa - ther, Gos - pel of His God.
Sold him for a coin, _____ sold Him for a coin.
Nailed Him to the tree, _____ nailed Him to the tree.
Placed it in a tomb, _____ placed it in a tomb.
Burst the bonds of death, _____ burst the bonds of death.

Je - sus born in Beth - 'ny and in a man - ger lay.
Je - sus went a - preach - in' the Gos - pel of his God.
Ju - das did be - tray him and sold Him for a coin.
peo - ple cru - ci - fied him and nailed Him to the tree.
Jo - seph begged His bod - y and placed it in a tomb.
Tomb, it would not hold Him, He burst the bonds of death.

Additional Lyrics

7. Early, then, one morning, before the break of day,

8. Mary came a-weeping, "They've stole my Lord away."

9. Jesus has arisen and gone to Galilee.

10. Jesus then ascended up to His Father's home.

JAY GOULD'S DAUGHTER

American Hobo Song

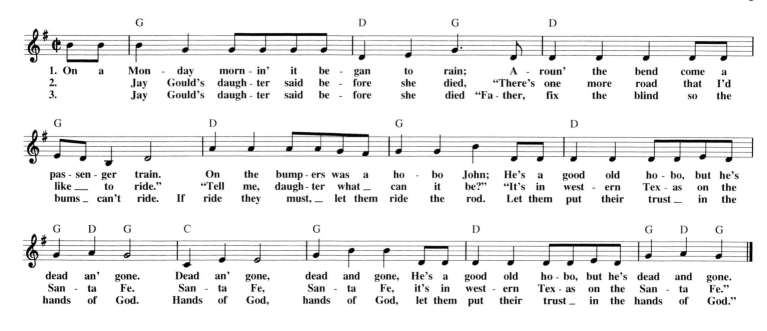

1. On a Mon - day morn - in' it be - gan to rain; A - roun' the bend come a
2. Jay Gould's daugh - ter said be - fore she died, "There's one more road that I'd
3. Jay Gould's daugh - ter said be - fore she died "Fa - ther, fix the blind so the

pas - sen - ger train. On the bump - ers was a ho - bo John; He's a good old ho - bo, but he's
like ___ to ride." "Tell me, daugh - ter what ___ can it be?" "It's in west - ern Tex - as on the
bums ___ can't ride. If ride they must, ___ let them ride the rod. Let them put their trust ___ in the

dead an' gone. Dead an' gone, dead and gone, He's a good old ho - bo, but he's dead and gone.
San - ta Fe. San - ta Fe, San - ta Fe, it's in west - ern Tex - as on the San - ta Fe."
hands of God. Hands of God, hands of God, let them put their trust ___ in the hands of God."

JENNY JENKINS

18th Century American, from New England

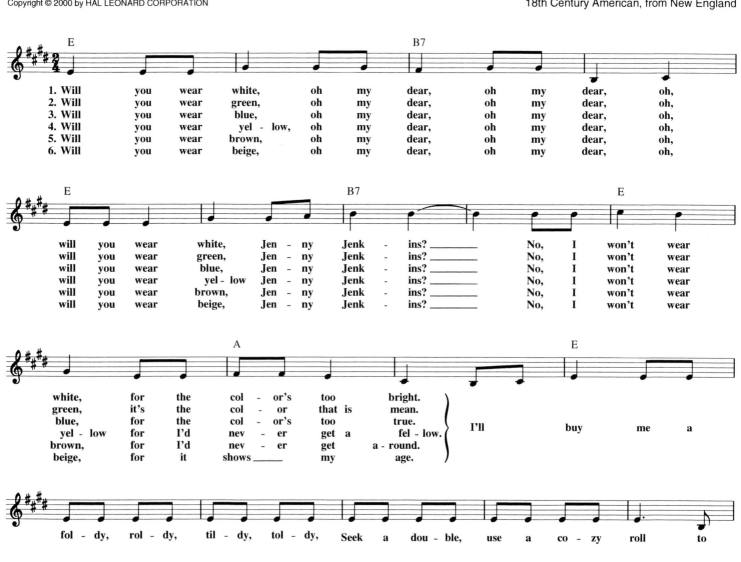

1. Will you wear white, oh my dear, oh my dear, oh,
2. Will you wear green, oh my dear, oh my dear, oh,
3. Will you wear blue, oh my dear, oh my dear, oh,
4. Will you wear yel - low, oh my dear, oh my dear, oh,
5. Will you wear brown, oh my dear, oh my dear, oh,
6. Will you wear beige, oh my dear, oh my dear, oh,

will you wear white, Jen - ny Jenk - ins? _____ No, I won't wear
will you wear green, Jen - ny Jenk - ins? _____ No, I won't wear
will you wear blue, Jen - ny Jenk - ins? _____ No, I won't wear
will you wear yel - low Jen - ny Jenk - ins? _____ No, I won't wear
will you wear brown, Jen - ny Jenk - ins? _____ No, I won't wear
will you wear beige, Jen - ny Jenk - ins? _____ No, I won't wear

white, for the col - or's too bright.
green, it's the col - or that is mean.
blue, for the col - or's too true.   I'll buy me a
yel - low for I'd nev - er get a fel - low.
brown, for I'd nev - er get a - round.
beige, for it shows ___ my age.

fol - dy, rol - dy, til - dy, tol - dy, Seek a dou - ble, use a co - zy roll to

find me. Roll, _____ Jen - ny Jenk - ins, roll. _____

JERRY RYAN

Logging song from Newfoundland

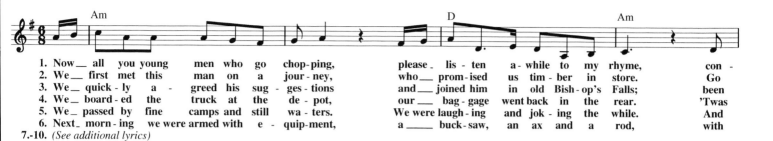

1. Now__ all you young men who go chop-ping, please__ lis-ten a-while to my rhyme, con -
2. We__ first met this man on a jour-ney, who__ prom-ised us tim-ber in store. Go
3. We__ quick-ly a-greed his sug-ges-tions and__ joined him in old Bish-op's Falls; been
4. We__ board-ed the truck at the de-pot, our__ bag-gage went back in the rear. 'Twas
5. We__ passed by fine camps and still wa-ters. We were laugh-ing and jok-ing the while. And
6. Next__ morn-ing we were armed with e-quip-ment, a_____ buck-saw, an ax and a rod, with

7.-10. *(See additional lyrics)*

cern-ing the year I was work - ing with that fore-man, well known Jer - ry Ryan.
up to camp boys, __ they're o - pen, and__ stay till the job is all o'er.
ea - ger for work and em - ploy-ment so scarce, not __ know-ing the wag - es were small.
lit - tle we thought as we jour-neyed a - long; the __ hard-ships you go through up there.
then with a bound__ he brought her a-round, say-ing, "Boys, we are up thir - ty miles."
for - ty - nine men to make wag - es, with__ on - ly scrub spruce on a bog.

Additional Lyrics

7. It is hard for a man to make money,
   When there's only scrub spruce to be found;
   And if you refuse a bad chance on scale,
   The word is you got to go down.

8. Seventy cents they would charge for a buck-saw,
   And seventy cents a day for your board;
   And then there's a fee for the doctor,
   Out of one dollar-twenty a cord.

9. We found no complaints with this foreman,
   I think he is honest and square;
   But it fell to our lot, like cattle were brought,
   And yoked to a buck-saw up there.

10. And when you lay down on your pillow,
    No matter if you're asleep or awake;
    You will think on the time you spent with Jerry Ryan,
    On the borders of old Rocky Lake.

JESUS LOVES ME

Words by Anna B. Warner
Music by William B. Bradbury

1. Je - sus loves me! this I know, For the Bi - ble tells me so;
2. Je - sus loves me! He who died Heav - en's gates to o - pen wide!
3. Je - sus loves me! loves me still, Tho' I'm ver - y weak and ill;
4. Je - sus loves me! He will stay Close be - side me all the way;

Lit - tle ones to Him be - long; They are weak, but He is strong.
He will wash a - way my sin, Let His lit - tle child come in.
From His shin - ing throne on high, Comes to watch me where I lie.
If I love Him, when I die He will take me home on high.

Yes, Je - sus loves me, Yes, Je - sus loves me,

Yes, Je - sus loves me, The Bi - ble tells me so.

JESUS, THE CHRIST, IS BORN

Hymn from Tennessee

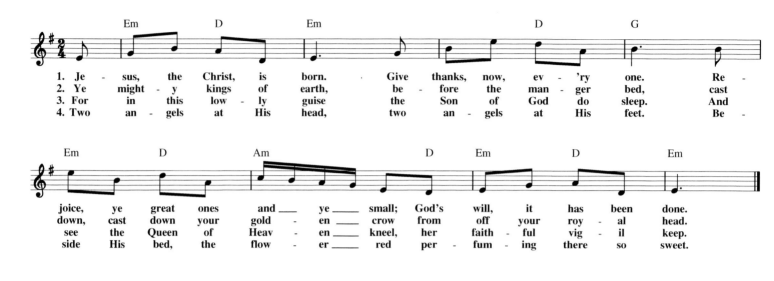

1. Je - sus, the Christ, is born. Give thanks, now, ev - 'ry one. Re -
2. Ye might - y kings of earth, be - fore the man - ger bed, cast
3. For in this low - ly guise the Son of God do sleep. And
4. Two an - gels at His head, two an - gels at His feet. Be -

joice, ye great ones and ye small; God's will, it has been done.
down, cast down your gold - en crow from off your roy - al head.
see the Queen of Heav - en kneel, her faith - ful vig - il keep.
side His bed, the flow - er red per - fum - ing there so sweet.

JOHN BROWN'S BODY

Words by the men of the
Massachusetts Volunteer Militia, circa 1861
Tune based on a hymn by William Steffe

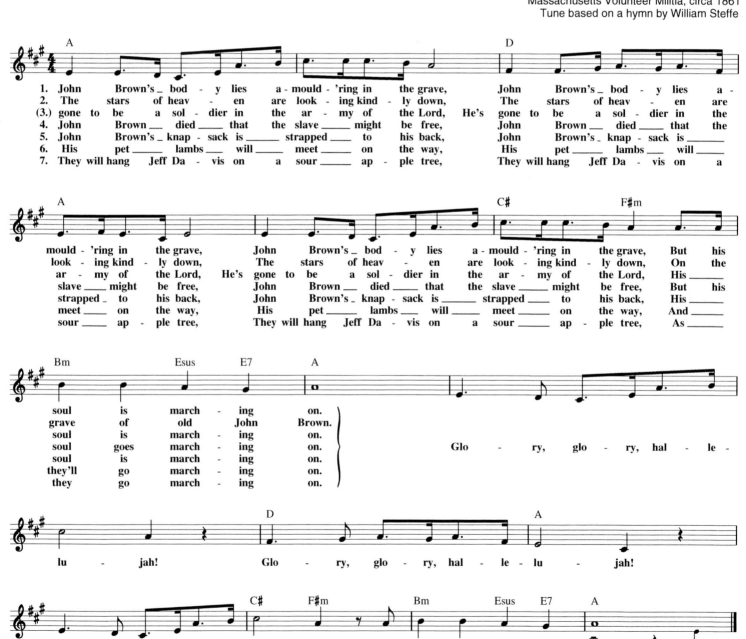

1. John Brown's bod - y lies a - mould - 'ring in the grave, John Brown's bod - y lies a -
2. The stars of heav - en are look - ing kind - ly down, The stars of heav - en are
(3.) gone to be a sol - dier in the ar - my of the Lord, He's gone to be a sol - dier in the
4. John Brown died that the slave might be free, John Brown died that the
5. John Brown's knap - sack is strapped to his back, John Brown's knap - sack is
6. His pet lambs will meet on the way, His pet lambs will
7. They will hang Jeff Da - vis on a sour ap - ple tree, They will hang Jeff Da - vis on a

mould - 'ring in the grave, John Brown's bod - y lies a - mould - 'ring in the grave, But his
look - ing kind - ly down, The stars of heav - en are look - ing kind - ly down, On the
ar - my of the Lord, He's gone to be a sol - dier in the ar - my of the Lord, His
slave might be free, John Brown died that the slave might be free, But his
strapped to his back, John Brown's knap - sack is strapped to his back, His
meet on the way, His pet lambs will meet on the way, And
sour ap - ple tree, They will hang Jeff Da - vis on a sour ap - ple tree, As

soul is march - ing on.
grave of old John Brown.
soul is march - ing on.
soul goes march - ing on.
soul is march - ing on.
they'll go march - ing on.
they go march - ing on.

Glo - ry, glo - ry, hal - le -

lu - jah! Glo - ry, glo - ry, hal - le - lu - jah!

Glo - ry, glo - ry, hal - le - lu - jah! His soul is march - ing on. (3. He's)

JIM FISK

American Ballad
circa 1872

1. If   you'll   lis - ten   a   while,   I   will   sing   you   a
2. If   you've   plen - ty   of   stamps   you   can   hold   up   your
3. In   the   tri - als   for   mur - der   we've   had   now - a -
4. Let   me   sing   of   a   man   who's   now   dead   in   his
5. We _____   know _____   he   loved   both _____   wom - en   and
6. If   a   man   was   in   trou - ble   Fisk   helped   him   a-

7.-12. *(See additional lyrics)*

song   of   the   glo - ri - ous   land   of   the   free, _____
head   and   walk   out   from   your   own   pris - on   door. _____
days   the _____   rich   ones   get   off   swift   and   sure. _____
grave,   a _____   good   man   as   ev - er   was   born. _____
wine,   but   his   heart   it   was   right,   I   am   sure. _____
long   to _____   drive   the   grim   wolf   from   the   door. _____

_____   and   the   dif - f'rence   I'll   show   'twixt   the   rich   and   the
_____   But   they'll   hang   you   up   high   if   you've   no   friends   or
_____   While   they've   thou - sands   to   pay   to   the   ju - ry   and
_____   Jim   Fisk   he   was   called   and   his   mon - ey   he
_____   Though   he   lived   like   a   prince   in   a   pal - ace   so
_____   He _____   strove   to   do   right,   though   he   may   have   done

poor   in   a   tri - al   by   ju - ry,   you   see. _____
gold.   Let   the   rich   go   but   hang   up   the   poor. _____
judge,   you   can   bet   they'll   go   back   on   the   poor. _____
gave   to   the   out - cast,   the   poor   and   for - lorn. _____
fine,   yet   he   nev - er   went   back   on   the   poor. _____
wrong,   but   he   nev - er   went   back   on   the   poor. _____

Additional Lyrics

7. Jim Fisk was a man wore his heart on his sleeve,
   No matter what people might say,
   And he did all his deeds, (both the good and the bad)
   In the broad open light of the day.

8. With his grand six-in-hand on the beach at Long Branch
   He cut a big dash, to be sure.
   But Chicago's great fire showed the world that Jim Fisk
   With his wealth still remembered the poor.

9. When the telegram came that the homeless that night
   Were starving to death, slow but sure,
   His "Lightning Express," manned by noble Jim Fisk,
   Flew to feed all her hungry and poor.

10. Now what do you think of the trial of Stokes,
    Who murdered this friend of the poor?
    When such men get free, is there anyone safe
    If they step from outside their own door?

11. Is there one law for the poor and one for the rich?
    It seems so, at least so I say.
    If they hang up the poor, why, surely the rich
    Ought to swing up the very same way.

12. Don't show any favor to friend or to foe,
    The beggar or prince at his door.
    The big millionaire you must hang up also
    But never go back on the poor.

JOHN JACOB JINGLEHEIMER SCHMIDT

Traditional Game Song

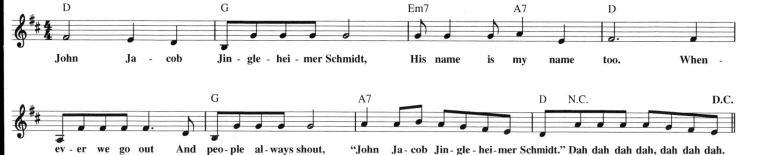

John   Ja - cob   Jin - gle - hei - mer Schmidt,   His   name   is   my   name   too.   When -

ev - er   we   go   out   And   peo - ple   al - ways   shout,   "John   Ja - cob   Jin - gle - hei - mer Schmidt." Dah dah dah dah, dah dah dah.

JOE BOWERS

American Miners' Song, circa 1860

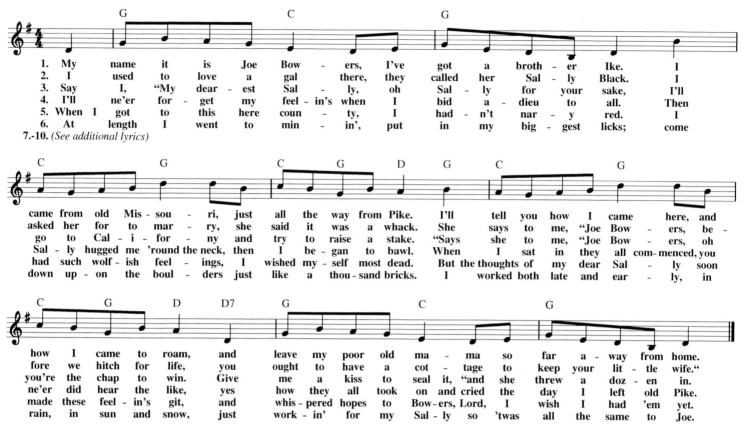

1. My name it is Joe Bow - ers, I've got a broth - er Ike. I
2. I used to love a gal there, they called her Sal - ly Black. I
3. Say I, "My dear - est Sal - ly, oh Sal - ly for your sake, I'll
4. I'll ne'er for - get my feel - in's when I bid a - dieu to all. Then
5. When I got to this here coun - ty, I had - n't nar - y red. I
6. At length I went to min - in', put in my big - gest licks; come

7.-10. *(See additional lyrics)*

came from old Mis - sou - ri, just all the way from Pike. I'll tell you how I came here, and
asked her for to mar - ry, she said it was a whack. She says to me, "Joe Bow - ers, be -
Sal - ly hugged me 'round the neck, then I be - gan to bawl. "Says she to me, "Joe Bow - ers, oh
had such wolf - ish feel - ings, I wished my - self most dead. When I sat in they all com - menced, you
down up - on the boul - ders just like a thou - sand bricks. I worked both late and ear - ly, in

how I came to roam, and leave my poor old ma - ma so far a - way from home.
fore we hitch for life, you ought to have a cot - tage to keep your lit - tle wife."
you're the chap to win. Give me a kiss to seal it, "and she threw a doz - en in.
ne'er did hear the like, yes how they all took on and cried the day I left old Pike.
made these feel - in's git, and whis - pered hopes to Bow - ers, Lord, I wish I had 'em yet.
rain, in sun and snow, just work - in' for my Sal - ly so 'twas all the same to Joe.

Additional Lyrics

7. I made a very lucky strike, as the gold itself did tell,
And saved it for my Sally, the gal I loved so well,
I saved it for my Sally, that I might pour it at her feet,
That she might kiss and hug me and call me something sweet.

8. But one day I got a letter from my dear, kind brother Ike,
It came from old Missouri, sent all the way from Pike;
It brought me the gol-darndest news as ever you did hear;
My heart is almost busted, so pray excuse this tear.

9. It said my Sal was fickle, that her love for me had fled,
That she'd married with a butcher, those hair was awful red;
It told me more than that— oh, it's enough to make one swear!
It said Sally had a baby, and the baby had red hair.

10. Now I've told you all that I could tell about the sad affa'r,
'Bout Sally marryin' the butcher, and the butcher had red ha'r.
Whether it was a boy or gal child, the letter never said,
It only said its cussed hair was inclinèd to be a red.

JOHNNY HAS GONE FOR A SOLDIER

Song from the American Revolutionary War
Based on a 17th Century Irish Tune

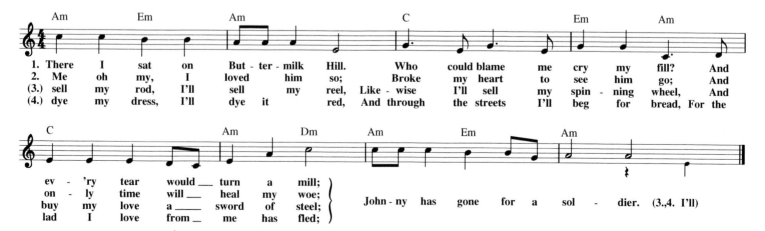

1. There I sat on But - ter - milk Hill. Who could blame me cry my fill? And
2. Me oh my, I loved him so; Broke my heart to see him go; And
(3.) sell my rod, I'll sell my reel, Like - wise I'll sell my spin - ning wheel, And
(4.) dye my dress, I'll dye it red, And through the streets I'll beg for bread, For the

ev - 'ry tear would __ turn a mill;
on - ly time will __ heal my woe;
buy my love a __ sword of steel; } John - ny has gone for a sol - dier. (3.,4. I'll)
lad I love from __ me has fled;

JOHN HARDY

19th Century Southern American

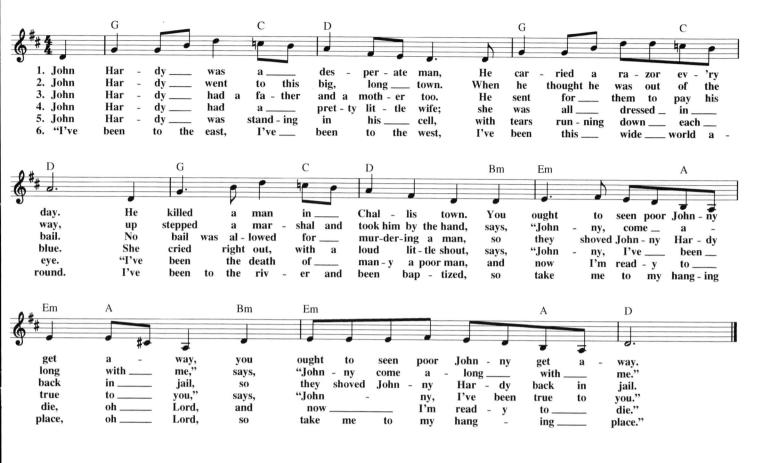

1. John Har - dy ___ was a ___ des - per - ate man, He car - ried a ra - zor ev - 'ry
2. John Har - dy ___ went to this big, long ___ town. When he thought he was out of the
3. John Har - dy ___ had a fa - ther and a moth - er too. He sent for ___ them to pay his
4. John Har - dy ___ had a ___ pret - ty lit - tle wife; she was all ___ dressed __ in ___
5. John Har - dy ___ was stand - ing in his ___ cell, with tears run - ning down ___ each ___
6. "I've been to the east, I've ___ been to the west, I've been this ___ wide ___ world a -

day. He killed a man in ___ Chal - lis town. You ought to seen poor John - ny
way, up stepped a mar - shal and took him by the hand, says, "John - ny, come ___ a -
bail. No bail was al - lowed for ___ mur-der-ing a man, so they shoved John - ny Har - dy
blue. She cried right out, with a loud lit - tle shout, says, "John - ny, I've ___ been ___
eye. "I've been the death of ___ man - y a poor man, and now I'm read - y to ___
round. I've been to the riv - er and been bap - tized, so take me to my hang - ing

get a - way, you ought to seen poor John - ny get a - way.
long with ___ me," says, "John - ny come a - long ___ with ___ me."
back in ___ jail, so they shoved John - ny Har - dy back in jail.
true to ___ you," says, "John - ny, I've been true to you."
die, oh ___ Lord, and now ___ I'm read - y to ___ die."
place, oh ___ Lord, so take me to my hang - ing ___ place."

JOHN PEEL

Words by John W. Graves
circa 1820
Tune based on an 18th Century Scottish Folksong

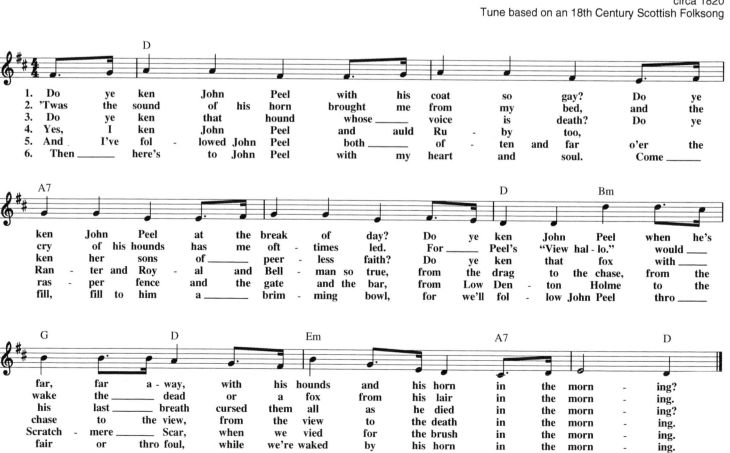

1. Do ye ken John Peel with his coat so gay? Do ye
2. 'Twas the sound of his horn brought me from my bed, and the
3. Do ye ken that hound whose ___ voice is death? Do ye
4. Yes, I ken John Peel and auld Ru - by too,
5. And I've fol - lowed John Peel both ___ of - ten and far o'er the
6. Then ___ here's to John Peel with my heart and soul. Come ___

ken John Peel at the break of day? Do ye ken John Peel when he's
cry of his hounds has me oft - times led. For ___ Peel's "View hal - lo." would ___
ken her sons of ___ peer - less faith? Do ye ken that fox with ___
Ran - ter and Roy - al and Bell - man so true, from the drag to the chase, from the
ras - per fence and the gate and the bar, from Low Den - ton Holme to the
fill, fill to him a ___ brim - ming bowl, for we'll fol - low John Peel thro ___

far, far a - way, with his hounds and his horn in the morn - ing?
wake the ___ dead or a fox from his lair in the morn - ing.
his last ___ breath cursed them all as he died in the morn - ing?
chase to the view, from the view to the death in the morn - ing.
Scratch - mere ___ Scar, when we vied for the brush in the morn - ing.
fair or thro foul, while we're waked by his horn in the morn - ing.

JOHNNY, COME DOWN TO HILO

African-American Sea Chantey

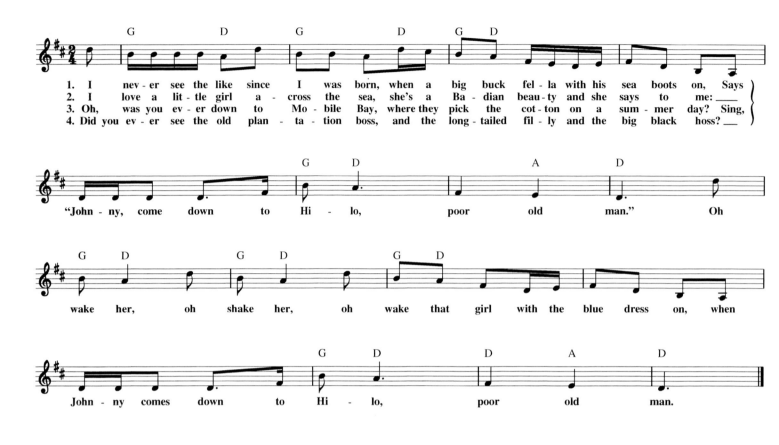

1. I nev-er see the like since I was born, when a big buck fel-la with his sea boots on, Says
2. I love a lit-tle girl a-cross the sea, she's a Ba-dian beau-ty and she says to me: ___
3. Oh, was you ev-er down to Mo-bile Bay, where they pick the cot-ton on a sum-mer day? Sing,
4. Did you ev-er see the old plan-ta-tion boss, and the long-tailed fil-y and the big black hoss? ___

"John-ny, come down to Hi-lo, poor old man." Oh

wake her, oh shake her, oh wake that girl with the blue dress on, when

John-ny comes down to Hi-lo, poor old man.

JOHN HENRY

Folk Ballad from West Virginia
circa 1870s

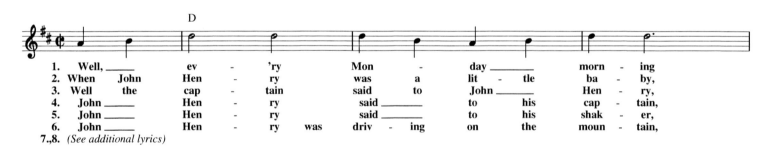

1. Well, ___ ev-'ry Mon-day ___ morn-ing
2. When John Hen-ry was a lit-tle ba-by,
3. Well the cap-tain said to John Hen-ry,
4. John ___ Hen-ry said ___ to his cap-tain,
5. John ___ Hen-ry said ___ to his shak-er,
6. John ___ Hen-ry was driv-ing on the moun-tain,
7.,8. *(See additional lyrics)*

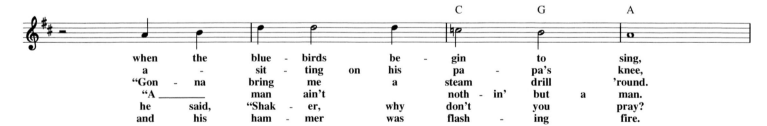

when the blue-birds be-gin to sing,
a- sit-ting on his pa-pa's knee,
"Gon-na bring me a steam drill 'round.
"A ___ man ain't noth-in' but a man.
he said, "Shak-er, why don't you pray?
and his ham-mer was flash-ing fire.

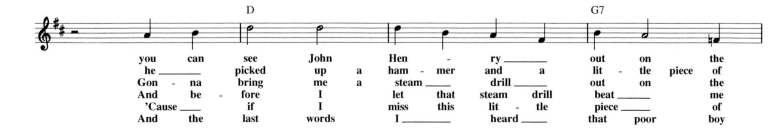

you can see John Hen-ry ___ out on the
he ___ picked up a ham-mer and a lit-tle piece of
Gon-na bring me a steam ___ drill ___ out on the
And be-fore I let that steam drill beat ___ me
'Cause ___ if I miss this lit-tle piece ___ of
And the last words I ___ heard ___ that poor boy

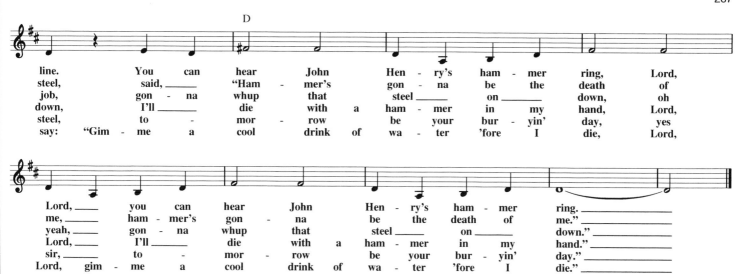

Additional Lyrics

7. John Henry, he drove fifteen feet,
The steam drill only made nine.
But he hammered so hard that he broke his poor heart,
And he laid down his hammer and he died . . .

8. They took John Henry to the graveyard
And they buried him in the sand.
And every locomotive comes a-roaring by says,
"There lies a steel-driving man". . .

JOHNNY I HARDLY KNEW YE

19th Century Irish

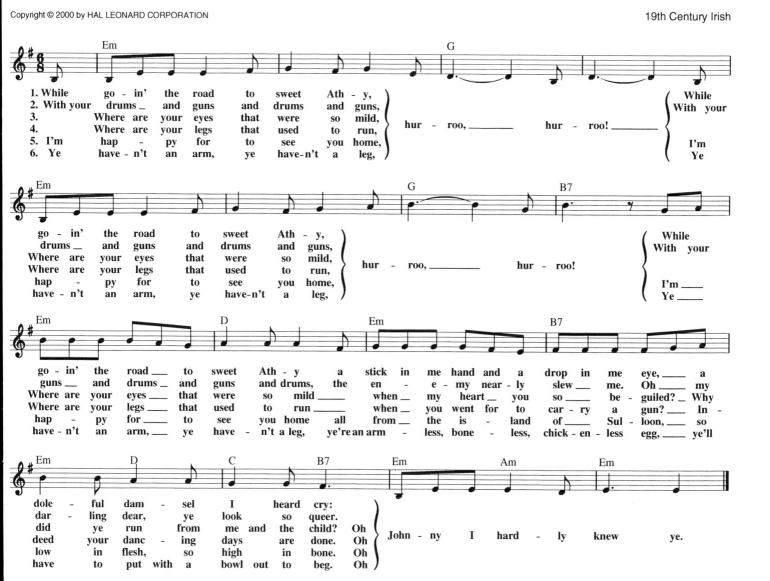

JOHN RILEY (I)

Irish

1. Fair young maid all in her gar - den, ___ Strange young man come rid - ing ___ by. ___ Said, "Fair maid, ___ will you mar - ry me?" ___ This then, sir, ___ was ___ her re - ply. ___
2. Oh, kind sir, I can - not mar - ry, ___ I've a love who sails the deep sea. ___ He's been gone ___ for these sev - en years, ___ Still no man ___ shall ___ mar - ry me. ___
3. What if he's in bat - tle slain, ___ Or drowned in the deep salt ___ sea? ___ What if he's ___ found an - oth - er love, ___ And that they ___ both ___ mar - ried be. ___
4. If he's in some bat - tle slain, ___ I'll die when the moon doth ___ wane. ___ If he's drowned ___ in the deep salt sea, ___ I'll be true ___ to his mem - o - ry. ___
5. If he's found an - oth - er love, ___ And if they both mar - ried ___ be, ___ Then I wish ___ them both hap - pi - ness, ___ Where they dwell ___ a - cross the sea. ___
6. Then he picked her up in his arms, ___ Kiss - es gave her one, two ___ three. ___ Weep no more ___ my ___ own true love, ___ I'm your long ___ lost ___ John Ri - ley. ___

JOHN RILEY (II)

Folksong from Kentucky

1. On walk - ing out one ___ sum - mer morn - ing to take the cool and pleas - ant air, I spied a fair and most beau - ti - ful dam - sel; her cheeks were like some ___ lil - y fair.
2. I walk - ed up and ___ spoke with cau - tion, "Oh, would you be a sail - or's wife?" "Oh no, kind sir," she ___ quick - ly an - swered, "my mind is to live a sin - gle life."
3. I said, "Fair maid, what ___ makes you dif - fer from all the rest of wom - an - kind? You are so fair, you ___ are ___ so three long years a - go, all to a man whom they called ___ John hand - some. To mar - ry you I ___ would in - cline."
4. "Kind sir, kind sir, I ___ could have mar - ried some two or me to a dis - tant shore. We'll sail o'er to a man whom they called ___ John Ri - ley, who was the cause of my o - ver - throw."
5. "Oh leave off think - ing ___ of John Ri - ley, and come with you to a dis - tant shore. My mind is with him, I can - not for va - nia, where John Ri - ley lives for ev - er - more."
6. "I'll not leave think - ing ___ of John Ri - ley, nor go with gave her were one, two, three. "I am the man whom they call ___ John sake him, though his face I may nev - er see an - y - more."
7. Then I walk - ed up to ___ her sweet kiss - es, the kiss - es I Ri - ley. I've just re - turned to ___ mar - ry thee."

JOHNNY TODD

19th Century English Ballad from Liverpool

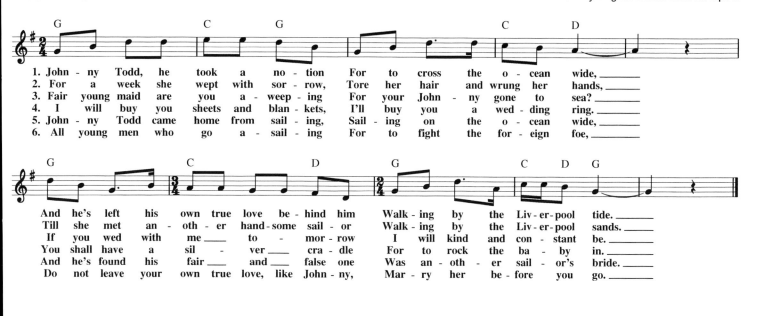

1. John - ny Todd, he took a no - tion For to cross the o - cean wide, _____
2. For a week she wept with sor - row, Tore her hair and wrung her hands, _____
3. Fair young maid are you a - weep - ing For your John - ny gone to sea? _____
4. I will buy you sheets and blan - kets, I'll buy you a wed - ding ring. _____
5. John - ny Todd came home from sail - ing, Sail - ing on the o - cean wide, _____
6. All young men who go a - sail - ing For to fight the for - eign foe, _____

And he's left his own true love be - hind him Walk - ing by the Liv - er-pool tide. _____
Till she met an - oth - er hand-some sail - or Walk - ing by the Liv - er-pool sands. _____
If you wed with me ____ to - mor - row I will kind and con - stant be. _____
You shall have a sil - ver ____ cra - dle For to rock the ba - by in. _____
And he's found his fair ____ and ____ false one Was an - oth - er sail - or's bride. _____
Do not leave your own true love, like John - ny, Mar - ry her be - fore you go. _____

JOHNSON BOYS

19th Century American

1. John - son boys were boys of hon - or, They knew how to court a maid;
2. John - son boys had skill and cour - age, And their sight was nev - er poor.
3. John - son boys were reb - el scouts, and They were known both far and wide.

They knew how to kiss and hug 'em, Hop up, pret - ty girls, don't be a - fraid.
Then they joined their coun - try's ser - vice In that ter - ri - ble Civ - il ____ War.
When the Yan - kees saw them com - ing They throw down all their guns and ____ hide

Hop up, pret - ty girls, don't be a - fraid. Hop up, pret - ty girls, don't be a - fraid. ____
In that ter - ri - ble Civ - il ____ War, In that ter - ri - ble Civ - il ____ War. ____
They throw down all their guns and ____ hide. They throw down all their guns and ____ hide. ____

THE JOLLY MILLER

Early 18th Century English

1. There was a jol - ly mil - ler once Lived on the riv - er Dee, _____ He worked and sang from
2. I live by my mill, she is to me Like par - ent, child and wife! _____ I would not change my

morn till night, No lark more blithe than he. _____ And ___ this the bur - den of his song For
sta - tion For an - y oth - er in life. _____ No ___ law - yer, sur - geon, doc - tor Ev - er

ev - er used to be. _____ "I care for no - bod - y, no, not I, And no - bod - y cares for me." _____
had a groat from me, _____ "I care for no - bod - y, no, not I, And no - bod - y cares for me" _____

JOIN THE BRITISH ARMY

19th Century English

1. When I was young I used to be as fine a man as you could see. The
2. When Sar - ah Com - den baked a cake, 'twas all for Cor - p'ral Slat - t'ry's sake, I
3. Now Cor - p'ral Duff's got such a drought just give him a cou - ple of jars of stout, He'll
4. Now Cap - tain Da - ley's gone a - way; his wife got in the fam - 'ly way, And

Prince of Wales, he said to me, "Come join the Brit - ish ar - my."
threw me - self in - to the lake, pre - tend - ing I was barm - y.
kill the en - e - my with his mouth and save the Brit - ish ar - my.
all the words that she would say was "Blame the Brit - ish ar - my."

Too - ra loo - ra - loo ra - loo,
'twas the on - ly thing that I could do To
me curs - es on the La - bour crew. They
I've made up me mind just what to do, I'll

they're look - ing for mon - keys in the zoo, And

if I had a face like you, I'd join the Brit - ish ar - my.
work my tick - et home to you and leave the Brit - ish ar - my.
took your dar - lin' boy from you to join the Brit - ish ar - my.
work my tick - et home to you and leave the Brit - ish ar - my.

JORDAN AIN'T A HARD ROAD TO TRAVEL

Words by Ossian E. Dodge
Music by Daniel Decatur Emmett
1855

1. As we're liv - ing in an age, when ev - 'ry - thing is new, We've
2. A _____ man can please the la - dies, if he is hon - est in his heart, No
3. An _____ hon - est - heart - ed man, is the no - blest work of God, For
4. A _____ man can drive a bar - gain, when he's trad - ing with the poor, And
5. If _____ spir - its act as guard - ians and see us work for love, Our en -

made our cal - cu - la - tions all ac - cord - in'
mat - ter if he is - n't worth a - farth - in'.
hap - pi - ness is all he is a - ward - in'.
drive a - way all hon - es - ty ac - cord - in'.
deav - ors they'll be cheer - ful - ly re - ward - in'.

To sing a new song that will
But if they should dis - cov - er that he
With a pret - ty lit - tle wife and a
But when he leaves this world they'll _____
And if we all are broth - er - ly when

give a dif - f'rent hue To a song called the "Oth - er Side of Jor - dan."
wears a dou - ble face He'll _____ nev - er get the oth - er side of Jor - dan.
ba - by in her arms He _____ hap - pi - ly will jour - ney on to Jor - dan.
drive him from the shore Of a land called the oth - er side of Jor - dan.
we are called a - bove, We'll _____ sing to - geth - er t'oth - er side of Jor - dan.

Then

sing boys, sing, with a mer - ry, mer - ry ring, Nor med - dle with the cares of a

neigh-bor, If man'll mind his own and let oth-er folks a-lone, Then Jor-dan ain't a hard road to trav-el, not at all.

JOSHUA (FIT THE BATTLE OF JERICHO)

African-American Spiritual

Josh-ua fit the bat-tle of ___ Jer-i-cho, ___ Jer-i-cho, ___ Jer-i-cho. ___

Josh-ua fit the bat-tle of ___ Jer-i-cho ___ and the walls came tum-blin' down.

1. You may
2. 'Way ___
3. Then the

talk a-bout your man of Gid-e-on, you may talk a-bout your man of Saul; there's none like good old
up ___ to the walls of Jer-i-cho he ___ marched with a spear in hand. "Go blow the ram's horn,"
lamb, ram, ___ sheep horns be-gan to blow and the trum-pets ___ be-gan to sound; and Josh-ua com-mand-ed the

Josh-u-a ___ at the bat-tle of Jer-i-cho. ___
Josh-ua cried, ___ " 'cause the bat-tle is in my hands." ___
chil-dren to shout ___ and the walls ___ came tum-blin' down. ___

down.

THE JUNIPER TREE

Party Song from Arkansas

1. Oh, sis-ter Phoe-be, how mer-ry were we the
2. Hat on your head ___ will keep your head warm, and
3. Go choose a part-ner, so choose you a one. Go

night we sat un-der the jun-i-per tree, the jun-i-per tree, hi-
one or two kiss-es will do you no harm, will do you no harm, I
choose you the fair-est that ev-er you can. Now rise you up, gal, and

o, hi-o, the jun-i-per tree, hi-o.
know, I know, will do you no harm, I know.
go and go. Now rise you up, gal, and go.

JUG OF PUNCH

Irish

1. 'Twas ver - y ear - ly in the month of June I was sit - ting with my ___
2. What more di - ver - sion can a man de - sire, Than to court a girl by a
3. All ye mor - tal Lords drink your nec - tar wine And the no - ble folks drink their
4. Oh, but when I'm dead and in my grave, No ___ cost - ly tomb - stone ___

glass and spoon A small bird sat on an i - vy bunch, And the song he sang was "The
neat turf fire? A Ker - ry pip - pin and the crack and crunch, And on the ta - ble a
clar - et fine. I'll give them all the grapes in the bunch For a jol - ly pull at the
will I crave. Just lay me down in my na - tive peat With a jug of punch at my

Jug of Punch." }
jug of punch. } Too - rah - loo - rah - loo, too - rah - loo - rah lay. Too - rah -
jug of punch. }
head and feet. }

loo - rah - loo, too - rah - loo - rah lay.

{ A small bird sat on an
{ A Ker - ry pip - pin and the
{ I'll give them all the grapes
{ Just lay me down in my

i - vy bunch, and the song he sang was "The Jug of Punch."
crack and crunch, And ___ on the ta - ble a jug of punch.
in the bunch For a jol - ly pull at the jug of punch.
na - tive peat With a jug of punch at my head and feet.

JUST BEFORE THE BATTLE, MOTHER

Words and Music by
George F. Root, 1863

1. Just be - fore the bat - tle, Moth - er, I am think - ing most of you,
2. Oh I long to see you, Moth - er, And the lov - ing ones at home,
3. Hark! I hear the bu - gles sound - ing, 'Tis the sig - nal for the fight,

While up - on the field we're watch - ing, With the en - e - my in view.
But I'll nev - er leave our ban - ner, Till in hon - or I can come.
Now may God pro - tect us, Moth - er, As he ev - er does the right.

Com - rades brave are round me ly - ing, Filled with thoughts of home and God; For
Tell the trai - tors, all a - round you, That their cru - el words, we know, In
Hear the "Bat - tle - Cry of Free - dom," How it swells up - on the air, Oh,

well they know that on the mor - row, Some will sleep be - neath the sod.
ev - 'ry bat - tle kill our sol - diers By the help they give the foe.
yes we'll ral - ly round the stan - dard, Or we'll per - ish no - bly there.

Fare - well, Moth - er, you may nev - er Press me to your heart a - gain; But

O, you'll not for - get me, Moth - er, If I'm num-ber'd with the slain.

JUST A CLOSER WALK WITH THEE

American

1. I am weak but Thou art strong. Je - sus, keep me from all wrong. ___ I'll be sat - is - fied as
2. Thro' this world of toil and snares, If I fal - ter, Lord, who cares? ___ Who with me my bur - den
3. When my fee - ble life is o'er, Time for me will be no more. ___ Guide me gen - tly, safe - ly

long ___ as I walk, let me walk close to Thee.
shares? ___ None but Thee, dear Lord, none but Thee. { Just a clos - er walk with Thee,
o'er ___ to Thy king - dom shore, to Thy shore. }

Grant it, Je - sus, is my plea. ___ Dai - ly walk-ing close to Thee, ___ Let it be, dear Lord, let it be.

KRISHNA

Folksong from India

"Krish - na, Krish - na, Krish - na" sing the peo - ple as they go each day.
"Krish - na, Krish - na, Kris - na" yen - du ha - da - na - di sa - gu va!

"Krish - na, Krish - na, Krish - na" let this chant for ev - er guide our way.
"Krish - na, Krish - na, Krish - na" yen - du ha - da - na - di ba - lu va!

KATY CLINE

Southern American

KATY CRUEL

Early 18th Century American

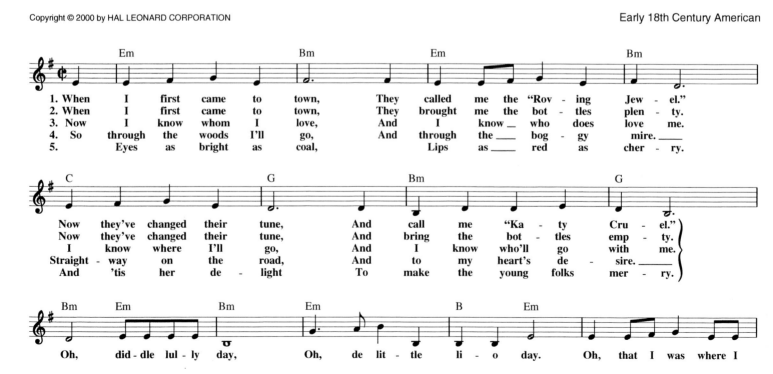

would be, Then should I be where I am not; Here I am where I must be, Where I
would be I can not; Oh, did-dle lul-ly day, Oh, de lit-tle li-o day.

KITTY OF COLERAINE

Irish

1. As beau-ti-ful Kit-ty one morn-ing was ___ trip-ping with a
2. I sat down be-side her and gen-tly did ___ chide her that ___

pitch-er of milk from the fair ___ of ___ Cole-raine: When she saw me, she
such a mis-for-tune should give ___ her ___ such ___ pain. A ___ kiss then I

stum-bled. The pitch-er, it ___ tum-bled, and all the sweet but-ter-milk
gave her, and be-fore I did ___ leave her she vowed for such pleas-ure she'd

wa-tered the plain. "Oh, ___ what shall I do now? 'Twas look-ing at
break it a-gain. 'Twas ___ hay-mak-ing sea-son. I can't tell the

you, now! Sure, sure, such a pitch-er I'll ne'er meet a-gain. 'Twas the
rea-son. Mis-for-tune will nev-er come sin-gle, 'tis plain. For ___

pride of my dai-ry. Oh, Bar-ney Mc-Clear-y, you're
ver-y soon af-ter poor Kit-ty's di-sas-ter there

sent as a plague to the girls of Cole-raine!"
was not a pitch-er found whole in Cole-raine!

KUMBAYA

Folksong from the Congo

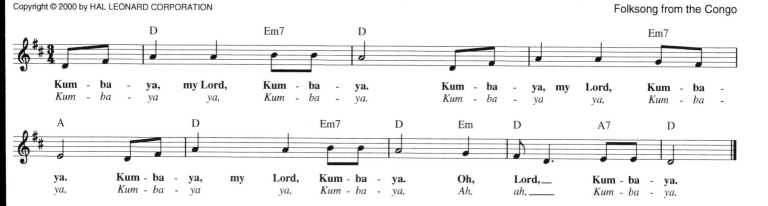

Kum-ba-ya, my Lord, Kum-ba-ya. Kum-ba-ya, my Lord, Kum-ba-
Kum-ba-ya ya, Kum-ba-ya. Kum-ba-ya ya, Kum-ba-

ya. Kum-ba-ya, my Lord, Kum-ba-ya. Oh, Lord, ___ Kum-ba-ya.
ya, Kum-ba-ya ya, Kum-ba-ya, Ah, ah, ___ Kum-ba-ya.

KENTUCKY BABE

Words by Richard Henry Buck
Music by Adam Giebel
1896

KEVIN BARRY

Irish
Anonymous Words, 20th Century
English Folk Melody, "Rolling Home to Merry England"

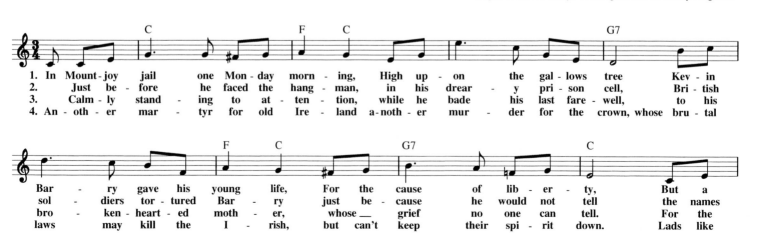

lad | of | eight - een | sum - mers, | Yet ____ | no | one | can | de -
of | his | brave com - pan - ions and | oth - er | things | they | wished | to
cause | he | proud - ly | cher - ished, | this | sad | part - ing | had | to
Bar - ry | are | no | cow - ards, | from the | foe | they | will | not

ny | As he | walked | to | death that | morn - ing, | He | proud - ly | held | his | head on | high.
know. | "Turn in - form - er | or | we'll | kill | you," __ | Ke - vin | Bar - ry | an - swered | "No."
be. | Then to | death | walked | soft - ly | smil - ing, ____ | that | old | Ire - land might | be | free.
fly. | Lads like | Bar - ry will | free | Ire - land, __ | for | her | sake | they'll | live and | die.

THE KEYS TO CANTERBURY

18th Century English

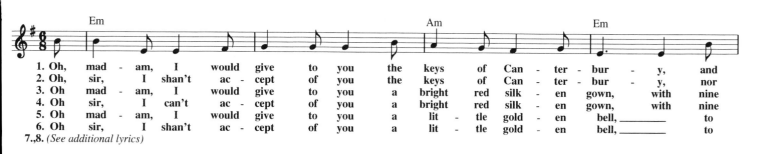

1. Oh, mad - am, I | would give to | you the | keys of Can - ter - bur - y, | and
2. Oh, sir, I | shan't ac - cept of | you the | keys of Can - ter - bur - y, | nor
3. Oh mad - am, I | would give to | you a | bright red silk - en gown, | with nine
4. Oh sir, I | can't ac - cept of | you a | bright red silk - en gown, | with nine
5. Oh mad - am, I | would give to | you a | lit - tle gold - en bell, _____ | to
6. Oh sir, I | shan't ac - cept of | you a | lit - tle gold - en bell, _____ | to

7.,8. *(See additional lyrics)*

all the bells of Lon - don will | ring to make us mer - ry, | if you will be my
all the bells of Lon - don won't | ring to make me mer - ry. | I will not be your
yards a - trail - ing and a - droop - ing on the | ground, | if you will be my
yards a - trail - ing and a - droop - ing on the | ground. ___ | I will not be your
ring for all your ser - vants that they | may serve you well, _____ | if you will be my
ring for all my ser - vants that they | may serve me well, _____ | I will not be your

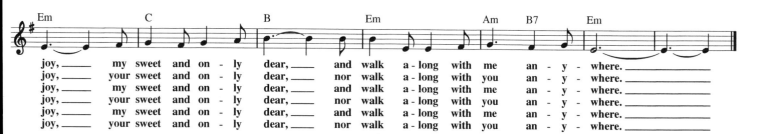

joy, ____ my sweet and on - ly dear, ____ and walk a - long with me an - y - where. _____
joy, ____ your sweet and on - ly dear, ____ nor walk a - long with you an - y - where. _____
joy, ____ my sweet and on - ly dear, ____ and walk a - long with me an - y - where. _____
joy, ____ your sweet and on - ly dear, ____ nor walk a - long with you an - y - where. _____
joy, ____ my sweet and on - ly dear, ____ and walk a - long with me an - y - where. _____
joy, ____ your sweet and on - ly dear, ____ nor walk a - long with you an - y - where. _____

Additional Lyrics

7. Oh madam, I would give to you the keys to my heart;
Oh keep them forever and we will never part;
If you will be my joy, my sweet and only dear
And walk along with me anywhere.

8. Oh sir, I shall accept of you the keys to your heart,
And keep them forever and never we will part.
And I will be your joy, your sweet and only dear
And walk along with you anywhere.

KITTY ALONE AND I (I)

Southeastern United States

1. Saw a crow a-flyin' low,
2. First came in a lit-tle bat,
3. Next came in a hon-ey bee,
4. Next came in two lit-tle ants,
5. Next came in was lit-tle Pete,
6. Bye-o, bye-o, ba-by-o,

Kit-ty a-lone, Kit-ty a-lone.

Saw a crow a-flyin' low,
First came in a lit-tle bat,
Next came in a hon-ey bee,
Next came in two lit-tle ants,
Next came in was lit-tle Pete,
Bye-o, bye-o, ba-by-o,

Kit-ty a-lone, a-lye.

Saw a crow a-flyin' low and a cat a-spin-nin' tow.
First came in a lit-tle bat with some but-ter and some fat.
Next came in a hon-ey bee with his fid-dle 'cross his knee.
Next came in two lit-tle ants, fix-in' for to have a dance.
Next came in was lit-tle Pete, fix-in' for to go to sleep.
Bye-o, bye-o, ba-by-o, bye-o, bye-o, ba-by-o.

Kit-ty a-lone, a-lye. Rock-a-ma-rye, ree.

KITTY ALONE AND I (II)

Appalachian Folksong

1. There was a frog lived in the well,
2. He rode up to Miss Mouse-'s door,
3. "Gen-tle-man Frog, won't you step in?"
4. He took Miss Mouse up-on his knee,
5. "In-deed, I can't con-sent to that,"
6. Un-cle Rat gave his con-sent,

Kit-ty a-lone, Kit-ty a-lone.

There
He

He
"In-

was a frog lived in the well,
rode up to Miss Mouse-'s door,
"Gen-tle-man Frog, won't you step in?"
took Miss Mouse up-on his knee,
deed I can't con-sent to that,"
Un-cle Rat gave his con-sent,

Kit-ty a-lone and I.

There
He

He
"In-

was	a	frog	lived	in	the	well	and	in	the	mill	a	mouse did dwell.
rode	up	to	Miss	Mouse - 's	door,	and	there	he	did	both	stop	and call.
"Gen - tle - man	Frog,	won't	you	step	in	and	sit	by the	fire	and	watch	me spin?"
took	Miss Mouse	up - on	his	knee,	"I	will	have	you	if	you'll	have	me."
deed	I	can't	con - sent	to	that	un - til	I	ask	my	Un - cle	Rat."	
Un - cle	Rat	gave	his	con - sent,	and	that's	the	way	the	wed - ding	went.	

Cal - lum - a - car - ey Kit - ty a - lone, Kit - ty a - lone and I._____

THE KNIGHT AND THE SHEPHERD'S DAUGHTER

16th Century English

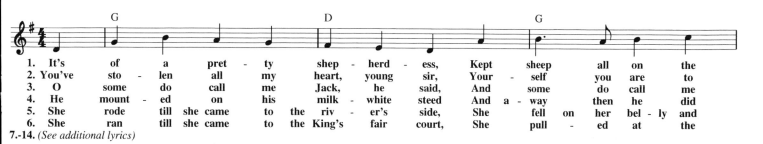

1. It's of a pret - ty shep - herd - ess, Kept sheep all on the
2. You've sto - len all my heart, young sir, Your - self you are to
3. O some do call me Jack, he said, And some do call me
4. He mount - ed on his milk - white steed And a - way then he did
5. She rode till she came to the riv - er's side, She fell on her bel - ly and
6. She ran till she came to the King's fair court, She pull - ed at the

7.-14. *(See additional lyrics)*

plain;	Who	should	ride	by	but ____	Knight	Wil - liam	And ____
blame;	So	if	your	vows	are ____	made	in truth,	Pray ____
John;	But	when	I'm	in	the ____	fair	King's court	My ____
ride;	She	tied	a	hand - ker - chief	round	her	waist	And ____
swam;	And	when	she	came	to	the	oth - er side	She ____
ring:	There	was	none so	read - y	as	the	King him - self	To ____

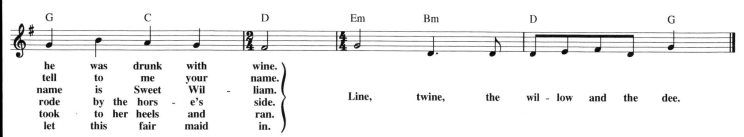

he	was	drunk	with	wine.
tell	to	me	your	name.
name	is	Sweet	Wil -	liam.
rode	by	the hors -	e's	side.
took	to	her heels	and	ran.
let	this	fair	maid	in.

Line, twine, the wil - low and the dee.

Additional Lyrics

7. Good morning to you, my pretty maid.
   Good morning, sir, said she;
   You have a knight all in your court
   This day has a-robbed me.

8. O has he robbed you of your gold,
   Or any of your fee?
   Or has he robbed you of the rarest branch
   That grows in your body?

9. He has not robbed me of my gold,
   Nor any of my fee;
   But he has robbed me of the rarest branch
   That grows in my body.

10. Here's twenty pounds for you, he said,
    All wrap-ped in a glove;
    And twenty pounds for you, he said,
    To seek some other love.

11. I will not have your twenty pounds,
    Nor any of your fee;
    But I will have the king's fair knight
    This day to marry me.

12. The king called up his merry men all,
    By one, by two, by three—
    Young William once the foremost was,
    But now behind came he.

13. He mounted on his milk-white steed,
    And she on her pony grey;
    He threw the bugle round his neck
    And together they rode away.

14. The very next town that they came to
    The wedding bells did ring;
    And the very next church that they came to
    There was a gay wedding.

LA CUCARACHA

Mexican Revolutionary Folksong

LADIES OF BRISBANE

Australian

1. Fare - well and a - dieu to you, sweet Bris - bane la - dies, Fare - well and a -
2. The first camp we make, we shall call it the Quart - pot, Ca - bool - ture, then
3. Then on to Tar - o - me - o and Yar - ra - man Creek, _ lads, It's there we shall
4. Then on to Nan - an - go, that hard - bit - ten town - ship, Where the out - of - work
5. The girls of Too - man - cey, they look so en - tranc - ing; Those young bawl - ing
6. Then fill up your glass - es and drink to the lass - es; We'll drink this town

dieu to you girls of Too - wong, For we've sold all our cat - tle, and
Kil - coy and Col - in - ton's hut. We'll pull up at the Stone House, Bob
make our next camp for the day, Where the wa - ter and grass are both
sta - tion hands sit in the dust, And the shear - ers get shorn by old
heif - ers are out for their fun, With the waltz and the pol - ka and
dry, then fare - well to them all. And _ when we've got back to the

have _ to be mo - ving, But we hope we shall see _ you a - gain be - fore
Wil - liam - son's pad - dock, And _ ear - ly next morn - ing we cross the Black -
plen - ty and sweet, _ lads, And _ may - be we'll butch - er a fat lit - tle
Tim _ the con - trac - tor; Oh, I would - n't go near there, but I flam - ing well
all _ kinds of danc - ing To the rack - et - y old ban - jo of Bob An - der -
Au - ga - thel - la Sta - tion, We'll _ hope you come by _ there and pay us a

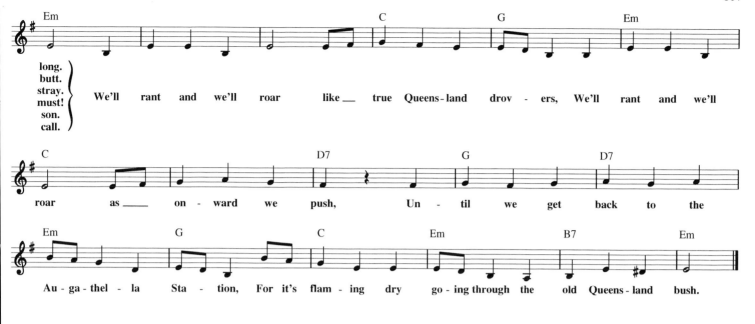

long.
butt.
stray.
must!
son.
call.

We'll rant and we'll roar like ___ true Queens-land drov-ers, We'll rant and we'll

roar as ___ on-ward we push, Un - til we get back to the

Au - ga-thel - la Sta - tion, For it's flam - ing dry go - ing through the old Queens-land bush.

LADY GAY

American

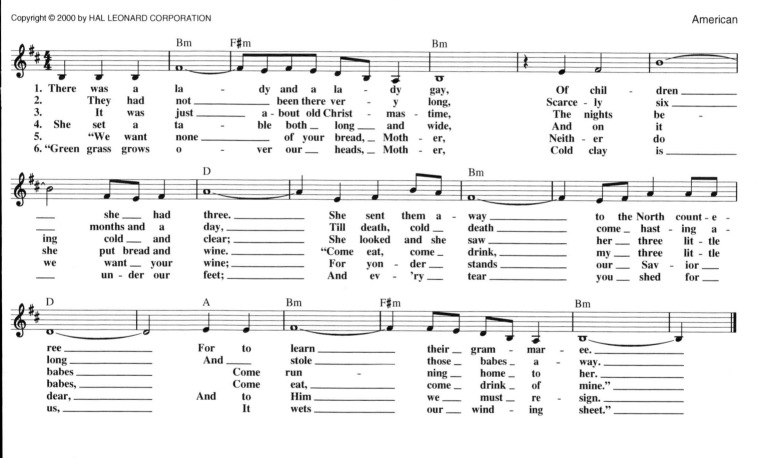

1. There was a la - dy and a la - dy gay, Of chil - dren ___
2. They had not ___ been there ver - y long, Scarce - ly six ___
3. It was just ___ a-bout old Christ - mas - time, The nights be -
4. She set a ta - ble both ___ long ___ and wide, And on it
5. "We want none ___ of your bread, ___ Moth - er, Neith - er do
6. "Green grass grows o - ver our ___ heads, ___ Moth - er, Cold clay is ___

___ she ___ had three. ___ She sent them a - way ___ to the North count - e -
___ months and a day, ___ Till death, cold ___ death ___ come ___ hast - ing a -
ing cold ___ and clear; ___ She looked and she saw ___ her ___ three lit - tle
she put bread and wine. ___ "Come eat, come ___ drink, ___ my ___ three lit - tle
we want ___ your wine; ___ For yon - der ___ stands ___ our ___ Sav - ior ___
___ un - der our feet; ___ And ev - 'ry ___ tear ___ you ___ shed for ___

ree ___ For to learn ___ their ___ gram - mar - ee. ___
long ___ And ___ stole ___ those ___ babes a - way. ___
babes ___ Come run - ning home ___ to her.
babes, ___ Come eat, ___ come ___ drink ___ of mine."
dear, ___ And to Him ___ we ___ must ___ re - sign. ___
us, ___ It wets ___ our ___ wind - ing sheet." ___

LAVENDER'S BLUE

Traditional American

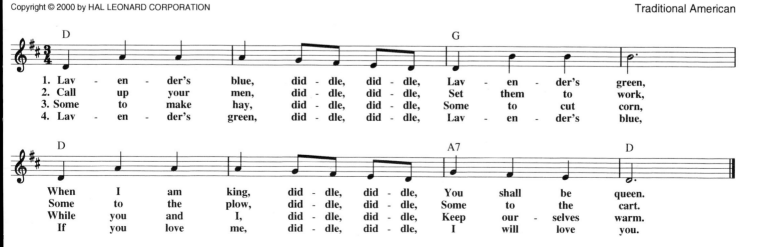

1. Lav - en - der's blue, did - dle, did - dle, Lav - en - der's green,
2. Call up your men, did - dle, did - dle, Set them to work,
3. Some to make hay, did - dle, did - dle, Some to cut corn,
4. Lav - en - der's green, did - dle, did - dle, Lav - en - der's blue,

When I am king, did - dle, did - dle, You shall be queen.
Some to the plow, did - dle, did - dle, Some to the cart.
While you and I, did - dle, did - dle, Keep our - selves warm.
If you love me, did - dle, did - dle, I will love you.

LADY ISABEL AND THE ELF KNIGHT

English

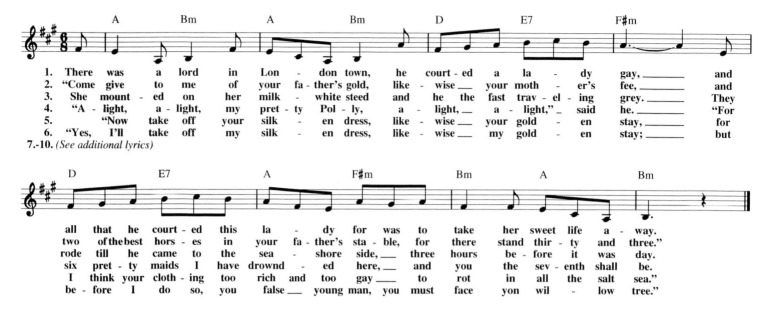

1. There was a lord in Lon - don town, he court - ed a la - dy gay, _____ and
2. "Come give to me of your fa - ther's gold, like - wise ___ your moth - er's fee, _____ and
3. She mount - ed on her milk - white steed and he the fast trav - el - ing grey. _____ They
4. "A - light, a - light, my pret - ty Pol - ly, a - light, ___ a - light," _ said he. _____ "For
5. "Now take off your silk - en dress, like - wise ___ your gold - en stay, _____ for
6. "Yes, I'll take off my silk - en dress, like - wise ___ my gold - en stay; _____ but

7.-10. *(See additional lyrics)*

all that he court - ed this la - dy for was to take her sweet life a - way.
two of the best hors - es in your fa - ther's sta - ble, for there stand thir - ty and three."
rode till he came to the sea - shore side, ___ three hours be - fore it was day.
six pret - ty maids I have drownd - ed here, ___ and you the sev - enth shall be.
I think your cloth - ing too rich and too gay ___ to rot in all the salt sea."
be - fore I do so, you false ___ young man, you must face yon wil - low tree."

Additional Lyrics

7. Then he turned his back around
And faced yon willow tree.
She caught him around the middle so small
And throwed him into the sea.

8. And as he rose and as he sank
And as he rose, said he,
"O give me your hand, my pretty Polly,
My bride forever you'll be."

9. "Lie there, lie there, you false young man,
Lie there instead of me,
For six pretty maids you've drownded here,
And the seventh one has drownded thee."

10. She lighted on her milk-white steed
And led the fast traveling grey,
And rode till she came to her father's outside
One hour before it was day.

LADY OF CARLISLE

English

1. Down in Car - lisle _____ there lived a la - dy, _____ be - ing most beau - ti - ful and
2. Un - less it were _____ a man of hon - or, _____ a man of hon - or and high de -
3. One be - ing a _____ brave lieu - ten - ant, _____ a brave lieu - ten - ant and a man of
4. Then up spoke this _____ fair young la - dy, say - ing, "I can't be _____ but one man's
5. She or - dered her _____ a span of hors - es, _____ a span of hors - es at her com -
6. There she stopped _____ and there she halt - ed, _____ these two sol - diers stood gaz - ing

7.-11. *(See additional lyrics)*

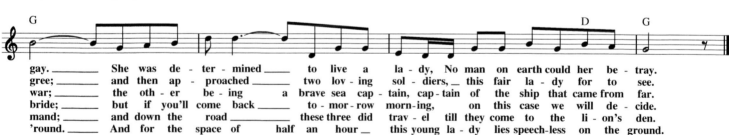

gay. _____ She was de - ter - mined _____ to live a la - dy, No man on earth could her be - tray.
gree; _____ and then ap - proached _____ two lov - ing sol - diers, _ this fair la - dy for to see.
war; _____ the oth - er be - ing a brave sea cap - tain, cap - tain of the ship that came from far.
bride; _____ but if you'll come back _____ to - mor - row morn - ing, on this case we will de - cide.
mand; _____ and down the road _____ these three did trav - el till they come to the li - on's den.
'round. _____ And for the space of half an hour _ this young la - dy lies speech - less on the ground.

Additional Lyrics

7. And when she did recover,
Threw her fan down in the lions' den;
Saying, "Which of you to gain a lady
Will return her fan again?"

8. Then up spoke the brave lieutenant,
Raised his voice both loud and clear,
Saying, "You know I am a dear lover of women,
But I will not give my life for love."

9. Then up spoke this brave sea captain,
He raised his voice both loud and high,
Saying, "You know I am a dear lover of women,
I will return her fan or die."

10. Down in the lions' den, he boldly entered,
The lions being both wild and fierce;
He marched around and in among them,
Safely returned her fan again.

11. And when she saw her true lover coming,
Seeing no harm had been done to him,
She threw herself against his bosom,
Saying, "Here is the prize that you have won."

LANDLORD, FILL THE FLOWING BOWL

English

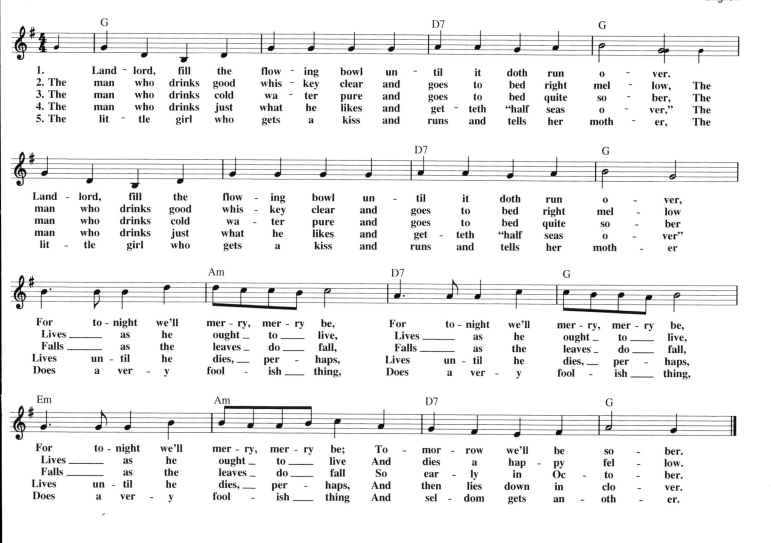

THE LARK IN THE CLEAR AIR

Irish
Words and Music by
Sir Samuel Ferguson, circa 1850

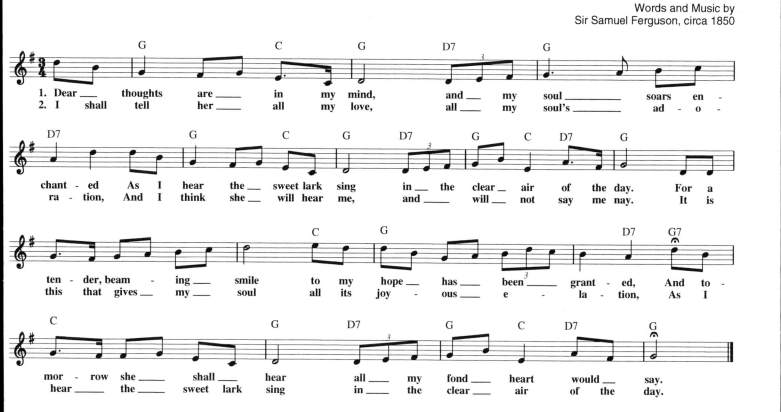

THE LARK IN THE MORN

English

1. As I _____ was a - walk - ing one morn - ing in the Spring, I met ___ a young
2. The lark ___ in the morn ___ she will rise up from her nest, And mount _ in the

dam - sel, so sweet - ly she did sing. And as we were a _ walk - ing these
air _____ with the dew all on her breast. And like the pret - ty plough - boy she will

words _ she did say: ___ There's no life ___ like a plough - boy's all in the month of May.
whis - tle and sing, ___ And at night _ she'll re - turn ___ to her own nest back a - gain.

THE LAST REQUEST

American

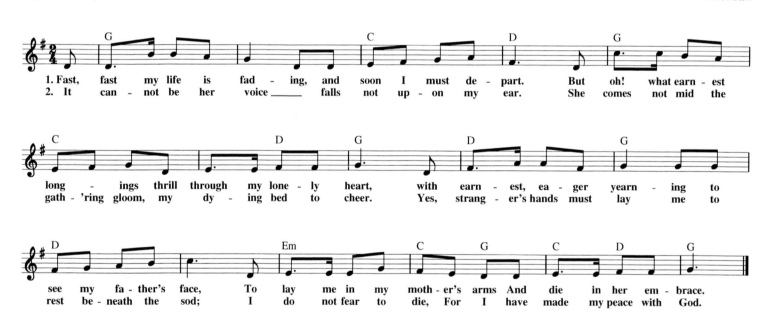

1. Fast, fast my life is fad - ing, and soon I must de - part. But oh! what earn - est
2. It can - not be her voice _____ falls not up - on my ear. She comes not mid the

long - ings thrill through my lone - ly heart, with earn - est, ea - ger yearn - ing to
gath - 'ring gloom, my dy - ing bed to cheer. Yes, strang - er's hands must lay me to

see my fa - ther's face, To lay me in my moth - er's arms And die in her em - brace.
rest be - neath the sod; I do not fear to die, For I have made my peace with God.

LAZY MARY, WILL YOU GET UP?

Children's Play Song

La - zy Mar - y, will you get up? Will you get up? Will you get up?

La - zy Mar - y, will you get up? Will you get up to - day? _____

LEATHERWING BAT

Folksong from Vermont

1. Hi! said the lit - tle leath - er - wing bat, I'll tell you ____ the rea - son that, the
2. Hi! said the wood - peck - er, sit - tin' on a fence, once I court - ed a hand - some wench. ____
3. Hi! said the blue - bird as ____ he flew, if I were a young man ____ I'd have two. If
4. Hi! said the rob - in as ____ he flew, when I was young ____ I had two. If
5. Hi! said the black - bird, sit - ting on a bench, once I court - ed a hand - some wench. ____
6. Hoot! said the owl with eyes ____ so bright, a lone - some day, ____ a lone - some night. ____
7. Oh, no ____ no, said the tur - tle dove, that's no way ____ to gain your love. If

rea - son that I fly in the night is be - cause I lost my heart's de - light.
She got sauc - y and from me ____ fled; ____ and ev - er since then my head's been red.
one got sauc - y and want - ed to go, ____ I'd have a new string for my bow.
one wouldn't love me the oth - er ____ would. ____ Now don't you think my no - tion's good.
Then one day she turned her ____ back, ____ and ev - er since I've dressed in black.
Thought I heard a pret - ty gal ____ say, ____ court all night and sleep all day.
you would have you heart's de - light, ____ keep them a - wake both day and night.

How - dee, dow - dee did - dle - o - day; how - dee, dow - dee did - dle - o - day;

how - dee, dow - dee did - dle - o - day; ho - lo - lee - dee did - dle - dee doe. ____

LET ERIN REMEMBER THE DAYS OF OLD

Irish Folk Melody, "The Red Fox"
Words by Thomas Moore

1. Let E - rin re - mem - ber the days of old, Ere her faith - less sons be -
2. On Lough Ne - agh's bank as the fish - er - man strays, when the clear, cold eve's de -

tray'd her; When Mal - a - chi wore the ____ col - lar of gold, Which he won from her proud in -
clin - ing, he sees the round tow - ers of oth - er days, in the wave be - neath him

va - der; When her kings with stand - ards of green un - furl'd, Led the Red - Branch Knights to
shin - ing! Thus shall mem - 'ry of - ten, in dreams sub - lime, catch a glimpse of the days that are

dan - ger: Ere the em - 'rald gem of the west - ern ____ world Was ____ set in the crown of a stran - ger.
o - ver. Thus, ____ sigh - ing, look through the waves of ____ time for the long fad - ed glo - ries they cov - er!

LET ME FLY

African-American Spiritual

1. Way down yon-der in the mid-dle of the field, an-gel work-in' at the
2. I got a moth-er in the Prom-ised ___ Land, ain't gon-na stop ___ till I
3. Meet that hyp-o-crite ___ on ___ the ___ street, first thing he'll do ___ is to

char-iot wheel. Not so par-tic-u-lar 'bout work-in' at the wheel, but I
shake her hand. Not so par-tic-u-lar 'bout shak-in' her hand, but I
show his teeth. Next thing he'll do ___ is to tell ___ a ___ lie, and the

just wan-na see how the char-iot feels.
just wan-na go up in the Prom-ised Land. Now let me fly, ___ now let me fly. ___
best thing to do is ___ pass him by.

___ Now let me fly ___ in-to Mount Zi-on, Lord, Lord. ___

LIKES LIKKER BETTER THAN ME

American

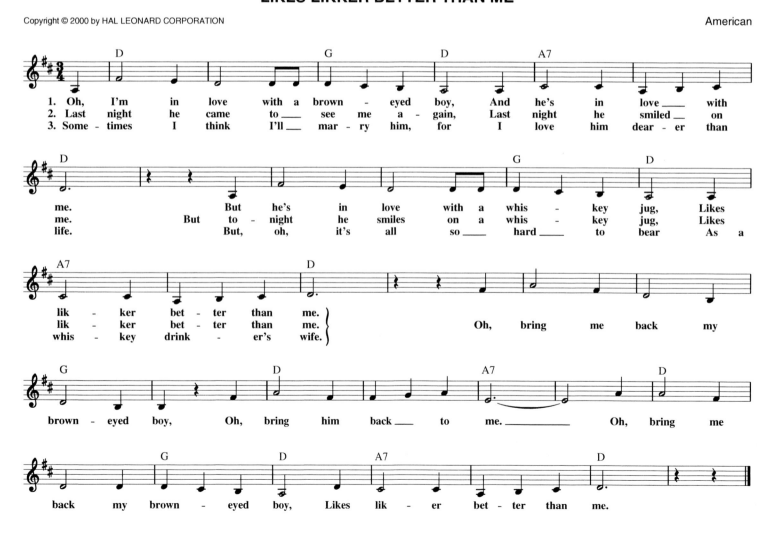

1. Oh, I'm in love with a brown-eyed boy, And he's in love ___ with
2. Last night he came to ___ see me a-gain, Last night he smiled ___ on
3. Some-times I think I'll ___ mar-ry him, for I love him dear-er than

me. But he's in love with a whis-key jug, Likes
me. But to-night he smiles on a whis-key jug, Likes
life. But, oh, it's all so ___ hard ___ to bear As a

lik-ker bet-ter than me.
lik-ker bet-ter than me. Oh, bring me back my
whis-key drink-er's wife.

brown-eyed boy, Oh, bring him back ___ to me. ___ Oh, bring me

back my brown-eyed boy, Likes lik-er bet-ter than me.

LET US ALL BE JOYFUL NOW
(Gaudeamus Igitur)

Student Drinking Song from Germany

Let us all be joy - ful now while we're young and full of life.
Gau - de - a - mus i - gi - tur ju - ve - nes dum su - mus

Af - ter youth has run its dis - tance, at the end of our ex - is - tence, In the grave we shall
Post ju - cun - dam ju - ven - tu - tem post mo - les - tam se - nec - tu - tem, Nos ha - be - bit ___

end our strife, In the grave we shall end our strife.
hu - mus, Nos ha - be - bit ___ hu - mus.

LILY OF THE WEST

American

1. When first I came to Lou - is - ville, ___ some pleas - ure
2. I court - ed love - ly Flo - ra, ___ and to her I
3. Way down in yon - der shad - y grove, ___ a man of
4. I stepped up to my ri - val, ___ my dag - ger
5. I had to stand my tri - al, ___ I had to

there to find, ___ a dam - sel there from Lex - ing - ton ___ was
was so kind. ___ But she went to an - oth - er man, ___ which
high de - gree ___ con - vers - ing with my Flo - ra there, ___ it
in my hand. ___ I seized him by the col - lar and ___ I
make my plea. ___ They placed me in a crim - i - nal box and

pleas - ing to my mind. ___ Her ros - y cheeks, her ru - by lips ___
sore dis - tressed my mind. ___ She robbed me of my lib - er - ty, ___
seemed so strange to me. ___ And the an - swer that she gave to him, ___
bold - ly bade him stand. ___ Be - ing mad to des - per - a - tion, ___
then com - menced on me. ___ Al - though she swore my life a - way, ___

___ like ar - rows pierced my breast, ___ and the name she
___ de - prived me of my rest; ___ be - trayed was
___ it sore did me op - press; ___ be - trayed was
___ I pierced him in the breast. ___ Be - trayed was
___ de - prived me of my rest, ___ still I love my

bore was Flo - ra, ___ the Lil - y of the West. ___
I by Flo - ra, ___ the Lil - y of the West. ___
I by Flo - ra, ___ the Lil - y of the West. ___
I by Flo - ra, ___ the Lil - y of the West. ___
faith - less Flo - ra, ___ the Lil - y of the West. ___

LET US BREAK BREAD TOGETHER

African-American Spiritual

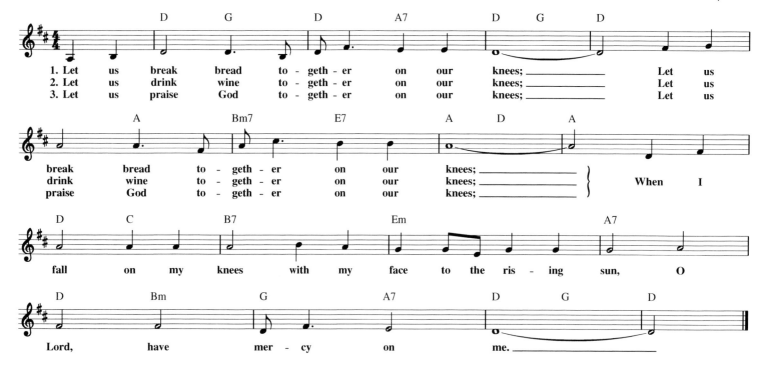

1. Let us break bread to - geth - er on our knees; Let us
2. Let us drink wine to - geth - er on our knees; Let us
3. Let us praise God to - geth - er on our knees; Let us

break bread to - geth - er on our knees; When I
drink wine to - geth - er on our knees; When I
praise God to - geth - er on our knees;

fall on my knees with my face to the ris - ing sun, O

Lord, have mer - cy on me.

LI'L LIZA JANE

American Folk Ballad
possibly from Maryland

1. I know a gal that I a - dore, Li'l Li - za Jane. 'Way down south in
2. Down where she lives the po - sies grow, Li'l Li - za Jane. Chick - ens 'round the
3. I would-n't care how far we roam, Li'l Li - za Jane. Where she's at is

Bal - ti - more, Li'l Li - za Jane. Oh, E - li - za,
kitch - en door, Li'l Li - za Jane.
home sweet home, Li'l Li - za Jane.

Li'l Li - za Jane! Oh, E - li - za, Li'l Li - za Jane.

LIFE'S RAILWAY TO HEAVEN

Words by M.E. Abbey
Music by Charles D. Tillman
1890

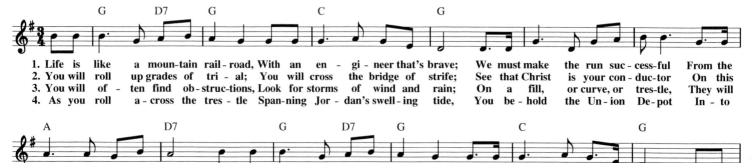

1. Life is like a moun-tain rail-road, With an en - gi - neer that's brave; We must make the run suc - cess-ful From the
2. You will roll up grades of tri - al; You will cross the bridge of strife; See that Christ is your con - duc-tor On this
3. You will of - ten find ob-struc-tions, Look for storms of wind and rain; On a fill, or curve, or tres-tle, They will
4. As you roll a - cross the tres - tle Span-ning Jor - dan's swell-ing tide, You be-hold the Un - ion De-pot In - to

cra - dle to the grave; Watch the curves, the fills, the tun - nels, Nev - er fal - ter, nev - er quail; Keep your
light - ning train of life; Al - ways mind - ful of ob - struc-tion, Do your du - ty, nev - er fail; Keep your
al - most ditch your train; Put your trust a - lone in Je - sus, Nev - er fal - ter nev - er fail; Keep your
which your train will glide; There you'll meet the Su-p'rin - ten - dent, God the Fa - ther, God the Son; With the

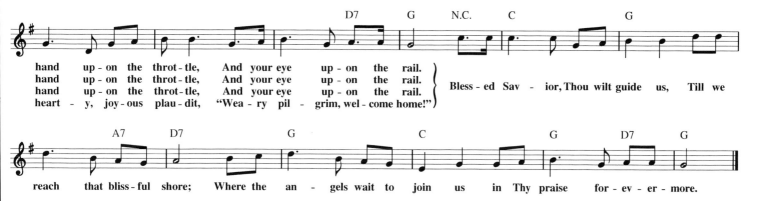

hand up-on the throt-tle, And your eye up-on the rail.
hand up-on the throt-tle, And your eye up-on the rail.
hand up-on the throt-tle, And your eye up-on the rail.
heart-y, joy-ous plau-dit, "Wea-ry pil-grim, wel-come home!"
Bless-ed Sav-ior, Thou wilt guide us, Till we

reach that bliss-ful shore; Where the an-gels wait to join us in Thy praise for-ev-er-more.

LIMERICK IS BEAUTIFUL

Words by Michael Scanlon
Irish

1. Oh, Lim-er-ick is beau-ti-ful, as ev-'ry-bod-y knows. The
2. 'Tis not for Lim-er-ick that I sigh, though I love her in my soul, Though
3. Oh, she I love is beau-ti-ful, and world-wide is her fame, She
4. I loved her in my boy-hood and now in man-hood's noon, The

Riv-er Shan-non full of fish through-out the cit-y flows. It's
times will change and friends will die and man will not con-trol, No,
dwells down by the rush-ing tide, and Eire is her name; And
vi-sion of my life is still to dry thy tears, a-roon, I'd

not the riv-er or the fish that weighs up-on my mind, Or
not for friends long passed a-way, or days for-ev-er flown, The
dear-er than my ver-y life her glanc-es are to me, The
sing un-to the tomb or dance be-neath the gal-lows tree, To

with the town of Lim-er-ick have I an-y fault to find.
But the maid-en I a-dore is sad in Gar-ry-owen.
light that guides my wea-ry soul a-cross life's storm-y sea.
see her on the hills once more proud pas-sion-ate and free.

LITTLE ANNIE ROONEY

Michael Nolan
1890

She's my sweet-heart I'm her beau, She's my An-nie,
I'm her Joe Soon we'll mar-ry nev-er to
part, Lit-tle An-nie Roo-ney is my sweet-heart.

THE LINCOLNSHIRE POACHER

English

1. When I was bound _ ap - pren - tice in fa - mous Lin - coln - shire, _____ full well I served my
2. As me and my ___ com - pan - ions were set - ting of a snare, _____ 'twas then we spied the
3. As me and my ___ com - pan - ions were set - ting four or five _____ and tak - ing on 'em
4. I threw him on _____ my shoul - der and then we trudged _ home. _____ We took him to a
5. Suc - cess to ev - 'ry gen - tle - man that lives in Lin - coln - shire, _____ suc - cess to ev - 'ry

mas - ter for more than se - ven years _____ till I took up to poach - ing, as
game - keep - er, for him we did ___ not care. _____ For we can wres - tle and fight, my boys, and
up a - gain, we caught a hare _ a - live. _____ We took a hare a - live, my boys, and
neigh - bor's house and sold him for ___ a crown. _____ We sold him for a crown, my boys, but
poach - er that wants to sell ___ a hare. _____ Bad luck to ev - 'ry game - keep - er that

you shall quick - ly hear.
jump out an - y - where.
through the woods _ did steer. } Oh, 'tis my de - light of a shin - y night in the sea - son of the
I did not tell you where.
will not sell _ his deer.

year. Oh, 'tis my de - light of a shin - y night in the sea - son of the year. _____

LINSTEAD MARKET

Jamaican

1. Car - ry me ack - ee go a Lin - stead Mar - ket, not a quat - ty wut sell. Oh, _____
2. Ev - 'ry - bod - y come _ feel up, feel up, not a quat - ty wut sell. Oh, _____
3. Mek _ me call _ i' lou - da, "Ack - ee, ack - ee, red an' pret - ty dem tan. Oh, _____
4. All _ de pick - ney come _ ling - a - ling, _____ fe weh dem Ma - ma no bring. Oh, _____

car - ry me ack - ee go a Lin - stead Mar - ket, not a quat - ty wut sell.
ev - 'ry - bod - y come _ feel up, feel up, not a quat - ty wut sell. }
la - dy, buy _ yuh Sun - day maw - nin' break - fus', rice an' ack - ee nyam gran." Oh,
all _ de pick - ney come _ ling - a - ling _____ fe weh dem Ma - ma no bring.

Lawd! Not a mite, not a bite, Wat a Sat - i - day night! Oh

Lawd! Not a mite, Not a bite, Wat a Sat - i - day night!

LISTEN TO THE MOCKINGBIRD

Southern American Folksong
Words and Music by Alice Hawthorne, 1854
(pen name for Septimus Winner)

1. I'm dream - ing now of _____ Hal - lie, _____ sweet _ Hal - lie, _____ sweet _ Hal - lie, _____ I'm
2. Ah, well I yet re - mem - ber, _____ re - mem - ber, _____ re - mem - ber, _____ Ah,

dream - ing now of _____ Hal - lie, _____ for the thought of her is one that nev - er dies. She's
well I yet re - mem - ber _____ when we gath-er'd in the cot - ton side by side. 'Twas

sleep - ing in the _____ val - ley, _____ the _____ val - ley, _____ the _____ val - ley, _____ She's
in the mild Sep - tem - ber, _____ Sep - tem - ber, _____ Sep - tem - ber, _____ 'Twas

sleep - ing in the _____ val - ley, _____ and the mock - ing - bird is sing - ing where she
in the mild Sep - tem - ber, _____ and the mock - ing - bird was sing - ing far and

lies.)
wide. } Lis - ten to the mock - ing - bird, lis - ten to the mock - ing - bird, The

mock - ing - bird still sing - ing o'er her grave. Lis - ten to the mock - ing - bird, lis - ten to the

mock - ing - bird, Still sing - ing where the weep - ing wil - lows wave.

LITTLE MAGGIE

American

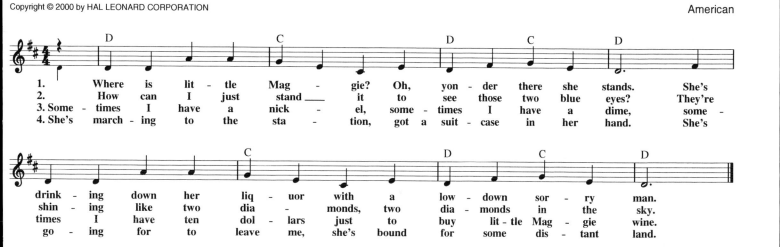

1. Where is lit - tle Mag - gie? Oh, yon - der there she stands. She's
2. How can I just stand _____ it to see those two blue eyes? They're
3. Some - times I have a nick - el, some - times I have a dime, some -
4. She's march - ing to the sta - tion, got a suit - case in her hand. She's

drink - ing down her liq - uor with a low - down sor - ry man.
shin - ing like two dia - monds, two dia - monds in the sky.
times I have ten dol - lars just to buy lit - tle Mag - gie wine.
go - ing for to leave me, she's bound for some dis - tant land.

LITTLE BROWN DOG

American Children's Song

1. I buyed _ me a lit - tle dog, it's col - or it was brown. I learned _ him to
2. I buyed _ me a lit - tle bull a - bout four inch - es high. Ev - 'ry - bod - y
3. I buyed _ me a flock of sheep; I thought they were all weth - ers. Some - times they yield - ed
4. I buyed _ me a lit - tle box a - bout four a - cres square. I filled _ it with
5. I buyed _ me a lit - tle hen, all speck - led, gay and fair. I sat her on an

whis - tle, _____ sing, dance and run. His legs they were four - teen yards long, his
feared him that ev - er heard him cry. When he be - gan to bel - low, it made
wool, some - times they yield - ed feath - ers. I think mine are the best of sheep for
guin - ea and sil - ver so fair. Oh, now I'm bound for Tur - key, I'll
oys - ter shell; she hatched me out a hair. The hair it sprang a hand - some horse full

ears they were broad. A - round the world in half a day, and
yield - ing me in - crease, for ev - 'ry full and change of the moon they
trav - el like an ox, in my breech - es pock - et I'll car -
fif - teen hands - full high, and him that tells a big - ger tale would

on him I could ride.
tum - bling to the ground.
bring both lambs and geese. } Sing tad - dle - o day. _____
ry my lit - tle box.
have to tell a lie.

LITTLE BROWN JUG

Words and Music by
Joseph E. Winner

1. My wife and I lived all a - lone in a lit - tle log hut we
2. 'Tis you who makes my friend my foes, 'tis _ you _ who makes me
3. When I got toil - ing to my farm, I take lit - tle brown jug un -
4. If I'd a cow that gave such milk, I'd _ clothe _ her in the
5. The rose is red, my nose is too, the _ vi - o - let's blue and

called our own, She loved gin and I loved rum; I tell you what, we'd lots of fun!
wear old clothes, Here you are so near my nose, so tip her up and down she goes!
der my arm. I place it un - der a shad - y tree; _ lit - tle brown jug, 'tis you and me.
fin - est silk, I'd feed her on the choic - est hay and milk her for - ty times a day.
so are you. And yet I guess, be - fore I stop I'd bet - ter take an - oth - er drop. }

Ha, ha, ha, you and me, lit - tle brown jug, don't I love thee!

Ha, ha, ha, you and me, lit - tle brown jug don't I love thee!

LITTLE DAVID PLAY ON YOUR HARP

African-American Spiritual

THE LITTLE ORPHAN GIRL

American

LITTLE MOHEE

American

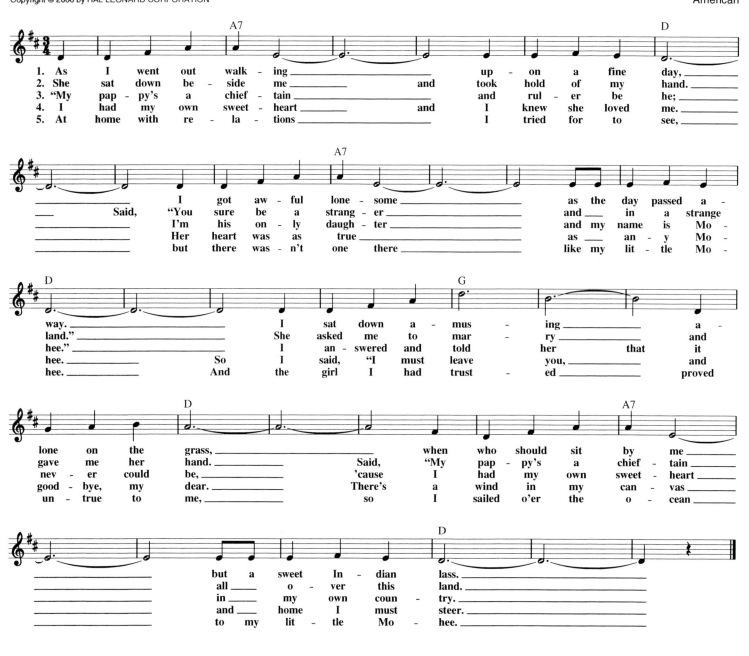

LITTLE JOE, THE WRANGLER

Western American Cowboy Song

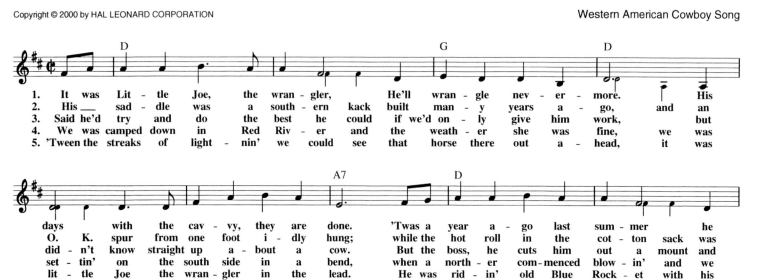

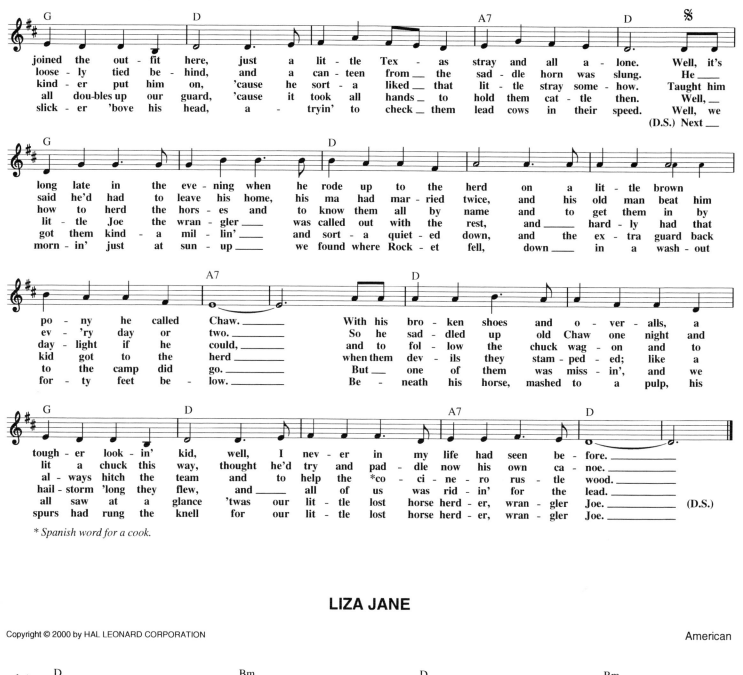

joined the out-fit here, just a lit-tle Tex-as stray and all a-lone. Well, it's
loose-ly tied be-hind, and a can-teen from the sad-dle horn was slung. He
kind-er put him on, 'cause he sort-a liked that lit-tle stray some-how. Taught him
all dou-bles up our guard, 'cause it took all hands to hold them cat-tle then. Well,
slick-er 'bove his head, a-tryin' to check them lead cows in their speed. Well, we
(D.S.) Next

long late in the eve-ning when he rode up to the herd on a lit-tle brown
said he'd had to leave his home, his ma had mar-ried twice, and his old man beat him
how to herd the hors-es and to know them all by name and to get them in by
lit-tle Joe the wran-gler was called out with the rest, and hard-ly had that
morn-in' just at sun-up we found where Rock-et fell, down in a wash-out

po-ny he called Chaw. With his bro-ken shoes and o-ver-alls, a
ev-'ry day or two. So he sad-dled up old Chaw one night and
day-light if he could, and to fol-low the chuck wag-on and to
kid got to the herd when them dev-ils they stam-ped-ed; like a
to the camp did go. But one of them was miss-in', and we
for-ty feet be-low. Be-neath his horse, mashed to a pulp, his

tough-er look-in' kid, well, I nev-er in my life had seen be-fore.
lit a chuck this way, thought he'd try and pad-dle now his own ca-noe.
al-ways hitch the team and to help the *co-ci-ne-ro rus-tle wood.
hail-storm 'long they flew, and all of us was rid-in' for the lead.
all saw at a glance 'twas our lit-tle lost horse herd-er, wran-gler Joe. (D.S.)
spurs had rung the knell for our lit-tle lost horse herd-er, wran-gler Joe.

* Spanish word for a cook.

LIZA JANE

American

1. I'll go up on the moun-tain top and plant me a patch of cane. I'll
2. I'll go up on the moun-tain top, put up my moon-shine still. I'll
3. I went to see my Li-za Jane, she was stand-ing in the door, her
4. Head is like a cof-fee pot, nose is like a spout, her
5. Hard-est work that I ev-er did was a-brak-in' on the train. The

make me a jug of mo-las-ses for to sweet-en lit-tle Li-za Jane.
make you a quart of old moon-shine for just one dol-lar bill.
shoes and stock-ings in her hand and her feet all o-ver the floor.
mouth is like an old fire-place with the ash-es all raked out.
eas-i-est work that I ev-er did was a-hug-gin' lit-tle Li-za Jane.

Oh, po' Li-za, po' gal, oh, po' Li-za Jane.

Oh, po' Li-za, po' gal, She died on the train.

LITTLE OLD SOD SHANTY ON MY CLAIM

American Pioneer Song

1. I'm look - ing rath - er seed - y now while hold - ing down my claim, and my
2. I rath - er like the nov - el - ty of liv - ing in this way, though my
3. Oh, when I left my East - ern home, a bach - e - lor so gay, _____ to
4. My clothes are plas - tered o'er with dough, I'm look - ing like a fright, _____ and
5. Still, I wish that some kind - heart - ed girl would pit - y on me take and re -
6. And if kind - ly fate should bless us _____ with, now and then, an heir _____ to

vit - tles are not al - ways served the best, _____ and the mice play shy - ly
bill of fare is al - ways rath - er tame. _____ But I'm hap - py as a
try and win my way to wealth and fame, _____ I _____ lit - tle thought I'd
ev - 'ry - thing is scat - tered 'round the room, _____ but I would - n't give the
lieve me from the mess that I am in. _____ The _____ an - gel, how I'd
cheer our hearts with hon - est pride of fame, _____ oh, _____ then we'd be con -

'round me as I nes - tle down to rest in my lit - tle old sod
clam _____ on the land of Un - cle Sam in my lit - tle old sod
come down _____ to burn - ing twist - ed hay in the lit - tle old sod
free - dom that I have out in the West for the ta - ble of the
bless her _____ if this her home she'd make in the lit - tle old sod
tent - ed for the toil that we had spent in the lit - tle old sod

shan - ty in the West. _____
shan - ty on my claim. _____
shan - ty on my claim. _____
East - ern man's old home. _____
shan - ty on my claim. _____
shan - ty on our claim. _____

Oh, the hin - ges are of leath - er and the

win - dows have no glass; the boards, they let the howl - ing bliz - zard in. _____

_____ You can see the hun - gry coy - ote as he slinks up in the

grass 'round my lit - tle old sod shan - ty on my claim.

LITTLE SANDY GIRL

Folksong from Tobago

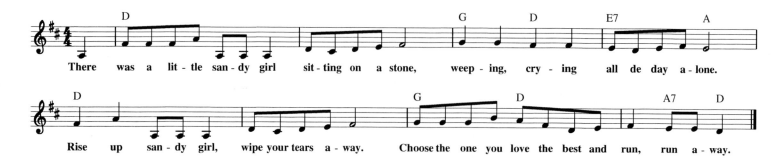

There was a lit - tle san - dy girl sit - ting on a stone, weep - ing, cry - ing all de day a - lone.

Rise up san - dy girl, wipe your tears a - way. Choose the one you love the best and run, run a - way.

THE LITTLE SAUCEPAN
(Sospan Vach)

Welsh

1. My dear Mary Ann's cut her fin - ger, And Da - vid the but - ler's feel - ing
2. My dear Ma - ry Ann's feel - ing bet - ter, And Da - vid the but - ler's dead and

1. My beese Mar - y Ann wed - dee bree'oo - oh, Ah Dahv - ith uh gwas ___ thim un
2. My beese Mar - y Ann wed - dee goo - eh - lluh, Ah Dahv - ith uh gwas ___ un i

weak; And the ba - by's wail - ing loud in its cra - dle, The cat's claws are scratch - ing John - ny's
gone; And the ba - by's qui - et now in his cra - dle, The cat seems to want to get a -

yach. My - ur bah - bahn un uh creed un ___ cree - oh, Ahr gath wed - dee crahv - ee John - ny
vaith. My - ur bah - bahn un uh creed wed - dee teh - wee, Ahr gath wed - ee hee - no meh - oon

cheek. }
long. }
bach. }
haith. }

Sos - pan fach is boil - ing on the fire, Sos - pan fawr boils
Sos - pan vach un bare - we ar uh tahn, Sos - pan vow'r un

o - ver on the floor, { 1. The cat's claws are scratch - ing John - ny's cheek. }
{ 2. The cat seems to want to get a - long. }

bare - we ar uh llauer, { 1. Ahr gath wed - dee crahv - ee John - ny bach. }
{ 2. Ahr gath we - dee hee - no me - own haith. }

Da - vid's a sol - dier, Da - vid's a sol - dier,
Die bach uh soul - joor, Die bach uh soul - joor,

Da - vid's a sol - dier, His shirt - tail's fall - ing out.
Die ___ bach uh soul - joor, Ah choot - ee greese eh mahs.

LONDON BRIDGE

Nursery Rhyme Song

1. Lon - don Bridge is fall - ing down, fall - ing down, fall - ing down,
2. Take the key and lock her up, lock her up, lock her up,
3. Build it up with silver and gold, silver and gold, silver and gold,

Lon - don Bridge is fall - ing down, }
Take the key and lock her up, }
Build it up with silver and gold, }

My fair la - dy - O.

LITTLE SNOWBALL BUSH
(Kalinka)

Russian

LOCH LOMOND

Scottish

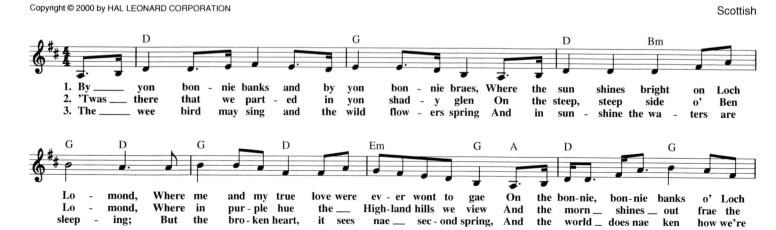

gloam - ing.) Oh, ___ ye'll take the high road and I'll take the low, road, And I'll be in Scot - land a -
greet - ing;)

fore ye, But me an' my true love will nev - er meet a - gain On the bon - nie, bon - nie banks o' Loch Lo - mond.

LOOBY LOO

American Play Party Song

Here we go Loo - by Loo, _____ Here we go

loo - by light. _____ Here we go Loo - by

Loo, _____ All on a Sat - ur - day night. _____

1. I
2. I
3. I
4. I
5. I
6. I

put my right hand in, _____ I take my
put my left hand in, _____ I take my
put my right foot in, _____ I take my
put my left foot in, _____ I take my
put my big head in, _____ I take my
put my whole self in, _____ I take my

right hand out; _____ I give my right hand a
left hand out; _____ I give my left hand a
right foot out; _____ I give my right foot a
left foot out; _____ I give my left foot a
big head out; _____ I give my big head a
whole self out; _____ I give my whole self a

shake, shake, shake, and turn my - self a - bout. _____
shake, shake, shake, and turn my - self a - bout. _____
shake, shake, shake, and turn my - self a - bout. _____
shake, shake, shake, and turn my - self a - bout. _____
shake, shake, shake, and turn my - self a - bout. _____
shake, shake, shake, and turn my - self a - bout. _____

LONESOME VALLEY

Traditional American Spiritual

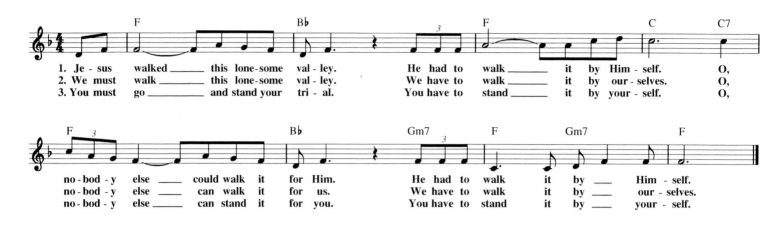

1. Je - sus walked _____ this lone-some val - ley. He had to walk _____ it by Him - self. O,
2. We must walk _____ this lone-some val - ley. We have to walk _____ it by our - selves. O,
3. You must go _____ and stand your tri - al. You have to stand _____ it by your - self. O,

no - bod - y else _____ could walk it for Him. He had to walk it by ___ Him - self.
no - bod - y else _____ can walk it for us. We have to walk it by ___ our - selves.
no - bod - y else _____ can stand it for you. You have to stand it by ___ your - self.

LOOK DOWN THAT LONESOME ROAD

Virginia Folksong

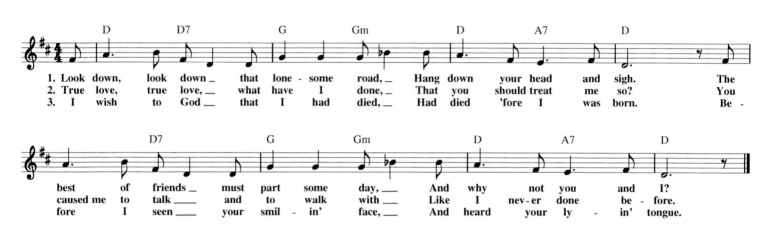

1. Look down, look down _ that lone - some road, _ Hang down your head and sigh. The
2. True love, true love, _ what have I done, _ That you should treat me so? You
3. I wish to God _ that I had died, _ Had died 'fore I was born. Be -

best of friends _ must part some day, _ And why not you and I?
caused me to talk _____ and to walk with _ Like I nev - er done be - fore.
fore I seen _____ your smil - in' face, And heard your ly - in' tongue.

LORD, I WANT TO BE A CHRISTIAN

African-American Spiritual

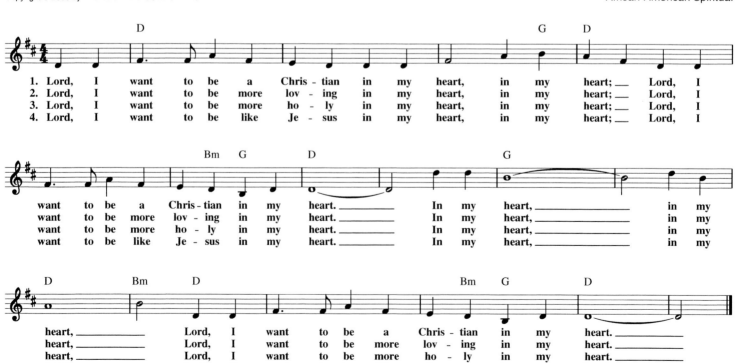

1. Lord, I want to be a Chris - tian in my heart, in my heart; ___ Lord, I
2. Lord, I want to be more lov - ing in my heart, in my heart; ___ Lord, I
3. Lord, I want to be more ho - ly in my heart, in my heart; ___ Lord, I
4. Lord, I want to be like Je - sus in my heart, in my heart; ___ Lord, I

want to be a Chris - tian in my heart. _____ In my heart, _____ in my
want to be more lov - ing in my heart. _____ In my heart, _____ in my
want to be more ho - ly in my heart. _____ In my heart, _____ in my
want to be like Je - sus in my heart. _____ In my heart, _____ in my

heart, _____ Lord, I want to be a Chris - tian in my heart. _____
heart, _____ Lord, I want to be more lov - ing in my heart. _____
heart, _____ Lord, I want to be more ho - ly in my heart. _____
heart, _____ Lord, I want to be like Je - sus in my heart. _____

LORD RENDAL

English

1. Where have you been all the day, Ren - dal, my son? Where have you been all the day, my pret - ty one? I've
2. What have you been eat - ing, Ren - dal, my son? What have you been eat - ing, my pret - ty one? O
3. Where_ did she get them from, Ren - dal, my son? Where_ did she get them from, my pret - ty one? From
4. What was the col - or on their skin, Ren - dal, my son? What was the col - or on their skin, my pret - ty one? O
5. What will you leave your fa - ther, Ren - dal, my son? What will you leave your fa - ther, my pret - ty one? My
6. What will you leave your moth - er, Ren - dal, my son? What will you leave your moth - er, my pret - ty one? My
7. What will you leave your broth - er, Ren - dal, my son? What will you leave your broth - er, my pret - ty one? My
8. What will you leave your lov - er, Ren - dal, my son? What will you leave your lov - er, my pret - ty one? A

been to my sweet - heart, moth - er, I've been to my sweet - heart, moth - er._____
eels and_ eel broth, moth - er, O eels and_ eel broth, moth - er._____
hed - ges and ditch - es, moth - er, From hed - ges and ditch - es, moth - er._____
spick - it and spark - it, moth - er, O spick - it and spark - it, moth - er._____
land and_ hous - es, moth - er, my land and_ hous - es, moth - er._____
gold and_ sil - ver, moth - er, my gold and_ sil - ver, moth - er._____
cows and_ hors - es, moth - er, my cows and_ hors - es, moth - er._____
rope to_ hang her, moth - er, a rope to_ hang her, moth - er._____

Make my bed soon, for I'm sick to my heart and I fain would lie down.

THE LOW, LOW LANDS OF HOLLAND

18th Century English

1. The ver - y day ___ I was mar - ried, That __ night I lay on my bed; A
2. But Hol - land is ___ a ___ cold ___ place, A ___ place where grows no ___ green, And
3. I'll build my love ___ a ___ gal - lant ship, A ___ ship of not - ed ___ fame, With
4. Says the moth - er to ___ the ___ daugh - ter: What ___ makes you to la - ment? O
5. There's not a swaithe_ goes ___ round my waist, Nor a comb goes in my ___ hair, Nei - ther

press - gang came _ to ___ my bed - side, These_ words to me ___ they said: A -
Hol - land is ___ a ___ cold ___ place For my love to wan - der in. Though _
four and twen - ty ___ sea - men bold To ___ box her on ___ the main. They'll _
there are lords_ and ___ dukes and squires Can _ ease your heart's _ con - tent. But ___
fire - light _ nor ___ can - dle - light Can _ ease my heart's _ des - pair. And ___

rise, a - rise, _ a - rise, young man, _ And _ come a - long _ with me, with me, To the
mon - ey had been as ___ plen - ti - ful _ As ___ leaves up - on ___ the tree, the tree, Yet be -
rant and roar _ in ___ spar - kling glee _ Where-so - ev - er they _ do go, do go, To the
nev - er will _ I ___ mar - ried be ___ Un - til the day _ I die, I die, Since the
nev - er will _ I ___ mar - ried be ___ Un - til the day _ I die, I die, Since the

LULLABY
(Komoriuta)

Japanese

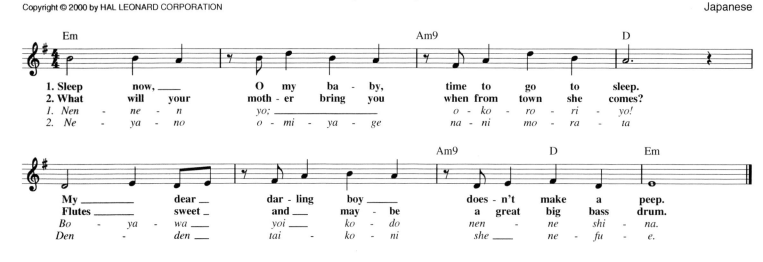

1. Sleep now, O my ba - by, time to go to sleep.
2. What will your moth - er bring you when from town she comes?
1. Nen - ne - n yo; o - ko - ro - ri - yo!
2. Ne - ya - no o - mi - ya - ge na - ni mo - ra - ta

My dear dar - ling boy does - n't make a peep.
Flutes sweet and may - be a great big bass drum.
Bo - ya - wa yoi ko - do nen - ne shi - na.
Den - den tai - ko - ni she ne - fu - e.

LULLABY, MY BABY
(Arroro Mi Niño)

Argentinian

1. Lul - la - by, my ba - by, Lul - la - by, my sun, Lul - la - by, my sweet - heart,
1. Ar - ro - ro mi ni - ño, Ar - ro - ro mi sol, Ar - ro - ro pe - da - zo,

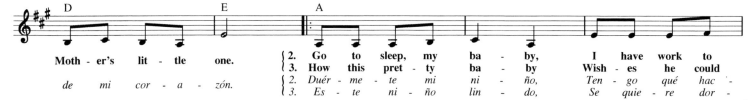

Moth - er's lit - tle one. 2. Go to sleep, my ba - by, I have work to
de mi cor - a - zón. 3. How this pret - ty ba - by Wish - es he could
2. Duér - me - te mi ni - ño, Ten - go qué hac -
3. Es - te ni - ño lin - do, Se quie - re dor -

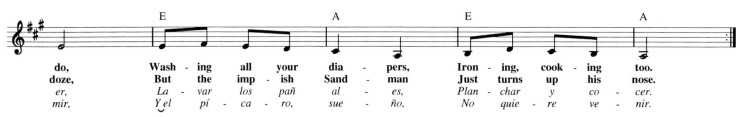

do, Wash - ing all your dia - pers, Iron - ing, cook - ing too.
doze, But the imp - ish Sand - man Just turns up his nose.
er, La - var los pañ - al - es, Plan - char y co - cer.
mir, Y el pí - ca - ro, sue - ño, No quie - re ve - nir.

MacPHERSON'S FAREWELL

18th Century Scottish

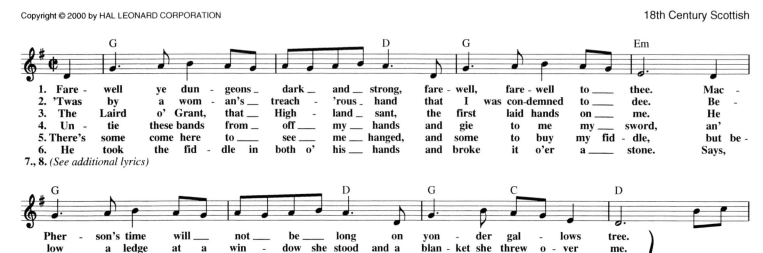

1. Fare - well ye dun - geons dark and strong, fare - well, fare - well to thee. Mac -
2. 'Twas by a wom - an's treach - 'rous hand that I was con - demned to dee. Be -
3. The Laird o' Grant, that High - land sant, the first laid hands on me. He
4. Un - tie these bands from off my hands and gie to me my sword, an'
5. There's some come here to see me hanged, and some to buy my fid - dle, but be -
6. He took the fid - dle in both o' his hands and broke it o'er a stone. Says,
7., 8. *(See additional lyrics)*

Pher - son's time will not be long on yon - der gal - lows tree.
low a ledge at a win - dow she stood and a blan - ket she threw o - ver me.
played the cause on Pe - ter Broon to let Mac - Pher - son dee.
there's not a man in all Scot - land but I'll brave him at a word.
fore that I do part with her, I'll break her through the mid - dle.
there's nae ith - er hand shall play on thee when I'm dead and gone.
Sae

rant - in' - ly, ___ sae ___ wan - ton - ly, sae ___ daunt - in' - ly, ___ gaed ___ he. He

played a tune ___ and he danced a - roon' be - low the gal - lows tree.

Additional Lyrics

7. O little did my mother think
When first she cradled me,
That I would turn a rovin' boy
And die on the gallows tree.

8. The reprieve was comin' o'er the brig o' Banff
To let MacPherson free,
But they pit the clock a quarter afore
And hanged him to the tree.

THE MAID ON THE SHORE

English

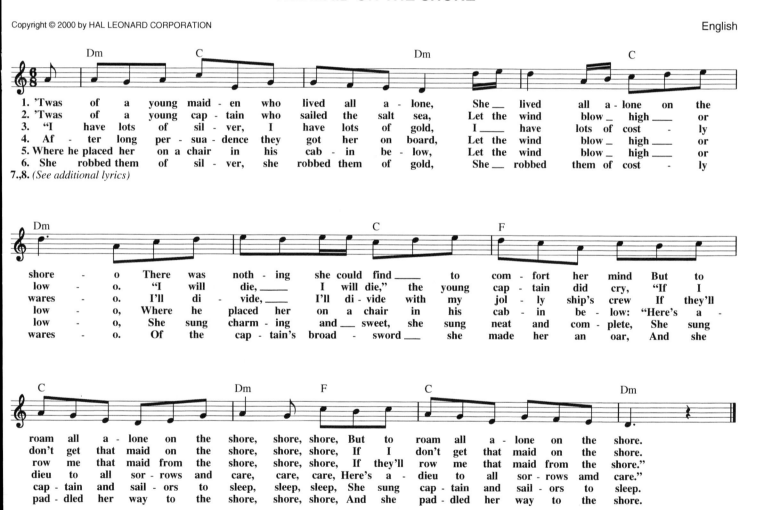

1. 'Twas of a young maid - en who lived all a - lone, She ___ lived all a - lone on the
2. 'Twas of a young cap - tain who sailed the salt sea, Let the wind blow _ high ___ or
3. "I have lots of sil - ver, I have lots of gold, I ___ have lots of cost - ly
4. Af - ter long per - sua - dence they got her on board, Let the wind blow _ high ___ or
5. Where he placed her on a chair in his cab - in be - low, Let the wind blow _ high ___ or
6. She robbed them of sil - ver, she robbed them of gold, She ___ robbed them of cost - ly
7.,8. *(See additional lyrics)*

shore - o There was noth - ing she could find ___ to com - fort her mind But to
low - o. "I will die, ___ I will die," the young cap - tain did cry, "If I
wares - o. I'll di - vide, ___ I'll di - vide with my jol - ly ship's crew If they'll
low - o, Where he placed her on a chair in his cab - in be - low: "Here's a -
low - o, She sung charm - ing and ___ sweet, she sung neat and com - plete, She sung
wares - o. Of the cap - tain's broad - sword ___ she made her an oar, And she

roam all a - lone on the shore, shore, shore, But to roam all a - lone on the shore.
don't get that maid on the shore, shore, shore, If I don't get that maid on the shore.
row me that maid from the shore, shore, shore, If they'll row me that maid from the shore."
dieu to all sor - rows and care, care, care, Here's a - dieu to all sor - rows amd care."
cap - tain and sail - ors to sleep, sleep, sleep, She sung cap - tain and sail - ors to sleep.
pad - dled her way to the shore, shore, shore, And she pad - dled her way to the shore.

Additional Lyrics

7. "My men must be crazy, my men must be mad,
My men must be deep in despair-o
To let her go 'way with her beauty so gay,
And paddle her way to the shore, shore, shore,
And paddle her way to the shore."

8. "Your men was not crazy, your men was not mad,
Your men was not deep in despair-o;
I deluded the sailors as well as yourself;
I'm a maiden again on the shore, shore, shore,
I'm a maiden again on the shore."

THE MAID FREED FROM THE GALLOWS

English

MAKE ME A BED ON THE FLOOR

American

MAMA DON'T 'LOW

American

Ma - ma don't 'low no
1. gui - tar pick - in'
2. ban - jo play - in'
3. ci - gar smok - in'
4. talk - in' __
'round here. _____ Ma - ma don't 'low no

gui - tar pick - in'
ban - jo play - in'
ci - gar smok - in'
talk - in' __
'round here. _____ I don't care what Ma - ma don't 'low, Gon - na

pick my gui - tar
play my ban - jo
smoke my ci - gar
shoot my mouth off
an - y - how, Ma - ma don't 'low no
gui - tar pick - in'
ban - jo play - in'
ci - gar smok - in'
talk - in' __
'round here. _____

MAMA, HAVE YOU HEARD THE NEWS

American

1. Ma - ma, Ma - ma, Ma - ma, have you heard the news? Dad - dy got killed on the C B and Q's.
2. Ear - ly in the morn-ing when it looked like rain, A - round the curve came a grav - el train.
3. All the way __ by the last __ board he passed, Thir - ty - five min-utes late with the U. S. mail.
4. When __ Ca-sey's fam - i - ly heard of his death, Ca - sey's daugh - ter ____ fell on her knees:

Shut your eyes __ and __ hold your breath, for we'll all draw a pen-sion on your pa - pa's death.
On the train __ was __ Ca - sey Jones; he's a good old ____ round-er but he's dead __ and gone.
Ca - sey Jones __ to his fire - man said, "We'll make it in - to Can-ton or leave the rail.
"Ma - ma, Ma - ma, how __ can it be, Pa - pa got killed __ on the old __ I. C.?"

On your pa - pa's death, on your pa - pa's death, we will all draw a pen-sion on your pa-pa's death.
But he's dead and gone, but he's dead and gone, he's a good old round-er but he's dead __ and __ gone.
Or __ leave the rail, or __ leave the rail, we'll make it in - to Can-ton or __ leave the rail.
"O ___ hush your mouth and __ hold your breath, we will all draw a pen-sion from __ Ca-sey's death.

MAN GOIN' ROUND

American

There's a man go - in' round tak - in' names, There's a man go - in' round tak - in' names, And he

took my
1. moth-er's
2. fa - ther's
3. sis - ter's
4. broth-er's
name, And he left my heart in pain, There's a man go - in' round tak - in' names.

THE MAN ON THE FLYING TRAPEZE

Words by George Leybourne
Music by Alfred Lee

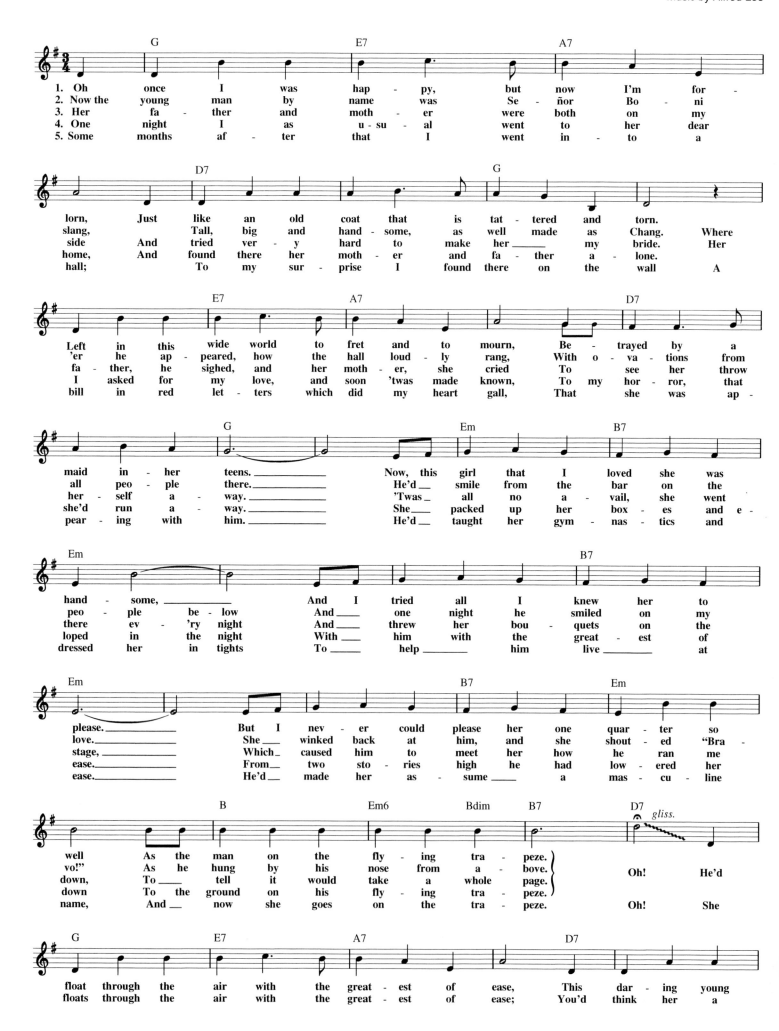

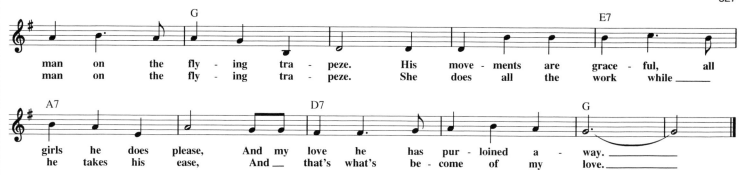

man on the fly - ing tra - peze. His move - ments are grace - ful, all
man on the fly - ing tra - peze. She does all the work while _____

girls he does please, And my love he has pur - loined a - way. _____
he takes his ease, And ___ that's what's be - come of my love. _____

MARY ANN

Canadian version
of an Irish Folksong

1. They ___ fare thee well, my own true ___ love, then ___ fare thee well for a while, For the
2. Oh, ___ don't you see that pret-ty tur-tle dove, ___ sit - ting on a ____ pine? He's ___
3. The ___ lob - ster boil-ing in the ___ pot and the cray - fish on the ___ line, they're ___
4. Oh, ___ had I but a bot - tle of gin and a sug - ar here for ___ two and a

ship is a - wait-ing and the wind blows free, and I am bound ___ a way to the sea, Mar - y
mourn - ing the loss ___ of his own true love as I now mourn ___ for mine, my ___ dear Mar - y
suf - f'ring ___ long, ___ but it's noth - ing like the ache I bear ___ for you, my ___ dear Mar - y
great big ___ bowl ___ for to mix it in, I'd fix a drink ___ for you, my ___ dear Mar - y

Ann, and ____ I am bound ___ a way to the sea, Mar - y Ann.
Ann, as ____ I now mourn ___ for mine, my ____ dear Mar - y Ann.
Ann, the ____ ache I bear ___ for you, my ____ dear Mar - y Ann.
Ann, I'd ____ fix a drink ___ for you, my ____ dear Mar - y Ann.

A MAN WITHOUT A WOMAN

19th Century American

A man _____ with - out a wom - an _____ is like a ship _____ with - out a

sail, _____ is like a boat with - out a rud - der, _____ is like a fish with - out a

tail. A man _____ with - out a wom - an _____ is like a use - less, emp - ty

can, _____ but if there's one thing worse in the u - ni - verse, it's a

wom - an, _____ I said a wom - an, _____ it's a wom - an with - out a man. ___

MANDOLINA

Mexican Serenade

MARCHING THROUGH GEORGIA

Civil War Song
Words and Music by Henry Clay Work

1. Bring the good old bu - gle, boys, we'll sing an - oth - er song.   Sing it with a spir - it that will
2. How the peo - ple shout - ed when they heard the joy - ful sound!   How the tur - keys gob - bled which our
3. Yes, and there were Un - ion men who wept with joy - ful tears   When they saw the hon - ored flag they
4. "Sher - man's dash - ing Yan - kee boys will nev - er reach the coast!"   So the sauc - y Reb - els said, and
5. So we made a thor - ough - fare for Free - dom and her train,   Six - ty miles in lat - i - tude, three

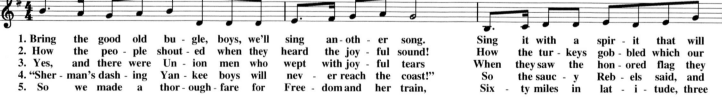

start the world a - long.   Sing it as we used to sing it, fif - ty thou - sand strong,
com - mis - sar - y found!   How the sweet po - ta - toes e - ven start - ed from the ground
had not seen for years.   Hard - ly could they be re - strained from break - ing forth in cheers
'twas a hand - some boast;   Had they not for - got, a - las! to reck - on with the host,
hun - dred to the main.   Trea - son fled be - fore us, for re - sis - tence was in vain

While we were march - ing through Geor - gia. Hur - rah! Hur - rah! We

bring the ju - bi - lee! Hur - rah! Hur - rah! The flag that makes you free!

So we sang the cho - rus from At - lan-ta to the sea, While we were march - ing through Geor - gia.

MARIANNE

Jamaican

1. Mar - i - anne, oh Mar - i - anne, oh you're the girl for me, e - ven though your
2. When I met sweet Mar - i - anne, her moth - er said to me, "Would you care to

dear old ma - ma will not say "si, si". Mar - i - anne, oh Mar - i - anne, oh
tell me where you stand fi - nan - cial - ly?" She does not ap - prove of me 'cause

won't you please a - gree? You and I should mar - ry, raise a fam - i - ly.
I'm no mil - lion - aire, but I love her daugh - ter more than I can bear.

All day, all night, Mar - i - anne, down by the sea - side

sift - in' sand. All the lit - tle chil - dren love Mar - i - anne,

down by the sea - side sift - in' sand.

MARY HAD A LITTLE LAMB

Words by Sarah Josepha Hale
Nursery Rhyme Song

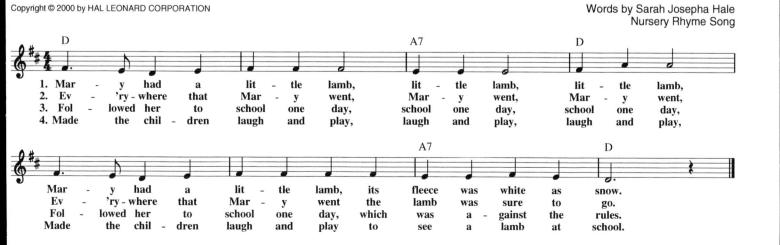

1. Mar - y had a lit - tle lamb, lit - tle lamb, lit - tle lamb,
2. Ev - 'ry - where that Mar - y went, Mar - y went, Mar - y went,
3. Fol - lowed her to school one day, school one day, school one day,
4. Made the chil - dren laugh and play, laugh and play, laugh and play,

Mar - y had a lit - tle lamb, its fleece was white as snow.
Ev - 'ry - where that Mar - y went the lamb was sure to go.
Fol - lowed her to school one day, which was a - gainst the rules.
Made the chil - dren laugh and play to see a lamb at school.

MARY HAD A BABY

African-American Spiritual

1. Mar - y Had A Ba - by,
2. What __ did she name Him?
3. She __ called Him Je - sus,
4. Where_ was He born?__
5. Born__ in a sta - ble,
6. Where_ did they lay Him?
7. Laid Him in a man - ger,

Oh Lord; __

Mar - y Had A Ba - by,
What __ did she name Him?
She __ called Him Je - sus,
Where_ was He born?__
Born__ in a sta - ble,
Where_ did they lay Him?
Laid Him in a man - ger,

Oh my __ Lord;

Mar - y Had A Ba - by,
What __ did she name Him?
She __ called Him Je - sus,
Where_ was He born?__
Born__ in a sta - ble,
Where_ did they lay Him?
Laid Him in a man - ger,

Oh Lord; ___ The peo - ple keep a - com - ing and the train_ done gone.

MAY SONG
(Canción de Maja)

Andalusian

1. Fool - ish lov - ers, cease to lan - guish, Cease to
2. Sil - ly fel - lows, vain your pas - sion, Dan - gling
1. De que sir - ve à las U - si - as Ca - me -
2. Un se - ñor cur - ra - ta - qui - llo Me quie -

wea - ry ___ and com - plain. Leave your sigh - ing,
'round me ev - 'ry - where, Dressed in all the
lar à ___ lo se - ñor, Si ca - ra - cen
re á ___ mi jon - ja - bar, Y se vis - te

leave your an - guish, Nought to me a - vails your_____
lat - est fash - ion, Such con - ceits I _____ can - not_____
de zan - dun - ga A la me - jor _____ o - ca -
de mil mo - dós Pa - ra po - der - me agra -

pain. All your wiles ig - nor - ing, Free as bird I'm soar - ing,
bear. Such fan - tas - tic pac - ing, Bow - ing and grim - ac - ing,
sion? A - si di ma - jo - ta Quie - ro siem-pre an - dar, _____
dar. To - do es dar sal - ti - tos Los pies ar - ra - strar, _____

All your sweet al - lure - ments Light - ly I dis - dain._____ Gay I'm
Emp - ty flat-tering speech - es, Curled and scent - ed hair._____ Gay I'm
Que esel ma - ne - ji - llo De der - ra - mar sal, _____ Y yo le
Re - frun - cir la bo - ca, El pe - lo pei - nar; _____ Y yo le

sing - ing, "Go, poor lov - ers, _____ come not_____ near, _____
sing - ing, "Go, vain lov - ers, _____ come not_____ near, _____
di - go: Ar - ri - ma - te _____ pa - ra a - llá, _____
di - go: Ar - ri - ma - te _____ pa - ra a - llá, _____

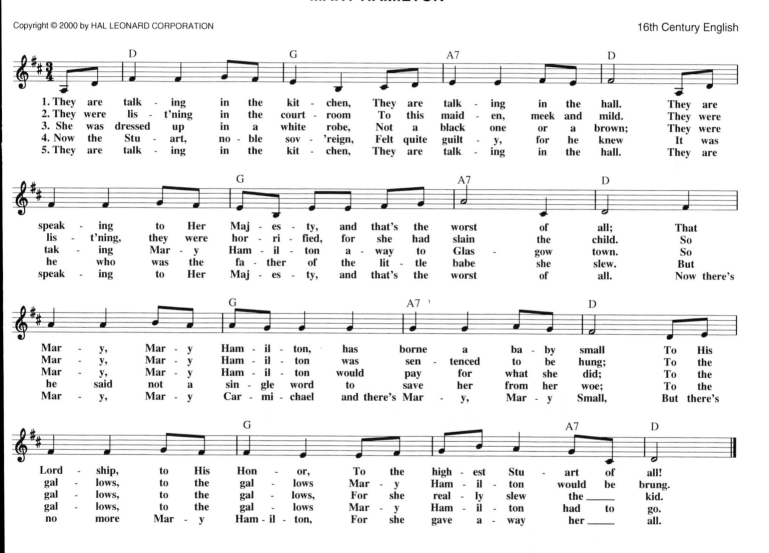

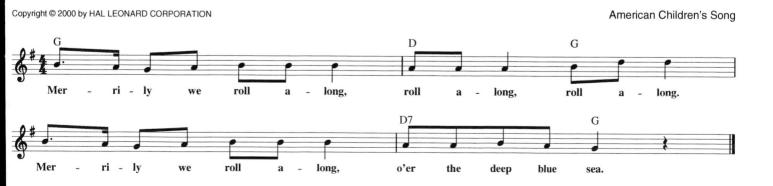

MATILDA

West Indian Calypso

Ma - til - da, _____ Ma - til - da, _____

Ma - til - da, she take me mon - ey and run Ven - e - zue - la! _____

1. That
2. I
3.
4.

wom - an made a wreck of me, what she done to me you ought to see. ____
save up, gon - na make her my wife, but she want - a live an - oth - er kind of life. ____
We were sleep - ing in me bed, when she found the mon - ey me had hid. ____
What to do and where to go? Nev - er trust a wom - an with your dough. _

Ma - til - da, she take me mon - ey and gone Ven - e - zue - la! _____

ME FATHER'S A LAWYER IN ENGLAND

English

1. Me fa - ther's a law - yer in Eng - land, Me moth - er's a jus - tice of
2. Me fa - ther's a hed - ger and ditch - er, Me moth - er does noth - ing but
3. Me wife, she is dirt - y, she's nas - ty, She's lous - y and itch - y and
4. My fa - ther's an ap - ple pie bak - er, My moth - er makes syn - thet - ic
5. My broth - er's a street mis - sion - ar - y, He saves lit - tle girl - ies from

peace, Me sis - ter's a Shak - er and an ap - ple pie bak - er, She
spin, Me sis - ter's a Shak - er and an ap - ple pie bak - er; She
black, She is a dev - il for ____ fight - ing and scold - ing; Her
gin, My sis - ter sells sin to the ____ sail - ors; _____ My
sin. He'll save you a blonde for a ____ dol - lar; _____ My

makes them of tal - ler and grease. O how the mon - ey comes in!
tongue ____ goes click - et - y - clack. God, how the mon - ey rolls in!
God, how the mon - ey rolls in!

To - me - fang, to - me - fang, fang - o -

lear - y, To - me - fang, to - me - fang, fang - o - lay, To - me

hoot - te - toot, toot - te - toot, lar - ry. To - me - whack, fal - dee - did - dle al - a -

day, To - me - whack, fal - dee - did - dle al - de - day.

MEN OF HARLECH
(Rhyfelgyrch Gwyr Harlech)

Words by Ceriog
Welsh Folk Melody

See the flames of fires like hell there, Fie - ry tongues that ache and swell there.
Well - uh goil - kairth wen un flam - yo, Ah thav - ode - i tahn un bloyth - yo,

Hear the brave man's bat - tle yell there: On - ward as we go.
Ahr eer dew - rion thod ee dah - ro, Een - wythe et on een.

Hear the war cries, ar - mor clash - ing, Chief - tains urge the right - eous thrash - ing,
Gahn - von - llev i tuh - ois - og - yon, Llice gel - on - yon, troost ar - vog - yon

Sol - diers ride on hors - es dash - ing, On - ward as we go.
Ah char - lom - yod uh march - og - yon, Creig - ar grieg ah green!

Ar - fon sings on al - ways, Of her might and glo - ry.
Ahr - von beeth nee or - veeth, Ken - eer un dra - guh weeth,

Wales will be as Wales has been, So great in free - dom's sto - ry. These
Cum - ree veeth vel Cum - ree vee, Un glode - ees um mus gled - eeth. Ung

sac - ri - fic - es light the fi - res, Brave men are dy - ing, Wales in - spi - res,
ween ohl - i - neer goil - kerth ak - oo, Tros wev - ees - i Cum - rone mah - roo,

Free - dom drives us ev - er high - er, Welsh - men must be free.
On - nee - bun - yeith seeth un gal - oo, Am i day - rav deen!

MICHAEL ROW THE BOAT ASHORE

Traditional American

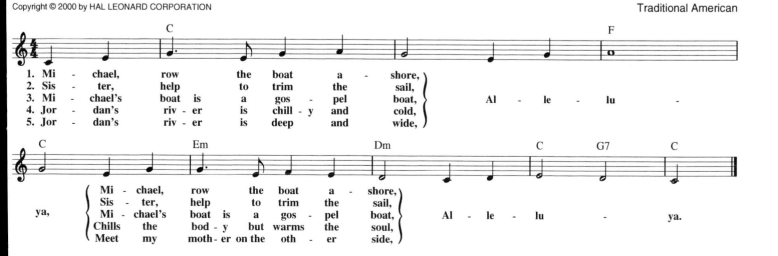

1. Mi - chael, row the boat a - shore,
2. Sis - ter, help to trim the sail,
3. Mi - chael's boat is a gos - pel boat,
4. Jor - dan's riv - er is chill - y and cold,
5. Jor - dan's riv - er is deep and wide,

Al - le - lu -

ya,

Mi - chael, row the boat a - shore,
Sis - ter, help to trim the sail,
Mi - chael's boat is a gos - pel boat,
Chills the bod - y but warms the soul,
Meet my moth - er on the oth - er side,

Al - le - lu - ya.

McCAFFERY

Irish

1. When I was bare-ly eigh-teen years of age, to join the arm-y I did en-gage. I
2. To Ful-wood Bar-racks I then did go, To spend some time in that de-pot. But
3. It hap-pened that I was on guard one day; Three ser-geants' chil-dren came out to play. I
4. At Ful-wood guard-room I did ap-pear, But Cap-tain Han-som my case would not hear. So
5. For thir-teen weeks my ha-tred grew; It filled my bod-y all through and through, Un-
6. Ear-ly one morn-ing on the bar-rack square, Cap-tain Han-som was walk-ing with Colo-nel Blair. I

7.-9. *(See additional lyrics)*

left the fac-to-ry with true in-tent, To join the for-ty-sec-ond reg-i-ment.
for-tu-nate I was not to be, For Cap-tain Han-som took a dis-like to me.
took one's name in-stead of all three; With ne-glect of du-ty they did charge me.
to my fate I was re-signed, And in Ful-wood guard-room I was con-fined.
til the deed I re-solved one night Was to shoot Cap-tain Han-som dead on sight.
raised my ri-fle, I shot to kill, But I shot my colo-nel a-gainst my will.

Additional Lyrics

7. I done the deed, I shed the blood.
   At Liverpool Assizes my trial I stood.
   Judge says to me, "McCaffery,
   Prepare yourself for the gallows tree."

8. I had no father to take my part,
   Likewise no mother to break her heart.
   Only one pal and a girl was she—
   She'd have laid down her life for McCaffery.

9. Come all you young Irishmen, come listen to me,
   Have nothing to do with the British Army.
   For only lies and tyranny
   Made a murderer out of McCaffery.

THE MEN OF THE WEST

Irish
By William Rooney

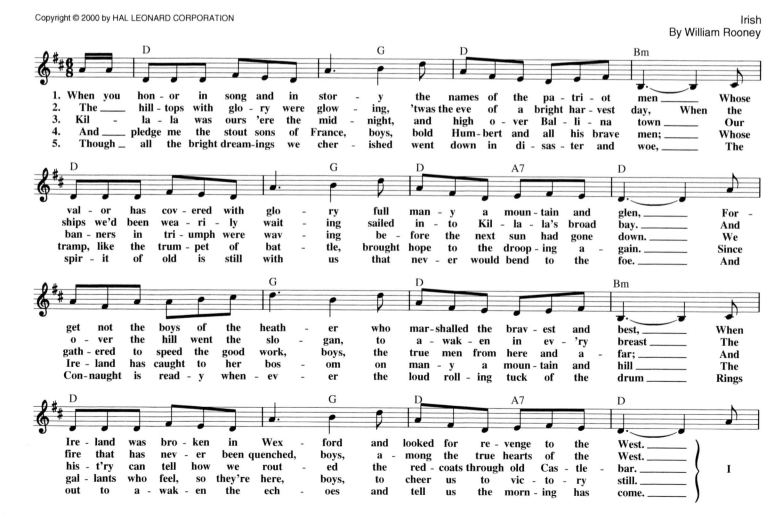

1. When you hon-or in song and in stor-y the names of the pa-tri-ot men Whose
2. The hill-tops with glo-ry were glow-ing, 'twas the eve of a bright har-vest day, When the
3. Kil-la-la was ours 'ere the mid-night, and high o-ver Bal-li-na town Our
4. And pledge me the stout sons of France, boys, bold Hum-bert and all his brave men; Whose
5. Though all the bright dream-ings we cher-ished went down in di-sas-ter and woe, The

val-or has cov-ered with glo-ry full man-y a moun-tain and glen, For
ships we'd been wea-ri-ly wait-ing sailed in-to Kil-la-la's broad bay. And
ban-ners in tri-umph were wav-ing be-fore the next sun had gone down. We
tramp, like the trum-pet of bat-tle, brought hope to the droop-ing a-gain. Since
spir-it of old is still with us that nev-er would bend to the foe. And

get not the boys of the heath-er who mar-shalled the brav-est and best, When
o-ver the hill went the slo-gan, to a-wak-en in ev-'ry breast The
gath-ered to speed the good work, boys, the true men from here and a-far; And
Ire-land has caught to her bos-om on man-y a moun-tain and hill The
Con-naught is read-y when-ev-er the loud roll-ing tuck of the drum Rings

Ire-land was bro-ken in Wex-ford and looked for re-venge to the West.
fire that has nev-er been quenched, boys, a-mong the true hearts of the West.
his-t'ry can tell how we rout-ed the red-coats through old Cas-tle-bar.
gal-lants who feel, so they're here, boys, to cheer us to vic-to-ry still. I
out to a-wak-en the ech-oes and tell us the morn-ing has come.

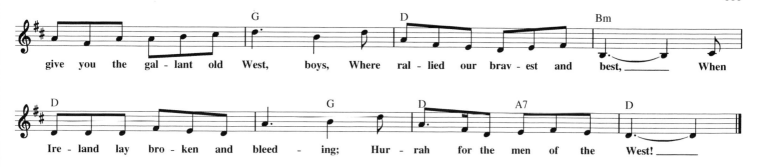

give you the gal - lant old West, boys, Where ral - lied our brav - est and best, _____ When Ire - land lay bro - ken and bleed - ing; Hur - rah for the men of the West! _____

MERMAID SONG

18th Century Irish Sea Chantey

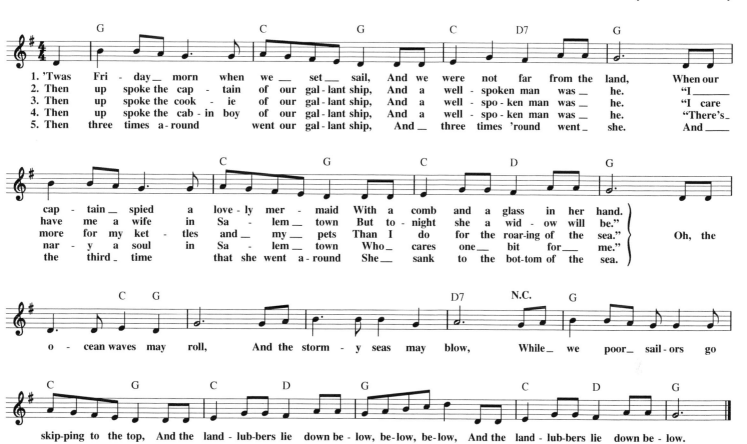

1. 'Twas Fri - day_ morn when we _ set _ sail, And we were not far from the land, When our
2. Then up spoke the cap - tain of our gal - lant ship, And a well - spoken man was _ he. "I _____
3. Then up spoke the cook - ie of our gal - lant ship, And a well - spo - ken man was _ he. "I care
4. Then up spoke the cab - in boy of our gal - lant ship, And a well - spo - ken man was _ he. "There's_
5. Then three times a - round went our gal - lant ship, And _ three times 'round went _ she. And _____

cap - tain _ spied a love - ly mer - maid With a comb and a glass in her hand.
have me a wife in Sa - lem _ town But to - night she a wid - ow will be."
more for my ket - tles and _ my _ pets Than I do for the roar-ing of the sea." Oh, the
nar - y a soul in Sa - lem _ town Who_ cares one _ bit for_ me."
the third _ time that she went a - round She_ sank to the bot-tom of the sea.

o - cean waves may roll, And the storm - y seas may blow, While_ we poor_ sail - ors go

skip-ping to the top, And the land - lub-bers lie down be - low, be-low, be-low, And the land - lub-bers lie down be - low.

MOLLY BANN

Kansas version of an English Folksong

1. Mol - ly Bann went _____ walk - ing, Walk - ing a -
2. She got un - der some bush - es, The show - ers to
3. I _____ killed a fair maid - en, The joy of my
4. Then _____ up spoke my fa - ther, His locks were turn - ing
5. The _____ day of my tri - al, Mol - ly's ghost did ap -

lone. Mol - ly Bann went _____ walk - ing When the show - ers come on.
shun. With her a - pron pinned 'round her, I shot her for a fawn.
life; I had al - ways in - tend - ed For to make her my wife.
grey, Say - ing, "Jim - my, oh, Jim - my, Do _ not run a - way."
pear, Say - ing, "Gen - tle - men of the ju - ry, Let my true love go clear."

MICHAEL FINNEGAN

American

There was an old man named Mi - chael Fin - ne - gan. He had whisk - ers on his chin - ne - gan.
He cut 'em off but they grew in a - gain. Poor old Mi - chael Fin - ne - gan. Be - gin a - gain. There
was an old man named Mi - chael Fin - ne - gan. He went fish - ing with a pin a - gain. Caught a fish but it
flopped back in a - gain. Poor old Mi - chael Fin - ne - gan. Be - gin a - gain. There was an old man named
Mi - chael Fin - ne - gan. Ran a race and tried to win a - gain. He fell down and bumped his shin a - gain.
Poor old Mi - chael, poor old Mi - chael, poor old Mi - chael Fin - ne - gan. Don't be - gin a - gain.

MICHAEL ROY OF BROOKLYN CITY

Irish

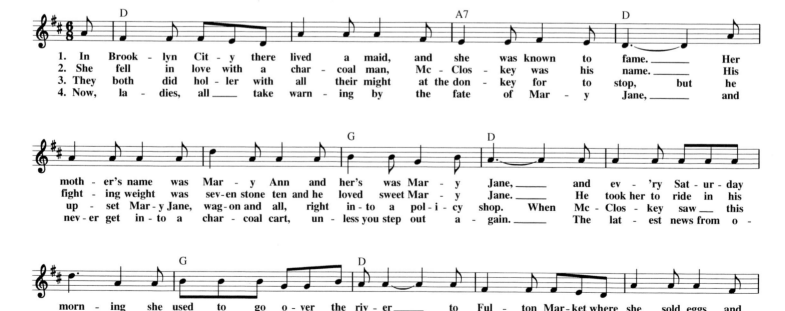

1. In Brook - lyn Cit - y there lived a maid, and she was known to fame. _____ Her
2. She fell in love with a char - coal man, Mc - Clos - key was his name. _____ His
3. They both did hol - ler with all their might at the don - key for to stop, but he
4. Now, la - dies, all _____ take warn - ing by the fate of Mar - y Jane, _____ and

moth - er's name was Mar - y Ann and her's was Mar - y Jane, _____ and ev - 'ry Sat - ur - day
fight - ing weight was sev - en stone ten and he loved sweet Mar - y Jane. _____ He took her to ride in his
up - set Mar - y Jane, wag - on and all, right in - to a pol - i - cy shop. When Mc - Clos - key saw _____ this
nev - er get in - to a char - coal cart, un - less you step out a - gain. _____ The lat - est news from o -

morn - ing she used to go o - ver the riv - er _____ to Ful - ton Mar - ket where she sold eggs and
char - coal cart on a fine _____ St. Pat - rick's day, _ but the don - key took fright at a Jer - sey man, and
cruel thing, his heart _____ was moved _ to pit - y, so he stabbed his don - key with a piece of char - coal and
ver the plain comes straight _ from Salt _ Lake Cit - y: _____ Mc - Clos - key, he was for - ty - five wives and is

MORE PRETTY GIRLS THAN ONE

American

There's more pret-ty girls than one, There's more pret-ty girls than one. For ev-'ry town I ram-bled a-round, There's more pret-ty girls than one.

My ma-ma told me last night,
Look down that lone-some road,
Look down that lone-some road

She gave me good ad-vice:
Hang down your lit-tle head and cry,
Be-fore you trav-el on.

Bet-ter stop your ram-bling
For think-ing of those
I'm leav-ing you this

'round, pret-ty boy, And mar-ry you a lov-ing wife.
pret-ty lit-tle girls And hop-ing you nev-er will die.
lone-some song To sing when I am gone.

D.C.
Last time D.C. al Fine

MOTHERLESS CHILDREN

African-American Spiritual

1. Moth-er-less chil-dren have a hard time when Moth-er is dead.
2. Some peo-ple say, "Sis-ter will do when your moth-er is dead."
3. Your wife or your hus-band may be good to you when your moth-er is dead.
4. Some peo-ple say, "Your aunt-ie will do when your moth-er is dead."
5. Je-sus will be a Fa-ther to you when your moth-er is dead.

Moth-er-less chil-dren have a hard time when Moth-er is dead.
Some peo-ple say, "Sis-ter will do when your moth-er is dead."
Your wife or your hus-band may be good to you when your moth-er is dead.
Some peo-ple say, "Your aunt-ie will do when your moth-er is dead."
Je-sus will be a Fa-ther to you when your moth-er is dead.

Wan-d'rin' 'round from door to door, They don't have no place to go.
Some peo-ple say, "Your sis-ter will do;" Soon as she mar-ries, turn her back on you.
Wife or your hus-band may be good to you; No-bod-y treat you like your moth-er do.
Some peo-ple say, "Your aunt-ie will do;" Make a start, then prove un-true.
Je-sus will be a Fa-ther to you, Through pain and sor-row lead you through.

Moth-er-less chil-dren have a hard time when Moth-er is dead.

MORRISSEY AND THE RUSSIAN SAILOR

Irish

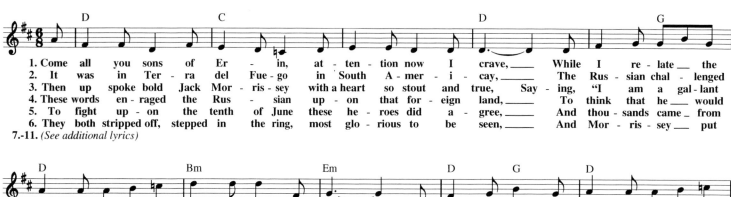

1. Come all you sons of Er - in, at - ten - tion now I crave, ____ While I re - late ____ the
2. It was in Ter - ra del Fue - go in South A - mer - i - cay, ____ The Rus - sian chal - lenged
3. Then up spoke bold Jack Mor - ris - sey with a heart so stout and true, Say - ing, "I am a gal - lant
4. These words en - raged the Rus - sian up - on that for - eign land, To think that he ____ would
5. To fight up - on the tenth of June these he - roes did a - gree, ____ And thou - sands came ____ from
6. They both stripped off, stepped in the ring, most glo - rious to be seen, ____ And Mor - ris - sey ____ put

7.-11. *(See additional lyrics)*

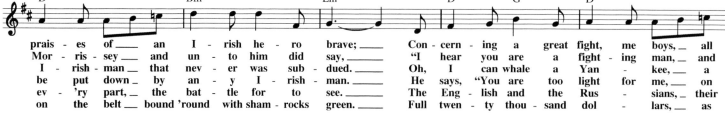

prais - es of ____ an I - rish he - ro brave; ____ Con - cern - ing a great fight, me boys, ____ all
Mor - ris - sey ____ and un - to him did say, ____ "I hear you are a fight - ing man, ____ and
I - rish - man ____ that nev - er was sub - dued. ____ Oh, I can whale a Yan - kee, ____ a
be put down ____ by an - y I - rish - man. ____ He says, "You are too light for me, ____ on
ev - 'ry part, ____ the bat - tle for to see. ____ The Eng - lish and the Rus - sians, ____ their
on the belt ____ bound 'round with sham - rocks green. ____ Full twen - ty thou - sand dol - lars, ____ as

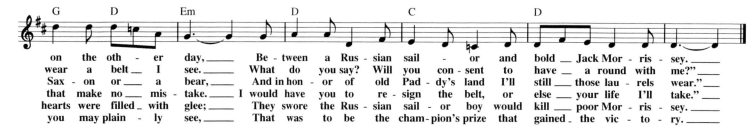

on the oth - er day, ____ Be - tween a Rus - sian sail - or and bold ____ Jack Mor - ris - sey. ____
wear a belt ____ I see. ____ What do you say? Will you con - sent to have ____ a round with me?" ____
Sax - on or ____ a bear, ____ And in hon - or of old Pad - dy's land I'll still ____ those lau - rels wear." ____
that make no ____ mis - take. ____ I would have you to re - sign the belt, or else ____ your life I'll take." ____
hearts were filled ____ with glee; ____ They swore the Rus - sian sail - or boy would kill ____ poor Mor - ris - sey. ____
you may plain - ly see, ____ That was to be the cham - pion's prize that gained ____ the vic - to - ry. ____

Additional Lyrics

7. They both shook hands, walked round the ring, commencing then to fight.
It filled each Irish heart with joy for to behold the sight.
The Russian, he floored Morrissey up to the eleventh round,
With English, Russian and Saxon cheers the valley did resound.

8. A minute and a half our hero lay before he could rise.
The word went all around the field: "He's dead," were all their cries.
But Morrissey raised manfully, and raising from the ground,
From that until the twentieth the Russian he put down.

9. Up to the thirty-seventh round 'twas fall and fall about,
Which made the burly sailor to keep a sharp lookout.
The Russian called his second and asked for a glass of wine.
Our Irish hero smiled and said, "The battle will be mine."

10. The thirty-eighth decided all. The Russian felt the smart
When Morrissey, with a fearful blow, he struck him o'er the heart.
A doctor he was called on to open up a vein.
He said it was quite useless, he would never fight again.

11. Our hero conquered Thompson, the Yankee Clipper too;
The Benicia boy and Shepherd he nobly did subdue.
So let us fill a flowing bowl and drink a health galore
To brave Jack Morrissey and Paddies evermore.

MOUNTAIN DEW

American Bluegrass

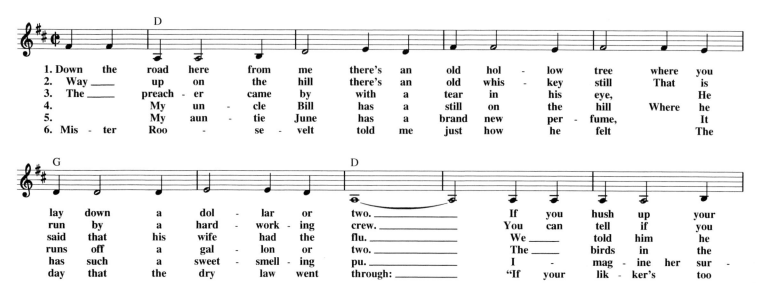

1. Down the road here from me there's an old hol - low tree where you
2. Way ____ up on the hill there's an old whis - key still That is
3. The ____ preach - er came by with a tear in his eye, He
4. My un - cle Bill has a still on the hill Where he
5. My aun - tie June has a brand new per - fume, It
6. Mis - ter Roo - se - velt told me just how he felt The

lay down a dol - lar or two. ____ If you hush up your
run by a hard - work - ing crew. ____ You can tell if you
said that his wife had the flu. ____ We ____ told him he
runs off a gal - lon or two. ____ The ____ birds in the
has such a sweet - smell - ing pu. ____ I - mag - ine her sur -
day that the dry law went through: ____ "If your lik - ker's too

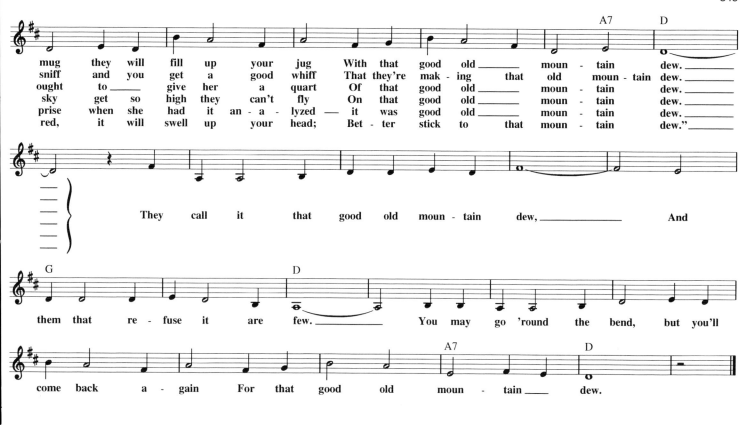

mug they will fill up your jug With that good old _____ moun - tain dew. _____
sniff and you get a good whiff That they're mak - ing that old moun - tain dew. _____
ought to _____ give her a quart Of that good old _____ moun - tain dew. _____
sky get so high they can't fly On that good old _____ moun - tain dew. _____
prise when she had it an - a - lyzed — it was good old _____ moun - tain dew. _____
red, it will swell up your head; Bet - ter stick to that moun - tain dew." _____

They call it that good old moun - tain dew, _____ And

them that re - fuse it are few. _____ You may go 'round the bend, but you'll

come back a - gain For that good old moun - tain _____ dew.

MOUNTAINS OF MOURNE

Words by Percy French, 1896
Traditional Irish Melody

1. Oh Mar - y, this Lon - don's a won - der - ful sight, with peo - ple here
2. I be - lieve that when writ - ing a wish you ex - pressed as to how the fine
3. There's beau - ti - ful girls here, oh nev - er you mind, with beau - ti - ful

work - ing by day and by night. They don't plant po - ta - toes nor bar - ley nor
la - dies in Lon - don were dressed. Well, if you'll be - lieve me, when asked to a
shapes na - ture nev - er de - signed. And love - ly com - plex - ions all ros - es and

wheat, but there's gangs of them dig - ging for gold in the street. At
ball, they don't wear no top to their dress - es at all. Oh, I've
cream, but let me re - mark with re - gard to the same, that

least when I asked them, that's what I was told, so I just took a
seen them me - self, and you could not in truth say that if they were
if that those ros - es you ven - ture to sip, the _____ col - ors might

hand at this dig - ging for gold. But for all that I've found there, I
bound for a ball or a bath. Don't be start - ing them fash - ions, now,
all come a - way on your lip. So I'll wait for the wild rose that's

might as well be where the moun - tains of Mourne _____ sweep down to the sea.
Mar - y Mc - Cree, where the moun - tains of Mourne _____ sweep down to the sea.
wait - ing for me in the place where the dark Mourne sweeps down to the sea.

MOWING THE BARLEY

English

MY BONNIE LIES OVER THE OCEAN

Scottish

MUST I GO BOUND?

American

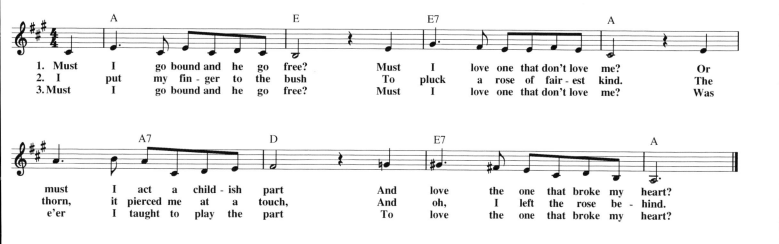

1. Must I go bound and he go free? Must I love one that don't love me? Or must I act a child-ish part And love the one that broke my heart?
2. I put my fin-ger to the bush To pluck a rose of fair-est kind. The thorn, it pierced me at a touch, And oh, I left the rose be-hind.
3. Must I go bound and he go free? Must I love one that don't love me? Was e'er I taught to play the part To love the one that broke my heart?

MY OLD KENTUCKY HOME

Words and Music by
Stephen C. Foster

1. The sun shines bright in my old Ken-tuck-y home, 'Tis sum-mer, the folks there are gay. The corn top's ripe and the mead-ow's in the bloom, While the birds make mu-sic all the day. The young folks roll on the lit-tle cab-in floor, All mer-ry, all hap-py and bright. By'n by hard times come a-knock-ing at the door,
2. They hunt no more for the 'pos-sum and the 'coon, On mead-ow, the hill and the shore, They sing no more by the glim-mer of the moon, On the bench by that old cab-in door. The day goes by like a shad-ow o'er the heart, With sor-row where all was de-light. The time has come when the old friends have to part,
3. The head must bow and the back will have to bend, Where-ev-er the poor folks may go. A few more days and the trou-ble all will end, In the field where sug-ar canes grow; A few more days for to tote the wea-ry load, No mat-ter, 'twill nev-er be light. A few more days till we tot-ter on the road,

Then my old Ken-tuck-y home, good night.

Weep no more, my la-dy, Oh, weep no more to-day. We will sing one song for the old Ken-tuck-y home, For the old Ken-tuck-y home far a-way.

THE MULBERRY BUSH

American Game Song

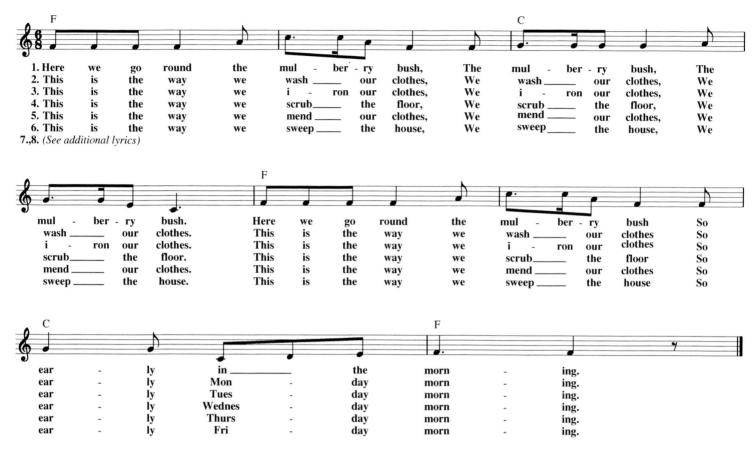

1. Here we go round the mul - ber - ry bush, The mul - ber - ry bush, The
2. This is the way we wash ___ our clothes, We wash ___ our clothes, We
3. This is the way we i - ron our clothes, We i - ron our clothes, We
4. This is the way we scrub ___ the floor, We scrub ___ the floor, We
5. This is the way we mend ___ our clothes, We mend ___ our clothes, We
6. This is the way we sweep ___ the house, We sweep ___ the house, We
7.,8. *(See additional lyrics)*

mul - ber - ry bush. Here we go round the mul - ber - ry bush So
wash ___ our clothes. This is the way we wash ___ our clothes So
i - ron our clothes. This is the way we i - ron our clothes So
scrub ___ the floor. This is the way we scrub ___ the floor So
mend ___ our clothes. This is the way we mend ___ our clothes So
sweep ___ the house. This is the way we sweep ___ the house So

ear - ly in ___ the morn - ing.
ear - ly Mon - day morn - ing.
ear - ly Tues - day morn - ing.
ear - ly Wednes - day morn - ing.
ear - ly Thurs - day morn - ing.
ear - ly Fri - day morn - ing.

Additional Lyrics

7. This is the way we bake our bread, etc.
   So early Saturday morning.

8. This is the way we got to church, etc.
   So early Sunday morning.

MY DAME HAD A LAME TAME CRANE

American

My dame had a lame, tame crane, ___ My dame had a

crane that was lame. ___ Come, Mis - tress Jane, can my dame's lame

tame crane Fly and re - turn a - gain? ___

* May be sung as a four-part round.

MY DAYS HAVE BEEN SO WONDROUS FREE

American
By Francis Hopkinson, 1759

My days have been so won - drous __ free, the lit - tle birds that fly with care - less ease from __ tree __ to tree, were but as blest as __ I, were __ but as blest as I. Ask the glid - ing wa - ters __ if __ a __ tear __ of __ mine in - creased their stream, and ask the breath - ing gales if ev - er I lent a __ sigh to them, _____ if I lent __ a _____ sigh to them.

MY HEART'S TONIGHT IN TEXAS

Western American

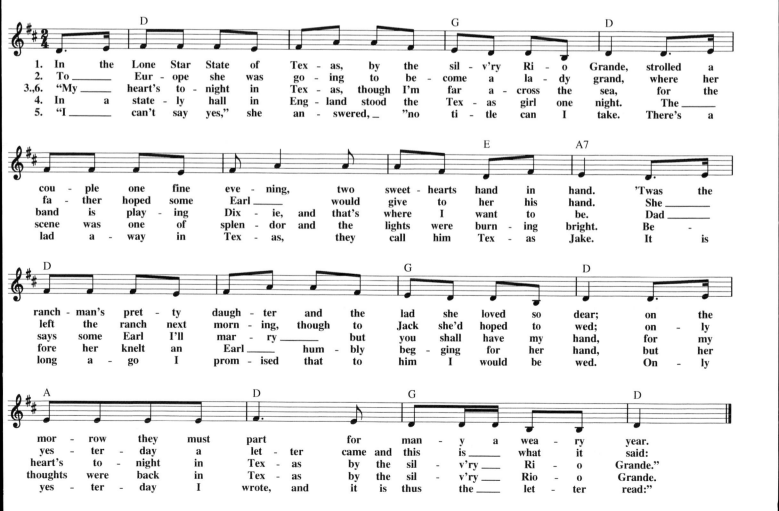

1. In the Lone Star State of Tex - as, by the sil - v'ry Ri - o Grande, strolled a cou - ple one fine eve - ning, two sweet - hearts hand in hand. 'Twas the ranch - man's pret - ty daugh - ter and the lad she loved so dear; on the mor - row they must part for man - y a wea - ry year.

2. To _____ Eur - ope she was go - ing to be - come a la - dy grand, where her fa - ther hoped some Earl _____ would give to her his hand. She _____ left the ranch next morn - ing, though to Jack she'd hoped to wed; on - ly yes - ter - day a let - ter came and this is _____ what it said:

3.,6. "My _____ heart's to - night in Tex - as, though I'm far a - cross the sea, for the band is play - ing Dix - ie, and that's where I want to be. Dad _____ says some Earl I'll mar - ry _____ but you shall have my hand, for my heart's to - night in Tex - as by the sil - v'ry _____ Ri - o Grande."

4. In a state - ly hall in Eng - land stood the Tex - as girl one night. The _____ scene was one of splen - dor and the lights were burn - ing bright. Be - fore her knelt an Earl _____ hum - bly beg - ging for her hand, but her thoughts were back in Tex - as by the sil - v'ry _____ Rio - o Grande.

5. "I _____ can't say yes," she an - swered, _ "no ti - tle can I take. There's a lad a - way in Tex - as, they call him Tex - as Jake. It is long a - go I prom - ised that to him I would be wed. On - ly yes - ter - day I wrote, and it is thus the _____ let - ter read:"

MY HOME'S ACROSS THE SMOKY MOUNTAINS

Appalachian Folksong

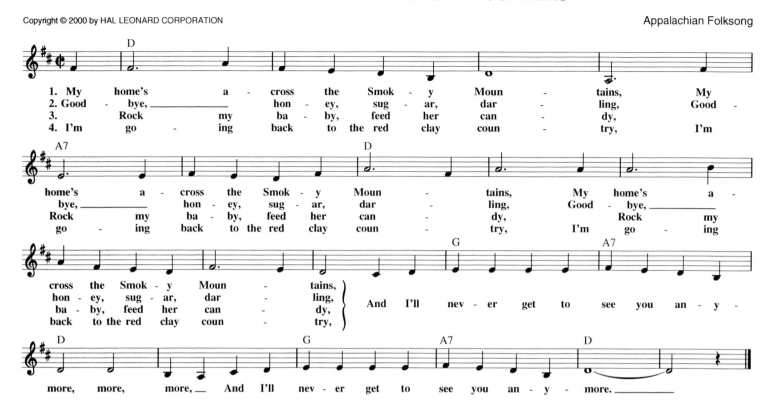

1. My home's a - cross the Smok - y Moun - tains, My home's a - cross the Smok - y Moun - tains, My home's a - cross the Smok - y Moun - tains,
2. Good - bye, hon - ey, sug - ar, dar - ling, Good - bye, hon - ey, sug - ar, dar - ling, Good - bye, hon - ey, sug - ar, dar - ling,
3. Rock my ba - by, feed her can - dy, Rock my ba - by, feed her can - dy, Rock my ba - by, feed her can - dy,
4. I'm go - ing back to the red clay coun - try, I'm go - ing back to the red clay coun - try, back to the red clay coun - try,

And I'll nev - er get to see you an - y - more, more, more, — And I'll nev - er get to see you an - y - more. ___

MY LORD, WHAT A MORNING

African-American Spiritual

My Lord, what a morn - ing; my Lord, what a morn - ing; oh, ___
my Lord, what a morn - ing, when the stars be - gin to fall.

1. You'll
2. You'll

hear the trum - pet sound ___ to wake the na - tions un - der - ground,
hear the sin - ners moan, ___ look - ing to my God's right hand, when the stars be - gin to fall.

MY LUVE IS LIKE A RED, RED ROSE

Words by Robert Burns
Scottish Folk Melody, circa 1745

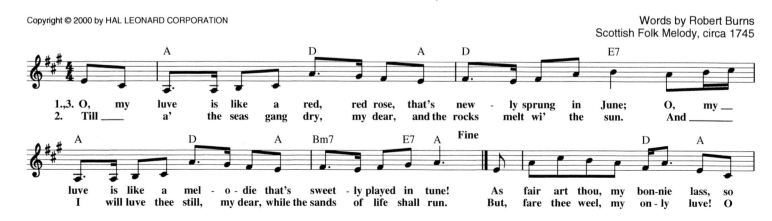

1.,3. O, my luve is like a red, red rose, that's new - ly sprung in June; O, my ___
2. Till ___ a' the seas gang dry, my dear, and the rocks melt wi' the sun. And ___

luve is like a mel - o - die that's sweet - ly played in tune! As fair art thou, my bon - nie lass, so
I will luve thee still, my dear, while the sands of life shall run. But, fare thee weel, my on - ly luve! O

MY MOTHER'S OLD RED SHAWL

American

MY SWEETHEART'S A MULE

American Work Song

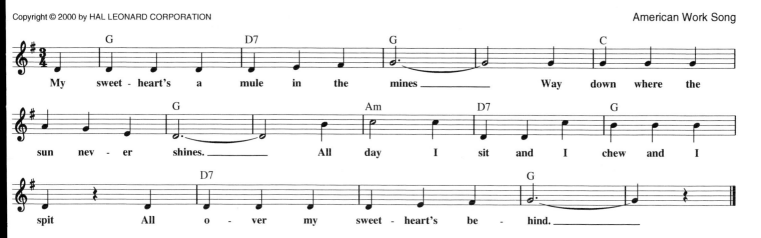

MY LOVE IS A RIDER

American Cowboy Song

1. My love is a rid - er, wild hors - es be breaks, But he's prom - ised to
2. The first time I met him, 'twas ear - ly in spring; He was rid - ing a
3. The next time I saw him, 'twas some - time that fall, Swing - ing the
4. He made me some pres - ents, a - mong them a ring. The re - turn that I
5. My love has a gun, and that gun he can use, But he's quit his gun
6. Lis - ten, all you young maid - ens, where - e'er you re - side: Ride __ shy of the

quit it now just for my sake. He ties one foot up and the
bron - co, a high - head - ed thing. He tipped me a wink as he
girls __ at Tom - lin - son's hall. He laughed and he talked as we
made him was a far bet - ter thing: 'Twas a young maid - en's heart, __ I'd
fight - ing as well as his booze. And he's sold him his sad - dle, his
cow - boy who swings the raw - hide. He'll court you and pet you and

sad - dle puts on; With a run and a jump he is mount - ed and gone.
gai - ly did go, For he wished me to no - tice his buck - ing bron - co.
danced to and fro, And __ prom - ised he'd nev - er ride on an - oth - er bron - co.
have you all know; He'd __ won it by rid - ing his buck - ing bron - co.
spurs and his rope, And there's no more cow - punch - ing, and that's what I hope.
leave you and go Up the trail in the spring on his buck - ing bron - co.

MY MOTHER CHOSE MY HUSBAND

American

1. My moth - er chose my hus - band, a law - yer's son was he, When
2. When on the wed - ding night he came to bed with me, He
3. He bit me on the shoul - der and al - most broke my knee, I
4. I called my wait - ing wom - an, "Come quick - ly, Mar - jor - ie! Go
5. "Go tell Ma - ma I'm dy - ing; bid her come hast - i - ly." Came
6. Came Ma - ma to my bed - side be - fore I could count three: "Cheer

7.-10. (See additional lyrics)

on the wed - ding night he came to bed with me.
bit me on the shoul - der and al - most broke my knee.
called my wait - ing wom - an, "Come quick - ly, Mar - jor - ie!"
tell Ma - ma I'm dy - ing; bid her come hast - i - ly.
Ma - ma to my bed - side be - fore I could count three.
up, my girl, what ails you will nev - er kill," said she.

Ah, ah, ah! That's no way to... Ah, ah, ah! That can't be!

Additional Lyrics

7. "Cheer up, my girl, what ails you will never kill," said she.
   "If I had died of that, child, God knows where you would be.

8. "If I had died of that, child, God knows where you would be.
   So if you die, my daughter, I'll grave you splendidly.

9. "So if you die, my daughter, I'll grave you splendidly.
   Then carve upon your tombstone, where everyone can see...

10. "Then carve upon your tombstone, where everyone can see:
   'The only girl who couldn't survive that malady.'"

MY OLD HEN

American

My old hen's a good old hen, she lays eggs for the farm - er men. Some - times one, some - times two, some - times 'nough for the whole darn crew! Cluck, old hen, cluck, I tell you. Cluck, old hen, or I'm a goin' to sell you. Cluck, old hen, cluck, I say. Cluck, old hen, I'll give you a - way.

MY WHITE HORSE
(Mi Caballo Blanco)

Chilean

1. He's my white horse so hand - some, Shin - ing just like the dawn.
2. When hap - py wings trans - port me, He flies a - long so free,
3. I pray for God's pro - tec - tion: "Health for my steed pro - vide."
1. Es mi ca - ba - llo blan - co, Co - mo un a - man - e - cer,
2. En a - las de u - na di - cha Mi ca - ba - llo co - rrió,
3. Has - ta que a Dios le pi - do Que lo ten - ga muy bien,

He is a friend so faith - ful; Bud - dies, we trav - el on.
And when my heart is heav - y, He al - ways car - ries me.
But when I go to heav - en, On my white horse I'll ride.
Siem - pre jun - ti - tos va - mos, Es mi a - mi - go más fiel.
Y en bra - zos de u - na pe - na Tam - bién él me lle - vó.
Si a su la - do me lla - ma, En mi blan - qui - to i - ré.

My hand - some horse, my hand - some horse, gal - lop - ing a - way,
Mi ca - ba - llo, mi ca - ba - llo, gal - o - pan - do va,

My hand-some horse, my hand-some horse rac - es all day. Ah _____
Mi ca - ba - llo, mi ca - ba - llo, se va y se va. Ah _____

ah _____ ah _____ ah ah. _____
ah ah ah ah.

MY WILD IRISH ROSE

Words and Music by
Chauncey Olcott

NASSAU BOUND

Sea Chantey from the Bahamas

Chorus

1. We sailed on the Sloop John B. My grand - fa - ther, and
up with the John B's sails, See how the main - sail
first mate he___ got drunk and broke up the la - dies'
Cook - ie he___ got fits and throw 'way all the

me. 'Round Nas - sau Town we ___ did roam;
set. Send for the Cap-tain a - shore, Lem - me go home;
trunks. The con - sta - ble he come on board to take him a - way.
grits. Then he take and throw 'way ___ all the corn.

Drink - in' all night. Got in - to a fight, I feel so break up,
Oh Sher - iff John - stone Won't you let me a - lone I feel so break up,
Oh Sher - iff John - stone, please let me a - lone. I feel so break up,
Oh Sher - iff John - stone, please let me a - lone. I feel so break up,

I wan - na go home.___
I wan - na go home.___
I wan - na go home.___
I wan - na go home.___

To Coda

Verse

There's no bet - ter place than a
We car - ried ___ la - dies to
We eat a - board the___

sail - ing ship, To get an Ed - u - ca - tion. You learn to tar the
Nas - sau,___ Like oth - er sail - ing bo - ats There were twen - ty trunks down
Sloop John B., just like the ver - y best.___ But Cook - ie nev - er

Last time D.S. al Coda

CODA

rat - lines down, While drink - in' ___ your rum ra - tion. 2. An it's
in the hold, All full of ___ pet - ti - coats.___ 3. But the
calls it food, he on - ly calls it a mess. ___ 4. Then___

NIGHTINGALE WITH THE DARK BEAK
(Rouxinol do Pico Preto)

Brazilian

1. Night - in - gale with the dark beak, ___ night - in - gale with the dark beak, ___ please leave the
2. Let the ba - by rest his head, ___ let the ba - by rest his head. ___ At long ___
3. Rest, oh rest, my ba - by, ___ rest, oh rest, my ba - by. ___ Your ___
4. She has left to wash your clothes, ___ she has left to wash your clothes ___ on ___ the

1. Roux - in - ol do pic - o pre - to, roux - in - ol do pic - o pre - to, de - i - xa a
2. Deix - a dor - mir o men - i - no, deix - a dor - mir o men - i - no. Que stá no
3. Dor - me, dor - me, meu men - i - no, dor - me, dor - me, meu men - i - no. Que a maez -
4. Foi la - var os cuer - in - hos, ___ foi la - var os cuer - in - hos ___ a ri - beir -

ber - ries of the lau - rel bush. ___ Oh, oh! ___ Oh, oh! ___
last, ___ he is rest - ing. Oh, oh! ___ Oh, oh! ___
ma - ma ___ will re - turn soon. Oh, oh! ___ Oh, oh! ___
shores of ___ Be - lém. ___ Oh, oh! ___ Oh, oh! ___

Ba - ga ___ do lou - eir - o. O, o! ___ O, o! ___
so - no ___ prim - eir - o. O, o! ___ O, o! ___
in - ha ___ lo - go vem. ___ O, o! ___ O, o! ___
a de ___ Be - lém. ___ O, o! ___ O, o! ___

NEARBY TO MY DEAR ONE
(Auprès de ma Blonde)

French

1. Now in my fa-ther's gar-den, The li-lacs flow-er
1. Dans les jar-dins d'mon pè-re, Les li-las sont fleu-

2.-6. *(See additional lyrics)*

there, _____ Now in my fa-ther's gar-den, The li-lacs flow-er
ris, _____ Dans les jar-dins d'mon pè-re, Les li-las sont fleu-

there, _____ The birds from all the earth are en-chant-ing in the
ris, _____ Tous les oi-seaux du mon-de Vienn't y fai-re leurs

air. _____ Near-by to my dear one, How I love to
nids, _____ Au-près de ma blon-de, Qu'il fait bon, fait

be, to be, Near-by to my dear one, How I love to be. _____
bon, fait bon, Au-près de ma blon-de, Qu'il fait bon dor-mir. _____

Additional Lyrics

2. The quail, the grey woodpigeon,
And speckled partridge come,
The quail, the grey woodpigeon,
And speckled partridge come.
My little dove, my dearest,
That night and day doth croon.
Refrain

3. It's comforting the maidens
Unmarried and alone,
It's comforting the maidens,
Unmarried and alone.
Sweet dove, don't sing for me then,
A man, I have my own.
Refrain

4. O tell us, tell us lady,
Where is your husband gone?
O tell us, tell us lady,
Where is your husband gone?
In Holland he's a prisoner,
The Dutch have taken him.
Refrain

5. What would you give, my beauty,
To have your husband home?
What would you give, my beauty,
To have your husband home?
Versailles I'd gladly give them,
And Paris and Notre Dame.
Refrain

6. Versailles I'd gladly give them,
And Paris and Notre Dame;
Versailles I'd gladly give them,
And Paris and Notre Dame,
Saint Denis's Cathedral,
And our church-spire at home.
Refrain

2. *La caill', la tourterelle,*
Et la jolie perdrix,
La caill', la tourterelle,
Et la jolie perdrix,
Et ma jolie colombe
Qui chante jour et nuit.
Refrain

3. *Qui chante pour les filles*
Qui n'ont pas de mari,
Qui chante pour les filles
Qui n'ont pas de mari.
Pour moi, ne chante guère,
Car j'en ai un joli,
Refrain

4. *Dites-nous donc, la belle,*
Où donc est vot' mari?
Dites-nous donc, la belle,
Où donc est vot' mari?
Il est dans la Hollande,
Les Hollandais l'ont pris,
Refrain

5. *Que donneriez-vous, belle,*
Pour avoir votre ami?
Que donneriez-vous, belle,
Pour avoir votre ami?
Je donnerais Versailles,
Paris et Saint-Denis,
Refrain

6. *Je donnerais Versailles,*
Paris et Saint-Denis,
Je donnerais Versailles,
Paris et Saint-Denis,
Les tours de Notre-Dame,
Et l'clocher d'mon pays;
Refrain

NELLY WAS A LADY

Stephen C. Foster
1849

1. Down on the Mis - sis - sip - pi float - ing, Long time I trav - el on the way, _____ All night the cot - ton - wood a - tot - ing, Sing for my true love all the day. _____
2. Now I'm un - hap - py and I'm weep - ing, Can't tote the cot - ton - wood no more; _____ Last night, while Nel - ly was a - sleep - ing, Death came a - knock - ing at the door. _____
3. When I saw my Nel - ly in the morn - ing, Smile till she o - pened up her eyes, _____ Seemed like the light of day a - dawn - ing, Just be - fore the sun be - gan to rise. _____
4. Close by the mar - gin of the wa - ter, Where the lone weep - ing wil - low grows, _____ There lived Vir - gin - ny's love - ly daugh - ter, There she in death may find re - pose. _____
5. Down in the mead - ow 'mong the clo - ver, Walk with my Nel - ly by my side; _____ Now all them hap - py days are o - ver, Fare - well my sweet Vir - gin - ny bride. _____

Nel - ly was a la - dy Last night she died, Toll the bell for love - ly Nell, My sweet Vir - gin - ny bride.

NEW YORK GIRLS (CAN'T YOU DANCE THE POLKA?)

19th Century American

1. Oh, ship - mates, lis - ten un - to me, I'll tell you in my song of things that hap - pened to me when I come home from Hong Kong. ___
2. As I walked down to Chat - ham Street, a fair maid I did meet, who asked me please to see her home; she lived on Bleeck - er Street. ___
3. "Now if you'll on - ly come with me, _____ you can have a treat. You can have a glass of bran - dy and some - thing to eat. _____
4. Be - fore we sat _____ down to eat _____ we had sev - 'ral drinks. The liq - uor was so aw - ful strong I quick - ly fell a - sleep. _____
5. When I a - woke next morn - ing _____ I had an ach - ing head. My gold watch and my pock - et - book and la - dy friend had fled. _____
6. On look - ing 'round this lit - tle room, ___ noth - ing could I see but a wom - an's shoes and a - pron, _____ which now be - long to me. _____
7. Now dressed in a la - dy's a - pron, _____ I wan - dered most for - lorn, till Mar - tin Chur - chill took me in and sent me 'round Cape Horn. ___

To me way, you San - ty, my dear An - nie. Oh, you New York girls, can't you dance the pol - ka?

NEW RIVER TRAIN

American

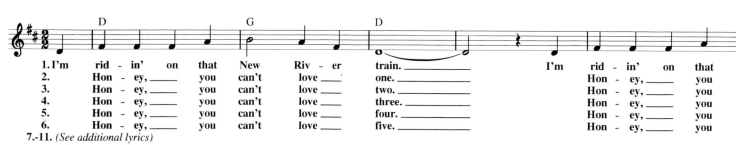

1. I'm rid - in' on that New Riv - er train. _____ I'm rid - in' on that
2. Hon - ey, _____ you can't love ____ one. _____ Hon - ey, _____ you
3. Hon - ey, _____ you can't love ____ two. _____ Hon - ey, _____ you
4. Hon - ey, _____ you can't love ____ three. _____ Hon - ey, _____ you
5. Hon - ey, _____ you can't love ____ four. _____ Hon - ey, _____ you
6. Hon - ey, _____ you can't love ____ five. _____ Hon - ey, _____ you
7.-11. *(See additional lyrics)*

New Riv - er train. _____ The same old train that ____ brought me
can't love ____ one. _____ You can't love one and have an - y
can't love ____ two. _____ You can't love two and ____ still be
can't love ____ three. _____ You can't love three 'cause you'll be up a
can't love ____ four. _____ You can't love four or you'll be want - ing
can't love ____ five. _____ You can't love five and still be a -

here, gon - na car - ry me home a - gain. _____
fun. Hon - ey, you can't love ____ one. _____
true. Hon - ey, you can't love ____ two. _____
tree. Hon - ey, you can't love ____ three. _____
more. Hon - ey, you can't love ____ four. _____
live. Hon - ey, you can't love ____ five. _____

Additional Lyrics

7. Honey, you can't love six,
You can't love six, or you'll be in a fix.
Honey, you can't love six.

8. Honey, you can't love seven,
You can't love seven and still go to heaven.
Honey, you can't love seven.

9. Honey, you can't love eight,
You can't love eight and meet them at the gate.
Honey, you can't love eight.

10. Honey, you can't love nine,
You can't love nine and still be mine.
Honey, you can't love nine.

11. Honey, you can't love ten,
You can't love ten and sing it all again.
Honey, you can't love ten.

THE NEXT MARKET DAY

Irish

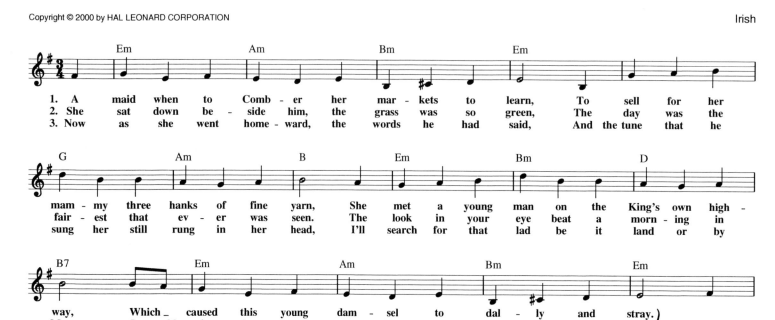

1. A maid when to Comb - er her mar - kets to learn, To sell for her
2. She sat down be - side him, the grass was so green, The day was the
3. Now as she went home - ward, the words he had said, And the tune that he

mam - my three hanks of fine yarn, She met a young man on the King's own high -
fair - est that ev - er was seen. The look in your eye beat a morn - ing in
sung her still rung in her head, I'll search for that lad be it land or by

way, Which _ caused this young dam - sel to dal - ly and stray.
May, I could sit by your side till the next mar - ket day.
sea, Till he learns me the tune to "The Next Mar - ket Day." } Come

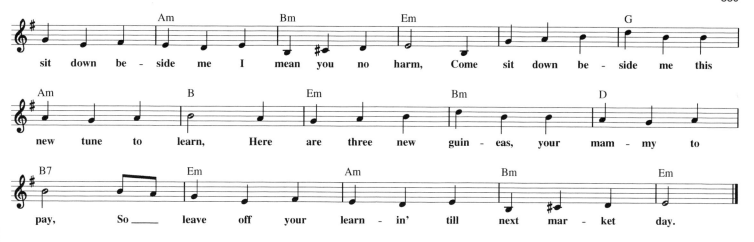

sit down be - side me I mean you no harm, Come sit down be - side me this
new tune to learn, Here are three new guin - eas, your mam - my to
pay, So ___ leave off your learn - in' till next mar - ket day.

NIGHT HERDING SONG

American Cowboy Song

1. Oh, slow up do - gies, quit mov - ing a - round, You have wan - dered and
2. Oh say, lit - tle do - gies, when you goin' to lay down? And ___ give up this
3. Lay still, lit - tle do - gies, since you have laid down, And ___ stretch a - way

tram - pled all o - ver the ground. Oh, graze a - long do - gies and feed kind of
shift - ing and rov - ing a - round? My horse is leg - wea - ry and I'm aw - ful
out on the big o - pen ground. Snore loud, lit - tle do - gies, and drown the wild

slow, And don't for - ev - er be on the go. Move slow, lit - tle
tired, But if you get a - way I am sure to get fired. Lay down, lit - tle
sound That will go a - way when the day rolls a - round. Lay still, lit - tle

do - gies, move slow, _____
do - gies, lay down, _____   Hi - o, hi - o, _____ hi - o. _____
do - gies, lay still, _____

NO HIDING PLACE

American

1. No hid - ing place down there,   No hid - ing place down
2. The rock cried, "I'm burn - ing too."   The rock cried, "I'm burn - ing
3. Sin - ner man he stum - bled and he fell. Sin - ner man he stum - bled and he

there,   Ran to the rock to hide my face,)
too.   I   want to go to heav - en the same as you." } The
fell.   Want - ed to go to heav - en but he had to go to hell.)

rock cried out, "No hid - ing place." No hid - ing place down there.

NINE HUNDRED MILES

American Blues

NINE MILES FROM GUNDAGAI

19th Century Australian

NINE POUND HAMMER

American

1. This nine - pound ham - mer _____ is a lit - tle too heav - y _____
2. Up on the moun - tain _____ just to see ___ my hon - ey _____
3. Ain't no - bod - y's ham - mer _____ in ___ this moun - tain _____
4. It rings like sil - ver _____ and ___ shines ___ like gold, _____
5. It's a long way to Haz - ard, _____ it's a long ___ way to Har - len _____

Hon - ey for my size, _____ hon - ey for my size.
And I ain't com - ing back, _____ Lord, I ain't com - ing back.
That ___ rings like mine, _____ that ___ rings like mine.
It ___ rings like sil - ver _____ and ___ shines like gold.
Just to get a lit - tle booze, _____ just to get a lit - tle booze.

So roll on bud - dy _____ Don't you roll ___ so slow.

How can I roll _____ When the wheels won't go.

NO MORE BOOZE

American Nonsense Song

1. There was a lit - tle man and he had a lit - tle can, And he used to rush the
2. The cham - ber - maid came ___ to _____ my ___ door, "Get ___ up, you la - zy

growl - er; He went to the sa - loon on a Sun - day af - ter - noon, And you
sin - ner, We need _____ those ___ sheets for _____ ta - ble - cloths, And it's

ought to heard the bar - ten - der hol - ler: _____ No more booze, no more booze,
al - most ___ time for _____ din - ner." _____

no more booze on Sun - day; No more booze, no more booze, Got to get your can filled

Mon - day. She's the on - ly girl I love, _____ With a face like a horse and bug - gy.

Lean - ing up a - gainst the lake, O fire - man! save ___ my child!

NO IRISH NEED APPLY

Irish

1. I'm a de-cent boy just land-ed from the town of Bal-ly
2. I _____ start-ed out to find the house, I got it might-y
3. I _____ could-n't stand it long-er so a-hold of him I

fad, _____ I want a sit-u-a-tion, yes, I want it ver-y
soon, _____ There I found the old chap seat-ed, he was read-ing the Tri-
took, _____ And gave him such a welt-ing as he'd get at Don-ny-

bad. I have seen em-ploy-ment ad-ver-tised, "'tis just the thing," says
bune. I _____ told him what I came for, when he in a rage did
brook. He _____ hol-lered, "Mil-lia, Mur-ther," and to get a-way did

I, _____ But the dirt-y spal-peen end-ed with, "No I-rish need ap-
fly, _____ "No," he says, "You are a Pad-dy, and no I-rish need ap-
try, _____ And swore he'd nev-er write a-gain, "No I-rish need ap-

ply." "Whoa!" says I, "but that's an in-sult, tho' to get the place I'll
ply." Then I gets my dan-der ris-ing And I'd like to black his
ply." Well, he made a big a-pol-o-gy, I bid him then good-

try," _____ So I went to see this black-guard with his "No I-rish need ap-
eye, _____ To tell an I-rish gen-tle-man, ___ "No I-rish need ap-
bye, Say-ing when next you want a beat-ing, write ___ "No I-rish need ap-

ply."
ply." } Some do count it a mis-for-tune to be chris-tened Pat or Dan, But to
ply."

me it is an hon-or to be born an I-rish-man. _____

NORAH O'NEALE

Irish, County Derry

I'm _____ lone-ly to-night, love, with-out you, _____ And my

love I can nev-er con-ceal, For they say there's a charm, love a-

NONE CAN LOVE LIKE AN IRISHMAN

Irish

NOBODY KNOWS THE TROUBLE I'VE SEEN

African-American Spiritual

NOBODY'S BUSINESS

Jamaican

O HOW I LOVE JESUS

American
Words by Frederick Whitfield

O SOLDIER

English

O NO, JOHN!

English

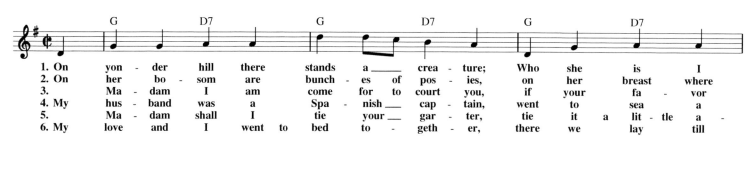

1. On yon - der hill there stands a _____ crea - ture; Who she is I
2. On her bo - som are bunch - es of pos - ies, on her breast where
3. Ma - dam I am come for to court you, if your fa - vor
4. My hus - band was a Spa - nish _____ cap - tain, went to sea a
5. Ma - dam shall I tie your _____ gar - ter, tie it a lit - tle a -
6. My love and I went to bed to - geth - er, there we lay till

do not know. I'll go and court her for her ___ beau - ty, She must an - swer
flow - ers grow. If I should chance to touch that ___ pos - y, She must an - swer
I can gain. If you ___ will but en - ter - tain me, per - haps then I might
month; a - go. The ver - y last time we kissed and ___ part - ed, bid me al - ways
bove your knee? If my hand should slip a lit - tle ___ far - ther, would you think it a -
cocks did crow. Un - close your arms my dear - est ___ jew - el, un - close your arms and

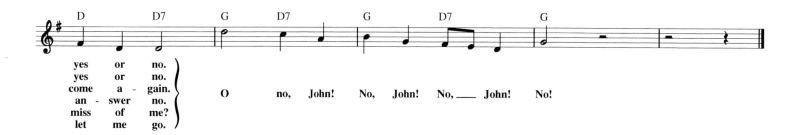

yes or no.
yes or no.
come a - gain. } O no, John! No, John! No, ___ John! No!
an - swer no.
miss of me?
let me go.

O WALY, WALY
(The Water Is Wide)

English

1. The wa - ter is wide, I can - not get o'er _____ and nei - ther
2. I put my ___ hand in - to one soft bush, _____ think - ing the
3. I leaned my ___ back up a - gainst some oak, _____ think - ing it
4. Must I be _____ bound, O, and he go free, _____ must I love
5. O love is _____ hand - some and love is fine, _____ and love is

have I wings to fly. _____ O go and get me
sweet - est flow'r to _____ find. _____ I prick'd my ___ fin - ger
was a trust - y _____ tree. _____ But first he ___ bend - ed
one that don't love ___ me! _____ Why should I _____ act such a
charm - ing when it is true. _____ As it grows ___ old - er it

some lit - tle boat _____ to car - ry o'er my true love and I. _____
to the ___ bone, _____ and left the sweet - est flow'r a - lone. _____
and then he broke, _____ so did my love prove false to ___ me. _____
child - ish ___ part, _____ and love a man that will break my ___ heart. _____
grow - eth ___ cold - er and fades a - way like the morn - ing dew. _____

O'DONNELL ABOO

Michael Joseph McCann
Irish, circa 1840s

THE OAK AND THE ASH

17th Century English

OATS, PEAS, BEANS AND BARLEY GROW

American Game Song

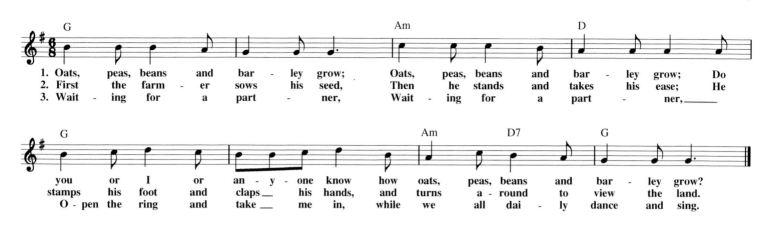

1. Oats, peas, beans and bar - ley grow; Oats, peas, beans and bar - ley grow; Do
2. First the farm - er sows his seed, Then he stands and takes his ease; He
3. Wait - ing for a part - ner, Wait - ing for a part - ner,___

you or I or an - y - one know how oats, peas, beans and bar - ley grow?
stamps his foot and claps __ his hands, and turns a - round to view the land.
O - pen the ring and take __ me in, while we all dai - ly dance and sing.

OH, BRANDY, LEAVE ME ALONE

South African

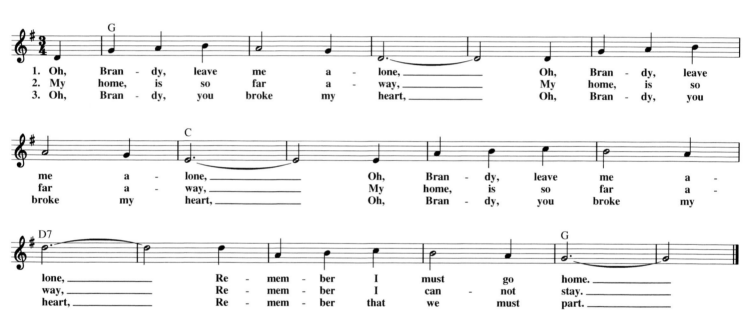

1. Oh, Bran - dy, leave me a - lone, ___ Oh, Bran - dy, leave
2. My home, is so far a - way, ___ My home, is so
3. Oh, Bran - dy, you broke my heart, ___ Oh, Bran - dy, you

me a - lone, ___ Oh, Bran - dy, leave me a -
far a - way, ___ My home, is so far a -
broke my heart, ___ Oh, Bran - dy, you broke my

lone, ___ Re - mem - ber I must go home. ___
way, ___ Re - mem - ber I can - not stay.
heart, ___ Re - mem - ber that we must part.

OH, DADDY BE GAY

American version of an English Folksong

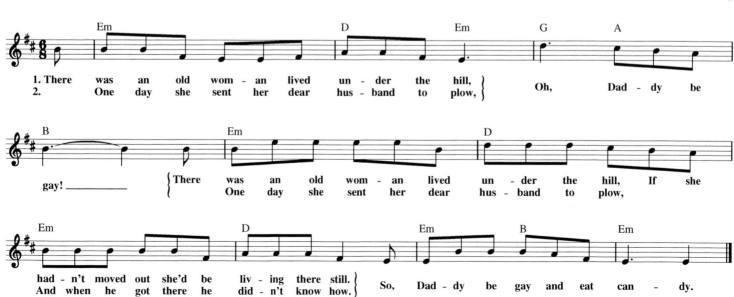

1. There was an old wom - an lived un - der the hill, } Oh, Dad - dy be
2. One day she sent her dear hus - band to plow, }

gay! ___ { There was an old wom - an lived un - der the hill, If she
One day she sent her dear hus - band to plow,

had - n't moved out she'd be liv - ing there still. } So, Dad - dy be gay and eat can - dy.
And when he got there he did - n't know how. }

OH DEAR! WHAT CAN THE MATTER BE?

369

Traditional American

Oh, dear! What can the mat-ter be? Dear, dear, what can the mat-ter be?

Oh, dear! What can the mat-ter be? John-ny's so long at the fair.
1. He
2. He

prom-ised to buy me a trin-ket to please me, and then for a smile, oh he vowed he would tease me; he
prom-ised to bring me a bas-ket of po-sies, a gar-land of lil-ies, a gar-land of ros-es, a

prom-ised to bring me a bunch of blue rib-bons to tie up my bon-nie brown hair.
lit-tle straw hat to set off the blue rib-bons that tie up my bon-nie brown hair.

OH! SUSANNA

Words and Music by
Stephen C. Foster
First published 1848

1. I come from Al-a-bam-a with a ban-jo on my knee. I'm
2. I had a dream the oth-er night when ev-'ry-thing was still. I

goin' to Lou'-si-an-a my Su-san-na for to see. It
thought I saw Su-san-na a-com-ing down the hill. The

rained all night the day I left, the weath-er it was dry. The
buck-wheat cake was in her mouth, the tear was in her eye. Say

sun so hot I froze to death, Su-san-na don't you cry.
I, "I'm com-ing from the south, Su-san-na don't you cry.

Oh! Su-san-na, oh don't you cry for me, for I

come from Al-a-bam-a with a ban-jo on my knee.

OH, FREEDOM

African-American Spiritual

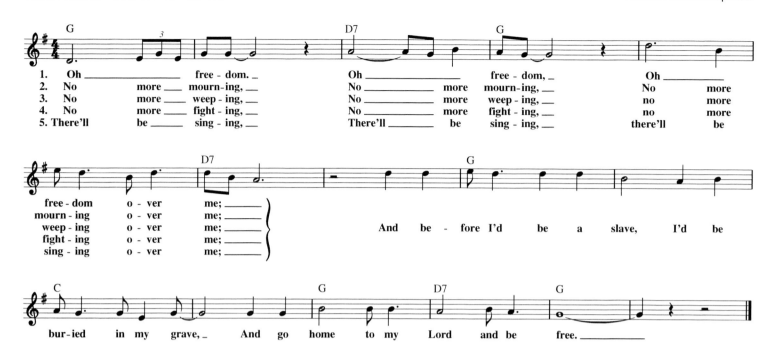

1. Oh _____ free - dom. _
2. No more _____ mourn-ing, _
3. No more _____ weep - ing, _
4. No more _____ fight - ing, _
5. There'll be _____ sing - ing, _

Oh _____ free - dom, _
No _____ more mourn-ing, _
No _____ more weep - ing, _
No _____ more fight - ing, _
There'll _____ be sing - ing, _

Oh _____
No more
no more
no more
there'll be

free - dom o - ver me; _____
mourn - ing o - ver me; _____
weep - ing o - ver me; _____
fight - ing o - ver me; _____
sing - ing o - ver me; _____

And be - fore I'd be a slave, I'd be

bur-ied in my grave, _ And go home to my Lord and be free. _____

OH HOW LOVELY IS THE EVENING

American Camp Song

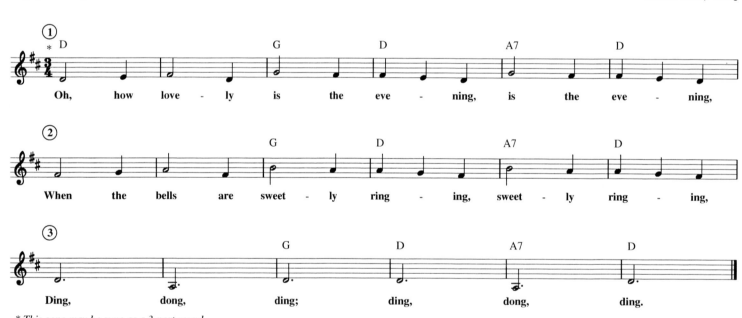

Oh, how love - ly is the eve - ning, is the eve - ning,

When the bells are sweet - ly ring - ing, sweet - ly ring - ing,

Ding, dong, ding; ding, dong, ding.

This song may be sung as a 3-part round.

OH MARY, DON'T YOU WEEP

American Gospel Song

Oh Mar - y, don't you weep, don't you mourn, Oh Mar - y, don't you

weep, don't you mourn. Phar-aoh's ar - my got drown - ded, Oh Mar - y, don't you weep.

371

1. If I could I sure-ly would _ Stand on the rock where Mo - ses stood.
2. Won-der what Sa - tan's grum-blin' 'bout, _ Chained in _____ Hell and he can't get out.
3. Sa - tan's mad and I am glad, _ Missed that _____ soul he thought he had.
4. I went down in the val - ley to pray, My soul got hap-py and stayed all day.

Phar-aoh's ar - my got drown - ded. Oh, Mar - y, don't you weep.

OH, THEM GOLDEN SLIPPERS

Copyright © 2000 by HAL LEONARD CORPORATION

Words and Music by
James A. Bland, 1879

1. Oh, my gold - en slip - pers are ___ laid a - way, 'Cause I don't 'spect to wear 'em 'til my
2. Oh, my old ban - jo ___ hangs _ on the wall, 'Cause it ain't been _ tuned _ since _
3. So, it's good - bye chil - dren, I will have to go, Where the rain don't _ fall ___ and the

wed - ding day, And my long - tailed coat that I love so well, I will
way last fall, But the folks all say we will have a good time, when we
wind don't blow, And your uls - ter coats, why, you will not need, when you

wear up in the char - iot in the morn; And my long white robe ___ that I
ride up in the char - iot in the morn; There's old Bro - ther Ben ___ and ___
ride up in the char - iot in the morn; But your gold - en slip - pers must be

bought last June, I'm ___ goin' to get changed 'case it fits too soon, And the
Sis - ter Luce, They will tele - graph the news to un - cle 'Bac - co Juice, What a
nice and clean, And our age must _ be just ___ sweet six - teen, And you're

ole gray horse that I used to drive, I will hitch him to the char - iot in the
great camp meetin' there will be that day, When we ride up in the char - iot in the
white kid gloves you will have to wear, When you ride up in the char - iot in the

morn.
morn. Oh, them gold - en slip-pers! Oh, them gold - en slip-pers! Gold - en slip-pers I'm
morn.

goin' to wear be - cause they look so neat; Oh, them gold - en slip-pers! Oh, them

gold - en slip-pers! Gold - en slip-pers I'm goin' to wear, to walk the gold - en street.

OH ROWAN TREE

Scottish
Words by Lady Carolina Nairne

1. Oh_ row-an tree, oh row-an tree, thou'lt aye be dear to me,__ En - twin'd thou art wi' mo-ny ties, o'
2. How. fair wert thou in sim-mer time, wi' all thy clus-ters white,_ how_ rich and gay thy au-tumn dress, wi'
3. We_ sat a-neath thy spread-ing shade, the bair-nies round thee ran.__ They_ pu'd thy bon-nie ber-ries red and
4. Oh,_ there a-rose my fa-ther's pray'r in ho - ly eve-ning's calm,_ how_ sweet was then my mith-er's voice__

hame and in - fan-cy. Thy leaves were aye the first of spring, thy flow'rs the sim-mer's pride;_ There_
ber - ries red and bright. On thy fair stem were mo - ny names which now nae mair_ I_ see.__ But,__
neck-lac - es they strang. My mith - er oh, I see her still, she smild our sports_ to_ see. __ Wi'__
in the mar - tyr's psalm. Now a' are gane! We meet nae mair a - neath the row - an_ tree.__ But__

was nae sic a bon - nie tree, in all the coun - try side.
there en - grav - en on my heart, for - got they ne'er can be.
lit - tle Jean - nie on her lap, wi' Ja - mie at her knee.
hal - lowed thoughts a - round thee twine o' hame and in - fan-cy.

Oh _ row - an tree!

OH, SINNER MAN

African-American Spiritual

1. Oh, sin - ner man, where you gon - na run to, Oh, sin - ner
2. Run to the rock, the rock was a - melt - ing, Run to the
3. Run to the sea, the sea was a - boil - ing, Run to the
4. Run to the moon, the moon was a - bleed - ing, Run to the
5. Run to the Lord, Lord, ___ won't you hide me, Run to the
6. Oh, sin - ner man, you ought - ta been a - pray - ing, Oh, sin - ner

man, where you gon - na run to, Oh, sin - ner man,
rock, the rock was a - melt - ing, Run to the rock,
sea, the sea was a - boil - ing, Run to the sea,
moon, the moon was a - bleed - ing, Run to the moon,
Lord, Lord, ___ won't you hide me, Run to the Lord,
man, you ought - ta been a - pray - ing, Oh, sin - ner man, you

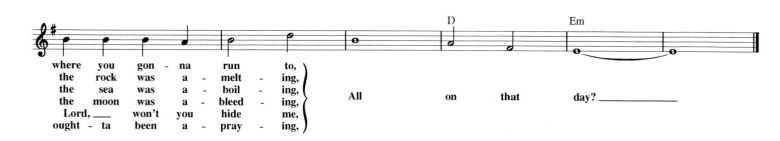

where you gon - na run to,
the rock was a - melt - ing,
the sea was a - boil - ing,
the moon was a - bleed - ing,
Lord, ___ won't you hide me,
ought - ta been a - pray - ing,

All on that day? ___

OH WHERE, OH WHERE HAS MY LITTLE DOG GONE

American

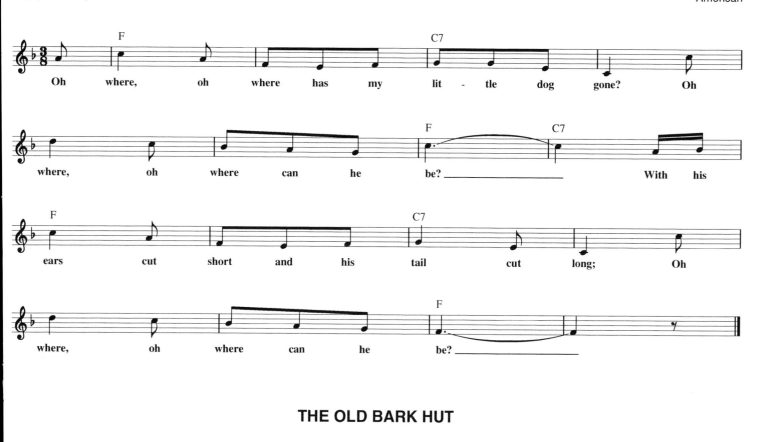

THE OLD BARK HUT

Australian

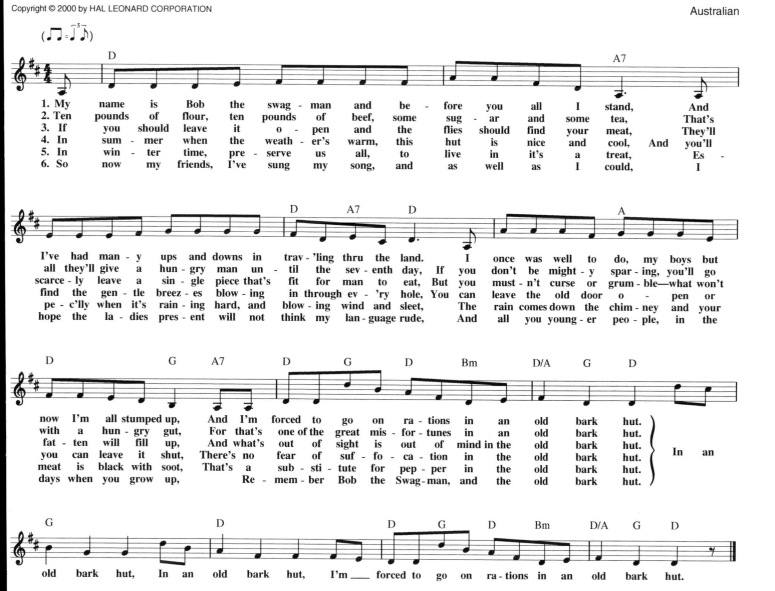

OH, WON'T YOU SIT DOWN?

African-American Spiritual

Oh, won't you sit down? Lord, I can't sit down. _ Oh, won't you sit down? Lord, I

can't sit down. _ Oh, won't you sit down? Lord, I can't sit down, _ 'Cause I just got to heav-en, goin' to

look a - round. ___
1. Who's that yon - der dressed in red? _ Must be the chil-dren that _
2. Who's that yon - der dressed in blue? _ Must be the chil-dren that are

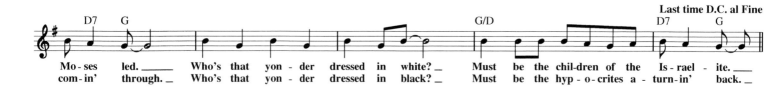

Mo - ses led. ___ Who's that yon - der dressed in white? _ Must be the chil-dren of the Is - rael - ite. ___
com-in' through. _ Who's that yon - der dressed in black? _ Must be the hyp - o-crites a - turn-in' back. _

THE OLD ARK'S A-MOVERIN'

African-American Spiritual

Oh the old ark's a - mov - er - in', a - mov - er - in', a - mov - er - in', The

old ark's a - mov - in' by the spir - it of God. Oh the old ark's a - mov - er - in', a -

mov - er - in', a - mov - er - in'. The old ark's a - mov - er - in' and I thank God.

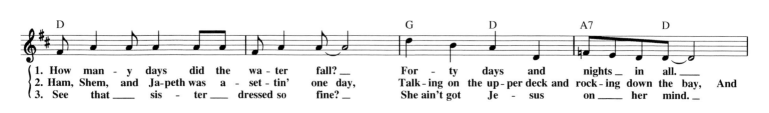

1. How man - y days did the wa - ter fall? _ For - ty days and nights _ in all. ___
2. Ham, Shem, and Ja-peth was a - set - tin' one day, Talk-ing on the up-per deck and rock-ing down the bay, And
3. See that _ sis - ter _ dressed so fine? _ She ain't got Je - sus on _ her mind. _

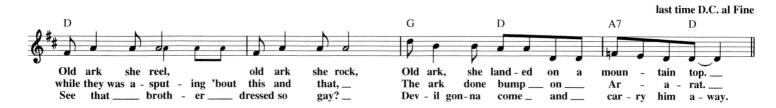

Old ark she reel, old ark she rock, Old ark, she land - ed on a moun - tain top. _
while they was a - sput - ing 'bout this and that, _ The ark done bump _ on _ Ar - a - rat. _
See that _ broth - er _ dressed so gay? _ Dev - il gon-na come _ and _ car - ry him a - way.

OLD AUNT KATE

American Children's Song

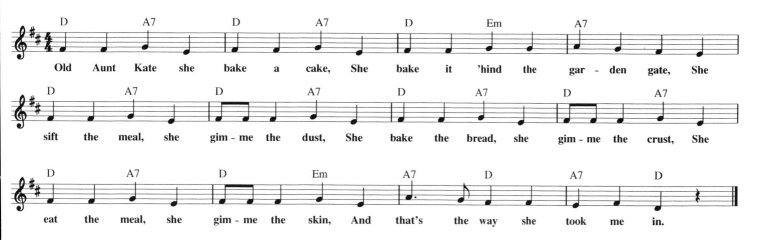

Old Aunt Kate she bake a cake, She bake it 'hind the gar - den gate, She
sift the meal, she gim - me the dust, She bake the bread, she gim - me the crust, She
eat the meal, she gim - me the skin, And that's the way she took me in.

OLD BLUE

19th Century Southern American

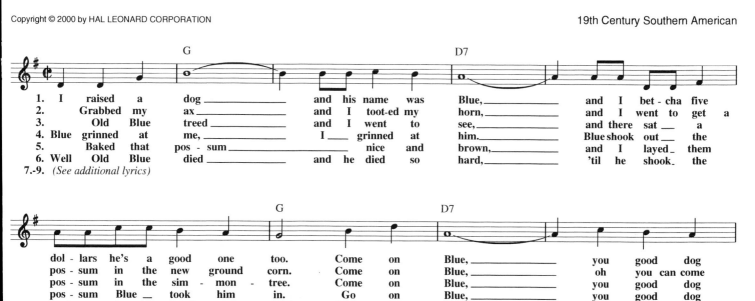

1. I raised a dog _____ and his name was Blue, _____ and I bet - cha five
2. Grabbed my ax _____ and I toot - ed my horn, _____ and I went to get a
3. Old Blue treed _____ and I went to see, _____ and there sat __ a
4. Blue grinned at me, _____ I __ grinned at him. _____ Blue shook out __ the
5. Baked that pos - sum _____ nice and brown, _____ and I layed_ them
6. Well Old Blue died _____ and he died so hard, _____ 'til he shook. the

7.-9. *(See additional lyrics)*

dol - lars he's a good one too. Come on Blue, _____ you good dog
pos - sum in the new ground corn. Come on Blue, _____ oh you can come
pos - sum in the sim - mon - tree. Come on Blue, _____ you good dog
pos - sum Blue _ took him in. Go on Blue, _____ you good dog
sweet po - ta - toes round and round. Come on Blue, _____ you can have some
ground _ in _ my back - yard. Go on Blue, _____ you good dog

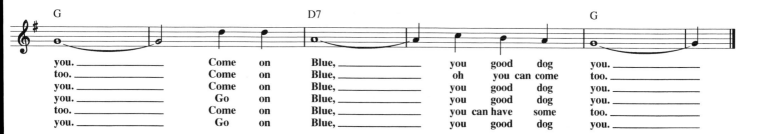

you. _____ Come on Blue, _____ you good dog you. _____
too. _____ Come on Blue, _____ oh you can come too. _____
you. _____ Come on Blue, _____ you good dog you. _____
you. _____ Go on Blue, _____ you good dog you. _____
too. _____ Come on Blue, _____ you can have some too. _____
you. _____ Go on Blue, _____ you good dog you. _____

Additional Lyrics

7. Old Blue died and I layed him in the shade.
   I dug his grave with a silver spade.
   Go on Blue, you good dog you. *(2 times)*

8. Lowered him down with a golden chain,
   And link by link slipped through my hand.
   Go on Blue, you good dog you. *(2times)*

9. There's just one thing disturbs my mind,
   Old Blue's gone to heaven and left me behind.
   Go on Blue I'm comin' too. *(2 times)*

OLD BLACK JOE

Stephen C. Foster
1860

1. Gone are the days when my heart was young and gay, gone are my friends from the
2. Why do I weep when my heart should feel no pain, why do I sigh that my
3. Where are the hearts once so hap - py and so free, The chil - dren so dear that I

cot - ton fields a - way, gone from the earth to a bet - ter land I know.
friends come not a - gain, griev - ing for forms now de - part - ed long a - go?
held up - on my knee? Gone to the shore where my soul has longed to go.

I

hear their gen - tle voic - es call - ing "Old Black Joe." I'm com - ing, I'm com - ing, for my

head is bend - ing low; I hear those gen - tle voic - es call - ing "Old Black Joe."

THE OLD CHISHOLM TRAIL

Texas Cowboy Song

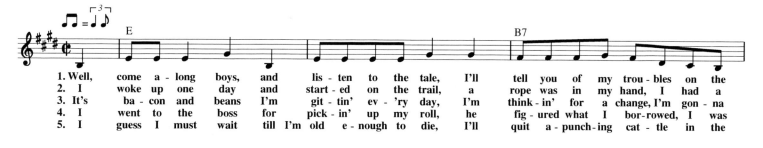

1. Well, come a - long boys, and lis - ten to the tale, I'll tell you of my trou - bles on the
2. I woke up one day and start - ed on the trail, a rope was in my hand, I had a
3. It's ba - con and beans I'm git - tin' ev - 'ry day, I'm think - in' for a change, I'm gon - na
4. I went to the boss for pick - in' up my roll, he fig - ured what I bor - rowed, I was
5. I guess I must wait till I'm old e - nough to die, I'll quit a - punch - ing cat - tle in the

old Chis - holm trail,
cow by the tail.
eat prai - rie hay.   Come-a ti yi yip - py, yip - py yay, yip - py yay, Come-a ti yi yip - py, yip - py yay.
nine in the hole.
sweet by and by.

THE OLD COW DIED

American

The old cow ___ died, Sail a - round, The old cow ___ died,

Sail a - round, The old cow ___ died, Sail a - round, The

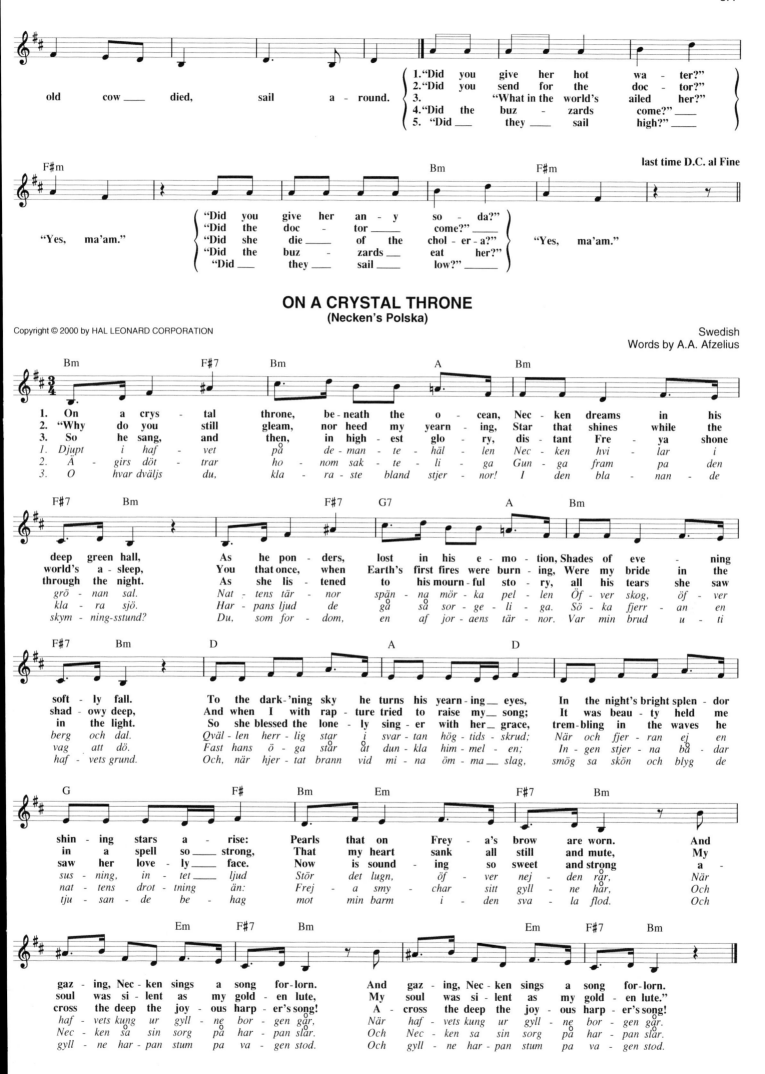

old cow___ died, sail a - round.

1. "Did you give her hot wa - ter?"
2. "Did you send for the doc - tor?"
3. "What in the world's ailed her?"
4. "Did the buz - zards come?"___
5. "Did___ they___ sail high?"___

"Yes, ma'am."

last time D.C. al Fine

"Did you give her an - y so - da?"
"Did the doc - tor___ come?"
"Did she die___ of the chol - er - a?"
"Did the buz - zards___ eat her?"
"Did___ they___ sail___ low?"___

"Yes, ma'am."

ON A CRYSTAL THRONE
(Necken's Polska)

Copyright © 2000 by HAL LEONARD CORPORATION

Swedish
Words by A.A. Afzelius

1. On a crys - tal throne, be - neath the o - cean, Nec - ken dreams in his
2. "Why do you still gleam, nor heed my yearn - ing, Star that shines while the
3. So he sang, and then, in high - est glo - ry, dis - tant Fre - ya shone

1. Djupt i haf - vet på de - man - te - häl - len Nec - ken hvi - lar i
2. Ä - girs döt - trar ho - nom sak - te - li - ga Gun - ga fram pa den
3. O hvar dväljs du, kla - ra - ste bland stjer - nor! I den bla - nan - de

deep green hall, As he pon - ders, lost in his e - mo - tion, Shades of eve - ning
world's a - sleep, You that once, when Earth's first fires were burn - ing, Were my bride in the
through the night. As she lis - tened to his mourn - ful sto - ry, all his tears she saw

grö - nan sal. Nat - tens tär - nor spän - na mör - ka pel - len Öf - ver skog, öf - ver
kla - ra sjö. Har - pans ljud de gå så sor - ge - li - ga. Sö - ka fjerr - an en
skym - ning-sstund? Du, som for - dom, en af jor - dens tär - nor. Var min brud u - ti

soft - ly fall. To the dark-'ning sky he turns his yearn - ing___ eyes, In the night's bright splen - dor
shad - owy deep, And when I with rap - ture tried to raise my___ song; It was beau - ty held me
in the light. So she blessed the lone - ly sing - er with her___ grace, trem-bling in the waves he

berg och dal. Qväl - len herr - lig star i svar - tan hög - tids - skrud; När och fjer - ran ej en
vag att dö. Fast hans ö - ga star åt dun - kla him - mel - en; In - gen stjer - na bå - dar
haf - vets grund. Och, när hjer - tat brann vid mi - na öm - ma___ slag, smög sa skön och blyg de

shin - ing stars a - rise: Pearls that on Frey - a's brow are worn. And
in a spell so___ strong, That my heart sank all still and mute, My
saw her love - ly___ face. Now is sound - ing so sweet and strong a -

sus - ning, in - tet___ ljud Stör det lugn, öf - ver nej - den rar, När
nat - tens drot - tning än: Frej - a smy - char sitt gyll - ne har, Och
tju - san - de be - hag mot min barm i den sva - la flod. Och

gaz - ing, Nec - ken sings a song for-lorn. And gaz - ing, Nec - ken sings a song for-lorn.
soul was si - lent as my gold - en lute, My soul was si - lent as my gold - en lute."
cross the deep the joy - ous harp - er's song! A - cross the deep the joy - ous harp - er's song!

haf - vets kung ur gyll - ne bor - gen går, När haf - vets kung ur gyll - ne bor - gen går.
Nec - ken sa sin sorg på har - pan slar. Och Nec - ken sa sin sorg på har - pan slar.
gyll - ne har - pan stum pa va - gen stod. Och gyll - ne har - pan stum pa va - gen stod.

OLD DAN TUCKER

American

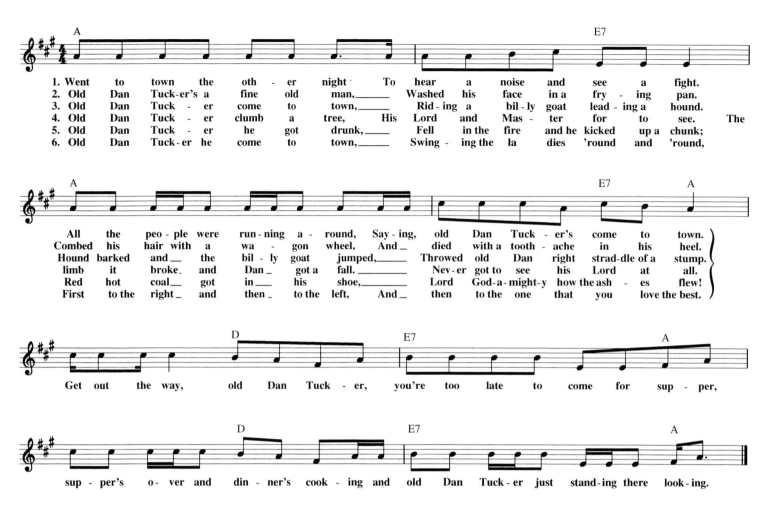

1. Went to town the oth - er night To hear a noise and see a fight.
2. Old Dan Tuck-er's a fine old man,____ Washed his face in a fry - ing pan.
3. Old Dan Tuck - er come to town,____ Rid - ing a bil - ly goat lead - ing a hound.
4. Old Dan Tuck - er clumb a tree, His Lord and Mas - ter for to see. The
5. Old Dan Tuck - er he got drunk,____ Fell in the fire and he kicked up a chunk;
6. Old Dan Tuck-er he come to town,____ Swing - ing the la dies 'round and 'round,

All the peo - ple were run - ning a - round, Say - ing, old Dan Tuck - er's come to town.
Combed his hair with a wa - gon wheel, And _ died with a tooth - ache in his heel.
Hound barked and _ the bil - ly goat jumped,____ Throwed old Dan right strad-dle of a stump.
limb it broke. and Dan _ got a fall. ____ Nev - er got to see his Lord at all.
Red hot coal _ got in _ his shoe,____ Lord God-a-might-y how the ash - es flew!
First to the right _ and then _ to the left, And _ then to the one that you love the best.

Get out the way, old Dan Tuck - er, you're too late to come for sup - per,

sup - per's o - ver and din - ner's cook - ing and old Dan Tuck - er just stand-ing there look - ing.

OLD DOG TRAY

Stephen C. Foster
1853

1. The morn of life is past, and eve - ning comes at last; it
2. The forms I called my own have van - ished one by one, the
3. When thoughts re - call the past, his eyes are on me last; I

brings me a dream of a once hap - py day, of mer - ry forms I've
lov'd ones, the dear ones have all passed a - way. Their hap - py smiles have
know that he feels what my break-ing heart would say. Al - though he can - not

seen up - on the vil - lage green, sport - ing with my old dog Tray.____
flown, their gen - tle voic - es gone; I've noth - ing left but old dog Tray.____
speak, I'll vain - ly, vain - ly seek a bet - ter friend than old dog Tray.____

Old dog Tray's ev - er faith - ful, grief can - not

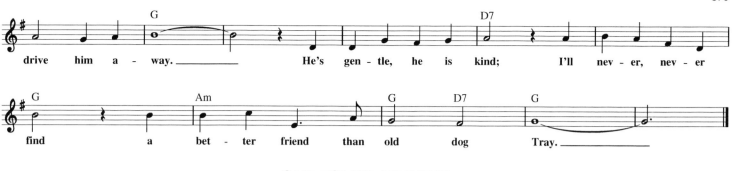

drive him a - way. _____ He's gen - tle, he is kind; I'll nev - er, nev - er

find a bet - ter friend than old dog Tray. _____

OLD FOLKS AT HOME

Words and Music by
Stephen C. Foster
1851

1. Way down up - on the Swan - ee riv - er, Far, far a - way,
2. All 'round the lit - tle farm I wan - der'd, When I was young;
3. One lit - tle hut a - mong the bush - es, One that I love,

There's where my heart is turn - ing ev - er; There's where the old folks stay. All up and down the
Then man - y hap - py days I squan - der'd, Man - y the songs I sung. When I was play - ing
Still sad - ly to my mem - 'ry rush - es, No mat - ter where I rove. When shall I see the

whole cre - a - tion, Sad - ly I roam, Still long - ing for the old plan - ta - tion,
with my broth - er, Hap - py was I, Oh, take me to my kind old moth - er,
bees a hum - ming, All 'round the comb? When shall I hear the ban - jo strum - ming,

And for the old folks at home.)
There let me live and _ die.) All the world is sad and drear - y Ev - 'ry - where I
Down in my good old _ home.)

roam, Oh, how my heart is grow - ing wea - ry, Far from the old folks at home. _____

THE OLD GRAY MARE

Tennessee Folksong

Oh the old gray mare, she ain't what she used to be, Ain't what she used to be, Ain't what she used to be. The

old gray mare, She ain't what she used to be, man - y long years a - go.

Man - y long years a - go, Man - y long years a - go, Oh the

THE OLD GOSPEL SHIP

American Gospel Song

1. I have good news to bring and that is why I sing, All my joys with
2. O I can scarce-ly wait, I know I'll not be late, For I'll spend my
3. If you're a-shamed of me, you have no cause to be, For with Christ I

you ____ I'll share; _____ I'm going to take a trip in the Old Gos-pel
time ____ in prayer; _____ And when my ship comes in I will leave this world of
am ____ an heir; _____ If too much fault you find, you will sure be left be-

ship and go sail - ing through the air. _____ O
sin and go sail - ing through the air. _____
hind, While I go sail - ing through the air. _____

I'm gon-na take a trip in the good Old Gos-pel Ship, I'm go-ing far be-

yond ____ the sky; _____ O I'm gon-na shout and sing un-

til the heav-ens ring, When I'm bid-ding this world good - by. _____

OLD JOE CLARK

Tenessee Folksong

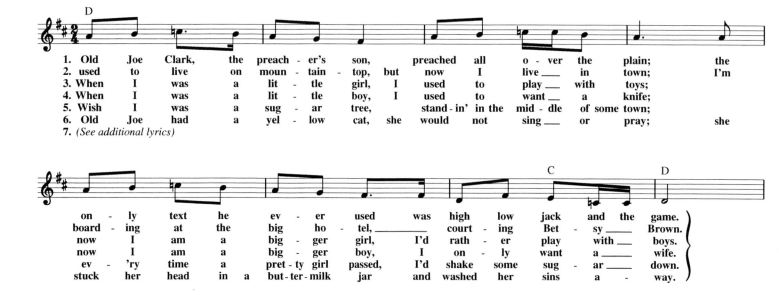

1. Old Joe Clark, the preach-er's son, preached all o-ver the plain; the
2. used to live on moun-tain-top, but now I live ____ in town; I'm
3. When I was a lit-tle girl, I used to play ____ with toys;
4. When I was a lit-tle boy, I used to want ____ a knife;
5. Wish I was a sug-ar tree, stand-in' in the mid-dle of some town;
6. Old Joe had a yel-low cat, she would not sing ____ or pray; she
7. *(See additional lyrics)*

on - ly text he ev - er used was high low jack and the game.
board - ing at the big ho - tel, _____ court - ing Bet - sy ____ Brown.
now I am a big - ger girl, I'd rath - er play with ____ boys.
now I am a big - ger boy, I on - ly want a ____ wife.
ev - 'ry time a pret-ty girl passed, I'd shake some sug - ar ____ down.
stuck her head in a but-ter-milk jar and washed her sins a - way.

Chorus

'Round and a - round, Old Joe Clark, 'round and a - round, I say; He'd
fol - low me ten thou - sand miles to hear my fid - dle play. (2.) I play.

Additional Lyrics

7. I wish I had a sweetheart;
   I'd set her on the shelf,
   And ev'ry time she'd smile at me
   I'd get up there myself.
   Chorus

OLD MacDONALD HAD A FARM

American Folksong

1. Old Mac - Don - ald had a farm E - I - E - I - O! And
2.-10. *(See additional lyrics)*

on this farm he had a duck, E - I - E - I - O! With a

quack - quack here, and a quack - quack there, Here a quack, there a quack, Ev - 'ry-where a quack, quack.

Old Mac - Don - ald had a farm, E - I - E - I - O!

Additional Lyrics

2. Old MacDonald had a farm,
   E - I - E - I - O!
   And on this farm he had a chick,
   E - I - E - I - O!
   With a chick, chick here
   And a chick, chick there,
   Here a chick, there a chick,
   Everywhere a chick, chick
   Old MacDonald had a farm,
   E - I - E - I - O!

Other verses:

3. Cow — moo, moo
4. Dogs — bow, bow
5. Pigs — oink, oink
6. Rooster — cock-a-doodle, cock-a-doodle
7. Turkey — gobble, gobble
8. Cat — meow, meow
9. Horse — neigh, neigh
10. Donkey — hee-haw, hee-haw

OLD OAKEN BUCKET

Words by Samuel Woodworth
Music by Edwin Krallmark

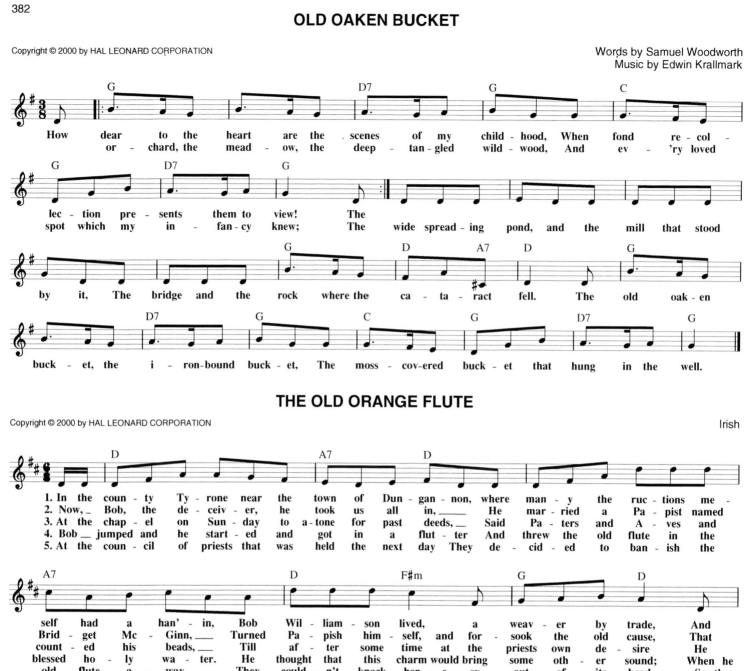

How dear to the heart are the scenes of my child - hood, When fond re - col -
or - chard, the mead - ow, the deep - tan - gled wild - wood, And ev - 'ry loved

lec - tion pre - sents them to view! The
spot which my in - fan - cy knew; The wide spread - ing pond, and the mill that stood

by it, The bridge and the rock where the ca - ta - ract fell. The old oak - en

buck - et, the i - ron-bound buck - et, The moss - cov-ered buck - et that hung in the well.

THE OLD ORANGE FLUTE

Irish

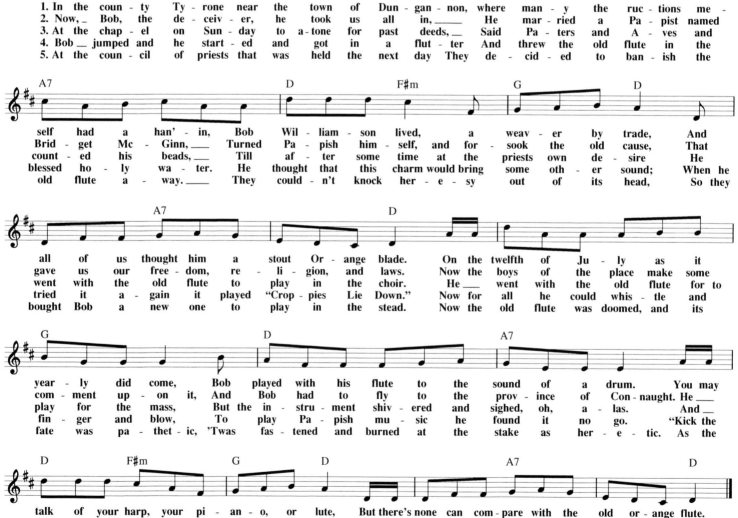

1. In the coun - ty Ty - rone near the town of Dun - gan - non, where man - y the ruc - tions me -
2. Now, Bob, the de - ceiv - er, he took us all in, He mar - ried a Pa - pist named
3. At the chap - el on Sun - day to a - tone for past deeds, Said Pa - ters and A - ves and
4. Bob jumped and he start - ed and got in a flut - ter And threw the old flute in the
5. At the coun - cil of priests that was held the next day They de - cid - ed to ban - ish the

self had a han' - in, Bob Wil - liam - son lived, a weav - er by trade, And
Brid - get Mc - Ginn, Turned Pa - pish him - self, and for - sook the old cause, That
count - ed his beads, Till af - ter some time at the priests own de - sire He
blessed ho - ly wa - ter. He thought that this charm would bring some oth - er sound; When he
old flute a - way. They could - n't knock her - e - sy out of its head, So they

all of us thought him a stout Or - ange blade. On the twelfth of Ju - ly as it
gave us our free - dom, re - li - gion, and laws. Now the boys of the place make some
went with the old flute to play in the choir. He went with the old flute for to
tried it a - gain it played "Crop - pies Lie Down." Now for all he could whis - tle and
bought Bob a new one to play in the stead. Now the old flute was doomed, and its

year - ly did come, Bob played with his flute to the sound of a drum. You may
com - ment up - on it, And Bob had to fly to the prov - ince of Con - naught. He
play for the mass, But the in - stru - ment shiv - ered and sighed, oh, a - las. And
fin - ger and blow, To play Pa - pish mu - sic he found it no go. "Kick the
fate was pa - thet - ic, 'Twas fas - tened and burned at the stake as her - e - tic. As the

talk of your harp, your pi - an - o, or lute, But there's none can com - pare with the old or - ange flute.

OLD RATTLER

American

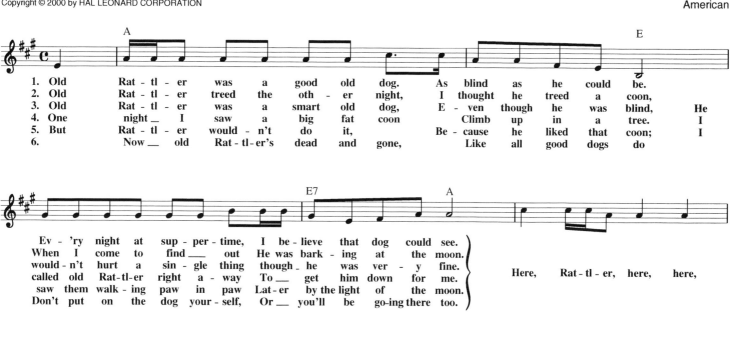

1. Old Rat - tl - er was a good old dog. As blind as he could be.
2. Old Rat - tl - er treed the oth - er night, I thought he treed a coon,
3. Old Rat - tl - er was a smart old dog, E - ven though he was blind, He
4. One night __ I saw a big fat coon Climb up in a tree. I
5. But Rat - tl - er would - n't do it, Be - cause he liked that coon; I
6. Now __ old Rat - tl - er's dead and gone, Like all good dogs do

Ev - 'ry night at sup - per - time, I be - lieve that dog could see.
When I come to find __ out He was bark - ing at the moon.
would - n't hurt a sin - gle thing though __ he was ver - y fine.
called old Rat - tl - er right a - way To __ get him down for me.
saw them walk - ing paw in paw Lat - er by the light of the moon.
Don't put on the dog your - self, Or __ you'll be go - ing there too.

Here, Rat - tl - er, here, here,

Here, Rat - tl - er, here, Call old Rat - tl - er from the barn, __ Here, Rat - tl - er, here.

ON A MONDAY

American

1. On a Mon - day, Mon - day I was ar - rest - ed, On a Tues - day
2. On a Fri - day me and my ba - by was a - walk - in', On a Sat - ur - day she
3. Take these stripes, __ stripes from a - round my shoul - der, Take these chains, __

locked up in jail. On a We'ns - day my trial was at - test - ed,
locked me out of doors. On a Sun - day we were sit - tin' down a - talk - in',
chains from a - round my leg. Lord, these stripes, __ stripes they sure don't wor - ry me,

On a Thurs - day __ no - bod - y would - n't go my bail. Well it's all,
On a Mon - day __ she __ pawned off all my clothes. __
But these chains __ chains __ gon - na kill me dead. __

al - most done. Well it's all, al - most done. Well it's

all, al - most done, And I ain't gon - na see them __ pret - ty girls no more.

OLD SOLDIERS NEVER DIE

American Army Song

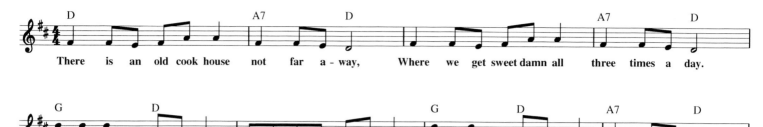

There is an old cook house not far a-way, Where we get sweet damn all three times a day.

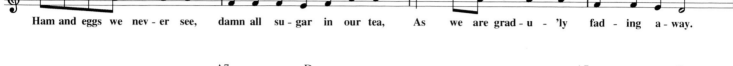

Ham and eggs we nev-er see, damn all su-gar in our tea, As we are grad-u-'ly fad-ing a-way.

Old sol-diers nev-er die, nev-er die, nev-er die, Old sol-diers nev-er die, They just fade a-way.

THE OLD TURF FIRE

Irish

1. Oh, the old turf fire ___ and the hearth swept clean, There is no one half so hap-py as my-
2. Oh, the man that I work for is a rich-er man than me, But ___ some-how in this world, ___ faith, we
3. I have got a lit-tle house ___ and a ti-dy bit of land. You would nev-er see a bet-ter one this

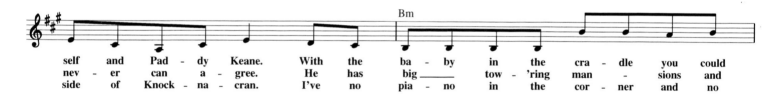

self and Pad-dy Keane. With the ba-by in the cra-dle you could
nev-er can a-gree. He has big ___ tow-'ring man-sions and
side of Knock-na-cran. I've no pia-no in the cor-ner and no

hear her mam-my say, "Would-n't you go to sleep, a-lan-na, till I wet your dad-dy's tay."
cas-tles o-ver all, But ___ sure I would-n't ex-change with him my lit-tle mar-ble hall.
pic-tures on the wall, But I'm ___ some-how quite con-tent-ed in my lit-tle mar-ble hall.

THE OLD WOMAN WHO WENT TO MARKET

New England version of an English Folksong

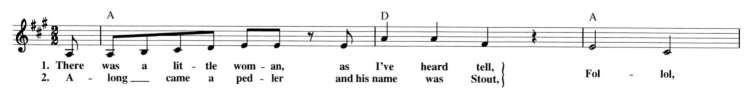

1. There was a lit-tle wom-an, as I've heard tell, Fol - lol,
2. A-long ___ came a ped-ler and his name was Stout,

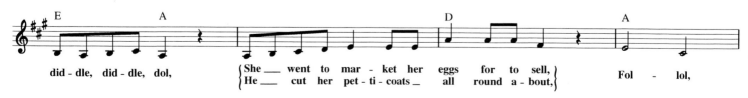

did-dle, did-dle, dol, She ___ went to mar-ket her eggs for to sell, Fol - lol,
He ___ cut her pet-ti-coats ___ all round a-bout,

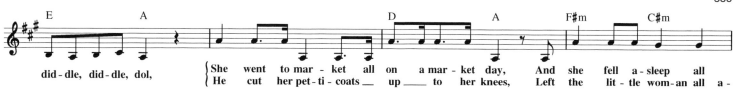

did - dle, did - dle, dol,

She went to mar - ket all on a mar - ket day, And she fell a - sleep all
He cut her pet - ti - coats __ up __ to her knees, Left the lit - tle wom - an all a -

on the King's high - way.
lone __ for to freeze.

Fol de rol de lol lol, lol lol lol, Fol - lol, did - dle, did - dle, dol.

THE OLE GREY GOOSE

19th Century American

1. Mon - day was my wed - ding day, Tues - day I was mar - ried, Wednes - day night my
2. Wednes - day night my wife took sick, de - spair of death come o'er her, Some did cry but

wife took sick, Sat' - day she was bur - ied.
I did laugh to see that death go from her.

Oh! Look - y here! Oh! Look - y where?

Look right o - ver yan - der. Don't you see the ole grey goose Smil - ing at the gan - der?

OLEANNA

Norwegian

Oh, to be in O - le - an - na, oh, the place for you and me. In O - le - an - na

we will live as if we are no - bil - i - ty. O - le, O - le - an - na.

O - le, O - le - an - na, O - le, O - le, O - le, O - le, O - le - an - na.

OMIE WISE

Folksong from North Carolina

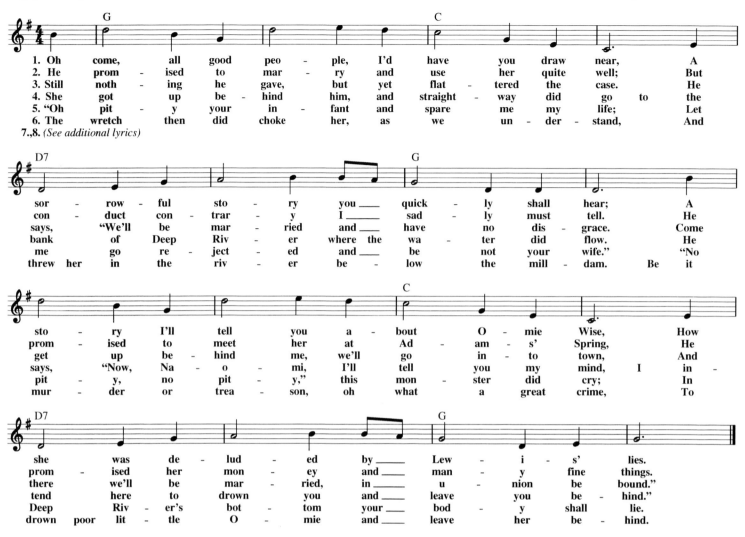

1. Oh come, all good peo - ple, I'd have you draw near, A
2. He prom - ised to mar - ry and use her quite well; But
3. Still noth - ing he gave, but yet flat - tered the case. He
4. She got up be - hind him, and straight - way did go to the
5. "Oh pit - y your in - fant and spare me my life; Let
6. The wretch then did choke her, as we un - der - stand, And
7.,8. (See additional lyrics)

sor - row - ful sto - ry you ___ quick - ly shall hear; A
con - duct con - trar - y I ___ sad - ly must tell. He
says, "We'll be mar - ried and ___ have no dis - grace. Come
bank of Deep Riv - er where the wa - ter did flow. He
me go re - ject - ed and ___ be not your wife." "No
threw her in the riv - er be - low the mill - dam. Be it

sto - ry I'll tell you a - bout O - mie Wise, How
prom - ised to meet her at Ad - am - s' Spring, He
get up be - hind me, we'll go in - to town, And
says, "Now, Na - o - mi, I'll tell you my mind, I in -
pit - y, no pit - y," this mon - ster did cry; In
mur - der or trea - son, oh what a great crime, To

she was de - lud - ed by ___ Lew - i - s' lies.
prom - ised her mon - ey and ___ man - y fine things.
there we'll be mar - ried, in ___ u - nion be bound."
tend here to drown you and ___ leave you be - hind."
Deep Riv - er's bot - tom your ___ bod - y shall lie.
drown poor lit - tle O - mie and ___ leave her be - hind.

Additional Lyrics

7. Omie was missing they all did well know,
   And hunting for her to the river did go;
   And there found her floating on the water so deep,
   Which caused all the people to sigh and to weep.

8. The neighbors were sent for to see the great sight,
   While she lay floating all that long night;
   So early next morning the inquest was held;
   The jury correctly the murder did tell.

ON JORDAN'S STORMY BANKS

Traditional American melody
Words by Samuel Stennett

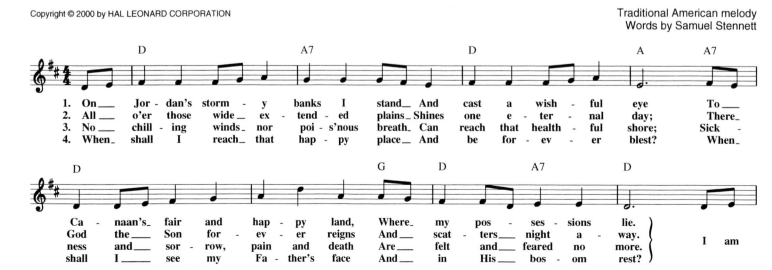

1. On ___ Jor - dan's storm - y banks I stand ___ And cast a wish - ful eye To ___
2. All ___ o'er those wide ___ ex - tend - ed plains ___ Shines one e - ter - nal day; There ___
3. No ___ chill - ing winds, nor poi - s'nous breath ___ Can reach that health - ful shore; Sick -
4. When ___ shall I reach ___ that hap - py place ___ And be for - ev - er blest? When ___

Ca - naan's ___ fair and hap - py land, Where ___ my pos - ses - sions lie.
God the ___ Son for - ev - er reigns And ___ scat - ters ___ night a - way.
ness and ___ sor - row, pain and death Are ___ felt and ___ feared no more.
shall I ___ see my Fa - ther's face And ___ in His ___ bos - om rest?

I am

bound for the Prom - ised Land,_____ I am bound for the Prom - ised Land. O ___

who will __ come and go with me? I am bound for the Prom - ised Land.

ON MONDAYS I NEVER GO TO WORK

English

On Mon - days I nev - er go to work. On Tues - days I

stay at home. On Wednes - days I nev - er feel in - clined. Work is the last thing

on my mind. On Thurs - days it's a hol - i - day, and Fri - days I de - test. It's too

late to make a start on Sat - ur - day and Sun - day is the day of rest.

ONCE I HAD A SWEETHEART

Southern Appalachian

1. Once I had a sweet - heart, now I have none. Once I had a
2. He was such a sweet - heart, oh! hap - py hours. When it was my
3. Once I had a sweet - heart, what have I now? Twen - ty doz - en

sweet - heart, now I have none.
birth - day, he brought me flow'rs.   } He's gone and left __ me, he's
mem - 'ries, one bro - ken vow.

gone and left __ me, he's gone and leaves me to sor - row and moan.

ON THE PARIS WAY
(Passant par Paris)

18th Century French Sea Chantey

1. On the Par - is way, Drink - ing all the way there, On the
2. "John, look out, look out, Some - one's got your girl there, John, go
3. She gave me her heart, None can take my place there, She gave
1. Pas - sant par Pa - ris, Vi - dant la bou - teil - le, Pas - sant
2. "Jean, prends garde à toi, L'on cour - tis' ta bel - le: Jean, prends
3. J'ai eu de son coeur La fleur la plus bel - le, J'ai eu

4.,5. *(See additional lyrics)*

Par - is way, drink - ing all the way there, Saw a pal from
home right now, some - one's got your girl there. I say, let it
me her heart, None can take my place there. In our big white
par Pa - ris, Vi - dant la bou - teil - le, Un de mes a -
garde à toi, L'on cour - tis' ta bel - le: Cour - tis' qui vou -
de son coeur La fleur la plus bel - le. Dans un grand lit

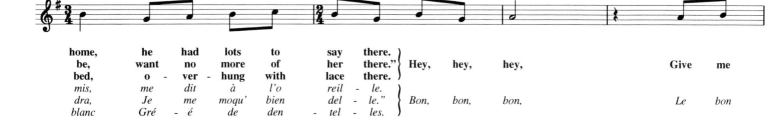

Refrain

home, he had lots to say there. ⎫
be, want no more of her there." ⎬ Hey, hey, hey, Give me
bed, o - ver - hung with lace there. ⎭
mis, me dit à l'o reil - le. ⎫
dra, Je me moqu' bien del - le." ⎬ Bon, bon, bon, Le bon
blanc Gré - é de den - tel - les. ⎭

wine to sleep, Love will wake me ear - ly, Give me wine to
vin m'en - dort, L'a - mour me ré - veil - le, Le bon vin m'en -

sleep, _____ Love will wake me up a - gain.
dort, _____ L'a - mour me ré - veille en - core.

Additional Lyrics

4. She gave me three sons,
   Captains one and all-o
   She gave me three sons,
   Captains one and all-o,
   At Bordeaux there's one,
   One at La Rochelle-o,
   Refrain

5. And the youngest there,
   Through the world does stray-o,
   And the youngest there,
   Through the world does stray-o,
   Like his father here,
   Drinking all the way-o,
   Refrain

4. *J'ai eu trois garçons,*
   Tous trois capitaines,
   J'ai eu trois garçons
   Tous trois capitaines,
   L'un est à Bordeaux,
   L'autre à La Rochelle,
   Refrain

5. *L'troisième à Paris,*
   Qui f'ra comm' son père,
   L'troisième à Paris,
   Qui f'ra comm' son père,
   Ira d'ville en bourg,
   Toujours buvant bouteille,
   Refrain

ON THE BANKS OF ALLAN WATER

Scottish

1. On the banks of Al - lan Wa - ter, When the sweet spring - time did fall, _____ Was the
2. On the banks of Al - lan Wa - ter, When the au - tumn spread its store, _____ There I
3. On the banks of Al - lan Wa - ter, When the win - ter snow fell fast, _____ Still was

mill - er's love - ly daugh - ter, Fair - est of them all. For his
saw the mill - er's daugh - ter, But she smiled no more. For the
seen the mill - er's daugh - ter, Chill - ing blew the blast. But the

bride a sol - dier sought her, And a win - ning tongue had he. _____ On the
sum - mer, grief had brought her, And the sol - dier, false was he. _____ On the
mill - er's love - ly daugh - ter, Both from cold and care was free, _____ On the

banks of Al - lan Wa - ter, So mis - led was she.
banks of Al - lan Wa - ter, Left a - lone was she.
banks of Al - lan Wa - ter, In a grave lay she.

OPHELIA LETTER BLOW 'WAY

Folksong from Trinidad

1. O - phe - lia let - ter blow 'way, _ it blow 'way in A - ri - ma. O -
2. O - phe - lia whe' you let - ter?_ it blow 'way in A - ri - ma. O -
3. O - phe - lia whe' you let - ter?_ it blow 'way in Cas - ta - ra. O -

phe - lia let - ter blow 'way, _ it blow 'way in A - ri - ma. It
phe - lia whe' you let - ter?_ it blow 'way in A - ri - ma. It
phe - lia whe' you let - ter?_ it blow 'way in Cas - ta - ra. It

blow 'way in A - ri - ma, it blow 'way in A - ri - ma. It
blow 'way in A - ri - ma, it blow 'way in A - ri - ma. It
blow 'way in Cas - ta - ra, it blow 'way in Cas - ta - ra. It

blow 'way in A - ri - ma, It blow 'way in A - ri - ma.
blow 'way in A - ri - ma, It blow 'way in A - ri - ma.
blow 'way in Cas - ta - ra, It blow 'way in Cas - ta - ra.

ON TOP OF OLD SMOKY

Kentucky Mountain Folksong

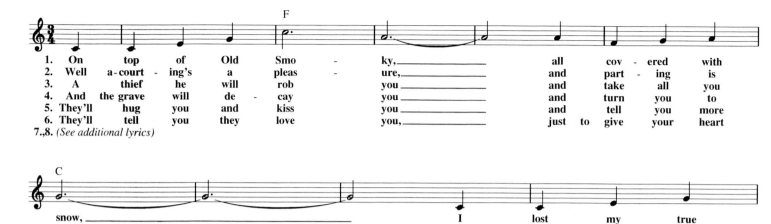

1. On top of Old Smo - ky, _____ all cov - ered with
2. Well a-court - ing's a pleas - ure, _____ and part - ing is
3. A thief he will rob you _____ and take all you
4. And the grave will de - cay you _____ and turn you to
5. They'll hug you and kiss you _____ and tell you more
6. They'll tell you they love you, _____ just to give your heart

7.,8. *(See additional lyrics)*

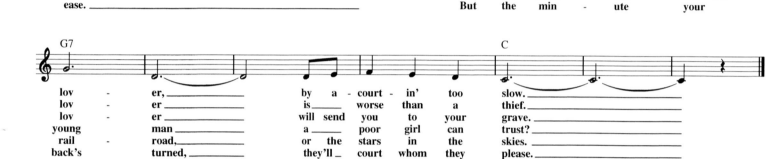

snow, _____ I lost my true
grief. _____ But a false - heart - ed
have, _____ but a false - heart - ed
dust. _____ And where is the
lies _____ than the cross - ties on the
ease. _____ But the min - ute your

lov - er, _____ by a - court - in' too slow. _____
lov - er _____ is _____ worse than a thief. _____
lov - er _____ will send you to your grave. _____
young man _____ a _____ poor girl can trust? _____
rail - road, _____ or the stars in the skies. _____
back's turned, _____ they'll _ court whom they please. _____

Additional Lyrics

7. So come all you young maidens
   And listen to me.
   Never place your affection
   On a green willow tree.

8. For the leaves they will wither
   And the roots they will die,
   And your true love will leave you,
   And you'll never know why.

ONE MAN SHALL MOW MY MEADOW

English Counting Song

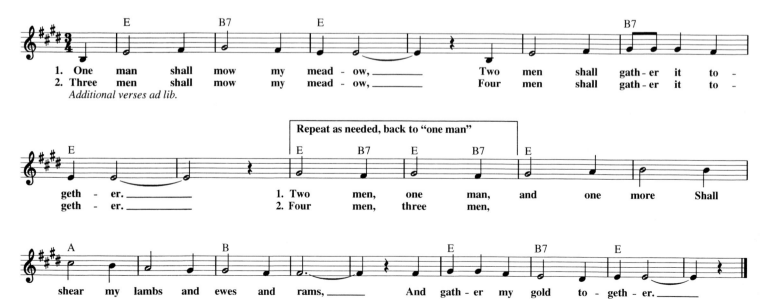

1. One man shall mow my mead - ow, _____ Two men shall gath - er it to -
2. Three men shall mow my mead - ow, _____ Four men shall gath - er it to -

Additional verses ad lib.

Repeat as needed, back to "one man"

geth - er. _____ 1. Two men, one man, and one more Shall
geth - er. _____ 2. Four men, three men,

shear my lambs and ewes and rams, _____ And gath - er my gold to - geth - er. _____

ONE MORE RIVER

American Gospel Song

1. Old No - ah once he built the Ark } There's one more riv - er to
   patched it up with hick - 'ry bark }

2.-13. *(See additional lyrics)*

cross. And cross.

Chorus
One more riv - er, _____ and that's the riv - er of Jor - dan, One more riv - er, _____ There's one more riv - er to cross.

Additional Lyrics

2. The animals went in one by one...
   The elephant chewing a caraway bun...
   Chorus

3. The animals went in two by two...
   The rhinoceros and the kangaroo...
   Chorus

4. The animals went in three by three...
   The bear, the flea and the bumble bee...
   Chorus

5. The animals went in four by four...
   Old Noah got mad and hollered for more...
   Chorus

6. The animals went in five by five...
   With Saratoga trunks they did arrive...
   Chorus

7. The animals went in six by six...
   The hyena laughed at the monkey's tricks...
   Chorus

8. The animals went in seven by seven...
   Said the ant to the elephant, who are you a-shovin'...
   Chorus

9. The animals went in eight by eight...
   They came with a rush 'cause 'twas so late...
   Chorus

10. The animals went in nine by nine...
    Old Noah shouted, "Cut that line!"
    Chorus

11. The animals went in ten by ten...
    The Ark she blew her whistle then...
    Chorus

12. And then the voyage did begin...
    Old Noah pulled the gang-plank in...
    Chorus

13. They never knew where they were at...
    Till the old Ark bumped on Ararat...
    Chorus

ONE MORE DAY

Sea Chantey

1. Oh ___ have you heard the news, my John - ny? one more ___ day! We're home - ward bound to -
2. Oh ___ heave and sight the an - chor, John - ny, one more ___ day! Oh heave and sight the
3. I'm ___ bound a - way to leave you, John - ny, one more ___ day! But I will not de -

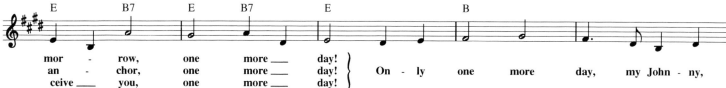

mor - row, one more ___ day! On - ly one more day, my John - ny,
an - chor, one more ___ day!
ceive ___ you, one more ___ day!

one more ___ day, oh rock and row me o - ver, one more ___ day.

OVER THE MOUNTAINS
(Love Will Find Out the Way)

17th Century English

1. O - ver the ___ moun - tains And ___ o - ver the waves,
2. When there is ___ no place For the glow - worm to lie,
3. You may es - teem him A ___ child ___ for his might;
4. Some think to lose him By ___ hav - ing him con - fined;
5. If earth it should part him, He would gal - lop it o'er;
6. There is no ___ striv - ing To ___ cross ___ his in - tent;

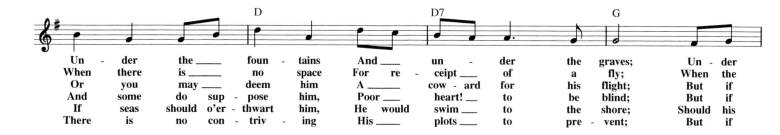

Un - der the ___ foun - tains And ___ un - der the graves; Un - der
When there is ___ no space For re - ceipt ___ of a fly; When the
Or you may ___ deem him A ___ cow - ard for his flight; But if
And some do sup - pose him, Poor ___ heart! ___ to be blind; But if
If seas should o'er - thwart him, He would swim ___ to the shore; Should his
There is no con - triv - ing His ___ plots ___ to pre - vent; But if

floods ___ that are deep - est, Which ___ Nep - tune o - bey, O - ver
midge ___ dares not ven - ture Lest her - self fast she ___ lay, If love
she whom love doth hon - or wall him, Be con - cealed from the ___ day, Set a
ne'er so close ye wall him, Do the best that ye ___ may, Blind
love be - come a swal - low, Through the bright air to ___ stray, Love will
once the mes - sage greet him That his true love doth ___ stay, If ___

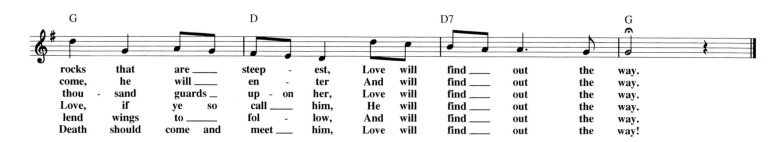

rocks that are ___ steep - est, Love will find ___ out the way.
come, he will ___ en - ter And will find ___ out the way.
thou - sand guards ___ up - on her, Love will find ___ out the way.
Love, if ye so call ___ him, He will find ___ out the way.
lend wings to ___ fol - low, And will find ___ out the way.
Death should come and meet ___ him, Love will find ___ out the way!

ONE MORNING IN MAY

American

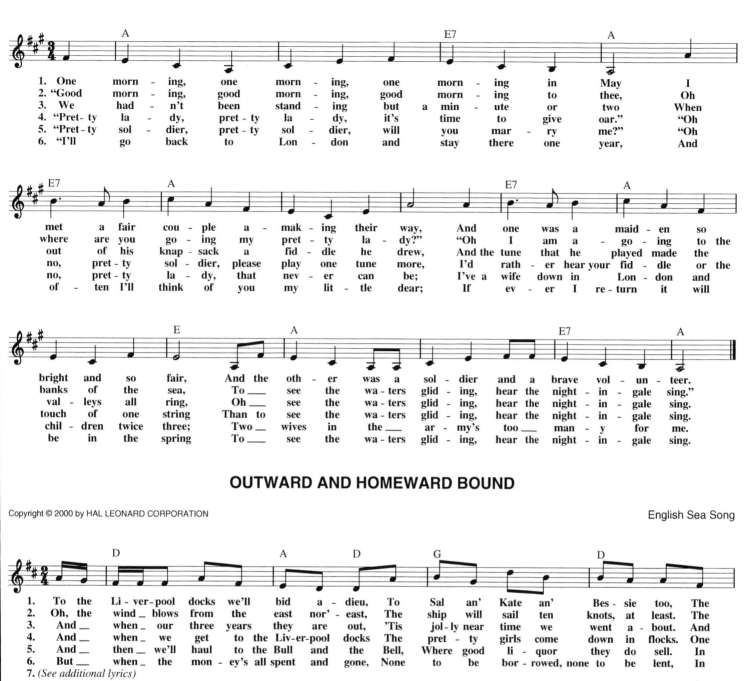

1. One morn - ing, one morn - ing, one morn - ing in May I
2. "Good morn - ing, good morn - ing, good morn - ing to thee, Oh
3. We had - n't been stand - ing but a min - ute or two When
4. "Pret - ty la - dy, pret - ty la - dy, it's time to give oar." "Oh
5. "Pret - ty sol - dier, pret - ty sol - dier, will you mar - ry me?" "Oh
6. "I'll go back to Lon - don and stay there one year, And

met a fair cou - ple a - mak - ing their way, And one was a maid - en so
where are you go - ing my pret - ty la - dy?" "Oh I am a - go - ing to the
out of his knap - sack a fid - dle he drew, And the tune that he played made the
no, pret - ty sol - dier, please play one tune more, I'd rath - er hear your fid - dle or the
no, pret - ty la - dy, that nev - er can be; I've a wife down in Lon - don and
of - ten I'll think of you my lit - tle dear; If ev - er I re - turn it will

bright and so fair, And the oth - er was a sol - dier and a brave vol - un - teer.
banks of the sea, To ___ see the wa - ters glid - ing, hear the night - in - gale sing."
val - leys all ring, Oh ___ see the wa - ters glid - ing, hear the night - in - gale sing.
touch of one string Than to see the wa - ters glid - ing, hear the night - in - gale sing.
chil - dren twice three; Two ___ wives in the ___ ar - my's too ___ man - y for me.
be in the spring To ___ see the wa - ters glid - ing, hear the night - in - gale sing.

OUTWARD AND HOMEWARD BOUND

English Sea Song

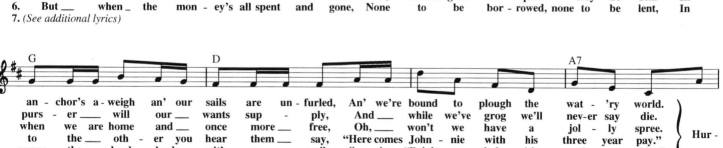

1. To the Li - ver - pool docks we'll bid a - dieu, To Sal an' Kate an' Bes - sie too, The
2. Oh, the wind ___ blows from the east nor' - east, The ship will sail ten knots, at least. The
3. And ___ when ___ our three years they are out, 'Tis jol - ly near time we went a - bout. And
4. And ___ when ___ we get to the Liv - er - pool docks The pret - ty girls come down in flocks. One
5. And ___ then ___ we'll haul to the Bull and the Bell, Where good li - quor they do sell. In
6. But ___ when ___ the mon - ey's all spent and gone, None to be bor - rowed, none to be lent, In

7. (See additional lyrics)

an - chor's a - weigh an' our sails are un - furled, An' we're bound to plough the wat - 'ry world.
purs - er ___ will our ___ wants sup - ply, And ___ while we've grog we'll nev - er say die.
when we are home and ___ once more ___ free, Oh, ___ won't we have a jol - ly spree.
to the ___ oth - er you hear them ___ say, "Here comes John - nie with his three year pay."
comes the ___ land - lord ___ with a ___ smile, Say - ing, "Drink up lads, it's worth your while."
comes the ___ land - lord ___ with a ___ frown, Say - ing, "Get up Jack, let John sit down."

Hur -

rah, we're out - ward bound, _____ Hur - rah, we're out - ward bound!

Additional Lyrics

7. Then poor old Jack must understand
   There's ships in port all wanting hands.
   He goes on board as he did before
   And he bids adieu to his native shore.

OTTO WOOD

Folksong from North Carolina

1. Step up bud - dies and listen to my song, I'll sing it to you right but you may sing it
2. He stepped in a pawn-shop on a rain - y day, And then he had a quar-rel with the clerk, they
3. They spread the news as fast as they could, The sher - iff served a war - rant on Ot - to
4. He was a man who could - n't run, For he al - ways tot - ed a for - ty - four
5. They put him in the pen but it did no good, 'Cause it would-n't hold a man they call Ot - to
6. He ram-bled out west and he ram-bled all a - round, Till he met two sher-iffs in a South - ern
7., 8. *(See additional lyrics)*

wrong. / say. / Wood. / gun. / Wood. / town.

The song a - bout a man they call Ot - to Wood. I
He pulled out his pis - tol and struck a fa - tal blow, And
The ju - ry said mur - der in the sec - ond de - gree, And the
He loved the wom - en and hat - ed the law, He
It was - n't ver - y long till he slipped out - side, Pulled a
They said, "Ot - to, step to the way, For

can't tell you all but I wish I could.
this is the way the sto - ry goes.
judge passed sen-tence to the pen - i-ten - tia - ry.
just did - n't take no - bod - y's jaw.
gun on the guard, said, "Take me for a ride."
we've been ex - pect - ing you ev - 'ry day."

Ot - to, why did - n't you run

Ot - to's done dead and gone.

Ot - to, why

did - n't you run when the sher - iff pulled out that for - ty - four gun.

Additional Lyrics

7. The second time they caught him was way out West
   In a holdup game he got shot through the breast
   They brought him back and when he got well
   They locked him down in a dungeon cell.

8. He pulled out his gun and then he said,
   "Make a crooked move and you both fall dead.
   You better crank up your car and take me out of town."
   But a few minutes later he was graveyard bound.

OVER THE RIVER AND THROUGH THE WOODS

19th Century American

O - ver the riv - er and thro' the woods, To grand - fa - ther's house we
O - ver the riv - er and thro' the woods, To have a first - rate
O - ver the riv - er and thro' the woods, And straight thro' the barn - yard

go; / play; / gate,

The horse knows the way to car - ry the sleigh, Thro' the
Oh hear the bells ring, "Ting - a - ling - ling!" Hur -
We seem to go ex - treme - ly slow It

D7 **G** **C**

white and drift - ed snow. _____ O - ver the riv - er and
rah for Thanks - giv - ing Day. _____ O - ver the riv - er and
is so hard to wait! _____ O - ver the riv - er and

F **C**

thro' the woods, Oh how the wind does blow! _____ It
thro' the woods, Trot fast my dap - ple gray! _____ Spring
thro' the woods, Now grand-moth - er's cap I spy! _____ Hur -

F **F#dim7** **C/G** **F** **Fm** **C** **G7** **C**

stings the toes. And bites the nose, As o - ver the ground we go. _____
o - ver the ground, Like a hunt - ing hound! For this is Thanks-giv - ing Day. _____
rah for the fun! Is the pud - ding done? Hur - rah for the pump - kin pie! _____

OVER THE WAVES

Juventino Rosas
1880

G **D7**

G

Am **G**

D7 **G** **Fine**

D7

G **E7**

Am **G** **D7** **G** **D.C. al Fine**

THE OX-DRIVING SONG

American

1. I pop my whip and I bring the blood, I make my lead - ers take the mud, ___
2. On the four - teenth day of Oc - to - ber - o, I hitched my team in or - der - o, ___
3. When I got there the ___ hills were steep, A ten - der - heart - ed per - son'd weep ___
4. When I get home I'll ___ have re - venge, I'll land my fam - i - ly a - mong my friends. ___

___ I grab the wheel _____ and I turn them a - round, _____ One
___ To drive the hills _____ of Sal - u - di - o, _____ To my
___ To hear me cuss _____ and ___ pop my ___ whip, _____ To
___ I'll bid a - dieu _____ to the whip and ___ line, _____ And

long, long pull and we're on high ground. }
roll, to my roll, to my ride - e - o. } To my roll, to my roll, to my ride - e - o, To my
see my ox - en ___ pull and slip. }
drive no more in the win - ter - time. }

roll, to my roll, to my ride - e - o, _____ To my ride - e - o, _____

___ to my ride - e - o, _____ To my roll, to my roll, to my ride - e - o.

PADDY AND THE WHALE

Sea Chantey from Newfoundland

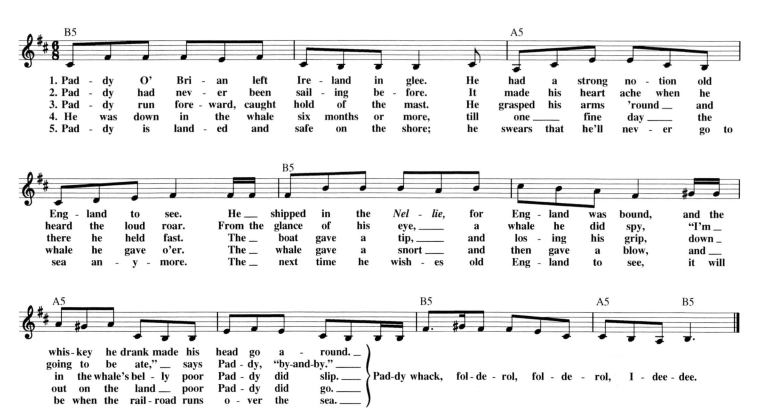

1. Pad - dy O' Bri - an left Ire - land in glee. He had a strong no - tion old
2. Pad - dy had nev - er been sail - ing be - fore. It made his heart ache when he
3. Pad - dy run fore - ward, caught hold of the mast. He grasped his arms 'round and
4. He was down in the whale six months or more, till one ___ fine day ___ the
5. Pad - dy is land - ed and safe on the shore; he swears that he'll nev - er go to

Eng - land to see. He ___ shipped in the *Nel - lie,* for Eng - land was bound, and the
heard the loud roar. From the glance of his eye, ___ a whale he did spy, "I'm
there he held fast. The ___ boat gave a tip, ___ and los - ing his grip, down ___
whale he gave o'er. The ___ whale gave a snort ___ and then gave a blow, and ___
sea an - y - more. The ___ next time he wish - es old Eng - land to see, it will

whis - key he drank made his head go a - round. _ }
going to be ate," ___ says Pad - dy, "by-and-by." ___ }
in the whale's bel - ly poor Pad - dy did slip. ___ } Pad - dy whack, fol - de - rol, fol - de - rol, I - dee - dee.
out on the land ___ poor Pad - dy did go. ___ }
be when the rail - road runs o - ver the sea. ___ }

PAPER OF PINS

19th Century American adaptation of an Irish Folksong

1. I'll give to you a pa - per of pins, and that's the way that love be - gins,
2. I'll give to you a coach __ and four, that you may ride from door to door,
3. I'll give to you a lit - tle lap dog to car - ry with you when you go a - broad,
4. I'll give to you a pac - ing horse that paced these hills from cross to cross,
5. I'll give to you a coach __ and six, with ev - 'ry horse as black as pitch,
6. I'll give to you a gown __ of green, that you may shine as an - y queen,

if

7.-13. *(See additional lyrics)*

you will mar - ry me, if you will mar - ry me. __

I'll
I'll
I'll
I'll
I'll
I'll

not ac - cept a pa - per of pins, if that's the way that love be - gins,
not ac - cept a coach __ and four, that I may ride from door to door,
not ac - cept a lit - tle lap dog to car - ry with me when I go a - broad,
not ac - cept a pac - ing horse that paced these hills from cross to cross,
not ac - cept a coach __ and six with ev - 'ry horse as black as pitch,
not ac - cept a gown __ of green, that I may shine as an - y queen,

and

I won't mar - ry you, and I won't mar - ry you. __

Additional Lyrics

7. I'll give to you a dress of red,
   All bound around with golden thread, *etc.*

8. I'll give to you a blue silk gown,
   With golden tassels all around, etc.

9. I'll give to you my hand and heart,
   That we may marry and never part, *etc.*

10. I'll give to you the keys of my chest,
    That you may have gold at your request,
    If you will marry me,
    If you will marry me.

11. Oh, yes, I'll accept the key to your chest,
    That I may have gold at my request,
    And I will marry you,
    And I will marry you.

12. And now I see that money is all,
    And woman's love is nothing at all;
    So I'll not marry you,
    So I'll not marry you.

13. I'm determined to be an old maid,
    Take my stool and live in the shade,
    And marry no one at all,
    And marry no one at all.

THE PAW PAW PATCH

Southern American Singing Game Song

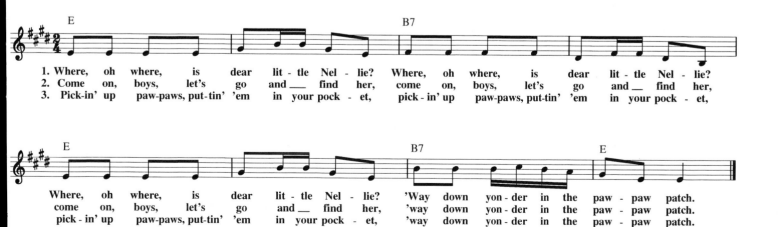

1. Where, oh where, is dear lit - tle Nel - lie? Where, oh where, is dear lit - tle Nel - lie?
2. Come on, boys, let's go and __ find her, come on, boys, let's go and __ find her,
3. Pick - in' up paw-paws, put - tin' 'em in your pock - et, pick - in' up paw-paws, put - tin' 'em in your pock - et,

Where, oh where, is dear lit - tle Nel - lie? 'Way down yon - der in the paw - paw patch.
come on, boys, let's go and __ find her, 'way down yon - der in the paw - paw patch.
pick - in' up paw-paws, put - tin' 'em in your pock - et, 'way down yon - der in the paw - paw patch.

THE PARTING GLASS

Irish

PAT-A-PAN
(Willie, Take Your Little Drum)

French
Words and Music by
Bernard de La Monnoye

PAY ME MY MONEY DOWN

Caribbean Work Song

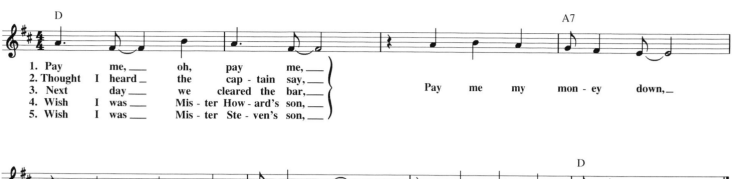

1. Pay me, ___ oh, pay me, ___
2. Thought I heard ___ the cap - tain say, ___
3. Next day ___ we cleared the bar, ___
4. Wish I was ___ Mis - ter How - ard's son, ___
5. Wish I was ___ Mis - ter Ste - ven's son, ___

Pay me my mon - ey down, ___

Pay me or go to jail, ___
'Mor - row is our sail - ing day, ___
He knocked me down with the end of a spar, ___
Sit in the house and drink all the rum, ___
Sit in the shade and watch all the work done, ___

Pay me my mon - ey down, ___

PEANUT SAT ON A RAILROAD TRACK

American Children's Song

A pea - nut sat on a rail - road track; his heart was all a - flut - ter. A -

long came a choo - choo train. (Instrumental)

Pea - nut ___ but - ter. (Instrumental)

PETER, PETER, PUMPKIN EATER

Nursery Rhyme Song

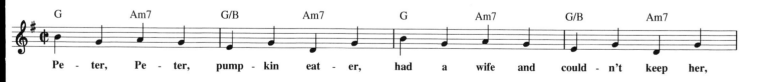

Pe - ter, Pe - ter, pump - kin eat - er, had a wife and could - n't keep her,

put her in a pump - kin shell, and there he kept her ver - y well.

PO' BOY

Southern American

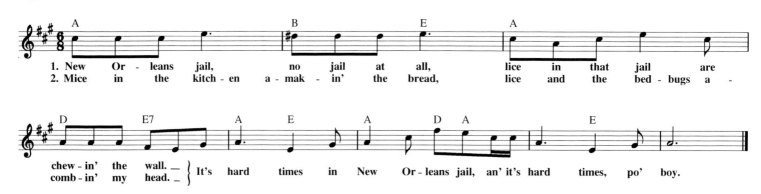

1. New Orleans jail, no jail at all, lice in that jail are
2. Mice in the kitchen a-makin' the bread, lice and the bedbugs a-

chewin' the wall. — } It's hard times in New Orleans jail, an' it's hard times, po' boy.
combin' my head. —

POLLY, PUT THE KETTLE ON

American Game Song

Polly, put the kettle on, Polly, put the kettle on,

Polly, put the kettle on, We'll all have tea.

Sukey, take it off again, Sukey, take it off again,

Sukey, take it off again, They've all gone away.

POLLY WOLLY DOODLE

Southern American

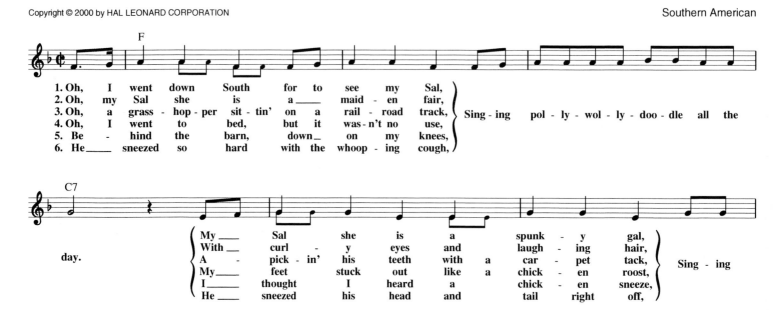

1. Oh, I went down South for to see my Sal,
2. Oh, my Sal she is a maiden fair,
3. Oh, a grasshopper sittin' on a railroad track,
4. Oh, I went to bed, but it wasn't no use,
5. Behind the barn, down on my knees,
6. He sneezed so hard with the whooping cough,

Singing polly-wolly-doodle all the day.

My Sal she is a spunky gal,
With curly eyes and laughing hair,
A-pickin' his teeth with a carpet tack,
My feet stuck out like a chicken roost,
I thought I heard a chicken sneeze,
He sneezed his head and tail right off,

Singing

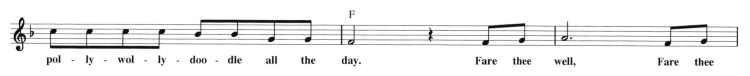

pol - ly - wol - ly - doo - dle all the day. Fare thee well, Fare thee

well, Fare thee well, my fair - y fay, For I'm goin' to Lou' - si - an - a for to

see my Su - zi - an - na, Sing - ing pol - ly - wol - ly - doo - dle all the day.

PREGUNTALES A LAS ESTRELLAS

Latin American

POOR BOY

American

1. As I went down to the riv - er, poor boy, to see the ships go by, _____ my
2. I fol - lowed her _____ for months _ and months; she of - fered me her hand. _____ We
3. He came at me with a big _____ jack - knife; I went for him with lead. _____ And
4. They took me to _____ the big _____ jail - house, the months and months rolled by. _____ The
5. "Oh do you bring _ me par - don, poor boy, to turn _____ me a - loose?" _____ "I
6. And yet they call _____ this jus - tice, poor boy, then jus - tice let it be. _____ I

sweet-heart stood on the deck of one where she waved to me _____ good - bye. _____
were just a - bout to be mar - ried, when she ran off with a gam - blin' man. _____
when _ the fight was o - ver, poor boy, he lay on the ground cold and dead. _____
ju - ry found me guil - ty, poor boy; the judge said you _____ must die. _____
bring _ you noth - ing," said _ the man, "ex - cept a hang - man's noose." _____
on - ly killed a man _ who was a - fix - in' to _____ kill me. _____

} Hang

down your head and cry, poor boy, Hang down your head and cry. _____ Stop

think - ing a - bout the wom - an you love. Hang down your head _ and cry. _____

POOR LAZARUS

Southern American

1. High Sher - iff told the dep - u - ty, "Go out and bring me _____
2. Oh bad man Laz - 'rus done broke in the com - mis - sar - y _____
3. Oh, dep - u - ty be - gin to won - der, where in the world he could
4. Oh, they found poor _____ Laz - 'rus way out be - tween two _____
5. Poor Laz - 'rus told the dep - u - ty he had nev - er been ar -
6. So they shot poor _____ Laz - 'rus, shot him with a great big _____

Laz - 'rus." High Sher - iff told the dep - u - ty, "Go out an' bring me _____
win - dow. Oh bad man Laz - 'rus done broke in the com - mis - sar - y _____
find him. Oh the dep - u - ty be - gin to won - der, where in the world he could
moun - tains. Oh, they found poor _____ Laz - 'rus way out be - tween two _____
rest - ed. Old Laz - 'rus told the dep - u - ty he had nev - er been ar -
num - ber. So they shot poor _____ Laz - 'rus, shot him with a great big _____

Laz - 'rus. Bring him dead or a - live. Lawd! Lawd! Bring him dead or a - live."
win - dow. Well _ he been paid off. Lawd! Lawd! Well he been paid _ off.
find him. Well _ I don't know. _ Lawd! Lawd! Well I just don't _ know.
moun - tains. And they blowed him down. _ Lawd! Lawd! And they blowed him _ down.
rest - ed by _____ no one man. _ Lawd! Lawd! By _____ no one _ man.
num - ber: num - ber for - ty - five. _____ Lawd! Lawd! Num - ber for - ty _____ five.

POOR LONESOME COWBOY

American

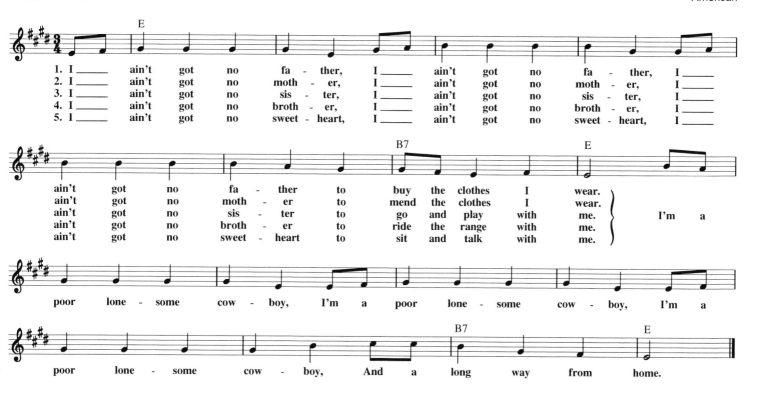

1. I _____ ain't got no fa - ther, I _____ ain't got no fa - ther, I _____
2. I _____ ain't got no moth - er, I _____ ain't got no moth - er, I _____
3. I _____ ain't got no sis - ter, I _____ ain't got no sis - ter, I _____
4. I _____ ain't got no broth - er, I _____ ain't got no broth - er, I _____
5. I _____ ain't got no sweet - heart, I _____ ain't got no sweet - heart, I _____

ain't got no fa - ther to buy the clothes I wear.
ain't got no moth - er to mend the clothes I wear.
ain't got no sis - ter to go and play with me.
ain't got no broth - er to ride the range with me.
ain't got no sweet - heart to sit and talk with me. } I'm a

poor lone - some cow - boy, I'm a poor lone - some cow - boy, I'm a

poor lone - some cow - boy, And a long way from home.

PRETTY POLLY

Mountain Song from Kentucky

1. I court - ed pret - ty Pol - ly the live - long _____ night, I court - ed pret - ty Pol - ly the
2. Pret - ty Pol - ly, pret - ty Pol - ly come go a - long with me. Pret - ty Pol - ly, pret - ty Pol - ly
3. She jumped on be - hind him and a - way they did go. She jumped on be - hind him and a -
4. They went a lit - tle furth - er and what did they spy. They went a lit - tle furth - er and
5. Oh, Wil - lie, oh _____ Wil - lie I'm a - fraid of your way. Oh, Wil - lie, oh _____ Wil - lie I'm a -
6. Pret - ty Pol - ly, pret - ty Pol - ly you've guessed a - bout right. Pret - ty Pol - ly, pret - ty Pol - ly

7.-11. *(See additional lyrics)*

live - long night, then left her next morn - ing be - fore it was light.
come go a - long with me, be - fore we get mar - ried some pleas - ures to see.
way they did go, o - ver the hills and the val - ley be - low.
what did they spy, a new dug _____ grave with a spade lay - ing by.
fraid of your way, I'm a - fraid you will lead my poor bod - y a - stray.
you've guessed a - bout right, for I slept on your grave the best part of last night.

Additional Lyrics

7. He throwed her on the ground and she broke into tears;
He throwed her on the ground and she broke into tears;
She throwed her arms around him and trembled with fear.

8. There's no time to talk now, there's no time to stand;
There's no time to talk now, there's no time to stand;
He drew out his knife all in his right hand.

9. He stabbed her in the heart and the blood it did flow;
He stabbed her in the heart and the blood it did flow,
And into the grave pretty Polly did go.

10. He put on a little dirt and he started for home;
Throwed on a little dirt and he started for home,
Leaving no one behind but the wild birds to moan.

11. A debt to the devil Willie must pay;
A debt to the devil Willie must pay;
For killing pretty Polly and running away.

POP GOES THE WEASEL

American Ring Game Song

1. All a - round the cob - bler's bench, The mon - key chased the wea - sel. The
2. Ru - fus has the whoop - ing cough, And Sal - ly has the mea - sles, And

mon - key thought 'twas all _____ in fun, }
that's the way the doc - tor goes, }
Pop! goes the wea - sel. A

pen - ny for a spool _____ of thread, A pen - ny for _____ a nee - dle.

That's the way the mon - ey goes, Pop! goes the wea - sel.

THE PRATIES, THEY GROW SMALL

Irish

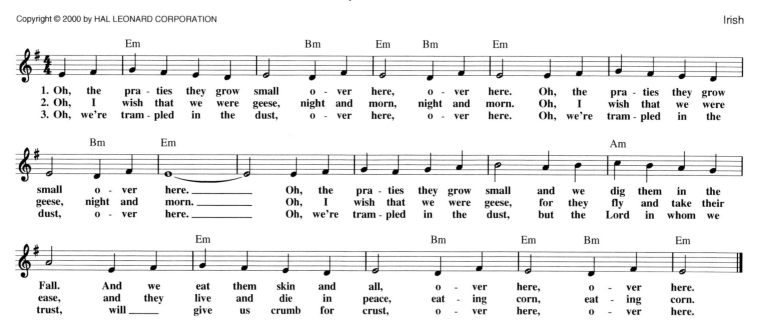

1. Oh, the pra - ties they grow small o - ver here, o - ver here. Oh, the pra - ties they grow
2. Oh, I wish that we were geese, night and morn, night and morn. Oh, I wish that we were
3. Oh, we're tram - pled in the dust, o - ver here, o - ver here. Oh, we're tram - pled in the

small o - ver here. _____ Oh, the pra - ties they grow small and we dig them in the
geese, night and morn. _____ Oh, I wish that we were geese, for they fly and take their
dust, o - ver here. _____ Oh, we're tram - pled in the dust, but the Lord in whom we

Fall. And we eat them skin and all, o - ver here, o - ver here.
ease, and they live and die in peace, eat - ing corn, eat - ing corn.
trust, will _____ give us crumb for crust, o - ver here, o - ver here.

THE PRETTY GIRL MILKING HER COW

Irish
Words by Thomas Moore

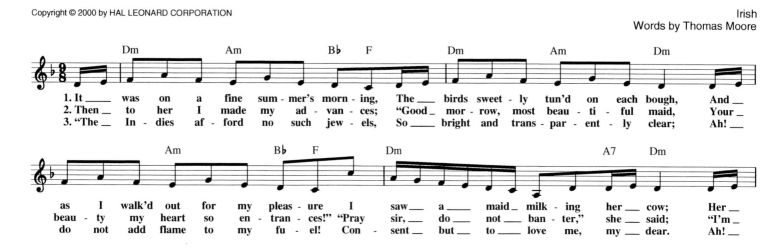

1. It _____ was on a fine sum - mer's morn - ing, The _____ birds sweet - ly tun'd on each bough, And _____
2. Then _ to her I made my ad - van - ces; "Good_ mor - row, most beau - ti - ful maid, Your _
3. "The _ In - dies af - ford no such jew - els, So _____ bright and trans - par - ent - ly clear; Ah! _____

as I walk'd out for my pleas - ure I saw_ a _ maid_ milk - ing her _ cow; Her _
beau - ty my heart so en - tran - ces!" "Pray sir, _ do _ not ban - ter," she _ said; "I'm _
do not add flame to my fu - el! Con - sent _ but to _ love me, my _ dear. Ah! _

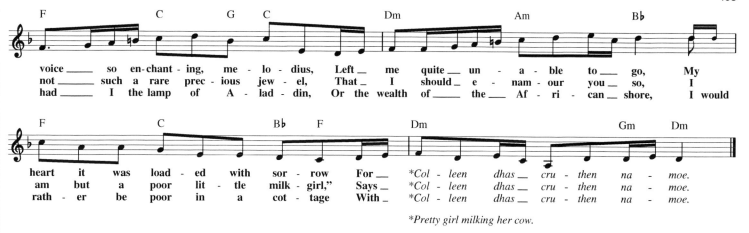

voice	so en-chant-ing,	me-lo-dius,	Left me	quite un-a-ble	to go,	My
not	such a rare prec-ious	jew-el,	That I	should e-nam-our	you so,	I
had	I the lamp of A-lad-din,	Or the wealth of	the	Af-ri-can	shore,	I would

heart	it was load-ed with	sor-row	For	*Col-leen dhas cru-then na-moe.
am	but a poor lit-tle	milk-girl,"	Says	*Col-leen dhas cru-then na-moe.
rath-er	be poor in a	cot-tage	With	*Col-leen dhas cru-then na-moe.

*Pretty girl milking her cow.

PRETTY LITTLE GIRL WITH THE RED DRESS ON

American Children's Song

Poor old How-ard's dead and gone, left me here to sing this song. Who's been here since I been gone, pret-ty lit-tle girl with the red dress on. Pret-ty lit-tle girl with the red dress on, _____ pret-ty lit-tle girl with the red dress _ on, _____ pret-ty lit-tle girl with the red dress on, who knows? Pret-ty lit-tle girl with the red dress _ on. _____

PRETTY SARO

Southern Appalachian

1. Down in some lone val-ley in a lone-some place where the wild birds do
2. My love she won't have me so ___ I un-der-stand. She ___ wants a free-
3. If I were a mer-chant and could write a fine hand, I'd ___ write my love a

whis-tle and their notes do in-crease, fare-well ___ pret-ty Sa-ro I ___
hold-er who ___ owns house and land. I can-not main-tain her with ___
let-ter that ___ she'd un-der-stand. I'd write her by the riv-er, where the

bid you a-dieu. And I'll dream of pret-ty Sa-ro where-ev-er I go.
sil-ver and gold. And all of the ___ fine things a big ___ house ___ can hold.
wa-ters o'er-flow. But I'll dream of pret-ty Sa-ro wher-ev-er I go.

PRISON BOUND

American

1. It was ear - ly one morn - in', Lord, ___ the blues came fall - in' down.
2.-4. *(See additional lyrics)*

It was ear - ly one morn-in', the blues ___ came fall - in' down. _____ I'm

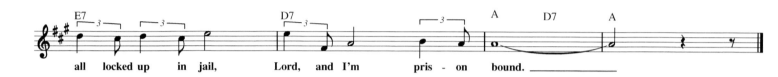

all locked up in jail, Lord, and I'm pris - on bound. _____

Additional Lyrics

2. It was all last night I sat in my cell and moaned.
It was all last night I sat in my cell and moaned.
Thinkin' about my baby, great God, and my happy home.

3. Now, baby, you will never see my smilin' face again.
Now, baby, you will never see my smilin' face again.
But you always can remember that your daddy has been your friend.

4. At my trial, baby, you could not be found.
At my trial, baby, you could not be found.
It's too late, mistreatin' woman, you know I'm prison bound.

A PRISONER FOR LIFE

American

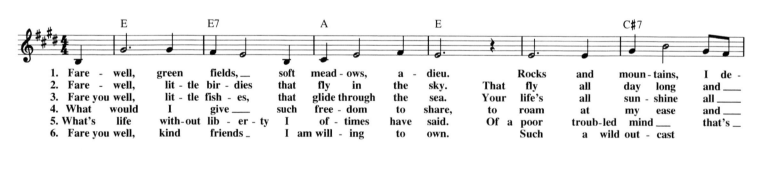

1. Fare - well, green fields, ___ soft mead - ows, a - dieu. Rocks and moun - tains, I de -
2. Fare - well, lit - tle bir - dies that fly in the sky. That fly all day long and ___
3. Fare you well, lit - tle fish - es, that glide through the sea. Your life's all sun - shine all ___
4. What would I give ___ such free - dom to share, to roam at my ease and ___
5. What's life with-out lib - er - ty I of - times have said. Of a poor troub-led mind ___ that's
6. Fare you well, kind friends ___ I am will - ing to own. Such a wild out - cast

part from ___ you. Nev - er - more shall my eyes by your beau - ty be
sing trou - bles by. I am doomed to this cell I ___ heave a deep
light, and all glee! Nev - er - more shall I watch your skill in the
breathe the fresh air. I would roam through the cit - ies, through the vil - lage and
al - ways in dread. No ___ sun, moon and stars can on me ___ now
nev - er was ___ known. I'm the down - fall of my fam - i - ly my ___ child - ren my

blest. Nev - er - more shall you soothe ___ my sad bos - om to rest.
sigh. My ___ heart sinks with - in me in ___ an - guish I die.
wave. I'll de - part from all friends ___ this ___ side of the grave.
dell. But I nev - er would re - turn to ___ my pri - son cell.
shine, no ___ change in my dan - ger from ___ day - light till dawn.
wife. God ___ pit - y and par - don the poor pris' - ner for life.

PUTTING ON THE STYLE

American

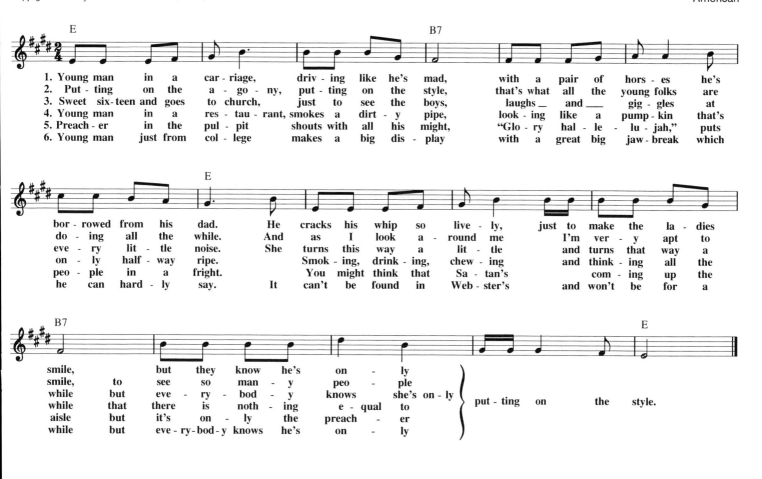

1. Young man in a car - riage, driv - ing like he's mad, with a pair of hors - es he's
2. Put - ting on the a - go - ny, put - ting on the style, that's what all the young folks are
3. Sweet six - teen and goes to church, just to see the boys, laughs __ and __ gig - gles at
4. Young man in a res - tau - rant, smokes a dirt - y pipe, look - ing like a pump - kin that's
5. Preach - er in the pul - pit shouts with all his might, "Glo - ry hal - le - lu - jah," puts
6. Young man just from col - lege makes a big dis - play with a great big jaw - break which

bor - rowed from his dad. He cracks his whip so live - ly, just to make the la - dies
do - ing all the while. And as I look a - round me I'm ver - y apt to
eve - ry lit - tle noise. She turns this way a lit - tle and turns that way a
on - ly half - way ripe. Smok - ing, drink - ing, chew - ing and think - ing all the
peo - ple in a fright. You might think that Sa - tan's com - ing up the
he can hard - ly say. It can't be found in Web - ster's and won't be for a

smile, but they know he's on - ly
smile, to see so man - y peo - ple
while but eve - ry - bod - y knows she's on - ly } put - ting on the style.
while that there is noth - ing e - qual to
aisle but it's on - ly the preach - er
while but eve - ry - bod - y knows he's on - ly

QUEEN JANE

English

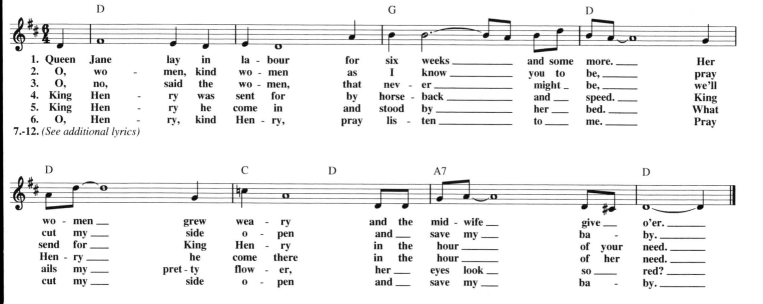

1. Queen Jane lay in la - bour for six weeks _____ and some more. ___ Her
2. O, wo - men, kind wo - men as I know _____ you to be, _____ pray
3. O, no, said the wo - men, that nev - er _____ might _ be, _____ we'll
4. King Hen - ry was sent for by horse - back _____ and __ speed. ___ King
5. King Hen - ry he come in and stood by _____ her __ bed. ___ What
6. O, Hen - ry, kind Hen - ry, pray lis - ten _____ to ___ me. ___ Pray

7.-12. *(See additional lyrics)*

wo - men ___ grew wea - ry and the mid - wife ___ give ___ o'er. _____
cut my ___ side o - pen and ___ save my ___ ba - by. _____
send for ___ King Hen - ry he come there in the hour _____ of your need. _____
Hen - ry ___ he come there in the hour _____ of her need. _____
ails my ___ pret - ty flow - er, her ___ eyes look ___ so ___ red? _____
cut my ___ side o - pen and ___ save my ___ ba - by. _____

Additional Lyrics

7. O, no, said King Henry, that never might be!
I'd lose my pretty flower to save my baby.

8. Queen Jane she turned over and fell in a swound,
They cut her side open, her baby was found.

9. How black was the mourning, how yellow her bed;
How white the bright shroud Queen Jane was laid in.

10. Six followed after, six bore her along.
King Henry come after, his head hanging down.

11. King Henry he wept 'til his hands were wrung sore,
Says, the flower of England is blooming no more.

12. That baby was christened the very next day;
His mother's poor body lay mouldering away.

QUEEN OF HEARTS

19th Century English Ballad

1. She's the queen of hearts, he's the king of ____ sor - row. Her love may
2. Oh I love my fath - er I ____ love my ____ moth - er. I love my
3. Thus he spoke one day when a trav - 'ling he start - ed. Now he's back
4. She's the queen of hearts, he's the king of ____ sor - row. Her love may

die be - fore ____ the mor - row. ____ Her love will van - ish and
sis - ter and ____ my bro - ther. ____ I love my home - town near
home so bro - ken - heart - ed. ____ He played his a - ces but
die be - fore ____ the mor - row. ____ Her love will van - ish and

nev - er come back. The queen of ____ hearts may be - long to a Jack. ____
mea - dows of green. I'd leave them ____ all for to be with my queen. ____
just could not win. His queen of ____ hearts did - n't let him come in. ____
nev - er come back. The queen of ____ hearts may be - long to a Jack. ____

THE QUEENSLAND DROVER

Australian

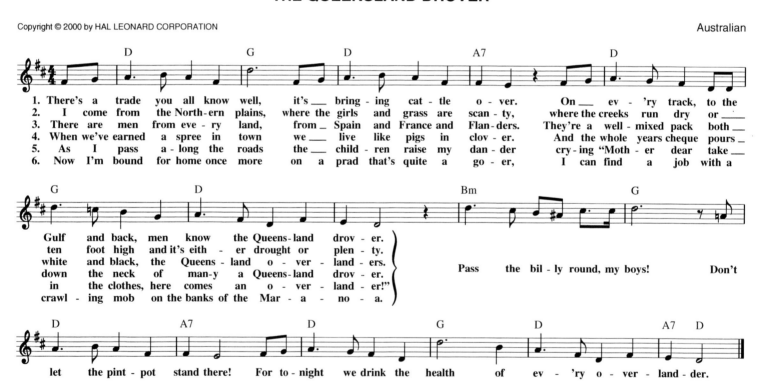

1. There's a trade you all know well, it's ____ bring - ing cat - tle o - ver. On ____ ev - 'ry track, to the
2. I come from the North-ern plains, where the girls and grass are scan - ty, where the creeks run dry or
3. There are men from eve - ry land, from ____ Spain and France and Flan - ders. They're a well - mixed pack both
4. When we've earned a spree in town we ____ live like pigs in clov - er. And the whole years cheque pours ____
5. As I pass a - long the roads the ____ child - ren raise my dan - der cry - ing "Moth - er dear take ____
6. Now I'm bound for home once more on a prad that's quite a go - er, I can find a job with a

Gulf and back, men know the Queens-land drov - er.
ten foot high and it's eith - er drought or plen - ty.
white and black, the Queens - land o - ver - land - ers.
down the neck of man - y a Queens-land drov - er.
in the clothes, here comes an o - ver - land - er!"
crawl - ing mob on the banks of the Mar - a - no - a.

Pass the bil - ly round, my boys! Don't

let the pint - pot stand there! For to - night we drink the health of ev - 'ry o - ver - land - der.

REUBEN AND RACHEL

American
Words and Music by
Harry Birch

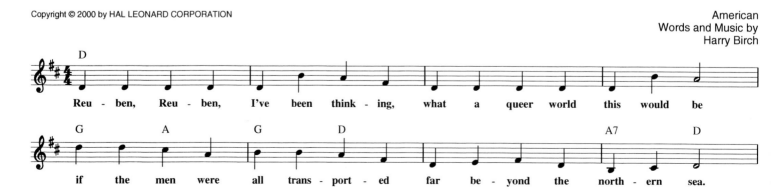

Reu - ben, Reu - ben, I've been think - ing, what a queer world this would be

if the men were all trans - port - ed far be - yond the north - ern sea.

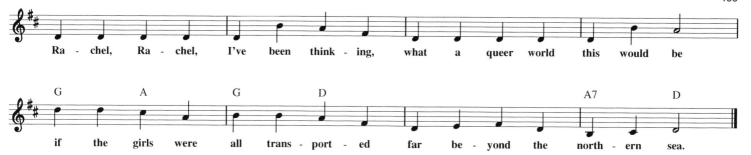

Ra - chel, Ra - chel, I've been think - ing, what a queer world this would be

if the girls were all trans - port - ed far be - yond the north - ern sea.

RAILROAD BILL

American

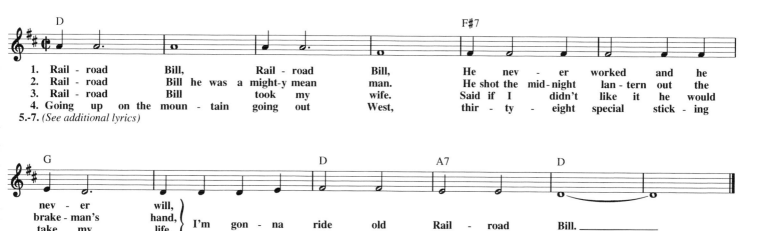

1. Rail - road Bill, Rail - road Bill, He nev - er worked and he
2. Rail - road Bill he was a might-y mean man. He shot the mid - night lan - tern out the
3. Rail - road Bill took my wife. Said if I didn't like it he would
4. Going up on the moun - tain going out West, thir - ty - eight special stick - ing
5.-7. *(See additional lyrics)*

nev - er will,
brake - man's hand,
take my life, } I'm gon - na ride old Rail - road Bill. _____
out of my vest,

Additional Lyrics

5. I've got a "thirty-eight special" on a "forty-four frame,"
   How in the world can I miss him when I've got dead aim...

6. Buy me a pistol just as long as my arm,
   Kill everybody ever done me harm...

7. Honey, honey, think I'm a fool,
   Think I would quit you when the weather is cool?...

A RAILROADER FOR ME

American

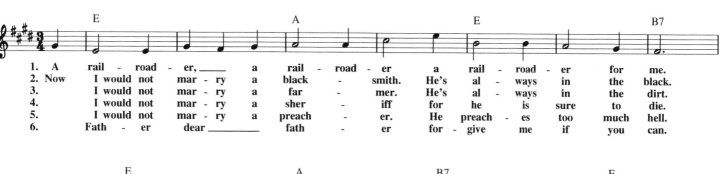

1. A rail - road - er, ____ a rail - road - er a rail - road - er for me.
2. Now I would not mar - ry a black - smith. He's al - ways in the black.
3. I would not mar - ry a far - mer. He's al - ways in the dirt.
4. I would not mar - ry a sher - iff for he is sure to die.
5. I would not mar - ry a preach - er. He preach - es too much hell.
6. Fath - er dear ____ fath - er for - give me if you can.

If ev - er I mar - ry in this wide world, a rail-road-er's bride _ I'll be.
I'd rath - er mar - ry an en - gi - neer that throws _ the throt - tle back.
I'd rath - er mar - ry an en - gi - neer that wears _ a striped ____ shirt.
But I would _ mar - ry a rail - road - er who has ____ them pret - ty blue eyes.
But I would _ mar - ry a rail - road - er who drives _ the for - ty nine.
If you ev - er see ____ your daugh - ter a - gain it'll be with a rail - road man.

RAISE A RUCKUS TONIGHT

Pre-Civil War African-American Song

1. My old mas-ter prom-ised me, raise a ruck-us to-night, that
2. My old mis-tress prom-ised me, raise a ruck-us to-night, "Sa-
3. Yes, they both done prom-ised me, raise a ruck-us to-night,

when he died he'd set me free, raise a ruck-us to-night. He
ra, I'm gon-na set you free," raise a ruck-us to-night. She
but their pa-pers did-n't set me free, raise a ruck-us to-night. A

lived un-til his head got bald, raise a ruck-us to-night, and
lived 'til her head got slick and bald, raise a ruck-us to-night, and the
dose of piz-in helped them a-long, raise a ruck-us to-night, may the

gave up think-in' 'bout dy-in' at all, raise a ruck-us to-night.
Lord could-n't kill her with a big green maul, raise a ruck-us to-night.
dev-il preach their fu-ner-al song, raise a ruck-us to-night.

Come a-long, lit-tle chil-dren, come a-long.

Come while the moon is shin-ing bright, _____

Come a-long, lit-tle chil-dren, come a-long, We're gon-na

raise a ruck-us to-night. _____

RAKE AND RAMBLING BOY

Irish

1. Well, __ I'm a rake _____ and a ram-bling __ boy,
2. My __ moth-er said _____ she's __ all a-lone.
3. When I die, _____ don't __ bur-y me at all,

there's man-y a cit-y _____ I did en-joy.
My sis-ter _____ said she has no home.
just place me a-way _____ in al-co-hol.

And now I mar - ried ___ me a pret - ty lit - tle wife,
My wife she wept ___ in sad des - pair
My for - ty - four ___ put by my feet,

and I love her dear - er than I love my life.
with an ach - ing heart and a ba - by fair.
tell eve - ry - one I'm just a sleep.

RAMBLING BLUES

American

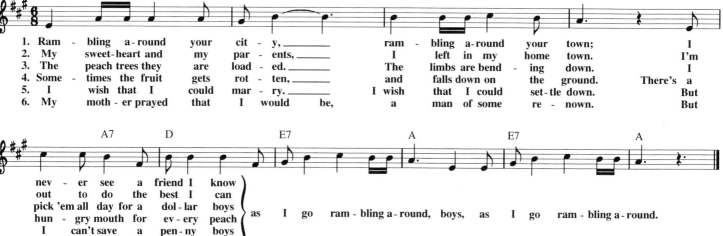

1. Ram - bling a - round your cit - y, ram - bling a - round your town; I
2. My sweet-heart and my par - ents, I left in my home town. I'm
3. The peach trees they are load - ed. The limbs are bend - ing down. I
4. Some - times the fruit gets rot - ten, and falls down on the ground. There's a
5. I wish that I could mar - ry. I wish that I could set - tle down. But
6. My moth - er prayed that I would be, a man of some re - nown. But

nev - er see a friend I know
out to do the best I can
pick 'em all day for a dol - lar boys   as I go ram - bling a - round, boys, as I go ram - bling a - round.
hun - gry mouth for ev - ery peach
I can't save a pen - ny boys
I am just a ref - u - gee

THE RAMBLING SAILOR

English Sea Chantey

1. I am a sail - or stout and bold, Long time I've ploughed the o - cean. I've
2. If you should want to know my name, My name it is young John - son. I've
3. The king's per - mis - sion grant - ed me To range the coun - try o - ver From

fought for king and coun - try too, Won hon - or and pro - mo - tion. I
got per - mis - sion from the king To court young girls and hand - some. I
Bris - tol Town to Liv - er - pool, From Ply - mouth Sound to Do - ver. And

said: My broth - er sail - or, I bid you a - dieu, No more to the sea will I go with you. I'll
said: My dear, what will you do? Here's ale and wine and bran - dy too, Be -
in what - ev - er town I went, To court young maid - ens I was bent; And

trav - el the coun - try through and through, And I'll be a ram - bling sail - or.
sides a pair of new silk shoes, To trav - el with a ram - bling sail - or.
mar - ry none was my in - tent, But live a ram - bling sail - or.

REAL OLD MOUNTAIN DEW

Irish

1. Let grass - es grow, and wa - ters flow, in a
2. At the foot of the hill there's a neat lit - tle still where the
3. Now learn - ed men who use the pen who've

free and eas - y way, but give me e - nough of the
smoke curls up to the sky. By the smoke and the smell you can
wrote your prais - es high, this sweet 'po - cheen' from

fine old stuff that's made near Gal - way Bay. Oh
plain - ly tell there's whis - key brew - ing near - by. For it
Ire - land's green dis - tilled from wheat and rye. Throw a -

peel - ers all, from Don - e - gal. Gal - way and E - trim too, we'll
fills the air with o - dor rare, and be - twixt both me and you, when
way your pills it'll cure all ills of pa - gan or Christ - ian, Jew.

give them the slip and we'll take a sip of the real old moun - tain dew.
home you roll you can take a bowl or a buck - et of moun - tain dew.
Take off your coat and free your throat with the real old moun - tain dew.

THE REBEL SOLDIER

Southern Appalachian Folksong

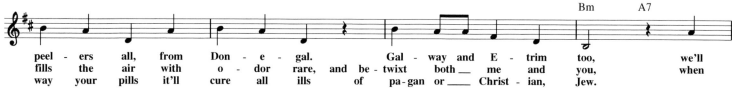
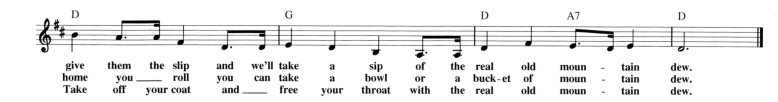

1. O, Pol - ly, O, Pol - ly, it's for your sake a - lone I've left my old
2. I'll eat when I'm hun - gry, I'll drink when I'm dry. If the Yan - kees don't

fa - ther, My coun - try and my home. I've left my old moth - er to
kill me, I'll live un - til I die. If the Yan - kees don't kill me and

weep and to mourn.
cause me to mourn. } I am a reb - el sol - dier and far from my home.

RED APPLE JUICE

American

1. I ain't got no use for your red ap - ple juice. Ain't got no hon - ey ba - by
2. Who'll rock the cra - dle, who'll sing this ___ song? Who'll rock the cra - dle when I'm
3. I'll rock the cra - dle, I'll sing this ___ song. I'll rock the cra - dle when you're
4. I've done all I can do, done all I can say. I can't ___ go on this - a
5. I've done all I can do, done all I can say. I'll sing it to your ma - ma next pay -

now, Lord, Lord. I ain't got no hon - ey ba - by now.
gone, Lord, Lord? Who'll rock the cra - dle when I'm gone?
gone, Lord, Lord. I'll rock the cra - dle when you're gone.
way, no, no. I can't ___ go on this - a way.
day, Lord, Lord. I'll sing it to your ma - ma next pay - day.

RED IRON ORE

American

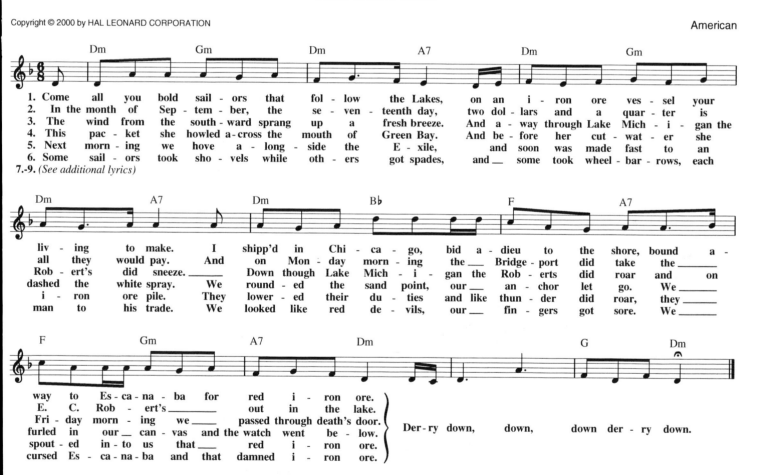

1. Come all you bold sail - ors that fol - low the Lakes, on an i - ron ore ves - sel your
2. In the month of Sep - tem - ber, the se - ven - teenth day, two dol - lars and a quar - ter is
3. The wind from the south - ward sprang up a fresh breeze. And a - way through Lake Mich - i - gan the
4. This pac - ket she howled a - cross the mouth of Green Bay. And be - fore her cut - wat - er she
5. Next morn - ing we hove a - long - side the E - xile, and soon was made fast to an
6. Some sail - ors took sho - vels while oth - ers got spades, and ___ some took wheel - bar - rows, each

7.-9. *(See additional lyrics)*

liv - ing to make. I shipp'd in Chi - ca - go, bid a - dieu to the shore, bound a -
all they would pay. And on Mon - day morn - ing the ___ Bridge - port did take the _____
Rob - ert's did sneeze. ___ Down though Lake Mich - i - gan the Rob - erts did roar and on
dashed the white spray. We round - ed the sand point, our ___ an - chor let go. We _____
i - ron ore pile. They lower - ed their du - ties and like thun - der did roar, they _____
man to his trade. We looked like red de - vils, our ___ fin - gers got sore. We _____

way to Es - ca - na - ba for red i - ron ore.
E. C. Rob - ert's _____ out in the lake.
Fri - day morn - ing we ___ passed through death's door. Der - ry down, down, down der - ry down.
furled in our ___ can - vas and the watch went be - low.
spout - ed in - to us that ___ red i - ron ore.
cursed Es - ca - na - ba and that damned i - ron ore.

Additional Lyrics

7. The tug Escanaba she towed out the Minch,
The Roberts she thought she had left in a pinch,
And as she passed by us she bid us good-bye,
Saying, "We'll meet you in Cleveland next Fourth of July!"

8. Through Louse Island it blew a fresh breeze;
We made the Foxes, the Beavers, the Skillagalees,
We flew by the Minch for to show her the way,
And she ne'er hove in sight till we were off Thunder Bay.

9. Across Saginaw Bay the Roberts did ride
With the dark and deep water rolling over her side.
And now for Port Huron the Roberts must go,
Where the tug Kate Williams she took us in tow.

THE RED LIGHT SALOON

American

1. It was ear - ly one morn - ing I strolled in - to town. For ____
2. I ____ bold - ly walked in and strolled up to the bar. A ____
3. Well, she mussed up my hair and sat down on my knee, say - ing,
4. She pro - ceed - ed to feel if my mus - cle was right. And I
5. Ear - ly next morn - ing I bid her good - bye. She ____
6. Well I cursed that young wo - man till the for - est turned blue. And with

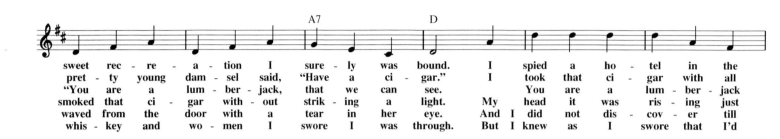

sweet rec - re - a - tion I sure - ly was bound. I spied a ho - tel in the
pret - ty young dam - sel said, "Have a ci - gar." I took that ci - gar with all
"You are a lum - ber - jack, that we can see. You are a lum - ber - jack
smoked that ci - gar with - out strik - ing a light. My head it was ris - ing just
waved from the door with a tear in her eye. And I did not dis - cov - er till
whis - key and wo - men I swore I was through. But I knew as I swore that I'd

mid af - ter - noon, it was sport - ing a sign, said the Red Light Sa - loon.
thanks for the boon. But she said, "That's our way in the Red Light Sa - loon."
that we all know. For your mus - cle is hard from your head to your toe."
like a bal - loon, from the treat - ment I got at the Red Light Sa - loon.
some - time next June, that she'd giv - en me a keep - sake from the Red Light Sa - loon.
give my for - tune just to be back once more in the Red Light Sa - loon.

RED RIVER VALLEY

19th Century American

1. Come and sit by my side if you love me, _____ Do not has - ten to
2. Won't you think of this val - ley you're leav - ing, _____ oh, how lone - ly, how
3. From this val - ley they say you are go - ing. _____ When you go, may your
4. I have prom - ised you, dar - ling, that nev - er _____ will a word from my

bid me a - dieu, _____ But re - mem - ber the Red Riv - er
sad it will be. _____ Oh, ____ think of the fond heart you're
dar - ling go, too? _____ Would you leave her be - hind un - pro -
lips cause you pain. _____ And my life, it will be yours for -

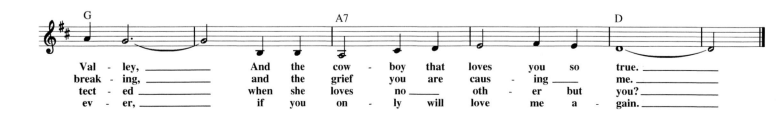

Val - ley, _____ And the cow - boy that loves you so true. _____
break - ing, _____ and the grief you are caus - ing ____ me. _____
tect - ed _____ when she loves no ____ oth - er but you? _____
ev - er, _____ if you on - ly will love me a - gain. _____

THE REGULAR ARMY, OH!

American

1. Three years a-go this ver-y day I went to Gov-er-nor's Isle, to stand fer-ninst the
2. We had our choice of go-ing to the ar-my or to ___ jail, or it's up the Hud-son
3. When we went out to Fort Ho-bo they run us in ___ the mill, and there they made us
4. The cap-tain's name was Murp — hy, of "da - cint Frinch _ des - cint," Sure he knew all the
5. The best of all the of - fi - cers is Se - cond Lie - ten-ant Mc - Duff of smok-ing cig - a -
6. There's corns u - pon me feet, me boy and bun - ions on me ___ toes, and lug-ging a gun in the

can - non in true mil - i - tar - y style. ___ Thir - teen A - mer-i - can dol - lars ___ each
Riv - er with a cop-per take a sail. So we pucker - ed up ___ our cour - age ___ and with
take a bath 'twas _ sure a - gainst our will. ___ But with three full meals _ with - in our belts each
ho - ly words in the He - brew tes - ta - ment. ___ And when he said to ___ Ho - gan, ___ "Just
rettes and sleep he ___ nev - er got e - nough. ___ Says the cap - tain, "All we want of you is to
red - hot sun puts _ freck - les on me nose. ___ And if you want ___ a fur-lough to the

month we sure - ly get, to car - ry a gun and bay - o - net with a mil - i - tar - y
bra - very we did go, and we cursed the day we marched a - way with the reg - u - lar ar - my
day, we had our fill, and we sat u - pon the dump cart ___ and ___ watched the ter - riers
move your feet a foot," sure Ho - gan _ jumped a half a mile on ___ Ser - geant Ril - ey's
go to rev - eil - le, and we'll ___ let the first ___ ser - geant _ run the com - pan -
cap - tain you do go. "Go to ___ bed and wait till you're dead in the reg - u - lar ar - my

step. ___
oh! ___
drill. ___ There's ser - geant John Mc - Caf - fer - ty and Cor - p'ral Don - a - hue, ___ they make us march up
boot. ___
y." ___
oh!" ___

to the crack in gal - lant com - p'ny Q. The drums they roll, up - on my soul, for that's the way we

go. ___ For - ty miles a day on beans and hay, in the reg - u - lar arm - y, Oh! ___

RIDING IN A BUGGY

American

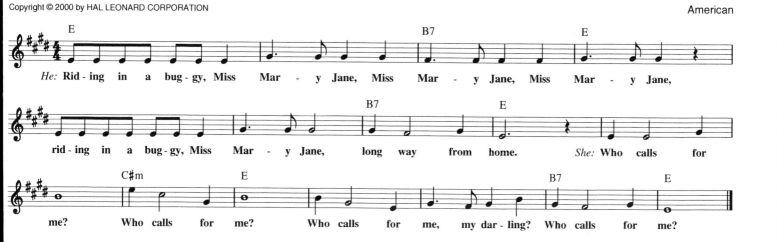

He: Rid - ing in a bug - gy, Miss Mar - y Jane, Miss Mar - y Jane, Miss Mar - y Jane,

rid - ing in a bug - gy, Miss Mar - y Jane, long way from home. *She:* Who calls for

me? Who calls for me? Who calls for me, my dar - ling? Who calls for me?

REUBEN'S TRAIN

American

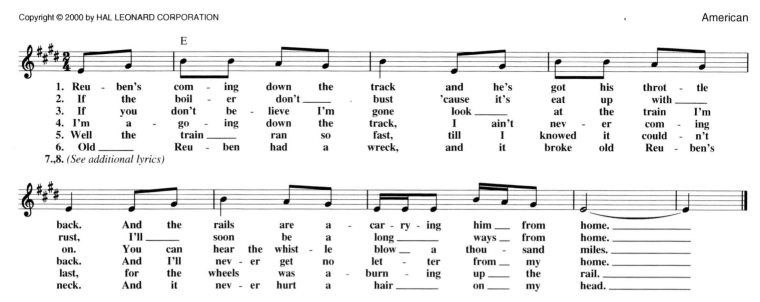

1. Reu - ben's com - ing down the track and he's got his throt - tle
2. If the boil - er don't _____ . bust 'cause it's eat up with _____
3. If you don't be - lieve I'm gone look _____ at the train I'm
4. I'm a - go - ing down the track, I ain't nev - er com - ing
5. Well the train _____ ran so fast, till I knowed it could - n't
6. Old _____ Reu - ben had a wreck, and it broke old Reu - ben's

7.,8. *(See additional lyrics)*

back. And the rails are a - car - ry - ing him ___ from home. _____
rust, I'll _____ soon be a long _____ ways ___ from home. _____
on. You can hear the whist - le blow ___ a thou - sand miles. _____
back. And I'll nev - er get no let - ter from ___ my home. _____
last, for the wheels was a - burn - ing up ___ the rail. _____
neck. And it nev - er hurt a hair _____ on ___ my head. _____

Additional Lyrics

7. Now I'm walking up the track,
   Hoping I'll get back;
   I'm a thousand miles away from home.

8. If I ever get back to you,
   You can beat me black and blue,
   For I'll never leave my shanty home again.

REVOLUTIONARY TEA

American

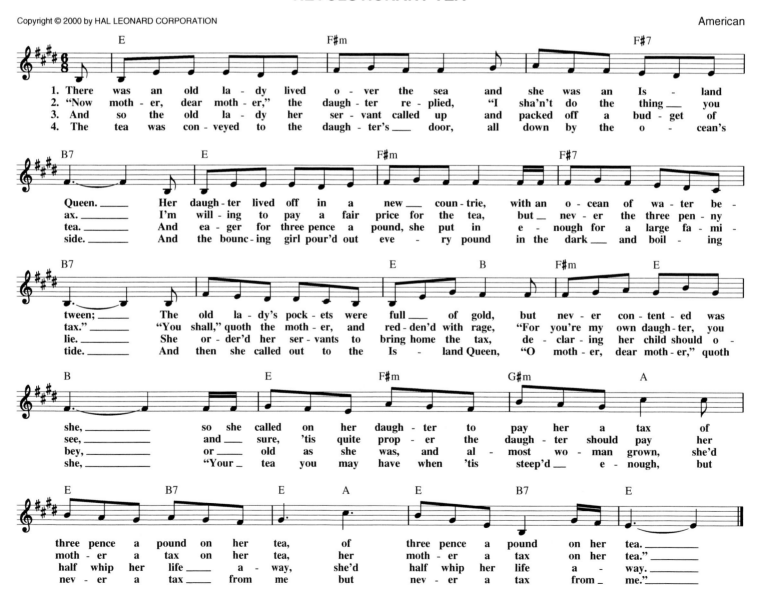

1. There was an old la - dy lived o - ver the sea and she was an Is - land
2. "Now moth - er, dear moth - er," the daugh - ter re - plied, "I sha'n't do the thing ___ you
3. And so the old la - dy her ser - vant called up and packed off a bud - get of
4. The tea was con - veyed to the daugh - ter's ___ door, all down by the o - cean's

Queen. _____ Her daugh - ter lived off in a new ___ coun - trie, with an o - cean of wa - ter be -
ax. _____ I'm will - ing to pay a fair price for the tea, but ___ nev - er the three pen - ny
tea. _____ And ea - ger for three pence a pound, she put in e - nough for a large fa - mi -
side. _____ And the bounc - ing girl pour'd out eve - ry pound in the dark ___ and boil - ing

tween; _____ The old la - dy's pock - ets were full ___ of gold, but nev - er con - tent - ed was
tax." _____ "You shall," quoth the moth - er, and red - den'd with rage, "For you're my own daugh - ter, you
lie. _____ She or - der'd her ser - vants to bring home the tax, de - clar - ing her child should o -
tide. _____ And then she called out to the Is - land Queen, "O moth - er, dear moth - er," quoth

she, _____ so she called on her daugh - ter to pay her a tax of
see, _____ and ___ sure, 'tis quite prop - er the daugh - ter should pay her
bey, _____ or ___ old as she was, and al - most wo - man grown, she'd
she, _____ "Your _ tea you may have when 'tis steep'd ___ e - nough, but

three pence a pound on her tea, of three pence a pound on her tea. _____
moth - er a tax on her tea, her moth - er a tax on her tea." _____
half whip her life _____ a - way, she'd half whip her life a - way. _____
nev - er a tax _____ from me but nev - er a tax from _ me." _____

A RICH IRISH LADY

Irish

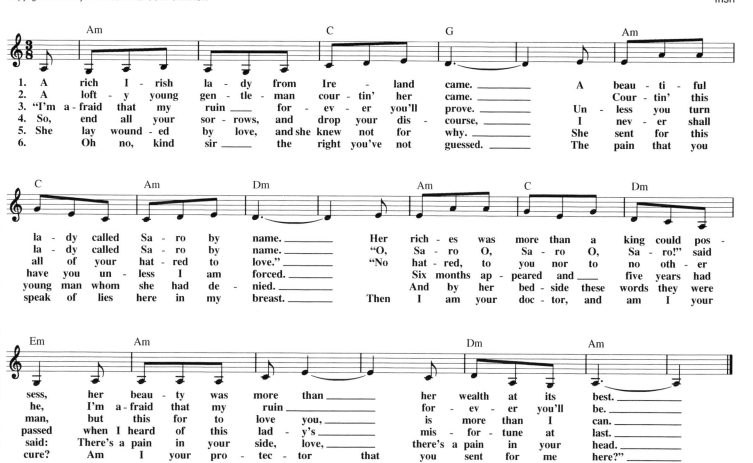

1. A rich I - rish la - dy from Ire - land came. _____ A beau - ti - ful
2. A loft - y young gen - tle - man cour - tin' her came. _____ Cour - tin' this
3. "I'm a - fraid that my ruin _____ for - ev - er you'll prove. _____ Un - less you turn
4. So, end all your sor - rows, and drop your dis - course, _____ I nev - er shall
5. She lay wound - ed by love, and she knew not for why. _____ She sent for this
6. Oh no, kind sir _____ the right you've not guessed. _____ The pain that you

la - dy called Sa - ro by name. _____ Her rich - es was more than a king could pos -
la - dy called Sa - ro by name. _____ "O, Sa - ro O, Sa - ro O, Sa - ro!" said
all of your hat - red to love." _____ "No hat - red, to you nor to no oth - er
have you un - less I am forced. _____ Six months ap - peared and _____ five years had
young man whom she had de - nied. _____ And by her bed - side these words they were
speak of lies here in my breast. _____ Then I am your doc - tor, and am I your

sess, her beau - ty was more than _____ her wealth at its best. _____
he, I'm a - fraid that my ruin _____ for - ev - er you'll be. _____
man, but this for to love you, _____ is more than I can. _____
passed when I heard of this lad - y's _____ mis - for - tune at last. _____
said: There's a pain in your side, love, _____ there's a pain in your head. _____
cure? Am I your pro - tec - tor that you sent for me here?" _____

RIG-A-JIG JIG

19th Century American Game Song

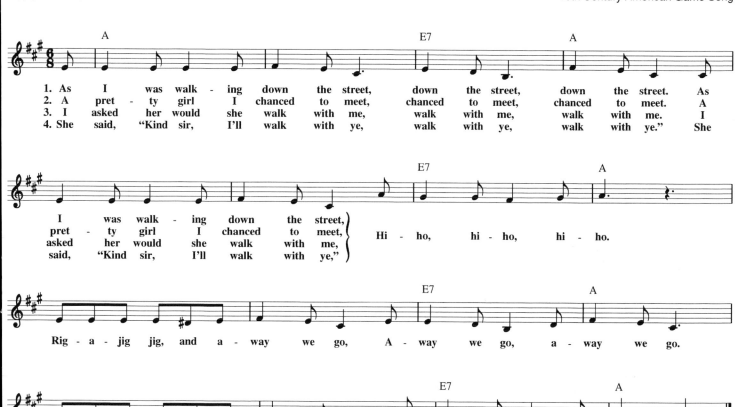

1. As I was walk - ing down the street, down the street, down the street. As
2. A pret - ty girl I chanced to meet, chanced to meet, chanced to meet. A
3. I asked her would she walk with me, walk with me, walk with me. I
4. She said, "Kind sir, I'll walk with ye, walk with ye, walk with ye." She

I was walk - ing down the street,
pret - ty girl I chanced to meet,
asked her would she walk with me,
said, "Kind sir, I'll walk with ye,"
Hi - ho, hi - ho, hi - ho.

Rig - a - jig jig, and a - way we go, A - way we go, a - way we go.

Rig - a - jig jig, and a - way we go, Hi - ho, hi - ho, hi - ho. _____

RICHMOND IS A HARD ROAD TO TRAVEL

Words by John Reuben Thompson
Music by Daniel Decatur Emmett
1863

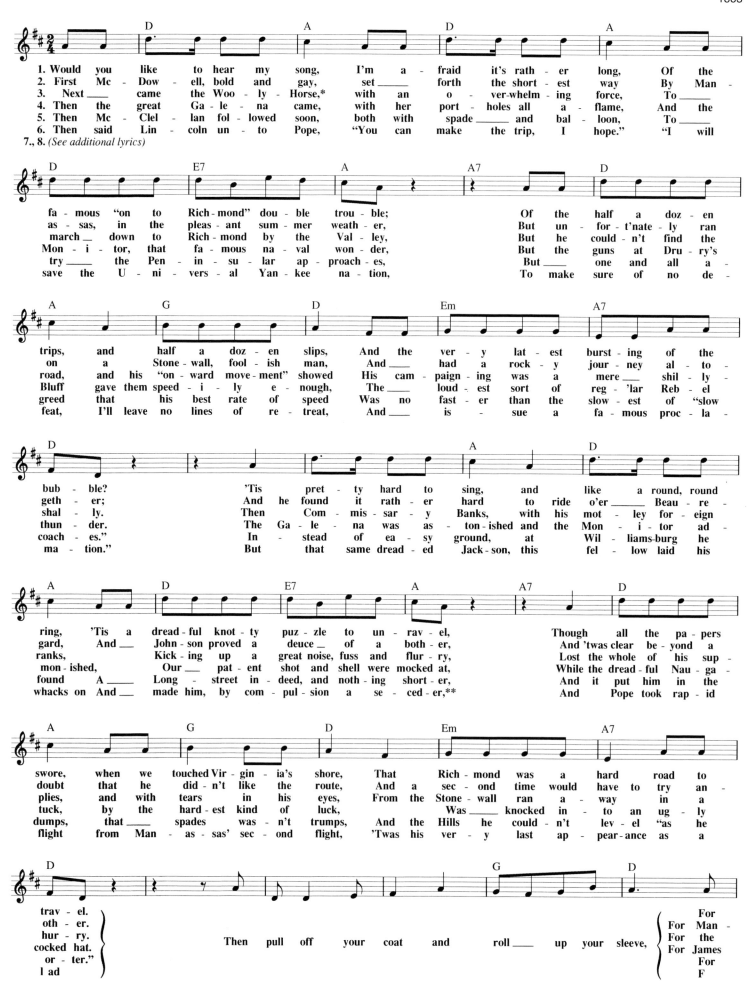

7., 8. *(See additional lyrics)*

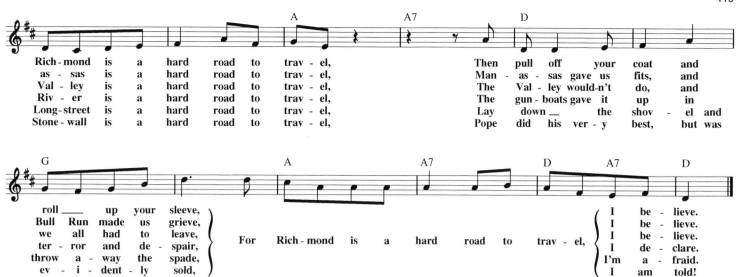

Rich-mond is a hard road to trav-el, Then pull off your coat and
as - sas is a hard road to trav-el, Man - as - sas gave us fits, and
Val - ley is a hard road to trav-el, The Val - ley would-n't do, and
Riv - er is a hard road to trav-el, The gun - boats gave it up in
Long-street is a hard road to trav-el, Lay down __ the shov - el and
Stone-wall is a hard road to trav-el, Pope did his ver - y best, but was

roll __ up your sleeve, } For Rich - mond is a hard road to trav-el, { I be - lieve.
Bull Run made us grieve, I be - lieve.
we all had to leave, I be - lieve.
ter - ror and de - spair, I de - clare.
throw a - way the spade, I'm a - fraid.
ev - i - dent - ly sold, I am told!

Additional Lyrics

7. Last of all the brave Burnside, with his pontoon bridges, tried
A road no one had thought of before him,
With two hundred thousand men for the Rebel slaughter pen
And the blessed Union flag waving o'er him;
But he met a fire like hell, of canister and shell,
That mowed his men down with great slaughter,
'Twas a shocking sight to view, that second Waterloo,
And the river ran with more blood than water.
Then pull off your coat and roll up your sleeve,
Rappahannock is a hard road to travel,
Burnside got in a trap, which caused him for to grieve
For Richmond is a hard road to travel, I believe!

8. We are very much perplexed to know who is the next
To command the new Richmond expedition,
For the Capital must blaze, and that in ninety days,
And Jeff, and his men be sent to perdition.
We'll take the cursed town, and then we'll burn it down,
And plunder and hang up each cursed Rebel;
Yet the contraband was right when he told us they would fight,
"Oh, yes, mister, they fight like the devil!"
Then pull off your coat and roll up your sleeve,
For Richmond is a hard road to travel,
Then pull off your coat and roll up your sleeve,
For Richmond is a hard road to travel, I believe!

RISE UP, SHEPHERD, AND FOLLOW

Southern American Folk Hymn

1. There's a star in the east on __ Christ-mas morn, } rise up, shep-herd, and fol-low. __ { It - 'll
2. If you take good __ heed to the an - gel's words, You'll for -

lead to the place where the Sav - ior's born __ } rise up, shep-herd, and fol-low.
get your __ flock, you'll for - get your herds, __

Leave your sheep and leave your lambs, rise up, shep-herd, and fol-low. Leave your ewes and

leave your rams, rise up, shep-herd, and fol-low. Fol - low, Fol - low, rise up, shep-herd, and

fol-low. Fol-low the star of Beth - le - hem, __ rise up, shep-herd, and fol-low.

THE RIFLE

Song from the American Revolutionary War

1. Why come ye hith-er, Red-coats your minds, what mad-ness fills? There is dan-ger in our
2. Ye ride a good-ly steed, ye may know an-oth-er mas-ter, Ye for-ward come with
3. Had ye no graves at home a-cross the brin-y wa-ter that hith-er ye must

val-ley and there's dan-ger in our hills. Oh hear ye not the sing-ing of the
speed, but ye'll learn to back much fas-ter. When you meet our moun-tain boys and their
come like bul-locks to the slaugh-ter? Well, if we the work must do, why, the

bu-gle, wild and free? Full soon you'll hear the ring-ing of the ri-fle from each
lead-er John-ny Stark lads who make but lit-tle noise lads who al-ways hit the
soon-er 'tis be-gun, if flint and pow-der hold but true, the soon-er 'twill be

tree.
mark. For the ri-fle, oh, the ri-fle, in our
done.

hands will prove no tri-fle. Oh, the ri-fle, oh the

ri-fle, in our hands will prove no tri-fle.

RING AROUND THE ROSIE

19th Century English Children's Game Song

Ring a-round the ros-y, a pock-et full of po-sies; ash-es, ash-es, we

all fall down. Lit-tle Sal-ly Wa-ters, sit-ting in a sau-cer,

weep-ing and a-moan-ing like a tur-tle dove. Rise, Sal-ly rise,

wipe your weep-ing eyes; fly to the east, fly to the

west, fly to the one that you love best.

RISE AND SHINE

American Gospel Song

1. Rise ___ and shine ___ and give God the glo - ry, glo - ry, Rise ___ and
2.-6. *(See additional lyrics)*

shine, ___ and give God the glo - ry, glo - ry, Rise and shine and

give God the glo - ry, glo - ry, Chil - dren of the Lord. ___

Additional Lyrics

2. The Lord said, "Noah, there's gonna be a floody, floody"...
   Get your children out of the muddy, muddy!"...

3. Noah, he built him, he built him an arky, arky...
   Made it out of hickory barky, barky...

4. The animals, they came, they came by twosy, twosy...
   Elephants and kangaroosy, roosy...

5. It rained and rained for forty daysy, daysy...
   Drove those animals nearly crazy, crazy...

6. The sun came out and dried up the landy, landy...
   Everyone felt fine and dandy...

THE RISING OF THE MOON

Irish
By John Keegan Casey

1. Oh! then tell me, Sean O' - Far - rell, tell me why you hur - ry so? Hush, a while, just
2. Oh! then tell me, Sean O' - Far - rell, where the gath - er - ing is to be? In the old spot
3. Out from man - y a mud - wall cab - in eyes were watch - ing through the night. Man - y a man - ly
4. There be - side the sing - ing riv - er that dark mass of men were seen. Far a - bove the

hush and lis - ten, and his cheeks were all a - glow. I bear or - ders ___ from the Cap - tain,
by the riv - er, right well known to you and me. One word more for ___ sig - nal to - ken
breast was throb - bing for the bles - sed warn - ing light. Mur - murs passed a - long the val - ley,
shin - ing wea - pons hung their own im - mor - tal green. Death to eve - ry ___ foe and trai - tor,

get you read - y quick and soon, for the pikes must be to - geth - er at the ris - ing of the moon!
whis - tle up the march - ing tune, with your pike up - on your shoul - der, by the ris - ing of the moon!
like the ban - shee's lone - ly croon, and a thou - sand blades were flash - ing at the ris - ing of the moon!
for - ward strike the march - ing tune, and, hur - rah, my boys for, free - dom, 'tis the ris - ing of the moon.

THE RIVER IN THE PINES

19th Century American

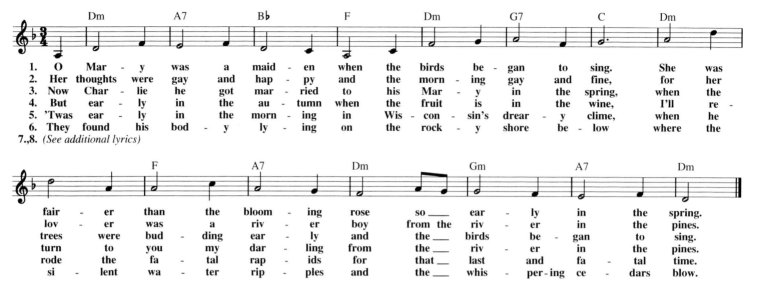

1. O Mar - y was a maid - en when the birds be - gan to sing. She was
2. Her thoughts were gay and hap - py and the morn - ing gay and fine, for her
3. Now Char - lie he got mar - ried to his Mar - y in the spring, when the
4. But ear - ly in the au - tumn when the fruit is in the wine, I'll re -
5. 'Twas ear - ly in the morn - ing in Wis - con - sin's drear - y clime, when he
6. They found his bod - y ly - ing on the rock - y shore be - low where the

7.,8. *(See additional lyrics)*

fair - er than the bloom - ing rose so ___ ear - ly in the spring.
lov - er was a riv - er boy from the riv - er in the pines.
trees were bud - ding ear - ly and the ___ birds be - gan to sing.
turn to you my dar - ling from the ___ riv - er in the pines.
rode the fa - tal rap - ids for that ___ last and fa - tal time.
si - lent wa - ter rip - ples and the ___ whis - per - ing ce - dars blow.

Additional Lyrics

7. Now every raft of lumber that comes from the Chippeway,
   There's a lonely grave that's visited by drivers on their way.

8. They plant wild flowers upon it in the morning fair and fine,
   'Tis the grave of two young lovers from the river in the pines.

THE ROAD TO GUNDAGAI

Australian

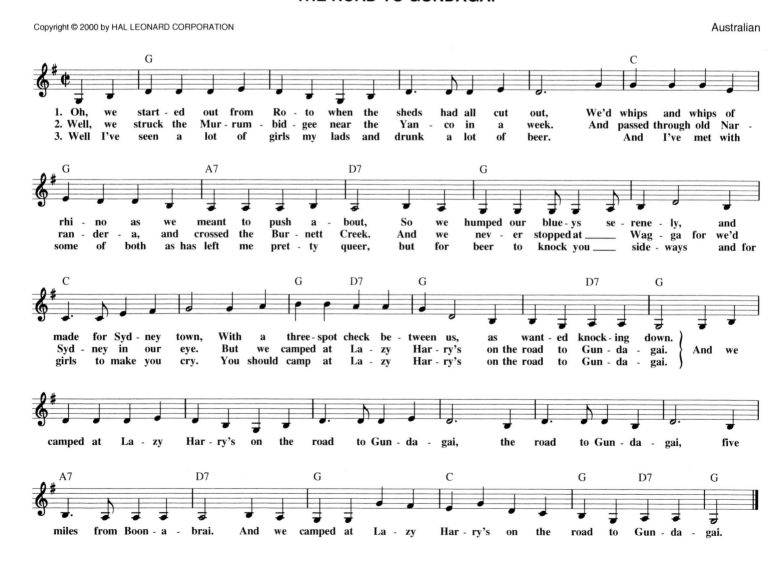

1. Oh, we start - ed out from Ro - to when the sheds had all cut out, We'd whips and whips of
2. Well, we struck the Mur - rum - bid - gee near the Yan - co in a week. And passed through old Nar -
3. Well I've seen a lot of girls my lads and drunk a lot of beer. And I've met with

rhi - no as we meant to push a - bout, So we humped our blue - ys se - rene - ly, and
ran - der - a, and crossed the Bur - nett Creek. And we nev - er stopped at ___ Wag - ga for we'd
some of both as has left me pret - ty queer, but for beer to knock you ___ side - ways and for

made for Syd - ney town, With a three - spot check be - tween us, as want - ed knock - ing down.
Syd - ney in our eye. But we camped at La - zy Har - ry's on the road to Gun - da - gai. } And we
girls to make you cry. You should camp at La - zy Har - ry's on the road to Gun - da - gai.

camped at La - zy Har - ry's on the road to Gun - da - gai, the road to Gun - da - gai, five

miles from Boon - a - brai. And we camped at La - zy Har - ry's on the road to Gun - da - gai.

RIVERS OF BABYLON

Jamaican

By the wa-ters of Ba-by-lon, __ where we sat down, and there we wept When we re-mem-ber'd Zi - on. But the wick - ed car-ried us a-way cap-ti - vi-ty, re-quire from us a song. __ How can we sing the Lord's __ own song __ in a strange land? when we re-mem-ber'd Zi - on. ____

THE ROAD TO THE ISLES

Scottish

1. A ____ far croon - in' is pull - in' me a - way As ____
2. It's by shiel wa - ter the track is to the west, By ____
3. The ____ blue is - lands are pull - in' me a - way, Their ____

take I wi' my cro-mack to the road. The ____ far Coo - lins are
Ail - lort and by Mor - ar to the sea. The ____ cool cress - es I am
laugh-ter puts the leap up - on the lame; The ____ blue is - lands from the

put - tin' love on me As step I with the sun - light for my load.)
think-in' of for pluck And brack-en for a wink on Moth - er knee.) Sure by
Sker-ries to the Lewis, Wi' heath-er hon - ey taste up - on each name.)

Tum-mel and Loch Ran-noch and Loch-a-ber I will go, by ____ heath-er tracks wi' heav-en in their

wiles; If it's think - in' in your in-ner heart the brag-gart's in my step, You've

nev - er smelled the tan - gle o' the Isles. Oh the far Coo - lins are

put - tin' love on me As step I wi' my cro-mack to the Isles.

ROBIN REDBREAST

J.M. Hubbard
American, 1859

1. Good - bye, good - bye to sum - mer, for the sum - mer's near - ly done, For the
2. Bright _ yel - low red and or - ange the _____ leaves come down in hosts, The _____
3. The _____ fire - side for the crick - et, the _____ wheat-stack for the mouse, The _____

sum - mer's near - ly done. The gar - den smil - ing faint - ly, cool _____
leaves come down in hosts. The trees are In - dian princ - es, but _____
wheat - stack for the mouse. When trem - bling night - winds whis - tle and _____

breez - es in _____ the _____ sun. The _____ thrush - es now are si - lent, our
soon they'll turn _ to _____ ghosts. The _____ leath - r'y pears and ap - ples hang
moan all 'round _ the _____ house. The _____ frost - y ways, like i - ron, the

swal - lows flown a - way, But Rob - bin's here in coat of brown and scar - let breast-knot gay. ⎫
rus - set on the bough, 'Tis au - tumn, au - tumn, au - tumn late, 'Twill soon be win - ter now. ⎬ Oh _____
branch - es plum'd with snow, A - las! in win - ter dead and dark, Where can poor Rob - in go? ⎭

Rob - in, Rob - in Red - breast, Oh Rob - in, Rob - in, dear, Oh Rob - in sings so

sweet - ly in the fall - ing of _____ the _____ year.

ROCK-A-MY SOUL

African-American Spiritual

Oh, rock - a - my soul _____ in the bos - om of A - bra - ham,

rock - a - my soul _____ in the bos - om of A - bra - ham, rock - a - my soul _____ in the

bo - som of A - bra - ham, oh, rock - a - my soul.

1. When
2. When
3. I
4. The

I went down to the val - ley to pray, oh, rock - a - my
I came home from the val - ley at night, oh, rock - a - my
felt so sad on the morn - ing be - fore, oh, rock - a - my
sun shines bright on the cloud - i - est day, oh, rock - a - my

soul,	my	soul	got	hap - py	and	I	stayed	all	day,
soul,	I	knew	that	ev - 'ry - thing	would	be	al - right,
soul,	I	found	the	peace	that	I	was	look - ing	for,
soul,	a	prayer	is	all	you	need	to	light	your	way,

oh, rock - a - my soul. Oh, soul.

ROCK-A-BYE, BABY

Traditional American Lullaby

1. Rock - a - bye, ba - by, on the tree top, When the wind blows the
2. When the bough breaks the cra - dle will fall, And

cra - dle will rock; down will come ba - by, cra - dle and all.

ROCK ABOUT MY SARO JANE

American

1. I've got a wife and - a five lit - tle chil - dren, be - lieve I'll make a trip on the
2. Boil - er bust - ed and the whis - tle done blowed, __ the head __ cap - tain done fell __
3. En - gine gave a crack and the whis - tle gave a squall, __ the en - gi - neer __ gone to the
4. Yank - ees built boats for to shoot them __ reb - els my mus - ket's __ load - ed and I'm

big __ Mac - mil - lan,
o - ver - board. __
hole __ in the wall. __
gon - na hold her lev - el.

O Sa - ro Jane! O there's noth - ing to do but to set down and

sing, and rock a - bout, my Sa - ro Jane. __ O rock a - bout my Sa - ro __

Jane. __ O rock a - bout, my Sa - ro Jane. O there's noth - ing to do but to

set down and sing and rock a - bout my Sa - ro Jane. __

THE ROCK ISLAND LINE

American

I say the Rock Is-land Line ___ is a might-y good road. ___ I say the Rock Is-land Line _ ___ is the road to ride. Oh, the Rock Is-land Line ___ is a might-y good road. _ ___ If you want to ride it, got to ride it like you're fly-in'. Buy your tick-et at the sta-tion on the Rock Is-land Line.

1. A, B, C, Dou-ble X, Y, Z, ___ cat's in the
2. Je-sus died to ___ save our sins. ___ Glo-ry be to
3. I may be right and I may be wrong. I know you're gon-na

1,2
3
D.S. al Fine

cup-board, but he can't see me. ___ } I say the
God, we're gon-na need Him a-gain. ___
miss me when I ___ have gone. _ ___ I say the

RODDY McCORLEY

Irish

1. Ho, ___ see the ___ fleet foot ___ hosts of men, ___ who speed with fac-es wan, from _
2. Up the ___ nar-row ___ street he stepped ___ smil-ing and proud and young, a -
3. When _ he last _ stepped up that street ___ his shin-ing pike in hand, be -
4. There is nev-er a ___ one of ___ all your dead ___ more brave-ly fell in fray, then _

farm-stead and from ___ fish-er's cot up-on the banks of Bann. They ___
bout the hemp-rope ___ on his neck the gold-en ring-lets clung. There's _
hind him marched in ___ grim ar-ray a stal-wart earn-est band! For ___
he who march-es ___ to his fate on the Bridge of Toome to-day. True ___

come with venge-ance ___ in their eyes, too late, too late are they. For
nev-er a tear in ___ his blue eyes both glad and bright are they. As } young
An-trim town for ___ An-trim town he led them to the fray. And }
to the last, true ___ to the last, he treads the up-ward way. And

Rod-dy M'-Cor-ley ___ goes to die on the Bridge of Toome to-day.

ROCKS AND GRAVEL

American

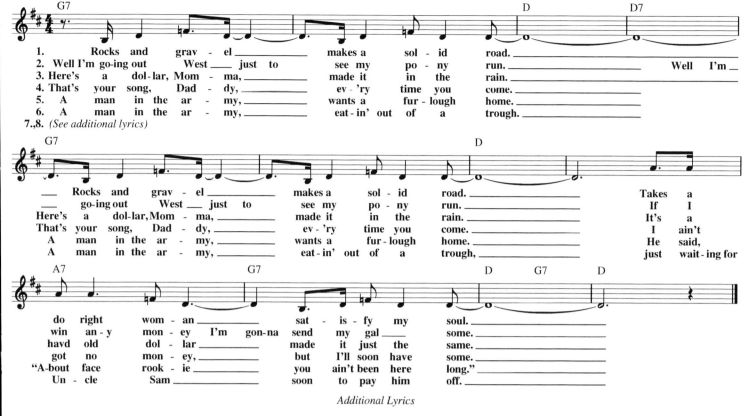

1. Rocks and grav-el _____ makes a sol-id road. _____
2. Well I'm go-ing out West ___ just to see my po-ny run. _____ Well I'm _
3. Here's a dol-lar, Mom-ma, _____ made it in the rain. _____
4. That's your song, Dad-dy, _____ ev-'ry time you come. _____
5. A man in the ar-my, _____ wants a fur-lough home. _____
6. A man in the ar-my, _____ eat-in' out of a trough. _____
7.,8. *(See additional lyrics)*

___ Rocks and grav-el _____ makes a sol-id road. _____ Takes a
___ go-ing out West ___ just to see my po-ny run. _____ If I
Here's a dol-lar,Mom-ma, _____ made it in the rain. _____ It's a
That's your song, Dad-dy, _____ ev-'ry time you come. _____ I ain't
A man in the ar-my, _____ wants a fur-lough home. _____ He said,
A man in the ar-my, _____ eat-in' out of a trough, _____ just wait-ing for

do right wom-an _____ sat-is-fy my soul. _____
win an-y mon-ey I'm gon-na send my gal ___ some. _____
havd old dol-lar _____ made it just the same. _____
got no mon-ey, _____ but I'll soon have some. _____
"A-bout face rook-ie _____ you ain't been here long." _____
Un-cle Sam _____ soon to pay him off. _____

Additional Lyrics

7. I got a girl in the country and she won't come to town.
   I got a girl in the country and she won't come to town.
   Got one in Louisiana and she's waterbound.

8. I can't see how you treat your Daddy mean.
   I can't see how you treat your Daddy mean.
   When you lays all night and your Daddy's on benzedrine.

ROLL, ALABAMA, ROLL

from the American Civil War

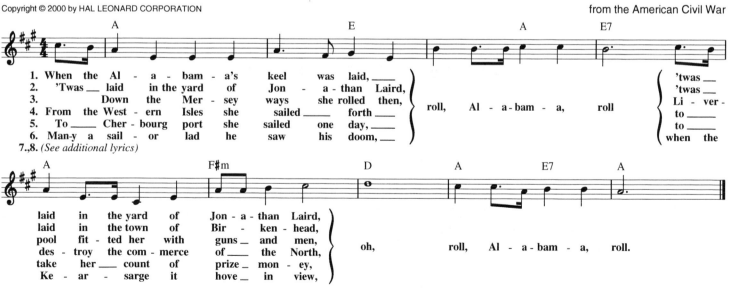

1. When the Al-a-bam-a's keel was laid, ___ roll, Al-a-bam-a, roll 'twas _
2. 'Twas ___ laid in the yard of Jon-a-than Laird, ___ 'twas _
3. Down the Mer-sey ways she rolled then, ___ Li-ver-
4. From the West-ern Isles she sailed ___ forth ___ to _
5. To ___ Cher-bourg port she sailed one day, ___ to _
6. Man-y a sail-or lad he saw his doom, ___ when the
7.,8. *(See additional lyrics)*

laid in the yard of Jon-a-than Laird, ___ oh, roll, Al-a-bam-a, roll.
laid in the town of Bir-ken-head,
pool fit-ted her with guns ___ and men,
des-troy the com-merce of the North,
take her ___ count of prize ___ mon-ey,
Ke-ar-sarge it hove ___ in view,

Additional Lyrics

7. Till a ball from the forward pivot that day,
   Roll Alabama roll.
   Shot the Alabama's stern away,
   Roll Alabama roll.

8. Off the three-mile limit in sixty-five,
   Roll Alabama roll.
   The Alabama went to her grave,
   Roll Alabama roll.

ROLL DOWN THE LINE

American Mining Song

1. Way back yon-der in Ten-nes-see they leased the con-victs out, to work in the
2. Ear-ly Mon-day morn-ing ___ they get you up on time, send you down to
3. Beans, they are ___ half done, you know, the bread is not so swell. Meat, it is all
4. Bank boss, he's ___ a hard man ___ a man you all know well, and if you don't get

coal mines a-gainst free la-bor stout. Free la-bor re-belled a-gainst it; to
Lone Rock, just to look in-to the mine. They send ___ you down to Lone Rock, just to
burned up, the cof-fee's black as hell. But when ___ you get your task done and
your task done he's gon-na give you hell. They car-ry you to the stock-ade, and

win it took some time. But while the lease was in ef-fect they made 'em rise and
look in-to that hole. The ver-y next thing the cap-tain says, "You'd bet-ter get your
on the floor you fall, well an-y-thing you get to eat it tastes good, done or
throw you in that hole. The ver-y next thing they say to you. "You'd bet-ter get your

shine.
pole."
raw.
pole. Bud-dy, won't you roll down the line? Bud-dy, won't you roll down the

line? Yon-der comes my dar-lin', com-in' down the line. Bud-dy, won't you

roll down the line? Bud-dy, won't you roll down the line?

Yon-der comes my dar-lin', com-in' down the line.

ROLL IN MY SWEET BABY'S ARMS

American

1. Ain't gon-na live in the coun-try. ___ Ain't gon-na live on the
2. Some-times there's a change in the o-cean. ___ Some-times there's a change in the
3. Ma-ma's a gin-ger cake ba-ker. ___ Sis-ter can weave and ___
4. They tell me your par-ents don't like me. ___ They have drove me a-way from your

farm. ___ Well, I'll lay 'round the shack 'till the mail train comes back, and I'll
sea. ___ Some-times there's a change in my own true ___ love, but there's
spin. ___ Dad's got an in-ter-est in that old cot-ton mill, just
door. ___ If I had all my time to do o-ver a-gain, I would

roll in my sweet ba - by's arms. _____
nev - er a change in ____ me. _____
watch that old mon - ey roll in. _____
nev - er go there an - y - more. _____

Roll in my sweet ba - by's

arms, _____ roll in my sweet ba - by's arms. _____ Lay 'round the

shack 'til the mail train comes back, then I'll roll in my sweet ba - by's arms. _____

ROLL ON THE GROUND

American

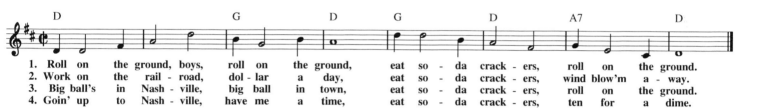

1. Roll on the ground, boys, roll on the ground, eat so - da crack - ers, roll on the ground.
2. Work on the rail - road, dol - lar a day, eat so - da crack - ers, wind blow'm a - way.
3. Big ball's in Nash - ville, big ball in town, eat so - da crack - ers, roll on the ground.
4. Goin' up to Nash - ville, have me a time, eat so - da crack - ers, ten for a dime.

ROLL OVER

American Children's Game Song

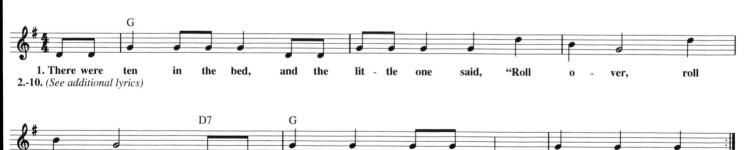

1. There were ten in the bed, and the lit - tle one said, "Roll o - ver, roll
2.-10. (See additional lyrics)

o - ver." So they all rolled o - ver and one fell out.

Additional Lyrics

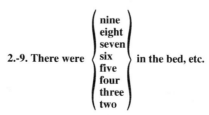

2.-9. There were { nine, eight, seven, six, five, four, three, two } in the bed, etc.

10. There was one in the bed
And the little one said,
(Spoken:) "Good night!"

ROLLING HOME

English Sea Chantey

1. Up a - loft, a - mid the rig - ging swift - ly blows the fa - v'ring gale, strong as
2. Now, it takes all hands to man the cap - stan, mis - ter, see your ca - bles clear! Soon you'll be
3. Full ten thou - sand miles be - hind us, and a thou - sand miles be - fore, an - cient

spring - time in its blos - som, fill - ing out each bend - ing sail. And the
sail - ing home - ward bound, sir, and for the chan - nel you will steer. See your
o - cean waves to waft us to the well - re - mem - bered shore. New born

waves we leave be - hind us seem to mur - mur as they rise. We have
sheets and crew - lines free, sir, all your bunt - lines o - ver - hauled. Are the
breez - es swell to send us to our child - hood wel - come skies, to the

tar - ried here to bear you to the land you dear - ly prize. } Roll - ing
sheer - poles and gear all read - y? For old Eng - land we will steer. }
glow of friend - ly fac - es and the glance of lov - ing eyes. }

home, roll - ing home, roll - ing home, a - cross the sea, roll - ing

home to dear old Eng - land, roll - ing home, _____ dear land, to thee.

ROSA

Flemish dance tune from the Netherlands

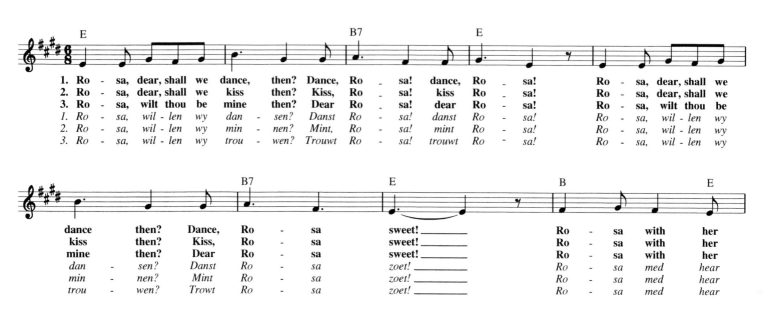

1. Ro - sa, dear, shall we dance, then? Dance, Ro - sa! dance, Ro - sa! Ro - sa, dear, shall we
2. Ro - sa, dear, shall we kiss then? Kiss, Ro - sa! kiss Ro - sa! Ro - sa, dear, shall we
3. Ro - sa, wilt thou be mine then? Dear Ro - sa! dear Ro - sa! Ro - sa, wilt thou be
1. Ro - sa, wil - len wy dan - sen? Danst Ro - sa! danst Ro - sa! Ro - sa, wil - len wy
2. Ro - sa, wil - len wy min - nen? Mint, Ro - sa! mint Ro - sa! Ro - sa, wil - len wy
3. Ro - sa, wil - len wy trou - wen? Trouwt Ro - sa! trouwt Ro - sa! Ro - sa, wil - len wy

dance then? Dance, Ro - sa sweet! _____ Ro - sa with her
kiss then? Kiss, Ro - sa sweet! _____ Ro - sa with her
mine then? Dear Ro - sa sweet! _____ Ro - sa with her
dan - sen? Danst Ro - sa zoet! _____ Ro - sa med hear
min - nen? Mint Ro - sa zoet! _____ Ro - sa med hear
trou - wen? Trowt Ro - sa zoet! _____ Ro - sa med hear

hat of flow - ers Ah! nei - ther wealth nor lands has she, But danc - es sweet - ly.
hat of flow - ers Ah! nei - ther wealth nor lands has she, But kiss - es sweet - ly.
hat of flow - ers Ah! nei - ther wealth nor lands has she, Wilt thou be mine?
bloe - men - hoed Zy had - de geld, maer wei - nig good, danst Ro - sa zoet!
bloe - men - hoed Zy had - de geld, maer wei - nig good, danst Ro - sa zoet!
bloe - men - hoed Zy had - de geld, maer wei - nig good, danst Ro - sa zoet!

Ro - sa dear, shall we dance, then? Dance, Ro - sa, dance, Ro - sa!
Ro - sa dear, shall we kiss, then? Kiss, Ro - sa, kiss Ro - sa!
Ro - sa, wilt thou be mine then? Dear Ro - sa, dear Ro - sa!
Ro - sa, wil - len wy dan - sen? Danst Ro - sa! danst Ro - sa,
Ro - sa, wil - len wy min - nen? Mint Ro - sa! mint Ro - sa!
Ro - sa, wil - len wy trou - wen? Trouwt Ro - sa! trouwt Ro - sa!

Ro - sa, dear, shall we dance then? Dance, Ro - sa sweet!
Ro - sa, dear, shall we kiss then? Kiss, Ro - sa sweet!
Ro - sa, wilt thou be mine then? Dear Ro - sa sweet!
Ro - sa, wil - len wy dan - sen? Danst Ro - sa zoet!
Ro - sa, wil - len wy min - nen? Mint Ro - sa zoet!
Ro - sa, wil - len wy trou - wen? Trouwt Ro - sa zoet!

ROSE, ROSE

16th Century English

Rose, Rose, Rose, Rose, shall I ev - er see thee wed.

I shall mar - ry at thy will, at thy will.

ROSEWOOD CASKET

Folksong from the Blue Ridge Mountains

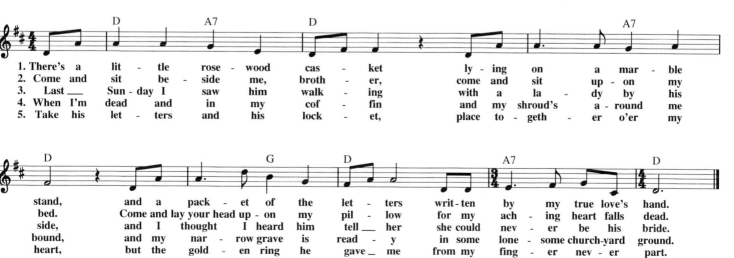

1. There's a lit - tle rose - wood cas - ket ly - ing on a mar - ble
2. Come and sit be - side me, broth - er, come and sit up - on my
3. Last Sun - day I saw him walk - ing with a la - dy by his
4. When I'm dead and in my cof - fin and my shroud's a - round me
5. Take his let - ters and his lock - et, place to - geth - er o'er my

stand, and a pack - et of the let - ters writ - ten by my true love's hand.
bed. Come and lay your head up - on my pil - low for my ach - ing heart falls dead.
side, and I thought I heard him tell her she could nev - er be his bride.
bound, and my nar - row grave is read - y in some lone - some church-yard ground.
heart, but the gold - en ring he gave me from my fing - er nev - er part.

THE ROSE OF TRALEE

Irish
Words by C. Mordaunt Spencer
Music by Charles W. Glover
1845

1. The pale moon was ris-ing a-bove the green moun-tain, the sun was de-clin-ing be-
2. The cool shades of eve-ning their man-tle were spread-ing, and Mar-y all smil-ing was

neath the blue sea, when I stray'd with my love to the pure crys-tal foun-tain that
list-'ning to me. The moon thro' the val-ley, her pale rays was shed-ding, when

stands in the beau-ti-ful vale of Tra-lee. She was love-ly and fair as the
I won the heart of the Rose of Tra-lee. Though love-ly and fair as the

rose of ___ the ___ sum-mer, yet 'twas not her beau-ty a-lone that won me. Oh, no! 'Twas the
rose of ___ the ___ sum-mer, yet 'twas not her beau-ty a-lone that won me. Oh, no! 'Twas the

truth in her eye ev-er dawn-ing, that made me love Mar-y, the Rose of Tra-lee.
truth in her eye ev-er dawn-ing, that made me love Mar-y, the Rose of Tra-lee.

ROSIN THE BEAU

Irish

1. I've trav-elled all o-ver this world, ___ And now to an-oth-er I
2. When I'm dead and laid out on the coun-ter, A voice you will hear from be-
3. Then get a half doz-en stout fel-lows, And stack them all up in a
4. Then get this half doz-en stout fel-lows, And let them all stag-ger and
5. Then get ye a cou-ple of bot-tles, Put one at me head and me
6. I've on-ly this one con-so-la-tion, As out of this world ___ I

go, ___ And I know that good quar-ters are wait-ing To
low, ___ Say-ing, "Send down a hogs-head of whis-key To
row, ___ Let them drink out of half gal-lon bot-tles To the
go, ___ And ___ dig a great hole in the mead-ow And
toe, ___ With ___ a dia-mond ring scratch up-on them The
go, ___ I ___ know that the next gen-er-a-tion Will re-

wel-come old Ros-in the Beau, ___ To wel-come old Ros-in the
drink with old Ros-in the Beau, ___ To drink with old Ros-in the
mem-'ry of Ros-in the Beau, ___ To the mem-'ry of Ros-in the
in it put Ros-in the Beau, ___ And in it put Ros-in the
name of old Ros-in the Beau, ___ The name of old Ros-in the
sem-ble old Ros-in the Beau, ___ Will re-sem-ble old Ros-in the

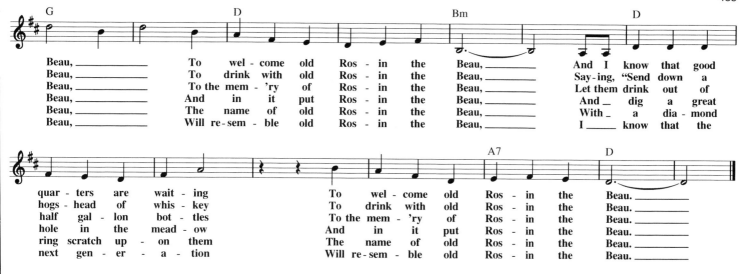

Beau, _____ To wel - come old Ros - in the Beau, _____ And I know that good
Beau, _____ To drink with old Ros - in the Beau, _____ Say-ing, "Send down a
Beau, _____ To the mem - 'ry of Ros - in the Beau, _____ Let them drink out of
Beau, _____ And in it put Ros - in the Beau, _____ And _ dig a great
Beau, _____ The name of old Ros - in the Beau, _____ With _ a dia - mond
Beau, _____ Will re-sem - ble old Ros - in the Beau, _____ I _____ know that the

quar - ters are wait - ing To wel - come old Ros - in the Beau. _____
hogs - head of whis - key To drink with old Ros - in the Beau. _____
half gal - lon bot - tles To the mem - 'ry of Ros - in the Beau. _____
hole in the mead - ow And in it put Ros - in the Beau. _____
ring scratch up - on them The name of old Ros - in the Beau. _____
next gen - er - a - tion Will re-sem - ble old Ros - in the Beau. _____

ROUND THE BAY OF MEXICO

Sea Chantey

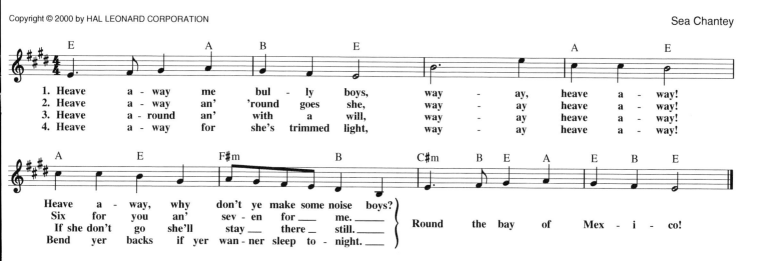

1. Heave a - way me bul - ly boys, way - ay, heave a - way!
2. Heave a - way an' 'round goes she, way - ay heave a - way!
3. Heave a - round an' with a will, way - ay heave a - way!
4. Heave a - way for she's trimmed light, way - ay heave a - way!

Heave a - way, why don't ye make some noise boys?
Six for you an' sev - en for ___ me.
If she don't go she'll stay ___ there _ still. ____
Bend yer backs if yer wan - ner sleep to - night. ___
Round the bay of Mex - i - co!

THE ROVING GAMBLER

American

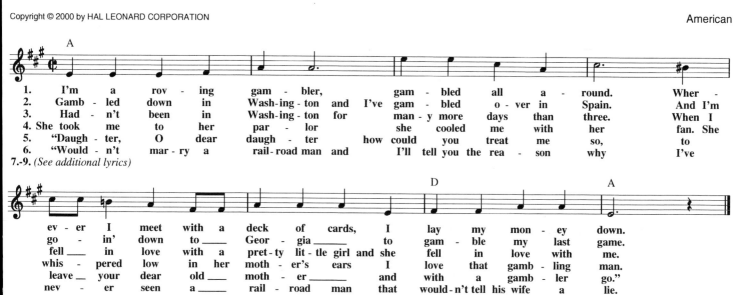

1. I'm a rov - ing gam - bler, gam - bled all a - round. Wher -
2. Gamb - led down in Wash-ing - ton and I've gam - bled o - ver in Spain. And I'm
3. Had - n't been in Wash-ing - ton for man - y more days than three. When I
4. She took me to her par - lor she cooled me with her fan. She
5. "Daugh - ter, O dear daugh - ter how could you treat me so, to
6. "Would - n't mar - ry a rail-road man and I'll tell you the rea - son why I've
7.-9. *(See additional lyrics)*

ev - er I meet with a deck of cards, I lay my mon - ey down.
go - in' down to ___ Geor - gia ___ to gam - ble my last game.
fell ___ in love with a pret - ty lit - tle girl and she fell in love with me.
whis - pered low in her moth - er's ears I love that gamb - ling man.
leave _ your dear old ___ moth - er ___ and with a gamb - ler go."
nev - er seen a ___ rail - road man that would-n't tell his wife a lie.

Additional Lyrics

7. "Wouldn't marry a farmer, he's always in the rain;
   The man I want to marry, wears a great, big, gold watch chain."

8. See the train a-comin', she's comin' 'round the curve,
   A-whistlin' and a-blowin', and a-strainin' ev'ry nerve."

9. "Mother, O dear mother, I'll tell you if I can;
   If you ever see me comin' back, I'll be with the gambling man."

ROW, ROW, ROW YOUR BOAT

American Folk Round

Row, row, row your boat, Gen - tly down the stream;

Mer - ri - ly, mer - ri - ly, mer - ri - ly, mer - ri - ly; Life is but a dream.

RUE

Folksong from Northern England

1. Come all you fair and ten - der girls that flour - ish in your
2. And when your thyme is past and gone he'll care no more for
3. A wom - an is a branch - ed tree and man a sing - ing

prime, __ prime. Be - ware, be - ware, make your gar - den __ fair, let no man steal __ your
you. __ And eve - ry day that your gar - den is waste will spread all o - ver with
wind. __ And from her branch - es __ care - less - ly he'll take what he __ can

thyme, ____ thyme.)
rue, ____ rue. } Let __ no man __ steal ____ your ____ thyme.
find, ____ find.)

RUN, CHILDREN, RUN

Southern American

Run, chil - dren, run, the pat - ter - roll - er catch you, Run, chil - dren, run! It's

al - most day. This child ran, this child flew,

This child lost his Sun - day shoe. Run, chil - dren, run, the

pat - ter - roll - er catch you, Run, chil - dren, run! It's al - most day.

RUSSIAN LULLABY

American version of a Russian Folksong

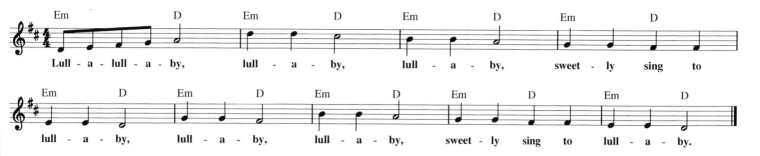

Lull - a - lull - a - by, lull - a - by, lull - a - by, sweet - ly sing to lull - a - by, lull - a - by, lull - a - by, sweet - ly sing to lull - a - by.

RYE WHISKEY

American

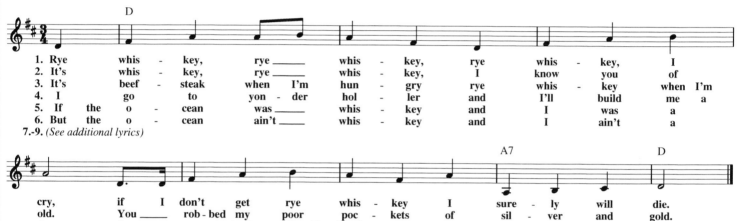

1. Rye whis - key, rye _____ whis - key, rye whis - key, I
2. It's whis - key, rye _____ whis - key, I know you of
3. It's beef - steak when I'm hun - gry rye whis - key when I'm
4. I go to yon - der hol - ler and I'll build me a
5. If the o - cean was _____ whis - key and I was a
6. But the o - cean ain't _____ whis - key and I ain't a

7.-9. *(See additional lyrics)*

cry, if I don't get rye whis - key I sure - ly will die.
old. You _____ rob - bed my poor poc - kets of sil - ver and gold.
dry. A _____ green - back when I'm hard up, oh, heav - en when I die.
still. And I'll give you a gal - lon for a five - dol - lar bill.
duck. I'd _____ dive to the bot - tom and nev - er come up.
duck. So I'll play Jack - o - Dia - monds and trust to my luck.

Additional Lyrics

7. Her parents don't like me,
They say I'm too poor,
And I'm unfit
To darken her door.

8. Her parents don't like me,
Well, my money's my own,
And them that don't like me
Can leave me alone.

9. Oh whiskey, you villain,
You're no friend to me,
You killed my poor pappy,
God-damn you, try me.

SABLE ISLAND SONG

Folksong from Nova Scotia

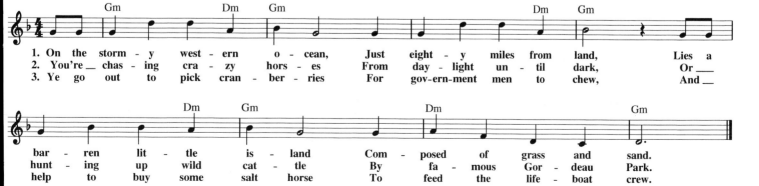

1. On the storm - y west - ern o - cean, Just eight - y miles from land, Lies a
2. You're _ chas - ing cra - zy hors - es From day - light un - til dark, Or _
3. Ye go out to pick cran - ber - ries For gov - ern - ment men to chew, And _

bar - ren lit - tle is - land Com - posed of grass and sand.
hunt - ing up wild cat - tle By fa - mous Gor - deau Park.
help to buy some salt horse To feed the life - boat crew.

SACRAMENTO

Sea Chantey

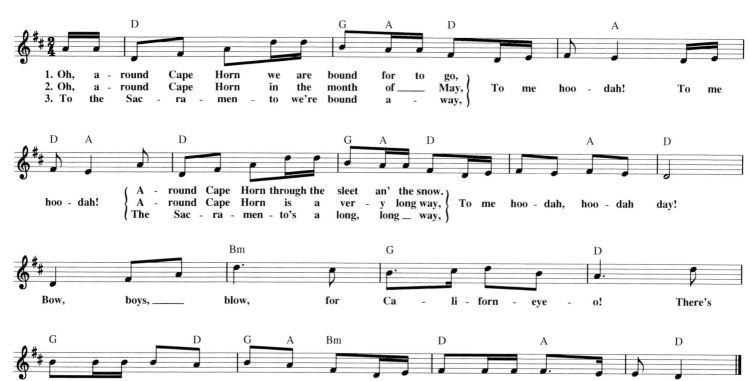

1. Oh, a - round Cape Horn we are bound for to go,
2. Oh, a - round Cape Horn in the month of ___ May,
3. To the Sac - ra - men - to we're bound a - way,
To me hoo - dah! To me hoo - dah!

A - round Cape Horn through the sleet an' the snow.
A - round Cape Horn is a ver - y long way,
The Sac - ra - men - to's a long, long ___ way,
To me hoo - dah, hoo - dah day!

Bow, boys, ___ blow, for Ca - li - forn - eye - o! There's

plen - ty o' gold, so I've been told, on the banks of the Sac - ra - men - to.

SAILING IN THE BOAT

American

1. Sail - ing in the boat when the tide runs high, Sail - ing in the boat when the tide runs high,
2. Here ___ she ___ comes, so ___ fresh and fair, Sky - blue ___ eyes and ___ curl - y hair,
3. Rose ___ in the gar - den for you, young man, Rose ___ in the gar - den for you, young man,
4. Choose ___ your ___ part - ner, ___ stay till day, Choose ___ your ___ part - ner, ___ stay till day,
5. Old ___ folks ___ say 'tis the ver - y best way, Old ___ folks ___ say 'tis the ver - y best way,

Sail - ing in the boat when the tide runs high, Wait - ing for the pret - ty girl to come by'n by.
Ros - y in cheek, dim - ple in her skin, Say, ___ young ___ man, ___ but you can't come in.
Rose in the gar - den, get it if you can, But ___ take ___ care not a frost - bit - ten one.
Choose ___ your ___ part - ner, ___ stay till day, And don't nev - er mind ___ what the old folks say.
Old ___ folks ___ say 'tis the ver - y best way, To ___ court all night ___ and ___ sleep all day.

SAILING, SAILING

Words and Music by
Godfrey Marks

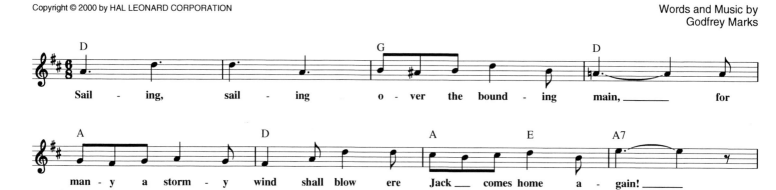

Sail - ing, sail - ing o - ver the bound - ing main, ___ for

man - y a storm - y wind shall blow ere Jack ___ comes home a - gain! ___

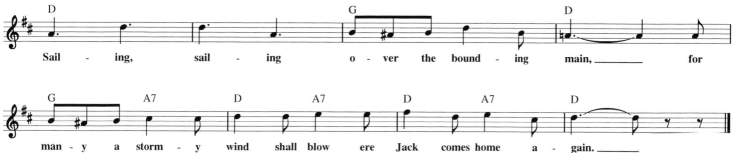

Sail - ing, sail - ing o - ver the bound - ing main, _____ for man - y a storm - y wind shall blow ere Jack comes home a - gain. _____

SAIL AWAY, LADIES

American

1. If ev - er I get my new house done, Sail a - way, la - dies, sail a - way, I'll
2. Ain't _ no use to sit and cry, Sail a - way, la - dies, sail a - way,
3. I've got __ a home in Ten - nes - see, Sail a - way, la - dies, sail a - way,
4. Come a - long, girls, and go with me, Sail a - way, la - dies, sail a - way,
5. Hush, lit - tle ba - by, don't you cry, Sail a - way, la - dies, sail a - way,

give the old one to my son, Sail a - way, la - dies, sail a - way.
You'll be an an - gel by and by, Sail a - way, la - dies, sail a - way.
That's the place I wan - na be, Sail a - way, la - dies, sail a - way.
We'll go down to Ten - nes - see, Sail a - way, la - dies, sail a - way.
You'll be an an - gel by and by, Sail a - way, la - dies, sail a - way.

Don't she rock 'em, die - di - o, Don't she rock 'em, die - di - o,

Don't she rock __ 'em, die - di - o, Don't she rock 'em, die - di - o.

SAILOR ON THE DEEP BLUE SEA

American

1. It was on one sum - mer's eve - ning, Just a - bout the hour _ of three, When my
2. Oh, he prom-ised to write me a let - ter, He __ said he'd write _ to me. But I've
3. Oh, my moth - er's dead and bur - ied, My __ pa's for - sak - en me, And I
4. Fare _ well to friends and re - la-tions, It's the last you'll see __ of me, For I'm

dar - ling start - ed to leave me For to sail up - on the deep blue __ sea.
not heard from my __ dar - ling Who is sail - ing on the deep blue __ sea.
have no one for to love me But the sail - or on the deep blue __ sea.
going to end my __ trou - bles By __ drown-ing in the deep blue __ sea.

SAILOR'S HORNPIPE

English

ST. JAMES INFIRMARY

Words and Music by
Joe Primrose

SAKURA
(Cherry Blossoms)

Japanese

Ka - su - mi ka ku - mo___ ka, Ni o - i - zo i - zu - ru.
Win - ter - time is fi - nally___ past, Now the spring is here at___ last.

I - za - ya! I - za - ya! Mi_____ ni_____ yu - kan.
Come with me! Come with me! Let us feel the sun - shine fair.

SAL GOT A MEATSKIN

American

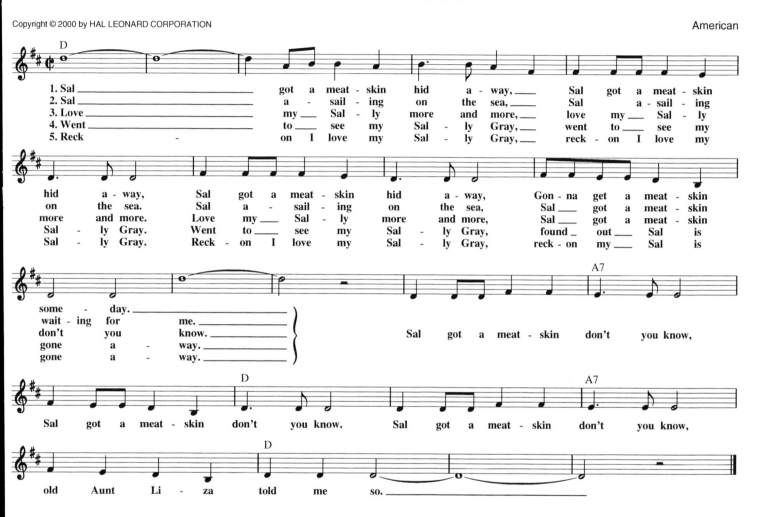

1. Sal___ got a meat - skin hid a - way,___ Sal got a meat - skin
2. Sal___ a - sail - ing on the sea,___ Sal a - sail - ing
3. Love___ my___ Sal - ly more and more,___ love my___ Sal - ly
4. Went___ to___ see my Sal - ly Gray,___ went to___ see my
5. Reck - on I love my Sal - ly Gray,___ reck - on I love my

hid a - way, Sal got a meat - skin hid a - way, Gon - na get a meat - skin
on the sea. Sal a - sail - ing on the sea, Sal___ got a meat - skin
more and more. Love my___ Sal - ly more and more, Sal___ got a meat - skin
Sal - ly Gray. Went to___ see my Sal - ly Gray, found___ out___ Sal is
Sal - ly Gray. Reck - on I love my Sal - ly Gray, reck - on my___ Sal is

some - day.____ Sal got a meat - skin don't you know,
wait - ing for me.____
don't you know.____
gone a - way.____
gone a - way.____

Sal got a meat - skin don't you know. Sal got a meat - skin don't you know,

old Aunt Li - za told me so.____

SALLY ANN

Southern Appalachian Folksong

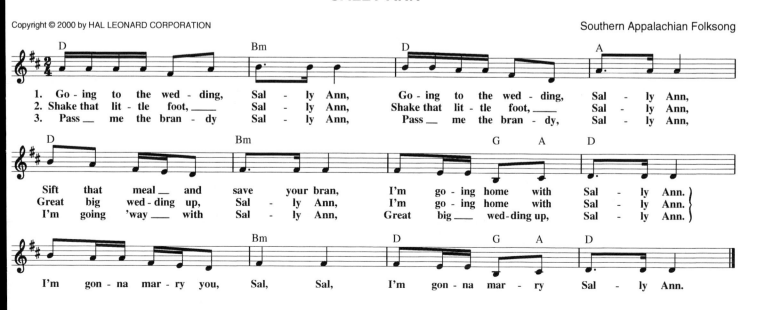

1. Go - ing to the wed - ding, Sal - ly Ann, Go - ing to the wed - ding, Sal - ly Ann,
2. Shake that lit - tle foot,___ Sal - ly Ann, Shake that lit - tle foot,___ Sal - ly Ann,
3. Pass___ me the bran - dy Sal - ly Ann, Pass___ me the bran - dy, Sal - ly Ann,

Sift that meal___ and save your bran, I'm go - ing home with Sal - ly Ann.
Great big wed - ding up, Sal - ly Ann, I'm go - ing home with Sal - ly Ann.
I'm going 'way___ with Sal - ly Ann, Great big___ wed - ding up, Sal - ly Ann.

I'm gon - na mar - ry you, Sal, Sal, I'm gon - na mar - ry Sal - ly Ann.

SALLY BROWN

Sea Chantey

1. Sal - ly Brown she's a bright mu - lat - ter,
2. Sal - ly Brown she ___ has a daugh - ter,
3. Sev - en long years I court - ed Sal - ly,
4. Sal - ly Brown I'm ___ bound to leave ___ you,
5. Sal - ly she's a ___ "Ba - dian" beau - ty,
6. Sal - ly lives on the old plan - ta - tion,

Way hey, _____ roll and go.

She drinks rum and chews ter - back - er,
Sent me sail - in' 'cross the wa - ter,
Sev - en long years I court - ed Sal - ly,
Sal - ly Brown, I'll not de - ceive you,
Sal - ly she's a "Ba - dian" beau - ty,
She be - longs to the Wild Goose Na - tion,

Spent my mon - ey on Sal - ly Brown.

SALLY GOODIN

Southern Appalachian Folksong

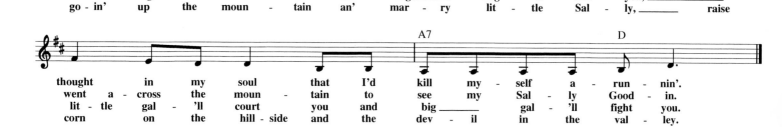

1. Had a piece of pie an' I had a piece of pud - din', an' I gave it all a - way just to
2. Love a 'ta - ter pie an' I love an ap - ple pud - din', an' I love a lit - tle gal that they
3. Sal - ly is my doo - zy and Sal - ly is my dai - sy; ___ when Sal - ly says she hates me, I
4. Rain - in' an' a - pour-in' an' the creek's ___ run - nin' mud - dy, ___ an' I'm so damn ___ drunk that I

see my Sal - ly Good - in. Well, I had a piece of pie an' I had a piece of pud - din', an' I
call ___ Sal - ly Good - in. Well, I love a 'ta - ter pie an' I love an ap - ple pud - din', an' I
think I'm go - in' cra - zy. ___ Well, Sal - ly is my doo - zy and Sal - ly is my dai - sy; ___ when
can't ___ stand ___ stead - y. Well, it's rain - in' an' a - pour-in' an' the creek's ___ run - nin' mud - dy, ___ and

gave it all a - way just to see my Sal - ly Good - in. Well, I looked down the road an' I
love a lit - tle gal that they call ___ Sal - ly Good - in. An' I dropped the 'ta - ter pie an' I
Sal - ly says she hates me, I think I'm go - in' cra - zy. Well, the lit - tle dog - 'll bark an' the
I'm so damn ___ drunk that I can't ___ stand ___ stead - y. Well, I'm go - in' up the moun - tain an'

seen my Sal - ly com - in', an' I thought in my soul that I'd kill my - self a - run - nin'. Well, I
left the ap - ple pud - din', but I went a - cross the moun - tain to see my Sal - ly Good - in'. An' I
big ___ dog - 'll bite you, _____ lit - tle gal - 'll court you and big ___ gal - 'll fight you. Well, the
mar - ry lit - tle Sal - ly, _____ raise corn on the hill - side an' the dev - il in the val - ley. Well, I'm

looked down the road an' I seen my Sal - ly com - in', an' I
dropped the 'ta - ter pie an' I left the ap - ple pud - din', but I
lit - tle dog - 'll bark an' the big _____ dog - 'll bite you, _____
go - in' up the moun - tain an' mar - ry lit - tle Sal - ly, _____ raise

thought in my soul that I'd kill my - self a - run - nin'.
went a - cross the moun - tain to see my Sal - ly Good - in.
lit - tle gal - 'll court you and big _____ gal - 'll fight you.
corn on the hill - side and the dev - il in the val - ley.

SALLY IN OUR ALLEY

English

1. Of all the girls that are so smart, there's none like pret-ty Sal-ly. She
2. Of all the days with-in the week, I dear-ly love but one day, and
3. My mas-ter and the neigh-bors all make game of me and Sal-ly, and

is the dar-ling of my heart and lives in our al-ley. There
that's the day that comes be-twixt a Sat-ur-day and Mon-day. Oh,
but for her I'd rath-er be a slave and row a gal-ley. But

is no la-dy in the land that's half as sweet as Sal-ly. She is the
then I'm dressed all in my best to walk a-broad with Sal-ly. She is the
when my sev-en years are out, oh, then I'll mar-ry Sal-ly. and then how

dar-ling of my heart and lives in our al-ley.
dar-ling of my heart and lives in our al-ley.
hap-pi-ly we'll live, but not in our al-ley.

SAM HALL

Words by C.W. Ross, circa 1850s
English

1. Now my name is Sam-uel Hall, Sam-uel Hall, Sam-uel Hall. Oh, my
2. Now I killed a man, they said, so they said, so they said. Oh, I
3. Now they put me in the quad, in the quad, in the quad. Oh, they
4. Now the preach-er he did come, he did come, he did come. Oh, the
5. Oh, it's up the rope I go, up I go, up I go. Oh, its
6. I must hang un-til I'm dead, till I'm dead, till I'm dead. I must

name is Sam-uel Hall, Sam-uel Hall. Oh, my name is Sam-uel
killed a man, they said, yes they said. Oh, I killed a man, they
put me in the quad, in the quad. Oh, they put me in the
preach-er, he did come, he did come. Oh, the preach-er he did
up the rope I go, up I go. Oh, it's up the rope I
hang un-til I'm dead, till I'm dead. I must hang un-til I'm

Hall and I hate you one and all, you're a bunch of muck-ers all, blast your
said, and I left him lay-in' dead 'cause I bashed his blood-y head, blast his
quad and they left me there, by God, fas-tened to a blood-y chain rod, blast their
come, and he looked so dog-gone glum as he talked of King-dom Come, blast his
go, while you crit-ters down be-low are say-ing, "Sam, I told you so," blast your
dead 'cause I killed a man, they said, and I left him lay-in' dead, blast his

eyes. You're a bunch of muck-ers all, blast your eyes.
eyes. 'Cause I bashed his blood-y head, blast his eyes.
eyes. Fas-tened to a blood-y chain rod, blast their eyes.
eyes. As he talked of King-dom Come, blast his eyes.
eyes. Say-in', "Sam, I told you so," blast your eyes.
eyes. And I left him lay-in' dead, blast his eyes.

SALTY DOG

American

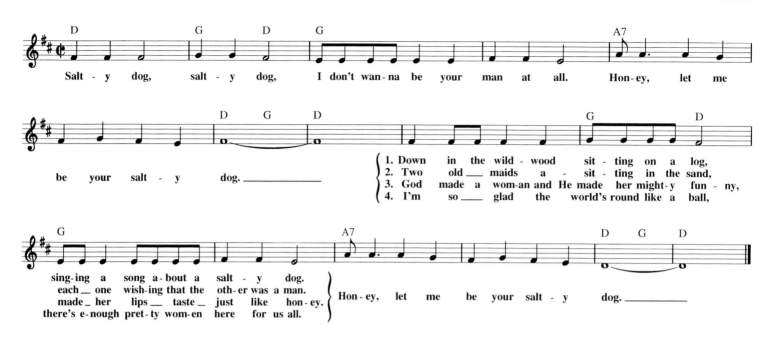

Salt-y dog, salt-y dog, I don't wan-na be your man at all. Hon-ey, let me

be your salt-y dog. _____

1. Down in the wild-wood sit-ting on a log,
2. Two old ___ maids a-sit-ting in the sand,
3. God made a wom-an and He made her might-y fun-ny,
4. I'm so ___ glad the world's round like a ball,

sing-ing a song a-bout a salt-y dog.
each ___ one wish-ing that the oth-er was a man.
made ___ her lips ___ taste ___ just like hon-ey.
there's e-nough pret-ty wom-en here for us all.

Hon-ey, let me be your salt-y dog. _____

SAMSON

Southern American

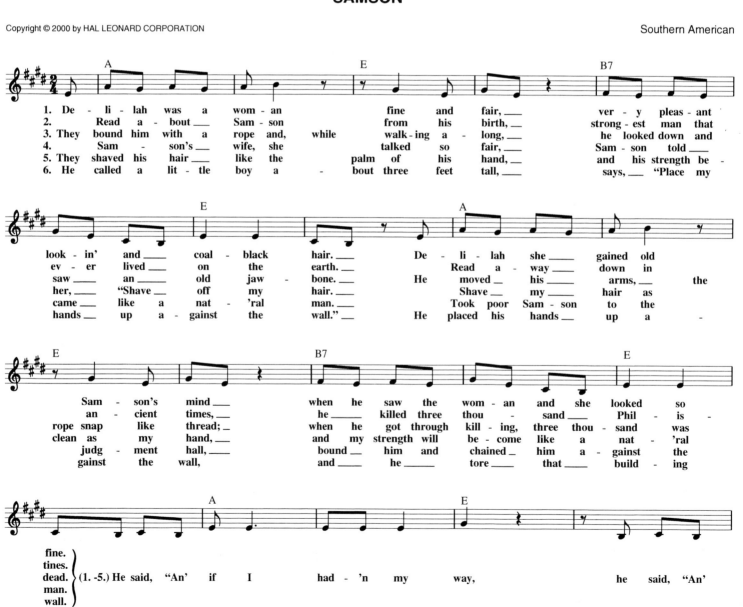

1. De-li-lah was a wom-an fine and fair, ___ ver-y pleas-ant
2. Read a-bout ___ Sam-son from his birth, ___ strong-est man that
3. They bound him with a rope and, while walk-ing a-long, ___ he looked down and
4. Sam-son's ___ wife, she talked so fair, ___ Sam-son told ___
5. They shaved his hair ___ like the palm of his hand, ___ and his strength be-
6. He called a lit-tle boy a-bout three feet tall, ___ says, ___ "Place my

look-in' and ___ coal-black hair. ___ De-li-lah she ___ gained old
ev-er lived ___ on the earth. ___ Read a-way ___ down in
saw ___ an old jaw-bone. ___ He moved ___ his ___ arms, ___ the
her, ___ "Shave ___ off my hair. ___ Shave ___ my ___ hair as
came ___ like a nat-'ral man. ___ Took poor Sam-son to the
hands ___ up a-gainst the wall." ___ He placed his hands ___ up a-

Sam-son's mind ___ when he saw the wom-an and she looked so
an-cient times, ___ he ___ killed three thou-sand ___ Phil-is-
rope snap like thread; ___ when he got through kill-ing, three thou-sand was
clean as my hand, ___ and my strength will be-come like a nat-'ral
judg-ment hall, ___ bound ___ him and chained ___ him a-gainst the
gainst the wall, and ___ he ___ tore ___ that ___ build-ing

fine.
tines.
dead. } (1.-5.) He said, "An' if I had-'n my way, he said, "An'
man.
wall.}
down. (6.) He said, "An' now I got ___ my way, he said, "An'

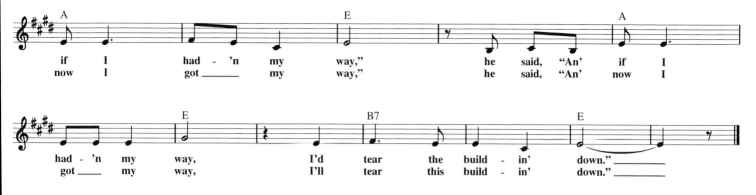

if I had-'n my way," he said, "An' if I
now I got_____ my way," he said, "An' now I

had-'n my way, I'd tear the build - in' down." _____
got_____ my way, I'll tear this build - in' down." _____

SAM BASS

American Cowboy Song

1. Sam Bass was born in In - di - an - a, it was his na - tive
2. Sam used to deal in race_____ stock,__ one called the Den - ton
3. Sam left the Col - lins ranch_____ in_____ the mer - ry month of
4. On their way back to Tex - as,_____ they robbed the U. P.
5. Sam made it back to Tex - as_____ all right side up with
6. Sam had_____ four com - pan - ions,_____ four bold and dar - ing

7.-10. *(See additional lyrics)*

home, and at the age of sev - en - teen, young Sam be - gan to
Mare. He matched her in scrub rac - es and took her to the
May with a herd of Tex - as cat - tle, the Black Hills for to
train, and then split up in cou - ples_____ and start - ed out a -
care, rode in - to the town of Den - ton_____ with all his friends to
lads. They were Rich - ard - son, Jack - son, Joe Col - lins and Old

roam. He came out to old Tex - as, _____ a cow - boy for to
Fair. Sam used to coin the mon - ey _____ and spend it just as
see. Sold out in Cus - ter Cit - y _____ and then got on a
gain. Joe Col - lins and his part - ner _____ were o - ver - tak - en
share. Sam's life was short in Tex - as, _____ three rob - b'ries he did
Dad. Four more bold and dar - ing cow - boys the rang - ers nev - er

be; a kind - er - heart - ed fel - low _____ you'll sel - dom ev - er see.
free. He al - ways drank good whis - key _____ wher - ev - er he might be.
spree; a hard - er set of cow - boys _____ you'll sel - dom ev - er see.
soon; with all their hard - earned mon - ey, _____ they had to meet their doom.
do: he robbed all the mail, pas - sen - ger _____ and ex - press cars too.
knew; they whipped the Tex - as rang - ers _____ and ran the boys in blue.

Additional Lyrics

7. Sam had another companion, called Arkansas for short;
Was shot by a Texas ranger by name of Thomas Floyd.
Oh, Tom, he's a big six-footer and thinks he's mighty fly,
But I can tell you this racket— he's a dead-beat on the sly.

8. Jim Murphy was arrested, and then released on bail;
He jumped his bond at Tyler and then took the train for Terrill.
But Major Jones had posted Jim, and that was all a stall;
'Twas only a plan to capture Sam before the coming fall.

9. Sam met his fate of Round Rock, July the twenty-third.
They pierced poor Sam with rifle balls and emptied out his purse.
Poor Sam, he is a corpse and six feet under clay,
And Jackson's in the bushes trying to get away.

10. Jim had borrowed Sam's good gold and didn't want to pay,
The only shot he saw was to give poor Sam away.
He sold out Sam and Barnes and left their friends to mourn—
Oh, what a scorching Jim will get when Gabriel blows his horn!

SANTY ANNA

Sea Chantey

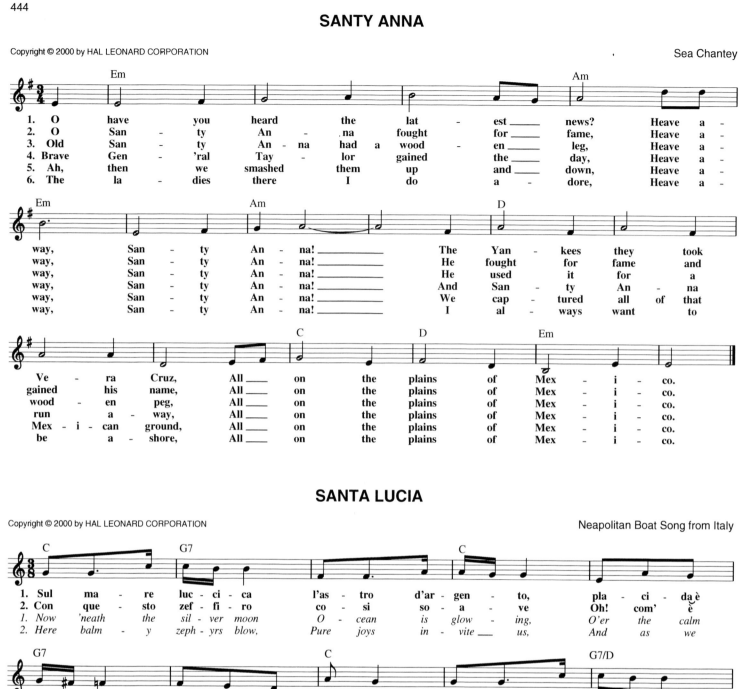

1. O have you heard the lat - est ____ news? Heave a-
2. O San - ty An - na fought for ____ fame, Heave a-
3. Old San - ty An - na had a wood - en ____ leg, Heave a-
4. Brave Gen - 'ral Tay - lor gained the ____ day, Heave a-
5. Ah, then we smashed them up and ____ down, Heave a-
6. The la - dies there I do a - dore, Heave a-

way, San - ty An - na! ____ The Yan - kees they took
way, San - ty An - na! ____ He fought for fame and
way, San - ty An - na! ____ He used it for a
way, San - ty An - na! ____ And San - ty An - na
way, San - ty An - na! ____ We cap - tured all of that
way, San - ty An - na! ____ I al - ways want to

Ve - ra Cruz, All ____ on the plains of Mex - i - co.
gained his name, All ____ on the plains of Mex - i - co.
wood - en peg, All ____ on the plains of Mex - i - co.
run a - way, All ____ on the plains of Mex - i - co.
Mex - i - can ground, All ____ on the plains of Mex - i - co.
be a - shore, All ____ on the plains of Mex - i - co.

SANTA LUCIA

Neapolitan Boat Song from Italy

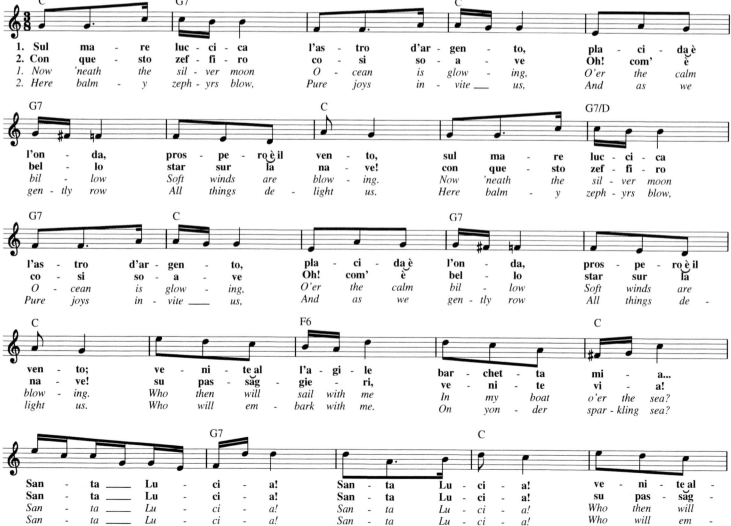

1. Sul ma - re luc - ci - ca l'as - tro d'ar - gen - to, pla - ci - da è
2. Con que - sto zef - fi - ro co - si so - a - ve Oh! com' è
1. Now 'neath the sil - ver moon O - cean is glow - ing, O'er the calm
2. Here balm - y zeph - yrs blow, Pure joys in - vite ____ us, And as we

l'on - da, pros - pe - ro è il ven - to, sul ma - re luc - ci - ca
bel - lo star sur la na - ve! con que - sto zef - fi - ro
bil - low Soft winds are blow - ing. Now 'neath the sil - ver moon
gen - tly row All things de - light us. Here balm - y zeph - yrs blow,

l'as - tro d'ar - gen - to, pla - ci - da è l'on - da, pros - pe - ro è il
co - si so - a - ve Oh! com' è bel - lo star sur la
O - cean is glow - ing, O'er the calm bil - low Soft winds are
Pure joys in - vite ____ us, And as we gen - tly row All things de -

ven - to; ve - ni - te al l'a - gi - le bar - chet - ta mi - a...
na - ve! su pas - sag - gie - ri, ve - ni - te vi - a!
blow - ing. Who then will sail with me In my boat o'er the sea?
light us. Who will em - bark with me. On yon - der spar - kling sea?

San - ta ____ Lu - ci - a! San - ta Lu - ci - a! ve - ni - te al
San - ta ____ Lu - ci - a! San - ta Lu - ci - a! su pas - sag
San - ta ____ Lu - ci - a! San - ta Lu - ci - a! Who then will
San - ta ____ Lu - ci - a! San - ta Lu - ci - a! Who will em -

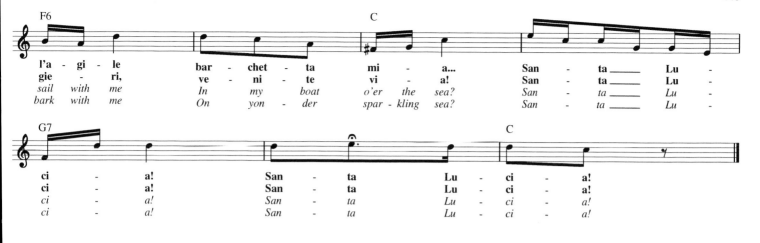

F6

l'a - gi - le bar - chet - ta mi - a... San - ta ___ Lu -
gie - ri, ve - ni - te vi - a! San - ta ___ Lu -
sail with me In my boat o'er the sea? San - ta ___ Lu -
bark with me On yon - der spar - kling sea? San - ta ___ Lu -

G7   **C**

ci - a! San - ta Lu - ci - a!
ci - a! San - ta Lu - ci - a!
ci - a! San - ta Lu - ci - a!
ci - a! San - ta Lu - ci - a!

SCHOOL DAYS

Words by Will D. Cobb
Music by Gus Edwards

G   **Am7   D7**   **G**

1. Noth - ing to do, Nel - lie Dar - ling, Noth - ing to do, you say? ___
2. 'Mem - ber the hill, Nel - lie Dar - ling, And the oak tree that grew on its brow? ___

D   G   **D7**

___ Let's take a trip on mem - or - y's ship, Back to the by - gone
They've built for - ty sto - ries up - on that old hill, And the oak's an old chest - nut

G   **Am7   D7**

days. ___ Sail to the old vil - lage school house, An - chor out -
now. ___ 'Mem - ber the mead - ows so green, dear, So fra - grant with

C   G   **A7**   **D   A7**   **D**

side the school door, ___ Look in and see, there's you and there's me, A
clo - ver and maize? ___ In - to new cit - y lots and pre - ferred bus - 'ness plots They've

A7   **D**   **G**   **D**

cou - ple of kids once more. ___ } School days, school
cut them up since those days. ___

G   **D7**

days, dear old gold - en rule days, Read - in' and 'rit - in' and

G

'rith - me - tic, Taught to the tune of a hick - 'ry stick. You were my

E7   A7   **D7**   **G**

queen in cal - i - co. I was your bash - ful, bare - foot beau, And you

C   **G   B   Em A7**   **D7**   **G**

wrote on my slate, "I love you, Joe," When we were a cou - ple of kids. ___

SCARBOROUGH FAIR

English

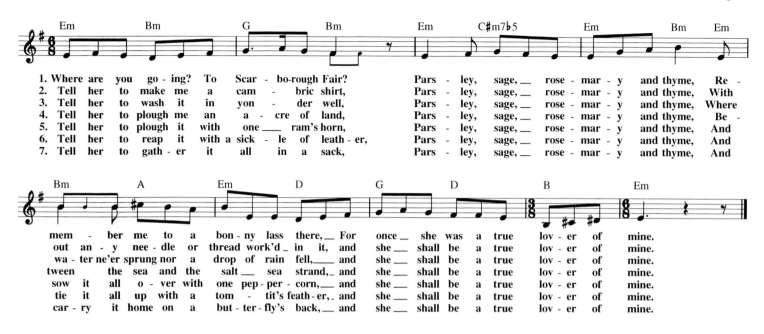

1. Where are you go-ing? To Scar-bo-rough Fair? Pars-ley, sage, __ rose-mar-y and thyme, Re-
2. Tell her to make me a cam-bric shirt, Pars-ley, sage, __ rose-mar-y and thyme, With
3. Tell her to wash it in yon-der well, Pars-ley, sage, __ rose-mar-y and thyme, Where
4. Tell her to plough me an a-cre of land, Pars-ley, sage, __ rose-mar-y and thyme, Be-
5. Tell her to plough it with one __ ram's horn, Pars-ley, sage, __ rose-mar-y and thyme, And
6. Tell her to reap it with a sick-le of leath-er, Pars-ley, sage, __ rose-mar-y and thyme, And
7. Tell her to gath-er it all in a sack, Pars-ley, sage, __ rose-mar-y and thyme, And

mem-ber me to a bon-ny lass there, __ For once __ she was a true lov-er of mine.
out an-y nee-dle or thread work'd _ in it, and she __ shall be a true lov-er of mine.
wa-ter ne'er sprung nor a drop of rain fell, __ and she __ shall be a true lov-er of mine.
tween the sea and the salt __ sea strand, _ and she __ shall be a true lov-er of mine.
sow it all o-ver with one pep-per-corn, __ and she __ shall be a true lov-er of mine.
tie it all up with a tom-tit's feath-er, _ and she __ shall be a true lov-er of mine.
car-ry it home on a but-ter-fly's back, __ and she __ shall be a true lov-er of mine.

SCOTLAND'S BURNING

16th Century English Round

Scot-land's burn-ing, Scot-land's burn-ing. Look out, look out.

Fire, fire, fire, fire. Pour on wa-ter, pour on wa-ter.

This song may be sung as a 4-part round.

SCOTS WHA HAE

Scottish
Words by Robert Burns

1. Scots wha hae wi' Wal-lace bled, Scots wham Bruce has of-ten led, __ Wel-come to your
2. Wha will be a trai-tor knave? Wha can fill a cow-ard's grave? _ Wha sae base as
3. By op-pres-sion's woes and pains, By your sons in ser-vile chains, _ We will drain our

gor-y bed Or to vic-to-ry! Now's the day and now's the hour,
be a slave? Let him turn and flee! Wha for Scot-land's king and law,
dear-est veins, But they shall be free. Lay the proud u-surp-ers low!

See the front o' bat-tle lour; See ap-proach proud Ed-ward's pow'r, Chains and slav-er-y.
Free-dom's sword will strong-ly draw, Free-man stand or free-man fa', Let him fol-low me!
Ty-rants fall in ev-'ry foe! Lib-er-ty's in ev-'ry blow! Let us do or die!

SEEING NELLIE HOME

Words by J. Fletcher
Music by Frances Kyle

1. In the sky the bright stars glit - tered, _____ on the bank the pale moon shone.
2. On my arm a soft hand rest - ed, _____ rest - ed light as o - cean foam.
3. On my lips a whis - per trem - bled, _____ trem - bled till it dared to come.
4. On my life new hopes were dawn - ing, _____ and those hopes have lived and grown.

It was from Aunt Di - nah's quilt - ing par - ty I was see - ing Nel - lie home. I was see - ing Nel - lie home, _____ I was see - ing Nel - lie home. It was from Aunt Di - nah's quilt - ing par - ty I was see - ing Nel - lie home.

SET DOWN, SERVANT

African-American Spiritual

"Set down, ser - vant." "I cain' set down." "Set down, ser - vant." "I cain' set down." _ "Set down, ser - vant." "I cain' set down. My soul's so hap - py that I cain' set down. My Lord, you _ know _____ that you prom - ise _ me, _ prom - ise me a long white robe _____ an' a { pair of shoes." / star - ry crown." / gold - en waist-band." }

"Go yon - der, _ an - gel, fetch me a { pair of shoes, _____ / star - ry crown. _____ / gold - en waist - band. _____ }

Last time D.C. al Fine

place them on - a my ser - vant's feet. }
place it on - a my ser - vant's head. } Now, ser - vant, please set down."
place it 'round _ my ser - vant's waist. }

THE SEVEN IRISHMEN

Irish

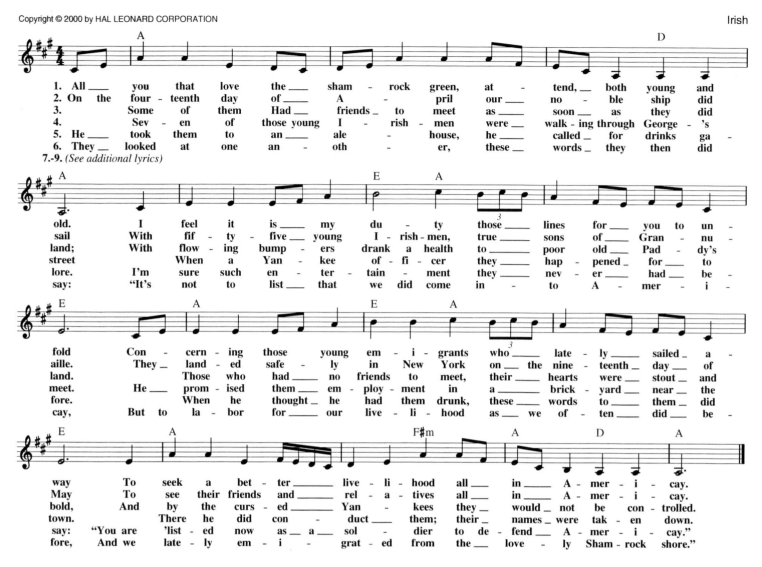

1. All ___ you that love the ___ sham - rock green, at - tend, ___ both young and
2. On the four - teenth day of ___ A - pril our ___ no - ble ship did
3. ___ Some of them Had ___ friends _ to meet as ___ soon ___ as they did
4. ___ Sev - en of those young I - rish - men were ___ walk - ing through George - 's
5. He ___ took them to an ___ ale - house, he ___ called _ for drinks ga -
6. They _ looked at one an - oth - er, these ___ words _ they then did

7.-9. *(See additional lyrics)*

old. I feel it is ___ my du - ty those ___ lines for ___ you to un -
sail With fif - ty - five ___ young I - rish-men, true ___ sons of ___ Gran - nu -
land; With flow - ing bump - ers drank a health to ___ poor old ___ Pad - dy's
street When a Yan - kee of - fi - cer they ___ hap - pened _ for ___ to
say: "It's not to list ___ that we did come in - to A - mer - i -

fold Con - cern - ing those young em - i - grants who ___ late - ly ___ sailed _ a -
aille. They _ land - ed safe - ly in New York on ___ the nine - teenth - day ___ of
land. Those who had ___ no friends to meet, their ___ hearts were ___ stout _ and
fore. When he thought _ he had them drunk, these ___ words to ___ them _ did
cay, But to la - bor for ___ our live - li - hood as ___ we of - ten ___ did ___ be -

way To seek a bet - ter ___ live - li - hood all ___ in ___ A - mer - i - cay.
May To see their friends and ___ rel - a - tives all ___ in ___ A - mer - i - cay.
bold, And by the curs - ed ___ Yan - kees they _ would _ not be con - trolled.
town. There he did con - duct ___ them; their _ names _ were tak - en down.
say: "You are 'list - ed now as _ a ___ sol - dier to de - fend ___ A - mer - i - cay."
fore, And we late - ly em - i - grat - ed from the ___ love - ly Sham - rock shore."

Additional Lyrics

7. Twelve Yankees dressed as soldiers came in without delay.
They said, "My lads, you must prepare with us to come away.
You signed with one of our officers, so you cannot now refuse,
So prepare, my lads, to join our ranks, for you must pay your dues."

8. The Irish blood began to rise, one of those heroes said,
"We have one only life to lose, therefore we're not afraid.
Although we are from Ireland, this day we'll let you see,
We'll die like Sons of Grannuaille and keep our liberty."

9. The Irish boys got to their feet, it made the Yankees frown.
As fast as they could strike a blow, they knocked the soldiers down.
With bloody heads and broken bones, they left them in crimson gore,
And proved themselves St. Patrick's Day throughout Columbus' shore.

SHAKE THAT LITTLE FOOT

Texas Play Party Song

1. Old Aunt Di - nah went to town Rid - ing a bil - ly goat, lead - ing a hound.
2. Hound dog barked and bil - ly goat jumped, Set Aunt ___ Di - nah strad - dle of a ___ stump.
3. Old Aunt Di - nah, sick to bed; sent for the doc - tor, doc - tor ___ said:
4. Get up, Di - nah, you ain't sick. All you ___ need ___ is a hick - o - ry stick.

Shake that lit - tle foot, Di - nah, O, Shake that lit - tle foot, Di - nah - o.

SHALL WE GATHER AT THE RIVER?

19th Century American
Words and Music by
Robert Lowry

1. Shall we gath-er at the riv-er, Where bright an-gel feet have trod;____
2. On the bos-om of the riv-er, Where the Sav-ior King we own,____
3. Ere we reach the shin-ing riv-er, Lay we ev-'ry bur-den down;____
4. Soon we'll reach the shin-ing riv-er, Soon our pil-grim-age will cease;____

With its crys-tal tide for-ev-er Flow-ing by the____ throne of____ God?
We shall meet, and sor-row nev-er 'Neath the glo-ry____ of the____ throne.
Grace our spir-its will de-liv-er, And pro-vide a____ robe and____ crown.
Soon our hap-py hearts will quiv-er With the mel-o-dy of____ peace.

Yes, we'll gath-er at the riv-er, The beau-ti-ful, the beau-ti-ful____ riv-er,

Gath-er with the saints____ at the riv-er That flows by the throne of____ God.

THE SHANTY-MAN'S LIFE

American Loggers' Song

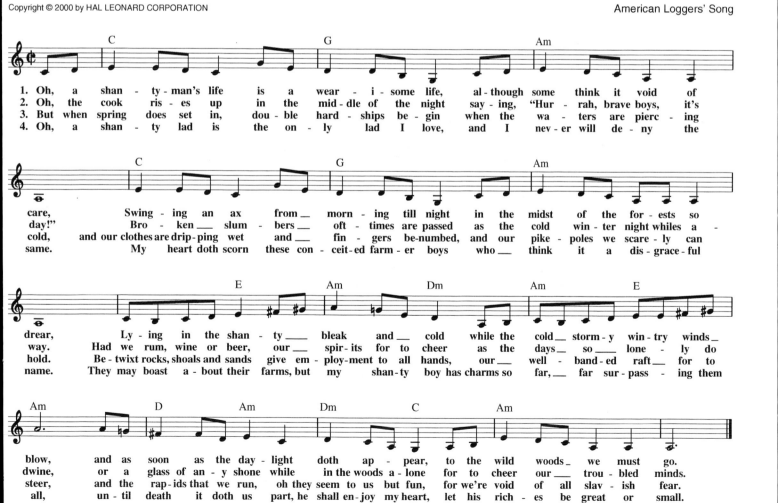

1. Oh, a shan-ty-man's life is a wear-i-some life, al-though some think it void of
2. Oh, the cook ris-es up in the mid-dle of the night say-ing, "Hur-rah, brave boys, it's
3. But when spring does set in, dou-ble hard-ships be-gin when the wa-ters are pierc-ing
4. Oh, a shan-ty lad is the on-ly lad I love, and I nev-er will de-ny the

care, Swing-ing an ax from____ morn-ing till night in the midst of the for-ests so
day!" Bro-ken____ slum-bers____ oft-times are passed as the cold win-ter night whiles a-
cold, and our clothes are drip-ping wet and____ fin-gers be-numbed, and our pike-poles we scare-ly can
same. My heart doth scorn these con-ceit-ed farm-er boys who____ think it a dis-grace-ful

drear, Ly-ing in the shan-ty____ bleak and____ cold while the cold____ storm-y win-try winds____
way. Had we rum, wine or beer, our____ spir-its for to cheer as the days____ so____ lone-ly do
hold. Be-twixt rocks, shoals and sands give em-ploy-ment to all hands, our____ well-band-ed raft____ for to
name. They may boast a-bout their farms, but my shan-ty boy has charms so far,____ far sur-pass-ing them

blow, and as soon as the day-light doth ap-pear, to the wild woods____ we must go.
dwine, or a glass of an-y shone while in the woods a-lone for to cheer our____ trou-bled minds.
steer, and the rap-ids that we run, oh they seem to us but fun, for we're void of all slav-ish fear.
all, un-til death it doth us part, he shall en-joy my heart, let his rich-es be great or small.

SHALOM CHAVEYRIM
(Shalom, My Friend)

Folksong from Israel

Sha - lom cha - vey - rim, sha - lom cha - vey - rim, sha - lom, sha -
Sha - lom, my ___ friend, sha - lom, my ___ friend, sha - lom, sha -

lom. L' - hit - ra - ot, l' - hit - ra - ot, sha - lom, sha - lom.
lom. We'll meet a - gain, we'll meet a - gain, sha - lom, sha - lom.

THE SHAN VAN VOCHT

Irish

1. O! the French are on the sea, ___ says the Shan Van Vocht. O! the French are on the
2. And where will they have their camp? ___ says the Shan Van Vocht. Where ___ will they have their
3. And what col - or will they wear? ___ says the Shan Van Vocht. What ___ col - or will they
4. And will Ire - land then be free? ___ says the Shan Van Vocht. Will ___ Ire - land then be

sea, ___ says the Shan Van Vocht. O! the French are in the Bay, ___ they'll be
camp? ___ says the Shan Van Vocht. On the Cur - ragh of Kil - dare ___ the ___
wear? ___ says the Shan Van Vocht. What ___ col - or should be seen ___ where our
free? ___ says the Shan Van Vocht. Yes! ___ Ire - land shall be free ___ from the

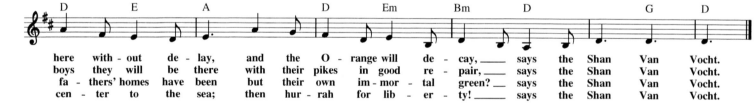

here with - out de - lay, and the O - range will de - cay, ___ says the Shan Van Vocht.
boys they will be there with their pikes in good re - pair, ___ says the Shan Van Vocht.
fa - thers' homes have been but their own im - mor - tal green? ___ says the Shan Van Vocht.
cen - ter to the sea; then hur - rah for lib - er - ty! ___ says the Shan Van Vocht.

SHADY GROVE

Southern Appalachian Folksong

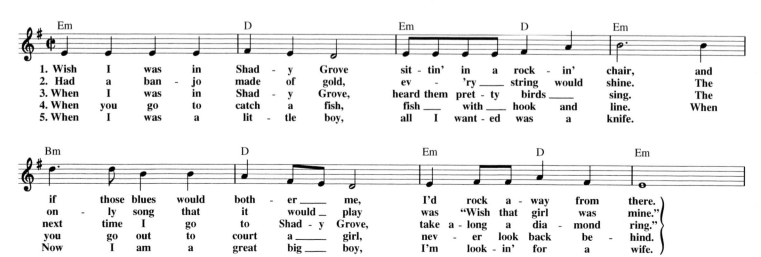

1. Wish I was in Shad - y Grove sit - tin' in a rock - in' chair, and
2. Had a ban - jo made of gold, ev - 'ry ___ string would shine. The
3. When I was in Shad - y Grove, heard them pret - ty birds ___ sing. The
4. When you go to catch a fish, fish with ___ hook and line. When
5. When I was a lit - tle boy, all I want - ed was a knife.

if those blues would both - er ___ me, I'd rock a - way from there.
on - ly song that it would ___ play was "Wish that girl was mine."
next time I go to Shad - y Grove, take a - long a dia - mond ring."
you go out to court a ___ girl, nev - er look back be - hind.
Now I am a great big ___ boy, I'm look - in' for a wife.

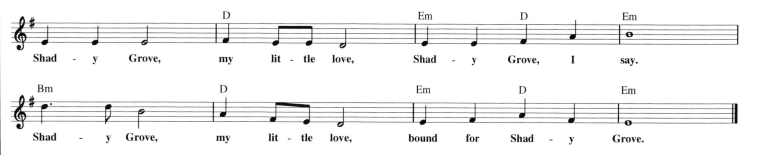

Shad - y Grove, my lit - tle love, Shad - y Grove, I say.

Shad - y Grove, my lit - tle love, bound for Shad - y Grove.

THE SHAVER

Sea Chantey

1. When I was a lit - tle ti - ny boy, I went to sea in Storm-y's em - ploy. I ____
2. Oh, they whacked me up and they whacked me down, the mate he cracked me on ____ the crown. They ____
3. When we lol-loped a - round ___ a - bout Cape Horn, I wished that I had nev - er been born. And I

sailed a - way _____ a - cross the sea. }
whacked me round ____ and round and round } when I was just a shav - er, a
wished I was home ____ all safe and sound }

shav - er. Oh, I was wea - ry of the sea when I ____ was just a shav - er.

SHE MOVED THROUGH THE FAIR

Words by Padraic Colum
Traditional Irish Melody

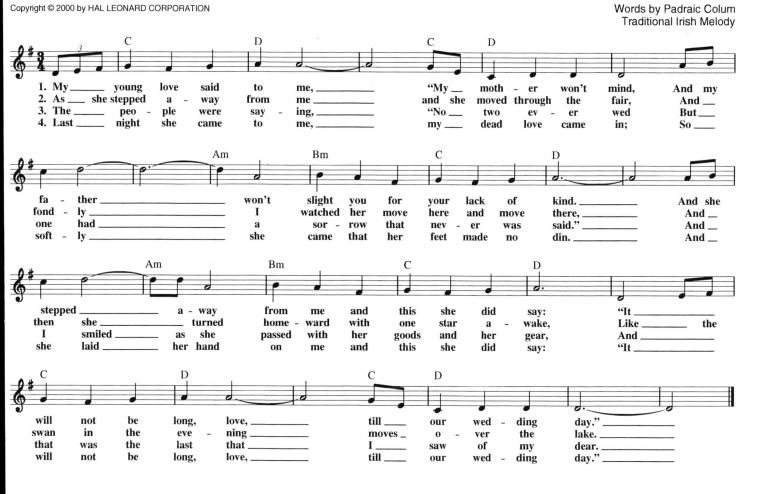

1. My _____ young love said to me, _____ "My __ moth - er won't mind, And my
2. As ___ she stepped a - way from me _____ and she moved through the fair, And __
3. The _____ peo - ple were say - ing, _____ "No __ two ev - er wed But__
4. Last _____ night she came to me, _____ my __ dead love came in; So ___

fa - ther _____ won't slight you for your lack of kind. _____ And she
fond - ly _____ I watched her move here and move there, _____ And __
one had _____ a sor - row that nev - er was said." _____ And __
soft - ly _____ she came that her feet made no din. _____ And __

stepped _____ a - way from me and this she did say: "It _____
then she _____ turned home - ward with one star a - wake, Like _____ the
I smiled _____ as she passed with her goods and her gear, And _____
she laid _____ her hand on me and this she did say: "It _____

will not be long, love, _____ till ____ our wed - ding day." _____
swan in the eve - ning _____ moves _ o - ver the lake. _____
that was the last that _____ I ____ saw of my dear. _____
will not be long, love, _____ till ____ our wed - ding day." _____

SHE'LL BE COMIN' 'ROUND THE MOUNTAIN

19th Century Western American

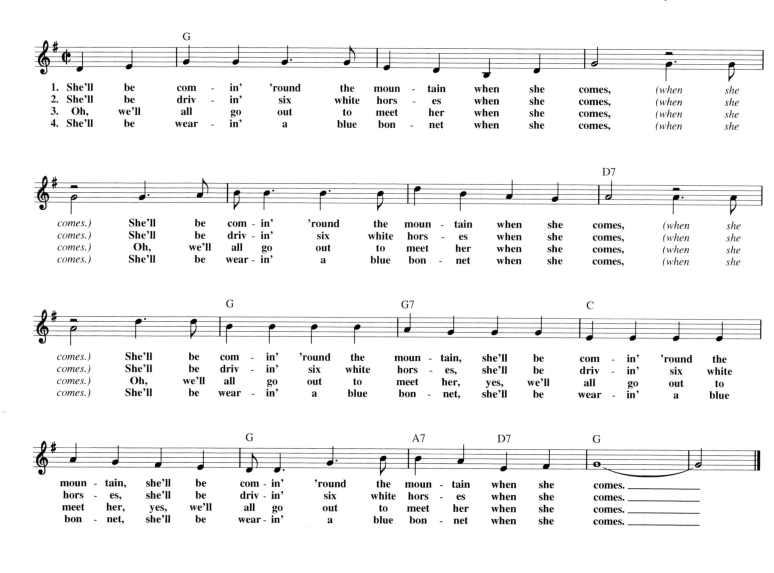

1. She'll be com - in' 'round the moun - tain when she comes, *(when she*
2. She'll be driv - in' six white hors - es when she comes, *(when she*
3. Oh, we'll all go out to meet her when she comes, *(when she*
4. She'll be wear - in' a blue bon - net when she comes, *(when she*

comes.) She'll be com - in' 'round the moun - tain when she comes, *(when she*
comes.) She'll be driv - in' six white hors - es when she comes, *(when she*
comes.) Oh, we'll all go out to meet her when she comes, *(when she*
comes.) She'll be wear - in' a blue bon - net when she comes, *(when she*

comes.) She'll be com - in' 'round the moun - tain, she'll be com - in' 'round the
comes.) She'll be driv - in' six white hors - es, she'll be driv - in' six white
comes.) Oh, we'll all go out to meet her, yes, we'll all go out to
comes.) She'll be wear - in' a blue bon - net, she'll be wear - in' a blue

moun - tain, she'll be com - in' 'round the moun - tain when she comes. ___
hors - es, she'll be driv - in' six white hors - es when she comes. ___
meet her, yes, we'll all go out to meet her when she comes. ___
bon - net, she'll be wear - in' a blue bon - net when she comes. ___

SHE WORE A YELLOW RIBBON

American
Words and Music by
George A. Norton

'Round her neck she wore a yel - low rib - bon; she wore it in the spring-time and

in the month of May. And if you asked her why the heck she wore it, she

says, "It's for my lov - er who is far, far a - way." Far a - way, ___

___ far a - way. ___ She wore it for her lov - er far a -

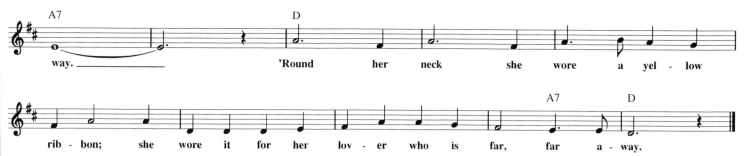

way. _____ 'Round her neck she wore a yel - low
rib - bon; she wore it for her lov - er who is far, far a - way.

SHE'S LIKE A SWALLOW

Canadian

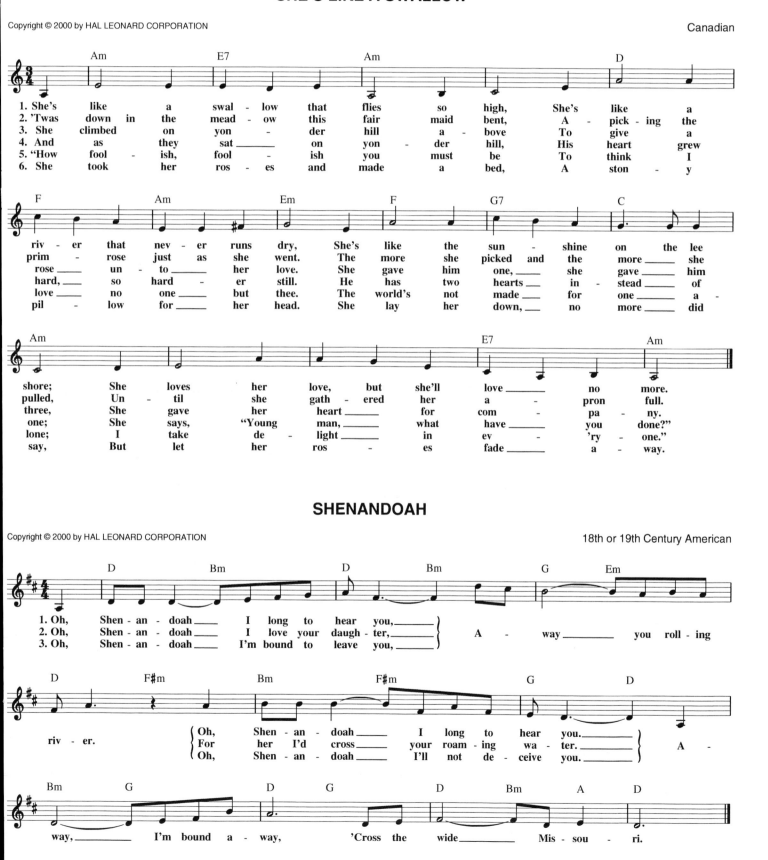

1. She's like a swal - low that flies so high, She's like a
2. 'Twas down in the mead - ow this fair maid bent, A - pick - ing the
3. She climbed on yon - der hill a - bove To give a
4. And as they sat on yon - der hill, His heart grew
5. "How fool - ish, fool - ish you must be To think I
6. She took her ros - es and made a bed, A ston - y

riv - er that nev - er runs dry, She's like the sun - shine on the lee
prim - rose just as she went. The more she picked and the more she
rose un - to her love. She gave him one, she gave him
hard, so hard - er still. He has two hearts in - stead of
love no one but thee. The world's not made for one a -
pil - low for her head. She lay her down, no more did

shore; She loves her love, but she'll love no more.
pulled, Un - til she gath - ered her a - pron full.
three, She gave her heart for com - pa - ny.
one; She says, "Young man, what have you done?"
lone; I take de - light in ev - 'ry - one."
say, But let her ros - es fade a - way.

SHENANDOAH

18th or 19th Century American

1. Oh, Shen - an - doah_____ I long to hear you,_____
2. Oh, Shen - an - doah_____ I love your daugh - ter,_____
3. Oh, Shen - an - doah_____ I'm bound to leave you,_____
A - way_____ you roll - ing

riv - er.
Oh, Shen - an - doah_____ I long to hear you._____
For her I'd cross_____ your roam - ing wa - ter._____
Oh, Shen - an - doah_____ I'll not de - ceive you._____
A -

way,_____ I'm bound a - way, 'Cross the wide_____ Mis - sou - ri.

THE SHIP THAT NEVER RETURNED

American
By Henry Clay Work

SHOO FLY, DON'T BOTHER ME

19th Century American Game Song

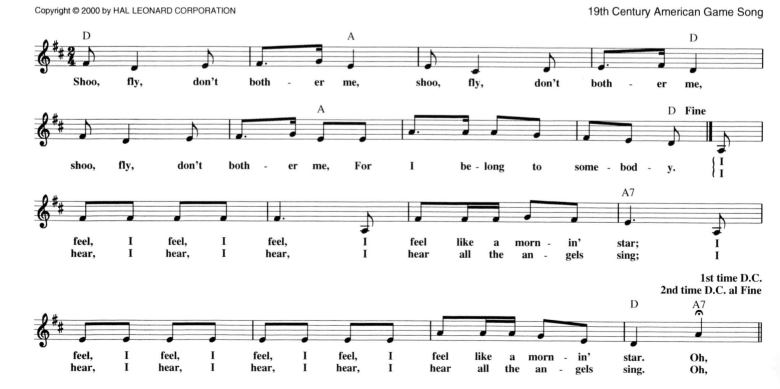

THE SIGN OF THE BONNY BLUE BELL

English

1. As I was a-walk-ing one morn-ing in Spring To
2. I stepped up to her and thus I did say: Pray
3. Six-teen, pret-ty maid? You are young for to mar-ry, I'll
4. On Mon-day night when I go there To
5. On a Tues-day morn-ing the bells they shall ring And

1. hear the birds whis-tle and the night-in-gale sing, I heard a fair
2. tell me your age and where you be-long. I be-long to the
3. leave you the oth-er four years for to tar-ry, You speak like a
4. pow-der my locks and to cur-dle my hair, There were three pret-ty
5. three pret-ty maid-ens so sweet-ly shall sing: So neat and so

1. dam-sel, so sweet-ly sang she; Say-ing: I will be mar-ried on a
2. sign of the Bon-ny Blue Bell; My age is six-teen and you
3. man with-out an-y skill; Four years I've been sin-gle a-
4. maid-ens for me a-wait-ing, Say-ing: I will be mar-ried on a
5. gay is my gold-en ring, Say-ing: I shall be mar-ried on a

1. Tues-day morn-ing, I heard a fair dam-sel, so sweet-ly sang
2. know ver-y well, I be-long to the sign of the Bon-ny Blue
3. gainst my own will, You speak like a man with-out an-y
4. Tues-day morn-ing, There were three pret-ty maid-ens for me a-wait-
5. Tues-day morn-ing, So neat and so gay is my gold-en

1. she; Say-ing: I will be mar-ried on a Tues-day morn-ing.
2. Bell; My age is six-teen and you know ver-y well.
3. skill; Four years I've been sin-gle a-gainst my own will.
4. ing, Say-ing: I will be mar-ried on a Tues-day morn-ing.
5. ring, Say-ing: I shall be mar-ried on a Tues-day morn-ing.

THE SILVER DAGGER

English

1. Sing no love songs, you'll wake my moth-er; she's sleep-ing here
2. You're the wrong one, so says my moth-er, I ought to wed
3. Go, my lov-er, go find a maid-en; my dear, sweet moth-

1. right by my side. And in her right hand there's a sil-ver dag-ger;
2. a man of wealth. So take your love songs, sing 'em to an-oth-er;
3. er must be o-beyed. That sil-ver dag-ger to pro-tect her daugh-ter

1. she says I nev-er can be your bride.
2. the sil-ver dag-ger no good for your health.
3. means on-ly one thing: I'll be an old maid.

SHOOT THE BUFFALO

American

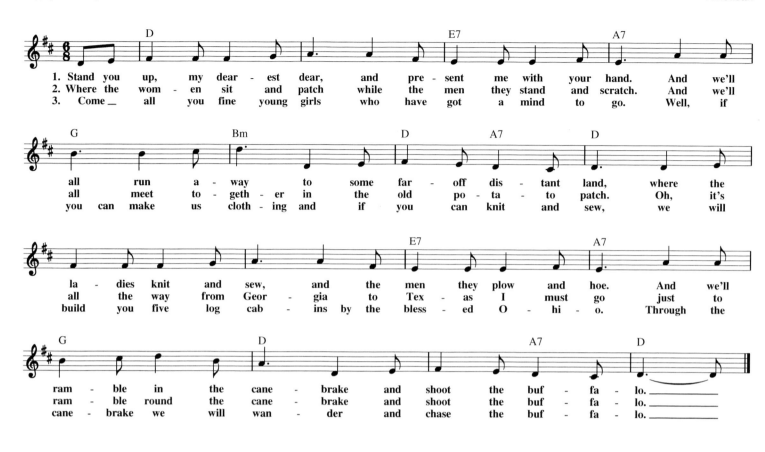

1. Stand you up, my dear-est dear, and pre-sent me with your hand. And we'll
2. Where the wom-en sit and patch while the men they stand and scratch. And we'll
3. Come _ all you fine young girls who have got a mind to go. Well, if

all run a-way to some far-off dis-tant land, where the
all meet to-geth-er in the old po-ta-to patch. Oh, it's
you can make us cloth-ing and if you can knit and sew, we will

la-dies knit and sew, and the men they plow and hoe. And we'll
all the way from Geor-gia to Tex-as I must go just to
build you five log cab-ins by the bless-ed O-hi-o. Through the

ram-ble in the cane-brake and shoot the buf-fa-lo. _____
ram-ble round the cane-brake and shoot the buf-fa-lo. _____
cane-brake we will wan-der and chase the buf-fa-lo. _____

SINCE I'VE BEEN IN THE ARMY

Irish
Traditional Scottish Melody
("Wha'll Be King but Charlie?")

1. I'm Pad-dy whack _ from Bal-ly-na-hack, not long a-go _____ turned sol-dier. In
2. The lots of girls _ my train un-furls _ would make a de-cent par-ty. There's
3. The roar-ing boys, _ they made a noise _ and whacked my like _ the div-il, and
4. My arms are bright, _ my heart is light, _ good hu-mor seems _ to warm me. I'm

grand at-tack, in storm or sack, none than will I _____ be bold-er. Wid
Ka-ty Lynch, a ti-dy wench, and Peg and Sue _____ Mc-Car-ty. There's
now be-come be-fore me dumb, or else they're might-y civ-il. There's
now be-come, wid ev-'ry chum, a fa-v'rite in _____ the ar-my. If

spir-its gay _____ I march a-way, _ I please each fair _____ be-hold-er. The
Sal-ly Maggs _ and Ju-dy Braggs _ and Mar-tha Scraggs, _ all storm me. And
Mur-phy Rourke, _ that of-ten broke _ my head, now dares-n't dare me, but
I go on _____ as I've be-gun, _ my com-rades all _____ in-form me, they

la-dies cry as me they spy, "Och! What a love-ly sol-dier!" In
Mol-ly Mag-ee, she's af-ter me since I've been in _____ the ar-my. The
bows and scrapes, and off he sneaks, since I've been in _____ the ar-my. An'
plain-ly see that I shall be a Gin-'ral in _____ the ar-my. De-

Lon - don der - ry or Lon - don mer - ry, ye la - dies all ___ I'll charm ___ ye, ___ an'
Kit - tys and Dol - lys, the Brid-gets and Pol - lys, in num - bers would _ a - larm ___ ye. E - ven
if one ne - glect to pay me re - spect, an' oth - er tips ___ the blar - ney ___ wid,
light - ful no - tion, to get pro - mo - tion! Ye la - dies thin ___ I'll charm ___ ye; for it's

down ye'll come whin I bate the drum to see me in ___ the ar - my.
Mrs. ___ White that's lost ___ her sight ad - mires me in ___ the ar - my.
"Whist, my friend, an' don't _ of - fend a gin - tle - man in the ar - my. } Wid my
my be - lief, Com - man - der - in - Chief, I soon shall be in the ar - my.

dub a dub dub dub, row dow dow dow, I live, ___ dear girls, ___ to charm ___ ye. ___ An'

down ye'll come whin I bate the drum to see me in ___ the ar - my.

THE SIOUX INDIANS

American Pioneer Song

1. I'll sing you a song, though it may be a sad one, of trials ___ and
2. I crossed the Mis - sou - ri and joined a large train ___ which bore us o'er
3. We heard of Sioux In - dians, all out on the plains, ___ a - kill - ing poor
4. We trav - eled three weeks till we came to the Platte, ___ a - pitch - ing our
5. While tak - ing re - fresh - ment, we heard a loud yell, ___ the whoops of Sioux
6. They made a bold dash and came near to our train, and the ar - rows fell
7.-9. (See additional lyrics)

trou - bles, and where first be - gun. I left my dear kin - dred, my friends and my
moun - tains, through val - ley and plain, and of - ten of eve - nings out hunt - ing we'd
driv - ers and burn - ing their trains, a - kill - ing poor driv - ers with ar - rows and
tents at the head of a flat. We spread down our blan - kets on the green grass - y
In - dians com-ing up from the dell. We sprang to our ri - fles with a flash in each
down just like hail and like rain. But with our long ri - fles we fed them cold

home, and we crossed the wide des - erts and moun - tains to roam.
go to ___ shoot the fleet an - te - lope and the wild buf - fa - lo.
bows; When ___ cap - tured by In - dians, no mer - cy they'd show.
ground where the mules and the hors - es were graz - ing a - round.
eye; "Boys," ___ says our brave lead - er, "we'll fight till we die."
lead, till ___ man - y a brave war - rior a - round us lay dead.

Additional Lyrics

7. In our little band there were just twenty-four,
And of the Sioux Indians five hundred or more.
We fought them with courage, we spoke not a word;
The whoop of Sioux Indians was all could be heard.

8. We shot their bold chief at the head of their band,
He died like a warrior with his bow in his hand.
When they saw their brave chief lie dead in his gore,
They whooped and they yelled and we saw them no more.

9. We hooked up our horses and started our train,
Three more bloody battles this trip on the plain.
And in our last battle three of our brave boys fell,
And we left them to rest in the green shady dell.

SHORT'NIN' BREAD

Plantation song from the American South

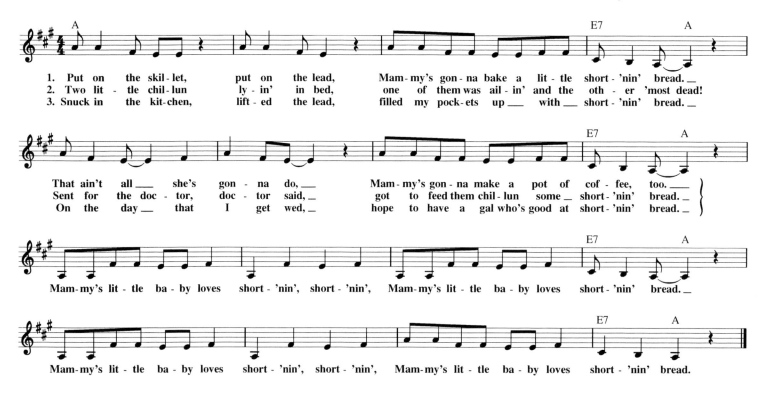

1. Put on the skil-let, put on the lead, Mam-my's gon-na bake a lit-tle short-'nin' bread. __
2. Two lit-tle chil-lun ly-in' in bed, one of them was ail-in' and the oth-er 'most dead!
3. Snuck in the kit-chen, lift-ed the lead, filled my pock-ets up __ with __ short-'nin' bread. __

That ain't all __ she's gon-na do, __ Mam-my's gon-na make a pot of cof-fee, too. __
Sent for the doc-tor, doc-tor said, __ got to feed them chil-lun some __ short-'nin' bread. __
On the day __ that I get wed, __ hope to have a gal who's good at short-'nin' bread. __

Mam-my's lit-tle ba-by loves short-'nin', short-'nin', Mam-my's lit-tle ba-by loves short-'nin' bread. __

Mam-my's lit-tle ba-by loves short-'nin', short-'nin', Mam-my's lit-tle ba-by loves short-'nin' bread.

SKIBBEREEN

19th Century Irish

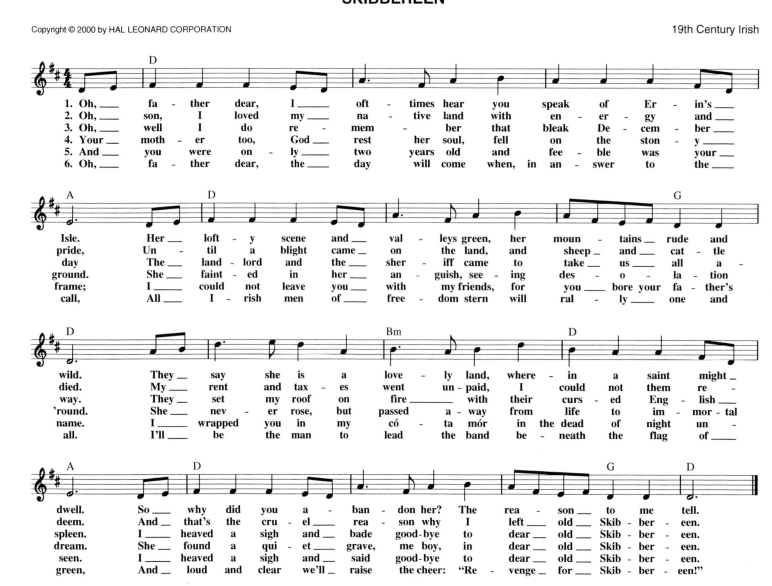

1. Oh, __ fa-ther dear, I __ oft-times hear you speak of Er-in's __
2. Oh, __ son, I loved my __ na-tive land with en-er-gy and __
3. Oh, __ well I do re-mem-ber that bleak De-cem-ber __
4. Your __ moth-er too, God __ rest her soul, fell on the ston-y __
5. And __ you were on-ly __ two years old and fee-ble was your __
6. Oh, __ fa-ther dear, the __ day will come when, in an-swer to the __

Isle. Her __ loft-y scene and __ val-leys green, her moun-tains __ rude and
pride, Un-til a blight came __ on the land, and sheep __ and __ cat-tle
day The __ land-lord and the __ sher-iff came to take __ us __ all a-
frame; I __ could not leave you __ with my friends, for you __ bore your fa-ther's
call, All __ I-rish men of __ free-dom stern will ral-ly __ one and

wild. They __ say she is a love-ly land, where-in a saint might __
died. My __ rent and tax-es went un-paid, I could not them re-
ground. She __ faint-ed in her an-guish, see-ing des-o-la-tion
name. I __ wrapped you in my có-ta mór in the dead of night un-
all. I'll __ be the man to lead the band be-neath the flag of __

dwell. So __ why did you a-ban-don her? The rea-son __ to me tell.
deem. And __ that's the cru-el __ rea-son why I left __ old __ Skib-ber-een.
spleen. I __ heaved a sigh and __ bade good-bye to dear __ old __ Skib-ber-een.
dream. She __ found a qui-et __ grave, me boy, in dear __ old __ Skib-ber-een.
seen. I __ heaved a sigh and __ said good-bye to dear __ old __ Skib-ber-een.
green, And __ loud and clear we'll __ raise the cheer: "Re-venge __ for __ Skib-ber-een!"

SHUCKIN' OF THE CORN

American

1. I have a ship on the o - cean _____ All lined with sil - ver and gold. _____ Be - fore I'd see my true love suf - fer, That ship should be an - chored and sold. _____

2. The wind blows cold in _____ Cai - ro, _____ The sun re - fus - es to shine. _____ Be - fore I'd see my true love suf - fer, I'd work all the sum - mer - time. _____

I'm a - go - in' to the shuck - in' of the corn, I'm a - go - in' to the shuck - in' of the corn, _____ A - shuck - in' of the corn and a - blow - in' of the horn, I'm a - go - in' to the shuck - in' of the corn. _____

SINGLE GIRL

American

1. When I was sin - gle, go dressed neat and fine. Now I am mar - ried, go rag - ged all the time.
2. When I was sin - gle, my shoes they did screak. Now I am mar - ried, my shoes they al - ways leak.
3. When I was sin - gle, I ate bis - cuit pie. Now I am mar - ried, eat corn-bread or _____ die.
4. Two lit - tle ba - bies all for to re - tain nei - ther one a - ble to help me one _____ grain.
5. One cry - ing "Ma - ma I want a piece of bread." One cry - ing "Ma - ma I want to go to bed."
6. Wash them and dress them and put them to bed, be - fore your man curs - es them and wish - es you were dead.

wish I were a sin - gle girl a - gain, Lord, Lord. I just wish I were a sin - gle girl a - gain.

SLEEP, MY BABY, PRECIOUS DARLING
(Duerme Niño Pequeñito)

Colombian

Sleep, my ba - by, pre - cious dar - ling, For the night is draw - ing nigh,
Duer - me ni - ño, peq - ue - ñi - to, Que la no - che vie - ne ya,

Slum - ber quick - ly, lit - tle ras - cal, As the wind sings its lull - a - by.
Duer - me pron - to mo - co - çit - o, Que el vien - to - te arul - la - rá.

Mm mm mm mm Mm mm mm mm mm _____ mm.

SHULE AGRA

17th Century Irish

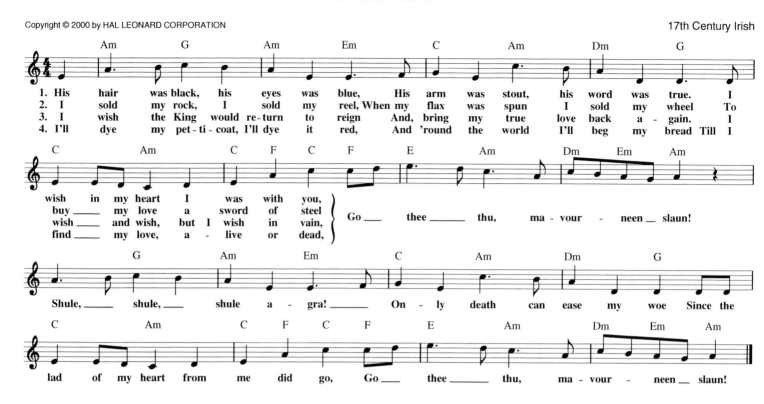

1. His hair was black, his eyes was blue, His arm was stout, his word was true. I
2. I sold my rock, I sold my reel, When my flax was spun I sold my wheel To
3. I wish the King would re-turn to reign And, bring my true love back a-gain. I
4. I'll dye my pet-ti-coat, I'll dye it red, And 'round the world I'll beg my bread Till I

wish in my heart I was with you,
buy ___ my love a sword of steel
wish ___ and wish, but I wish in vain,
find ___ my love, a-live or dead,

Go ___ thee ___ thu, ma-vour-neen ___ slaun!

Shule, ___ shule, ___ shule a-gra! On-ly death can ease my woe Since the

lad of my heart from me did go, Go ___ thee ___ thu, ma-vour-neen ___ slaun!

SING A SONG OF SIXPENCE

Nursery Rhyme Song

Sing a song of six-pence, a pock-et full of rye; Four and twen-ty black-birds

Baked in a pie. When the pie was o-pened, The birds be-gan to sing.

Was-n't that a dain-ty dish to set be-fore a king? The king was in the count-ing-house,

Count-ing out his mon-ey. The queen was in the par-lor, Eat-ing bread and hon-ey. The

maid was in the gar-den, Hang-ing out the clothes; A-long ___ came a black-bird And pecked ___ off her nose.

SIMPLE GIFTS

18th Century Shaker Hymn

'Tis the gift to be sim-ple, 'tis the gift to be free, 'tis the gift to come down

where we ought to be, and when we find our-selves in the place just right, 'twill

be in the val - ley of love and de - light. When true sim -

plic - i - ty is gained to bow and to bend we shan't be a-shamed, to turn, turn, will

be our de - light till by turn - ing, turn - ing we come round right.

SILKIE

Scottish
from the Orkney Islands

1. The silk - ie be a crea - ture strange; he ris - es
2. When he be man, he takes a wife; when he be
3. His love they will - ing - ly ac - cept, but af - ter
4. A maid - en from the Ork - ney Isles, a tar - get
5. And so, while Silk - ie kissed the lass, she rubbed his

from the sea to change in - to a man, a weird one
beast, he takes her life. La - dies, be - ware of him who
they have loved and slept, who is the mon - ster that they
for his charm, his smiles, ea - ger for love, no fool was
neck with Ork - ney grass. This had the mag - ic pow'r, you

he, whose home it is in Skule Sker - rie.
be a silk - ie come from Skule Sker - rie.
see? 'Tis "Silk - ie" come from Skule Sker - rie.
she; she knew the se - cret of Skule Sker - rie.
see, to slay the beast from Skule Sker - rie.

SKILLET GOOD AND GREASY

American

1. I'm go - in' down - town, gon - na get me a sack of flour, Gon - na
2. Well, if you say so, I'll nev - er work no more. I'll
3. I'm go - in' down - town, gon - na get me a jug of bran - dy. Gon - na

cook it ev - 'ry hour, keep my skil - let good and greas - y all the
bed down on your floor and I'll lay a - round your shan - ty all the
give it all to Nan - cy, keep her good and drunk and goos - y all the

time, time, time, skil - let good and greas - y all the time.
time, time, time, lay a - round your shan - ty all the time.
time, time, time, good and drunk and goos - y all the time.

SING AN' JUMP UP FOR JOY

Folksong from Antigua

SIX QUESTIONS

American

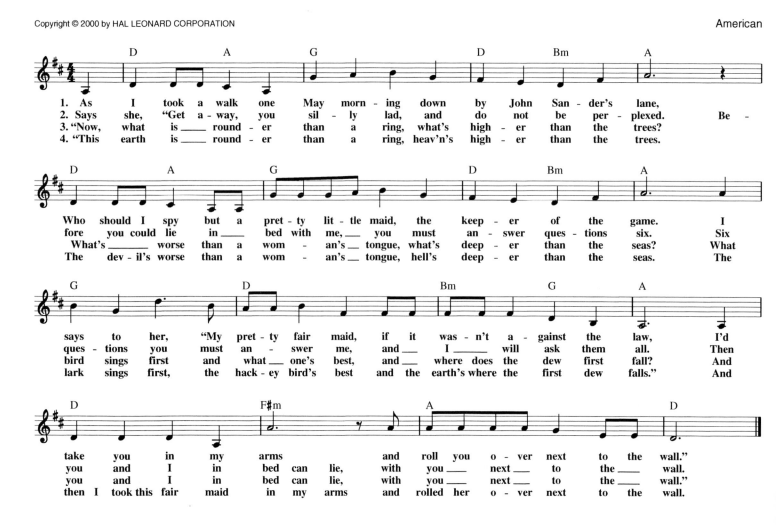

SKIP TO MY LOU

American Game Song

SLEEP, MY CHILD
(Aïnte)

Syrian, from Smyrna

SKYE BOAT SONG

Scottish Sea Chantey
Words by Sir Harold Boulton

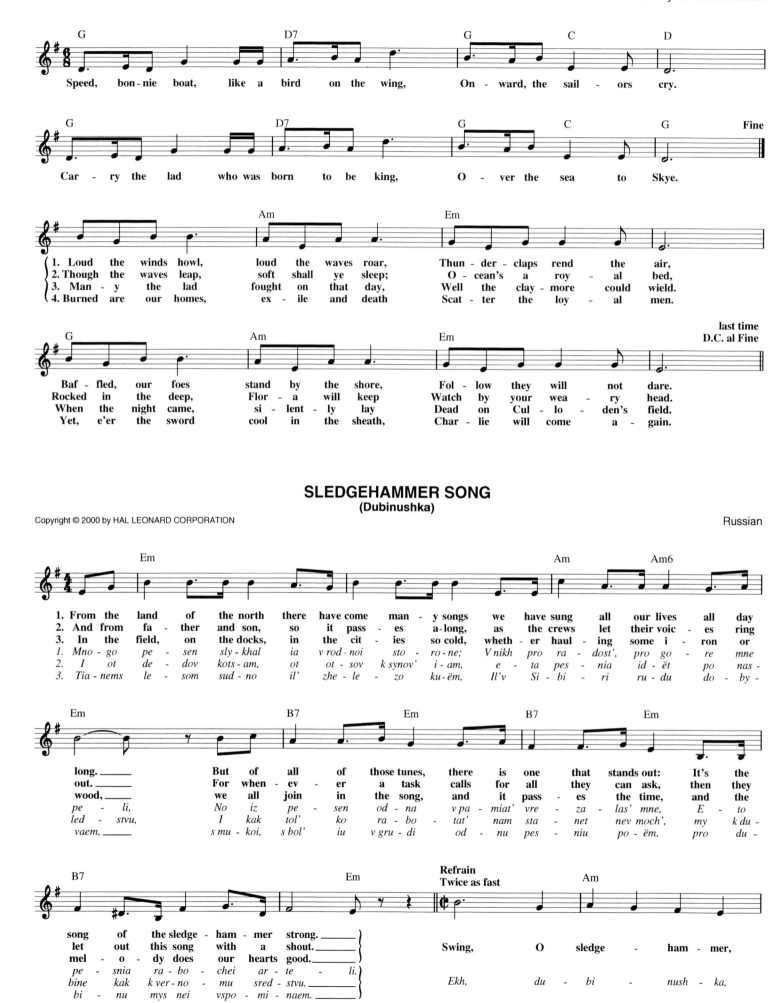

Speed, bon - nie boat, like a bird on the wing, On - ward, the sail - ors cry.
Car - ry the lad who was born to be king, O - ver the sea to Skye.

1. Loud the winds howl, loud the waves roar, Thun - der - claps rend the air,
2. Though the waves leap, soft shall ye sleep; O - cean's a roy - al bed,
3. Man - y the lad fought on that day, Well the clay - more could wield.
4. Burned are our homes, ex - ile and death Scat - ter the loy - al men.

Baf - fled, our foes stand by the shore, Fol - low they will not dare.
Rocked in the deep, Flor - a will keep Watch by your wea - ry head.
When the night came, si - lent - ly lay Dead on Cul - lo - den's field.
Yet, e'er the sword cool in the sheath, Char - lie will come a - gain.

SLEDGEHAMMER SONG
(Dubinushka)

Russian

1. From the land of the north there have come man - y songs we have sung all our lives all day
2. And from fa - ther and son, so it pass - es a - long, as the crews let their voic - es ring
3. In the field, on the docks, in the cit - ies so cold, wheth - er haul - ing some i - ron or

1. Mno - go pe - sen sly - khal ia v rod - noi sto - ro - ne; V nikh pro ra - dost', pro go - re mne
2. I ot de - dov kots - am, ot ot - sov k synov' i - am, e - ta pes - nia id - ёt po nas -
3. Tia - nems le - som sud - no il' zhe - le - zo ku - ём, Il'v Si - bi - ri ru - du do - by -

long. But of all of those tunes, there is one that stands out: It's the
out. For when - ev - er a task calls for all they can ask, then they
wood, we all join in the song, and it pass - es the time, and the
pe - li, No iz pe - sen od - na v pa - miat' vre - za - las' mne, E - to
led - stvu, I kak tol' ko ra - bo - tat' nam sta - net nev moch', my k du -
vaem, s mu - koi, s bol' iu v gru - di od - nu pes - niu po - ём, pro du -

song of the sledge - ham - mer strong.
let out this song with a shout.
mel - o - dy does our hearts good.
pe - snia ra - bo - chei ar - te - li.
bine kak k ver - no - mu sred - stvu.
bi - nu mys nei vspo - mi - naem.

Refrain
Twice as fast

Swing, O sledge - ham - mer,
Ekh, du - bi - nush - ka,

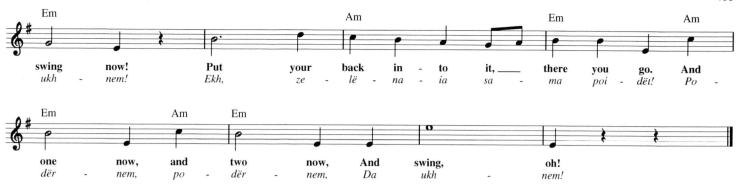

swing now! Put your back in - to it, ___ there you go. And
ukh - nem! Ekh, ze - lë - na - ia sa - ma poi - dët! Po -

one now, and two now, And swing, oh!
dër - nem, po - dër - nem, Da ukh - nem!

SLEEP, BABY, SLEEP

Pennsylvania Dutch Lullaby

Sleep, ba - by, sleep. ___ Your dad - dy's tend - ing the

sheep. ___
1. Your mom - my's tak - en the cows a - way And
2. Your mom - my's tend - ing the lit - tle ones;
3. Your mom - my's off too in gos - sip - ing flight and

won't be home 'til the break of day.
ba - by sleep as long as he wants. Sleep, ba - by, sleep.
won't be back ___ 'til late to - night.

SO EARLY IN THE MORNING

American

1. South Car - o - li - na's a sul - try clime where we used to work in the
2. When I was young I ___ used to wait on ___ Mas - ter's ta - ble, ___
3. Now Mas - ter's dead and ___ gone to rest; of ___ all the mas - ters ___

sum - mer - time. Mas - ter be - neath the shade would lay while we poor ser - vants
lay the plate, pass the ___ bot - tle when him dry, ___ brush a - way the
he were best. I nev - er seen the like since I was born, miss him now he's

toiled all day.
blue - tailed fly. So ___ ear - ly in the morn - ing. So ___ ear - ly in the
dead and gone.

morn - ing, so ___ ear - ly in the morn - ing be - fore the break of day.

SNAKE BAKED A HOECAKE

American

The snake baked a hoe-cake and set the frog to watch it. The frog fell a-doz-ing and the liz-ard came and took it. Bring back my hoe-cake, you long-tailed nan-y-O.

SOLDIER BOY

Appalachian Folksong

1.,4. We go walk-ing on the green grass thus, thus, thus. Come,
2. I would not mar-ry a doc-tor; he's al-ways kill-ing the sick. I'd
3. I would not mar-ry a farm-er; he's al-ways sell-ing his grain. I'd

all you pret-ty fair maids, come walk a-long with us. So pret-ty and so fair as you
rath-er mar-ry a sol-dier boy that march-es dou-ble quick. Sol-dier boy, O sol-dier boy,
rath-er mar-ry a sol-dier boy that march-es through the rain. Sol-dier boy, O sol-dier boy,

take your-selves to be, I'll choose you for a part-ner; come walk a-long with me.
sol-dier boy for me. If I ev-er get mar-ried, a sol-dier's wife I'll be.
sol-dier boy for me. If I ev-er get mar-ried, a sol-dier's wife I'll be.

SOLDIER, SOLDIER, WILL YOU MARRY ME?

American

1. "Sol-dier, sol-dier, will you mar-ry me with your mus-ket, fife and drum?" "Oh,
2. Then off to the cob-bler she did go as fast as she could run. She
3. "Now, sol-dier, sol-dier, will you mar-ry me with your mus-ket, fife and drum?" "Oh,
4. Then off to the tai-lor she did go as fast as she could run. She
5. "Now, sol-dier, sol-dier, will you mar-ry me with your mus-ket, fife and drum?" "Oh,

how can I mar-ry such a pret-ty lit-tle girl when I have no shoes to put on?"
brought him back the fin-est that was there, and the sol-dier put them on.
how can I mar-ry such a pret-ty lit-tle girl when I have no coat to put on?"
brought him back the fin-est that was there, and the sol-dier put it on.
how can I mar-ry such a pret-ty lit-tle girl when I wife and ba-by at home?"

SOMEBODY'S KNOCKING AT YOUR DOOR

African-American Spiritual

SOMETIMES I FEEL LIKE A MOTHERLESS CHILD

African-American Spiritual

THE SON OF A GAMBOLIER

Irish

1. I'm a ram - bling wretch of pov - er - ty, from Tip - p'ry town I came. 'Twas pov - er - ty com -
2. I once was tall and hand - some, and was so ver - y neat. They thought I was too
3. I'm a ram - bling wretch of pov - er - ty, from Tip - p'ry town I came. My coat I bought from an

pelled me first to go out in the rain. In all sorts of weath - er, be it wet or be it
good to live, most good e - nough to eat. But now I'm old, my coat is torn, and pov - er - ty holds me
old pawn shop way down in Maid - en Lane. My hat I got from a sail - or lad just eight - een years a -

dry, I am bound to get my live - li - hood, or lay me down and die.
fast, and ev - 'ry girl turns up her nose as I go wan - d'ring past.
go, and my shoes I picked from an old dust heap, I'll have you all to know.

Then com -

bine your hum - ble dit - ties as from tav - ern to tav - ern we steer. Like ev - 'ry hon - est

fel - low, I drinks my la - ger beer. Like ev - 'ry jol - ly fel - low, I

takes my whis - key clear; I'm a ram - bling wretch of po - ver - ty and the son of a gam - bo -

lier. I'm the son of a, son of a, son of a, son of a, son of a gam - bo - lier.

SONG OF THE VOLGA BOATMAN

Russian

THE SONS OF LIBERTY

18th Century Irish

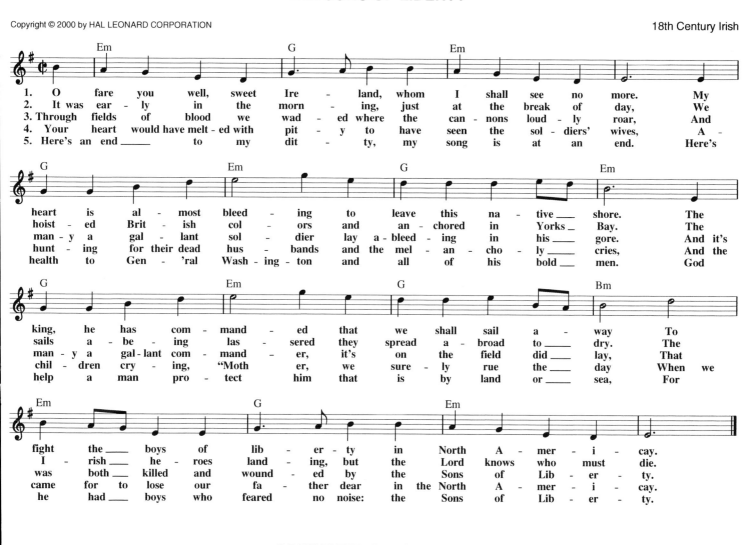

1. O fare you well, sweet Ire - land, whom I shall see no more. My
2. It was ear - ly in the morn - ing, just at the break of day, We
3. Through fields of blood we wad - ed where the can - nons loud - ly roar, And
4. Your heart would have melt - ed with pit - y to have seen the sol - diers' wives, A -
5. Here's an end ____ to my dit - ty, my song is at an end. Here's

heart is al - most bleed - ing to leave this na - tive ____ shore. The
hoist - ed Brit - ish col - ors and an - chored in Yorks _ Bay. The
man - y a gal - lant sol - dier lay a - bleed - ing in his ____ gore. And it's
hunt - ing for their dead hus - bands and the mel - an - cho - ly ____ cries, And the
health to Gen - 'ral Wash - ing - ton and all of his bold ____ men. God

king, he has com - mand - ed that we shall sail a - way To
sails a - be - ing las - sered they spread a - broad to ____ dry. The
man - y a gal - lant com - mand - er, it's on the field did ____ lay, That
chil - dren cry - ing, "Moth - er, we sure - ly rue the ____ day When we
help a man pro - tect him that is by land or ____ sea, For

fight the ____ boys of lib - er - ty in North A - mer - i - cay.
I - rish ____ he - roes land - ing, but the Lord knows who must die.
was both ____ killed and wound - ed by the Sons of Lib - er - ty.
came for to lose our fa - ther dear in the North A - mer - i - cay.
he had ____ boys who feared no noise: the Sons of Lib - er - ty.

SPRINGFIELD MOUNTAIN

18th Century American

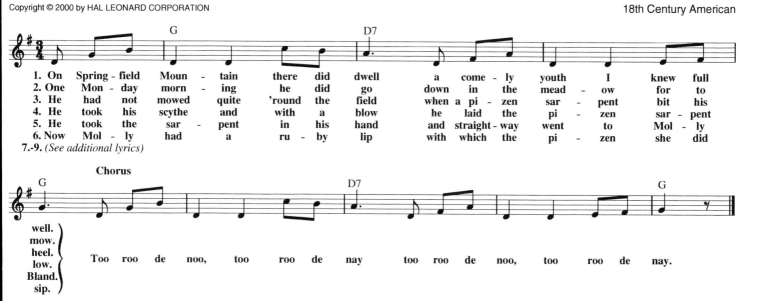

1. On Spring - field Moun - tain there did dwell a come - ly youth I knew full
2. One Mon - day morn - ing he did go down in the mead - ow for to
3. He had not mowed quite 'round the field when a pi - zen sar - pent bit his
4. He took his scythe and with a blow he laid the pi - zen sar - pent
5. He took the sar - pent in his hand and straight - way went to Mol - ly
6. Now Mol - ly had a ru - by lip with which the pi - zen she did

7.-9. *(See additional lyrics)*

Chorus

well. }
mow. }
heel. }
low. }
Bland. }
sip. }

Too roo de noo, too roo de nay too roo de noo, too roo de nay.

Additional Lyrics

7. But Molly had a rotten tooth,
   And so the pizen killed them both.
   Chorus

8. And all their friends both far and near
   Did cry and howl, they were so dear.
   Chorus

9. Now, all you maids, a warning take
   From Molly Bland and Tommy Blake.
   Chorus

SOON AH WILL BE DONE

African-American Spiritual

STANDING IN THE NEED OF PRAYER

African-American Spiritual

SOURWOOD MOUNTAIN

Southern Appalachian

1. Chick - ens a - crow - in' on Sour - wood Moun - tain,
2. I call my dar - ling a blue - eyed dai - sy,
3. Ducks go a - swim-ming a - cross the riv - er,
Hey! Hey! Dee - dee um day.

So man - y pret - ty girls I can't count 'em,
If she won't have me, I'll sure go cra - zy,
And in the win - ter we sure do shiv - er,
Hey! Hey! Dee - dee um day.

So man - y girls, I just can't count 'em, So man - y girls on Sour - wood Moun - tain.
I got to have my blue - eyed dai - sy. If she re - fus - es, I'll go cra - zy.
Ducks go a - swim - ming 'cross the riv - er, And in the win - ter, we sure shiv - er.

So man - y girls on Sour - wood Moun - tain,
I got to have my blue - eyed dai - sy,
I like _ liv - in' on Sour - wood Moun - tain,
Hey! Hey! Dee-dee um day. Dee-dee um day.

SOWING ON THE MOUNTAIN

African-American Spiritual

1. Sow - ing on the moun - tain, _____ reap - ing in the val - ley, _____
2. God __ gave __ No - ah _____ the __ rain - bow sign, _____
3. Won't _ be _____ wa - ter _____ but __ fire _____ next time, _____

__ Sow - ing on the moun - tain, _____ reap - ing in the val - ley, _____
__ God __ gave __ No - ah _____ the __ rain - bow _____ sign, _____
__ Won't _ be _____ wa - ter _____ but __ fire _____ next _____ time, _____

__ Sow - ing on the moun - tain, _____ reap - ing in the val - ley, _____
__ God __ gave __ No - ah _____ the __ rain - bow _____ sign; _____
__ Won't _ be _____ wa - ter _____ but __ fire _____ next _____ time; _____

__ You're gon - na reap _____ just what you __ sow. _____
__ It won't be wa - ter but fire next _____ time. _____
__ God __ gave __ No - ah the rain - bow __ sign. _____

THE SPORTING BACHELORS

American

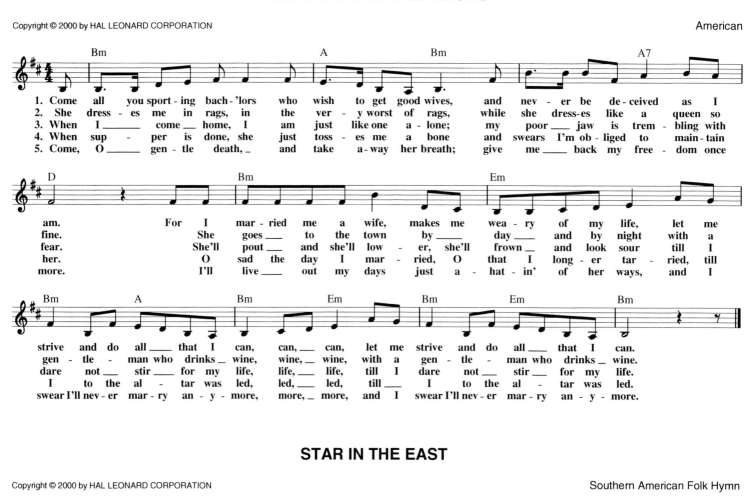

1. Come all you sport - ing bach - 'lors who wish to get good wives, and nev - er be de - ceived as I
2. She dress - es me in rags, in the ver - y worst of rags, while she dress - es like a queen so
3. When I _____ come ___ home, I am just like one a - lone; my poor ___ jaw is trem - bling with
4. When sup - per is done, she just toss - es me a bone and swears I'm ob - liged to main - tain
5. Come, O _____ gen - tle death, _ and take a - way her breath; give me ___ back my free - dom once

am. For I mar - ried me a wife, makes me wea - ry of my life, let me
fine. She goes ___ to the town by ___ day ___ and by night with a
fear. She'll pout ___ and she'll low - er, she'll frown ___ and look sour till I
her. O sad the day I mar - ried, O that I long - er tar - ried, till
more. I'll live ___ out my days just a - hat - in' of her ways, and I

strive and do all ___ that I can, can, _ can, let me strive and do all ___ that I can.
gen - tle - man who drinks _ wine, wine, _ wine, with a gen - tle - man who drinks _ wine.
dare not ___ stir ___ for my life, life, _ life, till I dare not ___ stir ___ for my life.
I to the al - tar was led, led, ___ led, till ___ I to the al - tar was led.
swear I'll nev - er mar - ry an - y - more, more, _ more, and I swear I'll nev - er mar - ry an - y - more.

STAR IN THE EAST

Southern American Folk Hymn

1. Hail the blest morn, see the great Me - di - a - tor Down from the re - gion of
2. Cold on His cra - dle the dew - drops are shin - ing; Low lies His bed, with the
3. Say, shall we yield Him, in cost - ly de - vo - tion, O - dors of E - den and
4. Vain - ly we of - fer each am - ple ob - la - tion, Vain - ly with gold we His

glo - ry de - scend. Shep - herds, go wor - ship the Babe in the man - ger;
beasts of the stall. An - gels a - dore Him in slum - ber re - clin - ing,
of - f'ring di - vine, Gems from the moun - tains and pearls from the o - cean,
fa - vor se - cure. Rich - er by far is the heart's ad - o - ra - tion,

Lo, for His guard the bright an - gels at - tend.)
Wise men and shep - herds be - fore Him do fall.)
Myrrh from the for - est and gold from the mine?)
Dear - er to God are the prayers of the poor.)

Bright - est and

best of the sons ___ of the morn - ing, Dawn on our dark - ness and

lend ___ us Thine aid. Star in the east, the ho - ri - zon a -

dorn - ing, Guide where our in - fant Re - deem - er was laid.

SOUTH AUSTRALIA

Sea Chantey

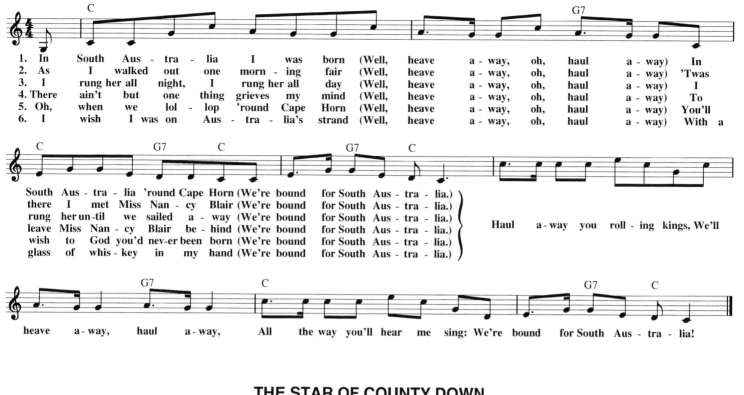

1. In South Aus - tra - lia I was born (Well, heave a - way, oh, haul a - way) In
2. As I walked out one morn - ing fair (Well, heave a - way, oh, haul a - way) 'Twas
3. I rung her all night, I rung her all day (Well, heave a - way, oh, haul a - way) I
4. There ain't but one thing grieves my mind (Well, heave a - way, oh, haul a - way) To
5. Oh, when we lol - lop 'round Cape Horn (Well, heave a - way, oh, haul a - way) You'll
6. I wish I was on Aus - tra - lia's strand (Well, heave a - way, oh, haul a - way) With a

South Aus - tra - lia 'round Cape Horn (We're bound for South Aus - tra - lia.)
there I met Miss Nan - cy Blair (We're bound for South Aus - tra - lia.)
rung her un - til we sailed a - way (We're bound for South Aus - tra - lia.)
leave Miss Nan - cy Blair be - hind (We're bound for South Aus - tra - lia.)
wish to God you'd nev-er been born (We're bound for South Aus - tra - lia.)
glass of whis - key in my hand (We're bound for South Aus - tra - lia.)

Haul a - way you roll - ing kings, We'll

heave a - way, haul a - way, All the way you'll hear me sing: We're bound for South Aus - tra - lia!

THE STAR OF COUNTY DOWN

Irish

1. Near to Ban - bridge town in the Coun - ty Down on a morn - ing in Ju - ly, Down a
2. As she on - ward sped, I scratched my head and I gazed with a feel - ing quare. There I
3. At the har - vest fair she'll sure - ly be there, so I'll dress in my Sun - day clothes. And I'll

bo - reen green came a sweet cai - leen, And she smiled as she passed me by. Oh, she
said, said I to a pas - ser - by, "Who's the maid with the nut - brown hair?" Oh, he
try sheep's eyes and de - lud - th'rin lies On the heart of the nut - brown Rose. No

looked so neat from her two white feet to the sheen of her nut - brown hair. Such a
smiled at me, and with pride says he, "That's the gem of Ire - land's crown, Young Ro -
pipe I'll smoke, no horse I'll yoke, though my plough with rust turn brown, Till a

coax - ing elf, had to shake my - self to make sure I was real - ly there.)
sie Mc - Cann from the banks of Bann; she's the star of the Coun - ty Down. }
smil - ing bridge by my own fire - side sits the star of the Coun - ty Down.)

Oh, from

Ban - try Bay up to Der - ry Quay, and from Gal - way to Dub - lin town, No

maid I've seen like the brown cai - leen that I met in the Coun - ty Down.

THE SOW TOOK THE MEASLES

Folksong from Arkansas

1. How do you think I be - gan in the world? I got me a sow and
sev - 'ral oth - er things. The sow took the mea - sles, and she died in the spring.

2. What do you think I made of her hide? The ver - y best sad - dle that you ev - er did ride.
3. What do you think I made of her nose? The ver - y best thim - bles that __ ev - er sewed clothes.
4. What do you think I made of her tail? The ver - y best whup __ that __ ev - er sought sail.
5. What do you think I made of her feet? The ver - y best pick - les that you ev - er did eat.

Sad - dle or bri - dle or an - y such thing,
Thim - ble or thread or an - y such thing,
Whup or whup sock - et an - y such thing,
Pick - les or glue or an - y such thing,
the sow took the mea - sles and she died in the spring.

STARVING TO DEATH ON MY GOVERNMENT CLAIM

American

1. My __ name is Tom Hight, an old bach - 'lor I am, __ you'll find me out west on the
2. My __ house, it is built __ of na - tion - al soil, __ its walls are e - rect - ed ac -
3. My __ clothes are all rag - ged, my lan - guage is rough, __ my bread is corn - dodg - ers, both
4. How __ hap - py am I when I crawl in - to bed; __ a rat - tle - snake hiss - es a
5. Now, __ all you claim hold - ers, I hope you will stay __ and chew your hard - tack till you're
6. Fare - well to Greer Coun - ty, fare - well to the west; __ I'll trav - el back east to the

coun - try of fame. __ You'll find me out west on an el - e - gant plain __ a -
cord - ing to Hoyle. __ Its roof has no pitch, but is lev - el and plain; __ I
sol - id and tough. __ But yet I am hap - py and live at my ease __ on
tune at my head. __ A gay lit - tle cen - ti - pede, all with - out fear, __ crawls
tooth - less and grey. __ But as for my - self, I'll no long - er re - main __ to
girl I love best. __ I'll trav - el to Tex - as and mar - ry a wife __ and

starv - in' to death on my gov - ern - ment claim.
al - ways get wet if it hap - pens to rain.
sor - ghum, mo - las - ses, ba - con and cheese.
o - ver my pil - low and in - to my ear.
starve like a dog on my gov - ern - ment claim.
quit __ corn - dodg - ers the rest of my life.
Hur - ray for Greer Coun - ty, the

land of the free, __ the land of the bed - bug, grass - hop - per and flea. __ I'll

sing of its prais - es, I'll tell of its fame, __ while starv - ing to death on my gov - ern - ment claim.

THE SQUID-JIGGIN' GROUND

Folksong from Newfoundland
Words by Arthur R. Scammel
Music by Larry O'Gaff

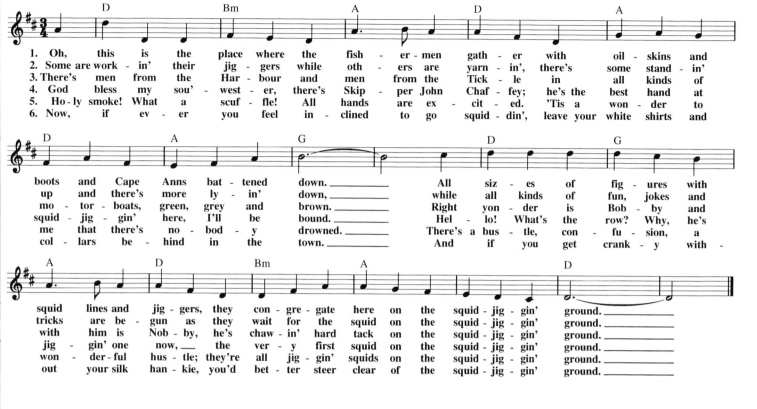

1. Oh, this is the place where the fish - er - men gath - er with oil - skins and
2. Some are work - in' their jig - gers while oth - ers are yarn - in', there's some stand - in'
3. There's men from the Har - bour and men from the Tick - le in all kinds of
4. God bless my sou' - west - er, there's Skip - per John Chaf - fey; he's the best hand at
5. Ho - ly smoke! What a scuf - fle! All hands are ex - cit - ed. 'Tis a won - der to
6. Now, if ev - er you feel in - clined to go squid - din', leave your white shirts and

boots and Cape Anns bat - tened down. _____ All siz - es of fig - ures with
up and there's more ly - in' down, _____ while all kinds of fun, jokes and
mo - tor - boats, green, grey and brown. _____ Right yon - der is Bob - by and
squid - jig - gin' here, I'll be bound. _____ Hel - lo! What's the row? Why, he's
me that there's no - bod - y drowned. _____ There's a bus - tle, con - fu - sion, a
col - lars be - hind in the town. _____ And if you get crank - y with -

squid lines and jig - gers, they con - gre - gate here on the squid - jig - gin' ground. _____
tricks are be - gun as they wait for the squid on the squid - jig - gin' ground. _____
with him is Nob - by, he's chaw - in' hard tack on the squid - jig - gin' ground. _____
jig - gin' one now, the ver - y first squid on the squid - jig - gin' ground. _____
won - der - ful hus - tle; they're all jig - gin' squids on the squid - jig - gin' ground. _____
out your silk han - kie, you'd bet - ter steer clear of the squid - jig - gin' ground. _____

THE STATE OF ARKANSAS

American

1. My name is Char - lie Bren - nan, from Charles - town I came, I've
2. I stepped be - hind the de - pot to dodge that bliz - zard wind,
3. I fol - lowed my con - duc - tor to his re - spect - ed place, where
4. I start - ed back to Tex - as a quar - ter af - ter five;
5. Fare - well, fare - well, Thom - as Quinn, and like - wise his dar - ling wife; I
6. Fare - well, fare - well, swamp an - gels, to cane - brakes and to chills, fare

trav - eled this wide world o - ver, and man - y a race I've run. I've
met a walk - ing skel - e - ton whose name was Thom - as Quinn. His
pit - y and star - va - tion was seen in ev - 'ry face. His
noth - ing was left but skin and bones, half dead and half a - live. I
know she will nev - er for - get me in the last days of her life. She
thee well to sage and sas - sa - fras tea and corn - dodg - er pills. If

trav - eled this wide world o - ver, and some ups and downs I've saw, but I
hair hung down in rat - tails on his long and lan - tern jaw, he in -
bread it was corn - dodg - er, his meat I could not chaw, but he
got me a bot - tle of whis - key, my mis - 'ry for to thaw, got
put her lit - tle hand in mine and tried to bite my jaw, and said,
I ev - er see that land a - gain, I'll give to you my paw; it

nev - er knew what mis - 'ry was _____ till I come to Ar - kan - sas. _____
vit - ed me to his ho - tel, _____ the best in Ar - kan - sas. _____
charged me half a dol - lar _____ in the state of Ar - kan - sas. _____
drunk as old A - bra - ham Lin - kern _____ when I left old Ar - kan - sas. _____
"Mis - ter Bren - nan, re - mem - ber me _____ when you leave old Ar - kan - sas. _____
will be through a tel - e - scope _____ from hell to Ar - kan - sas. _____

THE STRAWBERRY ROAN

American Cowboy Song

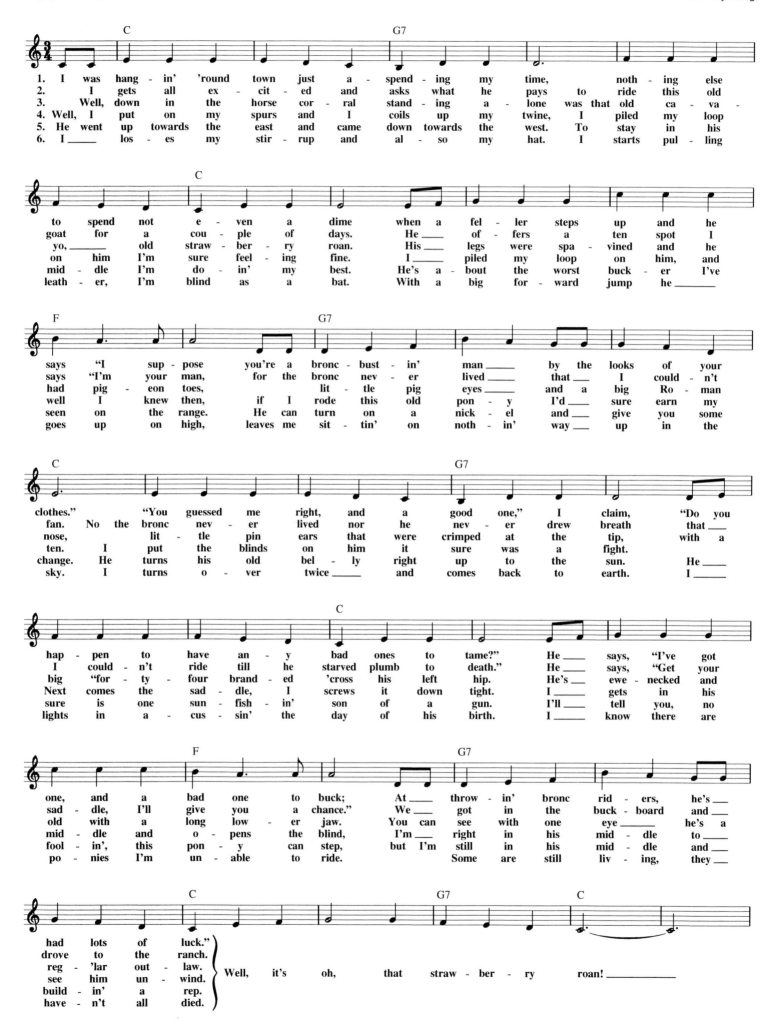

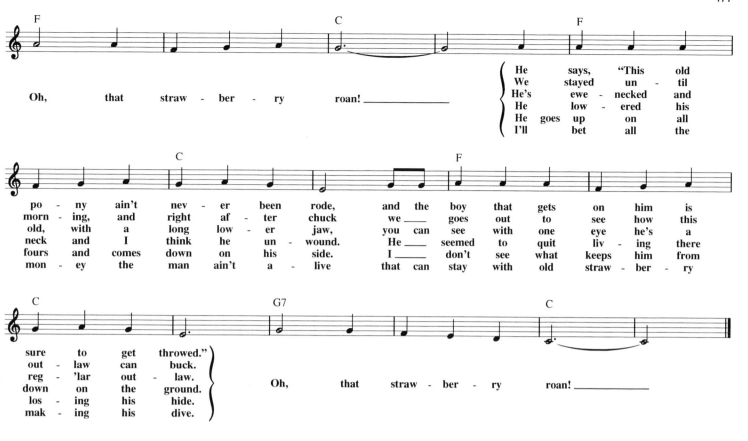

THE STREETS OF LAREDO

19th Century American
Based on the Irish Ballad "A Handful of Laurel"

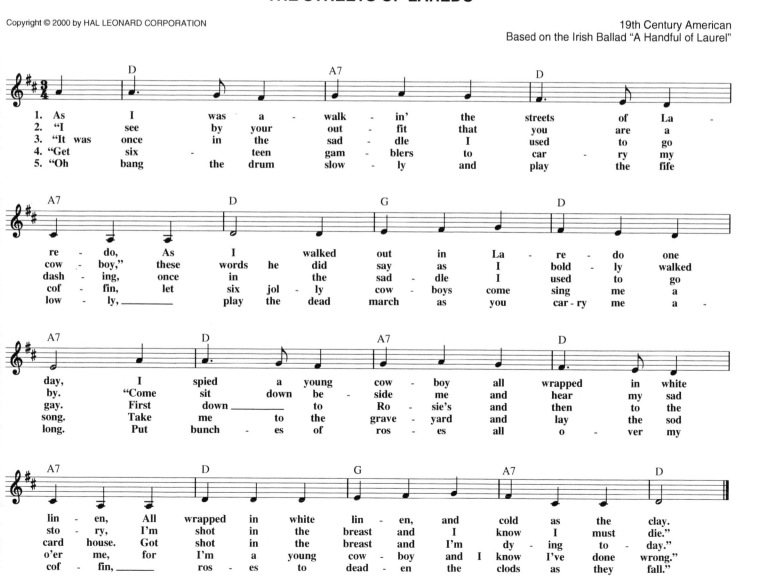

STIR THE PUDDING

19th Century American

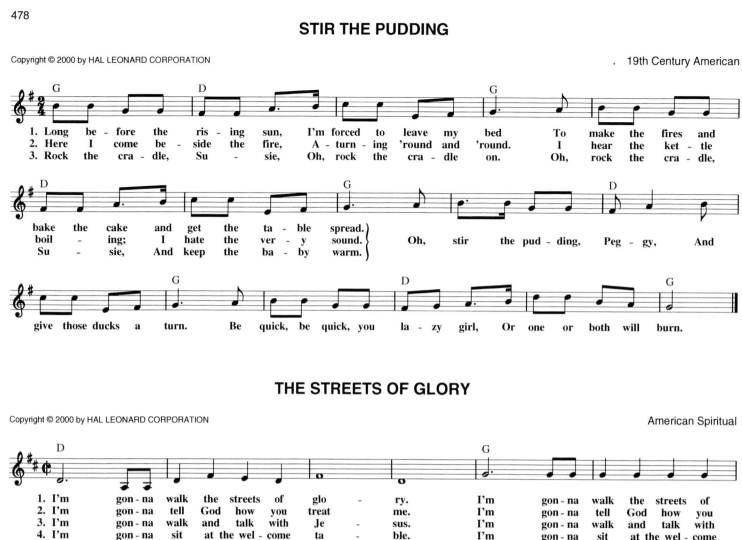

1. Long before the rising sun, I'm forced to leave my bed To make the fires and
2. Here I come beside the fire, A-turning 'round and 'round. I hear the ket-tle
3. Rock the cra-dle, Su-sie, Oh, rock the cra-dle on. Oh, rock the cra-dle,

bake the cake and get the ta-ble spread.)
boil-ing; I hate the ver-y sound. } Oh, stir the pud-ding, Peg-gy, And
Su-sie, And keep the ba-by warm.)

give those ducks a turn. Be quick, be quick, you la-zy girl, Or one or both will burn.

THE STREETS OF GLORY

American Spiritual

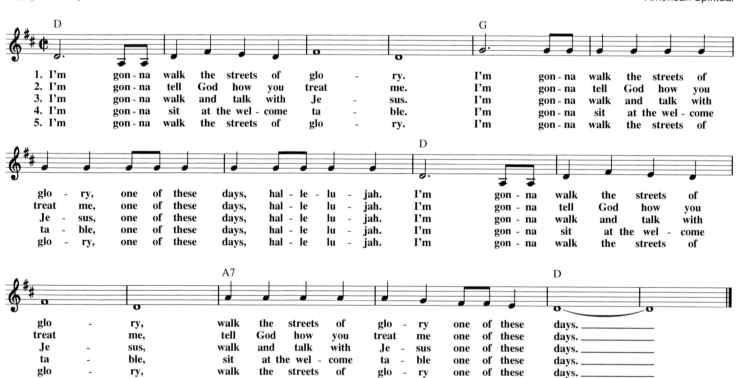

1. I'm gon-na walk the streets of glo-ry. I'm gon-na walk the streets of
2. I'm gon-na tell God how you treat me. I'm gon-na tell God how you
3. I'm gon-na walk and talk with Je-sus. I'm gon-na walk and talk with
4. I'm gon-na sit at the wel-come ta-ble. I'm gon-na sit at the wel-come
5. I'm gon-na walk the streets of glo-ry. I'm gon-na walk the streets of

glo-ry, one of these days, hal-le-lu-jah. I'm gon-na walk the streets of
treat me, one of these days, hal-le lu-jah. I'm gon-na tell God how you
Je-sus, one of these days, hal-le lu-jah. I'm gon-na walk and talk with
ta-ble, one of these days, hal-le lu-jah. I'm gon-na sit at the wel-come
glo-ry, one of these days, hal-le lu-jah. I'm gon-na walk the streets of

glo-ry, walk the streets of glo-ry one of these days. ___
treat me, tell God how you treat me one of these days. ___
Je-sus, walk and talk with Je-sus one of these days. ___
ta-ble, sit at the wel-come ta-ble one of these days. ___
glo-ry, walk the streets of glo-ry one of these days. ___

SUMER IS ICUMEN IN
(Summer Is A-Coming In)

13th Century English

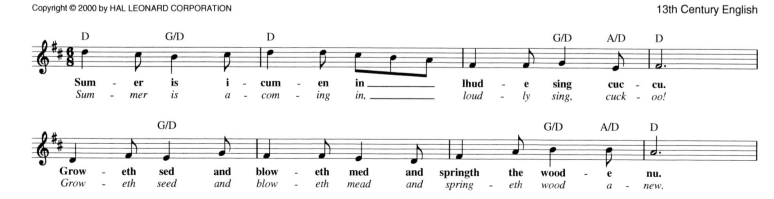

Sum-er is i-cum-en in___ lhud-e sing cuc-cu.
Sum-mer is a-com-ing in,___ loud-ly sing, cuck-oo!

Grow-eth sed and blow-eth med and springth the wood-e nu.
Grow-eth seed and blow-eth mead and spring-eth wood a-new.

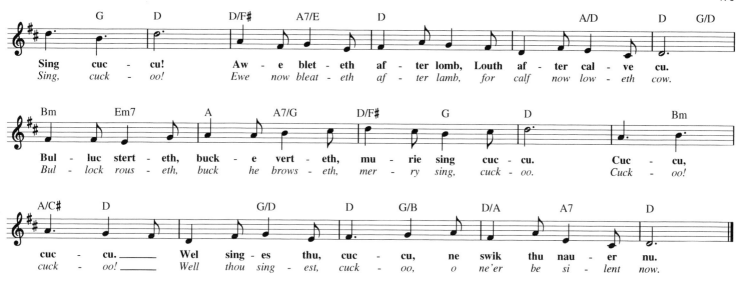

STEAL AWAY

African-American Spiritual

SUGAR BABY

Folksong from the Cumberland Mountains

SUN DON'T SET IN THE MORNIN'

Southern American Folk Hymn

THE SUN HANGS HIGH
(Charki Hidjaz)

Turkish

SWEET BETSY FROM PIKE

American

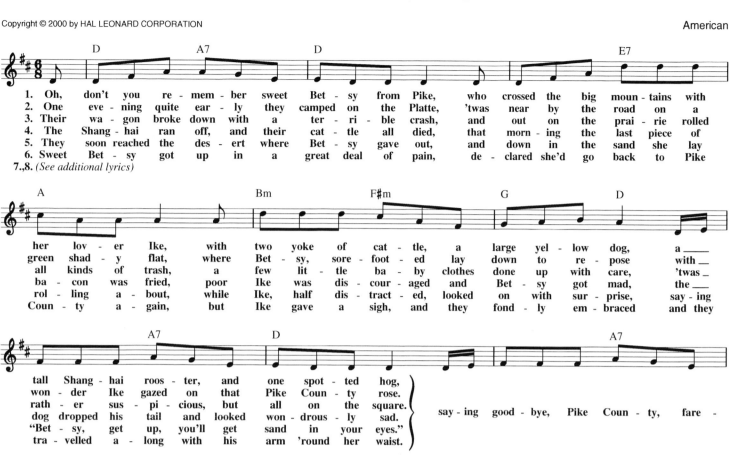

1. Oh, don't you re-mem-ber sweet Bet-sy from Pike, who crossed the big moun-tains with
2. One eve-ning quite ear-ly they camped on the Platte, 'twas near by the road on a
3. Their wa-gon broke down with a ter-ri-ble crash, and out on the prai-rie rolled
4. The Shang-hai ran off, and their cat-tle all died, that morn-ing the last piece of
5. They soon reached the des-ert where Bet-sy gave out, and down in the sand she lay
6. Sweet Bet-sy got up in a great deal of pain, de-clared she'd go back to Pike

7.,8. *(See additional lyrics)*

her lov-er Ike, with two yoke of cat-tle, a large yel-low dog, a _____
green shad-y flat, where Bet-sy, sore-foot-ed lay down to re-pose with __
all kinds of trash, a few lit-tle ba-by clothes done up with care, 'twas _
ba-con was fried, poor Ike was dis-cour-aged and Bet-sy got mad, the __
rol-ling a-bout, while Ike, half dis-tract-ed, looked on with sur-prise, say-ing
Coun-ty a-gain, but Ike gave a sigh, and they fond-ly em-braced and they

tall Shang-hai roos-ter, and one spot-ted hog,
won-der Ike gazed on that Pike Coun-ty rose.
rath-er sus-pi-cious, but all on the square.   say-ing good-bye, Pike Coun-ty, fare-
dog dropped his tail and looked won-drous-ly sad.
"Bet-sy, get up, you'll get sand in your eyes."
tra-velled a-long with his arm 'round her waist.

well for a-while. We'll _ come back a-gain when we've panned out our pile.

Additional Lyrics

7. They suddenly stopped on a very high hill,
   With wonder looked down upon old Placerville;
   Ike sighed when he said, and he cast his eyes down,
   "Sweet Betsy, my darling, we've got to Hangtown."

8. Long Ike and sweet Betsy attended a dance;
   Ike wore a pair of his Pike County pants;
   Sweet Betsy was dressed up in ribbons and rings;
   Says Ike,"You're an angel, but where are your wings?"

SWEET AND LOW

Poem by Alfred Tennyson
Music by Joseph Barnby

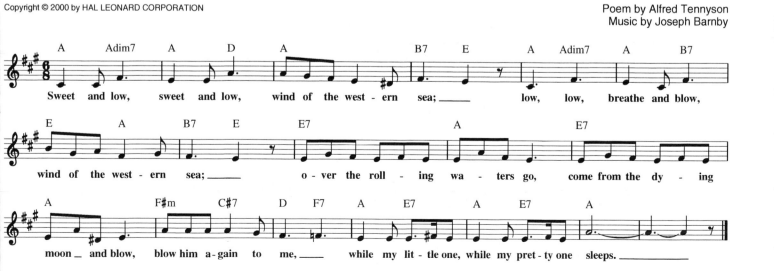

Sweet and low, sweet and low, wind of the west-ern sea; _____ low, low, breathe and blow,

wind of the west-ern sea; _____ o-ver the roll-ing wa-ters go, come from the dy-ing

moon _ and blow, blow him a-gain to me, _____ while my lit-tle one, while my pret-ty one, sleeps. _____

SWING A LADY

Dance Song from Kentucky

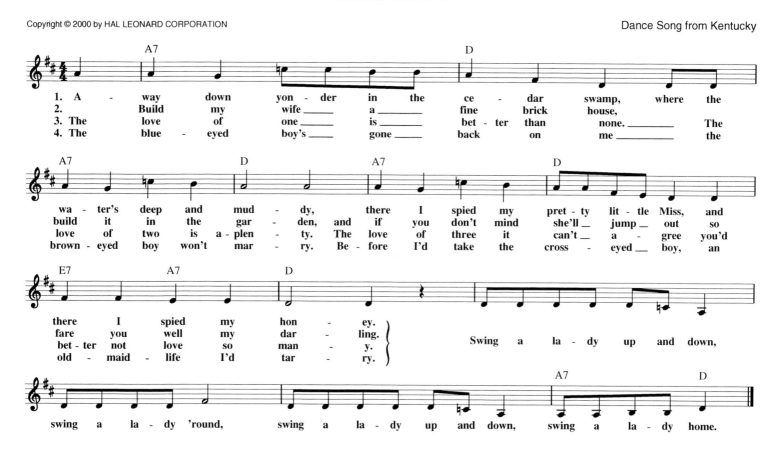

1. A - way down yon - der in the ce - dar swamp, where the
2. Build my wife ___ a ___ fine brick house,
3. The love of one ___ is ___ bet - ter than none. ___ The
4. The blue - eyed boy's ___ gone ___ back on me ___ the

wa - ter's deep and mud - dy, there I spied my pret - ty lit - tle Miss, and
build it in the gar - den, and if you don't mind she'll ___ jump ___ out so
love of two is a - plen - ty. The love of three it can't ___ a - gree you'd
brown - eyed boy won't mar - ry. Be - fore I'd take the cross - eyed ___ boy, an

there I spied my hon - ey.
fare you well my dar - ling.
bet - ter not love so man - y.
old - maid - life I'd tar - ry.   } Swing a la - dy up and down,

swing a la - dy 'round, swing a la - dy up and down, swing a la - dy home.

SWEET ROSIE O'GRADY

Irish-American, 1896
Words and Music by
Maud Nugent

1. Just down a - round the cor - ner of the street where I re - side, there
2. I nev - er shall for - get the day she prom - ised to be mine, as

lives the cut - est lit - tle girl that I have ev - er spied. Her
we sat tell - ing love - tales, in the gold - en sum - mer - time. 'Twas

name is Rose O' Gra - dy and, I don't mind tell - ing you, that
on her fing - er that I placed a small en - gage - ment ring, while

she's the sweet - est lit - tle Rose the gar - den ev - er grew.
in the trees, the lit - tle Rose birds this song they seemed to sing: }

Sweet Ro - sie O' Gra - dy, my dear lit - tle

Rose. ___ She's my stead - y la - dy,

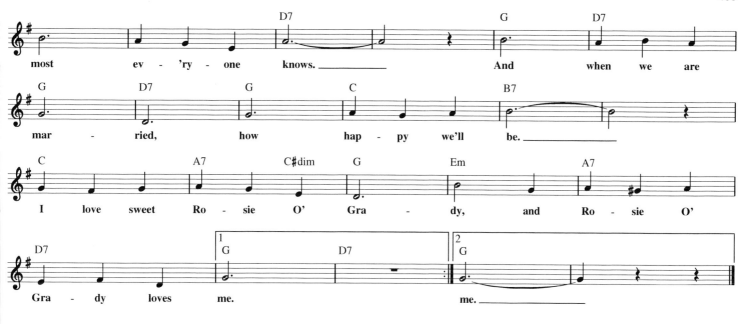

most ev-'ry-one knows. _____ And when we are mar-ried, how hap-py we'll be. _____ I love sweet Ro-sie O'Gra - dy, and Ro-sie O'Gra-dy loves me. me. _____

SWEET THE EVENING AIR OF MAY

Early English

Sweet the eve-ning air of May, soft my cheek ca-ress-ing.

Sweet the un-seen li-lacs spray with its scent-ed bless-ing.

White and ghost-ly in the gloom shine the ap-ple trees in bloom ap-ple trees in bloom.

SWING AND TURN, JUBILEE

19th Century American

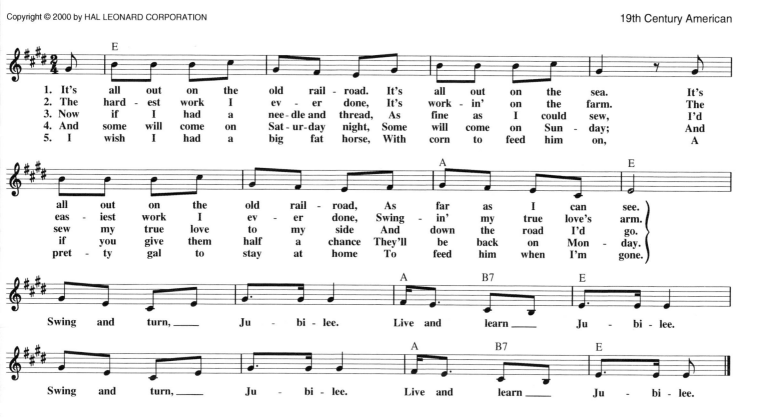

1. It's all out on the old rail-road. It's all out on the sea. It's
2. The hard-est work I ev-er done, It's work-in' on the farm. The
3. Now if I had a nee-dle and thread, As fine as I could sew, I'd
4. And some will come on Sat-ur-day night, Some will come on Sun-day; And
5. I wish I had a big fat horse, With corn to feed him on, A

all out on the old rail-road, As far as I can see.
eas-iest work I ev-er done, Swing-in' my true love's arm.
sew my true love to my side And down the road I'd go.
if you give them half a chance They'll be back on Mon-day.
pret-ty gal to stay at home To feed him when I'm gone.

Swing and turn, _____ Ju-bi-lee. Live and learn _____ Ju-bi-lee.

Swing and turn, _____ Ju-bi-lee. Live and learn _____ Ju-bi-lee.

484

SWANNANOA TUNNEL

American

Copyright © 2000 by HAL LEONARD CORPORATION

1. Ash - ville Junc - tion, Swan - na - no - a Tun - nel ____ all caved in babe, all caved in.
2. I'm goin' back to Swan - na - no - a Tun - nel ____ that's my home, hon - ey, that's my home.
3. When you hear that hoot __ owl __ squal - lin', ____ some - bod - y's dy - in' hon - ey some - bod - y's dy - in'.
4. When you hear that pis - tol __ growl ba - by an - oth - er man's gone an - oth - er man's gone.
5. If I could gam - ble like __ Tom __ Dou - ley ____ I'd leave my home, hon - ey, I'd leave my home.

SWING LOW, SWEET CHARIOT

African-American Spiritual

Copyright © 2000 by HAL LEONARD CORPORATION

Swing low, sweet char - i - ot, ____ Com - ing for to car - ry me home.

Swing __ low, sweet char - i - ot, ____ Com - ing for to car - ry me home.

looked o - ver Jor - dan and what did I see? __ Com - ing for to car - ry me home, A band __ of an - gels
you __ get there be - fore __ I do, __ Com - ing for to car - ry me home, Tell all __ my friends I'm

com - ing af - ter me, __ Com - ing for to car - ry me home.
com - ing __ too, __ Com - ing for to car - ry me home.

THE TAILOR AND THE MOUSE

English

Copyright © 2000 by HAL LEONARD CORPORATION

1. There was a tai - lor had a mouse, hi did - dle dum cum feed - a.
2. The tai - lor had a tall silk hat,
3. The tai - lor chased him o - ver the lea,

lived to - geth - er in one house, hi did - dle dum cum feed - a.
mouse, he ate it, fan - cy that,
last of that mouse he nev - er did see,

Hi did - dle dum cum, tin trum, tan trum, through the town of Ram - sey.

Hi did - dle dum, come o - ver the lea, hi did - dle dum cum feed - a.

TAKE ME OUT TO THE BALL GAME

Words by Jack Norworth
Music by Albert Von Tilzer

TAKING GAIR IN THE NIGHT

Folksong from Newfoundland

TAKE THIS HAMMER

Work Song from the American South

1. Take this ham - mer, *(huh!)* car - ry it to the cap - tain,
2. If he asks you *(huh!)* was __ I __ laugh - in',
3. If he asks you *(huh!)* was __ I __ run - nin',
4. I don't want no *(huh!)* cold __ i - ron shack - les,
5. I don't want no *(huh!)* corn - bread and mo - las - ses,

(huh!) Take this __ ham - mer *(huh!)* car - ry it to the cap - tain,
(huh!) If he __ asks you *(huh!)* was __ I __ laugh - in',
(huh!) If he __ asks you *(huh!)* was __ I __ run - in',
(huh!) I don't __ want no *(huh!)* cold __ i - ron shack - les,
(huh!) I don't __ want no *(huh!)* corn - bread and mo - las - ses,

(huh!) Take this ham - mer, *(huh!)* car - ry it to the cap - tain,
(huh!) If he asks you *(huh!)* was __ I __ laugh - in',
(huh!) If he asks you *(huh!)* was __ I __ run - in',
(huh!) I don't want no *(huh!)* cold __ i - ron shack - les,
(huh!) I don't want no *(huh!)* corn - bread and mo - las - ses,

(huh!) Tell him I'm gone, _____ *(huh!)* tell him I'm gone. *(huh!)*
(huh!) Tell him I was cry - in', _____ *(huh!)* tell him I was cry - in'. *(huh!)*
(huh!) Tell him I was fly - in', _____ *(huh!)* tell him I was fly - in'. *(huh!)*
(huh!) A - round my leg, _____ *(huh!)* a - round my leg. *(huh!)*
(huh!) They hurt my pride, _____ *(huh!)* they hurt my pride. *(huh!)*

TAM PIERCE

Scottish

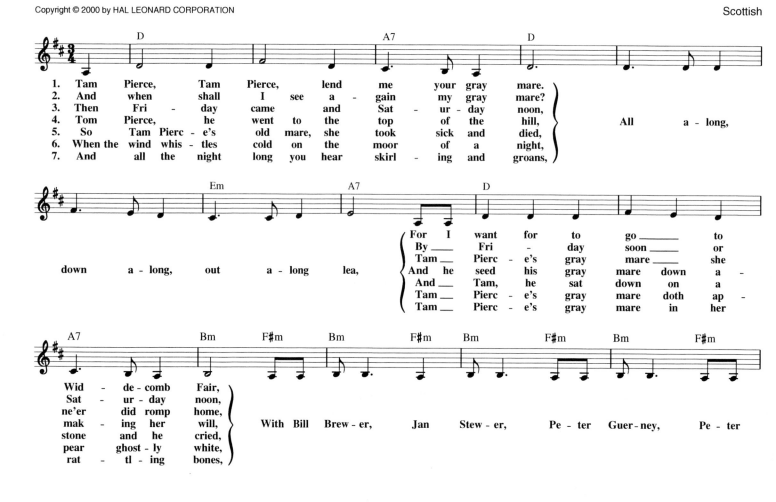

1. Tam Pierce, Tam Pierce, lend me your gray mare.
2. And when shall I see a - gain my gray mare?
3. Then Fri - day came and Sat - ur - day noon,
4. Tom Pierce, he went to the top of the hill,
5. So Tam Pierc - e's old mare, she took sick and died,
6. When the wind whis - tles cold on the moor of a night,
7. And all the night long you hear skirl - ing and groans,

All a - long, down a - long, out a - long lea,

For I want for to go _____ to
By __ Fri - day soon _____ or
Tam __ Pierc - e's gray mare _____ she
And he seed his gray mare down a -
And __ Tam, he sat down on a
Tam __ Pierc - e's gray mare doth ap -
Tam __ Pierc - e's gray mare in her

Wid - de - comb Fair,
Sat - ur - day noon,
ne'er did romp home,
mak - ing her will,
stone and he cried,
pear ghost - ly white,
rat - tl - ing bones,

With Bill Brew - er, Jan Stew - er, Pe - ter Guer - ney, Pe - ter

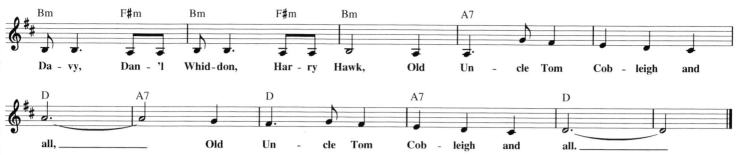

Da - vy, Dan - 'l Whid - don, Har - ry Hawk, Old Un - cle Tom Cob - leigh and

all, _____ Old Un - cle Tom Cob - leigh and all. _____

THE TANYARD SIDE

Irish

1. I am a ram - bling he - ro and by love I ___ am be - trayed, Near _
2. I cour - teous - ly sa - lut - ed her and I viewed her ___ o'er and o'er, I ___
3. Her gold - en hair in ring - lets rare fell ___ o'er her ___ snow - white neck. The _
4. For twelve long months we court - ed till at ___ length we ___ did a - gree For _
5. Fare - well my a - ged par - ents, to ___ you I ___ bid a - dieu, I'm _

to the town of Balt - in - glass there ___ dwells a ___ come - ly ___ maid. She's _
thought she was Au - ro - ra bright de - scend - ed ___ down so ___ low. "Oh _
ten - der glanc - es of her eyes would _ save a ___ ship from _ wreck. Her _
to ac - quaint her par - ents and ___ mar - ried ___ we would _ be. 'Twas _
cross - ing the main o - cean all ___ for the ___ sake of ___ you. And _

fair - er than Di - an - a bright, she's _ free from _ earth - ly ___ pride. She's a
no, kind sir, I'm a coun - try girl," she ___ mod - est - ly re - plied, "And I
two brown spar - kling eyes ___ and her teeth of ___ iv - 'ry ___ white Would _
then her cru - el fa - ther to ___ me did ___ prove un - kind, Which _
if I e'er re - turn a - gain I'll take you _ for my ___ bride, And I'll

love - ly maid and her dwell - ing place is ___ down by the tan - yard side.
la - bor dai - ly ___ for my bread down _ by the ___ tan - yard side.
make a man be - come her slave down _ by the ___ tan - yard side.
makes _ me sail a - cross the sea and ___ leave me ___ love be - hind.
roll you in my ___ arms my love, down _ by the ___ tan - yard side.

TEN LITTLE INDIANS

American Children's Counting Song

One lit - tle, two lit - tle, three lit - tle In - dians, Four lit - tle, five lit - tle, six lit - tle In - dians,
Ten lit - tle, nine lit - tle, eight lit - tle In - dians, Seven lit - tle, six lit - tle, five lit - tle In - dians,

Seven lit - tle, eight lit - tle, nine lit - tle In - dians, Ten lit - tle In - dian boys.
Four lit - tle, three lit - tle, two lit - tle In - dians, One lit - tle In - dian boy.

TARANTELLA

Italian

THE TARRY TROUSERS

Sea Chantey from Newfoundland

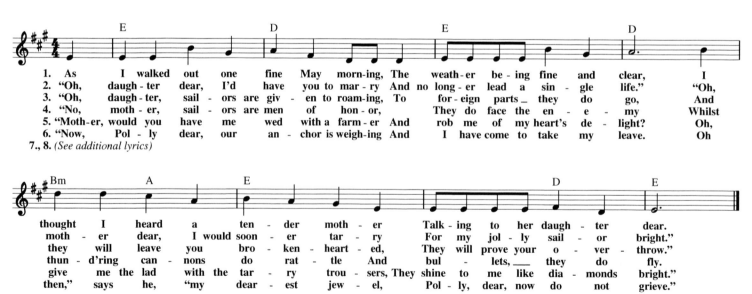

1. As I walked out one fine May morn-ing, The weath-er be-ing fine and clear, I
2. "Oh, daugh-ter dear, I'd have you to mar-ry And no long-er lead a sin-gle life." "Oh,
3. "Oh, daugh-ter, sail-ors are giv-en to roam-ing, To for-eign parts _ they do go, And
4. "No, moth-er, sail-ors are men of hon-or, They do face the en-e-my Whilst
5. "Moth-er, would you have me wed with a farm-er And rob me of my heart's de-light? Oh,
6. "Now, Pol-ly dear, our an-chor is weigh-ing And I have come to take my leave. Oh

7., 8. *(See additional lyrics)*

thought I heard a ten-der moth-er Talk-ing to her daugh-ter dear.
moth-er dear, I would soon-er tar-ry For my jol-ly sail-or bright."
they will leave you bro-ken heart-ed, They will prove your o-ver-throw."
thun-d'ring can-nons do rat-tle And bul-lets, ___ they do fly.
give me the lad with the tar-ry trou-sers, They shine to me like dia-monds bright."
then," says he, "my dear-est jew-el, Pol-ly, dear, now do not grieve."

Additional Lyrics

7. "Jimmy dear, may I go with you?
No foreign dangers do I fear."
Whilst he is in the height of battle
She cries, "fight on my jolly tar."

8. Come all you fair and beauteous maidens
Who know a sailor's your heart's delight,
I'd never have you wed with any other
For all their gold and silver bright.

TELL ME WHY

American

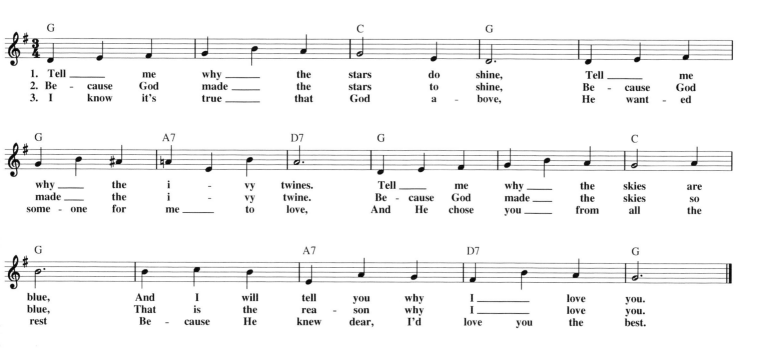

1. Tell me why the stars do shine, Tell me
2. Be - cause God made the stars to shine, Be - cause God
3. I know it's true that God a - bove, He want - ed

why the i - vy twines. Tell me why the skies are
made the i - vy twine. Be - cause God made the skies so
some - one for me to love, And He chose you from all the

blue, And I will tell you why I love you.
blue, That is the rea - son why I love you.
rest Be - cause He knew dear, I'd love you the best.

TENTING TONIGHT

Words and Music by
Walter Kittredge, 1863
From the American Civil War

1. We're tent - ing to - night on the old camp - ground. Give us a song to
2. We're tent - ing to - night on the old camp - ground, Think - ing of days gone
3. We're tent - ing to - night on the old camp - ground, The fires are flick - 'ring
4. A - las for those com - rades of days gone by Whose forms are missed to -
5. We're tired of war on the old camp - ground, Man - y are dead and
6. We've been fight - ing to - day on the old camp - ground, Man - y are ly - ing

cheer Our wea - ry hearts. A song of home And friends we love so dear.
by, Of the loved ones at home that gave the hand, And the tear that said, "Good - bye."
low. Still are the sleep-ers that lie a - round As the sent - 'nels come and go.
night. A - las for the young and true who lie Where the bat - tle flag braved the fight.
gone, Of the brave and true who've left their homes, Oth - ers been wound - ed long.
near. Some are dead and some are dy - ing, Man - y are in tears.

Man - y are the hearts that are wea - ry to - night Wish - ing for the war to cease.

Man - y are the hearts that are look - ing for the right to see the dawn of

peace. Tent - ing to - night, Tent - ing to - night, Tent - ing on the old camp - ground.

TEN THOUSAND CATTLE

American Cowboy Song

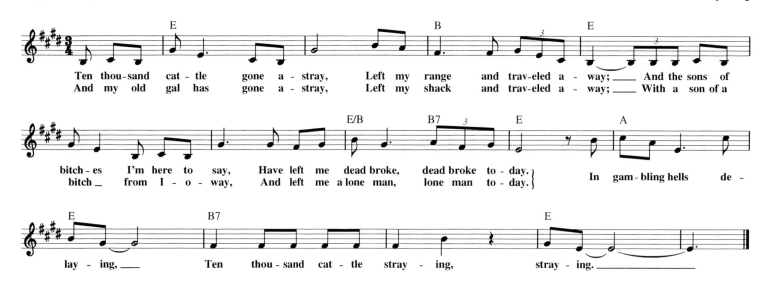

Ten thou-sand cat-tle gone a-stray, Left my range and trav-eled a-way;___ And the sons of
And my old gal has gone a-stray, Left my shack and trav-eled a-way;___ With a son of a

bitch-es I'm here to say, Have left me dead broke, dead broke to-day.
bitch___ from I-o-way, And left me a lone man, lone man to-day.

In gam-bling hells de-

lay-ing,___ Ten thou-sand cat-tle stray-ing, stray-ing.___

THE TEX-I-AN BOYS

American

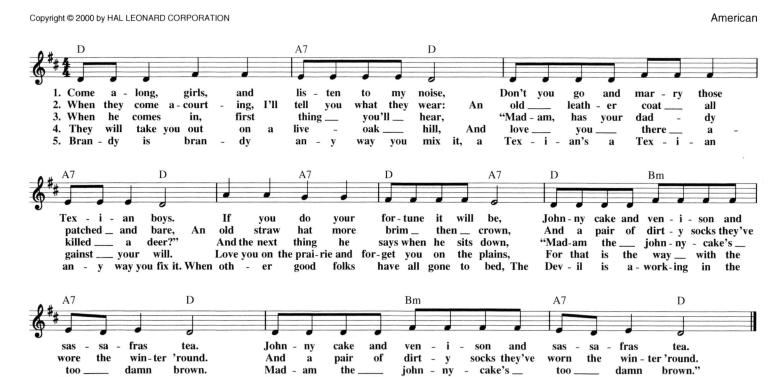

1. Come a-long, girls, and lis-ten to my noise, Don't you go and mar-ry those
2. When they come a-court-ing, I'll tell you what they wear: An old ___ leath-er coat ___ all
3. When he comes in, first thing ___ you'll ___ hear, "Mad-am, has your dad-dy
4. They will take you out on a live-oak ___ hill, And love ___ you ___ there ___ a-
5. Bran-dy is bran-dy an-y way you mix it, a Tex-i-an's a Tex-i-an

Tex-i-an boys. If you do your for-tune it will be, John-ny cake and ven-i-son and
patched ___ and bare, An old straw hat more brim ___ then ___ crown, And a pair of dirt-y socks they've
killed ___ a deer?" And the next thing he says when he sits down, "Mad-am the ___ john-ny-cake's ___
gainst ___ your will. Love you on the prai-rie and for-get you on the plains, For that is the way ___ with the
an-y way you fix it. When oth-er good folks have all gone to bed, The Dev-il is a-work-ing in the

sas-sa-fras tea. John-ny cake and ven-i-son and sas-sa-fras tea.
wore the win-ter 'round. And a pair of dirt-y socks they've worn the win-ter 'round.
too ___ damn brown. Mad-am the ___ john-ny-cake's ___ too ___ damn brown."
Tex-i-ans. For that is the way ___ with the Tex-i-ans.
Tex-i-an's head. The Dev-il is a-work-ing in the Tex-i-an's head.

THERE IS A BALM IN GILEAD

African-American Spiritual

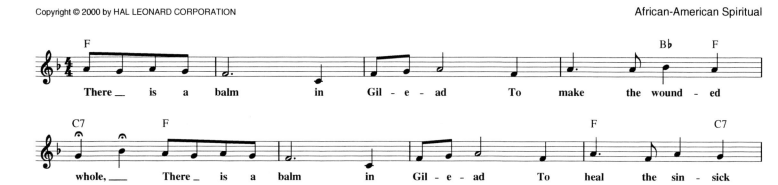

There ___ is a balm in Gil-e-ad To make the wound-ed

whole, ___ There ___ is a balm in Gil-e-ad To heal the sin-sick

THE TEXAS RANGERS

American Cowboy Song

Copyright © 2000 by HAL LEONARD CORPORATION

Additional Lyrics

7. 'Twas then I thought of mother, who to me in tears did say,
"To you they are all strangers, with me you had better stay."
I thought that she was childish, the best she did not know;
My mind was fixed on ranging and I was bound to go.

8. Perhaps you have a mother, likewise a sister too,
And maybe you have a sweetheart to weep and mourn for you;
If that be your situation, although you'd like to roam,
I'd advise you by experience, you had better stay at home.

9. I have seen the fruits of rambling, I know its hardships well;
I have crossed the Rocky Mountains, rode down the streets of hell;
I have been in the great Southwest where wild Apaches roam,
And I tell you from experience you had better stay at home.

10. And now my song is ended; I guess I have sung enough;
The life of a Rangers I am sure is very tough.
And here's to all you ladies, I am sure I wish you well,
I am bound to go a-ranging, so ladies, fare you well.

THAT CRAZY WAR

American
World War I version of "The Battleship of Maine"

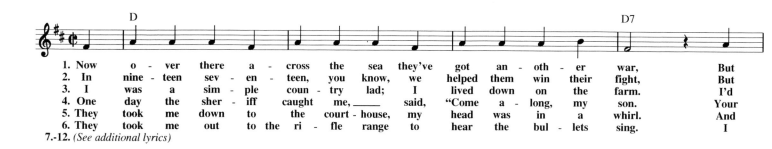

1. Now o - ver there a - cross the sea they've got an - oth - er war, But
2. In nine - teen sev - en - teen, you know, we helped them win their fight, But
3. I was a sim - ple coun - try lad; I lived down on the farm. I'd
4. One day the sher - iff caught me,___ said, "Come a - long, my son. Your
5. They took me down to the court - house, my head was in a whirl. And
6. They took me out to the ri - fle range to hear the bul - lets sing. I

7.-12. *(See additional lyrics)*

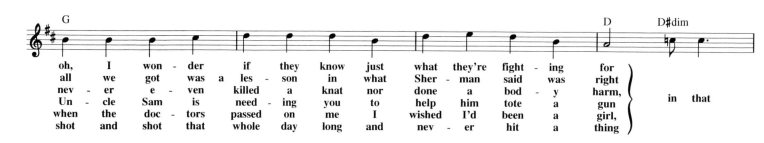

oh, I won - der if they know just what they're fight - ing for
all we got was a les - son in what Sher - man said was right
Unc - cle Sam is need - ing you to help him tote a gun   } in that
when the doc - tors passed on me I wished I'd been a girl,
shot and shot that whole day long and nev - er hit a thing

war,_____ that cra - zy war.

Additional Lyrics

7. The captain said to fire at will and I said, "Who is he?"
The old fool got so raving mad he fired his gun at me,
In that war, that crazy war.

8. When first we got to sunny France, I looked around with glee,
But rain and kilometers was all that I could see
In that war, that crazy war.

9. A cannonball flew overhead, I started home right then.
The corporal, he was after me but the general beat us in,
In that war, that crazy war.

10. And now we're back at home again from over there in France.
The enemy lost the battle, and we lost all our pants
In that war, that crazy war.

11. I run all over Europe a-trying to save my life.
If there will come another war, I'll send my darling wife,
In that war, that crazy war.

12. Well, wars may come and wars may go, but get this on your mind:
There will come another war, and I'll be hard to find
In that war, that crazy war.

THERE IS A TAVERN IN THE TOWN

English Drinking Song

1. There is a tav - ern in the town, in the town. And
2. He left me for a dam - sel dark, dam - sel dark. Each
3. And now I see him nev - er - more, nev - er - more. He
4. Oh, dig my grave both wide and deep, wide and deep. Put

there my dear love sits him down, sits him down, ___ And ___ drinks his
Fri - day night they used to spark, used to spark, ___ And ___ now my
nev - er knocks up - on my door, on my door. ___ Oh, ___ woe is
tomb - stones at my head and feet, head and feet. ___ And ___ on my

THERE WAS AN OLD SOLDIER

From the American Civil War

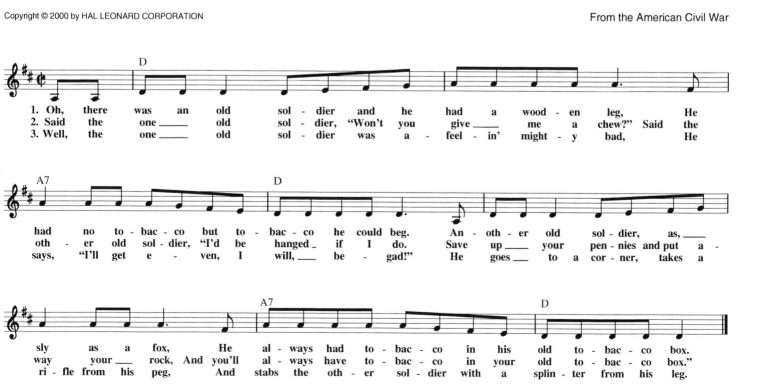

THERE'S A HOLE IN THE BOTTOM OF THE SEA

Traditional American Children's Song

1. There's a hole in the bot-tom of the sea. There's a hole in the bot-tom of the sea. There's a
2.-8. *(See additional lyrics)*

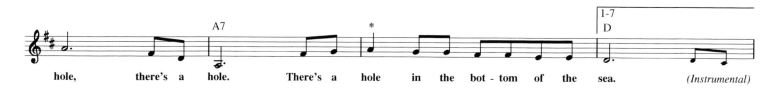

hole, there's a hole. There's a hole in the bot-tom of the sea. *(Instrumental)*

There's a sea. There's an eye on the flea, there's a

flea on the wing, there's a wing on the fly, there's a fly on the frog, there's a frog on the bump, there's a

bump on the log, there's a log in the hole in the bot-tom of the sea.

Additional Lyrics

(For each new verse, add 2 extra beats (keep repeating the first two beats) to the bars that are marked with an asterisk.)
(Extra beats are underlined below.)

2. There's a log in the hole in the bottom of the sea.
There's a log in the hole in the bottom of the sea.
There's a log, there's a log.
There's a log in the hole in the bottom of the sea.

3. There's a bump on the log in the hole in the bottom of the sea.
There's a bump on the log in the hole in the bottom of the sea.
There's a bump, there's a bump.
There's a bump on the log in the hole in the bottom of the sea.

4. There's a frog on the bump on the log in the
hole in the bottom of the sea.
There's a frog on the bump on the log in the
hole in the bottom of the sea.
There's a frog, there's a frog.
There's a frog on the bump on the log in the
hole in the bottom of the sea.

5. There's a fly on the frog on the bump on the log in the
hole in the bottom of the sea.
There's a fly on the frog on the bump on the log in the
hole in the bottom of the sea.
There's a fly, there's a fly.
There's a fly on the frog on the bump on the log in the
hole in the bottom of the sea.

6. There's a wing on the fly on the frog on the bump on the
log in the hole in the bottom of the sea.
There's a wing on the fly on the frog on the bump on the
log in the hole in the bottom of the sea.
There's a wing, there's a wing.
There's a wing on the fly on the frog on the bump on the
log in the hole in the bottom of the sea.

7. There's a flea on the wing on the fly on the frog on the
bump on the log in the hole in the bottom of the sea.
There's a flea on the wing on the fly on the frog on the
bump on the log in the hole in the bottom of the sea.
There's a flea, there's a flea.
There's a flea on the wing on the fly on the frog on the
bump on the log in the hole in the bottom of the sea.

8. There's an eye on the flea on the wing on the fly on the frog
on the bump on the log in the hole in the bottom of the sea.
There's an eye on the flea on the wing on the fly on the frog
on the bump on the log in the hole in the bottom of the sea.
There's an eye, there's an eye.
There's an eye on the flea on the wing on the fly on the frog
on the bump on the log in the hole in the bottom of the sea.

(ENDING)
There's an eye on the flea on the wing.
There's a wing on the fly on the frog.
There's a frog on the bump, there's a bump on the log.
There's a log in the hole in the bottom of the sea.

THERE'S A HOLE IN THE BUCKET

Southern American Folksong

1. There's a hole in the buck - et, dear Li - za, dear Li - za. There's a
2. Well then fix it, dear Hen - ry, dear Hen - ry, dear Hen - ry. Well, __
3. With __ what shall I fix it, dear Li - za, dear Li - za? With __
4. With a straw, _____ dear Hen - ry, dear Hen - ry, dear Hen - ry. With a
5. But the straw is too long, _____ dear Li - za, dear Li - za. but the
6. Then __ cut it, dear Hen - ry, dear Hen - ry, dear Hen - ry. Then __

7.-19. *(See additional lyrics)*

hole in the buck - et, dear Li - za, a hole!
fix it, dear Hen - ry, dear Hen - ry, fix it!
what shall I fix it, dear Li - za, with what?
straw, _____ dear Hen - ry, dear Hen - ry, a straw.
straw is too long, _____ dear Li - za, too long.
cut it, dear Hen - ry, dear Hen - ry, cut it.

Additional Lyrics

7. With what shall I cut it, dear Liza, etc.
8. With a knife, dear Henry, etc.

9. But the knife is too dull, dear Liza, etc.
10. Then sharpen it, dear Henry, etc.
11. With what shall I sharpen it, dear Liza, etc.
12. With a stone, dear Henry, etc.
13. But the stone is too dry, dear Liza, etc.

14. Then wet it, dear Henry, etc.
15. With what shall I wet it, dear Liza, etc.
16. With water, dear Henry, etc.
17. In what shall I carry it, dear Liza, etc.
18. In a bucket, dear Henry, etc.
19. There's a hole in the bucket, dear Liza, etc.

THERE'S A LITTLE WHEEL A-TURNING IN MY HEART

Appalachian Folksong

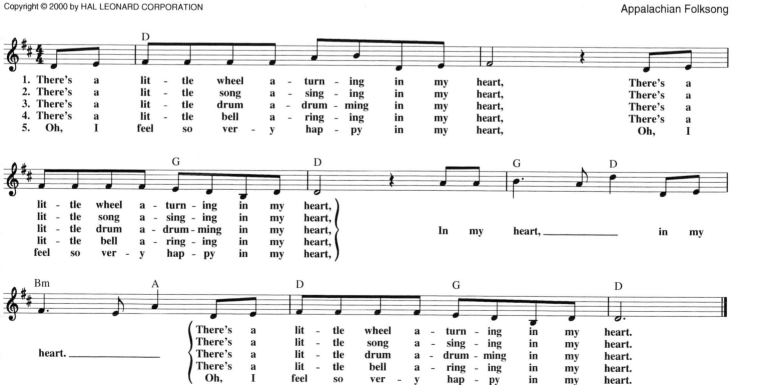

1. There's a lit - tle wheel a - turn - ing in my heart, There's a
2. There's a lit - tle song a - sing - ing in my heart, There's a
3. There's a lit - tle drum a - drum - ming in my heart, There's a
4. There's a lit - tle bell a - ring - ing in my heart, There's a
5. Oh, I feel so ver - y hap - py in my heart, Oh, I

lit - tle wheel a - turn - ing in my heart,
lit - tle song a - sing - ing in my heart,
lit - tle drum a - drum - ming in my heart,
lit - tle bell a - ring - ing in my heart,
feel so ver - y hap - py in my heart,

In my heart, _____ in my

heart. _____

There's a lit - tle wheel a - turn - ing in my heart.
There's a lit - tle song a - sing - ing in my heart.
There's a lit - tle drum a - drum - ming in my heart.
There's a lit - tle bell a - ring - ing in my heart.
Oh, I feel so ver - y hap - py in my heart.

THESE BONES GOIN' TO RISE AGAIN
(Dese Bones Gwine to Rise Again)

African-American Spiritual

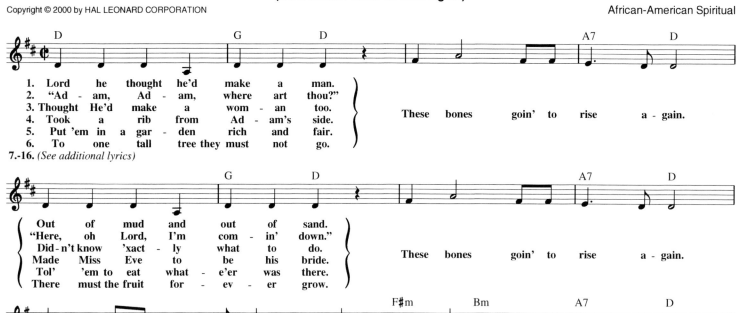

1. Lord he thought he'd make a man.
2. "Ad - am, Ad - am, where art thou?"
3. Thought He'd make a wom - an too.
4. Took a rib from Ad - am's side.
5. Put 'em in a gar - den rich and fair.
6. To one tall tree they must not go.

7.-16. *(See additional lyrics)*

These bones goin' to rise a - gain.

Out of mud and out of sand.
"Here, oh Lord, I'm com - in' down."
Did - n't know 'xact - ly what to do.
Made Miss Eve to be his bride.
Tol' 'em to eat what - e'er was there.
There must the fruit for - ev - er grow.

These bones goin' to rise a - gain.

I know it, yes I know it, These bones goin' to rise a - gain.

Additional Lyrics

7. Ol' Miss Eve come a-walkin' roun'...
   Spied that tree all loaded down...

8. Serpent he came round the trunk...
   At Miss Eve his eye he wunk...

9. First she took a little pull...
   Den she fulled her apron full...

10. Adam he come prowling 'round...
    Spied them peelings on the ground...

11. Then he took a little slice...
    Smack his lips and said 'twas nice...

12. Lord, he spoke with a mighty voice...
    Shook the heavens to the joists...

13. "Adam! Adam! Where are thou?"
    "Yes, Oh Lord, I'm a-comin' now."...

14. "You ate my apples, I believe?"...
    "Not me, Lord, but I 'spec 'twas Eve."...

15. Lord then rose up in his wrath...
    Tole 'em beat it down the path...

16. "Out of my garden you must git"...
    "For you and me has got to quit."...

THIS LITTLE LIGHT OF MINE

African-American Spiritual

This lit-tle light of mine, I'm gon-na let it shine; This lit-tle light of mine, I'm gon-na let it shine;

This lit-tle light of mine, I'm gon-na let it shine; let it shine, let it shine, let it shine.

1. Don't let Sa - tan phhh it out, I'm gon-na let it shine; Don't let Sa - tan phhh it out, I'm gon-na let it shine;
2. Hide it un-der a bush-el, NO! I'm gon-na let it shine; Hide it un-der a bush-el, NO! I'm gon-na let it shine;
3. Let it shine till Je - sus comes, I'm gon-na let it shine; Let it shine till Je - sus comes, I'm gon-na let it shine;

Don't let Sa - tan phhh it out, I'm gon-na let it shine; let it shine, let it shine, let it shine.
Hide it un-der a bush-el, NO! I'm gon-na let it shine; let it shine, let it shine, let it shine.
Let it shine till Je - sus comes, I'm gon-na let it shine; let it shine, let it shine, let it shine.

THIS OLD MAN

English Children's Game and Counting Song

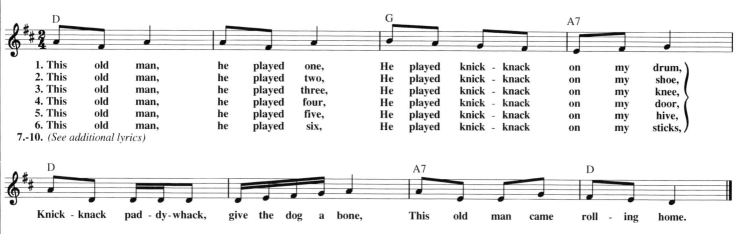

1. This old man, he played one, He played knick - knack on my drum,
2. This old man, he played two, He played knick - knack on my shoe,
3. This old man, he played three, He played knick - knack on my knee,
4. This old man, he played four, He played knick - knack on my door,
5. This old man, he played five, He played knick - knack on my hive,
6. This old man, he played six, He played knick - knack on my sticks,

7.-10. *(See additional lyrics)*

Knick - knack pad - dy - whack, give the dog a bone, This old man came roll - ing home.

Additional Lyrics

7. This old man, he played seven,
   He played knick-knack up to heaven,

8. This old man, he played eight,
   He played knick-knack at the gate,

9. This old man, he played nine,
   He played knick-knack on my line,

10. This old man, he played ten,
    He played knick-knack over again,

THIS TRAIN

American Gospel Song

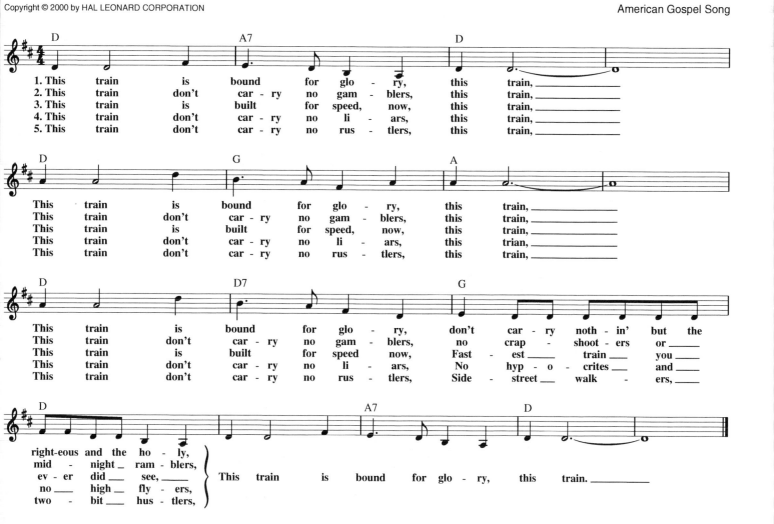

1. This train is bound for glo - ry, this train, _____
2. This train don't car - ry no gam - blers, this train, _____
3. This train is built for speed, now, this train, _____
4. This train don't car - ry no li - ars, this train, _____
5. This train don't car - ry no rus - tlers, this train, _____

This train is bound for glo - ry, this train, _____
This train don't car - ry no gam - blers, this train, _____
This train is built for speed, now, this train, _____
This train don't car - ry no li - ars, this trian, _____
This train don't car - ry no rus - tlers, this train, _____

This train is bound for glo - ry, don't car - ry noth - in' but the
This train don't car - ry no gam - blers, no crap - shoot - ers or _____
This train is built for speed now, Fast - est _____ train _____ you _____
This train don't car - ry no li - ars, No hyp - o - crites _____ and _____
This train don't car - ry no rus - tlers, Side - street _____ walk - ers, _____

right-eous and the ho - ly,
mid - night _ ram - blers,
ev - er did _ see, _____   This train is bound for glo - ry, this train. _____
no _____ high _ fly - ers,
two - bit _____ hus - tlers,

THREE BLIND MICE

Nursery Song Round

Three blind mice, Three blind mice, See how they run!

See how they run!____ They all ran af - ter the farm - er's wife, who cut off their tails with a

carv - ing knife, did you ev - er see such a sight in your life as three blind mice.

THREE LILIES
(Drei Lilien)

German

Three __ lil - ies, three lil - ies, I plant - ed on my tomb, then __
Drei __ Li - li - en, drei Li - li - en, die pflanzt' ich auf mein Grab, da __

came a horse - man __ proud and broke off each bloom. Ju - vi -
kam ein stol - zer __ Rei - ter und brach si ab. Ju - vi -

val - le - ral - le - ral - le - ral - le - ra, ____ ju - vi - val - le - ral - le - ral - le - ral - le
val - le - ral - le - ral - le - ral - le - ra, ____ ju - vi - val - le - ral - le - ral - le - ral - le

ra, ____ then came a horse - man __ proud and broke off each bloom.
ra, ____ da kam ein stol - zer __ Rei - ter und brach sie ab.

THE THREE RAVENS

Early 17th Century English

1. There were three ra - vens sat on a tree,
2. Down in yon - der green ____ field,
3. His hawks they fly so ea - ger - ly,
4. She lift - ed up his blood - y ____ head,
5. She bur - ied him be - fore the ____ prime,

Down a down, hey

down, hey down,

They were as black as black might be,
There lies a knight slain un - der his shield,
No oth - er foul dare come him nigh,
And kissed his wounds that were so red,
She was dead her - self ere e'en - song time,

With a down. ____

The one of them said to his mate, "Where shall we our
His hounds, they lie down at his feet, So well they do their
Down there comes a fal - low doe As heav - y with young as
She got him up up - on her back And car - ried him to
God send ev - 'ry gen - tle - man Such hawks, such hounds, and

break - fast take?"
mas - ter keep.
she might go.   With a down, der - ry, der - ry, der - ry down, down.
earth - en lake.
such le - man.

THE TRAIL TO MEXICO

American

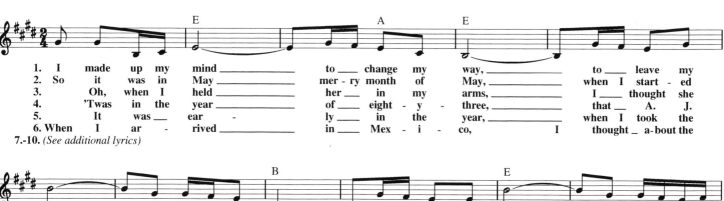

1. I made up my mind _____ to ____ change my way, _____ to ____ leave my
2. So it was in May _____ mer - ry month of May, _____ when I start - ed
3. Oh, when I held _____ her ____ in my arms, _____ I ____ thought she
4. 'Twas in the year _____ of ____ eight - y - three, _____ that ____ A. J.
5. It was ____ ear - ly ____ in the year, _____ when I took the
6. When I ar - rived _____ in ____ Mex - i - co, I thought ____ a-bout the

7.-10. *(See additional lyrics)*

crowd _____ that was ____ so gay. _____ To ____ leave my dar - ling girl ____ be -
for Tex - as far ____ a - way. _____ I ____ left my dar - ling girl ____ be -
had _____ ten thou - sand charms. Her ca - ress - es were soft, _____ her kiss - es were
Stin - son hir - ed me. _____ He ____ said: "Young man _____ I want ____ to ____
trail _____ to drive ____ those steer. _____ With ____ laugh - ter light _____ and a cow - boy's ____
girl _____ who loved ____ me so. _____ So I wrote a let - ter to ____ my ____

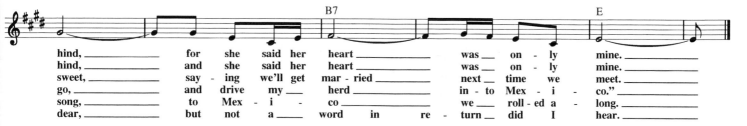

hind, _____ for she said her heart _____ was ____ on - ly mine. _____
hind, _____ and she said her heart _____ was ____ on - ly mine. _____
sweet, _____ say - ing we'll get mar - ried _____ next ____ time we meet. _____
go, _____ and drive my ____ herd _____ in - to Mex - i - co." _____
song, _____ to Mex - i - co _____ we ____ roll - ed a long. _____
dear, _____ but not a ____ word in re - turn ____ did I hear. _____

Additional Lyrics

7. So I started back to my once loved home;
Inquired for the girl who was my own;
They said, "Young man, she's wed a richer life,
Therefore young fellow you must seek another wife."

8. "Oh, curse your gold and silver too,
Oh, curse a girl who won't prove true,
I'll go right back to the Rio Grande
And get me a job with a cowboy band."

9. "Oh buddy, oh buddy, oh please stay home,
Don't be forever on the roam,
There's lots of girls more true than I,
So please don't go where the bullets fly."

10. "Yes, I'll go back where the girls are true,
And a false-hearted love I never knew,
I'll go right back where the bullets fly,
And stay on the cow trail till I die."

TIMBER
(Jerry the Mule)

American Lumberjack Song

1. Got to pull this tim - ber 'fore the sun goes down, ___ get ___ it 'cross the riv - er 'fore the boss ___ comes 'round, ___ drag it on down ___ that dust - y road. ___ Come on, Jer - ry, let's ___ dump ___ this load. ___

2. Well ___ my old Jer - ry is an Ar - kan - sas mule, ___ been ev - er - y - where ___ and he ain't ___ no fool. ___ Work is heav - y, ___ old Jer gets sore; ___ pull so much ___ and won't pull ___ no more. ___

3. Jer - ry's old shoul - der ___ is ___ six feet tall; ___ pull more ___ tim - ber than a freight ___ can haul. ___ Weighs nine hun - dred and twen - ty - two; ___ done most ev - 'ry - thing a poor mule can do. ___

4. Now the boss hit Jer - ry and it made him jump. ___ Jer - ry reared and kicked the boss ___ on ___ the rump. ___ My old Jer - ry, ___ such a good old mule; ___ had it been me, Lord, ___ I'd have killed ___ that fool. ___

5. Boss ___ tried to shoot ___ old Jer - ry in the head. ___ Jer - ry ducked that bul - let and he stomped ___ him dead. ___ Stomped ___ that boss, ___ till I want - ed to scream. Should - 've killed him my - self ___ 'cause he was so ___ damn mean. ___

Haul - in' tim - ber, ___ tim - ber, Lord, this tim - ber got - ta roll. Haul - in' tim - ber, ___ tim - ber, Lord, this tim - ber got - ta roll.

TIMES A-GETTING HARD, BOYS

American

1. Times a' - get - ting hard, boys, mon - ey's get - ting scarce. If time's don't get no bet - ter, boys, gon - na leave this place. Take my true love by the hand, lead her through the town, Say - ing good - bye to ev - 'ry - one, Good - bye to ev - 'ry - one.

2. Take my Bi - ble from the bed, shot - gun from the wall. Take old Sal and hitch her up, the wag - on for to haul. Pile the chairs and beds up high, let noth - ing drag the ground; Sal can ___ pull and we can push we're bound to leave this town.

3. Made a crop a year a - go, it with - ered to the ground. Tried to get some cred - it, but the bank - er turned me down. Goin' to Cal - i - forn - i - ay, where ev - 'ry - thing is green, Go - in' to have the best ___ farm that you have ev - er seen.

TIPPERARY RECRUITING SONG

19th Century Irish

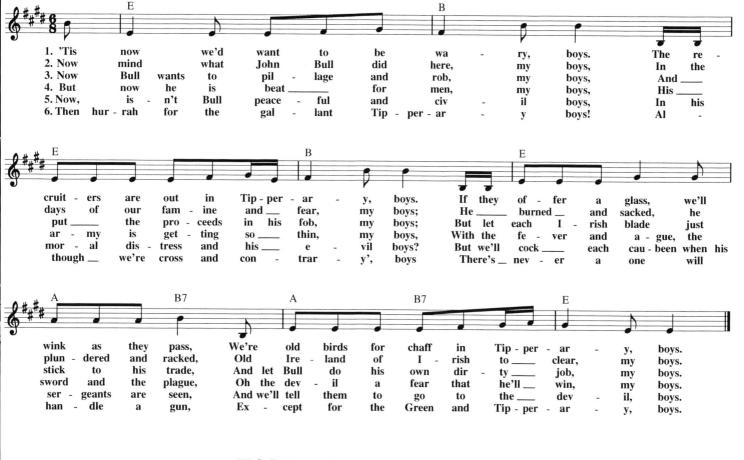

1. 'Tis now we'd want to be wa - ry, boys. The re-
2. Now mind what John Bull did here, my boys, In the
3. Now Bull wants to pil - lage and rob, my boys, And ___
4. But now he is beat ___ for men, my boys, His ___
5. Now, is - n't Bull peace - ful and civ - il boys, In his
6. Then hur - rah for the gal - lant Tip - per - ar - y boys! Al -

cruit - ers are out in Tip - per - ar - y, boys. If they of - fer a glass, we'll
days of our fam - ine and ___ fear, my boys; He ___ burned ___ and sacked, he
put ___ the pro - ceeds in his fob, my boys; But let each I - rish blade just
ar - my is get - ting so ___ thin, my boys, With the fe - ver and a - gue, the
mor - al dis - tress and his ___ e - vil boys? But we'll cock ___ each cau - been when his
though ___ we're cross and con - trar - y' boys There's ___ nev - er a one will

wink as they pass, We're old birds for chaff in Tip - per - ar - y, boys.
plun - dered and racked, Old Ire - land of I - rish to ___ clear, my boys.
stick to his trade, And let Bull do his own dir - ty ___ job, my boys.
sword and the plague, Oh the dev - il a fear that he'll ___ win, my boys.
ser - geants are seen, And we'll tell them to go to the ___ dev - il, boys.
han - dle a gun, Ex - cept for the Green and Tip - per - ar - y, boys.

'TIS THE LAST ROSE OF SUMMER

Words by Thomas Moore
circa 1805
Music by Richard Alfred Milliken

1. 'Tis the last rose ___ of ___ sum - mer, left ___ bloom - ing a - lone. All her
2. I'll not leave thee, ___ thou, ___ lone one, to ___ pine ___ on the stem; Since the
3. So ___ soon may ___ I ___ fol - low when ___ friend - ships de - cay, and from

love - ly ___ com - pan - ions are ___ fa - ded and ___ gone. No ___
love - ly ___ are ___ sleep - ing, go ___ sleep ___ thou with them. Thus ___
love's shin - ing ___ cir - cle the ___ gems ___ drop a - way. When ___

flow - er of her kin - dred, no ___ rose - bud is nigh, ___ to re -
kind - ly I'll scat - ter thy ___ leaves ___ on the bed, ___ where thy
true ___ hearts lie with - ered, and ___ fond ___ ones are flown, ___ Oh! ___

flect back ___ her blush - es, or ___ give ___ sigh for sigh!
mates of ___ the gar - den lie ___ scent - less and dead.
who would ___ in - hab - it this ___ bleak ___ world a - lone?

TO ALL GOOD CHEER
(Ein Prosit der Gemütlichkeit)

German Drinking Song

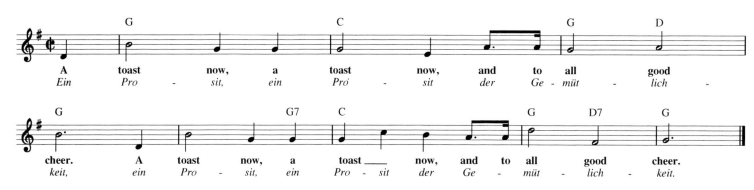

A toast now, a toast now, and to all good
cheer. A toast now, a toast now, and to all good cheer.

*Ein Pro - sit, ein Pro - sit der Ge - müt - lich -
keit, ein Pro - sit, ein Pro - sit der Ge - müt - lich - keit.*

TOBACCO UNION

Folksong from North Carolina

1. Come old and young and hear me tell How to - bac - co
2. Wom - en are nice, it is true, But they have learned to
3. Then the snuff box is pulled out, With their sticks they
4. Oft times in church you will see Some there that will
5. Oft times you'll see some five or six Out in the woods a -
6. To - bac - co is a nox - ious weed, From the dev - il it

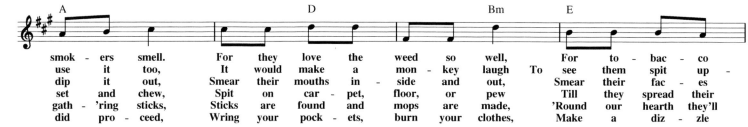

smok - ers smell. For they love the weed so well, For to - bac - co
use it too, It would make a mon - key laugh To see them spit up -
dip it out, Smear their mouths in - side and out, Smear their fac - es
set and chew, Spit on car - pet, floor, or pew Till they spread their
gath - 'ring sticks, Sticks are found and mops are made, 'Round our hearth they'll
did pro - ceed, Wring your pock - ets, burn your clothes, Make a diz - zle

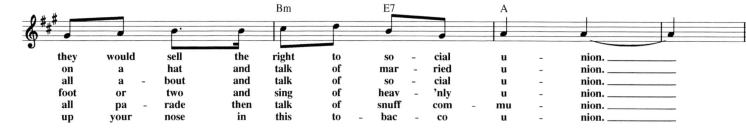

they would sell the right to so - cial u - nion. _____
on a hat and talk of mar - ried u - nion. _____
all a - bout and talk of so - cial u - nion. _____
foot or two and sing of heav - 'nly u - nion. _____
all pa - rade then talk of snuff com - mu - nion. _____
up your nose in this to - bac - co u - nion. _____

THE TITANIC

American

1. Oh, they built the ship Ti - tan - ic, to sail the o - cean blue, And they
2. Oh, they sailed ___ the ship from ___ Eng - land and were al - most to the shore, When then
3. The ___ boat was full of sin and the sides a - bout to burst, When the
4. Oh, they swung the life - boats out o'er the deep and rag - ing sea, When the

thought they had a ship that the wa - ter would nev - er go through, But the Lord's al - might - y hand said that
rich ___ re - fused to as - so - ci - ate with ___ the poor, So they put them down be - low, where they
cap ___ shout - ed, "A - wom - en and chil - dren first!" Oh, the cap - tain tried to wire, but the
band ___ struck ___ up with "A - Near - er My God ___ to Thee." Lit - tle chil - dren wept and cried as the

ship would nev - er stand,
were the first to go.
lines were all on fire.
waves swept o'er the side.
} It was sad ___ when the great ___ ship went down. It was

sad, it was sad, It was sad when that great ___ ship went down.

Hus - bands and wives, lit - tle chil - dren lost their lives; It was sad ___ when the great ___ ship went down.

TOBACCO'S BUT AN INDIAN WEED

Early 18th Century English

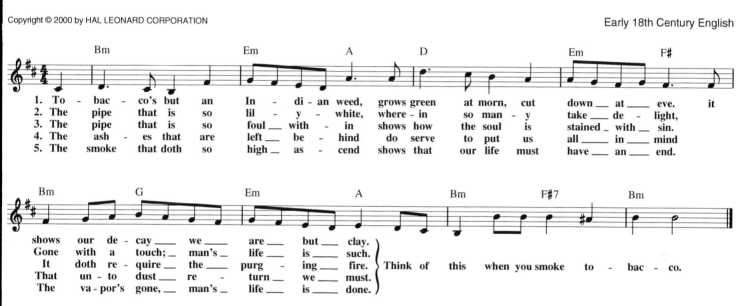

1. To - bac - co's but an In - di - an weed, grows green at morn, cut down ___ at ___ eve. it
2. The pipe that is so lil - y - white, where - in so man - y take ___ de - light,
3. The pipe that is so foul ___ with - in shows how the soul is stained ___ with ___ sin.
4. The ash - es that are left ___ be - hind do serve to put us all ___ in ___ mind
5. The smoke that doth so high ___ as - cend shows that our life must have ___ an ___ end.

shows our de - cay ___ we ___ are ___ but ___ clay.
Gone with a touch; ___ man's ___ life ___ is ___ such.
It doth re - quire ___ the ___ purg - ing ___ fire.
That un - to dust ___ re - turn ___ we ___ must.
The va - por's gone, ___ man's ___ life ___ is ___ done.
} Think of this when you smoke to - bac - co.

TOM CAT BLUES

American Blues

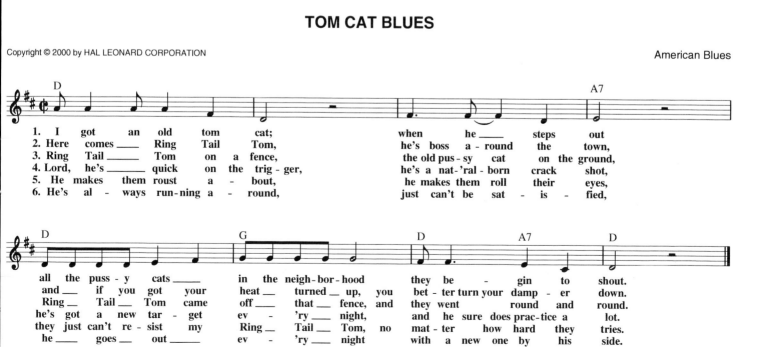

1. I got an old tom cat; when he ___ steps out
2. Here comes ___ Ring Tail Tom, he's boss a - round the town,
3. Ring Tail ___ Tom on a fence, the old pus - sy cat on the ground,
4. Lord, he's ___ quick on the trig - ger, he's a nat - 'ral - born crack shot,
5. He makes them roust a - bout, he makes them roll their eyes,
6. He's al - ways run - ning a - round, just can't be sat - is - fied,

all the puss - y cats ___ in the neigh - bor - hood they be - gin to shout.
and ___ if you got your heat ___ turned ___ up, you bet - ter turn your damp - er down.
Ring ___ Tail ___ Tom came off ___ that ___ fence, and they went round and round.
he's got a new tar - get ev - 'ry ___ night, and he sure does prac - tice a lot.
they just can't re - sist my Ring ___ Tail ___ Tom, no mat - ter how hard they tries.
he ___ goes ___ out ___ ev - 'ry ___ night with a new one by his side.

TOLD MY CAPTAIN

American Blues

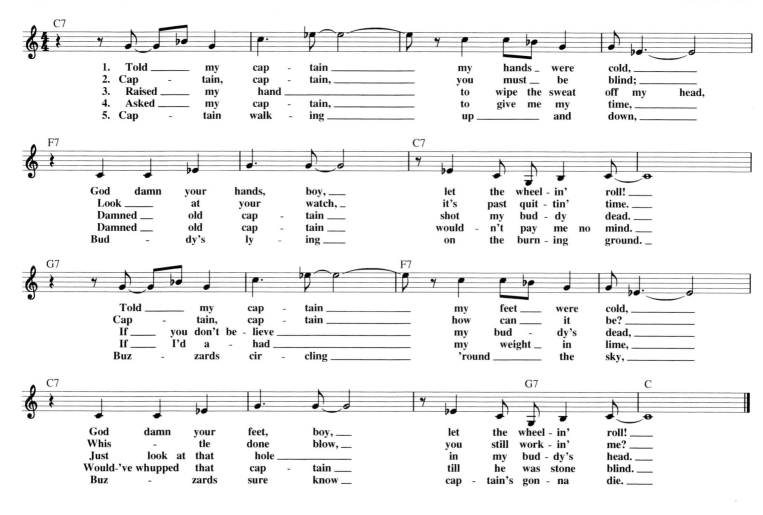

1. Told _____ my cap - tain _____ my hands _ were cold, _____
2. Cap - tain, cap - tain, _____ you must _ be blind; _____
3. Raised _____ my hand _____ to wipe the sweat off my head,
4. Asked _____ my cap - tain, _____ to give me my time, _____
5. Cap - tain walk - ing _____ up _____ and down, _____

God damn your hands, boy, ___ let the wheel - in' roll! ___
Look _____ at your watch, _ it's past quit - tin' time. ___
Damned _ old cap - tain _ shot my bud - dy dead. ___
Damned _ old cap - tain _ would - n't pay me no mind. ___
Bud - dy's ly - ing _____ on the burn - ing ground. _

Told _____ my cap - tain _____ my feet ___ were cold, _____
Cap - tain, cap - tain _____ how can ___ it be? _____
If _____ you don't be - lieve _____ my bud - dy's dead, _____
If _____ I'd a - had _____ my weight _ in lime, _____
Buz - zards cir - cling _____ 'round _____ the sky, _____

God damn your feet, boy, ___ let the wheel - in' roll! ___
Whis - tle done blow, _ you still work - in' me? ___
Just look at that hole _____ in my bud - dy's head. ___
Would - 've whupped that cap - tain _ till he was stone blind. ___
Buz - zards sure know _ cap - tain's gon - na die. _____

TOM DOOLEY

19th Century Southeastern American

Hang down your head, Tom Doo - ley, Hang down your head and cry,

You killed poor Lau - ra Fos - ter, Poor boy, you're go - ing to die. I

met her on the moun - tain, And there I took her life. I
This ___ time to - mor - row, Reck - on where I'll be?

met her on the moun - tain And I stabbed her with ___ my knife.
In some lone - some val - ley A - hangin' on a white ___ oak tree.

Hang down your head, Tom Doo - ley, Hang down your head and cry,

You killed poor Lau - ra Fos - ter, Poor boy you're go - ing to die.

TOM, TOM, THE PIPER'S SON

Nursery Rhyme Song

TOM'S GONE TO HILO

English Sea Chantey

TRAMP! TRAMP! TRAMP!

From the American Civil War
Words and Music by
George F. Root

TRAV'LIN' MAN

American

1. It was on one summer's eve - ning, _____ just a - bout the hour of three, _____ when my dar - ling start - ed to leave me, _____ to sail up - on the deep blue sea. _____ He's a trav' - lin' man, he's a trav' - lin' man, but when will he come trav' - lin' home to me? _____

2. He re - turned one au - tumn morn - ing. _____ I was filled with hap - pi - ness, _____ but at night, with hard - ly a warn - ing, _____ he hopped up - on the fast ex - press. _____

3. Christ - mas came, so nice and pleas - ant. _____ He was back from towns a - far. _____ And he took my kiss for a pres - ent. _____ A - las! He al - so took my car. _____

THE TREES ARE GETTING HIGH

18th Century English

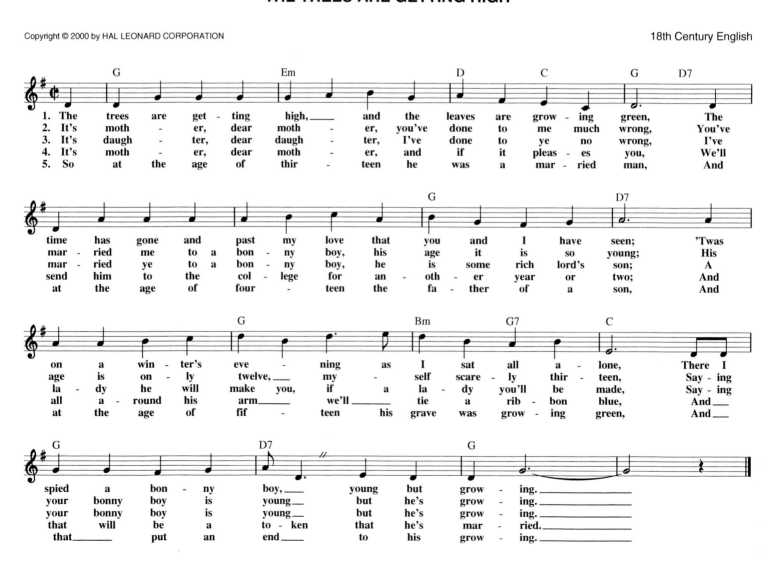

1. The trees are get - ting high, _____ and the leaves are grow - ing green, The time has gone and past my love that you and I have seen; 'Twas on a win - ter's eve - ning as I sat all a - lone, There I spied a bon - ny boy, _____ young but grow - ing. _____

2. It's moth - er, dear moth - er, you've done to me much wrong, The You've mar - ried me to a bon - ny boy, his age it is so young; His age is on - ly twelve, _____ my - self scare - ly thir - teen, Say - ing your bonny boy is young _____ but he's grow - ing. _____

3. It's daugh - ter, dear daugh - ter, I've done to ye no wrong, The I've mar - ried ye to a bon - ny boy, he is some rich lord's son; A la - dy he will make you, if a la - dy you'll be made, Say - ing your bonny boy is young _____ but he's grow - ing. _____

4. It's moth - er, dear moth - er, and if it pleas - es you, We'll send him to the col - lege for an - oth - er year or two; And all a - round his arm _____ we'll _____ tie a rib - bon blue, And _____ that will be a to - ken that he's mar - ried. _____

5. So at the age of thir - teen he was a mar - ried man, And at the age of four - teen the fa - ther of a son, And at the age of fif - teen his grave was grow - ing green, And _____ that _____ put an end _____ to his grow - ing. _____

TROIKA RUSHING
(Troika Mchitsia)

Russian
Words by P. Vyazemsky
Music by P. Bulakhov

1. Troi - ka quick - ly, troi - ka swift - ly, bring - ing forth the earth to rise.
2. Who is he that drives the hors - es, where's his jour - ney yet to come?
3. Cloud - ed by his true di - rec - tion, light to guide him miss - ing still.
1. Troi - ka mchit - sia, troi - ka ska - chet, V'ët - sia pyl' iz - pod ko - pyt.
2. Kto - sei put - nik i ot - ko - le? I da - lëk li put' e - mu?
3. Kak uz - nat'? Uzh on da - lë - ko. Me - siats v ob - la - ko nyr - nul.

Can you hear it fast ap - proach - ing, troi - ka guide__ my cu - rious eyes. ____
Fu - ri - ous pace with - out di - rec - tion, black sur - rounds__ him, day is done. ____
Ti - ny bell a - bove the hors - es, ring - ing toward__ a dis - tant hill. ____
Ko - lo - kol' - chik zvon - ko pla - chet, i kho - kho - chet, i zve - nit. _____
Po - ne - vo - le il' po vo - le mchit - sia on ____ v noch - nuiu t'mu? _____
I pu - stoi da - li glu - bo - ki ko - lo - kol' - chick uzh zas - nul. _____

Dash - ing quick - ly, cast - ing fate. My be - lov - ed I a - wait.
E - du, e - du, e - du k nei, E - du k liu - bush - ke mo - ei.

* *"Troika" is a Russian vehicle driven by a team of horses.*

THE TRUE LOVER'S FAREWELL

18th Century English

1. O ____ fare you well, I ____ must be gone And leave you for a ____
2. Ten ____ thou - sand miles, it ____ is so far To leave me here a -
3. The ____ crow that is so ____ black, my dear, Shall change his col - or ____
4. O ____ don't you see that ____ milk - white dove A - sit - ting on yon - der ____
5. The ____ riv - ers nev - er ____ will run dry, Nor the rocks melt with the ____

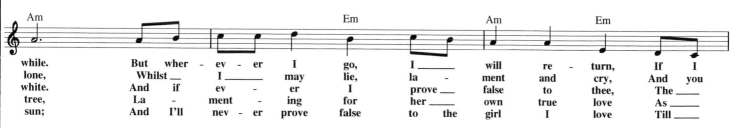

while. But wher - ev - er I go, I ____ will re - turn, If I
lone, Whilst ____ I ____ may lie, la - ment and cry, And you
white. And if ev - er I prove ____ false to thee, The ____
tree, La - ment - ing for her ____ own true love As ____
sun; And I'll nev - er prove false to the girl I love Till ____

go ten thou - sand mile, __ my ____ dear, If I go ten thou - sand mile.
will not hear my moan, __ my ____ dear, And you will not hear my moan.
day shall turn to night, __ my ____ dear, The ____ day shall turn to night.
I la - ment for thee, __ my ____ dear, As ____ I la - ment for thee?
all these things be done, __ my ____ dear, Till ____ all these things be done.

THE TROOPER AND THE MAID

Scottish Ballad

1. A troop - er lad cam' here ae nicht, and oh, but he was wea - ry. A
2. She's ta'en the horse by the hal - ter right and led it to the sta - ble. She's
3. She's ta'en the sod - ger by the lily - white hand and led him to her cham - ber. She's
4. She's made her bed baith lang and wide, she's made it like a la - dy. She's
5. And he's ta'en off his belt - ed coat, like - wise his hat and feath - er. And
6. They had-na been but an hour in bed, an hour but and a quar - ter. When the

7.-11. *(See additional lyrics)*

troop - er lad cam' here ae nicht when the moon was shin - ing clear - ly.
gi'en him oats and hay to eat as ___ muck-le as he was a - ble.
gi'en him stoup o' wine to drink, his ___ love it fleered like aim - ber.
ta'en her wee coat - ie ow - er her head' said ___ "Sod - ger, are you read - y?"
leaned his sword a - gainst the door, and ___ noo he's doon a - side her.
drum cam' sound - in' up the street and ___ il - ka beat was short - er.

Chorus

Bon - nie las - sie, will ye lie near me, bon - nie las - sie, will ___ ye lie

near me? An' I'll har a' your rib - bons reel in the morn ___ ere I leave ye.

Additional Lyrics

7. "It's up, up, up, and our colonel cries,
   It's up, up, up and away then;
   I maun sheathe my sword in its scabbard case,
   For tomorrow's our battle day then."
   Chorus

8. "And when will ye come back again,
   My ain dear sodger laddie?
   When will ye come back again,
   And be your bairn's daddie?
   Chorus

9. "O, haud your tongue, my bonnie wee lass,
   Dinna let this pairtin' grieve ye:
   When heather cowes grow ousen bows,
   Bonnie lassie, I'll come and see ye."
   Chorus

10. She's ta'en her wee coatie ower her heid,
    And followed him up to Stirlin',
    She's grown sae fu' that she couldna boo,
    And he's left her in Dunfermline.
    Chorus

11. It's breid and cheese for carles and dames,
    And oats and hay for horses;
    A cup of tea for auld maids,
    And bonnie lads for lasses.
    Chorus

TURKEY IN THE STRAW

American Minstrel Song

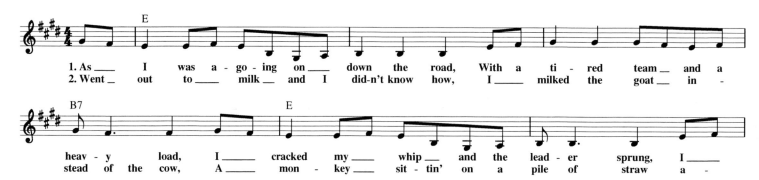

1. As ___ I was a - go - ing on ___ down the road, With a ti - red team ___ and a
2. Went ___ out to ___ milk ___ and I did-n't know how, I ___ milked the goat ___ in -

heav - y load, I ___ cracked my ___ whip ___ and the lead - er sprung, I ___
stead of the cow, A ___ mon - key ___ sit - tin' on a pile of straw a -

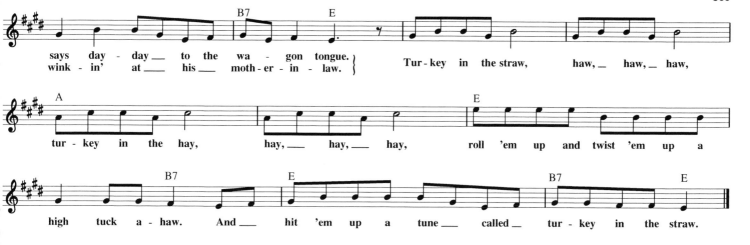

TUM BALALAIKA

Yiddish Folksong from Israel

TURKEY SONG

American

As I came o-ver yon-der hill I spied a might-y tur-key. He flapped his wings and he spread his tail, and his feet looked aw-ful dirt-y. Fol-link-a-ti-dy, fol-de-link-a-ti-dy-o, fol-link-a-ti-dy, and his feet looked aw-ful dirt-y.

THE TURTLE DOVE

American

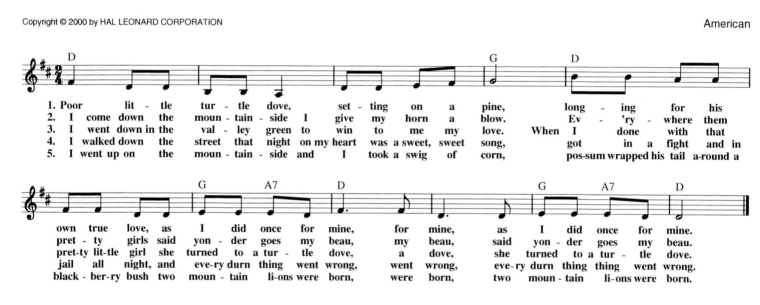

1. Poor lit-tle tur-tle dove, set-ting on a pine, long-ing for his own true love, as I did once for mine, for mine, as I did once for mine.
2. I come down the moun-tain-side I give my horn a blow. Ev-'ry-where them pret-ty girls said yon-der goes my beau, my beau, said yon-der goes my beau.
3. I went down in the val-ley green to win to me my love. When I done with that pret-ty lit-tle girl she turned to a tur-tle dove, a dove, she turned to a tur'tle dove.
4. I walked down the street that night on my heart was a sweet, sweet song, got in a fight and in jail all night, and eve-ry durn thing went wrong, went wrong, eve-ry durn thing thing went wrong.
5. I went up on the moun-tain-side and I took a swig of corn, pos-sum wrapped his tail a-round a black-ber-ry bush two moun-tain li-ons were born, were born, two moun-tain li-ons were born.

TWELVE GATES TO THE CITY

American

Oh, what a beau-ti-ful cit-y, oh, what a beau-ti-ful cit-y, oh, what a beau-ti-ful cit-y, twelve gates to the cit-y, hal-le-lu-jah.

Three gates to the east, three gates to the west, three gates to the north,

three gates _ to the south. There's twelve gates _ to the cit - y, hal - le - lu - jah.

Oh, what a beau - ti-ful cit - y, oh, what a beau - ti-ful cit - y, oh, what a

beau - ti-ful cit - y, twelve gates _ to the cit - y, hal - le - lu - jah. { Oh My When

who are those chil - dren dressed _ in red? _
God _ done just _____ what _ he said. _ } There's twelve gates _ to the cit - y, hal - le -
I _____ get to Heav'n _ gon - na sing ____ and shout. _

lu - jah. { It must be the chil - dren that Mo - ses led. _
He healed _ the sick and He raised _ the dead. _ } There's
Ain't no - bod - y there _ gon - na put ____ me out. _

twelve gates _ to the cit - y, hal - le - lu - jah. jah.

THE UTAH IRON HORSE

American

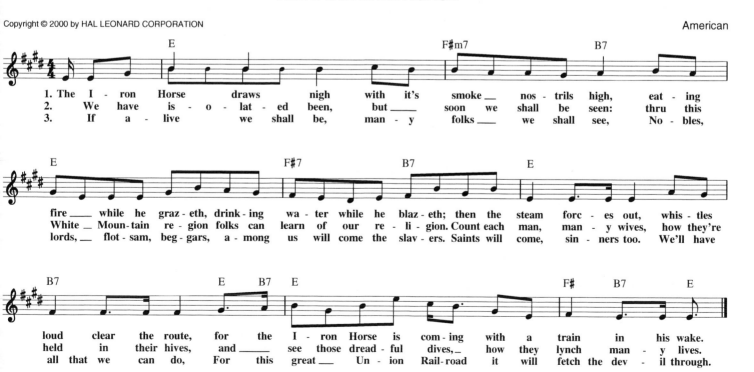

1. The I - ron Horse draws nigh with it's smoke _ nos - trils high, eat - ing
2. We have is - o - lat - ed been, but ____ soon we shall be seen: thru this
3. If a - live we shall be, man - y folks ____ we shall see, No - bles,

fire ____ while he graz - eth, drink - ing wa - ter while he blaz - eth; then the steam forc - es out, whis - tles
White _ Moun - tain re - gion folks can learn of our re - li - gion. Count each man, man - y wives, how they're
lords, _ flot - sam, beg - gars, a - mong us will come the slav - ers. Saints will come, sin - ners too. We'll have

loud clear the route, for the I - ron Horse is com - ing with a train in his wake.
held in their hives, and ____ see those dread - ful dives, _ how they lynch man - y lives.
all that we can do, For this great _ Un - ion Rail - road it will fetch the dev - il through.

TWINKLE, TWINKLE, LITTLE STAR
(Ah! Vous Dirai-je, Maman?)

French
French Words and Melody, 1761
English Words by Jane Taylor, 1806

1. Oh! dear ma - ma, shall I say what tor - ments me night and day?
*(Twin - kle, twin - kle, lit - tle star, how I won - der what you are,
1. Ah! vous di - rai - je, ma - man, Ce qui cau - se mon tour ment?
2.,3. (See additional lyrics)

Since the time I saw Ly - san - der, And I saw his look so ten - der,
Up a - bove the world so high Like a dia - mond in the sky.
De - puis que j'ai vu Li - san - dre Me re - gar - der d'un oeil ten - dre

My heart tells me ev - 'ry hour With - out love, life can - not flower.
Twin - kle, twin - kle lit - tle star, how I won - der what you are.)
Mon coeur dit à chaque ins - tant: Peut - on vi - vre sans a - mant?

*Traditional English lyric; it is not, however, a translation of the original French words.

Additional Lyrics

2. It was just the other day,
   That he brought me a bouquet;
   He was really very charming
   And he said to me: "My darling,
   No girl can compare with you,
   And I swear my love to you."

3. How I blushed! And, sad to say,
   Sighing gave my heart away.
   My poor heart with love was reeling
   And I could not hide my feeling;
   Then alas! Mama, his charms
   Led me straight into his arms.

2. *L'autre jour dans un bosquet,*
   De fleurs il fit un bouquet;
   Il en para ma houlette
   Me disant: "Chère brunette,
   Flore est moins belle que toi,
   L'amour moins tendre que moi."

3. *Je rougis et par malheur*
   Un soupir trahit mon coeur;
   Le cruel, avec adresse,
   Profita de ma faiblesse.
   Hélas! maman, un faux pas
   Me fit tomber dans ses bras.

TWO MAIDS WENT A-MILKING ONE DAY

17th Century English

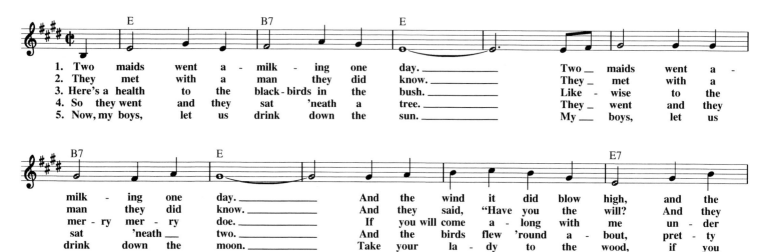

1. Two maids went a - milk - ing one day. _____ Two __ maids went a -
2. They met with a man they did know. _____ They __ met with a
3. Here's a health to the black - birds in the bush. _____ Like - wise to the
4. So they went and they sat 'neath a tree. _____ They __ went and they
5. Now, my boys, let us drink down the sun. _____ My __ boys, let us

milk - ing one day. _____ And the wind it did blow high, and the
man they did know. _____ And they said, "Have you the will? And they
mer - ry mer - ry doe. _____ If you will come a - long with me un - der
sat 'neath __ two. _____ And the birds flew 'round a - bout, pret - ty
drink down the moon. _____ Take your la - dy to the wood, if you

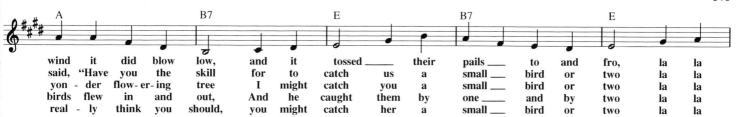

wind	it	did	blow	low,	and	it	tossed ___	their	pails ___	to	and	fro,	la	la
said,	"Have	you	the	skill	for	to	catch	us	a	small ___	bird	or	two	la	la
yon -	der	flow-er-ing	tree	I	might	catch	you	a	small ___	bird	or	two	la	la
birds	flew	in	and	out,	And	he	caught	them	by	one ___	and	by	two	la	la
real -	ly	think	you	should,	you	might	catch	her	a	small ___	bird	or	two	la	la

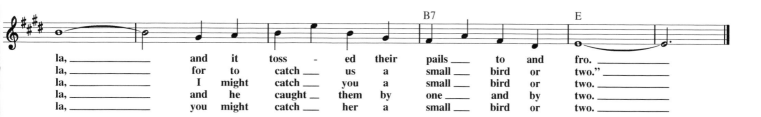

la, ___	and	it	toss -	ed	their	pails ___	to	and	fro. ___
la, ___	for	to	catch ___	us	a	small ___	bird	or	two." ___
la, ___	I	might	catch ___	you	a	small ___	bird	or	two. ___
la, ___	and	he	caught _	them	by	one ___	and	by	two. ___
la, ___	you	might	catch ___	her	a	small ___	bird	or	two. ___

TYIN' A KNOT IN THE DEVIL'S TAIL

American

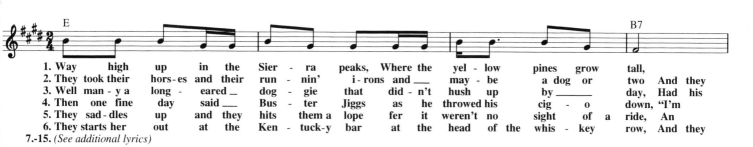

1. Way high up in the Sier - ra peaks, Where the yel - low pines grow tall,
2. They took their hors-es and their run - nin' i - rons and ___ may - be a dog or two And they
3. Well man - y a long - eared ___ dog - gie that did - n't hush up by ___ day, Had his
4. Then one fine day said ___ Bus - ter Jiggs as he throwed his cig - o down, "I'm
5. They sad - dles up and they hits them a lope fer it weren't no sight of a ride, An
6. They starts her out at the Ken - tuck-y bar at the head of the whis - key row, And they

7.-15. *(See additional lyrics)*

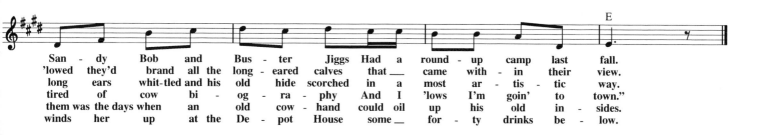

San -	dy	Bob	and	Bus -	ter	Jiggs	Had	a	round -	up	camp	last	fall.
'lowed	they'd	brand	all the	long -	eared	calves	that ___	came	with -	in	their	view.
long	ears	whit-tled	and his	old	hide	scorched	in a	most	ar -	tis -	tic	way.
tired	of	cow	bi -	og -	ra -	phy	And I	'lows	I'm	goin'	to	town."
them was	the days	when	an	old	cow -	hand	could oil	up	his	old	in -	sides.
winds	her	up	at the	De -	pot	House	some ___	for -	ty	drinks	be -	low.

Additional Lyrics

7. They sets her up and turns her around
And goes her the other way,
And to tell you the Lord forsaken truth
Them boys got drunk that day.

8. Well, as they was a-headin' back to camp
And packin' a pretty good load,
Who should they meet but the Devil, himself,
Come prancin' down the road.

9. Now the Devil he said: " You cowboy skunks,
You better go hunt your hole,
Cause I come up from the hell's rim-rock
To gather in your souls."

10. Said Buster Jiggs: "Now we're just from town
An' feelin' kind o' tight,
And you ain't gonna get no cowboy souls
Without some kind of a fight."

11. So he punched a hole in his old throw-rope
And he slings her straight and true,
And he roped the Devil right around the horns
He takes his dallies true.

12. Old Sandy Bob was a reata-man
With his rope all coiled up neat,
But he shakes her out and he builds him a loop
And he roped the Devil's hind feet.

13. They threw him down on the desert ground,
While the irons was a-gettin' hot,
They cropped and swallow-forked his ears
And branded him up a lot.

14. And they pruned him up with a dehorning saw
And knotted his tail for a joke,
Rode off and left him bellowing there,
Necked up to a lilac-jack oak.

15. Well, if you ever travel in the Sierra peaks
And you hear one helluva wail,
You'll know it's nothin' but the Devil, himself,
Raisin' hell about the knots in his tail.

THE UNQUIET GRAVE

English

1. How cold the wind doth blow dear love! How heav-y fall the
2. I'll do as much for my true love As ev-er in my
3. When this twelve-month was gone and past The ghost be-gan to
4. O what is it you want of me, Sweet-heart, or what of
5. "My lips they are so cold as clay, My breath it doth smell
6. "Cold though your lips in death, dear love, One kiss, one kiss is
7. How cold the wind doth blow dear love! How heav-y fall the

drops of ___ rain! I nev-er ___ had but ___ one true love, ___
pow'r doth ___ lay; I will sit and ___ mourn up-on his grave, ___
speak at ___ the last. "Why sit you ___ here all ___ on my grave, ___
me would ___ have? "One kiss, one ___ kiss from your snow-y white lips ___
earth-y ___ and strong; If you were to kiss my ___ snow-y white lips, ___
all I ___ crave. I care not ___ if I ___ kiss but thee ___
drops of ___ rain! I nev-er ___ had but ___ one true love, ___

___ And in the green-woods ___ he was slain.
___ Dear love, a twelve-month ___ and a day.
___ Sweet-heart and will ___ not ___ let me sleep?"
___ Is all I crave ___ from ___ you dear love."
___ Sweet-heart your time ___ would ___ not be long."
___ That I should share ___ thy grave."
___ And in the green-woods ___ he was slain.

UNTO A POOR BLIND LOVER
(A Un Niño Ciegocito)

Spanish

Un-to a poor blind lov-er I showed com-pas-sion, I showed com-pas -
A un ni-ño cie-go-ci-to Le diò aco-gi-da, le diò aco-gi

- sion;
da;

{ 1. I showed com-pas - sion Un-to a poor blind
{ 2. How mat-ters twist - ed: He soon was gaz-ing
{ *1. Le diò aco-gi - da, A un ni-ño cie-go-*
{ *2. Pe-rò el per-ver - so, Re-co-bran-do la*

lov
clear
ci
vi

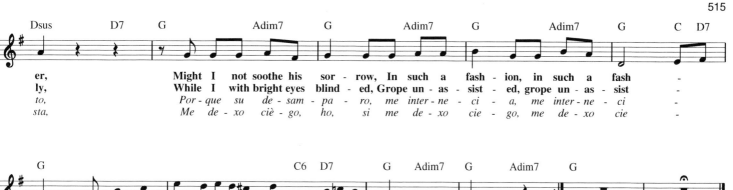

THE VICAR OF BRAY

English

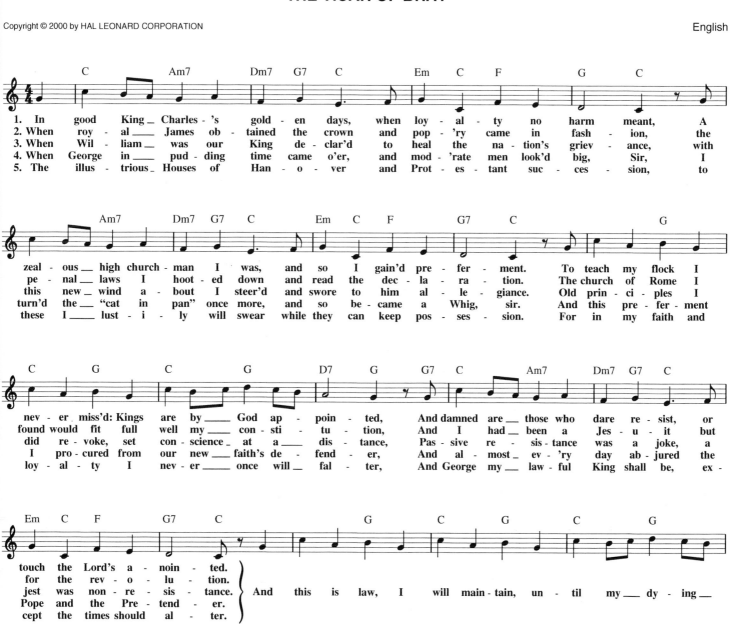

VICKSBURG BLUES

American

1. I've got the Vicks-burg blues, __ and I'm sing-in' it ev - 'ry where I go. _____
2.,3. *(See additional lyrics)*

I've got the Vicks-burg Blues _ and I'm sing-in' it ev - 'ry-where I go. _____

Now the rea-son I'm sing-in', my babe says she don't want me no more. _____

Additional Lyrics

2. I've got those Vicksburg Blues and I'm singing it everywhere I please
   I've got those Vicksburg Blues and I'm singing it everywhere I please
   Now, the reason I'm singing is to give my poor heart some ease.

3. Now, I don't like this place, mama, and I never will
   Now, I don't like this place, mama, and I never will
   I can sit right here in jail and look at Vicksburg on the hill.

VINE AND FIG TREE

Folksong from Israel

May ev-'ry-one 'neath their vine and fig tree, Now live in peace and har-mo-ny. May ev-'ry-
Now live in peace and un-a-

fraid. And in-to plough shares beat their swords, man-kind shall stud-y war no more. war no more.

* This song may be sung as a 2-part round.

THE WABASH CANNON BALL

American Hobo Song, circa 1880s

1. From the great At - lan - tic O - cean to the wide Pa - cif - ic's shore, From the ones we leave be -
2. Lis - ten to the rhyth - mic jin - gle and the rum - ble and the roar, As she glides a - long the
3. She was com - ing from At - lan - ta on a cold De - cem - ber day. As she rolled in - to the

hind us to the ones we see once more. She's might - y tall and hand - some, and
wood - lands thro' the hills and by the shore. You hear the might - y en - gine and
sta - tion, I could hear a wom - an say: "He's might - y big and hand - some, and

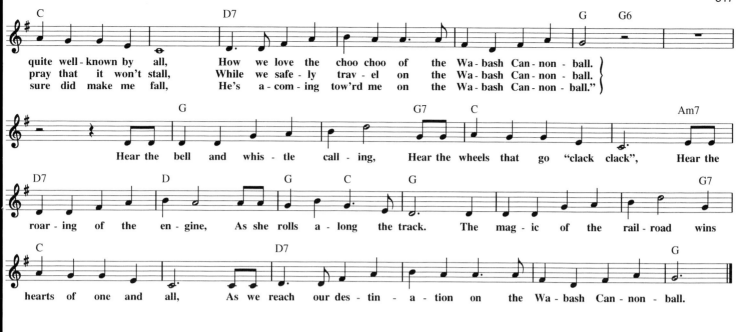

quite well-known by all, How we love the choo choo of the Wa-bash Can-non-ball.
pray that it won't stall, While we safe-ly trav-el on the Wa-bash Can-non-ball.
sure did make me fall, He's a-com-ing tow'rd me on the Wa-bash Can-non-ball."

Hear the bell and whis-tle call-ing, Hear the wheels that go "clack clack", Hear the

roar-ing of the en-gine, As she rolls a-long the track. The mag-ic of the rail-road wins

hearts of one and all, As we reach our des-tin-a-tion on the Wa-bash Can-non-ball.

WHISKEY, YOU'RE THE DEVIL

Irish

Whis-key, you're the dev-il,_____ you're lead-in' me a-stray O-ver hills and

moun-tains and to A-mer-i-cae. You're sweet-er, strong-er, de-cent-er, you're

spunk-i-er than tae; O_____ Whis-key, you're my dar-lin' drunk or so-

ber. Fine

1. Oh, now, brave boys, we're on the march And off to Por-tu-
2. The French are fight-ing bold - ly, Men dy-ing hot and
3. Said the moth-er, "Do not wrong___ me; Don't take my daugh-ter

gal and Spain. The drums are beat-ing, ban-ners fly-ing; The dev-il a-home will
cold - ly. Gives ev-'ry man his flask of pow-der, His far - lock on his
from___ me. For if you do, I will tor-ment you, And af-ter death a

come to-night.___ } Love, fare thee well with me tith-er-y eye, the doo-de-lum, the
shoul - der.___
ghost will haunt you." }

da, Me tith-er-y eye, the doo-de-lum, the da, Me

D.C.
last time D.C. al Fine

rikes fall, tour a lad-die, Oh, there's whis-key in the jar. Hey!

WAE'S ME FOR PRINCE CHARLIE

Scottish
Words by William Glen, circa 1825

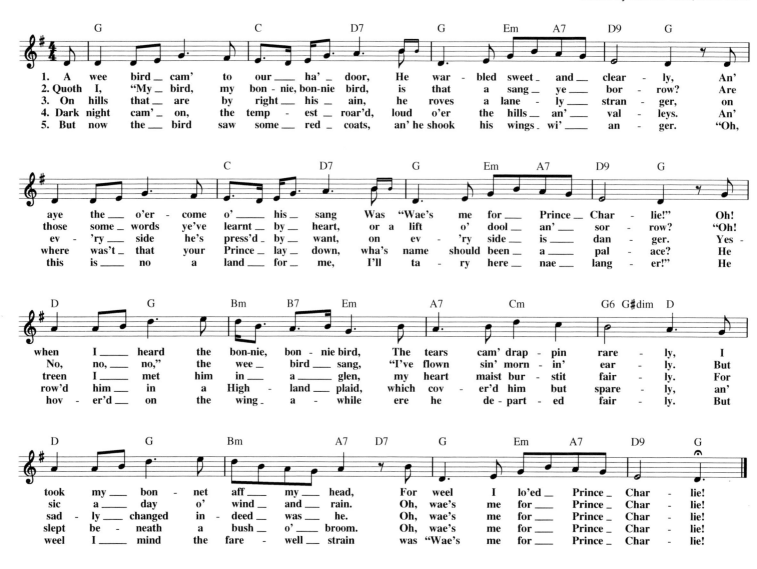

THE WEARING OF THE GREEN

18th Century Irish

WANDERIN'

American

WATER COME A ME EYE

Jamaican

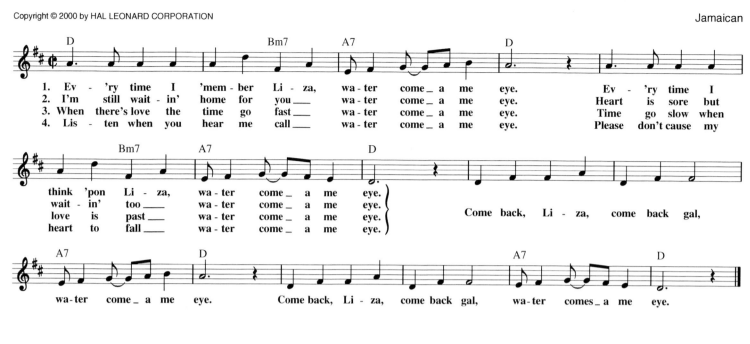

1. Ev - 'ry time I 'mem - ber Li - za, wa - ter come _ a me eye. Ev - 'ry time I
2. I'm still wait - in' home for you ___ wa - ter come _ a me eye. Heart is sore but
3. When there's love the time go fast ___ wa - ter come _ a me eye. Time go slow when
4. Lis - ten when you hear me call ___ wa - ter come _ a me eye. Please don't cause my

think 'pon Li - za, wa - ter come _ a me eye.
wait - in' too ___ wa - ter come _ a me eye.
love is past ___ wa - ter come _ a me eye.
heart to fall ___ wa - ter come _ a me eye.

Come back, Li - za, come back gal,

wa - ter come _ a me eye. Come back, Li - za, come back gal, wa - ter comes _ a me eye.

WATER IN ME RUM

Drinking Song from St. Thomas

1. One day I woke _ up feel - in' weak _ me head was ly - in' In the creek. _ Me
2. Now I was guest _ to a so - cial par - ty me host cried out "Boy drink heart - y." ___ I
3. When I was wed _ I had been told, _ to lift me bride 'cross the thresh - old. ___ So
4. Drank me cup of ___ rum one Sun - day, _ don't get home, till the foll - 'wing Mon - day.

bod - y was ___ on the hard stone ground. It was wa - ter in me rum had got me down. _
lift the keg ___ and drink it all. And right then I saw the night be - gin to fall. ___
for good luck, _ I drink one cup, and I spend the hon - ey-moon try - in' to raise she up. ___
I was blind, _ but I did not care, slept _ out ___ in the gut - ter, 'cause the weath - er was fair. ___

Wa - ter in me rum was what I found. _ Wa - ter in me rum was what I found. _

Wa - ter in me rum was what I found. _ Wa - ter in me rum ___ had got me down. _

WAYFARING STRANGER

Southern American

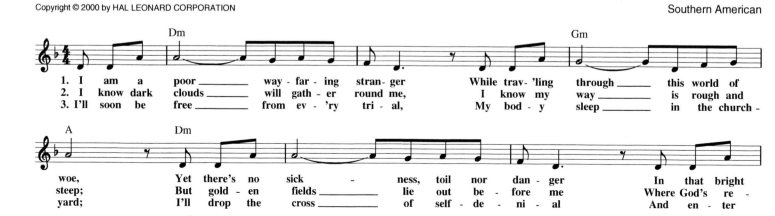

1. I am a poor _____ way - far - ing stran - ger While trav - 'ling through _____ this world of
2. I know dark clouds _____ will gath - er round me, I know my way _____ is rough and
3. I'll soon be free _____ from ev - 'ry tri - al, My bod - y sleep _____ in the church -

woe, Yet there's no sick - ness, toil nor dan - ger In that bright
steep; But gold - en fields _____ lie out be - fore me Where God's re -
yard; I'll drop the cross _____ of self - de - ni - al And en - ter

Gm — Dm — Bb — C7

world ____ to which I go. I'm go - ing there ____ to see my
deemed ____ shall ev - er sleep. I'm go - ing there ____ to see my
on ____ my great re - ward. I'm go - ing there ____ to see my

F — Bb — C7 — Dm

Fa - ther, I'm go - ing there ____ no more to roam;
moth - er, She said she'd meet ____ me when I come; } I'm on - ly
Sav - ior, To sing His praise ____ for - ev - er - more; }

Gm — Dm

go - ing o - ver Jor - dan, I'm on - ly go - ing o - ver home.

WE GATHER TOGETHER

Netherlands Folk Melody
Words from *Nederlandtsch Gedenckclanck,* 1626
Translated by Theodore Baker, 1894

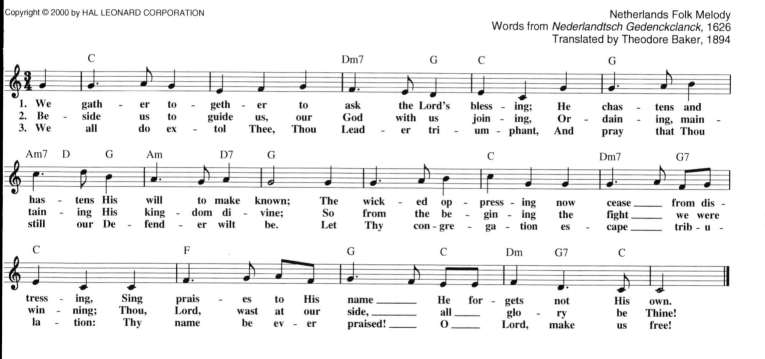

C — Dm7 — G — C — G

1. We gath - er to - geth - er to ask the Lord's bless - ing; He chas - tens and
2. Be - side us to guide us, our God with us join - ing, Or - dain - ing, main -
3. We all do ex - tol Thee, Thou Lead - er tri - um - phant, And pray that Thou

Am7 D — G Am — D7 G — C — Dm7 — G7

has - tens His will to make known; The wick - ed op - press - ing now cease ____ from dis -
tain - ing His king - dom di - vine; So from the be - gin - ing the fight ____ we were
still our De - fend - er wilt be. Let Thy con - gre - ga - tion es - cape ____ trib - u -

C — F — G — C — Dm G7 C

tress - ing, Sing prais - es to His name ____ He for - gets not His own.
win - ning; Thou, Lord, wast at our side, ____ all ____ glo - ry be Thine!
la - tion: Thy name be ev - er praised! ____ O ____ Lord, make us free!

WEAVING LILT

Scottish Work Song

D — A7 D G — D — G A7 D

1. Wait to - day, love, till ____ to - mor - row, Ho - ro e - ci - can a - rin hu - o,
2. Wait to - day un - til ____ to - mor - row. Ho - ro e - ci - can a - rin hu - o.
3. Shuttle I lent the King ____ of France, love, Ho - ro e - ci - can a - rin hu - o.

A7 — D

While I weave fine lin - en for thee, love, Lin - en for thee, fine lin - en for thee, love,
Sown is the lint, but och, will it grow, love? Lin - en for thee, fine lin - en for thee, love,
Loom, it grows in the wood of St. Pat - rick, Shut - tle, nor loom, have I ____ to weave, yet

G — D — G — A7 D — A7 D

While ____ I weave fine lin - en for thee, love, Wait to - day, love, till ____ to - mor - row.
Sure will it grow fine lin - en for thee, love? Wait to - day, love, till ____ to - mor - row.
wait till I weave fine lin - en for thee, love. Wait to - day, love, till ____ to - mor - row.

WEEL MAY THE KEEL ROW

Northeastern England, circa 1770

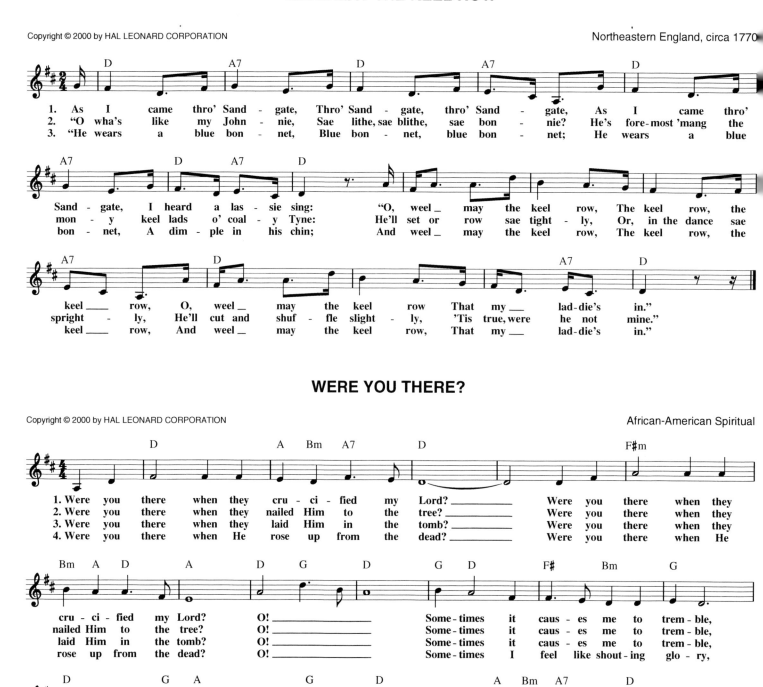

1. As I came thro' Sand-gate, Thro' Sand-gate, thro' Sand-gate, As I came thro' Sand-gate, I heard a las-sie sing: "O, weel_ may the keel row, The keel row, the keel_ row, O, weel_ may the keel row That my_ lad-die's in."

2. "O wha's like my John-nie, Sae lithe, sae blithe, sae bon-nie? He's fore-most 'mang the mon-y keel lads o' coal-y Tyne: He'll set or row sae tight-ly, Or, in the dance sae spright-ly, He'll cut and shuf-fle slight-ly, 'Tis true, were he not mine."

3. "He wears a blue bon-net, Blue bon-net, blue bon-net; He wears a blue bon-net, A dim-ple in his chin; And weel_ may the keel row, The keel row, the keel_ row, And weel_ may the keel row, That my_ lad-die's in."

WERE YOU THERE?

African-American Spiritual

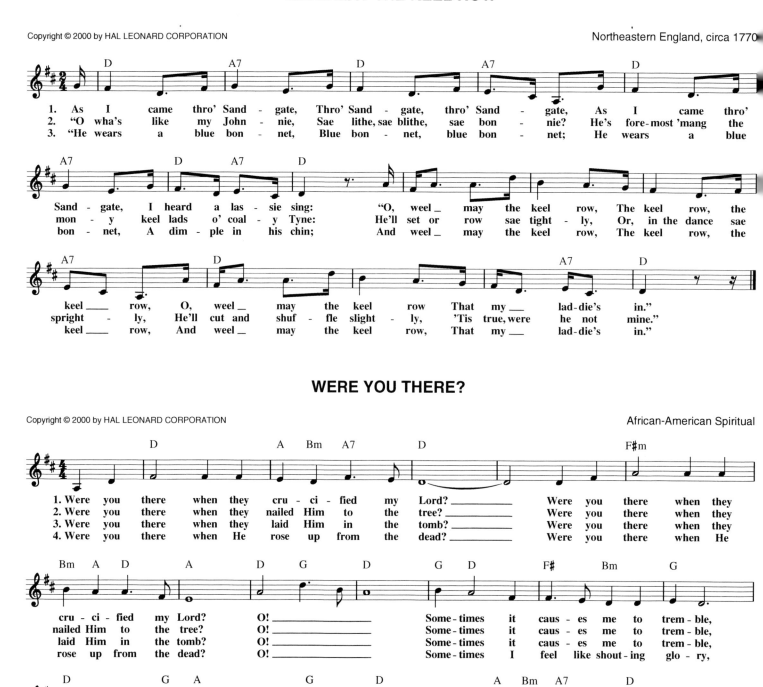

1. Were you there when they cru-ci-fied my Lord? Were you there when they cru-ci-fied my Lord? O! Some-times it caus-es me to trem-ble, trem-ble, trem-ble! Were you there when they cru-ci-fied my Lord?

2. Were you there when they nailed Him to the tree? Were you there when they nailed Him to the tree? O! Some-times it caus-es me to trem-ble, trem-ble, trem-ble! Were you there when they nailed Him to the tree?

3. Were you there when they laid Him in the tomb? Were you there when they laid Him in the tomb? O! Some-times it caus-es me to trem-ble, trem-ble, trem-ble! Were you there when they laid Him in the tomb?

4. Were you there when He rose up from the dead? Were you there when He rose up from the dead? O! Some-times I feel like shout-ing glo-ry, glo-ry, glo-ry! Were you there when He rose up from the dead?

WHITE CORAL BELLS

American Camp Song

White cor-al bells up-on a slen-der stalk, Lil-ies of the val-ley deck my gar-den walk.

Oh, don't you wish that you could hear them ring? That will hap-pen on-ly when the fair-ies sing.

WHAT TIME IS IT?
(Hoe Laat Is't?)

Folksong from the Netherlands

"The clock says it's twelve." to an - swer the maid. Where
Hoe laat is't? twaalf hur. Wie is bij? de meid. Waar

is she? in the kitch - en. She sits and she knits. For who? For
is zij? in de keu - ken. Wat doet zij? zij breit. Voor wie? Voor

who? For the ba - by, lit - tle ba - by, And the clock goes tick - tock.
wie? Voor de klei - ne pop - pe - dei - ne, En de groo - ten bim - bam.

WHEN COCKLESHELLS TURN SILVERBELLS

17th Century English

When cock - le - shells _____ turn sil - ver - bells, _____ And mus - sels grow _____
O had I wist _____ be - fore I kissed, _____ That love had been _____

_____ on ev - 'ry tree. _____ When blooms the rose _____ 'mongst frost and snows, _____
_____ so ill to win; _____ I'd locked my heart _____ in case of gold _____

_____ Then will my false _____ love prove true to me. _____
_____ And pinned it with _____ a sil - ver pin. _____ } O wa - ly,

wa - ly, but love is bon - nie, A lit - tle while _____ when it is

new. _____ But when it's old _____ it grow - eth cold, _____

_____ And fades a - way _____ like morn - ing dew. _____

WHEN ADAM WAS CREATED

Folksong from North Carolina

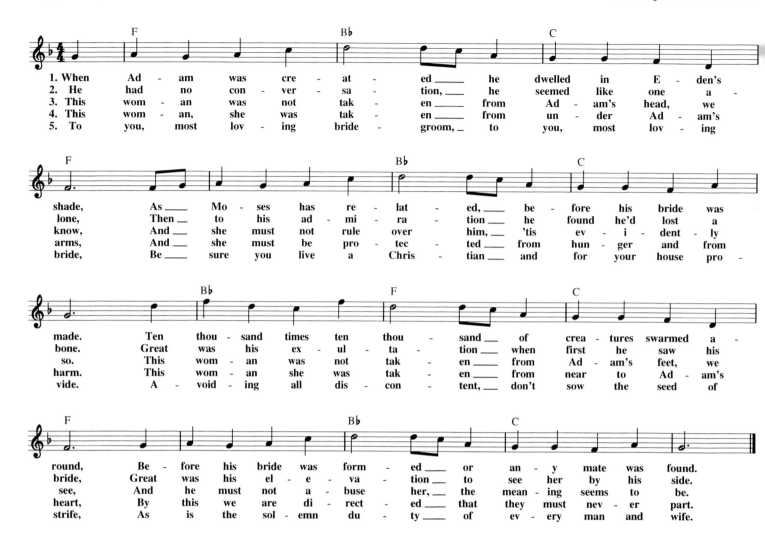

WHEN I CAN READ MY TITLE CLEAR

American
Music from *Kentucky Harmony*, 1816
Words by Isaac Watts

WHEN JOHNNY COMES MARCHING HOME

Words and Music by Louis Lambert, 1863
Melody adapted from an Irish Folksong

WHISKEY JOHNNY!

American

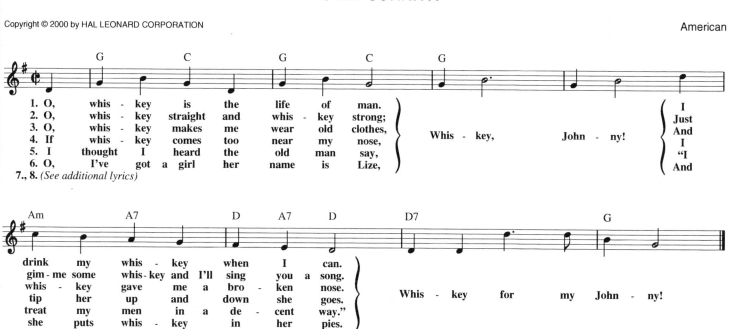

Additional Lyrics

7. Here somes the cook with a whiskey can;
Whiskey, Johnny!
A glass of grog for ev'ry man!
Whiskey for my Johnny!

8. A glass of grog for ev'ry man,
Whiskey, Johnny!
And a bottle full for the shanty man.
Whiskey for my Johnny!

WHEN THE SAINTS GO MARCHING IN

Words by Katherine E. Purvis
Music by James M. Black

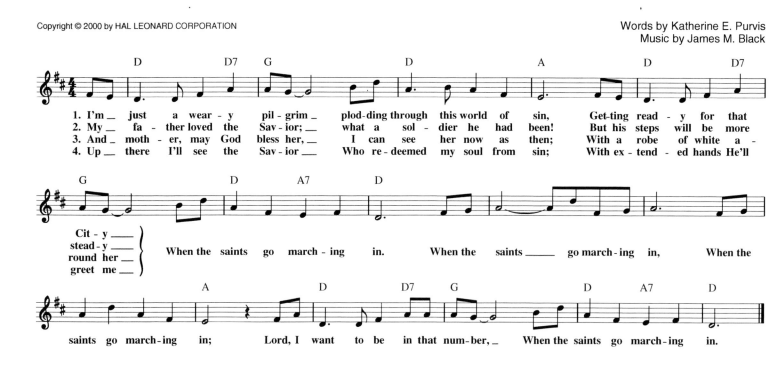

1. I'm _ just a wear - y pil - grim _ plod-ding through this world of sin, Get-ting read - y for that
2. My _ fa - ther loved the Sav - ior; _ what a sol - dier he had been! But his steps will be more
3. And _ moth - er, may God bless her, _ I can see her now as then; With a robe of white a -
4. Up _ there I'll see the Sav - ior _ Who re-deemed my soul from sin; With ex - tend - ed hands He'll

Cit - y ____)
stead - y ____) When the saints go march - ing in. When the saints _____ go march-ing in, When the
round her __)
greet me __)

saints go march-ing in; Lord, I want to be in that num-ber, _ When the saints go march-ing in.

WHISTLE, DAUGHTER, WHISTLE

American

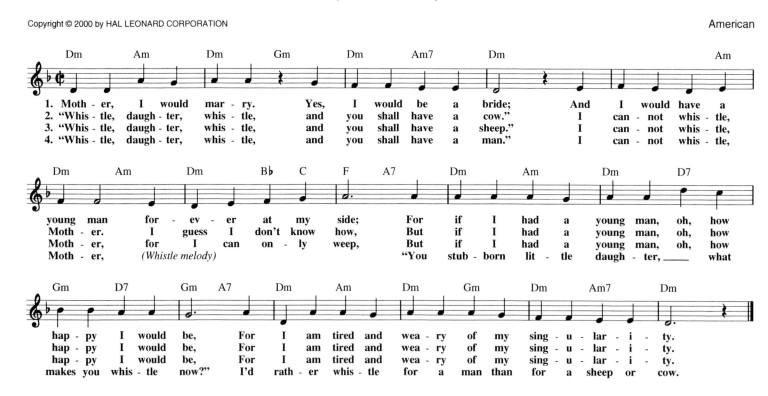

1. Moth - er, I would mar - ry. Yes, I would be a bride; And I would have a
2. "Whis - tle, daugh - ter, whis - tle, and you shall have a cow." I can - not whis - tle,
3. "Whis - tle, daugh - ter, whis - tle, and you shall have a sheep." I can - not whis - tle,
4. "Whis - tle, daugh - ter, whis - tle, and you shall have a man." I can - not whis - tle,

young man for - ev - er at my side; For if I had a young man, oh, how
Moth - er. I guess I don't know how, But if I had a young man, oh, how
Moth - er, for I can on - ly weep, But if I had a young man, oh, how
Moth - er, (Whistle melody) "You stub - born lit - tle daugh - ter, _____ what

hap - py I would be, For I am tired and wea - ry of my sing - u - lar - i - ty.
hap - py I would be, For I am tired and wea - ry of my sing - u - lar - i - ty.
hap - py I would be, For I am tired and wea - ry of my sing - u - lar - i - ty.
makes you whis - tle now?" I'd rath - er whis - tle for a man than for a sheep or cow.

THE WILD COLONIAL BOY

Australian

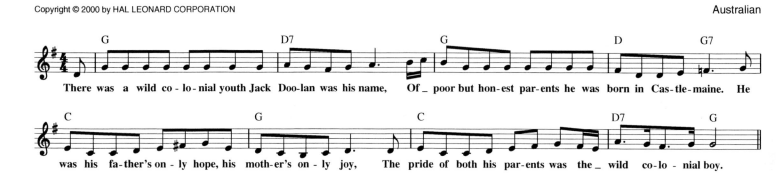

There was a wild co - lo - nial youth Jack Doo-lan was his name, Of _ poor but hon-est par-ents he was born in Cas-tle-maine. He

was his fa-ther's on - ly hope, his moth-er's on - ly joy, The pride of both his par-ents was the _ wild co-lo-nial boy.

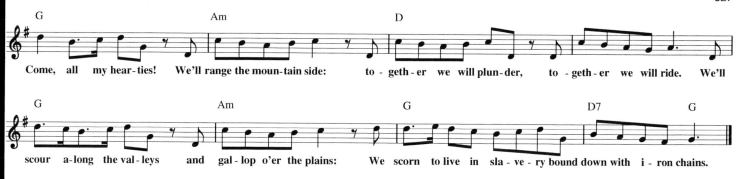

Come, all my hear-ties! We'll range the moun-tain side: to - geth - er we will plun-der, to - geth - er we will ride. We'll

scour a-long the val-leys and gal-lop o'er the plains: We scorn to live in sla-ve-ry bound down with i - ron chains.

WILL THE CIRCLE BE UNBROKEN

Words by Ada R. Habershon
Music by Charles H. Gabriel

1. I was stand - ing by my win - dow on one cold and cloud - y day, When I
2. Oh, I told the un - der - tak - er, "Un - der - tak - er, please drive slow, For this
3. I will fol - low close be - hind her, try to hold up and be brave; But I

saw the hearse come roll - ing, For to take my Moth - er a - way.
bod - y you are haul - ing, Lord, I hate to see her ___ go." Will the
could not hide my sor - row When they laid her in the ___ grave.

cir - cle be un - bro - ken by and by, Lord, by and by? There's a

bet - ter home a - wait - ing in the sky, in the sky.

WOOING
(Werbung)

Austrian

1. O - ver moun - tain, ___ through wood - land, Glad I wan - der ___ and ___
2. The ___ maid - en ___ I ___ long ___ for, With a pas - sion ___ un -
3. Sweet ___ maid ___ of ___ the ___ wood - land, O ___ hear ___ me, ___ please ___
1. Z'nächst ___ bin ___ i ___ halt ___ gan - ge Über's Ber - gel ___ im ___
2. Des ___ mer ___ gar ___ so ___ gut ___ g'fallt, Wie koi an - dre ___ so ___
3. Und ___ Di - an - del ___ vom ___ Wald, Geh' ___ sei ___ net ___ so ___

free, ___ Where the ech - oes ___ ring ___ sweet - ly, It is there ___ I ___ would ___ be.
told, ___ Black her eyes ___ are ___ deep ___ glanc - ing, Child no more, ___ but ___ not ___ old.
do; ___ I will wor - ship ___ you ___ al - ways, I will ev - er ___ be ___ true.
Wald, ___ Und da g'freut's ___ mi ___ zu ___ woh - ne, Weil's ___ Jo - deln ___ schön ___ hallt.
bald, ___ Und ___ schön ___ schwarz aug - et ___ ist Und net z'jung ___ und ___ net ___ z'alt.
kalt, ___ Nimm de z'samm'n ___ und ___ sag's ___ aus - ser, Ob mein Lieb' ___ dir ___ net ___ g'fallt!

WILL YE GO, LASSIE?

Irish

1. Oh, the summer time is coming, And the trees are sweetly blooming, And the
2. I will build my love a tower, Near yon pure crystal fountain, And on
3. If my true love she were gone, I would surely find another, Where the

wild mountain thyme _____ Grows around the blooming heather.)
it I will build _____ All the flowers of the mountain.) Will ye go, _____ lassie,
wild mountain thyme _____ Grows around the blooming heather.)

go? And we'll all go together, To pluck wild mountain

thyme, _____ All around the blooming heather. Will ye go, _____ lassie, go?

WILLIE THE WEEPER

American

1. Oh, hark to the story of Willie the Weeper, Willie the
2. He went into a joint _____ it was late one _____ night— Where he knew the
3. He rolled himself some _____ five or six pills, _____ That he knew
4. He started playin' poker when he lef' the land, An' he won a million
5. He went to a place that they called _____ Siam', An' he beat the
6. In Monte Carlo he _____ played _____ roulette; _____ Couldn't lose a
7.,8. *(See additional lyrics)*

Weeper was a chimmeney sweeper; Had a hop habit, an' he had it bad.
lights would be a-burnin' bright, _____ An' he says to the guy to give him some dope,
would cure up all 'is pains an' ills, An' he laid 'imself down an' he went to sleep, An' he
dollars on the very firs' hand' _____ An' when he seen _____ that the guys was broke,
King _____ with a royal flush han'. From the King _____ of Siam he won a million or more, An' he
nickel had 'e played on a bet. An' when he _____ saw _____ that the bank was broke, He

Listen to the story of a dream he had, An' of a dream he had. _____
So the guy laid out a tray of hops to smoke, A tray of hops to smoke. _____
dreamt he was a-sailin' on the ocean deep, Upon the ocean deep. _____
He laid 'imself down an' took another smoke, An' took another smoke. _____
went to Monte Carlo when the King got sore, _____ when the King got sore. _____
bought a million dollar's worth of hops to smoke, _ Worth of hops to smoke. _____

Additional Lyrics

7. He went to Paris, France, to buy up all the wine,
For a whole carload 'e paid a measly dime.
He bought a ruby bush an' a diamond tree,
For to tote back home to 'is family,
To 'is family.

8. Oh, that was the story of Willie the Weeper,
Willie the Weeper was a chimmeney sweeper,
Had a hop habit an' he had it bad,
An' that was the story of a dreamy lad,
An' of a dream he had.

WILL YE NO' COME BACK AGAIN?

Scottish

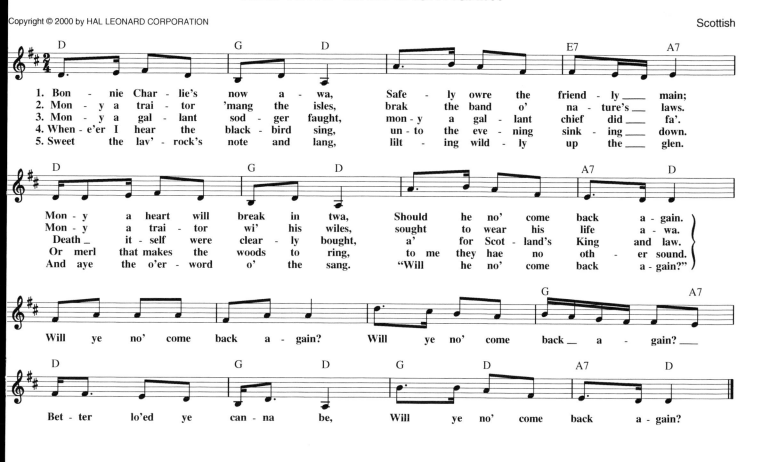

WONDROUS LOVE

Music from Walker's *Southern Harmony*, 1835
American Folk Hymn Text

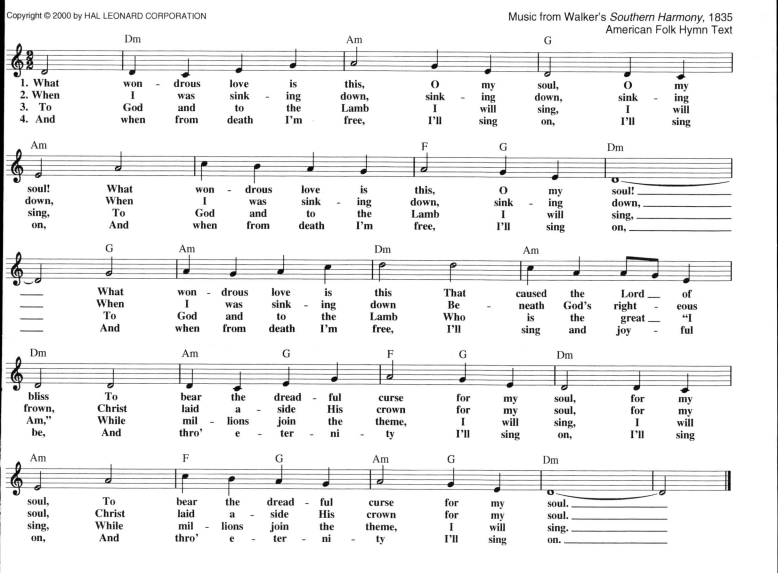

WILLIE MOORE

Southern Appalachian

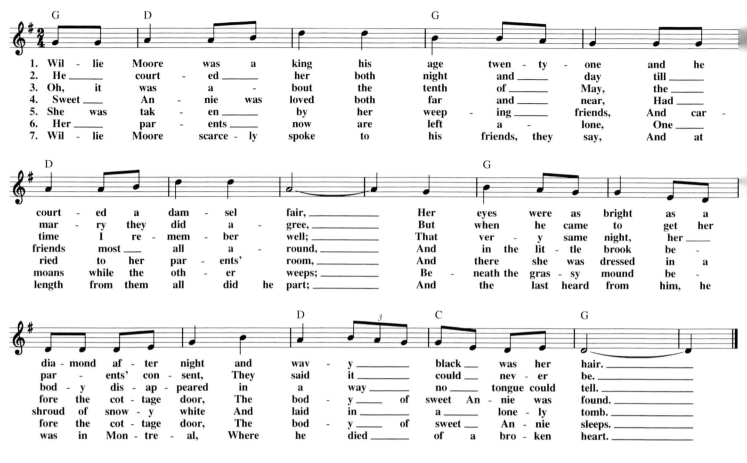

1. Willie Moore was a king his age twenty-one and he
2. He courted her both night and day till
3. Oh, it was about the tenth of May, the
4. Sweet Annie was loved both far and near, Had
5. She was taken by her weeping friends, And car-
6. Her parents now are left alone, One
7. Willie Moore scarcely spoke to his friends, they say, And at

courted a damsel fair, Her eyes were as bright as a
marry they did agree, But when he came to get her
time I remember well; That very same night, her
friends most all around, And in the little brook be-
ried to her parents' room, And there she was dressed in a
moans while the other weeps; Beneath the grassy mound be-
length from them all did he part; And the last heard from him, he

diamond after night and wavy black was her hair.
parents' consent, They said it could never be.
body disappeared in a way no tongue could tell.
fore the cottage door, The body of sweet Annie was found.
shroud of snowy white And laid in a lonely tomb.
fore the cottage door, The body of sweet Annie sleeps.
was in Montreal, Where he died of a broken heart.

WITH MY SWAG ALL ON MY SHOULDER

Australian

1. When first I left old Ireland's shore, the yarns that we were
2. When first we reached Port Melbourne we were all prepared to
3. We made our way into Gee-long, then north to Balla-
4. For many years I wandered round to each new field a-

told. Of how the folks in far Australia could pick up lumps of
slip. And bar the captain and the mate all hands abandoned
rat, where some of us grew mighty thin and some grew sleek and
bout, and made and spent full many a pound till al-luvial petered

gold! How gold-dust lay in all the streets and miner's right was
ship. And all the girls of Melbourne town threw up their arms with
fat. Some tried their luck at Bendigo and some at Fiery
out. And then for any job of work I was prepared to

free! "Hurrah!" I told my loving friends "That's just the place for
joy, hurrooing and exclaiming 'Here comes my Irish
Creek. I made my fortune in a day and blued it in a
try, but now I've found the tucker-track, I'll stay there till I

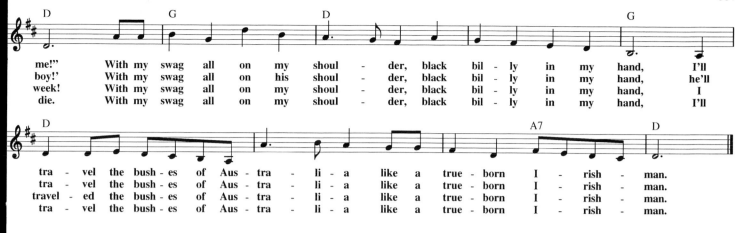

me!" With my swag all on my shoul - der, black bil - ly in my hand, I'll
boy!' With my swag all on his shoul - der, black bil - ly in my hand, he'll
week! With my swag all on my shoul - der, black bil - ly in my hand, I
die. With my swag all on my shoul - der, black bil - ly in my hand, I'll

tra - vel the bush - es of Aus - tra - li - a like a true - born I - rish - man.
tra - vel the bush - es of Aus - tra - li - a like a true - born I - rish - man.
travel - ed the bush - es of Aus - tra - li - a like a true - born I - rish - man.
tra - vel the bush - es of Aus - tra - li - a like a true - born I - rish - man.

THE WORK OF THE WEAVERS

Scottish

1. We're all met to - geth - er here, to sit and to crack. Wi' our glass - es in our hands and our
2. There's sol - diers and there's sail - ors and gla - ziers and all. There's doc - tors and there's min - is - ters and
3. Though weav - in' is a trade that nev - er can fail As long as we need clothes for to

work up - on our back. And there's nae a trade a - mong 'em that can ei - ther mend nor mak' if it
them that live by law. And our friends in South A - mer - i - ca tho' them we nev - er saw But we
keep an - oth - er hale. So let us all be mer - ry o'er a bick - er of good ale And we'll

was - na' for the work of the weav - ers.)
can they wear the work of the weav - ers.} If it was - na' for the weav - ers
drink to the health of the weav - ers.)

what would they do? We would - na' have cloth made of our wool. We would - na' have a coat,

nei - ther black nor blue, gin(if) it was - na' for the work of the weav - ers.

WORRIED MAN BLUES

American

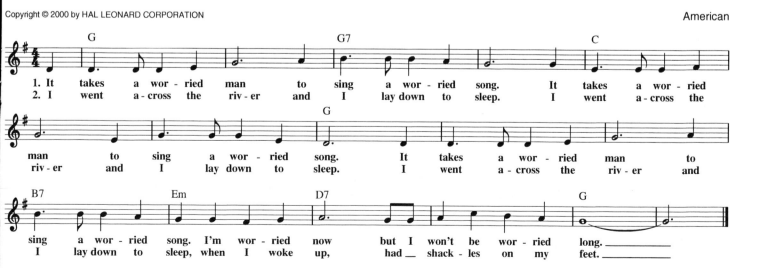

1. It takes a wor - ried man to sing a wor - ried song. It takes a wor - ried
2. I went a - cross the riv - er and I lay down to sleep. I went a - cross the

man to sing a wor - ried song. It takes a wor - ried man to
riv - er and I lay down to sleep. I went a - cross the riv - er and

sing a wor - ried song. I'm wor - ried now but I won't be wor - ried long.
I lay down to sleep, when I woke up, had shack - les on my feet.

WRAP ME UP IN MY TARPAULIN JACKET

Words attributed to G.I. Whyte-Melville
Music by Charles Coote

1. A tall stal-wart lan-cer lay dy-ing,_____ and as on his death-bed he lay,_____ to his friends who a-round him were sigh-ing_____ these last dy-ing words he did say:_____ Wrap me up in my tar-pau-lin jack-et_____ And say a poor duf-fer's laid low._____ Send for six salt-y sea-men to car-ry me_____ With steps mourn-ful, sol-emn and slow.

2. Oh, had I the wings of a lit-tle dove,_____ far, far a-way would I fly._____ Straight to the arms of my true love, and there I would lay me and die._____

3. Then get you two lit-tle white tomb-stones._____ Put them one at my head and my toe._____ And __ get you a pen-knife and scratch there: "Here lies a poor duf-fer be-low."_____

4. And get you six bran-dies and so-das,_____ and set them all out in a row._____ And __ get you six jol-ly good fel-lows to drink to this duf-fer be-low._____

5. And then in the calm of the twi-light,_____ when the soft winds are whis-per-ing low,_____ and the dark-en-ing shad-ows are fall-ing,_____ Some-times think of this duf-fer be-low._____

YANKEE DOODLE

18th Century American

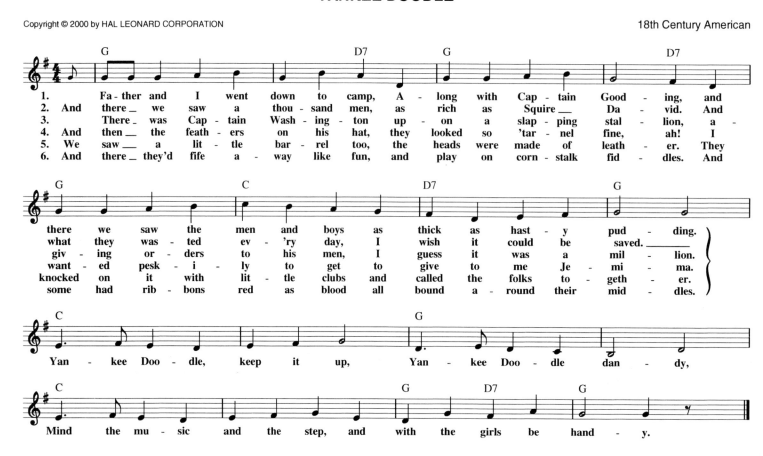

1. Fa-ther and I went down to camp, A-long with Cap-tain Good-ing, and there we saw the men and boys as thick as hast-y pud-ding.

2. And there _ we saw a thou-sand men, as rich as Squire __ Da-vid. And what they was-ted ev-'ry day, I wish it could be saved._____

3. There _ was Cap-tain Wash-ing-ton up-on a slap-ping stal-lion, a giv-ing or-ders to his men, I guess it was a mil-lion.

4. And then __ the feath-ers on his hat, they looked so 'tar-nel fine, ah! I want-ed pesk-i-ly to get to give to me Je-mi-ma.

5. We saw __ a lit-tle bar-rel too, the heads were made of leath-er. They knocked on it with lit-tle clubs and called the folks to-geth-er.

6. And there _ they'd fife a-way like fun, and play on corn-stalk fid-dles. And some had rib-bons red as blood all bound a-round their mid-dles.

Yan-kee Doo-dle, keep it up, Yan-kee Doo-dle dan-dy,

Mind the mu-sic and the step, and with the girls be hand-y.

YE BANKS AND BRAES O' BONNIE DOON

Words by Robert Burns
Melody attributed to Charles Miller, 1788

1. Ye banks and braes __ o' bon - nie Doon, __ How can __ ye bloom __ sae fresh __ and fair? How
2. Oft ha'e I roved __ by bon - nie Doon, __ to see __ the rose __ and wood - bine twine. And

can ye chant, __ ye lit - tle birds, __ and I _____ sae wear - y, fu' __ o' care! Ye'll
il - ka bird __ sang o' __ it's luve, __ and fond - ly sae __ did I _____ o' mine. Wi'

break my heart, __ ye war - bling bird, __ That wan - tons through __ the flow - 'ring thorn, Ye
light - some heart __ I stretch'd my hand, __ and pu'd __ a rose - bud from __ the tree. But

mind me o' _____ de - part - ed joys, __ De - part - ed nev - er to _____ re - turn.
my fause lov - er stole _ the rose, _____ and left _____ and left __ the thorn __ wi' me.

THE YELLOW ROSE OF TEXAS

Words and Music by J.K., 1858

1. There's a yel - low rose in Tex - as That __ I am goin' to see, No
2. Where the Ri - o Grande is flow - ing And the star - ry skies are bright, She
3. Oh, __ now I'm goin' to find her For my heart is full of woe, And we'll

oth - er fel - low loves her, No - bod - y, on - ly me. She cried so when I
walks a - long the riv - er In the qui - et sum - mer night. She thinks, if I re -
sing the song to - geth - er, That we sang so long a - go. We'll play the ban - jo

left her, It ____ like to broke my heart And if I ev - er find __ her, We
mem - ber, When we part - ed long a - go, I prom - ised to come back a - gain, And
gai - ly And we'll sing the songs of yore. And the Yel - low Rose of Tex - as Shall be

nev - er-more will part.
not to leave her so.
mine for ev - er - more.
She's the sweet - est rose of col - or This fel - low ev - er knew, Her

eyes are bright as dia - monds __ They spar - kle like the dew. You may talk a - bout your dear - est May, And

sing of Ro - sa Lee, But the Yel - low Rose of Tex - as beats the belles of Ten - nes - see.

YE PARLIAMENTS OF ENGLAND

American
circa War of 1812

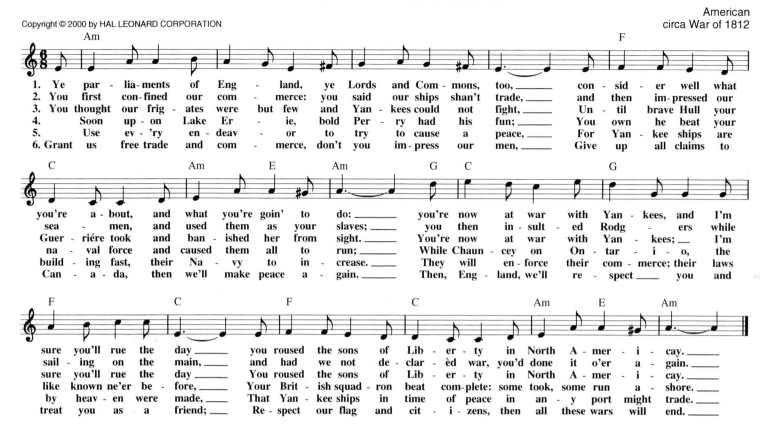

1. Ye par-lia-ments of Eng-land, ye Lords and Com-mons, too, _____ con-sid-er well what
2. You first con-fined our com-merce: you said our ships shan't trade, _____ and then im-pressed our
3. You thought our frig-ates were but few and Yan-kees could not fight, _____ Un-til brave Hull your
4. Soon up-on Lake Er-ie, bold Per-ry had his fun; _____ You own he beat your
5. Use ev-'ry en-deav-or to try to cause a peace, _____ For Yan-kee ships are
6. Grant us free trade and com-merce, don't you im-press our men, _____ Give up all claims to

you're a-bout, and what you're goin' to do: _____ you're now at war with Yan-kees, and I'm
sea-men, and used them as your slaves; _____ you then in-sult-ed Rodg-ers while
Guer-riére took and ban-ished her from sight. _____ You're now at war with Yan-kees; _____ I'm
na-val force and caused them all to run; _____ While Chaun-cey on On-tar-i-o, the
build-ing fast, their Na-vy to in-crease. _____ They will en-force their com-merce; their laws
Can-a-da, then we'll make peace a-gain. _____ Then, Eng-land, we'll re-spect _____ you and

sure you'll rue the day _____ you roused the sons of Lib-er-ty in North A-mer-i-cay. _____
sail-ing on the main, _____ and had we not de-clar-èd war, you'd done it o'er a-gain. _____
sure you'll rue the day _____ You roused the sons of Lib-er-ty in North A-mer-i-cay. _____
like known ne'er be-fore, _____ Your Brit-ish squad-ron beat com-plete: some took, some run a-shore. _____
by heav-en were made, _____ That Yan-kee ships in time of peace in an-y port might trade. _____
treat you as a friend; _____ Re-spect our flag and cit-i-zens, then all these wars will end. _____

YONDER STANDS A HANDSOME LADY

American version of an English Folksong

1. Yon-der _____ stands a _____ hand-some la-dy, Who she _____ is I _____ do not _____ know.
2. Mad-am, _____ I have _____ gold and sil-ver, Mad-am, _____ I have _____ house and _____ land,
3. What care _____ I for your gold and sil-ver, What care _____ I for your house and _____ land,
4. Mad-am, _____ do not _____ count on beau-ty, Beau-ty is a flow-er that will soon de-cay.
5. The sweet-est ap-ple _____ soon is rot-ten, The hot-test love now _____ soon is _____ cold.
6. A man may drink and _____ not be drunk-en. A man may fight and _____ not be _____ slain.

Shall I yon court her for her beau-ty? What was you Mad-am, "yes," or "no"?
Mad-am, I have a world of treas-ures. All shall _____ be at your com-mand.
What care I for your world of treas-ures? All I want is a hand-some man.
The bright-est flow-er in the midst of sum-mer, In the fall it will fade a-way.
A young man's word is soon for-got-ten; the cof-fin is the end of young and old.
A man may court a hand-some la-dy And be _____ wel-come there a-gain.

ZACCHAEUS

American Gospel Song

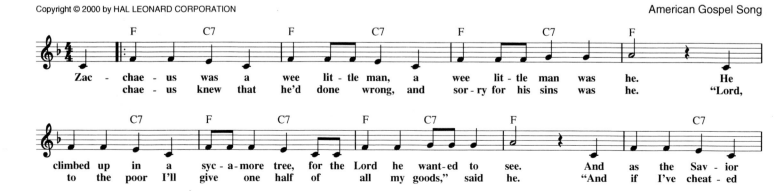

Zac-chae-us was a wee lit-tle man, a wee lit-tle man was he. He
chae-us knew that he'd done wrong, and sor-ry for his sins was he. "Lord,

climbed up in a syc-a-more tree, for the Lord he want-ed to see. And as the Sav-ior
to the poor I'll give one half of all my goods," said he. "And if I've cheat-ed

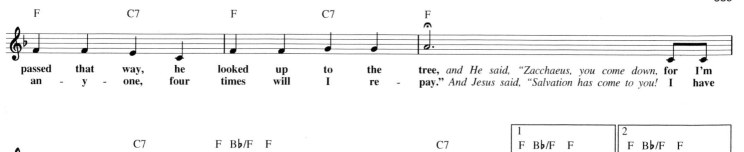

passed that way, he looked up to the tree, *and He said, "Zacchaeus, you come down, for I'm*
an - y - one, four times will I re - pay." *And Jesus said, "Salvation has come to you! I have*

go - ing to your house to - day, for I'm go - ing to your house to - day. Zac -
come _ to __ seek and save. I have come _ to __ seek and save."

THE YOUNG MAN WHO WOULDN'T HOE CORN

American

1. I'll sing you a song, __ and it's not ver - y long, a -
2. He went to the field, __ and he took a peep in: the
3. He went down ____ to ____ his _____ neigh - bor's door where
4. Well, here you _____ air a - want - in' for to _____ wed and
5. Now go down ____ to ____ that _____ cute lit - tle wid - der,

bout a young man who would - n't hoe corn. The rea - son why,
weeds and the grass was up to his chin, the weeds and the grass, they
he had been man - y times ___ be - fore; lit - tle miss, will you
can - not ____ make your own ____ corn bread. Pret - ty sin - gle I be, sin - gle
And I hope that you don't __ get her. She gave him the mit - ten as

I can't tell, for this young man was al - ways well. _____
were so high, they caused this young man for to sigh. _____
mar - ry me, Pret - ty lit - tle miss, what do you say? _____
I re - main; A la - zy man I won't main - tain. _____
sure as you're born, Be - cause this young man would - n't hoe corn. _____

ZUM GALI GALI

Folksong from Israel

Zum ga - li ga - li ga - li, Zum ga - li ga - li, Zum ga - li ga - li ga - li, Zum ga - li ga - li,

{ 1. He - cha - lutz le 'man a - vo - dah; A - vo - dah le 'man he - cha - lutz.
{ 2. A - vo - dah le 'man he - cha - lutz; He - cha - lutz le 'man a - vo - dah.

Translation: "The Pioneer is meant for work. Work is meant for the pioneer."

Guitar Chords

	Major	Minor	Sixth	Seventh
C				
C#/Db				
D				
D#/Eb				
E				
F				
F#/Gb				
G				
G#/Ab				
A				
A#/Bb				
B				